西安统计年鉴

XI'AN STATISTICAL YEARBOOK

2016

中英文对照 Chinese/English

中国统计出版社
China Statistics Press

西安市统计局
XI'AN MUNICIPAL BUREAU OF STATISTICS
国家统计局西安调查队
NBS SURVEY OFFICE IN XI'AN

图书在版编目（CIP）数据

西安统计年鉴. 2016 / 西安市统计局, 国家统计局西安调查队编. -- 北京 : 中国统计出版社, 2016.9
ISBN 978-7-5037-7877-3

Ⅰ. ①西… Ⅱ. ①西… ②国… Ⅲ. ①统计资料－西安市－2016－年鉴 Ⅳ. ①C832.411-54

中国版本图书馆CIP数据核字(2016)第184256号

西安统计年鉴—2016

作　　者/ 西安市统计局　国家统计局西安调查队
责任编辑/ 陈越月
装帧设计/ 西安力天世纪品牌策划设计有限公司
出版发行/ 中国统计出版社
地　　址/ 北京市丰台区西三环南路甲6号　邮政编码/100073
电　　话/ 邮购（010）63376909　书店（010）68783171
网　　址/ http://csp.stats.gov.cn
印　　刷/ 西安一印制版有限责任公司
经　　销/ 新华书店
开　　本/ 890mm×1240mm　1/16
字　　数/ 1533千字
印　　张/ 44.875
版　　别/ 2016年9月第1版
版　　次/ 2016年9月第1次印刷
定　　价/ 260元

如有印装差错，由本社发行部调换。

《西安统计年鉴—2016》编辑部

XI'AN STATISTICAL YEARBOOK-2016
EDITORLAL STAFF

编者说明

一、《西安统计年鉴—2016》系统收录了全市、区县及开发区2015年经济、社会各方面统计数据，以及重要历史年份主要统计数据，是一部全面记载西安市国民经济和社会发展情况的大型连续性统计文献资料和重要工具书。

二、本年鉴正文内容分为二十二个篇章：（一）综合；（二）基本单位；（三）国民经济核算；（四）人口、从业人员与职工工资；（五）固定资产投资；（六）财政；（七）物价指数；（八）人民生活；（九）城市公用事业；（十）环境保护；（十一）农业；（十二）工业；（十三）能源；（十四）建筑业；（十五）运输和邮电；（十六）国内贸易；（十七）对外经济贸易和旅游；（十八）服务业；（十九）金融业；（二十）教育和科技；（二十一）文化、体育、卫生、社会福利和其他；（二十二）企业调查。同时，为方便读者使用，各篇章前设有简要说明和主要统计指标，对本篇章的主要内容、资料来源、以及历史变动情况予以简要概述，篇末附有《主要统计指标解释》。

三、本年鉴统计资料的统计标准，按当时国家统计制度执行，有关指标的涵义、口径、范围、计算方法等，在不同时期可能有所不同，使用时请注意。如国民经济行业分类按GB/T4754—2011标准执行。

四、为便于国内外读者查阅，本年鉴全部内容均采用中英文对照编辑。

五、本年鉴中国民经济核算部分的2013年数据为全国第三次经济普查数据，2009-2012年数据为依据第三次经济普查修订数据；工业部分的2013年数据为第三次经济普查数据；国内贸易部分的2009—2013年为依据第三次经济普查调整后数据。

六、本年鉴中的部分指标合计数或相对数由于单位取舍不同产生的计算误差均未作机械调整。

七、本年鉴所使用的计量单位均依据2015年相关统计报表制度。

八、本年鉴使用的符号说明："空白"表示该项统计指标无数据或数据不详；"#"表示其中项；"*"表示另有注解。

感谢社会各界长期以来对《西安统计年鉴》的广泛关注和大力支持。为进一步做好工作，更好地为广大读者服务，希望社会各界提出宝贵意见。

PREFACE

I. Xi'an Statistical Yearbook 2016 is a periodical statistic yearbook which record economic and social development of Xi'an all-around in 2015 and some selected data series in historical important years. With its features of comprehensive and intensive information, this practically provides data covering the situation of social and economic developments in Xi' an. II. The book contains twenty-two parts, 1.General Survey; 2.Basic Unit; 3.National Economic Account; 4.Population, Employment and Wages; 5.Investment in Fixed Assets; 6.Government Finance; 7.Price Indices; 8.People's Livelihood; 9.Urban Public Utilities; 10.Environmental Protection; 11.Agriculture; 12.Industry; 13.Energy; 14.Construction; 15.Transportation, Post and Telecommunication Service; 16.Domestic Trade; 17.Foreign Trade; 18. Tertiary Industry; 19.Banking and Insurance; 20.Education, Science and Technology; 21.Culture, Sports, Public Health, Social Welfare Institutions and Other Social Activities; 22.Enterprises Investigation. As insert pages including statistical graphs and charts.

III. The data of various years in conformity to the statistical standards prescribed by national statistical system of the time. The meaning, scope and calculating method of indicators may have some difference in different periods, which readers must pay attention to. For example, national industries classification is carried out according to standard GB/T4754 -2011. For the sake of comparison of the old and new industry standards, we edit the division' s data in some major indicators according to standard GB/T4754 -2011.

IV. For the convenience of being consulted by foreigners, the book is Chinese-English bilingual edition.

V. In this yearbook, data from 2013 at the part of National Economic Account and Industry is the results of Third National Economic Census, the data from 2009 to 2012 at the part of National Economic Account and data from 2009 to 2013 at the part of Domestic Trade have adjusted by Third National Economic Census.

VI. Statistical discrepancies due to rounding are not adjusted automatically in this yearbook.

VII. Unit of measurement is used in this yearbook according to 2014 statistics system.

VIII. Explanations on symbols used in this yearbook:

(Blank) indicates the data not available;

# indicates the items of the total.

* indicates some other explanatory note.

Here we would like to express our sincere thanks to the people for their concerning and support to the Xi'an statistical yearbook. In order to do better and provide better service to readers, we hope that the whole society fields can propose constructive advices.

生产总值（亿元）
Gross Domestic Product(100 million yuan)

生产总值指数（以上年为100）
Indices of Gross Domestic Product (preceding year = 100)

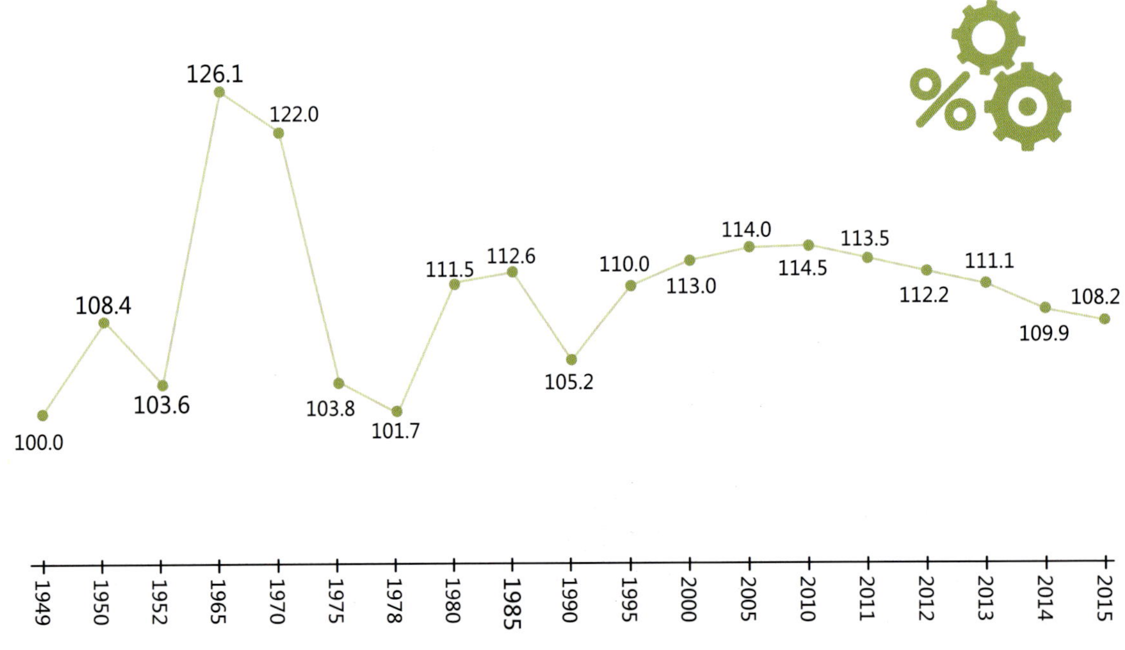

生产总值构成（%）
Composition of Gross Domestic Product (%)

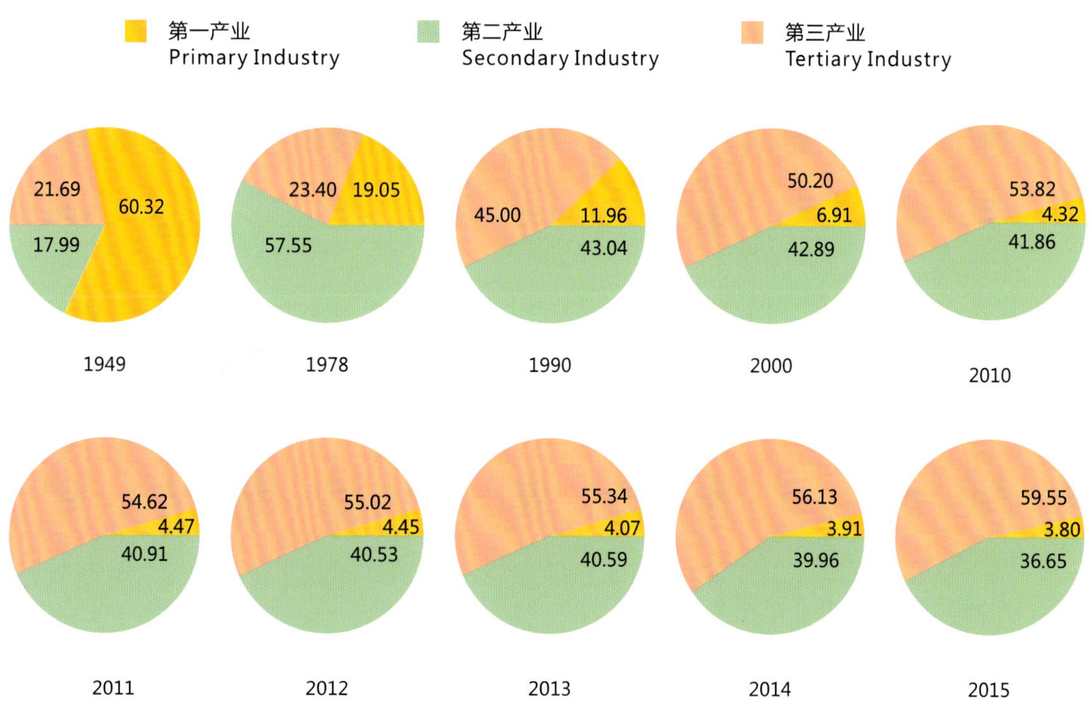

人均GDP（元/人）
Per Capita GDP(yuan/person)

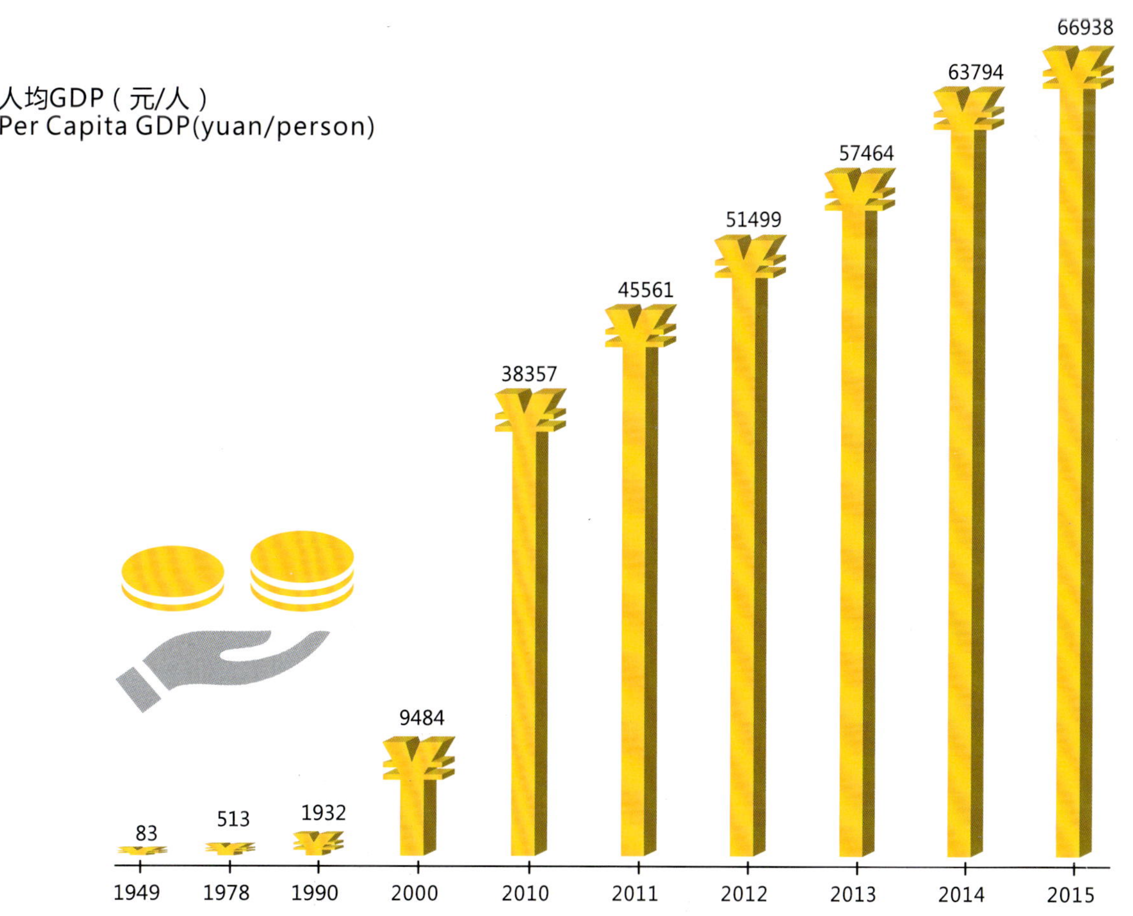

年末常住人口（万人）
Year-end Permanent population（10000 persons）

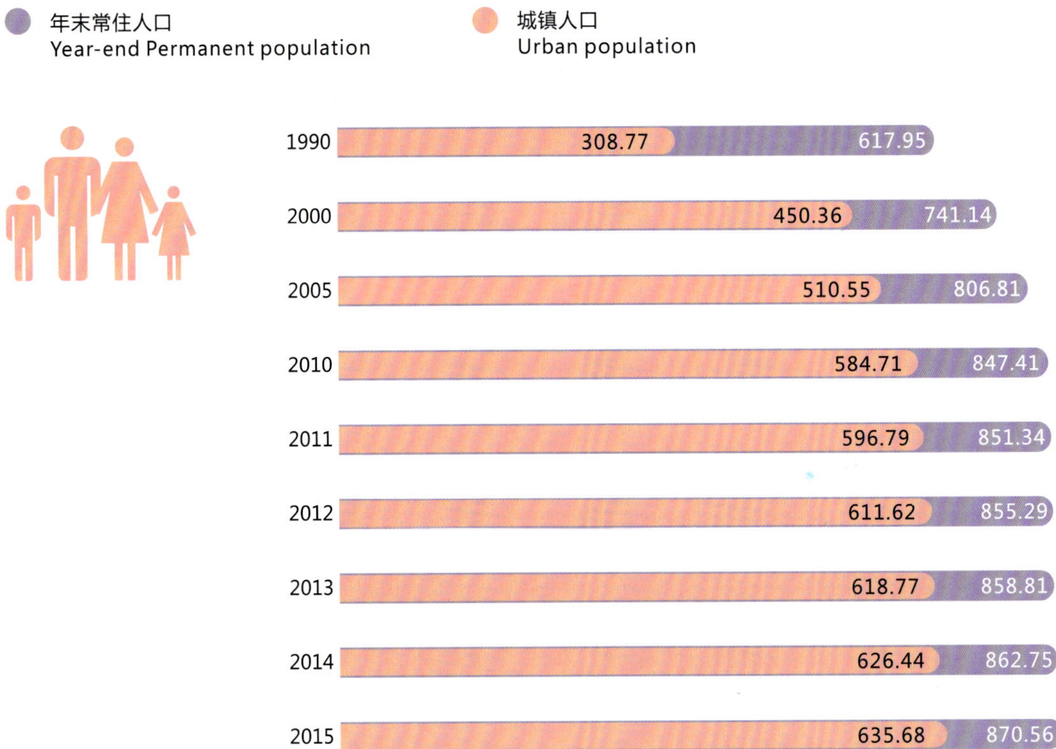

社会从业人数（万人）
Social Workers(10000 persons)

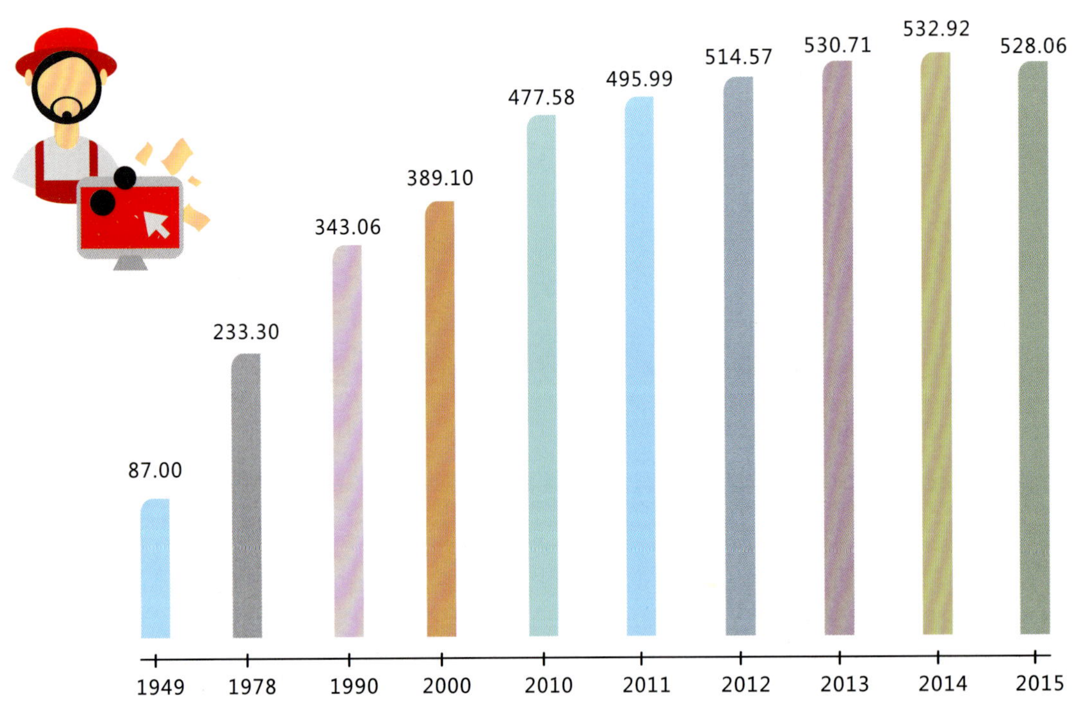

固定资产投资（亿元）
Investment in Fixed Assets(100 million yuan)

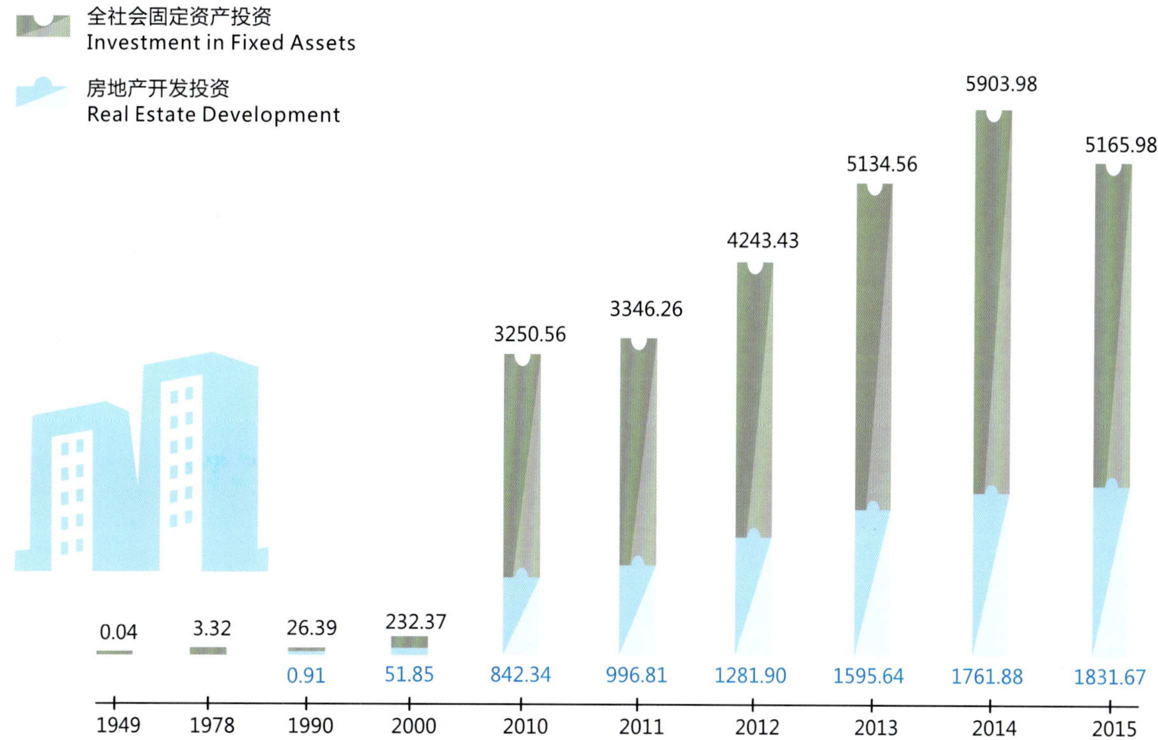

新增固定资产及住宅竣工面积
Newly Increased Fixed Assets and Residenctial Area of Completion

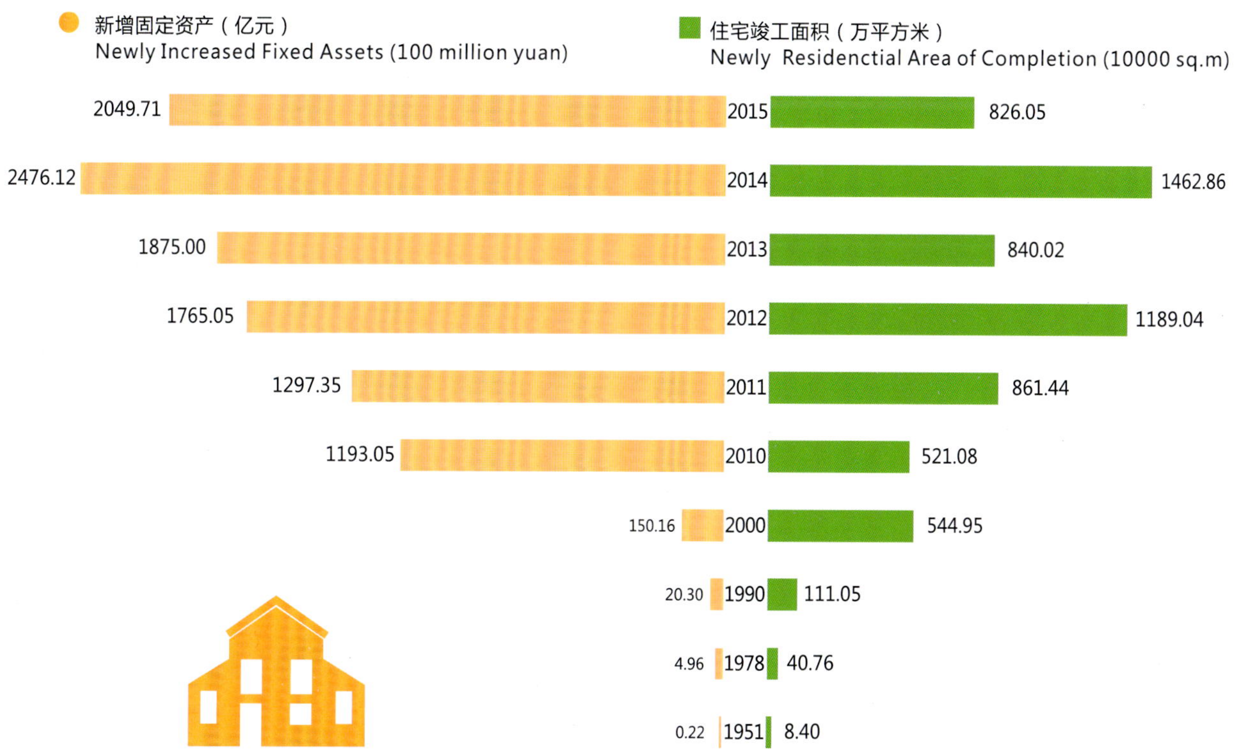

农林牧渔及服务业总产值（亿元）
Gross Output Value of Farming,Forestry, Animal Husbandry,Fishery and Service(100 million yuan)

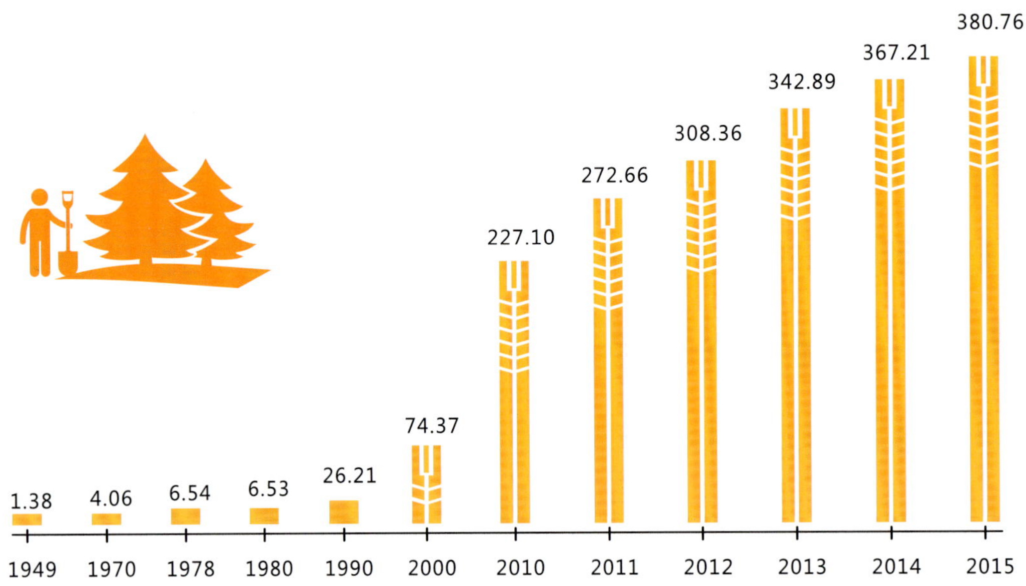

蔬菜产量（万吨）
Grain ,Vegetables Product(10000 ton)

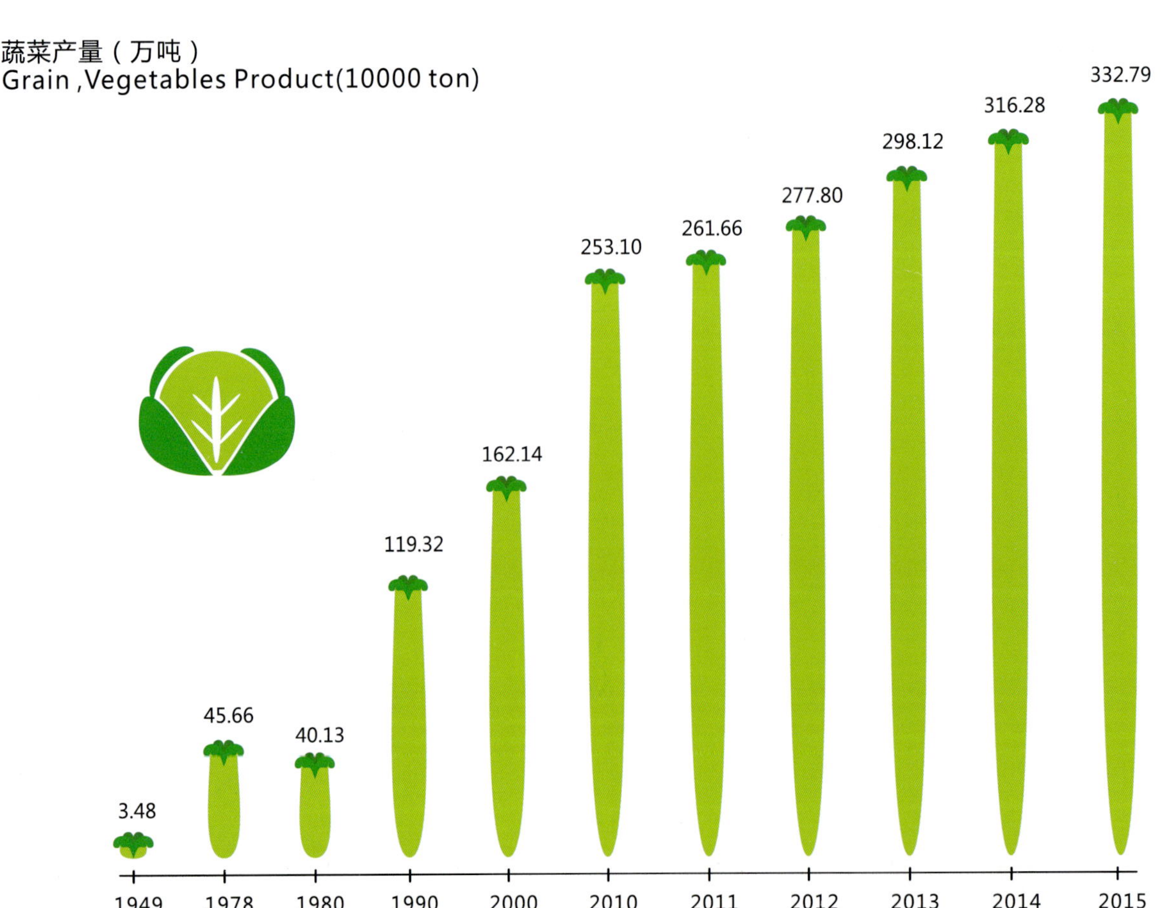

规模以上工业增加值（现价）（亿元）
Value Added of Industrial Enterprises Above Designated Size (100 million yuan)

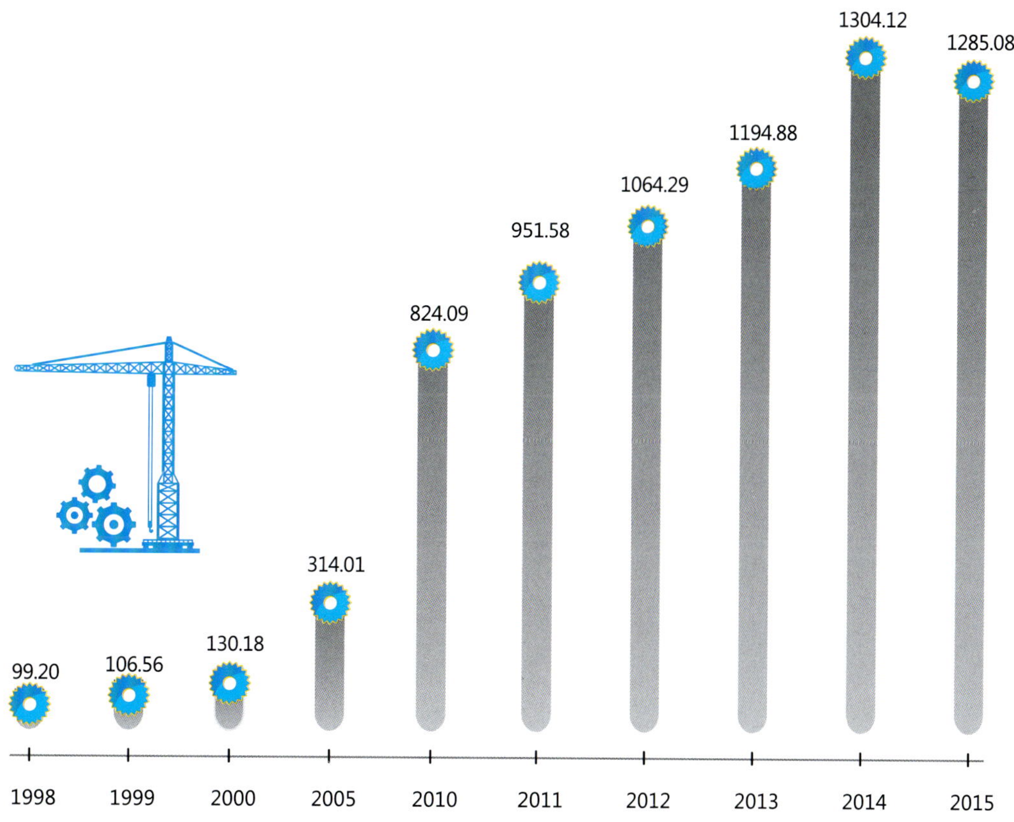

规模以上工业企业主要产品产量
Output of Major Industrial Products Of Enterprises Above Designated Size

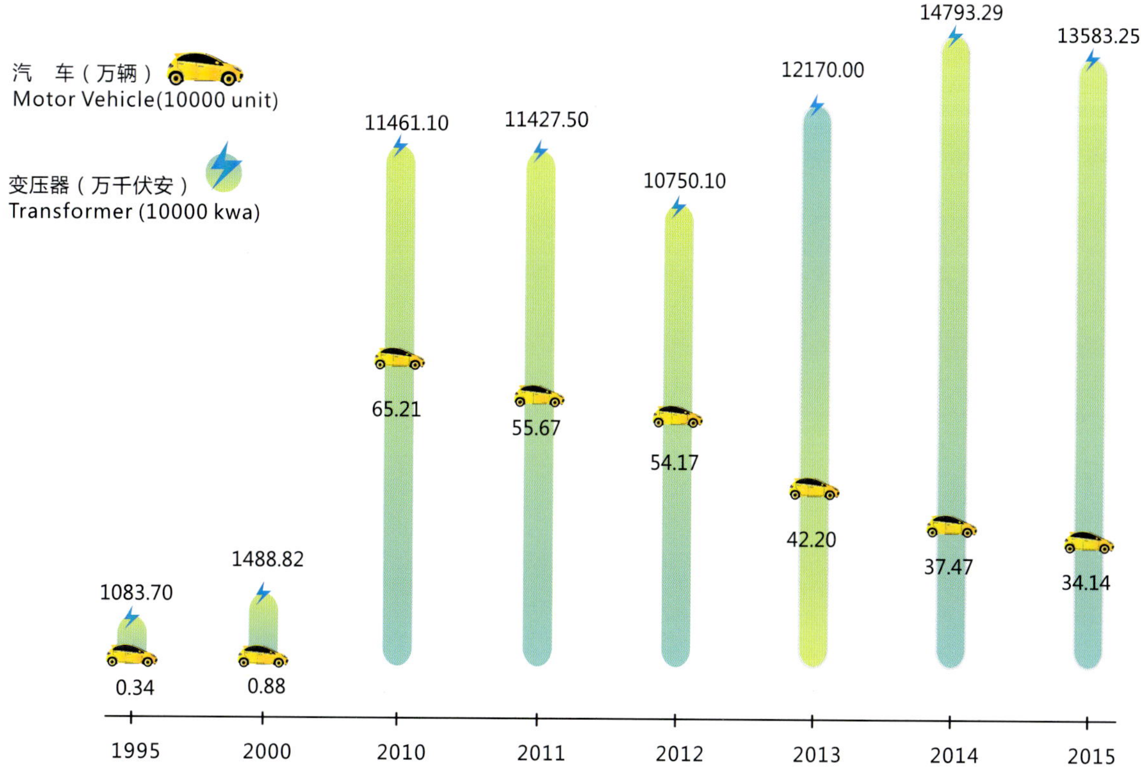

交通
Trafficed Size

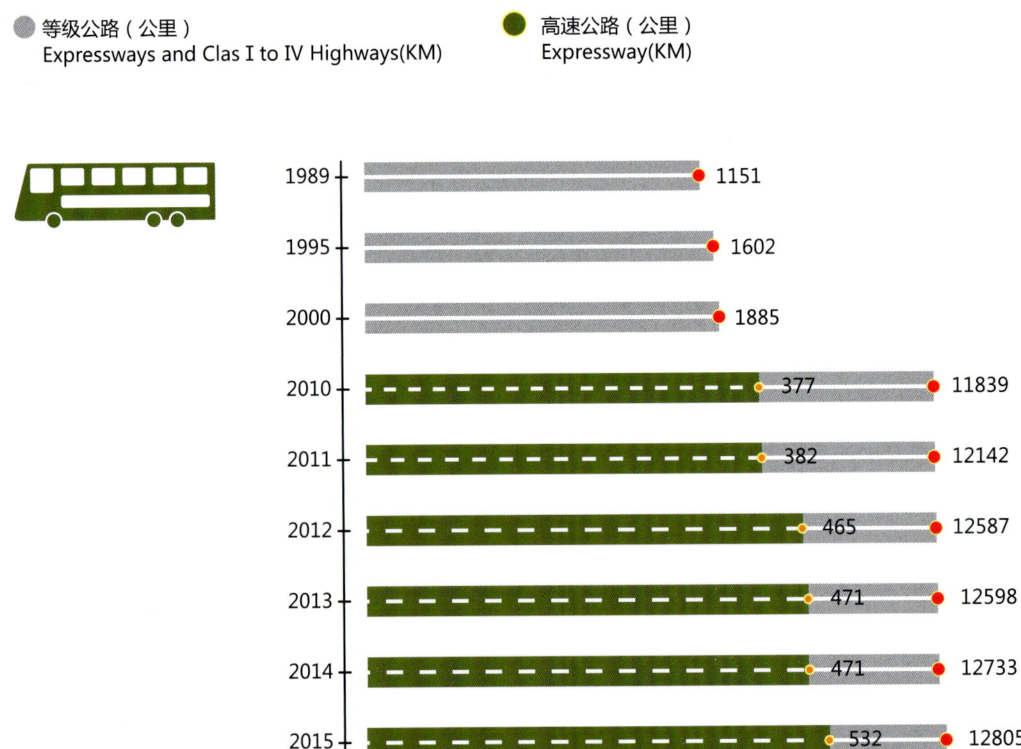

全社会车辆数（万辆）
Possession of Civil Vehicles(10000 unit)

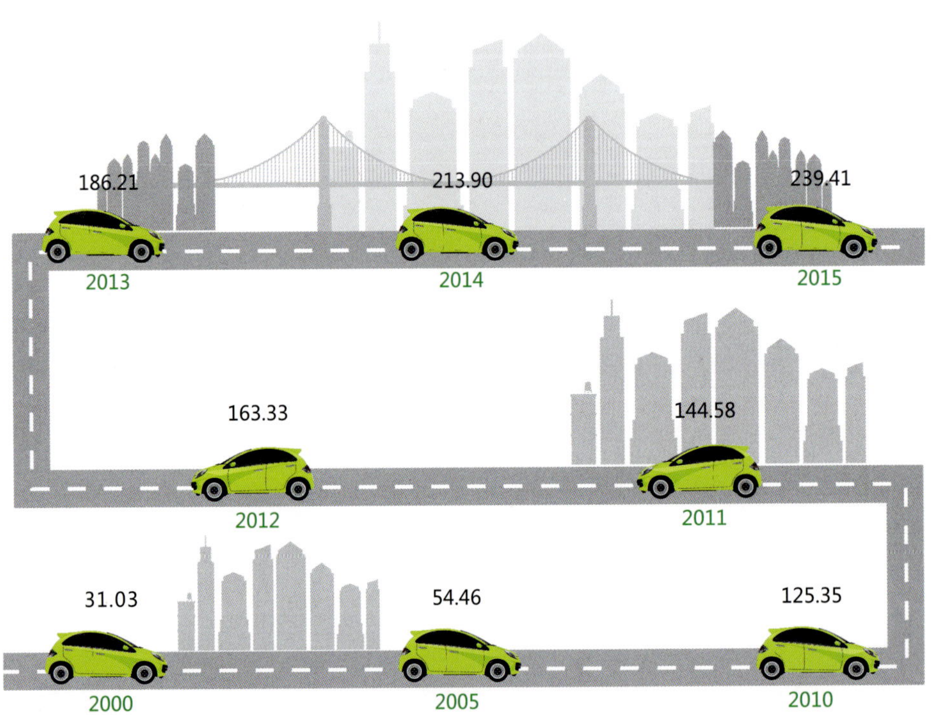

社会消费品零售总额（亿元）
Total Retail Sales of Consumer Goods(100 million yuan)

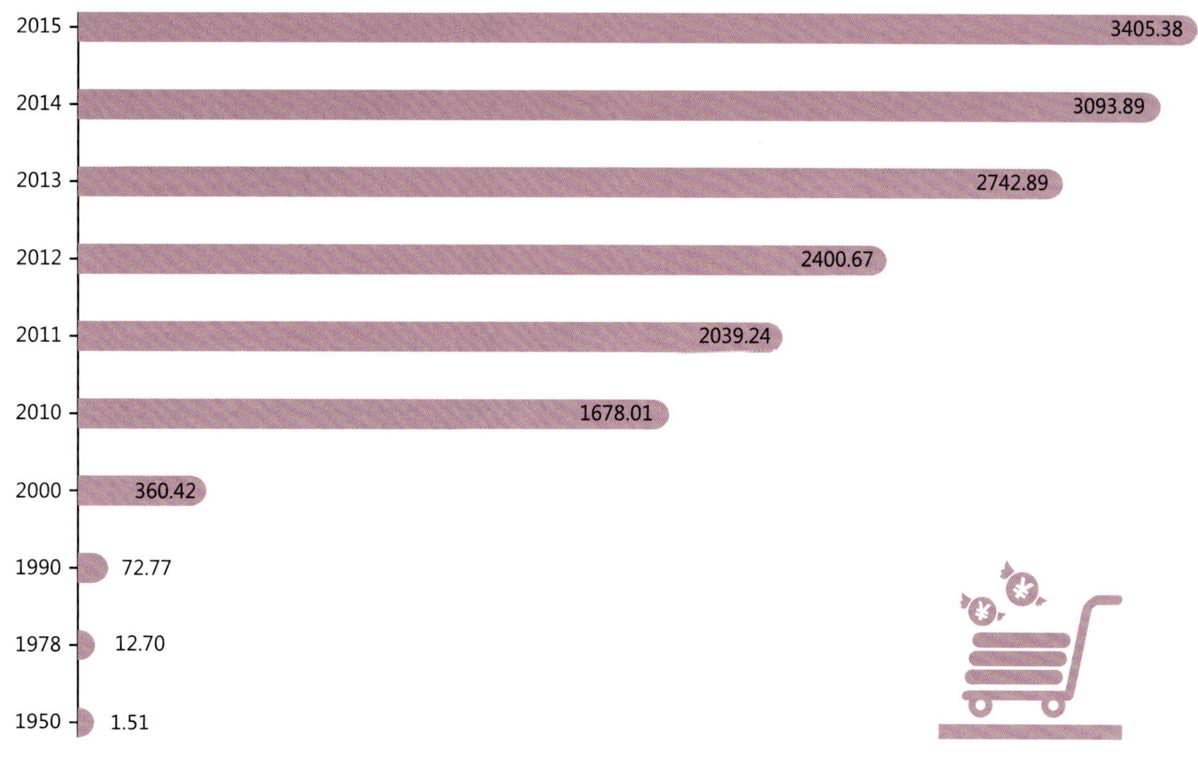

实际利用外商直接投资额（亿美元）
Foreign Direct Investment(USD 100 million)

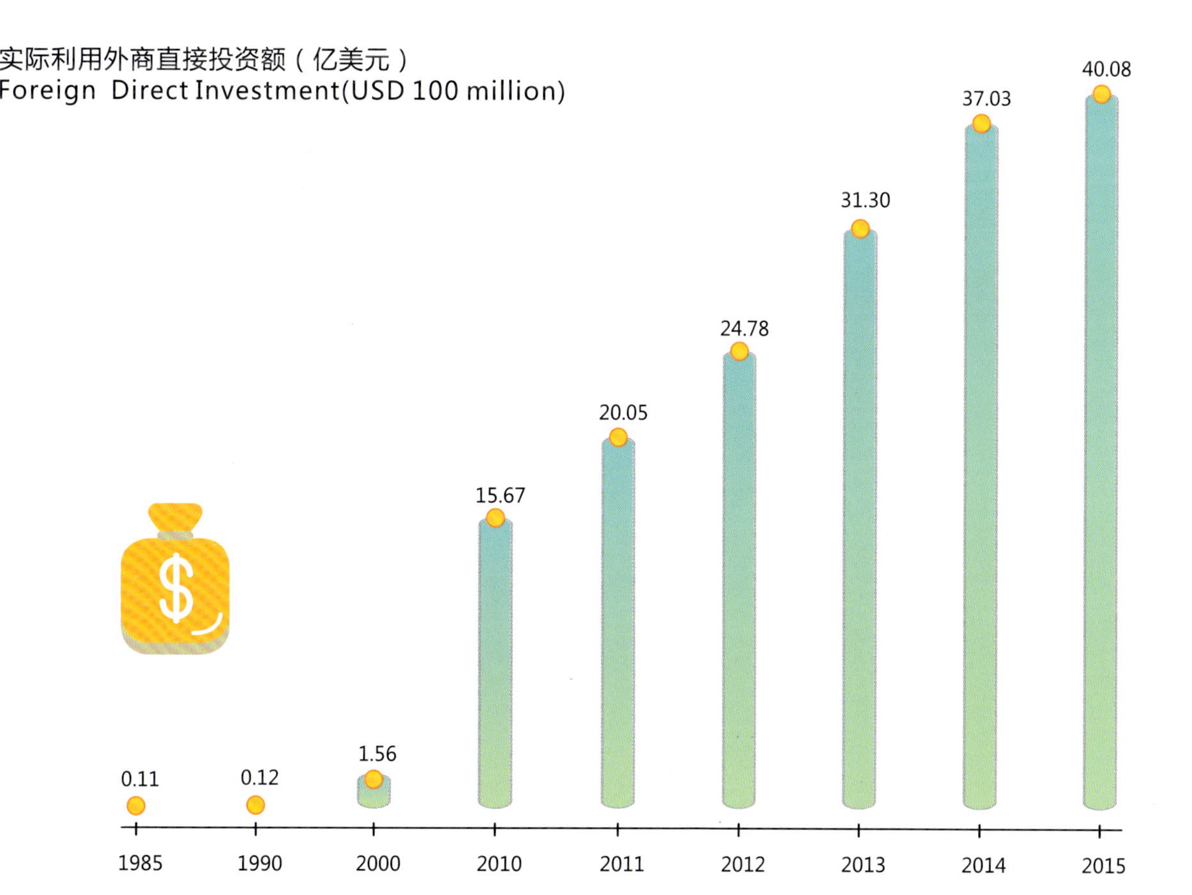

进出口总额（亿美元）
Total Value of Imports and Exports(USD 100 million)

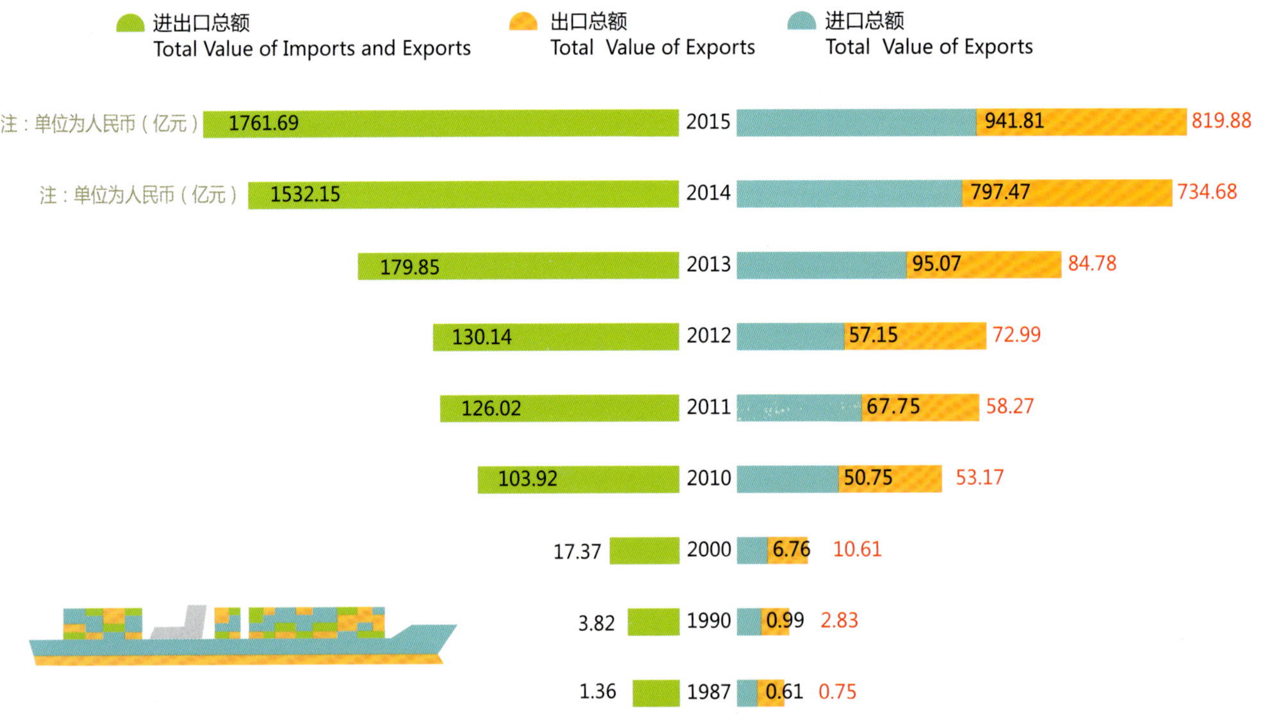

旅游人数及收入
Number of Tourists and Tourism Income

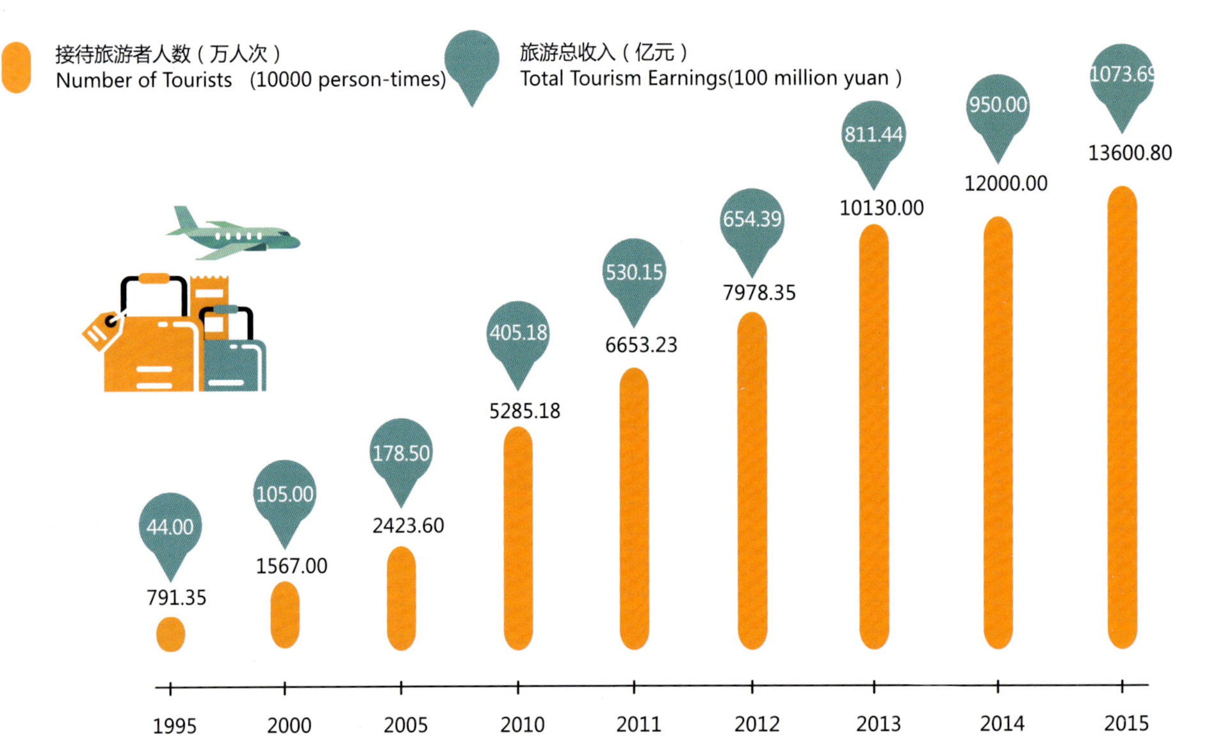

财政收支（亿元）
Govement Revenue and Expenditure(100 million yuan)

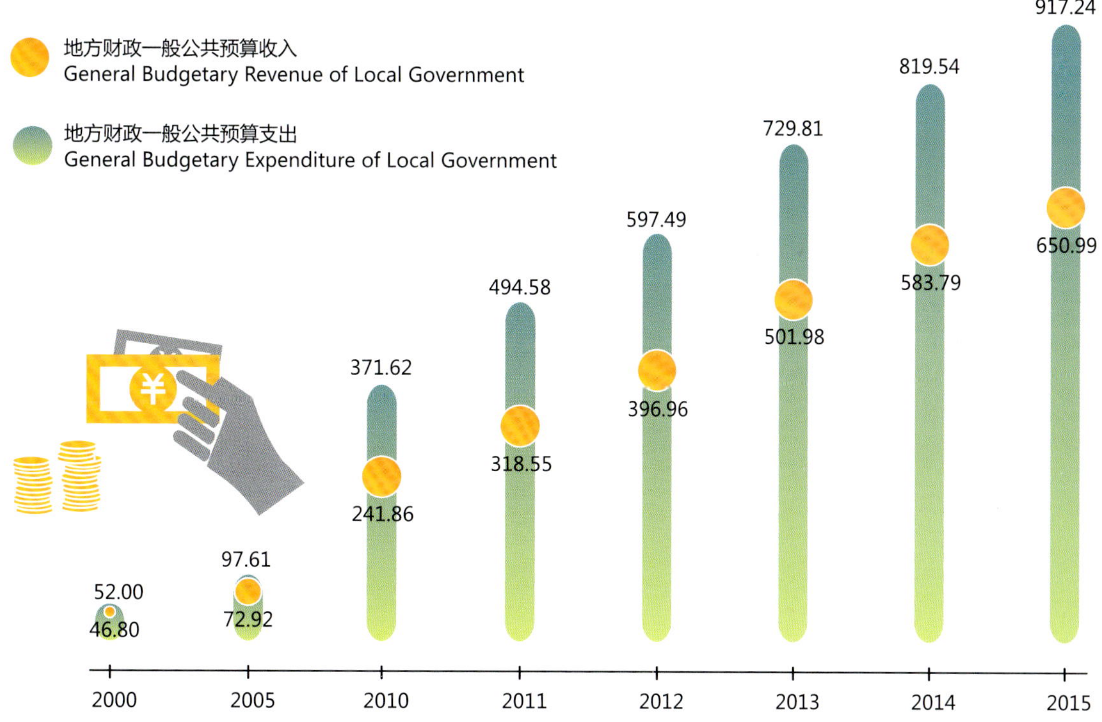

金融机构人民币存贷款年末余额（亿元）
Year-end Deposit and Loans in Financial Institutions (100 million yuan)

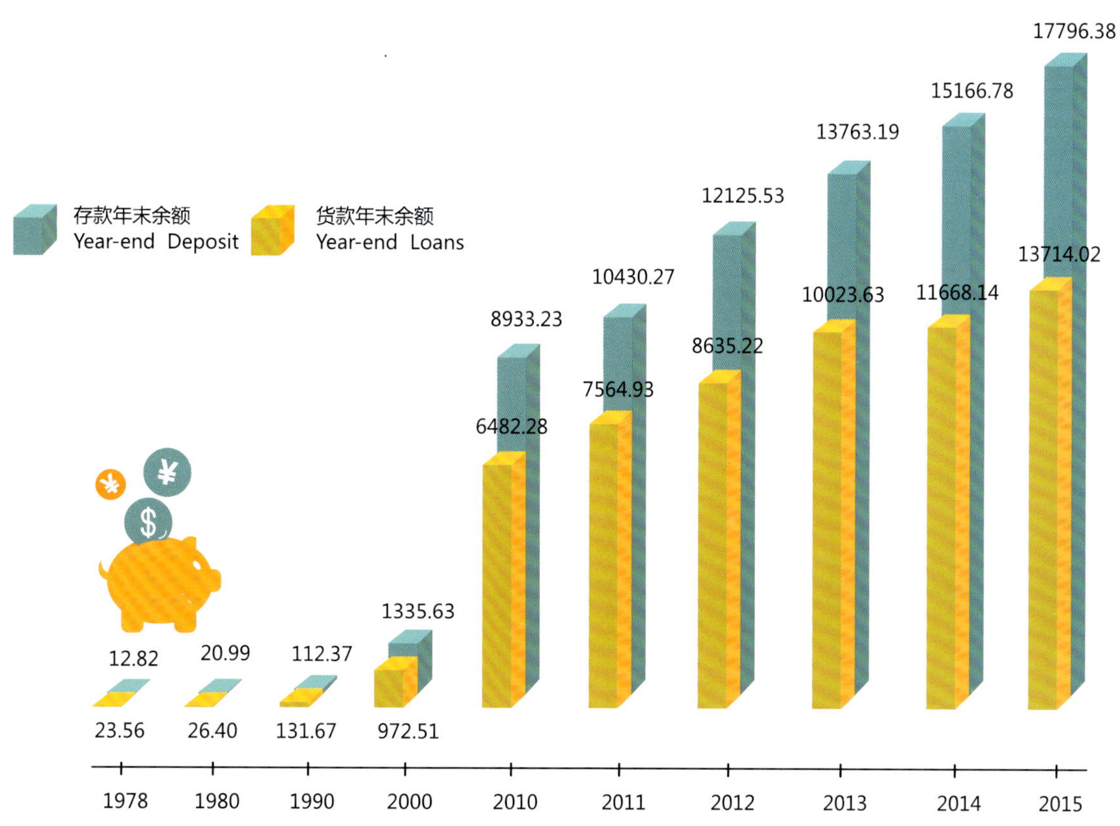

建成区面积（平方公里）
Area of Regions Built-up (sq.km)

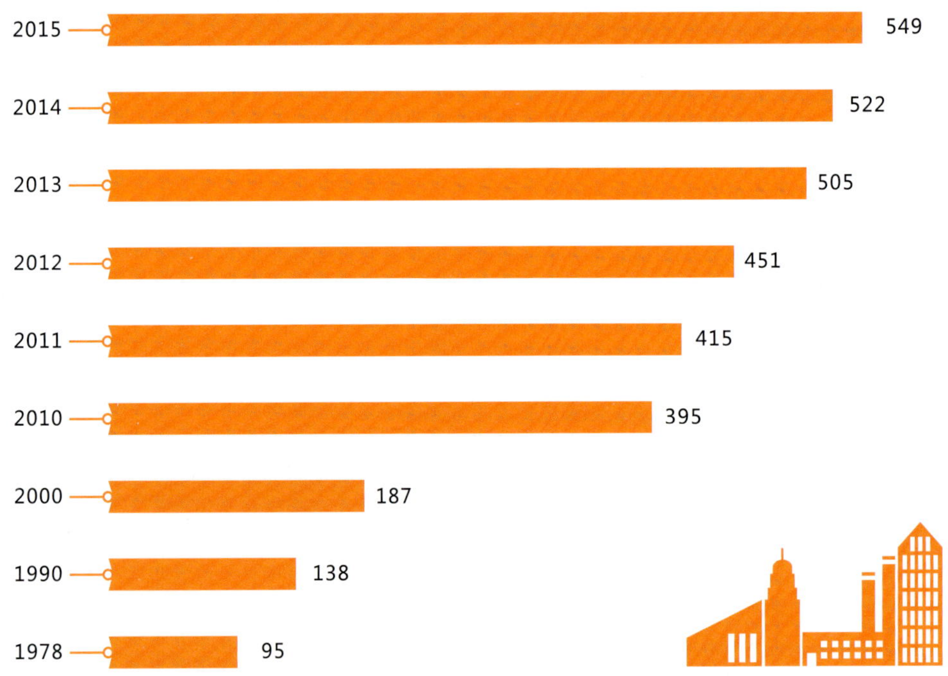

城市公共运营车辆（辆）
City Operating Vehicles(unit)

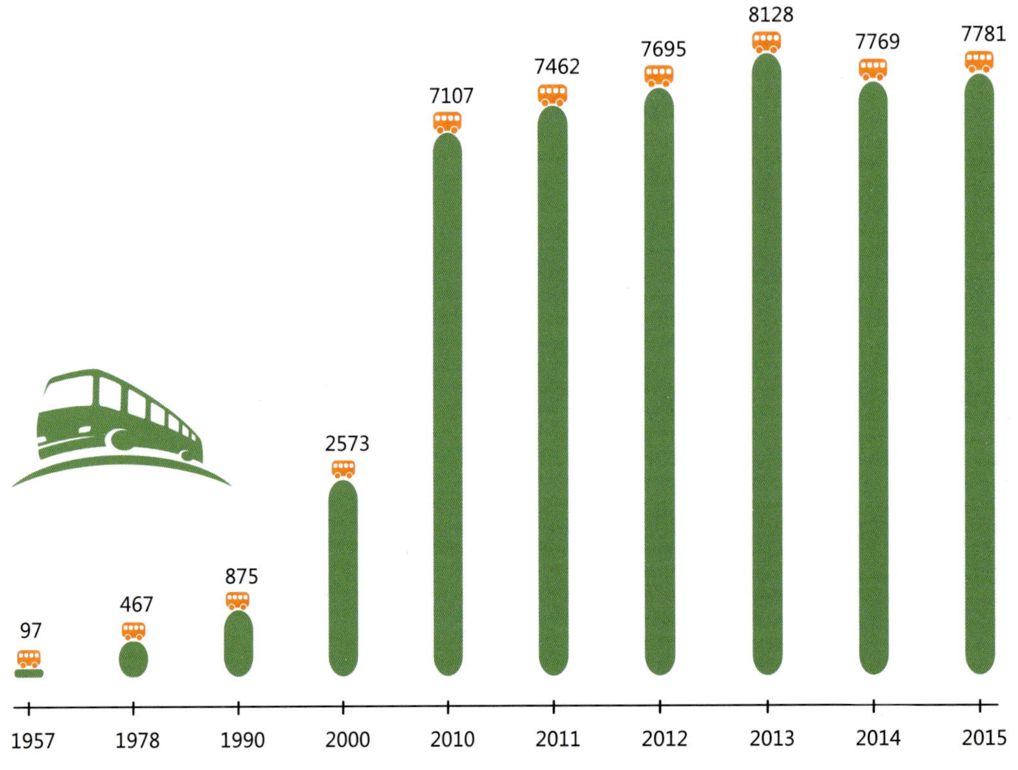

天然气供气总量（万立方米）
Total Natural Gas Supply(10000 cu.m)

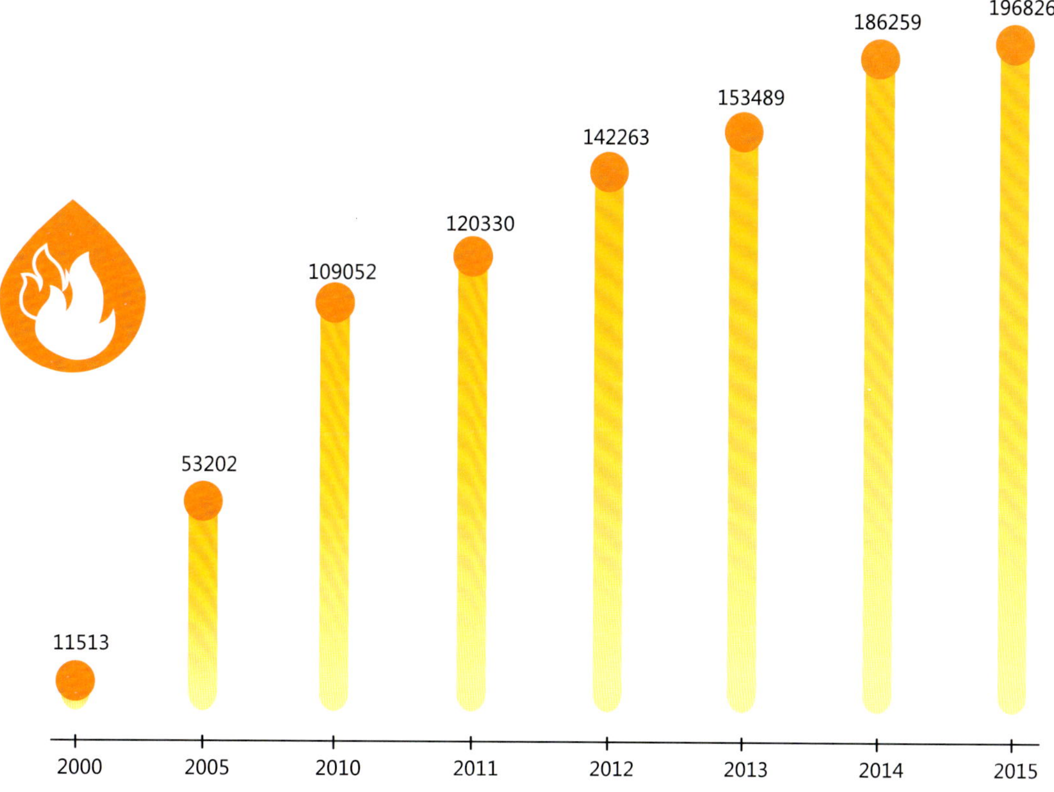

绿地面积（公顷）
Green Area (hectare)

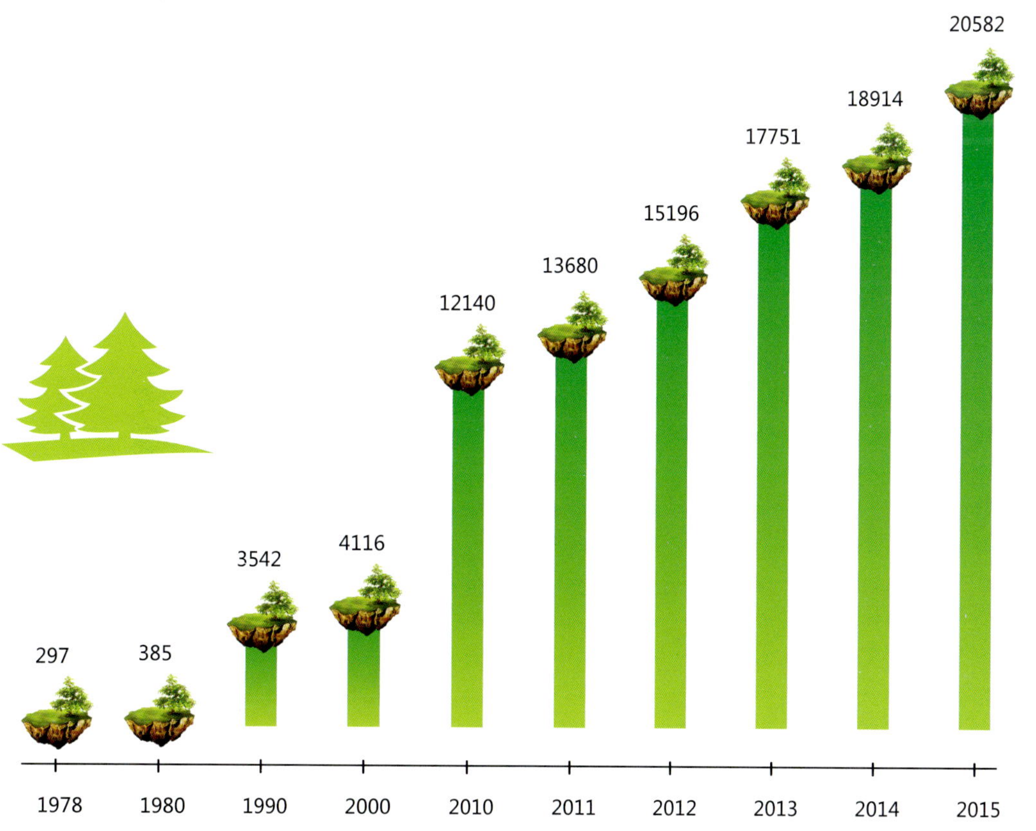

专任教师（万人）
Full-time Teachers（10000 persons）

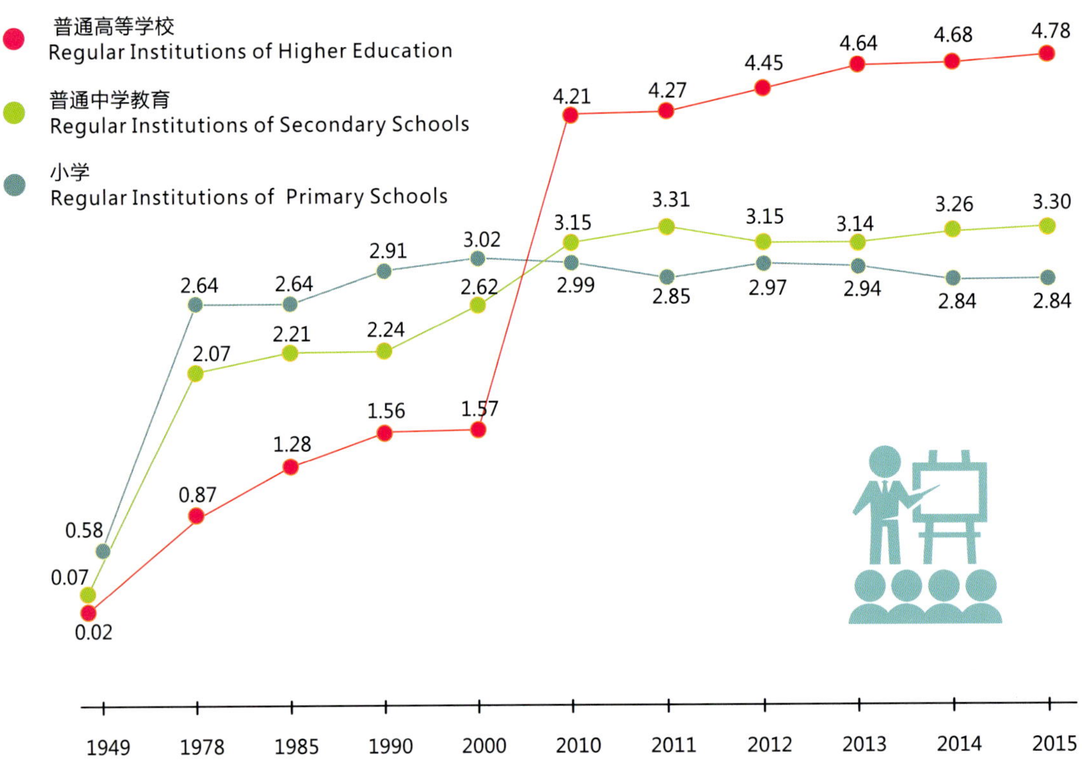

普通教育在校学生（万人）
Total Enrollment of Regular Education（10000 persons）

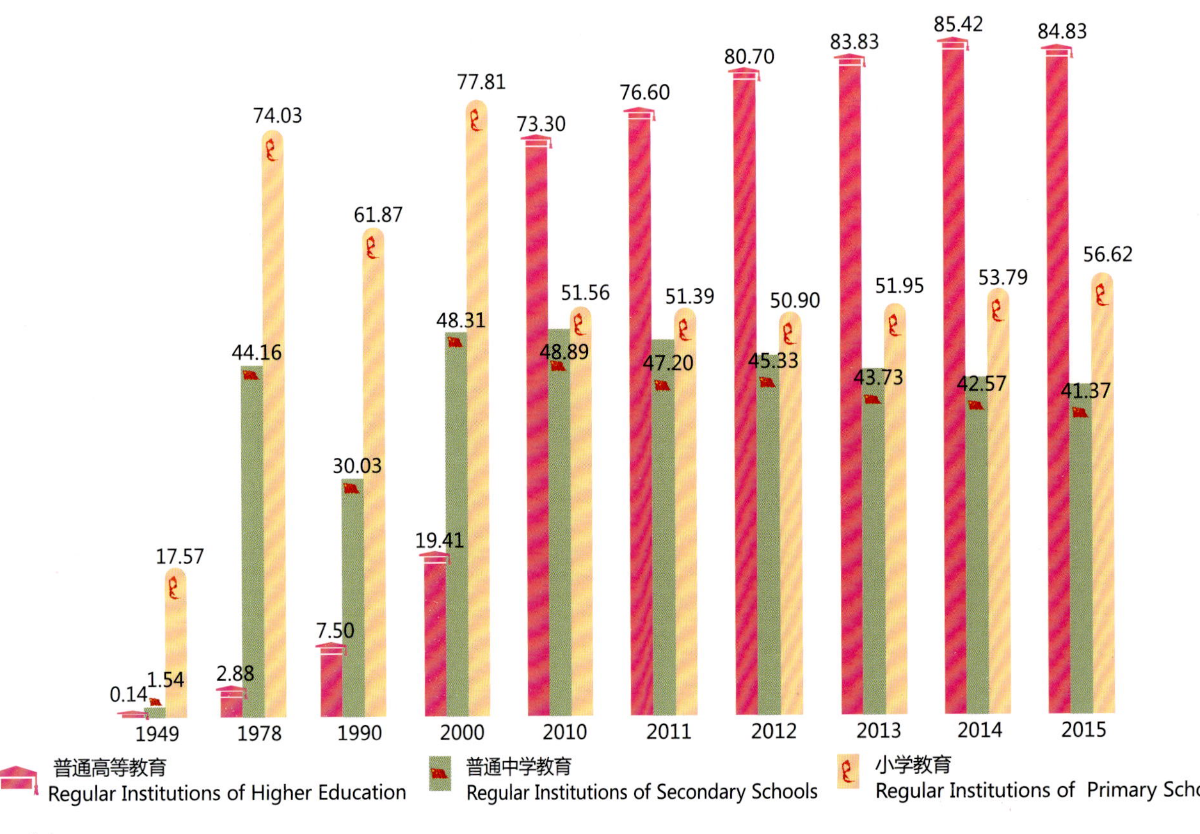

城乡居民收入（元）
The Income of Urban and Rural Residents (yuan)

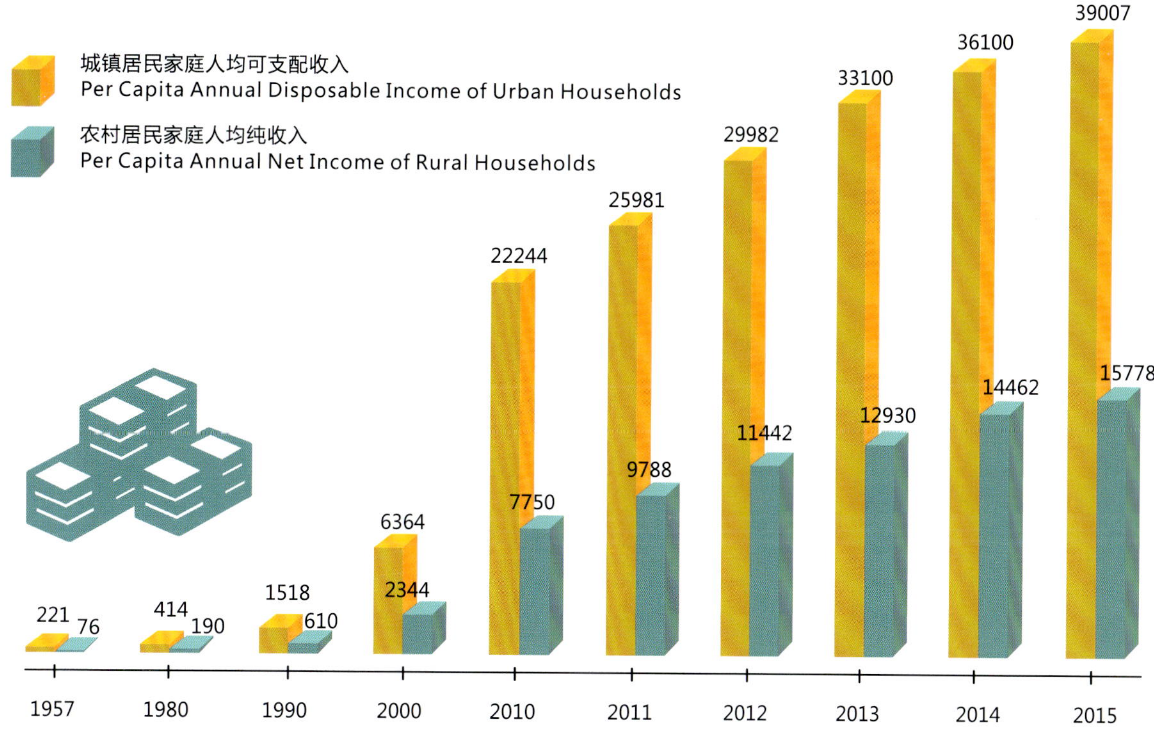

价格指数（以上年价格为100）
Price Indices(the price of preceding year=100)

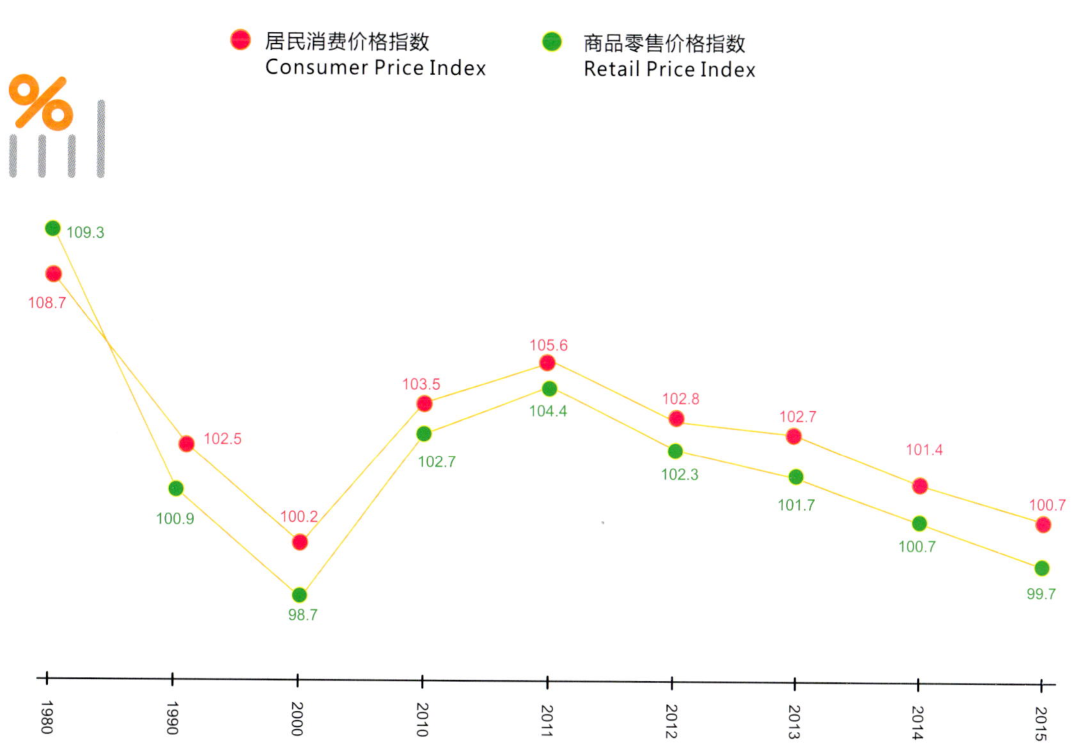

目　录

CONTENTS

一、综　合

GENERAL SURVEY

二、基本单位

BASIC UNIT

三、国民经济核算

NATIONAL ECONOMIC ACCOUNTS

四、人口、从业人员与职工工资

POPULATION EMPLOYMENT AND WAGES

五、固定资产投资

INVESTMENT IN FIXED ASSETS

六、财　政

GOVERNMENT FINANCE

七、物价指数

PRICE INDICES

八、人民生活

PEOPLE'S LIVELIHOOD

九、城市公用事业

URBAN PUBLIC UTLITIES

十、环境保护

ENVIRONMENT PROTECTION

十一、农　业
AGRICULTURE

十二、工　业

INDUSTRY

十三、能　源

ENERGY

十四、建筑业

CONSTRUCTION

十五、运输和邮电

TRANSPORT，POSTAL AND TELECOMMUNICATION SERVICE

十六、国内贸易

DOMESTIC TRADE

十七、对外经济贸易和旅游

FOREIGN TRADE AND ECONOMIC COOPERATION TOURISM

十八、服务业

TERTIARY INDUSTRY

十九、金融业

FINANCIAL INTERMEDIATION

二十、教育和科技

EDUCATION SCIENCE AND TECHNOLOGY

二十一、文化、体育、卫生、社会福利和其他

CULTURE, SPORTS, PUBLIC HEALTH, SOCIAL WELFARE INSTITUTIONS AND OTHER SOCIAL ACTIVITIES

二十二、企业调查

ENTERPRISES INVESTIGATION

西安市2015年国民经济和社会发展统计公报[1]

西安市统计局　国家统计局西安调查队

2016年3月4日

2015年，面对错综复杂的国际形势和艰巨繁重的国内改革发展稳定任务，市委、市政府坚持稳中求进工作总基调，主动适应引领新常态，全力推动中省市稳增长、调结构、促改革、惠民生、防风险各项政策落实，积极培育新机制、新动力，全市经济平稳较快发展、社会和谐稳定，实现了"十二五"圆满收官，为"十三五"经济社会发展和全面建成小康社会奠定了坚实基础。

一、综合

年末全市常住人口870.56万人，比上年末净增加7.81万人，其中，男性人口446.91万人，占51.3%；女性人口423.65万人，占48.7%，性别比为105.49（以女性为100，男性对女性的比例）。全年出生人口8.80万人，出生率为10.15‰；死亡人口4.78万人，死亡率为5.51‰；自然增长率为4.64‰。城镇人口635.68万人，占73.02%；乡村人口234.88万人，占26.98%。年末全市户籍总人口815.66万人，比上年增长0.05%。

初步核算，全年地区生产总值[2]（GDP）5810.03亿元，比上年增长8.2%。其中，第一产业增加值220.20亿元，增长5.0%；第二产业增加值2165.54亿元，增长6.8%；第三产业增加值3424.29亿元，增长9.5%。第一产业增加值占地区生产总值的比重为3.8%，第二产业增加值比重为37.3%，第三产业增加值比重为58.9%。

全年非公有制经济增加值3066.88亿元，占地区生产总值的比重为52.8%，比上年提高0.1个百分点。

图1　2011—2015年生产总值及其增长速度

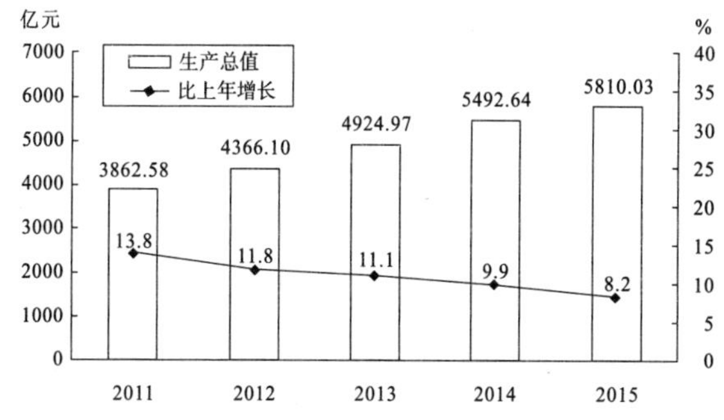

全年居民消费价格比上年上涨0.7%，其中，食品价格上涨0.5%。商品零售价格下降0.3%。工业生产者出厂价格下降1.5%。工业生产者购进价格下降5.5%。固定资产投资价格下降2.1%。新建住宅销售价格下降3.8%。

图2　2015年居民消费价格月度涨跌幅度

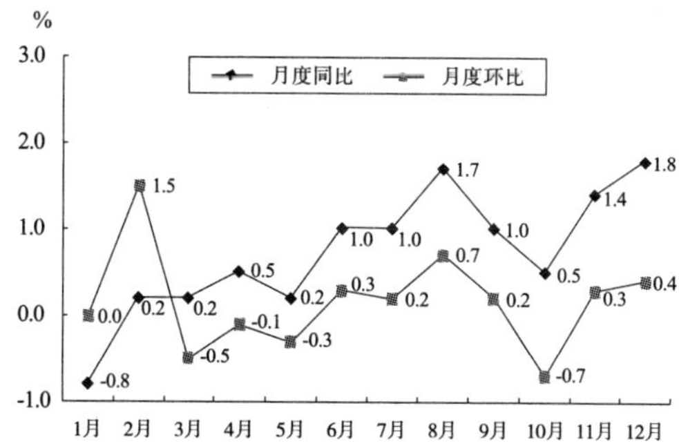

表1　2015年居民消费价格比上年涨跌幅度

指　标	涨跌幅度（%）
居民消费价格	0.7
食　品	0.5
其中：粮食	4.5
烟　酒	2.6
衣　着	3.3
家庭设备用品及维修服务	-0.3
医疗保健和个人用品	2.2
交通和通信	-1.2
娱乐教育文化用品及服务	1.3
居　住	-0.3

全年城镇新增就业12.85万人，城镇失业人员再就业5.80万人。年末城镇登记失业率为3.37%。

全年财政总收入1114.98亿元，比上年增长9.3%。全年地方财政一般公共预算收入650.99亿元，增长16.3%，其中，营业税下降5.3%，增值税、企业所得税和个人所得税分别增长0.8%、11.2%和22.6%。全年地方财政一般公共预算支出917.24亿元，比上年增长12.9%，其中，科学技术支出增长88.6%，城乡社区事务支出增长11.5%，社会保障和就业支出增长8.0%，节能环保支出增长55.9%，一般公共服务支出下降11.8%。

二、农业

全年粮食播种面积537.69万亩，比上年下降2.5%；油料播种面积6.83万亩，下降2.6%；蔬菜播种面积103.49万亩，增长1.9%；棉花播种面积0.33万亩，下降11.0%。全年粮食产量180.86万吨，比上年增长3.0%，其中，夏粮93.12万吨，增长5.8%；秋粮87.74万吨，增长0.2%。

表2　2015年主要农产品产量及其增长速度

产品名称	单位	产量	比上年增长（%）
粮食	万吨	180.86	3.0
油料	万吨	0.95	-3.1
蔬菜	万吨	332.79	5.2
瓜果	万吨	22.05	7.9
园林水果	万吨	105.20	5.6
肉类	万吨	16.13	-0.4
奶类	万吨	63.73	-3.1
禽蛋	万吨	14.02	3.7
大牲畜年末存栏数	万头	19.94	-8.2
#牛年末存栏数	万头	19.94	-7.8
猪年末存栏数	万头	92.49	-2.7
羊年末存栏数	万只	28.33	1.5
家禽年末存栏数	万只	1183.23	1.9

三、工业和建筑业

全年全部工业增加值1417.61亿元，比上年增长6.6%。规模以上工业增加值1174.67亿元，增长6.6%。在规模以上工业中，轻工业增加值290.09亿元，增长6.8%；重工业增加值884.58亿元，增长6.5%。

图3　2015年规模以上工业增加值增速（累计同比）

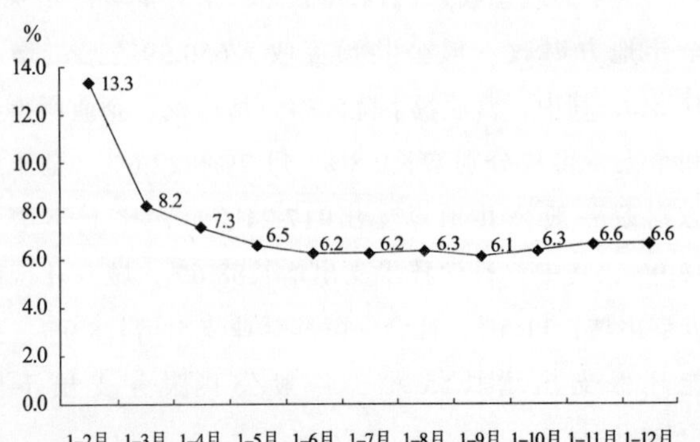

全年规模以上工业中，计算机、通信和其他电子设备制造业增加值比上年增长79.7%，仪器仪表制造业增长30.1%，汽车制造业下降10.1%，电气机械和器材制造业增长11.4%。六大高耗能行业[3]增长0.3%，其中，非金属矿物制品业增长13.0%，化学原料和化学制品制造业增长10.5%，有色金属冶炼和压延加工业增长16.5%，黑色金属冶炼和压延加工业下降1.0%，电力、热力生产和供应业下降4.1%，石油加工、炼焦和核燃料加工业下降58.6%。装备制造业[4]增加值增长10.1%，占规模以上工业增加值的比重为49.8%。

表3　2015年主要工业产品产量及其增长速度

产品名称	单位	产量	比上年增长（%）
发电量	亿千瓦小时	158.68	-11.6
原油加工量	万吨	28.16	-81.0
乳制品	万吨	107.01	-3.6
软饮料	万吨	269.24	31.3
商品混凝土	万立方米	2941.19	6.1
机制纸及纸板	万吨	12.22	8.7
交流电动机	万千瓦	671.02	-15.3
饲料	万吨	120.43	2.4
合成洗涤剂	万吨	9.07	-21.7
水泥	万吨	330.73	-19.8
风机	万台	0.98	66.5
汽车	万辆	34.14	-8.9
其中：轿车	万辆	24.01	-10.1
高压开关板	面	19037.00	-22.7
变压器	万千伏安	13583.25	-8.1
电力电缆	万千米	2.59	40.6
气体压缩机	万台	29.17	-28.9
电子元件	亿只	2.23	-10.0
单晶硅	吨	3412.13	7.2
集成电路圆片	万片	70.90	188.2

全年规模以上工业企业经济效益综合指数为283.6，比上年提高4.3个百分点。规模以上工业企业主营业务收入3683.70亿元，增长1.4%。实现利润总额

185.90亿元，增长10.9%。

全年全社会建筑业增加值770.28亿元，比上年增长7.4%。全市具有资质等级的总承包和专业承包建筑业企业实现总产值2650.41亿元，增长2.5%，其中，国有及国有控股企业2044.05亿元，增长5.2%；签订合同额6661.71亿元，增长15.8%；房屋建筑施工面积11979.16万平方米，增长7.1%。

图4　2011-2015年建筑业增加值及其增长速度

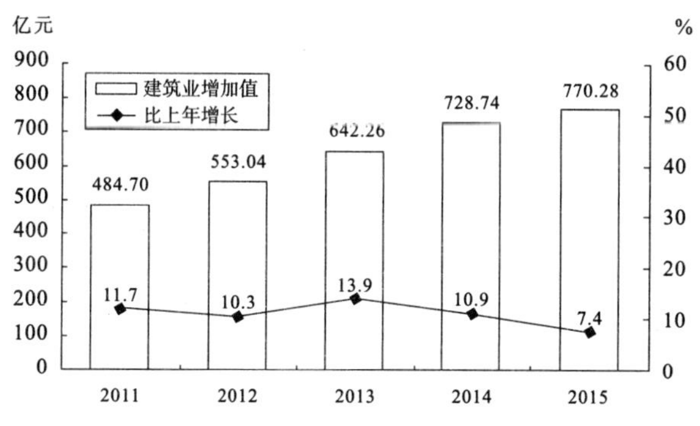

四、固定资产投资

全年全社会固定资产投资5165.98亿元，比上年下降12.5%，扣除价格因素，实际下降10.6%。其中，固定资产投资（不含农户）5086.93亿元，下降12.7%；农户投资79.05亿元，下降0.5%。

图5　2011—2015年全社会固定资产投资

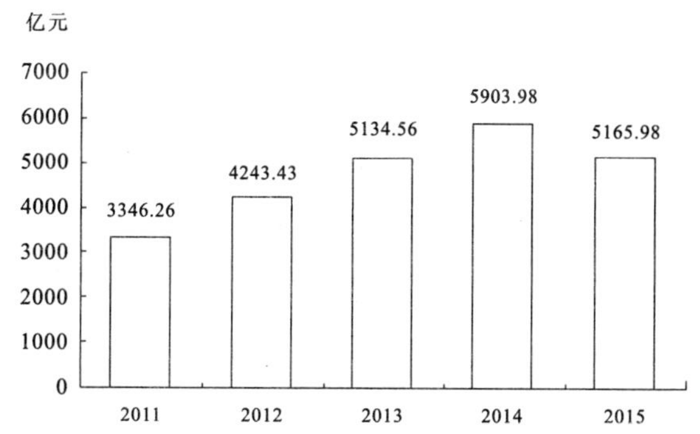

在固定资产投资（不含农户）中，第一产业投资99.78亿元，比上年增长32.8%；第二产业投资1158.30亿元，下降8.2%，其中，工业投资1135.87亿元，下降5.8%；第三产业投资3828.85亿元，下降14.7%。民间固定资产投资[5]2584.88亿元，下降16.1%，占固定资产投资（不含农户）的比重为50.8%。

表4　2015年主要行业固定资产投资（不含农户）及其增长速度

行　业	投资额（亿元）	比上年增长（%）
农、林、牧、渔业	117.29	36.3
制造业	1012.60	0.0
电力、热力、燃气及水的生产和供应业	123.30	-35.8
建筑业	22.44	-60.1
批发和零售业	144.77	-21.7
交通运输、仓储和邮政业	362.84	7.9
住宿和餐饮业	37.53	-58.6
信息传输、软件和信息技术服务业	108.21	58.0
房地产业	2351.70	-15.6
科学研究和技术服务业	33.62	-81.5
水利、环境和公共设施管理业	484.81	17.7
教育	88.72	6.1
卫生和社会工作	74.43	-22.8
文化、体育和娱乐业	36.47	2.1
公共管理和社会组织	23.16	-36.8

全年房地产开发投资1831.67亿元，比上年增长4.0%。其中，住宅投资1312.15亿元，下降1.7%；办公楼投资141.96亿元，增长69.0%；商业营业用房投资247.71亿元，增长17.9%。房屋施工面积13392.94万平方米，增长7.8%；房屋竣工面积976.64万平方米，下降36.3%。

表5　2015年房地产开发主要指标完成情况

指　标	单位	绝对量	比上年增长（%）
房地产开发投资	亿元	1831.67	4.0
其中：住宅	亿元	1312.15	-1.7
房屋施工面积	万平方米	13392.94	7.8
其中：住宅	万平方米	9777.23	0.5
房屋新开工面积	万平方米	2513.70	2.2
其中：住宅	万平方米	1458.14	-19.5
房屋竣工面积	万平方米	976.64	-36.3
其中：住宅	万平方米	766.58	-41.4

五、国内贸易

全年社会消费品零售总额3405.38亿元，比上年增长10.1%，扣除价格因素，实际增长10.4%。其中，限额以上企业（单位）消费品零售额2345.90亿元，增长4.5%，其中，限额以上企业（单位）网上零售额[6]

93.22亿元，增长112.8%。

按经营地统计，城镇消费品零售额3292.83亿元，增长9.9%；乡村消费品零售额112.55亿元，增长15.5%。按消费形态统计，商品零售额3146.45亿元，增长9.8%；餐饮收入额258.93亿元，增长13.2%。

图6 2015年社会消费品零售总额增速（累计同比）

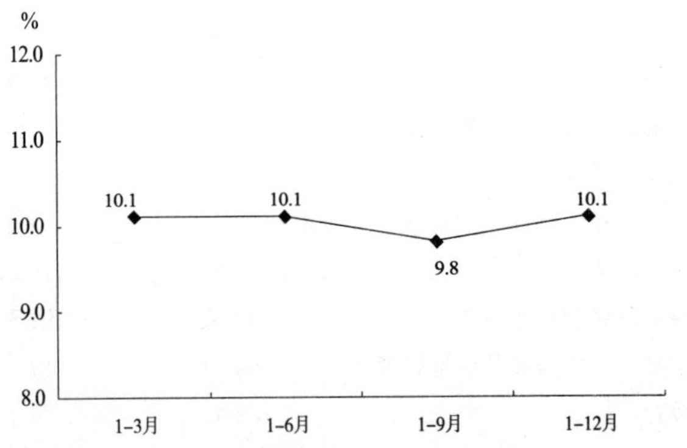

在限额以上企业（单位）商品零售额中，粮油、食品、饮料、烟酒类零售额比上年增长10.4%，服装、鞋帽、针、纺织品类增长6.0%，化妆品类增长5.5%，金银珠宝类下降5.7%，日用品类增长1.4%，体育、娱乐用品类增长28.9%，书报杂志类下降1.9%，家用电器和音像器材类增长16.9%，通讯器材类增长42.6%，家具类增长16.1%，石油及制品类下降3.2%，建筑及装潢材料类增长9.2%，汽车类下降3.3%。

六、对外经济

全年进出口总值1761.92亿元，比上年增长15.0%。其中，出口819.86亿元，增长11.6%；进口942.06亿元，增长18.1%。

在进出口总值中，加工贸易进出口1047.8亿元，增长14.3%，占进出口总额的59.5%；一般贸易进出口391.6亿元，增长1.5%，占进出口总额的22.2%。

主要进口商品有，机电产品进口772.7亿元，增长18.1%；精炼铜进口47.5亿元，增长2倍；矿砂进口22.8亿元，下降17.1%；医药品进口13.2亿元，增长18.9%。主要出口商品有，机电产品出口702.8亿元，增长20.6%；农产品出口19.8亿元，下降10.6%；纺织服装出口13.2亿元，下降7.4%；矿产品出口11.3亿元，下降33.1%。

全年批准外商直接投资项目73个，批准合同外资19.37亿美元，比上年下降24.1%；实际利用外商直接投资40.08亿美元，增长8.2%。

七、交通、邮电和旅游

全年货物运输总量4.63亿吨，比上年增长10.1%；货物运输周转量643.01亿吨公里，增长2.9%。旅客运输总量2.69亿人次，增长4.3%；旅客运输周转量324.15亿人公里，增长3.9%。

表6 2015年各种运输方式完成货物运输量及其增长速度

指标	单位	绝对数	比上年增长（%）
货物运输总量	万吨	46269.72	10.1
公路	万吨	45401	10.4
铁路	万吨	847.56	–5.8
民航（吞吐量）	万吨	21.16	13.5
货物运输周转量	亿吨公里	643.01	2.9
公路	亿吨公里	425.48	10.1
铁路	亿吨公里	216.40	–8.9
民航	亿吨公里	1.13	5.4

表7 2015年各种运输方式完成旅客运输量及其增长速度

指 标	单位	绝对数	比上年增长（%）
旅客运输总量	亿人次	2.69	4.3
公路	亿人次	1.96	1.8
铁路	亿人次	0.40	11.1
民航（吞吐量）	亿人次	0.33	12.7
旅客运输周转量	亿人公里	324.15	3.9
公路	亿人公里	108.89	2.0
铁路	亿人公里	68.41	–0.5
民航	亿人公里	146.84	7.6

年末全市机动车保有量239.41万辆，比上年末增长11.9%，其中，私人汽车保有量197.45万辆，增长15.8%。

全年邮政业务总收入30.70亿元,比上年增长43.5%。电信业务总收入134.37亿元，下降0.7%。年末全市固定电话用户292.08万户。移动电话用户1767.00万户，其中，4G移动电话用户[7]665.80万户。固定互联网宽带接入用户[8]289.39万户。

全年接待国内外游客13600.80万人次，比上年增长13.3%；旅游总收入1073.69亿元，增长13.0%。

八、金融

年末全市金融机构本外币存款余额18036.90亿元，比上年末增长14.4%。人民币存款余额17796.38亿元，增长14.0%，其中，住户存款余额6640.36亿元，增长6.1%。金融机构本外币贷款余额13965.64亿元，增长17.5%。人民币贷款余额13714.02亿元，增长17.5%。

全年证券市场各类证券交易总额53887.42亿元，比上年增长1.9倍。年末全市拥有上市股份公司32家，上市总股本415.65亿股，总市值5818.36亿元。

年末全市共有保险公司52家，其中，财产险25家，人寿险27家。保险专业中介机构116家。全年保费收入263.02亿元，比上年增长19.8%，其中，财产险保费收入83.55亿元，增长12.6%；人身险保费收入179.47亿元，增长23.5%。全年支付各类赔款给付87.62亿元，比上年增长8.5%，其中，财产险业务、人身险业务分别为40.65和46.97亿元，分别比上年增长9.0%和8.1%。

九、教育、科技、文化和体育

全市普通高校63所，在校学生75.75万人，毕业生20.72万人，另有研究生培养单位43个，在学研究生9.14万人，毕业生2.53万人；普通中学422所，在校学生41.37万人，毕业生13.92万人；小学1234所，在校学生56.62万人，毕业生7.85万人。小学、初中学龄人口入学率分别为99.98%和99.79%。

全年实施市级科技计划项目121项。重点扶持高新技术企业24家，支持建设农业科技示范园区22家。全年技术市场交易额657.44亿元。申请专利量60986件，专利授权量25103件。

全市博物馆113座，公共图书馆13个，群众艺术馆2个，文化馆14个，文化站183个。地市广播电视台2座，县级广播电视台6座。

全年举办各类群众体育展示表演和竞赛活动共计260项次，体育社团举办和承办体育赛事300项次，其中，国际性和全国性赛事25项次。新建城市社区全民健身器材配送工程91个，乡镇农民体育健身工程47个，新建和更新社区全民健身路径200个。全市新增社会体育指导员1627名。已有晨晚练点1600个，健身气功站点243个，在册练功人数8618人。

2015年，我市培养输送运动员参加国际、国内各项比赛获得金牌19枚、银牌16枚、铜牌13枚。

十、卫生和社会服务

年末全市共有各类卫生机构5802个，其中，医院295个，卫生院100个。各类卫生技术人员8.15万人，其中，执业（含助理）医师2.66万人。卫生机构床位5.47万张。

全市提供住宿的法定社会服务机构137个，床位2.5万张，年末收养人数1.4万人。年末城市低保对象3.3万户、5.9万人，发放低保金3.6亿元；农村低保对象4.3万户、13.1万人，发放低保金3.9亿元。4922人纳人农村五保供养[9]，发放供养金3655万元。全年民政部门直接医疗救助3.45万人次。

十一、人民生活和社会保障

全年全市居民人均可支配收入27845元，比上年名义增长8.77%，扣除价格因素实际增长8.01%。其中，城镇常住居民人均可支配收入33188元，比上年名义增长8.05%，扣除价格因素实际增长7.30%；农村常住居民人均可支配收入14072元，比上年名义增长9.10%，扣除价格因素实际增长8.34%。

年末全市城镇基本医疗保险参保人数419.52万人；城镇企业职工养老保险参保人数335.37万人；失业保险参保人数149.62万人；工伤保险参保人数149.22万人；职工生育保险参保人数110.04万人。年末农村新型合作医疗参保人数406.11万人，实际参合率99.22%。

十二、城市建设、环境和安全生产

全年完成市政公用设施投资392.70亿元。新建人行天桥8座，建设公交港湾65处，新建改造绿地广场60个。

全年城市环境空气质量好于国家二级标准（良好）以上的天数251天。二氧化硫年平均浓度为24微克/标立方米，比上年下降25.0%；二氧化氮年平均浓度为44微克/标立方米，下降6.4%；可吸入颗粒物年平均浓度为125微克/标立方米，下降15.0%。全市集中式饮用水源地的水质达标率为100%。区域环境噪声等效声级均值为54.7分贝，道路交通噪声等效声级均值为68.3分贝。

全年共发生各类安全生产事故[10]1260起，死亡195人，受伤620人，直接财产损失1972.02万元。

注释：

［1］本公报数据为初步统计数，部分数据因四舍五入的原因，存在着分项与合计不等的情况。

［2］生产总值、各产业增加值绝对数按现价计算，增长速度按不变价格计算。2013年地区生产总值及分行业增加值数据为第三次经济普查结果，以前年度未经修订；2014年数据为2014年年报最终核实数据。

［3］六大高耗能行业包括化学原料和化学制品制

造业，非金属矿物制品业，黑色金属冶炼和压延加工业，有色金属冶炼和压延加工业，石油加工炼焦和核燃料加工业，电力、热力生产和供应业。

[4] 装备制造业包括金属制品业，通用设备制造业，专用设备制造业，汽车制造业，铁路、船舶、航空航天和其他运输设备制造业，电气机械和器材制造业，计算机、通信和其他电子设备制造业，仪器仪表制造业，金属制品、机械和设备修理业。

[5] 民间固定资产投资是指具有集体、私营、个人性质的内资企事业单位以及由其控股（包括绝对控股和相对控股）的企业单位建造或购置固定资产的投资。

[6] 限额以上企业（单位）网上零售额是指限额以上企业（单位）通过公共网络交易平台（包括自建网站和第三方平台）实现的消费品零售额。

[7] 4G是指第四代移动通信系统（the 4th Generation mobile communication technology，简称4G），4G移动电话用户是指报告期末在计费系统拥有使用信息、占用4G网络资源的在网用户。

[8] 固定互联网宽带接入用户是指报告期末在电信企业登记注册，通过xDSL、FTTx+LAN、FTTH/0以及其他宽带接入方式和普通专线接入公众互联网的用户。

[9] 农村五保供养是指老年、残疾和未满16周岁的村民，无劳动能力、无生活来源又无法定赡养、抚养、扶养义务人，或者其法定赡养、抚养、扶养义务人无赡养、抚养、扶养能力的村民，在吃、穿、住、医、葬方面得到的生活照顾和物质帮助。

[10] 安全生产事故包括道路交通事故、火灾事故、农机事故和工矿商贸事故。

资料来源：本公报中物价数据来自国家统计局西安调查队；城镇新增就业、登记失业率、社会保障数据来自西安市人力资源和社会保障局；财政数据来自市财政局；进出口数据来自西安海关；利用外资数据来自市商务局；铁路运输数据来自西安铁路局；公路运输数据来自市交通运输局；民航运输数据来自西安咸阳国际机场；机动车数据来自市车管所；邮政业务数据来自市邮政局；电信数据来自中国移动西安分公司、中国电信西安分公司、中国联通西安分公司、陕西铁通西安分公司；旅游数据来自市旅游局；货币金融数据来自中国人民银行西安分行营业管理部；证券数据、保险业数据来自市金融办；教育数据来自市教育局；科技数据来自市科技局；艺术表演团体、公共图书馆、文化馆、广播、电视数据来自市文化广电新闻出版局；博物馆数据来自市文物局；体育数据来自市体育局；卫生、新农合数据来自市卫计委；社会服务、低保和五保供养数据来自市民政局；城市建设数据来自市城乡建设委员会；环境监测数据来自市环境保护局；安全生产数据来自市安全生产监督管理局；其他数据均来自市统计局。

Statistical Communique of Xi'an City on 2015 National Economic and Social Development [1]

Xi'an Municipal Bureau of Statistics and NBS Survey Office in Xi' an

Mar.1st, 2016

In 2015, faced with the complicated international situation and huge domestic tasks related to reform, development and stability, the Municipal Party Committee and Municipal Government of Xi'an insisted on the tone of maintaining stability of overall the work, strove to improve the quality and efficiency of economic operation, initiatively adapted to the new normal and guided it, strove to promote the practice of plan on steady growth, restructuring, promoting the reform, benefiting people' s livelihood and risk prevention, actively cultivated new mechanism and driving force. The city' s economic maintained a steady and fast growth while society maintained harmonious and steady. The successful ending of the 12th Five-Year Plan was achieved and laid a solid foundation for the 13th Five-Year economic and social development and building moderately prosperous society in all respects.

I. General Outlook

The resident population of Xi' an city at the end of 2015 was 8.7056 million, up by 78.1 thousand against the previous year, 4.4691 million male and 4.2365 million female, accounted for 51.3 percent and 48.7 percent respectively. The sex ratio was 105.49 (granted the female was 100) . The born population in the whole year was 88.0 thousand, and the birth rate was 10.15‰ ; the death population in the whole year was 47.8 thousand, and the death rate was 5.51‰; the natural growth rate was 4.64‰. The urban population was 6.3568 million, accounted for 73.02 percent; the rural population was 2.3488 million, accounted for 26.98 percent. The total household population was 8.1566 million, up by 0.05 percent by previous year .

In 2015, the gross domestic product [2] (GDP) preliminarily estimated was 581.003 billion Yuan, up by 8.2 percent against the previous year. Analyzed by different industries, the value added of the primary industry was 22.020 billion Yuan, up by 5.0 percent; the value added of the secondary industry was 216.554 billion Yuan, a rise of 6.8 percent; and the value added of the tertiary industry was 342.429 billion Yuan, up by 9.5 percent. The value added of the primary industry accounted for 3.8 percent of the GDP, that of the secondary industry accounted for 37.3 percent, the tertiary industry accounted for 58.9 percent.

The value added of non-public sectors of the economy is 306.688 billion, accounted for the proportion of GDP is 52.8 an increase of 0.1 percent over the previous year .

Table 1 the GDP and Growth Rate between 2011–2015

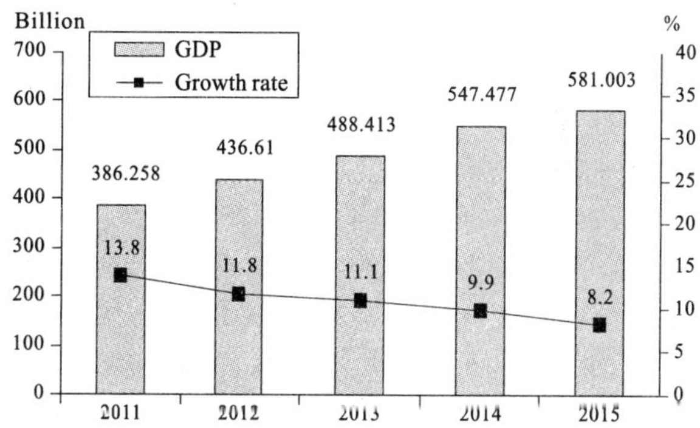

The general level of consumer prices in Xi'an was up by 0.7 percent against the previous year. Of this total, the prices for food went up by 0.5 percent. The retail prices for commodities went down by 0.3 percent. The producer prices for manufactured goods went down by 1.5 percent. The purchasing prices for manufactured goods went down by 5.5 percent. The fixed asset investment price went down by 2.1 percent and the price of newly founded house decreased by 3.8 percent.

Table 2 The rate of increase and decrease of CPI in 2015

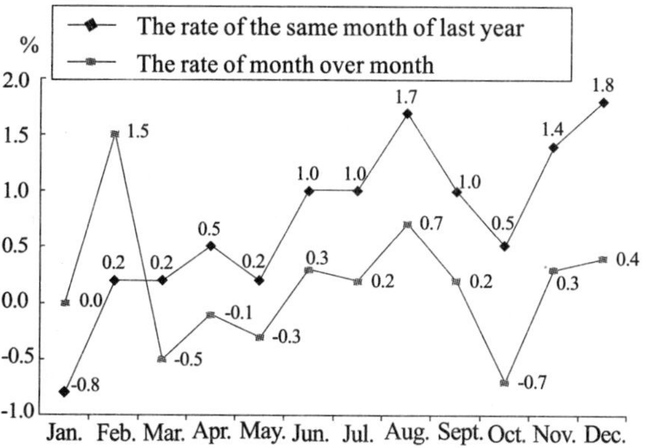

Sheet 1 Up and fall extent of Residents Consumer Price Indices with previous year (2015)

Item	2015(%)
Consumer Price Index	0.7
Food	0.5
#Grain	4.5
Tobacco and liquor	2.6
Clothing	3.3
Household facilities and maintaining services	-0.3
Medical, Health and Personal Articles	2.2
Transportation and Communication	-1.2
Recreation, Education and Cultural articles and Services	1.3
Residence	-0.3

In 2015, the newly increased employees in urban areas in Xi'an numbered 128.5 thousand. The number of reemployment of laid-off workers was 58.0 thousand, the urban unemployment rate through unemployment registration was 3.37 percent at the end of 2015.

The financial revenue totalled 111.498 billion Yuan, an increase of 9.3 percent compared with the previous year. The General Budget Revenue of Regional Finance reached 65.099 billion Yuan, up by 16.3 percent. Of this, business tax was down by 5.3 percent, the value added tax, income tax of enterprises and individual income tax were up by 0.8 percent, 11.2 percent and 22.6 percent respectively. The General Budget Expenditure of Regional Finance totalled 91.724 billion Yuan, up by 12.9 percent. Of this total expenditure, the expenditure on technology and science was up by 88.6 percent; that on urban and rural community affairs was up by 11.5 percent, that on social security and employment was up by 8.0 percent, that on environmental protection was up by 55.9 percent, that on general public service w ent d own 1 1.8 p ercent

II. Agricultur e

In 2015, the sown area of grain was 5376.9 thousand mu, a decrease of 2.5 percent compared with the previous year; the sown area of oil-bearing crops was 68.3 thousand mu, a decrease of 2.6 percent; the sown area of vegetables was 1034.9 thousand mu, up by 1.9 percent; the sown area of cotton was 3.3 thousand mu, a decrease of 11.0 percent. The total output of grain in 2015 was 1.8086 million tons, an increase of 3.0 percent. Of this, the output of summer crops was 0.9312 million tons, went up by 5.8 percent, and that of the autumn grain was 0.8774 million tons, an increase of 0.2 percent.

Sheet 2 Mail Product of Agriculture Production in 2015

Name of Product	Units	Output	Increase over the last year (%)
Grain	10,000 tons	180.86	3.0
Oil	10,000 tons	0.95	-3.1
Vegetable	10,000 tons	332.79	5.2
Melon	10,000 tons	22.05	7.9
Fruit	10,000 tons	105.20	5.6
Meat	10,000 tons	16.13	-0.4
Milk	10,000 tons	63.73	-3.1
Poultry eggs	10,000 tons	14.02	3.7
Year-end Cattle on hand	10,000 head	19.94	-8.2
#Year-end Ox on hand	10,000 head	19.94	-7.8
Year-end Pig on hand	10,000 head	92.49	-2.7
Year-end Sheep on hand	10,000 head	28.33	1.5
Year-end Fowl on hand	10,000 head	1183.23	1.9

III. Industry and Construction

In 2015, the value added by the industrial sectors was 141.761 billion Yuan, up by 6.6 percent over the previous year. The value added of industrial enterprises above the designated size was 117.467 billion Yuan, up by 6.6 percent. Of this, the value added of the light industry was 29.009 billion Yuan, up by 6.8 percent; that of the heavy industry was 88.458 billion Yuan up by 6.5 percent.

Table 3 Growth of Above-scale Industrial added Value in 2015

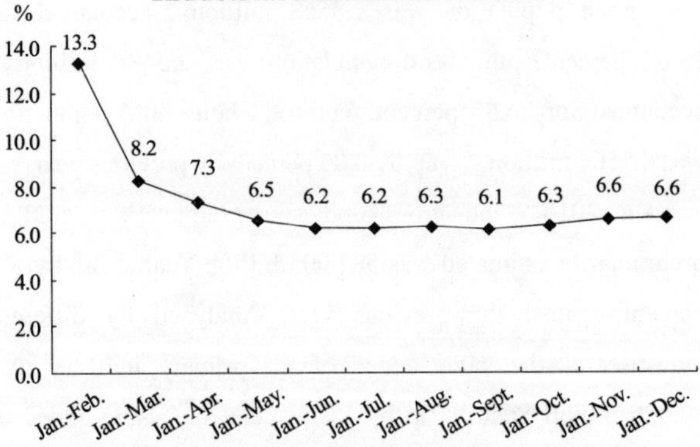

In 2015, of the industrial enterprises above designated size, the growth of value added for manufacture of

computer, communication and other electrical devices was up by 79.7 percent over the previous year; for manufacture of instruments up by 30.1 percent; for manufacture of car down by 10.1 percent; for manufacture of electrical machinery and equipment up by 11.4 percent. The growth of the value added for the major six high energy consuming industries [3] were 0.3 percent, of which, that of the manufacture of non-metallic mineral products was up by 13.0 percent, manufacture of raw chemical materials and chemical products up by 10.5 percent, smelting and pressing of ferrous metals up by 16.5 percent, smelting and pressing of non-ferrous metals down by 1.0 percent, production and supply of electric power and heat power down by 4.1 percent and 58.6 percent decrease for processing of petroleum, coking, processing of nuclear fuel. The growth of value added for equipment manufacturing industry [4] was up by 10.1 percent, accounted for 49.8 percent of the added value for industrial enterprises above designated s ize.

Sheet 3 Output of Major Industrial Products above designated size in Xi' an(2015)

Name of Product	Units	Output	Increase over the last year (%)
Electricity	100 million kilo watt-hour	156.68	-11.6
Crude Oil Processing	10,000 tons	28.16	-81.0
Dairy	10,000 tons	107.01	-3.6
Soft Drink	10,000 tons	269.24	31.3
Commercial Concrete	10,000 cubic meter	2941.19	6.1
Machine-made paper and Cardboard	10,000 tons	12.22	8.7
AC motors	10,000 Kilowatt	671.02	-15.3
Feed	10,000 tons	120.43	2.4
Synthetic deter gent	10,000 tons	9.07	-21.7
Cement	10,000 tons	330.73	-19.8
Draught fan	10,000 units	0.98	66.5
Motor vehicle	10,000 units	34.14	-8.9
#Car	10,000 units	24.01	-10.1
High voltage switch board	unit	19037.00	-22.7
Transformer	10,000 kilovolt amperes	13583.25	-8.1
Electric cable	10,000 km	2.59	40.6
Gas compressor	10,000 units	29.17	-28.9
Electronic component	100 million units	2.23	-10.0
Mono-crystalline silicon	ton	3412.13	7.2
Integrated circuit chip	10,000 chips	70.90	188.2

The composite index on economic benefits of the industrial enterprises above the designated size in 2015 was 283.6, an increase of 4.3 percent over the previous year. The main business income of the industrial enterprises above designated size is 368.370 billion Yuan, up by 1.4 percent over the previous year. The profit was 18.590 billion Yuan, up by 10.9 percent.

In 2015, the added value by construction sector was 77.028 billion Yuan, increased 7.4 percent over the pervious year. The total output value created by qualified contractors and professional building contractor companies was 265.041 billion Yuan, increased by 2.5 percent. Of it, the output of State-owned and State holding Corporations was 204.405 billion Yuan, increased by 5.2 percent; contract amount was 666.171 billion Yuan, increased by 15.8 percent; the housing construction area was 119.7916 million square meter, increased by 7.1 percent.

Table 4 the value added of construction and growth rate between 2011-2015

IV. Investment in F ixed Assets

The completed investment in fixed assets of the city in 2015 was 516.598 billion Yuan, down by 12.5 percent over the previous year. The real decline was 10.6 percent after deducting the price factors. Of the total investment in urban areas was 508.693 billion Yuan, down by 12.7 percent. Farmers' investment was 7.905 billion Yuan, down by 0.5 percent.

Table 5 Fixed Asset Investment of the city in 2015

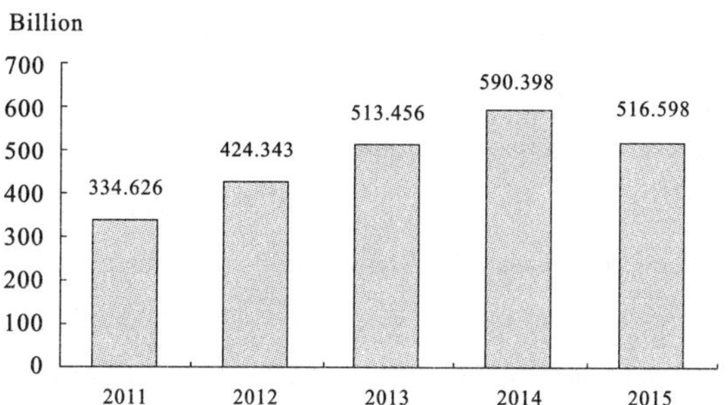

In whole investment, the investment in the primary industry was 9.978 billion Yuan, up by 32.8 percent against the previous year, in the secondary industry, it was 115.830 billion Yuan, down by 8.2 percent, of which industrial investment was 113.587 billion Yuan, down by 5.8 percent; in the tertiary industry, it was 382.885 billion Yuan, down by 14.7 percent. Private investment in fixed assets [5] was 258.488 billion Yuan, down by 16.1 percent, accounted for 50.8 percent of investment in fixed assets.

Sheet 4 the investment in fixed assets and growth rate in main industries in 2015

Industries	Investment (100 million Yuan)	Growth rate (%)
Agriculture, Forestry, Animal husbandry and fishery	117.29	36.3
Manufacturing	1012.60	0.0
Electricity, heat, gas and water production and supply industry	123.30	-35.8
Construction industry	22.44	-60.1
Wholesale and retail trade	144.77	-21.7
Transportation, storage and postal services	362.84	7.9
Hotels and catering services	37.53	-58.6
Information transmission, computer services and software industry	108.21	58.0
Real estate industry	2351.70	-15.6
Accommodation and catering industry	33.62	-81.5
Water Conservancy, environment and public facilities administration industry	484.81	17.7
Education	88.72	6.1
Sanitations, social security and social welfare	74.43	-22.8
Culture, sports and entertainment	36.47	2.1
Public administration and social organizations	23.16	-36.8

In 2015, the investment in real estate development was 183.167 billion Yuan, up by 4.0 percent. Of this, housing investment was 131.215 Yuan, down by 1.7 percent, office building investment was 14.196 billion Yuan, up by 69.0 percent; commercial and business building investment was 24.771 billion Yuan, up by 17.9 percent. Housing construction area was 133.9294 million square meters, up by 7.8 percent; floor space of commercial houses completed was 9.7664 million square meters, decreased by 36.3 percent.

Sheet 5 Mail Indicators of Real estate development and sales in 2015

Item	Units	Absolute Number	Increase over the last year(%)
Investment in Real Estate Development	100 million Yuan	1831.67	4.0
#Residential Building	100 million Yuan	1312.15	-1.7
Floor Space of Commercial Houses Construction	10,000 sq.m	13392.94	7.8
# Residential Building	10,000 sq.m	9777.23	0.5
Floor Space of Newly Construction	10,000 sq.m	2513.70	2.2
# Residential Building	10,000 sq.m	1458.14	-19.5
Floor Space of Commercial Houses Completed	10,000 sq.m	976.64	-36.3
# Residential Building	10,000 sq.m	766.58	-41.4

V. Domestic T rade

In 2015, the total retail sales of consumer goods reached 340.538 billion Yuan, a growth of 10.1 percent over the previous year or a real growth of 10.4 percent after deducting price factors. Of this, the total retail sales by wholesale and retail enterprises above designated size was 234.590 billion Yuan, up by 4.5 percent, of which the online sales by wholesale and retail enterprises [6] above designated size was 9.322 billion Yuan up by 1 12.8 percent.

An analysis on different areas showed that the retail sales of consumer goods in urban areas stood at 329.283 billion Yuan, up by 9.9 percent, and that in rural areas reached 11.255 billion Yuan, up by 15.5 percent. Grouped by consumption patterns, the income of retail sales of commodities was 314.645 billion Yuan, up by 9.8 percent; that of catering industry was 25.893 billion Yuan, up by 13.2 percent.

Table 6 The total retail sales of social consumer goods growth rate in 2015

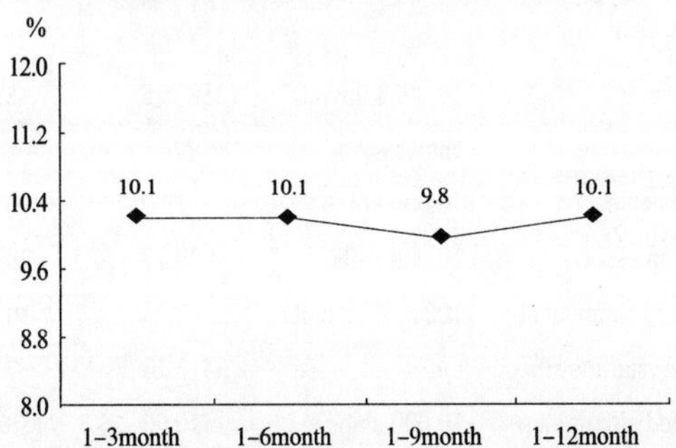

Of the total retail sales by wholesale and retail enterprises above designated size, the sales of food, beverage, wine and cigarette was up by 10.4 percent; clothing, shoes, hats and needle textiles up by 6.0 percent; cosmetics up by 5.5 percent; gold, silver and jewelry down by 5.7 percent; daily necessities up by 1.4 percent; sports-recreation up by 28.9 percent; books, newspapers and magazines down by 1.9 percent; electric and electronic appliances for household use and audio-video equipment up by 16.9 percent; telecommunication equipment up by 42.6 percent; furniture increased by 16.1 percent; oil and oil products down by 3.2 percent; building decoration materials up by 9.2 percent and motor vehicles down by 3.3 percent.

VI. Foreign Economic Relations

In 2015, the total value of imports and exports reached 176.192 billion Yuan, up by 15.0 percent over the previous year. Of this, the value of exports was 81.986 billion Yuan, up by 11.6 percent, and that of imports was 94.206 billion Yuan, increased by 18.1 percent.

In total imports and exports, the value of processing trade was 104.78 billion Yuan, up by 14.3 percent, accounted for 59.5 percent of import and export whole value of Xi' an region. The value of imports and exports of general trade was 39.16 billion Yuan, increased by 1.5 percent, accounted for 22.2 percent of import and export whole value of Xi' an region.

Among the main import commodities, the value of imports of electromechanical products was 77.27 billion Yuan, up by 18.1 percent; the value of imports of refined copper was 4.75 billion Yuan, up by 200 percent; the value of imports of ore sand was 2.28 billion Yuan, down by 17.1 percent; the value of imports of medical products was 1.32 billion Yuan, up by 18.9 percent. Among the main export commodities, the value of exports of electromechanical products was 70.28 billion Yuan, up by 20.6 percent; the value of exports of agricultural product was 1.98 billion Yuan, a decrease of 10.6 percent; the value of exports of textile products was 1.32 billion Yuan, a decrease of 7.4 percent; the value of exports of mineral products was 1.13 billion Yuan, down by 33.1 percent.

In 2015, there were 73 foreign direct investment projects approved in Xi'an and the contracted foreign direct investment was 1.937 billion US dollars, a decrease of 24.1 percent compared with the previous year; the realized foreign direct investment was 4.008 billion US dollars, up by 8.2 percent.

VII. Transportation, Post, Telecommunications and Tourism

In 2015, the total freight traffic reached 463 million ton, up by 10.1 percent over the previous year. The total goods transportation turnover reached 64.301 billion ton-kilometers, up by 2.9 percent over the previous year. The Total passenger transport reached 269 million, up by 4.3 percent over the previous year. The passenger transport turnover reached 32.415 billion person-kilometers, up by 3.9 percent over the previous year .

Sheet 6 The Total Freight Traffic and growth rate created by Kinds of transport Mode in 2015

Index	Unit	Amount	Growth rate (%)
The Total Freight Traffic	10,000 t ons	46269.72	10.1
Highway	10,000 t ons	45401	10.4
Railway	10,000 t ons	847.56	-5.8
Airway	10,000 t ons	21.16	13.5
Goods Transportation Turnover	100 m illion t on-kilometers	643.01	2.9
Highway	100 m illion t on-kilometers	425.48	10.1
Railway	100 m illion t on-kilometers	216.40	-8.9
Airway	100 m illion t on-kilometers	1.13	5.4

Sheet 7 The Total Passenger Traffic and growth rate created by Kinds of transport Mode in 2015

Index	Unit	Amount	Growth rate (%)
The Total Passenger	100 million person	2.69	4.3
Highway	100 million person	1.96	1.8
Railway	100 million person	0.40	11.1
Airway	100 million person	0.33	12.7
The passenger transport turnover	100 million person-kilometers	324.15	3.9
Highway	100 million person-kilometers	108.89	2.0
Railway	100 million person-kilometers	68.41	-0.5
Airway	100 million person-kilometers	146.84	7.6

The total number of motor vehicles for civilian use reached 2394.1 thousand by the end of 2015, up by 11.9 percent, of which private-owned vehicles numbered 1974.5 thousand, up by 15.8 percent. The revenue of post services totaled 3.070 billion Yuan, an increase of 43.5 percent over the previous year. That of telecommunication services was 13.437 billion Yuan, down by 0.7 percent. At the end of 2015, there were 2.9208 million fixed telephone users; there were 17.6700 million mobile phone users, of which the number of telecom and China Unicom 4G mobile phone users [7] was 6.6580 million. The number of fixed Internet broadband access users [8] was 2.8939 million.

The total of domestic and foreign tourists was 136.0080 million person-times, up by 13.3 percent. The revenue from tourism totaled 107.369 billion Yuan up by 13.0 percent.

VIII. F inancial Intermediation

Savings deposit in RMB and foreign currencies in all items of financial institutions totaled 1803.690 billion Yuan at the end of 2015, an increase of 14.4 percent compared with the end of the previous year. The savings deposit in RMB stood at 1779.638 billion Yuan, an increase of 14.0 percent, of which the household deposit was 664.036 billion Yuan, up by 6.1 percent. Loans in all items of financial institutions in RMB and foreign currencies reached 1396.564 billion Yuan, an increase of 17.5 percent as compared with the end of the previous year. The loans in RMB stood at 1371.402 billion Yuan, an increase of 17.5 percent.

The trading volume of stock exchange market was 5388.742 billion Yuan in 2015, an increase of 190 percent compared with the previous year. There were 32 listed companies in Xi'an at the end of 2015 of which the total capital stock was 41.565 billion shares, and the total market value was 581.836 billion Yuan.

By the end of 2015, there were 52 insurance institutions, of which the number of property insurance was 25, and that of life insurance was 27. There were 116 intermediary organs of insurance. The received by the insurance companies totaled 26.302 billion Yuan in 2015, up by 19.8 percent. Of this, the revenue from property insurance was 8.355 billion Yuan, up by 12.6 percent; that from life insurance was 17.947 billion Yuan, up by 23.5 percent. In total, insurance companies paid an indemnity worth of 8.762 billion Yuan, up by 8.5 percent over the previous year, of which the worth of property insurance and life insurance were 4.065 billion Yuan and 4.697 billion Yuan respectively, up by 9.0 percent and 8.1 percent respectively .

IX. Education、 Science& Technology and Cultur e

There were 63 general universities and colleges, with 757.5 thousand general tertiary education enrollments, including 207.2 thousand graduates; there were 43 post-graduate training units, with 91.4 thousand students in school and 25.3 thousand graduates. There were 422 general middle schools and high schools, with 413.7 thousand junior high education enrollments and 139.2 thousand graduates; there were 1234 primary schools, with 566.2 thousand primary education enrollments and 78.5 thousand graduates. The enrollment rates for school-age population of primary school and junior high school were 99.98 percent and 99.79 percent respectively.

121 science and technology projects were carried out in 2015. 24 high-tech enterprises were supported especially and 22 agricultural science and technology model gardens were supported to be constructed. The turnover in technology market reached 65.744 billion Yuan. 60986 patents were applied in 2015, including of 25103 patents accredited.

By the end of 2015, there were 113 museums, 13 public libraries, 2 mass art museums, 14 cultural centers, 183 culture stations. There were 2 city radio and television stations and county radio and television stations.

260 mass sports performances and competition activities were organized in 2015, and 300 sports competition were organized and host by sports associations, including 25 international and national sports competition. In 2015, there were 91 newly built fitness projects, 47 fitness projects for township farmers, and 200 public national fitness paths of community built. The number of social sports instructors had increased 1627. There were 1600 sites for morning and evening exercise and 243 sites for fitness Qigong, with 8618 taking part in fitness Qigong.

In 2015, the delegation of Xi'an won 19 gold medals、16 silver medals and 13 bronze medal in the National and international Games.

X. Health and P ublic Service

At the end of 2015, there were 5802 health institutions in Xi'an, including 295 general hospitals and 100 health centers. There were all 81.5 thousand health care workers, including 26.6 thousand practicing (assistant) doctors. General health centers in Xi'an possessed 54.7 thousand beds. There were 137 social welfare adoption class units, with a total of 25 thousand beds, and 14 thousand people were in them at the end of the year. There were 33 thousand of urban low-income households, with 59 thousand people, and 360 million Yuan were distributed to them. There were 43 thousand of village low-income households, with 131 thousand people, and 390 million Yuan were distributed to them. 4922 people were in the rural five guarantees [9] and 36.55 million Yuan were distributed. 34.5 thousand people gained medical relief directly from civil af fairs departments in 2015.

XI. Living Conditions and Social Security

In 2015, the annual per capita disposable income of all the city residents in Xi'an was 27845 Yuan, growth of 8.77 percent over the previous year, or a real increase of 8.01 percent when the factors of price increase were deducted. That of urban households was 33188 Yuan, growth of 8.05 percent over the previous year, or a real increase of 7.30 percent when the factors of price increase were deducted. And that of rural households was 14072 Yuan, growth of 9.10 percent over the previous year, or a real increase of 8.34 percent. By the end of 2015, a total of 4.1952 million people participated in urban basic health insurance program; a total of 3.3537 million people participated in basic pension program for staff and workers of enterprises; a total of 1.4962 million people participated in unemployment insurance programs; a total of 1.4922 million people participated in work accident insurance; a total of 1.1004 million people participated in maternity insurance programs for staff and workers. The number of farmers taking part in the new cooperative medical care system in rural areas reached 4.0611 million, with a participation rate of 99.22 percent covered.

XII. Urban Construction, Environment and W ork Safety

The total investment of municipal utilities was 39.270 billion Yuan. 8 pedestrian bridges, and 65 bus bays were newly built. 60 green squares were reformed and newly built.

In 2015, there were 251 days with air quality better than standard Grade II. The annual mean concentration of Sulfur dioxide, Nitrogen dioxide and respirable particulate matter was 0.024 Mg / cu.m, 0.044 Mg / cu.m and 0.125 Mg / cu.m, a decrease by 25.0 percent, 6.4 percent and 15.0 percent. All of water quality of reference water source reached the state standard. The average value of sound level equivalent of regional environmental noises was 54.7 decibel, and the average value of sound level equivalent of transportation noises was 68.3 decibel.

In 2015, various kinds of work accidents [10] amounted to 1260. Of this, there were 195 people dead and 620 people injured, the property losses was 19.7202 million Yuan.

Notes:

1. All figures in this Communique are preliminary statistics.

2. Gross domestic product (GDP) and value added as quoted in this Communique are calculated at current prices, whereas their growth rates are at constant prices. The statics of Gross Regional Product and added value of industries in 2013 were results of the third economic census, and statics in previous years without revision .Statics in 2014 were finally vertified r esults in annual r eport.

3. Six highly energy-consuming industries are: manufacture of raw chemical materials and chemical products, manufacture of non-metallic mineral products, smelting and pressing of ferrous metals, smelting and pressing of non-ferrous metals, oil processing, coking and nuclear fuel processing, and pr oduction and supply of electricity and heat.

4.Equipment manufacturing industry includes metal products industry, general equipment manufacturing industry, special equipment manufacturing industry, automobile manufacturing, railway, marine, aerospace and other transportation equipment manufacturing, electrical machinery and equipment manufacturing, computer, communications and other electronic equipment manufacturing, instrumentation manufacturing, metal products, machinery and equipment r epair industry .

5.Private investment in fixed assets is the construction or purchase of fixed assets investment by collective, private and individual domestic enterprises or institutions and enterprise units by its holdings (including absolute holdings and relative holdings).

6.Online sales by wholesale and retail enterprises above designated size are the wholesale and retail sales of consumer goods realized by enterprises above designated size through the public network trading platform (including self built website and the thir d-party platform).

7. 4G refers to the 4th Generation mobile communication technology(referred to as \ " 4G\"), the 4G mobile phone users refers to those who own using information in the billing system of the final report, and take up the 4G network resources in the network.

8.Fixed Internet broadband access users are people who have the registration of Telecom Enterprises at the end of the reporting period and access to the public Internet by xDSL、FTTx+LAN、FTTH/0 or other broadband access ways and common line access.

9. Rural five guarantees refer to the elderly, disabled, and those under the age of 16 villages, without labor ability, the source of life, and have no fixed support, raising, the obligation of maintenance, or its legal support, raising, the obligation of maintenance support, raising, the villages of bring up ability, who gain help in the car e of life and material.

10. Work accidents include traffic accidents, fire accidents, agricultural machinery accidents, mines and commercial and trade accidents.

Data Sour ces:

In this communique, data of price are from NBS Survey Office in Xi'an; data of newly increased employed people, unemployment rate through unemployment registration and social security are from the Xi'an Municipal Bureau of Human Resources and Social Security; financial data are from the Xi'an Municipal Bureau of Finance; data of imports and exports are from the Xi'an Customs; data of utilizing foreign capital are from the Xi'an Municipal Bureau of Business; data of railway transportation are from the Xi'an Municipal Bureau of Railways; data of highway transportation are from the Xi'an Municipal Bureau of Transport; data of air transport are from the Xi'an-Xian yang International Airport; data of motor vehicles for civilian use are from the Xi'an vehicle administration; data of post services are from the Xi'an Municipal Bureau of post; data of telecommunications are from Xi'an branch of China Mobile、China Unicom、China Telecom, and Shaanxi CTT; data of tourism are from the Xi'an Tourism Administration; data of monetary and financial are from business management department for Xi'an branch of the People's Bank of China; data of listed companies and insurance are from Xi'an Municipal Finance Office; data of education are from the Xi'an Municipal Bureau of Education; data of technology are from Xi'an Municipal Bureau of Technology; data of art-performing groups, public libraries, culture centers, radio and television are from the Xi'an Municipal Bureau of Culture, Radio, Press and Publication; data of museum are from Xi'an Municipal Bureau of Heritage; data of sports are from the Xi'an Municipal Bureau of Sport; data of health and new cooperative medical care system in rural areas are from the Xi'an Municipal Bureau of Health; data of central heating area and green area are from Xi'an Municipal Urban and Rural Construction Committee; data of sewage treatment in urban and environment monitoring are from the Xi'an Municipal Bureau of Environmental Protection; data of work safety are from the State Administration of Work Safety; all the other data ar e fr om Xi 'an Municipal Bur eau of Statistics.

1 综　合

GENERAL SURVEY

资料整理：栗海燕
Data management：Li Haiyan
数据审核：陈　英
Data audit：Chen Ying

第一部分　综合

一、简要说明

本章资料主要包括西安市行政区划、自然地理、自然资源、气象、国民经济和社会发展等综合资料，由西安市统计局综合处根据局内各专业处及有关部门统计资料进行整理和编辑。

二、主要指标

生产总值（亿元）	5801.20	比上年增长	8.2%
农林牧渔及服务业总产值（亿元）	380.76	比上年增长	5.1%
规模以上工业增加值（亿元）	1285.08	比上年增长	4.5%
全社会固定资产投资额（亿元）	5165.98	比上年下降	12.5%
社会消费品零售总额（亿元）	3405.38	比上年增长	10.1%
财政一般公共预算收入（亿元）	650.99	比上年增长	16.3%
财政一般公共预算支出（亿元）	917.24	比上年增长	12.9%
进出口总额（亿元）	1761. 69	比上年增长	15.0%
城镇居民人均可支配收入（元）	39007	比上年增长	8.1%
农村居民人均纯收入（元）	15778	比上年增长	9.1%

1　GENERAL SURVEY

Ⅰ.Brief Introduction

This chapter consists of mainly unified data of administrative divisions, natural geography, natural resources, meteorology, national economy and social development of Xi'an city. It is compiled by Integration Division according to the reported data from other divisions of the Xi'an Bureau of Statistics and other departments of the municipal government.

Ⅱ. Major Indicators

		Increase over Preceding Year
Gross Domestic Product (100 mil. Yuan)	5801.20	8.2%
Gross Output Value of Farming, Forestry, Animal, Husbandry and Fishery (100 mil. Yuan)	380.76	5.1%
Gross Industrial Added Value (100 mil. Yuan)	1285.08	4.5%
Investment Fulfilled In Fixed Assets (100 mil. Yuan)	5165.98	-12.5%
Total Retail Sales of Consumer Goods (100 mil. Yuan)	3405.38	10.1%
Local Government Public Revenue (100 mil. Yuan)	650.99	16.3%
Local Government Public Expenditures (100 mil. Yuan)	917.24	12.9%
Total Value of Exports and Imports(RMB 100 mil.Yuan)	1761. 69	15.0%
Per Capita Annual Disposable Income of Urban Households (Yuan)	39007	8.1%
Per Capita Net Income of Rural Residents (Yuan)	15778	9.1%

1-1 行政区划（2015年）

Administrative Division（2015）

单位：个 (unit)

地 区	Region	乡镇及街道办 Township and Urban Subdistrict Office	镇数 Town	街道办事处 Urban Subdistrict Office	村民委员会 Villagers' Committee	社区居委会 Neighbourhood Committee
西安市	**Xi'an**	**169**	**55**	**114**	**2925**	**856**
（一）市辖区	**Urban Area**	**111**	**5**	**106**	**1404**	**795**
新城区	Xincheng	9		9		103
碑林区	Beilin	8		8		100
莲湖区	Lianhu	9		9		134
灞桥区	Baqiao	9		9	209	51
未央区	Weiyang	10		10	95	110
雁塔区	Yanta	8		8	82	130
阎良区	Yanliang	7	2	5	80	23
临潼区	Lintong	23		23	284	41
长安区	Chang'an	22		22	567	95
高陵区	Gaoling	6	3	3	87	8
（二）三县	**Three Counties**	**53**	**50**	**3**	**1413**	**44**
蓝田县	Lantian	19	18	1	519	9
周至县	Zhouzhi	20	19	1	376	14
户县	Huxian	14	13	1	518	21
沣东新城	**Fengdongxincheng**	**5**		**5**	**108**	**17**

注：本表数据来源市民政局。

1-2 土地面积和常住人口密度（2015年）

Statistics on Land Area and Density of Permanent Population（2015）

地　区	Region	土地面积 Area 绝对数（平方公里）Absolute Value (sq.km)	比重（%）Proportion (%)	常住人口（万人）Total of Permanent Population (10 000 persons)	常住人口密度（人/平方公里）Density of Permanent Population (person/sq.km)
西安市	**Xi 'an**	**10096.81**	**100.0**	**870.56**	**862**
（一）市区	**Urban**	**3866.24**	**38.2**	**702.91**	**1818**
新城区	Xincheng	30.13	0.3	60.33	20023
碑林区	Beilin	23.37	0.2	62.89	26911
莲湖区	Lianhu	38.32	0.4	71.23	18588
灞桥区	Baqiao	324.50	3.2	61.39	1892
未央区	Weiyang	264.41	2.6	83.05	3141
雁塔区	Yanta	151.44	1.5	120.96	7987
阎良区	Yanliang	244.55	2.4	28.84	1179
临潼区	Lintong	915.97	9.1	67.62	738
长安区	Chang'an	1588.53	15.7	111.83	704
高陵区	Gaoling	285.03	2.8	34.77	1220
（二）三县	**Three Counties**	**6230.57**	**61.8**	**167.65**	**269**
蓝田县	Lantian	2005.95	19.9	52.53	262
周至县	Zhouzhi	2945.20	29.2	58.09	197
户　县	Huxian	1279.42	12.7	57.03	446

注：本表土地面积数据来源市国土资源局。

1-3　自然状况和资源（2015年）

Nature Conditions and Resources（2015）

指　标	Item	2015
一、自然状况	**Nature Conditions**	
土地总面积（平方公里）	Total Land Area (sq.km)	10096.81
#市区面积	Urban Area	3866.24
气候（市区）	Climate (Urban)	
年平均气温（℃）	Average Annual Temperature (℃)	15.2
年降水量（毫米）	Total Annual Precipitation (mm)	551.6
日照总时数（小时）	Total Sunshine Time (hour)	1795.9
平均风速（米/秒）	Average Wind-speed (m/sec.)	2.3
二、自然资源	**Natural Resources**	
年末实有耕地面积（千公顷）	Cultivated Area Year-end （1 000 hectare)	237.93
林业用地面积（千公顷）	Area of Forestry (1 000 hectare)	480.74
全市水面面积（千公顷）	Whole Water Area (1 000 hectare)	3.66
水资源总量（亿立方米）	Total Water Resource (0.1 billion cu.m)	22.48
#天然地表水资源总量	Total Savageness Surface Water Resource	18.74
地下水资源总量（亿立方米）	Total Ground Water Resource (0.1 billion cu.m)	11.37

注：全市水面面积包括湖泊、水库、鱼塘、城市段河流面积等。
本表数据来源市气象局、林业局、水务局等。

1-4 气象情况（2015年）

Climate Condition（2015）

地 区	Region	平均气温（℃）Average Temperature（℃）	日照时数（小时）Sunshine Time (hour)	降水天数（天）Raining days (day)	年降水量（毫米）Total Annual Precipitation (mm)	平均风速（米/秒）Average Wind-speed (m/second)
市 区	Urban	15.2	1795.9	86	551.6	2.3
临潼区	Lintong	14.8	2212.3	89	810.0	1.3
长安区	Chang'an	14.0	1606.9	109	683.4	1.3
高陵区	Gaoling	15.0	2092.7	93	573.3	1.6
蓝田县	Lantian	13.7	1947.8	113	704.8	1.2
周至县	Zhouzhi	13.9	1616.1	129	699.9	1.1
户 县	Huxian	14.2	2102.5	108	604.1	1.6

注：本表数据来源市气象局。

1-5 市区及县各月平均气温（2015年）

Average Temperature of Xi'an and the Districts of Each Month（2015）

单位：℃ (℃)

月 份	Month	市区 Urban	临潼 Lintong	长安 Chang'an	高陵 Gaoling	蓝田 Lantian	周至 Zhouzhi	户县 Huxian
一月	January	2.3	2.0	1.1	1.8	0.2	0.7	1.4
二月	February	5.6	5.3	3.9	5.3	3.4	3.7	4.2
三月	March	10.5	10.4	9.5	10.4	9.3	8.9	9.4
四月	April	16.3	16.0	15.2	16.1	14.7	14.7	15.1
五月	May	21.4	21.1	20.2	21.2	20.1	20.3	20.3
六月	June	24.3	24.0	23.2	24.3	22.9	23.2	23.7
七月	July	28.1	27.2	26.9	28.0	26.8	27.0	27.4
八月	August	26.0	25.0	24.5	25.7	24.5	24.6	24.8
九月	September	21.7	21.2	20.3	21.5	20.6	20.2	20.4
十月	October	15.0	14.5	13.8	14.6	13.4	13.8	14.2
十一月	November	8.2	7.8	7.4	7.9	7.5	7.6	7.7
十二月	December	3.1	3.0	1.9	2.6	1.2	2.1	2.1

注：本表数据来源市气象局。

1-6 市区及县各月日照时数（2015年）

Sunshine Duration of Xi'an and the Districts of Each Month（2015）

单位：小时 (hour)

月 份	Month	市区 Urban	临潼 Lintong	长安 Chang'an	高陵 Gaoling	蓝田 Lantian	周至 Zhouzhi	户县 Huxian
一月	January	127.0	143.1	117.9	141.8	125.5	100.7	145.4
二月	February	127.1	174.6	107.9	155.8	142.3	118.7	151.1
三月	March	144.3	176.3	143.3	151.4	145.5	127.7	164.8
四月	April	214.3	257.7	187.5	220.7	211.1	187.4	248.0
五月	May	200.4	260.5	178.4	209.3	271.7	197.7	270.9
六月	June	116.6	183.4	118.7	153.6	141.1	113.4	150.6
七月	July	257.1	316.0	243.6	288.4	289.0	255.4	289.7
八月	August	208.5	243.8	178.5	243.8	196.9	176.5	226.9
九月	September	119.8	145.6	99.6	154.8	130.9	82.0	124.1
十月	October	95.0	117.3	89.1	144.3	123.7	98.2	134.3
十一月	November	58.5	51.1	34.2	73.3	49.4	40.3	65.6
十二月	December	127.3	142.9	108.2	155.5	120.7	118.1	131.1

注：本表数据来源市气象局。

1-7 市区及县各月降水天数（2015年）

Precipitation Days of Xi'an and the Districts of Each Month（2015）

单位：天 (day)

月 份	Month	市区 Urban	临潼 Lintong	长安 Chang'an	高陵 Gaoling	蓝田 Lantian	周至 Zhouzhi	户县 Huxian
一月	January	3	4	5	4	6	6	5
二月	February	2	2	6	2	4	8	5
三月	March	6	8	12	7	10	14	13
四月	April	10	10	12	9	11	12	13
五月	May	8	9	11	9	11	15	14
六月	June	13	12	16	12	14	15	16
七月	July	6	4	4	7	8	3	4
八月	August	8	10	12	11	13	12	12
九月	September	13	13	11	13	14	16	14
十月	October	8	8	11	9	9	9	10
十一月	November	7	7	11	8	11	16	10
十二月	December	2	2	2	2	2	3	4

注：本表数据来源市气象局。

1-8 市区及县各月降水量（2015年）

Amount of Precipitation of Xi'an and the Districts of Each Month（2015）

单位：毫米 (mm)

月 份	Month	市区 Urban	临潼 Lintong	长安 Chang'an	高陵 Gaoling	蓝田 Lantian	周至 Zhouzhi	户县 Huxian
一月	January	3.3	2.2	3.4	7.6	3.8	7.1	4.0
二月	February	1.4	1.5	6.1	6.9	1.7	2.5	1.6
三月	March	42.6	51.6	55.0	49.8	42.3	55.5	42.4
四月	April	88.8	107.6	130.4	114.4	72.7	117.0	127.3
五月	May	50.2	65.0	68.6	65.4	54.9	43.1	70.7
六月	June	91.5	108.1	110.7	128.2	96.1	144.3	96.6
七月	July	20.8	26.6	41.3	40.8	17.0	4.4	6.6
八月	August	71.2	229.1	72.9	87.4	116.2	119.7	66.7
九月	September	90.9	91.8	106.9	88.3	76.4	99.8	88.8
十月	October	60.2	81.4	45.5	53.5	54.8	55.1	56.0
十一月	November	28.6	42.0	40.6	58.2	34.5	49.7	41.9
十二月	December	2.1	3.1	2.0	4.3	2.9	1.7	1.5

注：本表数据来源市气象局。

1-9 市区及县各月平均风速（2015年）

Average Wind Velocity of Xi'an and the Districts of Each Month（2015）

单位：米/秒 (m/s)

月 份	Month	市区 Urban	临潼 Lintong	长安 Chang'an	高陵 Gaoling	蓝田 Lantian	周至 Zhouzhi	户县 Huxian
一月	January	2.1	1.5	1.5	1.3	1.0	1.2	1.7
二月	February	2.9	1.7	1.5	1.9	1.4	1.4	1.8
三月	March	2.4	1.6	1.5	1.7	1.2	1.2	1.5
四月	April	2.3	1.8	1.5	1.7	1.4	1.6	1.8
五月	May	2.1	1.6	1.4	1.6	1.4	1.6	1.8
六月	June	2.5	1.7	1.1	1.9	1.2	1.2	1.7
七月	July	2.3	1.4	1.3	1.9	1.4	1.5	1.6
八月	August	2.2	1.5	1.2	1.5	1.2	1.3	1.5
九月	September	2.4	1.6	1.2	1.7	1.3	0.9	1.5
十月	October	1.9	1.3	1.2	1.2	1.0	0.3	1.4
十一月	November	2.1	1.2	1.0	1.3	0.9	0.3	1.3
十二月	December	2.0	1.4	1.4	1.2	1.1	1.0	1.5

注：本表数据来源市气象局。

1-10 主要年份国有土地使用权出让、划拨情况

The Transfer and Allocation of State-Owned Land Use Right in Representative Years

项　目	Item	2007	2008	2009	2010	2011	2012	2013	2014	2015
国有土地使用权出让	**Lease of the Use Right of State-owned Land**									
出让地块(宗)	Land leased (item)	333	278	297	386	474	581	550	506	416
协议	Agreement	171	119	100	173	133	80	90	109	72
招标	Invitation for Bid	1	3		3					
拍卖	Auction	3	5	1	11					
挂牌交易	Listed Transaction	158	149	196	199	341	500	460	397	344
出让面积（公顷）	Area of Totally Leased Land (hectare)	843	809	1047	1364	1386	1853	2195	1789	1294
土地使用权出让总收入（万元）	**Total Revenue from Leasing of the Use Right(10 000 yuan)**	**267666**	**309181**	**284405**	**358098**	**334069**	**218817**	**292945**	**183901**	**109116**
国有土地使用权划拨	**Administrative Allocation of the Use Right of State-owned Land**									
划拨地块（宗）	Land Allocated (item)	100	102	79	108	253	154	234	152	141
划拨面积（公顷）	Area of Land Allocated(hectare)	388	455	1721	1027	1426	1617	1986	1739	1209

注：本表数据来源市国土资源局。

1-11 主要年份国民经济和社会发展总量与速度指标

指 标	Item	总量指标 Total quantity index 1995	2000	2005	2010
人口与就业	Population and Employment				
人口	Population				
年底总人口(万人)	Population at the Year-end (10 000 persons)	648.21	688.01	741.73	782.73
城镇人口	Urban Population	255.71	285.79	333.14	374.64
乡村人口	Rural Population	392.50	402.22	408.59	408.09
男性人口	Male Population	334.75	355.18	382.02	398.80
女性人口	Female Population	313.46	332.83	359.71	383.93
就业	Employment				
全社会从业人员数(万人)	Employment(10 000 persons)	372.60	389.10	415.83	477.58
#全部单位在岗职工人数	Number of Employed Staff and Workers	141.17	109.62	119.73	130.70
城镇登记失业人数(万人)	Registered Unemployed in Urban Areas(10 000 persons)	5.92	3.85	8.45	10.46
宏观经济	Macroeconomic Indicator				
国民经济核算(亿元)	National Accounts(100 mil. yuan)				
生产总值(亿元)	Gross Domestic Product(100 mil. yuan)	330.35	646.13	1313.93	3242.86
第一产业	Primary Industry	41.40	44.65	66.01	140.06
第二产业	Secondary Industry	135.33	277.13	540.50	1357.53
第三产业	Tertiary Industry	153.62	324.35	707.42	1745.27
工业	Industry	112.50	218.44	420.00	954.38
建筑业	Construction			120.50	403.15
在生产总值中：最终消费	Total Consumption	239.64	413.43	766.62	1598.51
资本形成总额	Total Investment	151.55	287.82	839.01	2835.42
固定资产投资	Investment in Fixed Assets				
全社会固定资产投资总额(亿元)	Total Investment in Fixed Assets(100 mil. yuan)	103.42	232.37	835.10	3250.56
按类别分：	By classification:				
固定资产投资（不含农户）	Investment in Fixed Assets (excluding farmers)	88.50	203.01	776.33	3104.92
#房地产开发投资	Real Estate Investment	21.65	51.85	225.23	842.34
农户投资	Farmer Investment	14.92	29.36	58.77	145.64
按经济成分划分:	According to the Division of Economic Component				
国有经济	State-owned	69.08	159.60	373.70	1348.76
集体经济	Collective-Owned	9.78	14.65	59.23	326.44
个体经济	Self-employed Individual	11.13	24.40	79.04	54.73
其他经济	Other	13.43	33.72	323.13	1520.63
财政	Public Finance				
地方财政一般公共预算收入（亿元）	General Public Budgetary Revenue of Local Government (100 mil. yuan)	18.21	46.80	72.92	241.86
地方财政一般公共预算支出（亿元）	General Public Budgetary Expenditure of Local Government (100 mil. yuan)	18.42	52.00	97.61	371.62
物价指数(上年=100)	Price Indices(preceding year=100)				
商品零售价格指数	Retail Price Index	114.6	98.7	99.7	102.7
居民消费价格指数	Consumer Price Index	117.0	100.2	100.3	103.5
工业生产者出厂价格指数	Producer Price Indices (PPI) for Manufactured Goods	110.8	99.4	103.9	102.3
利用外资	Utilization of Foreign Capital				
利用外资签定协议额(万美元)	Amount of Foreign Capital for Utilization Through Signed Contracts or Agreements(USD 10 000)	28956	54123	121499	119689
外商实际直接投资额(万美元)	Amount of Foreign Capital Actually Utilized (USD 10 000)	18653	15633	57113	156653

注：国民经济核算2004—2008年为全国第二次经济普查修订数据。2009—2012年为三经普修订数据，2013年为全国第三次经济普查数据。2014—2015年为年报最终核实数。
2009年及以前年份财政收支为一般预算收支与基金预算收支之和。
由于2010年固定资产投资起报点的变化，指数和平均增长速度为可比口径计算。
2015年，市公安局提供户籍人口分类为“城镇人口”和“乡村人口”，2015年之前，分类为“非农业人口”和“农业人口”。
2015年，国家取消了城乡投资分组，“农户投资”2014年之前为原来的“农村投资”。

Total and Speed Index of National Economy and Social Development in Representative Years

2011	2012	2013	2014	2015	速度指标 Indices and Growth Rates						
					指数（2015比以下各年）(2015 as percentage of the following years)				平均增长速度（%）Average Annual Growth Rate（%）		
					2000	2005	2010	2014	2001-2005	2006-2010	2011-2015
791.83	795.98	806.93	815.29	815.66	118.6	110.0	104.2	100.0	1.5	1.1	0.8
391.31	392.04	409.82	418.16	545.95	191.0	163.9	145.7	130.6	3.1	2.4	7.8
400.52	403.94	397.11	397.13	269.71	67.1	66.0	66.1	67.9	0.3	-0.02	-7.9
402.52	397.58	408.78	412.46	412.23	116.1	107.9	103.4	99.9	1.5	0.9	0.7
389.31	398.40	398.15	402.83	403.43	121.2	112.2	105.1	100.1	1.6	1.3	1.0
495.99	514.57	530.71	532.92	528.06	135.7	127.0	110.6	99.1	1.3	2.8	2.0
154.33	155.28	183.60	183.22	181.86	165.9	151.9	139.1	99.3	1.8	1.8	6.8
10.37	9.60	10.13	10.84	10.74	279.0	127.1	102.7	99.1	17.0	4.4	0.5
3869.84	4394.47	4924.97	5492.64	5801.20	636.2	338.1	168.2	108.2	13.5	15.0	11.0
173.14	195.59	200.45	214.55	220.20	220.7	178.8	130.7	105.0	4.3	6.5	5.5
1583.21	1781.09	1998.82	2194.78	2126.29	666.6	328.7	165.2	105.6	15.2	14.8	10.6
2113.49	2417.79	2725.70	3083.31	3454.71	667.3	362.1	173.9	110.4	13.0	15.8	11.7
1098.51	1228.05	1376.74	1488.02	1376.72	617.2	309.3	164.6	104.8	14.8	13.4	10.5
484.70	553.04	642.26	728.74	770.29	855.9	398.1	167.1	107.4	16.5	19.0	10.8
1856.91	2092.97										
3264.83	3783.10										
3346.26	4243.43	5134.56	5903.98	5165.98	2807.2	781.1	200.7	87.5	29.2	31.2	14.9
3207.97	4107.54	4982.25	5682.42	5086.93	3204.5	838.0	209.5	89.5	30.8	31.9	15.9
996.81	1281.90	1595.64	1761.88	1831.67	3532.8	813.3	217.5	104.0	34.1	30.2	16.8
138.29	135.89	152.31	221.56	79.05	269.3	134.6	54.3	35.7	14.9	19.9	-11.5
1204.80	1661.22	1770.84	1916.31	1826.62	1144.8	617.1	171.0	95.3	18.5	29.3	11.3
258.15	194.71	219.88	203.35	158.14	1362.8	337.1	61.2	77.8	32.2	40.7	-9.4
74.64	82.72	84.43	83.28	80.47	416.3	128.5	185.6	96.6	26.5	-7.1	13.2
1808.67	2304.78	3059.41	3701.04	3100.75	11570.5	1207.4	256.6	83.8	57.1	36.6	20.7
318.55	396.96	501.98	583.79	650.99	1391.0	892.7	269.2	116.3	9.3	27.1	21.9
494.58	597.49	729.81	819.54	917.24	1763.9	939.7	246.8	112.9	13.4	30.7	19.8
104.4	102.3	101.7	100.7	99.7					-0.2	2.5	1.7
105.6	102.8	102.7	101.4	100.7					0.3	3.1	2.6
102.5	100.5	99.5	99.5	98.5					1.1	2.2	0.1
120083	360264	251874	255321	193684	357.9	159.4	161.8	75.9	17.6	-0.3	10.1
200522	247800	312994	370310	400833	2564.0	701.8	255.9	108.2	29.6	22.4	20.7

1-11 续表1

指 标	Item	总量指标 Total quantity index			
		1995	2000	2005	2010
产 业	**Industry**				
农业	**Agriculture**				
耕地面积(万亩)	Cultivated Areas(10 000 hectares)	463.97	443.37	400.17	383.32
农林牧渔及服务业总产值 (亿元)	Gross Output Value of Farming Forestry, Animal Husbandry and Fishery(100 mil yuan)	75.46	74.37	106.54	227.10
主要农产品产量(万吨)	Output of Major Farm Products(10 000 tons)				
粮 食	Grain	175.30	201.90	205.50	221.70
奶 类	Milk	13.29	24.59	42.22	63.37
油 料	Oil-bearing Crops	2.17	1.34	1.16	1.20
蔬 菜	Vegetables	133.60	162.14	195.70	253.10
水 果	Fruits	24.10	34.36	51.29	84.78
肉 类	Meat	12.78	14.76	18.20	13.65
水产品	Aquatic Products	0.85	1.14	0.94	1.19
工业	**Industry**				
全部工业总产值（亿元）	Gross industrial Output Value(100 mil. yuan)	405.90	639.48	1308.56	3562.88
规模以上工业企业主要经济指标（亿元）	Main Economic Indicators of All Industrial Enterprises State Ownership and Non-state-owned above Designated Size above Designated Size(100 mil. yuan)				
工业增加值	Value Added of Industrial		130.18	314.01	824.09
资产总计	Total Assets		958.05	1503.85	3592.13
主营业务收入	Revenue from Principal Business		420.42	980.97	3011.19
利润总额	Profits		16.11	28.72	245.37
从业人员年平均人数（万人）	Annual Average Employers(10 000 persons)		43.25	37.92	47.11
主要工业产品产量	Output of Major Industrial Products				
布(亿米)	Cloth(100 mil.m)	3.03	2.48	2.70	2.38
机制纸及纸板(万吨)	Machine-Made Paper(10 000ton)	36.44	5.47	22.19	49.60
发电量(亿千瓦时)	Electricity(100 million kwh)	22.00	19.00	48.00	96.94
钢材(万吨)	Steel Products(10 000ton)	31.44	10.00	24.02	110.77
汽车(万辆)	Motor Vehicle (10 000 units)	0.30	0.90	4.10	65.21
建筑业	**Construction**				
建筑业企业从业人数(人)	Number of Employed Persons(person)		136718	158311	539000
建筑业总产值(亿元)	Gross Output Value(100 mil. yuan)	42.55	105.93	326.65	1334.00
房屋建筑施工面积 (万平方米)	Floor Space of Buildings under Construction (10 000 sq.m)	601.70	793.30	1801.20	4592.57
房屋建筑竣工面积 (万平方米)	Floor Space of Buildings Completed (10 000 sq.m)	177.15	336.80	569.01	1391.91

注：规模以上工业2013年为全国第三次经济普查数据，依据第三次经济普查，对2009—2012年规模以上工业增加值数据进了修订。
由于2010年规模以上工业起报点的变化，指数和平均增长速度为可比口径计算。

continued 1

					速度指标 Indices and Growth Rates						
2011	2012	2013	2014	2015	指数（2015比以下各年） (2015 as percentage of the following years)				平均增长速度（%） Average Annual Growth Rate（%）		
					2000	2005	2010	2014	2001-2005	2006-2010	2011-2015
377.10	369.91	366.23	360.73	356.89	80.5	89.2	93.1	98.9	-2.0	-9.0	-1.4
272.66	308.36	342.89	367.21	380.76	228.7	182.8	130.9	105.1	4.6	6.8	5.5
182.04	192.55	183.12	175.61	180.86	89.6	88.0	81.6	103.0	0.4	1.5	-4.0
64.80	66.64	65.77	65.80	63.73	259.2	151.0	100.6	96.9	11.4	8.5	0.1
1.17	1.02	1.00	0.98	0.95	70.9	81.9	79.2	96.9	-1.6	0.0	-4.6
261.66	277.80	298.12	316.28	332.79	205.2	170.1	131.5	105.2	3.8	5.3	5.6
91.14	93.21	95.19	99.66	105.2	306.3	205.1	124.1	105.6	8.3	10.6	4.4
14.46	15.17	15.74	16.19	16.13	109.3	88.6	118.1	99.6	4.2	-5.6	3.4
1.18	1.40	1.42	1.42	1.42	124.5	151.0	119.2	99.9	-3.9	5.7	3.6
4093.32	4656.08	5042.64	5660.63	5159.91	739.7	378.8	145.0	91.2	14.3	21.2	7.7
951.58	1064.29	1194.88	1304.12	1285.08		356.0	168.0	4.5	15.9	16.2	10.9
3975.38	4775.92	5127.69	6048.34	6740.26	703.5	448.2	187.6	111.4	9.4	19.0	13.4
3381.27	3758.56	4171.21	4566.20	4374.11	1040.4	445.9	145.3	95.8	18.5	25.1	7.8
172.94	167.77	211.26	226.17	206.88	1284.2	720.3	84.3	91.5	12.3	53.6	-3.4
50.42	49.23	44.27	49.53	50.59	117.0	133.4	107.4	102.1	-2.6	4.4	1.4
1.63	1.43	1.40	1.12	1.04	41.9	38.5	43.7	92.9	1.7	-2.5	-15.3
49.79	27.61	16.00	11.24	12.22	223.4	55.1	24.6	108.7	32.3	17.5	-24.4
95.01	99.48	184.50	179.58	158.68	835.2	330.6	163.7	88.4	20.4	15.1	10.4
18.48	31.29	54.30	42.87	37.03	370.3	154.2	33.4	86.4	19.2	35.8	-19.7
55.67	54.17	42.20	37.47	34.14	3793.3	832.7	52.4	91.1	35.4	73.9	-12.1
372088	391199	577944	394070	596245	436.1	376.6	110.6	151.3	3.0	27.8	2.0
1619.09	1874.23	2228.41	2586.33	2650.41	2502.0	811.4	198.7	102.5	25.3	41.0	14.7
6218.70	7531.07	9753.45	11182.18	11979.16	1510.0	665.1	260.8	107.1	17.8	20.6	21.1
2392.39	1985.31	2229.97	2536.71	2712.01	805.2	476.6	194.8	106.9	11.1	19.6	14.3

1-11 续表2

指 标	Item	总量指标 Total quantity index 1995	2000	2005	2010
交通运输	**Transportation**				
货运量(万吨)	Freight Traffic(10 000 tons)	9590	6999	12051	34323
铁 路	Railways	3317	3101	540	706
公 路	Highways	6268	3890	11505	33610
民用航空	Civil Aviation	5	8	6	7
客运量(万人次)	Passenger Traffic(10 000 persons-times)	9069	8068	10479	30294
铁 路	Railways	2678	2130	1796	2781
公 路	Highways	6128	5578	8294	26536
民用航空	Civil Aviation	263	360	389	977
邮电通信业	**Post and Telecommunication Services**				
邮电业务总量(亿元)	Total Business Revenue(100 mil. yuan)	7.65	46.16	132.04	323.11
函 件(万件)	Number of Letters Delivered(10 000 pieces)	14647	8230	9526	8176
本地电话局用交换机容量 (万门)	Capacity of Local Office Telephone Exchanges (10 000 line)	58.3	204.8	457.3	449.0
本地电话年末用户(万户)	Local fixed telephone end users (10 000 subscribers)	29.95	124.26	321.48	261.77
城市电话用户	Urban Telephone Subscribers	29.11	107.24	271.40	228.26
乡村电话用户	Rural Telephone Subscribers	0.84	17.02	50.08	33.50
移动电话用户(万户)	Number of Mobile Telephone Subscribers (10 000 subscribers)		73.10	419.96	1423.08
互联网年末宽带用户(万户)	Number of Subscribers of Intemet Services (10 000 subscribers)			33.93	146.18
国内商业	**Domestic business**				
社会消费品零售总额 (亿元)	Total Retail Sales of Consumer Goods (100 mil. yuan)	186.60	360.42	670.56	1678.01
对外经济贸易	**Foreign Trade**				
进出口总额(万美元)	Total Exports and Imports(USD 10 000)	137510	173696	390146	1039273
出口额	Exports	110163	106062	263441	531729
进口额	Imports	27347	67634	126705	507544
旅游	**Tourism**				
旅游者人数(万人次)	Number of Tourists(10 000 persons)	791.35	1567.00	2423.60	5285.18
旅游收入(亿元)	Earnings from Tourism (100 mil. yuan)	44.00	105.00	178.50	405.18
金融业	**Financial Intermediation**				
金融机构（不含外资）人民币存款余额(亿元)	Balance of Deposits in Domestic Funded Financial Institutions (100 mil. yuan)	359.51	1335.63	3599.70	8863.36
金融机构（不含外资）人民币贷款余额 (亿元)	Balance of Loans in Domestic Funded Financial Institutions (100 mil. yuan)	334.50	972.52	2158.10	6420.72
保险公司保费收入(亿元)	Insurance premium income (100 million Yuan)	4.70	13.58	44.94	129.38
保险公司赔款及付给金额(亿元)	Indemnity Insurance and Amount Paid(100 million yuan)	1.70	1.39	9.50	26.39

注：2006年铁路数据按新口径统计；
2006年国际互联网络用户改为互联网宽带用户。
2009—2013年社会消费品零售总额为全国第三次经济普查修订数据。
2014年起，海关不发布美元口径数据，为了数据可持续性，使用年均汇率折算为美元口径。

continued 2

2011	2012	2013	2014	2015	速度指标 Indices and Growth Rates						
					指数（2015比以下各年）(2015 as percentage of the following years)				平均增长速度（%）Average Annual Growth Rate（%）		
					2000	2005	2010	2014	2001-2005	2006-2010	2011-2015
39239	44924	50119	42039	46270					11.5	23.3	
823	825	858	900	848					-29.5	5.5	
38399	44082	49243	41120	45401					24.2	23.9	
9	17	18	19	21					-5.6	3.1	
33375	36154	38289	25719	26904					5.4	23.7	
2861	2919	3071	3511	3982					-3.4	9.1	
29358	30893	32614	19282	19625					8.3	26.2	
1156	2342	2604	2926	3297					1.6	20.2	
200.50	216.21	247.94	292.20	331.53	718.2	251.1	102.6	113.5	23.4	19.6	0.5
3061	2769	2856	2112	1707	20.7	17.9	20.9	80.8	3.0	-3.0	-26.9
441.5	420.4	378.0	230.0	145.1	70.8	31.7	32.3	63.1	17.4	-0.4	-20.2
270.36	311.02	319.11	306.66	292.08	235.1	90.9	111.6	95.2	20.9	-4.0	2.2
238.35	277.43	286.05	269.38	261.44	243.8	96.3	114.5	97.1	20.4	-3.4	2.8
32.02	33.59	33.06	37.28	30.63	180.0	61.2	91.4	82.2	24.1	-7.7	-1.8
1614.15	1803.54	2160.67	2025.32	1767	2417.2	420.8	124.2	87.2	41.9	27.6	4.4
184.10	202.31	267.05	277.95	289.97		854.6	198.4	104.3		33.9	14.7
2039.24	2400.67	2742.89	3093.89	3405.38	944.8	507.8	202.9	110.1	13.2	19.5	15.2
1260179	1301446	1798534	2494223	2828479	1628.4	725.0	272.2	113.4	17.6	21.6	39.6
582662	729878	847819	1196005	1316350	1241.1	499.7	247.6	110.1	20.0	15.1	35.3
677517	571568	950715	1298218	1512129	2235.8	1193.4	297.9	116.5	13.4	32.0	43.9
6653.23	7978.35	10130.00	12000.00	13600.8	868.0	561.2	257.3	113.3	17.6	21.6	37.0
530.15	654.39	811.44	950.00	1073.69	1022.6	601.5	265.0	113.0	20.0	15.1	38.4
10350.80	12044.68	13665.89	15064.10	17682.94	1323.9	491.2	199.5	117.4	21.9	19.7	14.8
7496.25	8559.27	9930.04	11576.30	13604.89	1398.9	630.4	211.9	117.5	17.3	24.4	16.2
162.57	173.21	202.41	219.49	263.02	1936.8	585.3	203.3	119.8	27.0	23.6	15.2
37.14	47.55	66.49	80.77	87.62	6303.5	922.3	332.0	108.5	46.9	24.8	27.1

1-11 续表3

指 标	Item	总量指标 Total quantity index			
		1995	2000	2005	2010
教育、科技、文化	**Education, Science and Technology and Culture**				
教育	**Education**				
专任教师数(人)	Full-time Teachers(person)				
#普通高等学校	Institutions of Higher Education	15914	15679	29498	42098
普通中等专业学校	Regular Specialized Secondary Schools	2533	3172	2130	1845
普通中学	Regular Middk Schools	21984	26230	31094	31506
小 学	Primary Schools	30270	30215	29647	29944
在校学生数(万人)	Students Enrollment(10 000 person)				
#普通高等学校	Institutions of Higher Education	11.67	19.41	53.06	73.30
普通中等专业学校	Regular Specialized Secondary Schools	3.74	6.02	6.16	6.75
普通中学	Regular Schools	32.32	48.31	55.74	48.89
小 学	Primary Schools	79.36	77.81	60.47	51.56
科技	**Science and Technology**				
高新技术企业(个)	Hi-tech Enterprises (unit)				827
企事业单位累计授权专利数（件）	Accumulated patents awarded(unit)	3164	6139	11670	31999
文化	**Accumulated patents awarded(unit)**				
图书馆总藏量(千册件)	Total Collections in Library (1000 Volume-time)	2830	3214	3671	4465
文化馆、站（个)	Cultural Centers or Stations (unit)	201	251	192	197
电视节目制作时间(小时)	Time for TV Programs Production(hour)	5738	11871	27377	29626
家庭、生活、环境	**Family, People's Livelihood and Environment**				
家庭	**Family**				
家庭总户数户籍人口 (万户)	Total Number of Households(10 000 household)	171.25	187.08	203.04	226.71
城镇常住居民平均每户家庭人口(人)	Average Household Size in Urban Areas(person)	3.88	2.99	2.93	2.81
农村常住居民平均每户家庭人口(人)	The Total Number of Family Household of Domicile Population (person)	4.60	4.30	4.22	3.94
婚姻	**Marriages and Divorces**				
结婚(对)	Number of Marriages(couple)	47236	46415	49962	83645
离婚(对)	Number of Divorces(couple)	4296	5161	12747	19060
居住	**Housing**				
城镇居民人均现住房建筑面积 (平方米)	Per Capita Building Area of Urban Residents' (sq.m)	13.05	14.82	16.38	28.70
农村居民人均现住房建筑面积(平方米)	Per Capita Building Area of Rural Residents(sq.m)	21.77	28.31	36.73	66.73

注：2008年及以前图书馆总藏量为图书馆藏书量。

2005年以前城镇居民人均现住房总建筑面积为城镇人均住房使用面积。

2014年及以后城乡居民人均住房面积为城乡住户调查一体化改革后新口径数据，与往年不可比。

continued 3

2011	2012	2013	2014	2015	速度指标 Indices and Growth Rates						
					指数（2015比以下各年）(2015 as percentage of the following years)				平均增长速度（%）Average Annual Growth Rate（%）		
					2000	2005	2010	2014	2001-2005	2006-2010	2011-2015
42734	44487	46436	46766	47768	304.7	161.9	113.5	102.1	13.5	7.4	2.6
1723	1595	1474	1346	1228	38.7	57.7	66.6	91.2	-7.7	-2.8	-7.8
31675	31526	31419	32615	33014	125.9	106.2	104.8	101.2	3.5	0.3	0.9
29900	29651	29421	28395	28395	94.0	95.8	94.8	100.0	-0.4	0.2	-1.1
											2.8
76.60	80.73	83.83	85.42	84.83	437.0	159.9	115.7	99.3	22.3	6.7	3.0
6.11	5.43	4.66	4.07	3.47	57.6	56.3	51.4	85.3	0.7	1.9	-12.5
47.20	45.33	43.73	42.57	41.37	85.6	74.2	84.6	97.2	2.9	-2.6	-3.3
51.39	50.85	51.95	53.79	56.62	72.8	93.6	109.8	105.3	-4.9	-3.1	1.9
978	917	1026	1253	1316			159.1	105.0			9.7
41273	53118	69368	86639	103910	1692.6	890.4	324.7	119.9	13.7	22.4	26.6
4907	6123	6647	6285	6522	202.9	177.7	146.1	103.8	2.7	4.0	7.9
196	197	198	199	199	79.3	103.6	101.0	100.0	-5.4	0.6	0.2
43925	30091	46614	35182	43563	367.0	159.1	147.0	123.8	18.2	1.6	8.0
234.34	239.54	245.53	250.26	253.13	135.3	124.7	111.7	101.1	1.7	2.2	2.2
2.83	2.76	2.73	2.7	2.8	93.6	95.6	99.6	103.7	-0.4	-0.8	-0.1
3.97	4.09	4.09	3.5	3.6	83.7	85.3	91.4	102.9	-0.4	-1.6	-1.8
94398	89877	89136	91123	80790	174.1	161.7	96.6	88.7	1.5	10.9	-0.7
19421	18579	20304	21887	22748	440.8	178.5	119.3	103.9	19.8	8.4	3.6
28.90	32.98	33.43	32.06	32.1					2.0	11.9	
67	78	81	48.83	50.7					5.3	12.7	

1-11 续表4

指 标	Item	总量指标 Total quantity index			
		1995	2000	2005	2010
生活	**People's Livelihood**				
城镇居民人均可支配收入(元)	Per Capita Annual Disposable Income of Urban Households (yuan)	4153	6364	9628	22244
农村居民人均纯收入(元)	Per Capita Net Income of Rural Residents(yuan)	1353	2344	3460	7750
住户存款（亿元）	Household deposits(100 million yuan)	230.63	675.83	1716.76	3641.09
工资	**Wages and Welfare**				
在岗职工工资总额(亿元)	The Gross Salary of Workers (100 mil. yuan)	67.23	101.68	211.14	501.76
城镇非私营单位从业人员年平均工资(元)	Aunual Average Wage of Stuff and Workers in Urban Non-privite Enterprises(yuan)	4763	9179	17728	37870
卫生	**Health Care**				
医院、卫生院(个)	Number of Hospitals(unit)	368	426	479	412
执业（助理）医师（人）	Licensed (Assistant) Doctors (person)	18846	18750	17730	18763
医院、卫生院床位数(张)	Number of Hospital Beds(unit)	28265	28697	30087	36796
市政建设	**City Construction**				
自来水供应量(万立方米)	Volume of Tap Water Supply(10 000 cu.m)	35885	30273	35776	41089
自来水供水管道长度(公里)	Length of Water Supply Pipelines(km)	1066	2237	2315	2416
城市天然气供气量 (万立方米)	Volume of Natural Gas Supply in Urban Areas (10 000 cu.m)	8419	11513	53202	109052
公交运营汽(电)车总数(辆)	Total Number of Public Buses and Trolley Buses(unit)	977	2573	4762	7107
道路长度(公里)	Length of Paved Roads(km)	835	975	1382	2662
绿地面积(公顷)	Areas of Green Land(hectare)	5603	4116	4867	12140
环境、灾害	**Environment and Disaster**				
工业废水排放量(万吨)	Volume of Waste Water up to the Standard for Discharge(10 000 tons)	12479	9145	16969	13840
火灾发生数(起)	Number of Fire Disasters(case)	426	1040	2664	1825
火灾事故损失额（万元）	Fire Loss(10 000 yuan)	742.1	472.4	1565.5	2224.2
交通事故发生数（起）	Number of Traffic Accidents(case)	3065	4099	4903	2323
交通事故损失额（万元）	Loss of Traffic Accidents(10 000 yuan)	1103.2	1116.1	2024.4	736.6

注：城镇非私营单位从业人员年平均工资2012年前为城镇非私营单位在岗职工年平均工资。

continued 4

					速度指标 Indices and Growth Rates						
2011	2012	2013	2014	2015	指数（2015比以下各年）(2015 as percentage of the following years)				平均增长速度（%） Average Annual Growth Rate（%）		
					2000	2005	2010	2014	2001-2005	2006-2010	2011-2015
25981	29982	33100	36100	39007	612.9	405.1	175.4	108.1	8.6	18.2	15.1
9788	11442	12930	14462	15778	673.1	456.0	203.6	109.1	8.1	17.5	15.3
4155.65	4787.03	5357.05	5698.15	6571.18	972.3	382.8	180.5	115.3	16.5	13.3	12.5
629.35	742.16	987.80	1094.02	1202.01	1182.2	569.3	239.6	109.9	15.7	18.9	19.1
41679	44533	49350	54573	60557	659.7	341.6	159.9	111.0	14.1	16.4	9.8
368	376	381	381	395	92.7	82.5	95.9	103.7	2.4	-3.0	-0.8
21551	23051	23885	24820	26626	142.0	150.2	141.9	107.3	-1.1	1.1	7.3
37264	40585	44190	47075	51345	178.9	170.7	139.5	109.1	1.0	4.1	6.9
38934	45792	51372	53799	56055	185.2	156.7	136.4	104.2	3.4	2.8	6.4
2721	3208	3385	3500	4371	195.4	188.8	180.9	124.9	0.7	0.9	12.6
120330	142263	153489	186259	196826	1709.6	370.0	180.5	105.7	35.8	15.4	12.5
7462	7695	8128	7769	7781	302.4	163.4	109.5	100.2	13.1	8.3	1.8
2755	3119	3387	3461	3571	366.3	258.4	134.1	103.2	7.2	14.0	6.1
13680	15196	17751	18914	20582	500.0	422.9	169.5	108.8	3.4	20.1	11.1
13148	10224	8973	6340	5204	56.9	30.7	37.6	82.1	13.2	-4.0	-17.8
1920	2568	4062	3199	2590	249.0	97.2	141.9	81.0	20.7	-7.3	7.3
1587.2	2793.7	3011.9	4381.1	2401.5	508.4	153.4	108.0	54.8	27.1	7.3	1.5
2264	2446	2252	1970	2392	58.4	48.8	103.0	121.4	3.6	-13.9	0.6
611.9	1011.1	1143.9	1264.0	1470.2	131.7	72.6	199.6	116.3	12.6	-18.3	14.8

1-12 主要年份国民经济和社会发展结构指标

单位: %

指标	Item	1995	2000	2005
人口与就业	**Population and Employment**			
人口	**Population**			
城镇与农村结构	Structure			
农业人口	Agricultural Population	60.55	58.46	55.09
非农业人口	Non-agricultural Population	39.45	41.54	44.91
性别结构	Sexual Structure			
男	Male	51.64	51.62	51.50
女	Female	48.36	48.38	48.50
就业	**Employment**			
全社会从业人员产业结构	Industrial Structure of the Whole Society			
第一产业	Primary Industry	41.17	37.78	32.78
第二产业	Secondary Industry	29.43	27.57	27.46
第三产业	Tertiary Industry	29.40	34.65	39.76
宏观经济	**Macro Economy**			
国民经济核算	**National Accounting**			
生产总值产业结构	Industrial Structure			
第一产业	Primary Industry	12.53	6.91	5.02
第二产业	Secondary Industry	40.97	42.89	41.14
第三产业	Tertiary Industry	46.50	50.20	53.84
生产总值支出结构	Structure of Gross Domestic by Expenditures			
最终消费	Total Consumption	72.54	63.99	58.35
资本形成总额	Total Investment	45.88	44.55	63.85
货物和服务净出口	Net Export of Goods and Services	-18.42	-8.54	-22.20
投资	**Investment**			
全社会固定资产投资结构	Structure of Total Investment in Fixed Assets			
报表种类结构	By classification			
固定资产投资（不含农户）	Investment in Fixed Assets (excluding farmers)	85.57	87.36	92.96
#房地产开发投资	Real Estate Investment	20.93	22.31	27.00
农户投资	Farmer Investment	14.43	12.64	7.04
经济成分结构	Registion Status Composition			
国有经济	State-owned Enterprises Investment	66.79	68.68	44.75
集体经济	Collective-owned Enterprises Investment	9.46	6.30	7.09
个体经济	Self-employed Individual	10.76	10.50	9.46
其他经济	Other	12.99	14.51	38.69

注：2015年，市公安局提供户籍人口分类为“城镇人口”和“乡村人口”，2015年之前，分类为“非农业人口”和“农业人口”。

Structural Indicators of National Economic and Social Development in Representative Years

(%)

2007	2008	2009	2010	2011	2012	2013	2014	2015
53.70	52.88	52.58	52.14	50.58	50.75	49.21	48.71	33.07
46.30	47.12	47.42	47.86	49.42	49.25	50.79	51.29	66.93
51.35	51.22	51.08	50.95	50.83	49.95	50.66	50.59	50.54
48.65	48.78	48.92	49.05	49.17	50.05	49.34	49.41	49.46
30.55	28.50	26.40	25.65	24.41	22.33	20.81	19.71	20.39
28.66	29.10	28.45	29.65	30.51	31.55	28.55	28.49	24.53
40.79	42.40	45.15	44.70	45.08	46.12	50.64	51.80	55.08
4.44	4.46	4.05	4.32	4.48	4.48	4.07	3.91	3.80
42.12	42.34	42.01	41.86	40.99	40.79	40.59	39.96	36.65
53.44	53.20	53.94	53.82	54.72	55.38	55.34	56.13	59.55
53.60	51.02	51.51	49.31	48.07	47.93			
78.18	79.28	83.77	87.47	84.52	86.65			
-31.78	-30.30	-35.28	-36.78	-32.60	-34.58			
93.40	93.72	94.70	95.52	95.87	96.80	97.03	96.25	98.47
26.09	28.34	27.85	25.91	29.79	30.21	31.08	29.84	35.46
6.60	6.28	5.30	4.48	4.13	3.20	2.97	3.75	1.53
33.22	36.45	37.31	41.49	36.00	39.15	34.49	32.46	35.36
14.43	12.95	11.60	10.04	7.71	4.59	4.28	3.44	3.06
12.75	2.65	3.91	1.68	2.23	1.95	1.64	1.41	1.56
39.60	47.95	47.18	46.78	54.05	54.31	59.58	62.69	60.02

1-12 续表1

单位: %

指　标	Item	1995	2000	2005
财 政	**Government Finance**			
财政收入结构	Structure of Government Revenue			
中　央	Central Government		31.94	58.30
地　方	Local Governments		68.06	41.70
产　业	**Industrial**			
农 业	**Agriculture**			
农林牧渔及服务业总产值结构	Structure of Gross Output Value of Farming,Forestry,Animal Husbandry, Fishery and Service			
农　业	Farming	68.03	69.23	61.69
林　业	Forestry	0.96	1.14	1.23
牧　业	Animal Husbandry	30.29	28.58	30.96
渔　业	Fishery	0.72	1.05	0.69
农林牧渔服务业	Farming,Forestry,Animal Husbandry and Fishery			5.43
工 业	**Industry**			
工业总产值经济类型结构	Structure of Gross Output Value of Industry by Registion Status			
国有经济	State-owned Enterprises	51.04	43.00	45.21
集体经济	Collective-owned Enterprises	40.98	32.76	5.16
其他经济类型	Others	7.98	24.24	49.63
工业总产值轻重结构	Structure of Gross Output Value of Industry by Ligth Industry and Heavy Industry			
轻工业	Light Industry	40.31	48.81	31.17
重工业	Heavy Industry	59.69	51.19	68.83
工业总产值规模结构	Structure of Gross Output Value of Industry by Size of Enterprises			
大型企业	Large Enterprises	38.80	36.29	35.46
中型企业	Medium-sized Enterprises	9.14	5.14	24.67
小型企业	Small Enterprises	52.06	58.57	39.87

注：本表2008年以后财政收入结构中地方指地方财政一般公共预算收入。

continued 1

(%)

2007	2008	2009	2010	2011	2012	2013	2014	2015
60.40	39.49	39.68	37.28	35.78	32.37	30.80	29.61	28.94
39.60	44.87	45.32	47.36	49.02	52.71	55.60	57.25	58.39
59.50	56.85	59.42	63.36	63.42	62.69	63.38	64.37	64.19
1.18	1.13	1.27	1.18	1.27	2.02	2.34	2.37	2.57
30.58	33.52	30.56	27.72	27.68	26.61	25.19	23.95	23.30
0.68	0.66	0.66	0.56	0.55	0.65	0.66	0.65	0.51
8.06	7.84	8.09	7.18	7.09	8.04	8.42	8.66	9.43
51.41	52.26	51.07	51.52	50.46	52.20	50.29	48.32	48.47
1.85	1.85	1.38	1.22	0.92	0.81	0.64	0.59	0.31
46.74	45.89	47.55	47.26	48.62	46.99	49.07	51.09	51.22
37.03	25.17	23.47	22.01	21.97	21.95	18.44	18.32	19.55
62.97	74.83	76.53	77.99	78.03	78.05	81.56	81.68	80.45
42.18	43.85	43.54	42.11	41.15	48.46	34.49	43.95	51.33
21.07	20.96	21.88	23.96	15.17	13.41	14.42	15.47	16.34
36.75	35.19	34.58	33.93	43.68	38.13	51.09	40.58	32.33

1-12 续表2

单位: %

指 标	Item	1995	2000	2005
建筑业	**Construction**			
建筑业总产值结构	Structure of Gross Output Value of Construction Industry			
房屋建筑业	Building Construction	12.84	9.28	34.05
土木工程建筑业	Civil Engineering Construction	86.27	88.50	56.59
建筑安装业	Installation of Construction			
建筑装饰和其他建筑业	Decoration and others	0.89	2.22	9.36
交通运输业	**Transportation**			
客运量结构	Structure of Freight Traffic			
铁 路	Railways	29.53	26.40	17.14
公 路	Highways	67.57	69.14	79.15
民 航	Civil Aviation	2.90	4.46	3.71
货运量结构	Structure of Freight Traffic			
铁 路	Railways	34.59	44.30	26.92
公 路	Highways	65.36	55.58	73.04
民 航	Civil Aviation	0.05	0.12	0.04
国内贸易	**Domestic Trade**			
社会消费品零售总额结构	Composition of Retail Sales of Consumer Goods			
城 镇	Urban Area	88.95	87.99	90.17
农 村	Rural Area	11.05	12.01	9.83
国际旅游	**International Tourism**			
国际旅游人数结构	Structure of Tourists			
外国人	Foreigners	89.76	84.03	84.91
华侨及港澳台同胞	Overseas Chinese and Compatriots form Hong Kong, Macao and Taiwan	10.24	15.97	15.09
教育文化、卫生、人民生活	**Education and Culture，Health Care，People's Livelihood**			
教 育	**Education**			
在校学生结构	Structure of Student Enrollment			
#普通高等学校	Institutions of Higher Education	8.81	12.44	28.48
普通中等专业学校	Regular Specialized Secondary Schools	2.84	3.84	3.33
普通中学	Regular Schools	24.55	30.93	29.89
小 学	Primary Schools	59.91	49.89	32.45

continued 2

(%)

2007	2008	2009	2010	2011	2012	2013	2014	2015
32.44	29.80	25.50	24.63	36.81	43.03	43.03	41.58	38.41
57.78	59.14	67.14	68.61	53.75	47.57	47.86	49.43	51.84
			4.39	6.70	6.49	5.86	5.32	5.91
9.78	11.06	7.36	2.37	2.74	2.91	3.25	3.67	3.84
19.09	10.11	9.01	9.18	8.57	8.07	8.02	13.65	14.80
75.93	87.45	88.07	87.59	87.96	85.45	85.18	74.97	72.95
4.97	2.44	2.92	3.23	3.46	6.48	6.80	11.38	12.25
3.90	2.20	2.01	2.06	2.10	1.84	1.71	2.14	1.83
96.07	97.78	97.97	97.92	97.88	98.13	98.25	97.81	98.12
0.03	0.02	0.02	0.02	0.02	0.04	0.04	0.05	0.05
90.32	90.43	95.57	96.00	96.53	96.92	96.89	96.85	96.69
9.68	9.57	4.43	4.00	3.47	3.08	3.11	3.15	3.31
85.09	84.78	87.81	86.97	88.43	87.91	88.26		
14.91	15.22	12.19	13.03	11.58	12.08	11.74		
29.18	30.53	31.54	32.60	29.74	31.00	33.09	33.16	32.78
3.75	3.71	3.32	3.02	2.37	2.08	1.84	1.58	1.34
25.62	24.17	22.70	21.74	18.32	17.40	17.26	16.53	16.00
26.62	25.03	23.56	22.95	19.95	19.52	20.51	20.88	21.88

1-12 续表3

单位: %

指标	Item	1995	2000	2005
专任教师结构	Full-time Teachers by Type			
#普通高等学校	Institutions of Higher Education	21.25	19.89	29.93
普通中等专业学校	Regular Specialized Secondary Schools	3.38	4.02	2.16
普通中学	Regular Middk Schools	29.37	33.21	31.55
小 学	Primary Schools	40.41	38.34	30.08
人民生活	**People's Livelihood**			
城镇居民消费结构	Consumption Structure of Urban Residents			
食品烟酒	Food，Alcohol and Tobacco	44.68	36.46	37.04
衣 着	Clothing	12.67	8.13	9.03
家庭设备用品及服务	Household facilities,Articles and Services	13.75	11.33	4.73
医疗保健	Health Care	3.27	7.23	9.45
交通和通信	Transportation and Communication	5.58	6.93	9.67
教育文化娱乐服务	Recreation,Education and Culture Articles	9.05	13.74	17.18
居 住	Residence	6.49	11.23	9.10
杂项商品和服务	Articles for Daily Use and Others	4.51	4.95	3.80
农村居民消费结构	Consumption Structure of Rural Residents			
食品烟酒	Food，Alcohol and Tobacco	50.31	36.63	36.34
衣 着	Clothing	8.39	6.65	6.11
居 住	Residence	5.92	21.41	17.76
家庭设备用品及服务	Household facilities,Articles and Services	5.17	5.47	5.11
医疗保健	Health Care	1.78	6.93	8.19
交通和通讯	Transportation and Communication	8.09	4.21	8.19
文化娱乐用品及服务	Recreation,Education and Culture Articles	18.53	14.49	16.15
其它商品及服务	Articles for Daily Use and Others	1.81	4.21	2.15
卫 生	**Health Care**			
卫生技术人员结构	Medical Technical Personnel by Types			
执业（助理）医师	Licensed（Assistant） Doctors	45.42	44.82	41.96
注册护士	Registered Nurses	32.68	34.29	33.14
药 师	Junior Paramedics	8.78	8.31	7.30
技 师	Technicians	5.21	5.21	5.33
其 他	Others	7.91	7.37	12.27

注：2014年为城乡住户调查一体化改革后数据，居民消费结构与往年不可比。

continued 3

(%)

2007	2008	2009	2010	2011	2012	2013	2014	2015
30.72	31.63	31.90	32.47	31.97	32.96	33.91	33.87	34.52
1.68	1.55	1.35	1.42	1.29	1.18	1.08	0.97	0.89
26.25	25.53	24.68	24.30	23.70	23.36	22.95	23.62	23.86
25.55	24.68	23.83	23.10	22.37	21.97	21.49	20.57	20.52
36.61	36.40	32.43	31.29	31.29	32.48	32.44	29.21	29.59
9.41	10.25	10.98	11.11	12.27	12.17	12.02	9.09	8.78
5.91	6.33	7.28	7.56	8.11	7.87	7.80	7.21	7.42
8.40	9.67	9.65	9.50	9.00	8.52	7.99	7.32	7.92
11.35	10.37	11.33	12.06	12.81	14.26	14.01	14.16	13.31
14.52	14.35	14.34	14.66	14.27	14.33	14.17	12.60	12.48
10.18	8.81	8.86	9.33	8.26	8.47	7.82	17.89	17.78
3.62	3.82	5.13	4.49	4.00	1.91	3.76	2.53	2.72
38.15	36.95	35.81	32.54	31.89	33.83	32.96	29.93	28.18
6.09	6.52	6.40	6.55	7.20	7.42	7.87	7.44	7.12
22.72	19.39	19.47	24.41	23.92	21.91	19.82	21.99	23.28
5.66	7.02	6.97	6.53	7.10	7.46	7.76	6.97	6.60
7.61	8.05	8.50	8.54	8.65	8.85	8.41	11.07	10.68
7.58	7.84	9.83	8.45	9.01	10.19	9.86	10.66	10.70
10.44	12.43	11.13	11.20	10.43	10.20	10.56	10.26	11.68
1.75	1.80	1.89	1.78	1.80	0.14	2.77	1.68	1.76
39.51	38.09	37.34	33.16	35.17	34.46	33.58	32.66	32.69
35.09	36.23	39.05	40.01	40.87	41.61	42.13	42.28	42.74
6.19	5.74	5.45	5.36	5.10	5.05	4.99	4.88	4.86
6.97	6.68	6.49	8.11	5.91	5.91	5.75	5.63	5.76
12.24	13.26	11.67	13.36	12.95	12.97	13.55	14.56	13.97

1-13 主要年份国民经济和社会发展比例和效益指标

指　　标	Item	1995
人口与就业	**Population and Employment**	
人口	**Population**	
出生率(‰)	Birth Rate(‰)	11.95
死亡率(‰)	Death Rate(‰)	4.98
自然增长率(‰)	Natural Growth Rate(‰)	6.79
就业	**Employment**	
就业者负担人口	Dependency Ratio	1.7
三次产业就业者比例	Employment Ratio by Type of Industry	
(以第一产业为100)	(Employment in primary industry=100)	
第一产业	Primary Industry	100
第二产业	Secondary Industry	71.5
第三产业	Tertiary Industry	71.4
城镇登记失业率(%)	Unemployment Rate in Urban Areas(%)	3.1
宏观经济	**Macro Economy**	
国民经济核算	**National Accounting**	
三次产业增加值比例	Ratio of Value-added by Type of Industry	
(以第一产业为100)	(Employment in primary industry=100)	
第一产业	Primary Industry	100
第二产业	Secondary Industry	326.9
第三产业	Tertiary Industry	371.1
全社会劳动生产率(元／人)	Overall Labor Productivity(yuan/person)	8963
第一产业	Primary Industry	2698
第二产业	Secondary Industry	12404
第三产业	Tertiary Industry	14488
人均生产总值(元)	Per Capita GDP(yuan)	5131
固定资产投资	**Investment in Fixed Assets**	
全社会固定资产投资相当于生产总值比例(%)	Proportion of Investment in fixed Assets to GDP(%)	31.3
房屋建筑面积竣工率(%)	Rate of Floor Space of Buildings Completed in Construction(%)	33.4
固定资产交付使用率(%)	Rate of Fixed Assets Completed in Capital Construction and Put into Use(%)	70.7
建设项目建成投产率(%)	Rate of Projects Completed in Capital Construction and Put into Use(%)	43.7
财政	**Finance**	
财政总收入相当于生产总值比例(%)	Proportion of Local Government Revenue to GDP(%)	5.5
一般公共预算支出相当于生产总值比例(%)	Proportion of Local Government Public Expenditures to GDP(%)	5.6
利用外资	**Utilization of Foreign Capital**	
外商实际直接投资额相当于利用外资协议金额比例(%)	Proportion of Foreign Capital Actually Used to Total Amount of Foreign Capital for Utilization by Signed Contracts or Agreements (%)	64.4

注：本表财政收入数据2009年及以前为一般预算财政收入和基金收入之和。

Proportions of National Economic and Social Development and Benefit Index in Representative Years

2000	2005	2006	2007	2008	2009	2010	2011	2012	2013	2014	2015
13.07	9.58	9.98	10.00	10.15	10.08	9.73	9.71	10.13	9.57	10.11	10.15
5.96	5.16	5.46	5.48	5.57	5.63	5.34	5.38	5.57	5.37	5.47	5.51
7.11	4.42	4.52	4.52	4.58	4.45	4.39	4.33	4.56	4.20	4.64	4.64
1.8	1.8	1.8	1.9	1.9	1.9	1.8	1.7	1.7	1.6	1.6	1.6
100	100	100	100	100	100	100	100	100	100	100	100
73.0	83.8	85.9	93.8	101.9	107.7	124.0	125.0	141.3	137.2	144.6	120.3
91.7	121.3	126.5	133.5	148.6	171.0	183.3	184.7	206.5	243.3	262.9	270.1
3.4	4.3	4.3	4.3	4.2	4.3	4.2	3.9	3.5	3.4	3.4	3.4
100	100	100	100	100	100	100	100	100	100	100	100
620.7	818.8	916.6	947.7	948.8	1037.1	969.3	914.4	910.6	997.2	1023.0	965.6
726.4	1071.7	1168.2	1202.5	1192.0	1331.5	1246.1	1220.7	1236.2	1359.8	1437.1	1568.9
16367	31837	36730	43252	52422	59850	68990	79498	86971	94233	103281	109356
2960	4747	5191	6148	7921	8830	11701	14530	16578	17789	19915	20705
25443	47853	56073	64851	76899	87452	98027	106710	113561	127374	144703	151144
24024	44024	48938	56870	67031	73714	82377	96392	104914	107722	113188	121876
9484	16406	18890	22463	27794	32420	38357	45561	51499	57464	63794	66938
36.0	65.8	72.4	81.4	82.2	91.8	100.2	86.5	96.6	104.3	107.5	89.1
42.0	28.1	26.1	29.0	16.9	16.0	6.9	10.0	8.7	13.2	11.4	6.8
74.0	52.8	46.6	49.8	40.5	42.8	38.4	40.4	42.4	37.1	42.5	40.3
44.2	54.2	47.0	40.6	53.3	72.5	53.9	54.9	56.1	56.1	62.5	61
7.3	6.6	6.5	7.1	10.9	14.7	15.7	16.8	17.1	18.3	18.6	19.2
8.0	8.1	9.1	9.9	14.5	10.2	11.5	12.8	13.6	14.8	14.9	15.8
28.9	47.0	45.2	77.5	97.1	203.0	130.9	167.0	68.8	124.3	145.0	207.0

1-13 续表1

指　　标	Item	1995
能　　源	**Energy**	
单位生产总值能耗降低率(%)	Decreasing Rate of Energy Consumption per Unit GDP(%)	
规模以上工业单位工业增加值能耗降低率(%)	Decreasing Rate of Energy Consumption per Unit Industrial value-added of Industry Above Designated Size(%)	
单位生产总值电耗降低率(%)	Decreasing Rate of Electricity Consumption per Unit GDP(%)	
产　　业	**Industries**	
农业	**Agriculture**	
农业从业者人均耕地面积(公顷)	Cultivated Land per Agricultural Laborer(hectare)	0.20
每公顷耕地农业机械总动力(千瓦)	Total Power of Agricultural Machinery per Hectare of Cultivated Land(kw)	5.23
每公顷耕地化肥施用量(公斤)	Chemical Fertilizer Consumption per Hectare of Cultivated Land(kg)	536
每公顷耕地生产的农业总产值(元)	Agricultural Output Value per Hectare of Cultivated Land(yuan)	24396
每个农林牧渔及服务业劳动力农产品生产量(公斤)	Output of Farm Products per Farming,Forestry,Animal Husbandry,Fishery and Service Husbandry and Fishery Laborer (kg)	
粮食	Grain	1150
蔬菜	Vegetables	877
禽蛋	Poultry Eggs	93
肉类	Meat	84
水产品	Aquatic Products	6
每公顷播种面积农产品产量(公斤)	Output of Farm Crops per Hectare of Sown Area(kg)	
粮食	Grain	3806
油料	Oil-bearing Crops	1753
蔬菜	Vegetables	34800
工业	**Industrial**	
规模以上工业企业经济效益	**Economic Benefit of Industrial Enterprises above Designated Size**	
总资产贡献率(%)	Ratio of Total Assets to Industrial Output Value (%)	
资产负债率(%)	Assets-Liability Ratio (%)	
流动资产周转次数（次/年）	Rate of Annual Turnover Working Capitals(times/year)	
成本费用利润率(%)	Ratio of Profits to Cost (%)	
产品销售率(%)	Proportion of Industrial Products Sold(%)	
全员劳动生产率（元/人）	Overall Labor Productivity (yuan/person)	
建筑业	**Construction**	
机械装备率(元／人)	Value of Machinery per Laborer(yuan/person)	5990
产值利润率(%)	Ratio of Per-tax Profits to Gross Output Value (%)	3.5
全员劳动生产率(元／人)(按总产值计算)	Overall Labor Productivity(yuan/person) (in terms of gross output value per employee)	37689
邮电通信业	**Post and Communication Services**	
电话普及率(含移动电话）(部/百人)	Access to Telephones, National(include mobilphone) (set/100 persons)	7.9
移动电话普及率(部/百人)	Access to Mobilphones (set/100 persons)	0.48

continued 1

2000	2005	2006	2007	2008	2009	2010	2011	2012	2013	2014	2015
		4.15	5.75	6.65	5.56	2.06	3.56	3.51	3.57	5.89	3.20
		3.04	12.56	13.43	10.48	12.18	15.44	10.56	17.69	15.21	19.48
		4.48	6.94	6.93	5.33	1.00	4.43	2.92	2.26		
0.20	0.22	0.23	0.25	0.21	0.21	0.22	0.22	0.22	0.23	0.22	0.23
6.78	8.39	8.63	8.99	10.41	10.12	10.48	11.50	12.10	12.73	13.32	13.68
664	794	819	843	867	891	922	953	987	982	1045	1035
25161	39937	43261	51361	64593	69106	88869	108457	125041	140441	152695	160033
1382	1493	1569	1433	1695	1792	1901	1567	1700	1688	1592	1721
1110	1421	1536	1549	1752	1990	2171	2253	2452	2748	2867	3166
95	86	92	74	86	96	106	108	115	125	123	133
101	132	145	77	91	104	117	124	134	145	147	153
8	7	7	9	10	11	10	10	12	13	13	14
4342	4796	5025	4452	5102	5206	5349	4764	5045	4837	4777	5045
1526	1821	1880	1934	2008	1956	2004	1988	1987	1956	2097	2086
37797	35231	35916	33677	35723	38344	39667	40475	42607	44767	46713	48235
	8.4	7.8	10.2	8.6	11.3	12.2	8.6	7.7	8.5	7.4	5.7
65	65.0	64.3	64.6	62.6	61.1	57.6	57.7	59.4	59.5	59.7	57.3
1.0	1.3	1.4	1.6	1.5	1.7	1.7	1.5	1.5	1.5	1.4	1.3
4.2	3.1	5.5	7.3	4.6	8.1	8.8	5.2	4.5	5.2	5.2	4.8
97.1	97.5	98.2	96.8	96.1	97.6	97.1	97.4	96.7	95.7	94.9	94.5
29496	82815	97561	129706	150641	161289	188483	194105	230032	264324	275288	268182
6805	13332	13502	9079	12026	11928	9461	28669	12216	10339		12712
3.4	4.8	4.5	5.2	6.0	6.3	4.4	4.4	2.8	2.6	2.3	2.3
74347	206337	241887	203994	226669	285854	321340	334172	479232	354419	347000	406962
31.2	100.0	111.1	117.9	124.7	167.1	199.0	221.3	247.2	288.7	270.3	236.5
10.62	56.62	66.99	80.02	88.09	132.79	168.00	189.58	210.87	251.59	234.75	203.0

1-13 续表2

指　　标	Item	1995
国内贸易	**Domestic Trade**	
人均批发零售和住宿餐饮业消费品零售额(元)	Per Capita Retail Sales of Wholesale,Retail Trade and Accommodation Catering Trade (yuan)	1979
对外经济贸易	**Foreign Trade**	
进出口总额相当于生产总值比例(%)	Proportion of Total Imports & Exports to GDP(%)	34.76
旅游	**International Tourism**	
每一游客花费(元)	Expenditure per Tourist (yuan)	556
金融业	**Finance and Insurance**	
金融机构存款相当于生产总值比例(%)	Bank Deposits as Percentage of GDP(%)	108.83
金融机构贷款相当于生产总值比例(%)	Bank Loans as Percentage of GDP(%)	101.26
教育、科技、文化	**Education, Science and Technology and Culture**	
教育	**Education**	
毕业率(%)	Graduation Rate(%)	
小学	Primary Schools	
初中	Junior Schools	
学校教师负担系数	Student-teacher Ratio(in percentage)	
高等学校	Colleges and Universities	6.83
中等学校	Secondary Schools	14.42
小学	Primary Schools	26.22
文化	**Culture (unit)**	
每百万人有艺术表演团体	Number of Troupes per Million Persons	3.39
每百万人有公共图书馆	Number of Public Libraries per Million Persons	2.31
家庭、生活、环境	**Family, People's Livelihood and Environment**	
家庭	**Family**	
城市居民家庭	Urban Households	
平均每户就业面(%)	Percentage of Employees Per Household (%)	55.9
平均每一劳动力负担人口(人)	Persons Supported by Each Laborer (person)	1.8
农村居民家庭	Rural Households	
平均每一劳动力负担人口（人）	Persons Supported by Each Laborer(person)	1.6
卫生	**Health Care**	
每万人医院数（个）	Number of Hospitals per 10 000 Persons(unit)	0.60
每万人医生数(人)	Number of Doctors per 10 000 Persons(person)	29.10
每万人医院床位数(张)	Number of Hospital Beds per 10 000 Persons(unit)	43.60
市政建设	**City Construction**	
城市自来水普及率(%)	Percentage of Households with Access to Tap Water(%)	
城市用气普及率(%)	Percentage of Households with Access to Tap Gas (%)	
人均公园绿地面积(平方米)	Public Green Areas per 10 000 Persons(sq.m)	3.80

continued 2

2000	2005	2006	2007	2008	2009	2010	2011	2012	2013	2014	2015
4027	8795	9437	10932	13840	16638	19848	24007	28132	32004	35943	39293
22.25	24.79	22.01	22.21	21.97	18.16	21.22	20.52	18.61	22.27	27.89	30.37
645	737	746	761	753	757	767	797	820	801	792	789
206.71	283.41	275.92	259.80	264.31	273.69	273.32	267.47	274.09	277.48	274.26	304.82
150.51	169.91	159.11	152.16	149.22	162.81	198.00	193.71	194.77	201.63	210.76	234.52
						100.4	100.2	100.2	99.8	99.6	99.6
						99.7	100.6	98.7	99.3	99.9	98.3
12.38	17.99	17.36	16.97	17.13	17.32	17.41	17.92	18.15	18.05	18.27	17.76
17.84	18.47	20.51	19.99	18.97	18.27	17.78	16.91	16.43	15.07	14.01	13.88
25.75	20.38	19.78	18.61	17.99	17.32	17.22	18.06	17.15	17.66	18.94	19.94
3.20	2.56	2.31	2.16	2.15	2.13	1.53	3.52	2.22	2.10	2.09	2.07
2.18	2.02	1.82	1.81	1.79	1.78	1.77	1.76	1.75	1.75	1.74	1.49
45.7	47.4	48.3	47.8	47.9	53.2	53.7	54.8	54.0	54.6	76.9	76.9
2.2	2.1	2.1	2.1	2.1	1.9	1.9	1.8	1.9	1.8	1.3	1.3
1.6	1.6	1.6	1.6	1.5	1.5	1.5	1.5	1.5	1.5	1.4	1.4
0.57	0.59	0.58	0.55	0.52	0.49	0.49	0.43	0.44	0.44	0.44	0.45
25.30	21.98	21.89	20.79	21.57	22.86	22.14	25.31	26.95	27.81	28.77	30.58
38.72	37.29	37.49	37.11	39.40	41.38	43.42	43.77	47.45	51.45	54.56	58.98
98.95	99.00	99.09	100.01	111.22	100.00	98.77	99.95	100.00	100.00	100.00	100.00
81.51	91.30	92.62	98.60	97.66	98.15	97.02	97.46	98.19	98.68	98.71	98.79
5.12	5.63	7.59	7.61	7.80	7.90	9.11	9.89	10.22	10.70	11.22	11.47

1-14 主要年份平均每天主要社会经济活动

指　　标	Item	1995	2000
一、每天创造的财富	**Daily Production**		
生产总值(万元)	Gross Domestic Product(10 000 yuan)	9050.7	17702.2
第一产业	Primary Industry	1134.3	1223.3
第二产业	Secondary Industry	3707.7	7592.6
第三产业	Tertiary Industry	4208.8	8886.3
工业	Industry	3082.2	5984.7
建筑业	Construction	625.5	1608.0
批发和零售业	Wholesale and Retail Trade	909.6	1804.7
交通运输、仓储和邮政业	Transport, Storage, Post & Telecommunication Services	674.0	1178.4
住宿和餐饮业	Hotels and Catering Services		505.8
财政总收入(万元)	Total Government Revenue(10 000 yuan)	498.8	1304.0
财政一般预算支出(万元)	Government General Budgetary Expenditures(10 000 yuan)	504.7	1274.1
粮食(吨)	Grain(ton)	4801.0	5532.0
奶类(吨)	Milk(ton)	364	674
蔬菜(吨)	Vegetables(ton)	3660	4442
肉类(吨)	Meat(ton)	350	404
水产品(吨)	Aquatic Products(ton)	23	31
布(万米)	Cloth(10 000 m)	83	77
发电量(万千瓦小时)	Electricity(10 000 kwh)	610	534
钢材(吨)	Steel(ton)	861	274
汽车(辆)	Motor Vehicle(unit)	8	25
二、每天消费量	**Daily National Consumption**		
最终消费(万元)	Final Consumption Expenditure(10 000 yuan)	6565.5	11326.9
社会消费品零售总额(万元)	Total Retail Sales of Consumer Goods (10 000 yuan)	5112.3	9874.5
三、每天其他经济活动	**Other Daily Economic Activities**		
资本形成总额(万元)	Gross Capital Formation(10 000 yuan)	4152.1	7885.5
固定资本形成	Fixed Capital Formation		
存货增加	Changes in Stock		
竣工住宅面积(平方米)	Floor Space of Buildings Completed (sq.m)	6927	14930
货运量(万吨)	Freight Traffic(10 000 tons)	26.3	19.2
客运量(万人次)	Passenger Traffic(10 000 person-times)	24.8	22.1
邮电业务总量(万元)	Business Volume of Postal and Telecommunications Services(10 000 yuan)	209.6	1264.7
进出口总额(万美元)	Total Value of Imports and Exports (USD 10 000)	110.2	475.9
出口额	Exports	82.5	290.6
进口额	Imports	27.7	185.3
外商实际直接投资额(万美元)	Foreign Capital Actually Used(USD 10 000)	51.1	42.8
旅游者人数（人次）	Number of Tourists (person-time)	21681	42932
四、每天人口变动和婚姻	**Daily Population Changes and Marriages**		
出　生(人)	Births(person)	211	247
死　亡(人)	Deaths(person)	88	113
结　婚(对)	Marriages(couple)	129	129
离　婚(对)	Divorces(couple)	12	14

注：本表财政收入数据2009年及以前为一般预算财政收入和基金收入之和。

Major Social and Economic Activities in Representative Years

2005	2007	2008	2009	2010	2011	2012	2013	2014	2015
35998.1	50866.6	63510.7	74654.2	88845.5	106023.0	120396.4	134930.7	150483.3	158937.0
1808.5	2260.6	2834.3	3024.1	3837.3	4743.6	5358.6	5491.8	5878.1	6032.9
14808.2	21423.0	26892.6	31363.0	37192.6	43375.6	48797.0	54762.2	60131.0	58254.5
19381.4	27183.0	33783.8	40267.1	47815.6	57903.8	66240.8	74676.7	84474.2	94649.6
11506.9	16300.0	19764.4	22381.6	26147.7	30095.9	33644.9	37718.9	40767.7	37718.4
3301.4	5123.0	7128.2	8981.6	11045.2	13279.5	15151.8	17596.2	19965.5	21103.8
4032.9	5356.4	6655.1	8172.3	9654.0	12047.9	14053.7	15773.2	17360.3	18301.1
1816.4	2307.1	2716.7	3069.0	3717.8	4525.5	5272.9	5893.4	6454.2	7132.3
1381.9	1920.3	2346.6	2570.4	2816.4	3233.4	3550.1	3714.5	3949.3	4360.0
2300.6	3433.6	6417.8	9080.0	13991.5	17805.0	20632.1	24733.3	27936.7	30547.4
2819.6	4771.4	8679.2	11509.0	10181.4	13550.0	16369.6	19994.8	22453.2	25129.9
5631	5180	5874	5978	6074	4987	5275	5017	4811	4955
1157	1447	1616	1694	1736	1775	1826	1802	1803	1746
5362	5601	6069	6641	6934	7169	7611	8168	8665	9118
499	280	316	346	374	396	416	431	444	442
26	34	34	36	33	32	38	39	39	39
74.0	76.7	62.3	60.8	65.2	44.8	39.1	38.0	33.0	28.5
1316.3	1946.3	1964.1	2279.7	2655.9	2603.0	2725.5	5055	4920	4347
658	2157	1312	3028	3035	506	857	1488	1175	1015
112	468	734	1389	1787	1525	1484	1156	1027	935
21003.3	27266.3	32400.3	38441.1	43794.8	50874.2	57341.6			
18371.5	25649.6	32235.1	37838.9	44850.4	53862.5	62023.6	75147.7	84764.1	93298.1
22986.6	39766.3	50352.3	62518.1	77682.7	89447.4	103646.6			
20918.4	34795.6	45315.3	58878.9	72237.8	83395.6	97509.0			
2068.2	4970.7	5037.0	3639.2	5444.9	6051.8	6137.5			
16400	25466	18998	22537	12287	23601	24762	23014	40078	22632
33.0	41.4	75.5	83.9	94.0	107.5	123.1	137.3	115.2	126.8
28.7	34.2	72.6	78.6	83.0	91.4	99.1	104.9	70.5	73.7
3617.7	6212.7	7256.4	8189.6	8852.3	5494.8	5923.6	6793.0	8016.4	9083.1
1068.9	1468.9	1928.9	1985.3	2847.3	3452.5	3565.6	4927.5	6833.5	7749.3
721.8	951.0	1225.0	912.6	1456.8	1596.3	1999.7	2322.8	3276.7	3606.4
347.1	517.9	703.9	1072.6	1390.5	1856.2	1565.9	2604.7	3556.8	4142.8
156.5	305.7	314.4	333.9	429.2	549.4	678.9	857.5	1014.5	1098.2
66400	85425	88553	107652	144799	182280	218585	277534	328767	372625
210	226	232	232	225	226	237	225	238	241
63	124	127	130	124	125	130	126	129	131
137	185	213	241	229	259	246	244	250	221
35	43	43	43	52	53	51	56	60	62

1-15 各区县国民经济和社会发展主要指标（2015年）

指　标	Item	新城区 Xincheng	碑林区 Beilin
一、年底总人口（常住人口）（万人）	Population at the Year-end Permanent population(10 000 persons)	60.33	62.89
二、生产总值（亿元）	Gross Domestic Product(100 mil. yuan)	494.00	677.74
第一产业	Primary Industry		
第二产业	Secondary Industry	178.21	134.23
第三产业	Tertiary Industry	315.79	543.51
三、全社会固定资产投资总额（亿元）	Total Investment in Fixed Assets(100 mil. yuan)	289.25	199.98
#固定资产投资（不含农户）	Investment in Fixed Assets (excluding farmers)	289.25	199.98
#房地产	Real Estate	60.90	115.73
四、财政一般公共预算收入（亿元）	General Public Budgetary Revenue(100 mil. yuan)	37.07	45.33
财政一般公共预算支出（亿元）	General Public Budgetary Expenditure(100 mil. yuan)	34.15	32.20
五、农林牧渔及服务业总产值（万元）	Gross Output Value of Farming Forestry Animal Husbandry and Fishery(10 000 yuan)		
主要农产品产量（万吨）	Output of Major Farm Products(10 000 tons)		
粮食	Grain		
蔬菜	Vegetables		
瓜果	Melon and Fruit		
肉类(吨)	Meat (Ton)		
奶类(吨)	Milk (Ton)		
六、规模以上工业总产值（亿元）	Gross industrial Output Value(100 mil. yuan)	398.68	29.59
七、建筑业	Gross Output Value		
房屋建筑施工面积（万平方米）	Floor Space of Buildings under Construction (10 000 sq.m)	1091.29	3914.92
房屋建筑竣工面积（万平方米）	Total Retail Sales of Consumer Goods (100 mil. yuan)	260.95	800.72
八、社会消费品零售总额（亿元）	Floor Space of Buildings Completed(100 mil. yuan)	557.59	561.46
九、城镇居民人均可支配收入（元）	Per Capita Annual Disposable Income of Urban Households (yuan)	40014	40804
农村居民人均纯收入（元）	Per Capita Net Income of Rural Residents(yuan)		
十、医疗机构数（个）	Number of Health Care Institutions(unit)	271	388
卫生技术人员（人）	Number of Medical Technical Personnel (person)	10893	11946
床位数（张）	Number of Beds(unit)	6964	7486

Principal Indicators of National Economy and Social Development by Region（2015）

莲湖区 Lianhu	灞桥区 Baqiao	未央区 Weiyang	雁塔区 Yanta	阎良区 Yanliang	临潼区 Lintong	长安区 Chang'an	高陵区 Gaoling	蓝田县 Lantian	周至县 Zhouzhi	户 县 Huxian
71.23	61.39	83.05	120.96	28.84	67.62	111.83	34.77	52.53	58.09	57.03
573.60	312.87	720.22	1165.11	188.72	193.10	513.88	297.19	112.10	104.33	155.41
	18.74	1.34	0.14	22.37	30.27	36.53	27.70	26.00	29.54	27.57
183.47	124.24	357.71	365.07	102.71	81.20	261.90	215.02	32.89	25.01	64.61
390.13	169.89	361.17	799.90	63.64	81.63	215.45	54.47	53.21	49.78	63.23
283.10	505.92	927.05	812.15	287.21	186.31	726.53	432.08	196.68	168.95	150.77
283.10	500.12	924.62	810.00	283.80	174.56	709.46	429.12	185.18	156.72	141.01
191.48	256.50	520.01	462.01	14.61	23.14	124.52	31.71	6.22	10.28	14.57
49.16	25.42	37.80	50.17	12.83	13.74	37.78	14.13	4.26	3.93	9.14
41.05	29.54	28.24	34.75	22.06	39.22	53.43	25.54	30.10	34.17	33.89
	307940	25786	3205	368854	551556	584120	495452	465601	508904	496155
	5.40	0.19		8.82	32.87	34.59	19.28	26.04	23.17	30.50
	29.59	2.67		81.72	44.62	58.77	46.17	18.32	21.03	29.90
	0.67	0.04		24.55	7.11	8.36	3.29	4.18	0.50	5.64
	7532	2873	407	7514	43687	20973	10102	19856	28388	19922
	45863	8561	14	101007	317828	33627	51119	41075	13798	24448
402.62	175.89	839.29	677.00	321.23	263.29	720.87	869.60	49.32	41.25	135.94
1649.89	131.98	2049.99	2450.46	85.08	53.47	195.72	122.80	42.51	67.36	123.69
357.43	52.34	254.22	648.61	28.47	25.47	100.41	64.96	16.35	41.64	60.44
451.82	173.26	515.21	656.47	37.90	77.99	183.37	31.73	56.40	38.47	63.71
40802	38011	39397	41428	40533	32197	35048	30842	25834	26427	29153
	18521	20024		18572	14838	15502	14863	10835	10897	13310
349	453	385	492	162	534	810	230	640	475	613
10856	4212	7728	14353	2007	2648	6083	2322	1900	2637	3877
7350	3059	4873	8726	1422	2331	4953	1632	1256	1517	3139

主要统计指标解释

行政区划 指国家对行政区域的划分。根据有关法规规定，我国的行政区域划分如下：（1）全国分为省、自治区、直辖市；（2）省、自治区分为自治州、县、自治县、市；（3）自治州分为县、自治县、市；（4）县、自治县分为乡、民族乡、镇；（5）直辖市和较大的市分为区、县；（6）国家在必要时设立的特别行政区。

气候 指地球与大气之间长期能量交换与质量交换所形成的一种自然环境状态，它是多种因素综合作用的结果。气候既是人类生活和生产的环境要素之一，又是供给人类生活和生产的重要资源。气温、降水、湿度等气象要素的多年平均值是用来描述一个地区气候状况的主要参数，而各种气象要素某年、某月的平均值（或总量）则可以反映出该时期天气气候状况的重要特征。

自然资源 指人类可以直接从自然界获得，并用于生产和生活的物质资源。自然资源一般可以分成可再生资源和非再生资源两大类。可再生资源指在较短时间内可以再生、可以循环利用的资源，包括土地资源、水资源、气候资源、生物资源和海洋资源等。非再生资源指在使用后不能再生的资源，包括矿产资源和地热能源。

土地资源 土地指陆地的表层部分，它主要由岩石、岩石的风化物和土壤构成。土地资源按利用类型可以分为农用地、建筑用地和未利用地。农用地包括耕地、园地、林地、牧草地和水面。建筑用地包括居民点及工矿用地、交通用地和水利设施用地。未利用地指农用地和建筑用地以外的土地，包括滩涂、荒漠、戈壁、冰川和石山等。

耕地面积 指经过开垦用以种植农作物并经常进行耕耘的土地面积。包括种有作物的土地面积、休闲地、新开荒地和抛荒未满三年的土地面积。

森林面积 指由乔木树种构成，郁闭度0.2以上（含0.2）的林地或冠幅宽度10米以上的林带的面积，即有林地面积。森林面积包括天然起源和人工起源的针叶林面积、阔叶林面积、针阔混交林面积和竹林面积，不包括灌木林地面积和疏林地面积。

林业用地面积 指生长乔木、竹类、灌木、沿海红树林等林木的土地面积，包括有林地、灌木林、疏林地、未成林造林地、迹地、苗圃等。

水资源总量 指评价区内降水形成的地表和地下产水总量，即地表产流量与降水入渗补给地下水量之和，不包括过境水量。

地表水资源量 指评价区内河流、湖泊、冰川等地表水体中可以逐年更新的动态水量，即当地天然河川径流量。

地下水资源量 指评价区内降水和地表水对饱水岩土层的补给量，包括降水入渗补给量和河道、湖库、渠系、渠灌田间等地表水体的入渗补给量。

气温 指空气的温度，我国一般以摄氏度（℃）为单位表示。气象观测的温度表是放在离地面约1.5米处通风良好的百叶箱里测量的，因此，通常说的气温指的是离地面1.5米处百叶箱中的温度。其统计计算方法为：

月平均气温是将全月各日的平均气温相加，除以该月的天数而得。

年平均气温是将12个月的月平均气温累加后除以12而得。

降水量 指从天空降落到地面的液态或固态（经融化后）水，未经蒸发、渗透、流失而在地面上积聚的深度。其统计计算方法为：

月降水量是将全月各日的降水量累加而得。

年降水量是将12个月的月降水量累加而得。

日照时数 指太阳实际照射地面的时间。其统计方法与降水量相同。

平均增长速度 平均增长速度表明社会经济现象在一个较长的时期内逐期平均增长变化的程度，它不能根据各个环比增长速度直接求得，但与平均发展速度之间存在着一定的数量关系：平均增长速度 = 平均发展速度 - 1。

平均发展速度 是一种根据环比发展速度计算的序时平均数,由于各时期对比的基础不同，所以计算平均发展速度不能采用一般的序时平均数的计算方法，计算方法分为水平法和累计法。水平法，又称几何平均法，即将环比发展速度按连乘法用几何平均数公式计算。累计法，也称方程法，根据一段时期内各年发展水平总和与基期水平的关系，列出方程式计算平均发展速度。水平法着重考虑最后一年所达到的发展水平；累计法着重考虑整个时期累计发展水平的总量。

本《年鉴》内所列的平均增长速度，均用“水平法”计算。从某年到某年平均增长速度的年份，均不包括基期年在内。如建国六十年以来的平均增长速度是以1949年为基期计算的，则写为1950-2009年平均增长速度，其余类推。

Explanatory Notes on Main Statistical Indicators

Divisions of Administrative Areas refers to the division of administrative areas by the State. The relative laws stipulate that (1)the whole country is divided into provinces, autonomous regions and municipalities directly under the Central Government;(2)provinces and autonomous regions are further divided into autonomous prefectures, counties, autonomous counties and cities; (3)autonomous prefectures are further divided into counties, autonomous counties and cities; (4)counties and autonomous counties are further divided into townships, ethnic townships and towns; (5)municipalitics directly under the Central Government and large cities are divided into districts and counties, (6)the State shall, when necessary, establish special administrative regions.

Climate refers to the natural environmental status formed by the long-term exchange of energy and mass between the earth and the atmosphere, and is the result of interaction of many factors. Climate is both one of the environment factors and also the important resources for living and production activities of the human being. The average values across several years of meteorological factors such as temperature, rainfall and humidity are used as important parameters to describe the climate of a region, while the average values (or total values)of a given year or month of meteorological factors reflect the key characteristics of climate for that period of time.

Natural Resources refer to material resources that could be obtained from the nature by human being and used for production and living. Natural resources in general can be classified as renewable resources and non-renewable resources. Renewable resources refer to resources that could be renewed and recycled during a relatively short period of time, including land resource, water resource, climate resource, biology resource and marine resource. Non-renewable resources include resources that could not be renewed, such as minerals and geothermal resource.

Land Resource Land refers to the surface of the earth, consisting of mainly rocks and its whethering and earth. Land resource can be classified, by its utilization, as land for agriculture, land for construction and unused land. Land for agriculture includes cultivated land, plantation land, forestland, grassland and waters. Land for construction includes land for residential purpose, for manufacturing and mining, for transportation and for water-conservancy projects. Unused land refers to land other than land for agriculture and.construction, including beaches, deserts, Gobi, glaciers and rock mountains.

Area of Cultivated Land refers to area of land reclaimed for the regular cultivation of various farm crops, including crop-cover land, fallow, newly reclaimed land and land laid idle for less than 3 years.

Forest Area refers to the area of trees and bamboo grow with canopy density above 0.2, the area of shrubby tree according to regulations of the government, the area of forest land inside farm land and the area of trees planted by the side of villages, farm houses and along roads and rivers.

Area of Afforested Land refers to area for land for trees bamboo, bushes and mangrove, including forest-covered land, bush-covered land, sparse forest land, land planned for afforestation and nurseries of young trees.

Total Water Resources refers to total volume of water resources measured as run-off for surface water from rainfall and recharge for groundwater in a given area, excluding transit water.

Surface Water Resources refers to total renewable resources which exist in rivers, lakes, glaciers and other collectors from rainfall and are measured as run-off of rivers.

Groundwater Resources refers to replenishment of aquifers with rainfall and surface water.

Temperature refers to the air temperature. China uses centigrade as the unit. The thermometry used for weather observation is put in a breezy shutter, which is 1.5 meters high from the ground. Therefore, the commonly used temperature refers to the temperature in the breezy shutter 1.5 meters away from the ground. The calculation method is as follows:

Monthly average temperature is the summation of average daily temperature of one month divided by the actual days of that particular month.

Annual average temperature is the summation of monthly average of a year divided by 12 months.

Volume of Precipitation refers to the deepness of liquid state or solid state (thawed)water falling from the sky to the ground that has not been evaporated, infiltrated or run off. The calculation method is as follows:

Monthly precipitation is the summation of daily precipitation of a month.

Annual precipitation is the summation of 12 months precipitation of a year.

Sunshine Hours refer to the actual hours of sun irradiating the earth. The calculation method is the same as that of the precipitation.

Average Annual Growth Rate shows the average growth rate of social and economic development during a longer period. It can not be directly calculated by chain based growth rate. The relation is:

Average Annual Growth Rate=Average Speed of Development 1

Average speed of development is the time series average of speed which calculated by chain based.Because the reference bases during the different periods are not same, average speed of development can not be calculated by the general method. Level approach and accumulative approach for calculating average speed of development rate are applied. The "level approach" , or the method of calculating the geometric average, is derived by the formula of geometric average of the chain-based speeds of development, or comparing the level of the last year of the interval with that of the beginning year; the other is called the "accumulative approach" or the "algebraic average" , "equation" method, which is derived by the summation of the actual figure of each year in the interval divided by the figure in the base year. The level approach focuses on the level of the last year, while the accumulative approach emphasizes the aggregate development in the duration.

The average annual growth rates listed in the Yearbook are calculated by the level approach except for the growth rate of investment in fixed assets. The base year is not listed in the duration for which average annual growth rates are computed. For instance, the average annual growth rate of the 60 years since 1949 is shown as the average annual growth rate of 1950-2009 without showing the base year 1949.

2 基本单位

BASIC UNIT

资料整理：张　奇　张　斌
Data management：Zhang Qi　Zhang Bin
数据审核：张利民
Data audit：Zhang Limin

第二部分　基本单位

一、简要说明

本章资料主要包括法人单位、产业活动单位和企业一套表调查单位数等资料，由西安市统计局普查中心提供。本年统计年鉴一套表单位数为年报数，使用时请注意。

二、主要指标

法人单位数（个）	122726	比上年增长	10.5%
产业活动单位数（个）	135227	比上年增长	6.4%
规模以上工业企业数（个）	1117	比上年增长	0.4%
限额以上批发零售住宿餐饮业企业数（个）	1373	比上年增长	2.4%
资质内建筑业企业数（个）	706	比上年增长	31.0%
房地产开发经营企业数（个）	859	比上年增长	9.6%
规模以上服务业企业数（个）	1056	比上年增长	9.5%

2　BASIC UNIT

Ⅰ.Brief Introduction

This chapter consists of unified data of enterprises and industrial active unites and investigation unit in “Enterprises Data in One sheet”, provided by census center of Xi’an Municipal Bureau of statistics . Data of “Enterprises Data in One Sheet” in this Yearbook is the number of annual reports, please note that when used.

Ⅱ.Major Indicators

		Increase over Preceding Year
Number of Enterprises (unit)	122726	10.5%
Number of Industrial Active Units (unit)	135227	6.4%
Number of Industrial Enterprises above Designed Size (unit)	1117	0.4%
Number of Enterprises about Wholesale、Retail、Accommodation and Catering above Designed Size (unit)	1373	2.4%
Number of Qualified Construction Enterprises (unit)	706	31.0%
Number of Real Estate Development Enterprises (unit)	859	9.6%
Number of service Enterprises above Designed Size (unit)	1056	9.5%

2-1 按登记注册类型分法人单位数（2015年）

Impersonal Entities by Status of Registion（2015）

单位：个 (unit)

分 组	Classify	法人单位数 Number of Enterprises	企业 Enterprises
总 计	**Total**	**122726**	**106485**
#非公有制企业法人	Non-public corporate	100602	100602
按登记注册类型分	**Grouped by Status of Registion**		
（一）内资	Domestic Funded Enterprises	121883	105650
国有	State-owned Enterprises	7108	1692
集体	Collective-owned Enterprises	2687	1542
股份合作	Cooperative Enterprises	325	306
联营	Joint Ownership Enterprises	237	201
国有联营	State Joint Ownership Enterprises	31	24
集体联营	Collective Joint Ownership Enterprises	122	117
国有与集体联营	Joint State-collective Ownership Enterprises	17	11
其他联营	Other Joint Ownership Enterprises	67	49
有限责任公司	Limited Liability Corporations	44583	44465
国有独资公司	State Sole Funded Corporations	293	293
其他有限责任公司	Other Limited Liability Corporations	44290	44172
股份有限公司	Share-holding Corporations Limited	1086	1078
私营	Private Enterprises	52142	51891
私营独资企业	Private-funded Enterprises	11970	11801
私营合伙	Private Partnership Enterprises	1288	1247
私营有限责任公司	Private Limited Liability Corporations	37665	37626
私营股份有限公司	Private Share-holding Corporations Ltd.	1219	1217
其他	Other Domestic Funded Enterprises	13715	4475
（二）港、澳、台商投资企业	Enterprises with Funds from Hong Kong, Macao and Taiwan	264	263
与港、澳、台商合资经营	Joint-venture with Funds from Hong Kong,Macao and Taiwan	96	96
与港、澳、台商合作经营	Cooperative Enterprises with Funds from Hong Kong Macau and Taiwan	11	10
港澳台商独资经营	Enterprises with Sole Investment from Hong Kong Macau and Taiwan	138	138
港澳台商投资股份有限公司	Share-holding Corporations Ltd. with funds from Hong Kong, Macao & Taiwan	17	17
其他港澳台商投资	Other Enterprises with Funds from Hong Kong, Macao and Taiwan	2	2
（三）外商投资	Foreign Funded Enterprises	579	572
中外合资经营	Sino-foreign Joint Ventures	225	224
中外合作经营	Sino-Foreign Cooperation Enterprises	14	13
外资企业	Foreign Owned Enterprises	274	270
外商投资股份有限公司	Limited Company Funded by Foreign Investment	31	31
其他外商投资	Other Foreign Funded Enterprises	35	34

2-2 按国民经济行业分法人单位数（2015年）

Impersonal Entities by Industry of the National Economy（2015）

单位：个　　　　　　　　　　　　　　　　　　　　　　　　　　(unit)

分 组	Classify	法人单位数 Number of Enterprises	企业 Enterprises
总 计	**Total**	**122726**	**106485**
（一）农、林、牧、渔业	Agriculture,Forestry,Animal Husbandry and Fishery	3652	2667
农业	Farming	1760	1208
林业	Forestry	456	393
畜牧业	Animal Husbandry	1069	820
渔业	Fishery	62	53
农、林、牧、渔服务业	Services in Support of Agriculture	305	193
（二）采矿业	Mining	251	251
煤炭开采和洗选业	Mining and Washing of Coal	8	8
石油和天然气开采业	Extraction of Petroleum and Natural Gas	24	24
黑色金属矿采选业	Mining of Ferrous Metal Ores	12	12
有色金属矿采选业	Mining of Non-ferrous Metal Ores	23	23
非金属矿采选业	Mining and Processing of Nonmetal Ores	75	75
开采辅助活动	Mining of Other Ores	85	85
其他采矿业	Manufacturing	24	24
（三）制造业	Processing of Food from Agricultural Products	14167	14167
农副食品加工业	Manufacture of Foods	455	455
食品制造业	Manufacture of Beverages	440	440
酒、饮料和精制茶制造业	Manufacture of Tobacco	134	134
烟草制品业	Manufacture of Textile	2	2
纺织业	Manufacture of Textile Wearing	140	140
	Apparel, Footware and Caps		
纺织服装、服饰业	Manufacture of Leather, Fur,	137	137
	Feather and Related Products		
皮革、毛皮、羽毛及其	Processing of Timber,Manufacture of Wood,	35	35
制品和制鞋业	Bamboo,Rattan, its Froducts and Footwear		
木材加工和木、竹、藤、棕、	Plam and Straw Products	198	198
草制品业	and Straw Products		
家具制造业	Manufacture of Furniture	400	400
造纸及纸制品业	Manufacture of Paper and Paper Products	325	325
印刷和记录媒介复制业	Printing,Reproduction of Recording Media	544	544
文教、工美、体育和娱乐	Manufacture of Articles For Culture,	199	199
用品制造业	Education and Sport Activities		

2-2 续表1 continued 1

单位：个 (unit)

分 组	Classify	法人单位数 Number of Enterprises	企业 Enterprises
石油加工、炼焦和核燃料加工业	Processing of Petroleum, Coking, Processing of Nuclear Fuel	52	52
化学原料和化学制品制造业	Manufacture of Raw Chemical Materials and Chemical Products	679	679
医药制造业	Manufacture of Medicines	351	351
化学纤维制造业	Manufacture of Chemical Fibers	26	26
橡胶和塑料制品业	Manufacture of Rubber and Manufacture of Plastics	468	468
非金属矿物制品业	Manufacture of Non-metallic Mineral Products	1327	1327
黑色金属冶炼和压延加工业	Smelting and Pressing of Ferrous Metals	240	240
有色金属冶炼和压延加工业	Smelting and Pressing of Non-ferrous Metals	188	188
金属制品业	Manufacture of Metal Products	1003	1003
通用设备制造业	Manufacture of General Purpose Machinery	1883	1883
专用设备制造业	Manufacture of Special Equipment	1411	1411
汽车制造业	Manufacture of Motor Vehicle	180	180
铁路、船舶、航空航天和其他运输设备制造业	Railways,Shipbuilding,Aerospace and Other Transportation Equipment Manufacturing Industry	306	306
电气机械和器材制造业	Manufacture of Electric Equipment and Machinery	1407	1407
计算机、通信和其他电子设备制造业	Manufacture of Communication Equipment, Computers and other Electronic Equipment	751	751
仪器仪表制造业	Manufacture of Measuring Instruments and Machinery	547	547
其他制造业	Other Manufacturing	134	134
废弃资源综合利用	Recycling and Disposal of Waste	48	48
金属制品、机械和设备修理业	Metal Products,Machinery and Equipment Repair Industry	157	157
（四）电力、燃气及水的生产供应业	Production and Distribution of Electricity,Gas and Water	316	315
电力、热力生产和供应业	Production and Supply of Electric Power and Heat Power	185	185
燃气生产和供应业	Gas mining and supplying industry	46	46
水的生产和供应业	Production and Supply of Water	85	84
（五）建筑业	Construction	9099	9099
房屋建筑业	Construction of Building	1680	1680
土木工程建筑业	Civil Engineering	1772	1772
建筑安装业	Architectural Installation	1623	1623
建筑装饰和其他建筑业	Architectural Decoration and Other Construction	4024	4024
（六）批发和零售业	Wholesale and Retail Trades	39743	39743

2-2 续表2 continued 2

单位：个

分 组	Classify	法人单位数 Number of Enterprises	企业 Enterprises
批发业	Wholesale Trade	22278	22278
零售业	Retail Trade	17465	17465
（七）交通运输、仓储和邮政业	Traffic, Transport, Storage and Post	2213	2164
铁路运输业	Transport Via Railway	31	26
道路运输业	Transport Via Road	1228	1198
水上运输业	Water Transport	4	4
航空运输业	Air Transport	61	60
管道运输业	Transport Via Pipeline	8	8
装卸搬运和运输代理服务业	Loading, Unloading, Portage and Other Transport Services	478	476
仓储业	Storage	299	290
邮政业	Post	104	102
（八）住宿和餐饮业	Hotels and Catering Services	3331	3323
住宿业	Hotels	1313	1309
餐饮业	Catering Services	2018	2014
（九）信息传输、软件和信息技术服务业	Information Transmission, Computer Services and Software	5024	5002
电信、广播电视和卫星传输服务	Telecom & Other Information Transmission Services	217	213
互联网和相关服务	internet and relevant services	695	692
软件和信息技术服务	Software Industry	4112	4097
（十）金融业	Financial Intermediation	748	736
货币金融服务	Monetary and Financial Services	176	173
资本市场服务	Capital Market Services	332	330
保险业	Insurance	157	154
其他金融业	Other Financial Intermediation	83	79
（十一）房地产业	Real Estate	6612	6592
房地产业	Real Estate	6612	6592
（十二） 租赁和商务服务业	Leasing and Business Services	12073	11769
租赁业	Leasing	895	893
商务服务业	Business Services	11178	10876
（十三）科学研究和技术服务业	Scientific Research, Technical Sevice	5210	4615
研究与试验发展	Research and Experimental Development	543	455
专业技术服务业	Professional Technical Services	3513	3215

2-2 续表3 continued 3

单位：个 (unit)

分 组	Classify	法人单位数 Number of Enterprises	企业 Enterprises
科技推广和应用服务业	Services of Science and Technology Exchanges and Promotion	1154	945
（十四）水利、环境和公共设施管理业	Management of Water Conservancy, Environment and Public Facilities	984	786
水利管理业	Management of Water Conservancy	160	74
生态保护和环境治理业	Environmental Management	113	87
公共设施管理业	Management of Public Facilities	711	625
（十五）居民服务、修理和其他服务业	Services to Households and Other Services	2661	2598
居民服务业	Services to Households	926	871
机动车、电子产品和日用产品修理业	The repair service industry for motor vehicle、electronic	1110	1106
其他服务业	Other Services	625	621
（十六）教育	Education	3688	429
教育	Education	3688	429
（十七）卫生和社会工作	Health, Social Security	3254	245
卫生	Health	3041	223
社会工作	Social	213	22
（十八）文化、体育和娱乐业	Culture, Sports and Entertainment	2285	1978
新闻和出版业	Journalism and Publishing Activities	171	125
广播、电视、电影和影视录音制作业	Broadcasting, Movies, Television and Audiovisual Activities	365	348
文化艺术业	Cultural and Art Activities	699	500
体育	Sports Activities	162	128
娱乐业	Entertainment	888	877
（十九）公共管理、社会保障和社会组织	Public Management and Social Organizaion	7415	6
中国共产党机关	Organs of Communist Party of China	158	
国家机构	Government Agencies	2087	
人民政协、民主党派	People's Pc~litical Consultative Conference and Democratic Parties	32	
社会保障	Social Security	68	6
群众团体、社会团体和其他成员组织	Mass organizations、social groups and other members of the organization	1350	
基层群众自治组织	Grass-roots Mass Self-Government Organizations	3720	
（二十）国际组织	International Organizations		
国际组织	International Organizations		

2-3 按行政区划分法人单位数（2015年）

Impersonal Entities by Region（2015）

单位：个 (unit)

区 县	Region	法人单位数 Number of Enterprises	企业 Enterprises
总 计	**Total**	**122726**	**106485**
新城区	Xincheng	8491	7585
碑林区	Beilin	14188	13170
莲湖区	Lianhu	12145	11202
灞桥区	Baqiao	4943	3980
未央区	Weiyang	20082	19090
雁塔区	Yanta	32159	31116
阎良区	Yanliang	2701	2147
临潼区	Lintong	4420	2822
长安区	Chang'an	7848	5704
高陵区	Gaoling	3264	2441
蓝田县	Lantian	4119	2457
周至县	Zhouzhi	3400	1775
户 县	Huxian	4966	2996

2–4 按登记注册类型分产业活动单位数（2015年）

Industrial Active Units by Status of Registion（2015）

单位：个　　(unit)

分　组	Classify	产业活动单位数 Number of Industrial Active Units	企业 Enterprises
总计	**Total**	**135227**	**116157**
按登记注册类型分	Grouped by Status of Registion		
（一）内资	Domestic Funded Enterprises	133646	114584
国有	State-owned Enterprises	10385	2820
集体	Collective-owned Enterprises	3398	1949
股份合作	Cooperative Enterprises	599	579
联营	Joint Ownership Enterprises	330	288
国有联营	State Joint Ownership Enterprises	53	46
集体联营	Collective Joint Ownership Enterprises	152	143
国有与集体联营	Joint State-collective Ownership Enterprises	27	19
其他联营	Other Joint Ownership Enterprises	98	80
有限责任公司	Limited Liability Corporations	48070	47946
国有独资公司	State Sole Funded Corporations	319	319
其他有限责任公司	Other Limited Liability Corporations	47751	47627
股份有限公司	Share-holding Corporations Limited	2289	2281
私营	Private Enterprises	54278	54017
私营独资企业	Private-funded Enterprises	12415	12239
私营合伙	Private Partnership Enterprises	1377	1335
私营有限责任公司	Private Limited Liability Corporations	39170	39129
私营股份有限公司	Private Share-holding Corporations Ltd.	1316	1314
其他	Other Enterprises	14297	4704

2-4 续表 continued

单位：个 (unit)

分　组	Classify	产业活动单位数 Number of Industrial Active Units	企业 Enterprises
（二）港、澳、台商投资企业	Enterprises with Funds from Hong Kong,Macao and Taiwan	475	474
与港、澳、台商合资经营	Joint-venture with Funds from Hong Kong,Macao and Taiwan	124	124
与港、澳、台商合作经营	Cooperative Enterprises with Funds from Hong Kong Macau and Taiwan	23	22
港澳台商独资经营	Enterprises with Sole Investment from Hong Kong Macau and Taiwan	297	297
港澳台商投资股份有限公司	Share-holding Corporations Ltd. with funds from Hong Kong, Macao & Taiwan	23	23
其他港澳台商投资	Other Enterprises with Funds from Hong Kong,Macao and Taiwan	8	8
（三）外商投资	Foreign Funded Enterprises	1106	1099
中外合资经营	Sino-foreign Joint Ventures	335	334
中外合作经营	Sino-Foreign Cooperation Enterprises	26	25
外资企业	Foreign Owned Enterprises	555	551
外商投资股份有限公司	Limited Company Funded by Foreign Investment	118	118
其他外商投资	Other Foreign Funded Enterprises	72	71

2-5 按国民经济行业分产业活动单位数（2015年）

Industrial Active Units by Industry of the National Economy（2015）

单位：个 (unit)

分 组	Classify	产业活动单位数 Number of Industrial Active Units	企业 Enterprises
总 计	**Total**	**135227**	**116157**
（一）农、林、牧、渔业	Agriculture,Forestry,Animal Husbandry and Fishery	3671	2681
农业	Farming	1767	1215
林业	Forestry	462	395
畜牧业	Animal Husbandry	1073	824
渔业	Fishery	62	53
农、林、牧、渔服务业	Services in Support of Agriculture	307	194
（二）采矿业	Mining	264	264
煤炭开采和洗选业	Mining and Washing of Coal	9	9
石油和天然气开采业	Extraction of Petroleum and Natural Gas	27	27
黑色金属矿采选业	Mining of Ferrous Metal Ores	12	12
有色金属矿采选业	Mining of Non-ferrous Metal Ores	23	23
非金属矿采选业	Mining and Processing of Nonmetal Ores	75	75
开采辅助活动	Mining of Other Ores	94	94
其他采矿业	Manufacturing	24	24
（三）制造业	Processing of Food from Agricultural Products	14516	14516
农副食品加工业	Manufacture of Foods	464	464
食品制造业	Manufacture of Beverages	454	454
酒、饮料和精制茶制造业	Manufacture of Tobacco	141	141
烟草制品业	Manufacture of Textile	2	2
纺织业	Manufacture of Textile Wearing Apparel, Footware and Caps	144	144
纺织服装、服饰业	Manufacture of Leather, Fur, Feather and Related Products	141	141
皮革、毛皮、羽毛及其制品和制鞋业	Processing of Timber,Manufacture of Wood, Bamboo,Rattan its Froducts and Footwear	36	36
木材加工和木、竹、藤、棕、草制品业	Plam and Straw Products and Straw Products	204	204
家具制造业	Manufacture of Furniture	409	409
造纸及纸制品业	Manufacture of Paper and Paper Products	327	327
印刷和记录媒介复制业	Printing,Reproduction of Recording Media	561	561
文教、工美、体育和娱乐用品制造业	Manufacture of Articles For Culture, Education and Sport Activities	203	203

2-5 续表1 continued 1

单位：个 (unit)

分组	Classify	产业活动单位数 Number of Industrial Active Units	企业 Enterprises
石油加工、炼焦和核燃料加工业	Processing of Petroleum, Coking, Processing of Nuclear Fuel	52	52
化学原料和化学制品制造业	Manufacture of Raw Chemical Materials and Chemical Products	697	697
医药制造业	Manufacture of Medicines	360	360
化学纤维制造业	Manufacture of Chemical Fibers	26	26
橡胶和塑料制品业	Manufacture of Rubber and Manufacture of Plastics	475	475
非金属矿物制品业	Manufacture of Non-metallic Mineral Products	1362	1362
黑色金属冶炼和压延加工业	Smelting and Pressing of Ferrous Metals	244	244
有色金属冶炼和压延加工业	Smelting and Pressing of Non-ferrous Metals	190	190
金属制品业	Manufacture of Metal Products	1025	1025
通用设备制造业	Manufacture of General Purpose Machinery	1927	1927
专用设备制造业	Manufacture of Special Equipment	1440	1440
汽车制造业	Manufacture of Motor Vehicle	191	191
铁路、船舶、航空航天和其他运输设备制造业	Railways,Shipbuilding,Aerospace and Other Transportation Equipment Manufacturing Industry	312	312
电气机械和器材制造业	Manufacture of Electric Equipment and Machinery	1438	1438
计算机、通信和其他电子设备制造业	Manufacture of Communication Equipment, Computers and other Electronic Equipment	773	773
仪器仪表制造业	Manufacture of Measuring Instruments and Machinery	566	566
其他制造业	Other Manufacturing	139	139
废弃资源综合利用	Recycling and Disposal of Waste	52	52
金属制品、机械和设备修理业	Metal Products,Machinery and Equipment Repair Industry	161	161
（四）电力、燃气及水的生产供应业	Production and Distribution of Electricity,Gas and Water	404	400
电力、热力生产和供应业	Production and Supply of Electric Power and Heat Power	258	255
燃气生产和供应业	Gas mining and supplying industry	54	54
水的生产和供应业	Production and Supply of Water	92	91
（五）建筑业	Construction	9701	9701
房屋建筑业	Construction of Building	1976	1976
土木工程建筑业	Civil Engineering	1866	1866
建筑安装业	Architectural Installation	1692	1692
建筑装饰和其他建筑业	Architectural Decoration and Other Construction	4167	4167
（六）批发和零售业	Wholesale and Retail Trades	43299	43299

2-5 续表2 continued 2

单位：个 (unit)

分 组	Classify	产业活动单位数 Number of Industrial Active Units	企业 Enterprises
批发业	Wholesale Trade	22947	22947
零售业	Retail Trade	20352	20352
（七）交通运输、仓储和邮政业	Traffic, Transport, Storage and Post	2793	2707
铁路运输业	Transport Via Railway	66	56
道路运输业	Transport Via Road	1391	1341
水上运输业	Water Transport	5	5
航空运输业	Air Transport	67	66
管道运输业	Transport Via Pipeline	12	12
装卸搬运和运输代理服务业	Loading, Unloading, Portage and Other Transport Services	562	560
仓储业	Storage	319	310
邮政业	Post	371	357
（八）住宿和餐饮业	Hotels and Catering Services	4068	4058
住宿业	Hotels	1476	1470
餐饮业	Catering Services	2592	2588
（九）信息传输、软件和信息技术服务业	Information Transmission, Computer Services and Software	5455	5423
电信、广播电视和卫星传输服务	Telecom & Other Information Transmission Services	418	408
互联网和相关服务	internet and relevant services	745	741
软件和信息技术服务	Software Industry	4292	4274
（十）金融业	Financial Intermediation	2341	2319
货币金融服务	Monetary and Financial Services	1402	1391
资本市场服务	Capital Market Services	379	377
保险业	Insurance	467	463
其他金融业	Other Financial Intermediation	93	88
（十一）房地产业	Real Estate	6989	6963
房地产业	Real Estate	6989	6963
（十二） 租赁和商务服务业	Leasing and Business Services	12781	12412
租赁业	Leasing	933	931
商务服务业	Business Services	11848	11481
（十三）科学研究和技术服务业	Scientific Research, Technical Sevice	5525	4867
研究与试验发展	Research and Experimental Development	564	474
专业技术服务业	Professional Technical Services	3722	3405

2-5 续表3 continued 3

单位：个 (unit)

分 组	Classify	产业活动单位数 Number of Industrial Active Units	企业 Enterprises
科技推广和应用服务业	Services of Science and Technology Exchanges and Promotion	1239	988
（十四）水利、环境和公共设施管理业	Management of Water Conservancy, Environment and Public Facilities	1076	817
水利管理业	Management of Water Conservancy	198	77
生态保护和环境治理业	Environmental Management	121	88
公共设施管理业	Management of Public Facilities	757	652
（十五）居民服务、修理和其他服务业	Services to Households and Other Services	2977	2896
居民服务业	Services to Households	1129	1061
机动车、电子产品和日用产品修理业	The repair service industry for motor vehicle、electronic	1183	1179
其他服务业	Other Services	665	656
（十六）教育	Education	4302	507
教育	Education	4302	507
（十七）卫生和社会工作	Health, Social Security	3579	268
卫生	Health	3355	246
社会工作	Social	224	22
（十八）文化、体育和娱乐业	Culture, Sports and Entertainment	2452	2053
新闻和出版业	Journalism and Publishing Activities	186	134
广播、电视、电影和影视录音制作业	Broadcasting, Movies, Television and Audiovisual Activities	379	361
文化艺术业	Cultural and Art Activities	792	510
体育	Sports Activities	181	146
娱乐业	Entertainment	914	902
（十九）公共管理、社会保障和社会组织	Public Management and Social Organizaion	9034	6
中国共产党机关	Organs of Communist Party of China	175	
国家机构	Government Agencies	3522	
人民政协、民主党派	People's Pc~litical Consultative Conference and Democratic Parties	42	
社会保障	Social Security	102	6
群众团体、社会团体和其他成员组织	Mass organizations、social groups and other members of the organization	1466	
基层群众自治组织	Grass-roots Mass Self-Government Organizations	3727	
（二十）国际组织	International Organizations		
国际组织	International Organizations		

2-6 按行政区划分产业活动单位数（2015年）

Industrial Active Units by Region（2015）

单位：个 (unit)

区 县	Region	产业活动单位数 Number of Industrial Active Units	企业 Enterprises
总 计	**Total**	**135227**	**116157**
新城区	Xincheng	9469	8395
碑林区	Beilin	16353	15195
莲湖区	Lianhu	13631	12539
灞桥区	Baqiao	5782	4523
未央区	Weiyang	21263	20149
雁塔区	Yanta	33843	32652
阎良区	Yanliang	3037	2397
临潼区	Lintong	5311	3261
长安区	Chang'an	8482	6242
高陵区	Gaoling	3553	2688
蓝田县	Lantian	4931	2740
周至县	Zhouzhi	3992	1987
户 县	Huxian	5580	3389

2-7 按统计机构分企业一套表调查单位数（2015年）

Number of Survey Units by Statistical Agencies of "One Sheet" （2015）

单位：个 (unit)

区县、开发区	Region	合计 Total	规模以上工业 Industrial Enterprises above Designed Size	限额以上批发零售住宿餐饮业 Above wholesale and Retail Accommodation and Catering Industry	资质内建筑业 Qualified Construction Enterprises	房地产开发经营企业 Real Estate Development Enterprises	规模以上服务业 Service Enterprises above Designed Size
全 市	**Total**	**5111**	**1117**	**1373**	**706**	**859**	**1056**
新城区	Xincheng	287	10	136	50	32	59
碑林区	Beilin	537	12	211	101	88	125
莲湖区	Lianhu	415	28	135	62	79	111
灞桥区	Baqiao	227	77	51	34	35	30
未央区	Weiyang	224	25	71	31	47	50
雁塔区	Yanta	486	42	122	134	71	117
阎良区	Yanliang	125	52	19	19	27	8
临潼区	Lintong	138	55	31	24	8	20
长安区	Chang'an	205	40	72	28	43	22
高陵区	Gaoling	161	67	37	9	31	17
蓝田县	Lantian	71	27	14	9	13	8
周至县	Zhouzhi	103	39	23	11	20	10
户 县	Huxian	140	62	34	6	29	9
高新技术开发区	GaoXin	818	274	155	97	68	224
经济技术开发区	JingKai	623	215	161	69	57	121
曲江新区	Qujiang	189		27	8	77	77
阎良国家航空技术产业基地	Aviation Industry Base	43	29	2		8	4
国家民用航天产业基地	Aerospace Base	75	24	14	3	27	7
浐灞生态区	Chanba Eco-District	97		16	1	64	16
国际港务区	International Trade &Logistic Park	37	3	7	1	12	14
沣东新城	FengDongXinCheng	110	36	35	9	23	7
其他	other						

注：由于统计口径不同，一套表调查单位数与各专业有差异。

2-8 按行政区划分企业一套表调查单位数（2015年）

Number of Survey Units of "One Sheet" by Region（2015）

单位：个 (unit)

区 县	Region	合计 Total	规模以上工业 Industrial Enterprises above Designed Size	限额以上批发零售住宿餐饮业 Above wholesale and Retail Accommodation and Catering Industry	资质内建筑业 Qualified Construction Enterprises	房地产开发经营企业 Real Estate Development Enterprises	规模以上服务业 Service Enterprises above Designed Size
全 市	**Total**	**5111**	**1117**	**1373**	**706**	**859**	**1056**
新城区	Xincheng	291	10	137	50	35	59
碑林区	Beilin	543	13	212	101	92	125
莲湖区	Lianhu	420	29	136	62	80	113
灞桥区	Baqiao	327	83	67	35	86	56
未央区	Weiyang	910	200	269	110	153	178
雁塔区	Yanta	1372	237	292	235	197	411
阎良区	Yanliang	168	81	21	19	35	12
临潼区	Lintong	141	56	31	24	10	20
长安区	Chang'an	369	126	96	35	78	34
高陵区	Gaoling	235	133	41	9	31	21
蓝田县	Lantian	71	27	14	9	13	8
周至县	Zhouzhi	105	41	23	11	20	10
户 县	Huxian	159	81	34	6	29	9

2-9 按行政区划和国民经济法人单位数（2015年）

单位：个

区 县	Region	合计 Total	农、林、牧、渔业 Agriculture Forestry Animal Husbandry and Fishery	采矿业 Mining	制造业 Manufacturing	电力、燃气及水的生产和供应业 Production and Distribution of Electricity Gas and Water
全 市	**Total**	**122726**	**3652**	**251**	**14167**	**316**
新城区	Xincheng	8491	5	1	319	3
碑林区	Beilin	14188	2	7	256	9
莲湖区	Lianhu	12145	7	1	360	3
灞桥区	Baqiao	4943	117		1046	16
未央区	Weiyang	20082	72	42	2742	35
雁塔区	Yanta	32159	115	100	3365	109
阎良区	Yanliang	2701	226		640	18
临潼区	Lintong	4420	688	2	640	16
长安区	Chang'an	7848	505	14	1815	21
高陵区	Gaoling	3264	351	10	676	23
蓝田县	Lantian	4119	658	29	510	12
周至县	Zhouzhi	3400	379	22	249	27
户 县	Huxian	4966	527	23	1549	24

Impersonal Entities by Administrative Districts and Industry of the National Economy (2015)

(unit)

建筑业 Construction	批发和零售业 Wholesale and Retail Trades	交通运输、仓储和邮政业 Traffic Transport Storage and Post	住宿和餐饮业 Hotels and Catering Services	信息传输、软件和信息技术服务业 Information Transmission Software and Information Technology Services	金融业 Financial Intermediation
9099	**39743**	**2213**	**3331**	**5024**	**748**
425	4111	253	445	172	33
859	5905	124	651	541	111
838	5706	280	468	306	101
394	1153	201	101	53	7
1753	9201	518	363	331	67
3221	9169	243	715	3263	327
134	576	78	53	43	15
300	630	106	92	51	8
497	1114	85	209	194	45
203	581	101	58	21	9
246	534	45	86	21	12
86	660	105	38	10	3
143	403	74	52	18	10

2–9 续表

单位：个

区 县	Region	房地产业 Real Estate	租赁和商务服务业 Leasing and Business Services	科学研究和技术服务业 Scientific Research Technical Services	水利、环境和公共设施管理业 Management of Water Conservancy, Environment and Public Facilities
全 市	**Total**	**6612**	**12073**	**5210**	**984**
新城区	Xincheng	502	666	262	47
碑林区	Beilin	825	2326	886	77
莲湖区	Lianhu	771	1373	443	103
灞桥区	Baqiao	348	273	175	50
未央区	Weiyang	1111	1498	744	153
雁塔区	Yanta	2031	4725	1979	189
阎良区	Yanliang	96	158	56	33
临潼区	Lintong	86	269	174	55
长安区	Chang'an	396	375	232	86
高陵区	Gaoling	176	134	42	28
蓝田县	Lantian	71	101	38	43
周至县	Zhouzhi	80	42	73	57
户 县	Huxian	119	133	106	63

continude

(unit)

居民服务、修理和其他服务业 Services to Households Repairs and Other Services	教育 Education	卫生和社会工作 Health and Social Work	文化、体育和娱乐业 Culture Sports and Entertainment	公共管理、社会保障和社会组织 Public Administration Social Security and Social Organizations	国际组织 International Orgnizations
2661	**3688**	**3254**	**2285**	**7415**	
244	197	73	152	581	
369	339	107	322	472	
334	269	116	184	482	
120	268	66	80	475	
382	270	84	143	573	
757	463	148	781	459	
48	96	104	57	270	
74	251	353	106	519	
139	449	445	158	1069	
55	195	205	70	326	
55	237	563	83	775	
30	382	465	72	620	
54	272	525	77	794	

2-10 按行政区划和机构类型分法人单位数（2015年）

Impersonal Entities by Agencies Types of Legal Entities Corporate Units and Administrative Districts（2015）

单位：个 (unit)

区 县	Region	法人单位数 Number of Enterprises	企业法人 Business Entity	事业法人 Institution Entity	机关法人 Government Entity	社会团体 Social Organization	其他 other
全 市	**Total**	**122726**	**106485**	**4669**	**1211**	**1244**	**9117**
新城区	Xincheng	8491	7585	283	158	219	246
碑林区	Beilin	14188	13170	341	93	218	366
莲湖区	Lianhu	12145	11202	331	95	143	374
灞桥区	Baqiao	4943	3980	243	74	77	569
未央区	Weiyang	20082	19090	318	149	65	460
雁塔区	Yanta	32159	31116	328	96	70	549
阎良区	Yanliang	2701	2147	145	62	52	295
临潼区	Lintong	4420	2822	580	77	63	878
长安区	Chang'an	7848	5704	802	79	47	1216
高陵区	Gaoling	3264	2441	312	78	28	405
蓝田县	Lantian	4119	2457	220	107	72	1263
周至县	Zhouzhi	3400	1775	385	71	106	1063
户 县	Huxian	4966	2996	381	72	84	1433

2-11 按行政区划和登记注册类型分企业法人单位数（2015年）

The Corporate Units by Types of Corporate Registration and Adminstration Districts（2015）

单位：个 (unit)

区 县	Region	企业单位数 Number of Enterprises	内资企业 Domestic Investment Enterprises	国有企业 State-owned Enterprises	集体企业 Collective-owned Enterprises	股份合作企业 Share-holding Corperative Enterprises	联营企业 Joint Ownership Enterprises
全 市	Total	**106485**	**105650**	**1692**	**1542**	**306**	**201**
新城区	Xincheng	7585	7556	256	288	44	19
碑林区	Beilin	13170	13078	317	160	43	41
莲湖区	Lianhu	11202	11141	267	239	22	29
灞桥区	Baqiao	3980	3949	75	117	16	7
未央区	Weiyang	19090	18938	117	167	43	24
雁塔区	Yanta	31116	30781	199	91	42	19
阎良区	Yanliang	2147	2130	49	46	15	4
临潼区	Lintong	2822	2808	92	83	19	14
长安区	Chang'an	5704	5636	85	96	19	18
高陵区	Gaoling	2441	2422	54	33	15	7
蓝田县	Lantian	2457	2450	49	82	14	11
周至县	Zhouzhi	1775	1774	49	30	2	3
户 县	Huxian	2996	2987	83	110	12	5

2-11 续表

区 县	Region	有限责任公司 Limited Liability Corporations	股份有限公司 Share-holding Corperation Ltd.	私营企业 Private Enterprises	港、澳、台商投资企业 Enterprises with Funds from Hong Kong, Macao and Taiwan	外商投资企业 Enterprises with Foreign Investment
全 市	Total	**44465**	**1078**	**51891**	**263**	**572**
新城区	Xincheng	3934	91	2871	12	17
碑林区	Beilin	8115	156	3985	38	54
莲湖区	Lianhu	1347	78	8600	22	39
灞桥区	Baqiao	1702	36	1842	11	20
未央区	Weiyang	7695	149	10616	56	96
雁塔区	Yanta	16914	313	13103	83	252
阎良区	Yanliang	723	34	835	9	8
临潼区	Lintong	815	37	1344	3	11
长安区	Chang'an	1688	74	3151	22	46
高陵区	Gaoling	801	46	1191	3	16
蓝田县	Lantian	296	19	1360		7
周至县	Zhouzhi	104	9	821		1
户 县	Huxian	331	36	2172	4	5

主要统计指标解释

企业（单位）登记注册类型 是以在工商行政管理机关登记注册的各类企业为划分对象，以工商行政管理部门对企业登记注册的类型为依据，将企业登记注册类型分为内资企业、港澳台商投资企业和外商投资企业三大类。内资企业包括国有企业、集体企业、股份合作企业、联营企业、有限责任公司、股份有限公司、私营公司和其他企业；港澳台商投资企业和外商投资企业分别包括合资经营企业、合作经营企业、独资经营企业和股份有限公司。对不在工商行政管理部门进行登记注册的行政机关、事业单位和社会团体，主要按其经费来源和管理方式进行划分。

国有企业 指企业全部资产归国家所有，并按《中华人民共和国企业法人登记管理条例》规定登记注册的非公司制的经济组织。不包括有限责任公司中的国有独资公司。

集体企业 指企业资产归集体所有，并按《中华人民共和国企业法人登记管理条例》规定登记注册的经济组织。

股份合作企业 指以合作制为基础，由企业职工共同出资入股，吸收一定比例的社会资产投资组建，实行自主经营，自负盈亏，共同劳动，民主管理，按劳分配与按股分红相结合的一种集体经济组织。

联营企业 指两个及两个以上相同或不同所有制性质的企业法人或事业单位法人，按自愿、平等、互利的原则，共同投资组成的经济组织。联营企业包括国有联营企业、集体联营企业、国有与集体联营企业和其他联营企业。

有限责任公司 指根据《中华人民共和国公司登记管理条例》规定登记注册，由两个以上、五十个以下的股东共同出资，每个股东以其所认缴的出资额对公司承担有限责任，公司以其全部资产对其债务承担责任的经济组织。有限责任公司包括国有独资公司以及其他有限责任公司。

股份有限公司 指根据《中华人民共和国公司登记管理条例》规定登记注册，其全部注册资本由等额股份构成并通过发行股票筹集资本，股东以其认购的股份对公司承担有限责任，公司以其全部资产对其债务承担责任的经济组织。

私营企业 指由自然人投资设立或由自然人控股，以雇佣劳动为基础的营利性经济组织。包括按照《公司法》、《合伙企业法》、《私营企业暂行条例》规定登记注册的私营有限责任公司、私营股份有限公司、私营合伙企业和私营独资企业。

其他企业 指上述企业之外的其他内资经济组织。

与港澳台商合资经营企业 指港澳台地区投资者与内地企业依照《中华人民共和国中外合资经营企业法》及有关法律的规定，按合同规定的比例投资设立、分享利润和分担风险的企业。

与港澳台商合作经营企业 指港澳台地区投资者与内地企业依照《中华人民共和国中外合作经营企业法》及有关法律的规定，依照合作合同的约定进行投资或提供条件设立、分配利润和分担风险的企业。

港澳台商独资经营企业 指依照《中华人民共和国外资企业法》及有关法律的规定，在内地由港澳台地区投资者全额投资设立的企业。

港澳台商投资股份有限公司 指根据国家有关规定，经原外经贸部依法批准设立，其中港、澳、台商的股本占公司注册资本的比例达25%以上的股份有限公司。凡其中港、澳、台商的股本占公司注册资本的比例小于25%的，属于内资企业中的股份有限公司。

中外合资经营企业 指外国企业或外国人与中国内地企业依照《中华人民共和国中外合资经营企业法》及有关法律的规定，按合同规定的比例投资设立、分享利润和分担风险的企业。

中外合作经营企业 指外国企业或外国人与中国内地企业依照《中华人民共和国中外合作经营企业法》及有关法律的规定，依照合作合同的约定进行投资或提供条件设立、分配利润和分担风险的企业。

外资企业 指依照《中华人民共和国外资企业法》及有关法律的规定，在中国内地由外国投资者全额投资设立的企业。

外商投资股份有限公司 指根据国家有关规定，经原外经贸部依法批准设立，其中外资的股本占公司注册资本的比例达25%以上的股份有限公司。凡其中外资股本占公司注册资本的比例小于25%的，属于内资企业中的股份有限公司。

行政机关、事业单位和社会团体 参照企业登记注册类型，主要按其经费来源和管理方式划分。具体规定如下：

（1）行政机关：包括国家机关和政党机关，原则上均列为“国有”。但有特殊规定的，如供销社等，则列为“集体”。

（2）事业单位：包括经国家机构编制部门和有关业务主管部门批准成立的各类事业单位，不包括实行企业化管理的事业单位。事业单位的划分办法如下：

①由国家财政预算拨款或列入财政预算外资金管理以及经费主要来源于国有主管部门或国有上级单位的事业单位，列为“国有”。

②经费主要来源于集体单位的事业单位，列为“集体”。

③公民个人（或个人合伙）开办的事业单位，列为“私营”。

④上述以外的其他事业单位，如果其经费来源不明确，按管理方式进行归类。

（3）社会团体：包括经民政部门批准成立以及未纳入社会团体管理条例范围的工会、妇联等各类社会团体。社会团体的划分办法如下：

①未纳入民政部社会团体管理条例范围的工会、妇联、共青团、青联、工商联、科协、侨联等社会团体，国家拨款设立的基金会或基金管理组织以及经费主要来源于国有业务主管部门或国有上级单位的社会团体，列为“国有”。

②经费主要来源于集体单位的社会团体，列为“集体”。

③公民个人（或个人合伙）开办的社会团体，划为“私营”。

④上述以外的其他社会团体，如果其经费来源不明确，改按管理方式进行归类。

Explanatory Notes on Main Statistical Indicators

Registration Status of Enterprises Enterprises are classified into 3 categories, namely domestic-funded enterprises, enterprises with investment from Hong Kong, Macau and Taiwan, and enterprises with foreign investment, according to the registration status of an enterprise in industrial and commercial administration agencies. Domestic-funded enterprises include State- owned enterprises, collective-owned enterprises, cooperative enterprises, joint ownership enterprises, limited liability corporations, share-holding corporations Ltd., private enterprises and other enterprises. Included in the enterprises with investment from Hong Kong, Macau and Taiwan and enterprises with foreign investment are joint-venture enterprises, cooperative enterprises, sole investment enterprises and share-holding corporations Ltd. For government agencies, institutions and social organizations which are not registered in industrial and commercial administration agencies, they are classified mainly by their sources of funding and manner of management.

State–owned Enterprises refer to non-corporation economic units where the entire assets are owned by the State and which have been registered in accordance with the Regulation of the People's Republic of China on the Management of Registration of Corporate Enterprises. Not included from this category are solely State-funded corporations in the limited liability corporations.

Collective–owned Enterprises refer to economic units where the assets are owned collectively and which have been registered in accordance with the Regulation of the People's Republic of China on the Management of Registration of Corporate Enterprises.

Cooperative Enterprises refer to a form of collective economic units (enterprises)where capitals come mainly from employees as their shares, with certain proportion of capital from the outside, where production is organized on the basis of independent operation, independent accounting for profits and losses, joint work, democratic management, and a distribution system that integrates remuneration according to work with dividend according to capital share.

Joint Ownership Enterprises refer to economic units established by two or more corporate enterprises or corporate institutions of the same or different ownership, through joint investment on the basis of voluntary participation, equality, and mutual benefits. They include State joint ownership enterprises; collective joint ownership enterprises; joint State-collective enterprises; and other joint ownership enterprises.

Limited Liability Corporations refer to economic units established with investment from 2-50 investors and registered in accordance with the Regulation of the People's Republic of China on the Management of Registration of Corporations, each investor bearing limited liability to the corporation depending on its share of investment, and the corporation bearing liability to its debt to the maximum of its total assets. Limited liability corporations include solely State-funded limited liability corporations and other limited liability corporations.

Share–holding Corporations Ltd. refer to economic units registered in accordance with the Regulation of the People's Republic of China on the Management of Registration of Corporations, with total registered capital divided into equal shares and raised through issuing stocks. Each investor bears limited liability to the corporation depending on the holding of shares, and the corporation bears liability to its debt to the maximum of its total assets.

Private Enterprises refer to profit-making economic units invested and established by natural persons, or controlled by natural persons using employed labour~ Included in this category are private limited liability corporations, private share-holding corporations Ltd., private partnership enterprises and private-funded enterprises registered in accordance with the Company Law, the Law on Partnership Business and Interim Regulations on Private Enterprises.

Other Domestic–funded Enterprises refer to domestic-funded economic units other than those mentioned above.

Joint Venture Enterprises with Funds from Hong Kong, Macau and Taiwan are enterprises established by investors from Hong Kong, Macau and Taiwan with enterprises in the mainland of China in accordance with the Law of the People's Republic of China on Sino-foreign Equity Joint Ventures and other relevant laws, where the establishment of the investment and the sharing of profits and risks are stipulated under joint venture contracts.

Cooperative Enterprises with Funds from Hong Kong, Macan and Taiwan established by investors from Hong Kong, Macau and Taiwan with enterprises in the mainland of China in accordance with the Law of the People's Republic of China on Sino-foreign Contractual Joint Venture and other relevant laws, where the investment or provision of facilities and the sharing of profits and risks are stipulated under cooperative contracts.

Enterprises with Sole (exclusive)Investment from

Hong Kong, Macau and Taiwan refer to enterprises established in the mainland of China with exclusive investment from investors from Hong Kong, Macau and Taiwan in accordance with the Law of the People's Republic of China on Wholly Foreign-owned Enterprises and other relevant laws.

Share–holding Corporations Ltd. with Investment from Hong Kong, Macau and Taiwan refer to share- holding corporations Ltd. established with the approval from the former Ministry of Foreign Trade and Economic Relations in line with relevant State regulations, where the share of investment from Hong Kong, Macau or Taiwan businessmen exceeds 25% of the total registered capital of the corporation. In case the share of investmentfrom Hong Kong, Macau or Taiwan is less than 25% of thetotal registered capital, the enterprise is to be classified as domestic-funded share-holding corporation Ltd.

Joint Venture Enterprises with Foreign Investment refer to enterprises jointly established byforeign enterprises or foreigners with enterprises in themainland of China in accordance with the Law of thePeople's Republic of China on Sino-foreign Equity JointVentures and other relevant laws, where the sharing ofinvestment, profits and risks is stipulated under contract.

Cooperative Enterprises with Foreign Investment refer to enterprises jointly established by foreign enterprises or foreigners with enterprises in the mainland of China in accordance with the Law of the People's Republic of China on Sino-foreign Contractual Joint Venture and other relevant laws, where the investment or provision of facilities and the sharing of profits and risks are stipulated under cooperative contracts.

Enterprises with Sole (exclusive)Foreign Investment refer to enterprises established in the mainland of China with exclusive investment from foreign investors in accordance with the Law of the People's Republic of China on Wholly Foreign-owned Enterprises and other relevant laws.

Share–holding Corporations Ltd. with Foreign Investment refer to share-holding corporations Ltd. established with the approval from the former Ministry of Foreign Trade and Economic Relations in line with relevant State regulations, where the share of investment from foreign investors exceeds 25% of the total registered capital of the corporation. In case the share of foreign investment is less than 25% ofthe total registered capital, the enterprise is to be classified as domestic-funded share-holding corporation Ltd.

Government Agencies, Institutions and Social Organizations are classified into the following categories by source of funds and manner of management taking reference of thc registration status of enterprises:

(1)Government agencies: include State and party agencies, classified in principle as State-owned. There are exceptions, such as supply and marketing cooperatives which are classified as collective-owned.

(2)Institutions: include institutions of various types established with the approval by organization and staffing departments of the government, but exclude institutions where enterprise management system is introduced. Institutions are further classified as follows:

(a)Institutions for which their main budgets are from government budget appropriations or extra-budget funds, or allocated from the budget of their competent government agencies. Such institutions are classified as state-owned.

(b)Institutions for which their budget mainly come from collective units. Such institutions are classified as collective-owned.

(c)Social institutions established by individual or a group of citizens, which are classified as private.

(d)Institutions other than those mentioned above for which their sources of budget are not clear. Such institutions are classified by the manner of management.

(3)Social organizations: include social organizations established with the approval from the Ministry of Civil Affairs, and organizations that are not covered by social organization management regulations such as trade unions, women's federations etc.. Social organizations are further classified as follows:

(a)Social organizations that are not covered by social organization management regulations of the Ministry of Civil Affairs such as trade unions, women federations, communist youth leagues, youth associations, industrial and commerce associations, scientist associations, overseas Chinese associations, etc., foundations and fund management organizations established with funds from the state, and social organizations whose funds mainly come from the budget of their competent government agencies. Such institutions are classified as State-owned.

(b)Social organizations for which their budget mainly come from collective units. Such institutions are classified as collective-owned.

(c)Social organizations established by individual or a group of citizens, which are classified as private.

(d)Social organizations other than those mentioned above for which their sources of budget are not clear. Such organizations are classified by the manner of management.

3 国民经济核算

NATIONAL ECONOMIC ACCOUNTS

资料整理：吴　羽　徐　枫　段　斐
Data management：Wu Yu Xu Feng Duan Fei
数据审核：连　鹏
Data audit：Lian Peng

第三部分　国民经济核算

一、简要说明

本章资料包括西安市生产总值、构成和指数，分区县生产总值和指数，非公有制经济增加值及占比等。根据国家统计局的统一要求，2009年—2012年数据为第三次经济普查修订结果，2013年数据为第三次经济普查结果，2014年、2015年数据为年报最终核实数据；2013年（含）之后三次产业分类依据国家统计局2012年制定的新《三次产业划分规定》；2004年（含）之前人均GDP按户籍人口计算，2005年（含）之后按常住人口计算。资料由西安市统计局国民经济核算处提供。

生产总值（亿元）	5801.20	比上年增长	8.2%
第一产业	220.20	比上年增长	5.0%
第二产业	2126.29	比上年增长	5.6%
第三产业	3454.71	比上年增长	10.4%
人均生产总值（元/人）	66938	比上年增长	7.5%

3　NATIONAL ECONOMIC ACCOUNTS

Ⅰ.Brief Introduction

The data in this chapter consists of Xi'an GDP, composition, index, and sub-county gross production, index the added value of non-public-owned economics According to the uniform requirements of National Bureau of Statistics date between 2009 to 2012 were amended by the Third Economic Census, of 2013 data was revised by the Third Economic Census, data of 2014 and 2015 was the Annual Report final verification data. Three industrial classification after 2013 （included） based on the new "three industrial division rule" for mulated according to National Bureau of Statistics in 2012.per capita GDP was calculated on permanent population after 2005 （included）, had been calculated on register population before 2005.Data in this chapter is provided by National Economics Accounting Division of the Xi'an Bureau of Statistics.

		Increase over Preceding Year
Gross Domestic Product(100 mil. yuan)	5801.20	8.2%
Primary Industry	220.20	5.0%
Secondary Industry	2126.29	5.6%
Tertiary Industry	3454.71	10.4%
Per Capita Gross Domestic Product (yuan/person)	66938	7.5%

3-1 主要年份生产总值

Gross Domestic Product in Representative Years

(本表按当年价格计算)　　(Data in the table are calculated at current prices)

单位：亿元　　(100 million yuan)

年份 Year	生产总值 Gross Domestic Product	第一产业 Primary Industry	第二产业 Secondary Industry	第三产业 Tertiary Industry	人均生产总值 (元/人) Per Capita GDP (yuan/person)
1952	3.37	1.59	0.88	0.90	135
1965	12.76	2.62	7.22	2.92	323
1970	17.76	3.13	10.96	3.67	412
1975	21.33	4.14	12.63	4.56	448
1978	25.35	4.83	14.59	5.93	513
1980	31.66	4.73	18.69	8.24	623
1983	35.89	5.22	20.14	10.53	674
1984	44.14	7.45	24.17	12.52	817
1985	57.58	8.76	30.83	17.99	1049
1986	65.78	9.59	33.86	22.33	1178
1987	80.16	10.73	37.69	31.74	1409
1988	99.22	11.47	46.58	41.17	1711
1989	109.38	12.78	48.91	47.69	1861
1990	116.51	13.94	50.15	52.42	1932
1991	136.14	17.17	57.06	61.91	2224
1992	164.85	18.78	69.22	76.85	2662
1993	229.56	22.58	110.88	96.10	3661
1994	289.82	31.68	128.27	129.87	4363
1995	330.35	41.40	135.33	153.62	5131
1996	406.95	46.94	161.63	198.38	6246
1997	488.82	51.33	197.97	239.52	7424
1998	525.85	51.91	216.32	257.62	7906
1999	577.29	45.53	243.35	288.41	8599
2000	646.13	44.65	277.13	324.35	9484
2001	734.86	45.87	312.90	376.09	10628
2002	826.68	47.77	353.58	425.33	11831
2003	946.66	50.72	407.38	488.56	13341
2004	1102.39	60.21	476.92	565.26	15294
2005	1313.93	66.01	540.50	707.42	16406
2006	1538.94	70.44	645.65	822.85	18890
2007	1856.63	82.51	781.94	992.18	22463
2008	2318.14	103.45	981.58	1233.11	27794
2009	2724.88	110.38	1144.75	1469.75	32420
2010	3242.86	140.06	1357.53	1745.27	38357
2011	3869.84	173.14	1583.21	2113.49	45561
2012	4394.47	195.59	1781.09	2417.79	51499
2013	4924.97	200.45	1998.82	2725.70	57464
2014	5492.64	214.55	2194.78	3083.31	63794
2015	5801.20	220.20	2126.29	3454.71	66938

注：1.2004年（含）之前人均GDP按户籍人口计算，2005年（含）之后按常住人口计算。
2.2013年（含）之后三次产业分类依据国家统计局2012年制定的新《三次产业划分规定》。
3.2009年—2012年数据为第三次经济普查修订结果，2013年数据为第三次经济普查结果。
4.2014年、2015年数据为年报最终核实数据。（下同）

3-2 主要年份生产总值指数（上年＝100）

Indices of Gross Domestic Product in Representative Years(preceding year = 100)

(本表按可比价格计算) (Data in the table are calculated at constant prices)

年份	Year	生产总值 Gross Domestic Product	第一产业 Primary Industry	第二产业 Secondary Industry	第三产业 Tertiary Industry	人均生产总值 Per Capita GDP
1952		103.6	92.2	137.5	123.7	
1965		126.1	134.1	133.0	106.7	
1970		122.0	109.4	140.0	100.1	
1975		103.8	92.6	107.1	107.5	
1978		101.7	101.6	99.4	108.2	
1980		111.5	83.3	119.7	116.5	
1985		112.6	107.5	111.8	116.9	
1986		111.4	107.7	108.4	118.8	
1987		113.6	100.8	109.1	126.6	
1988		111.4	81.2	115.5	114.7	
1989		106.7	103.0	104.5	110.8	
1990		105.2	103.0	102.5	109.6	
1991		109.8	118.6	108.6	108.6	108.2
1992		115.6	109.4	118.1	115.0	114.3
1993		123.9	112.5	142.7	108.4	122.3
1994		110.3	98.4	110.6	113.2	108.8
1995		110.0	104.5	112.1	108.6	108.5
1996		114.9	106.8	118.8	111.7	113.5
1997		114.4	109.1	116.7	112.4	113.2
1998		113.3	106.5	117.5	108.8	112.1
1999		112.2	97.4	115.7	110.1	111.2
2000		113.0	103.5	115.1	111.5	111.4
2001		113.1	102.5	115.3	112.6	111.4
2002		113.3	103.1	115.0	113.0	112.1
2003		113.5	101.8	117.5	111.2	111.7
2004		113.5	106.7	115.9	112.0	111.7
2005		114.0	107.5	112.3	116.3	112.2
2006		114.0	107.1	113.7	114.9	112.9
2007		115.6	104.5	115.7	116.4	113.9
2008		116.3	107.6	116.4	116.9	115.3
2009		114.5	106.3	112.8	116.3	113.7
2010		114.5	106.9	115.2	114.5	113.8
2011		113.5	106.7	112.5	114.9	113.0
2012		112.2	106.0	112.0	112.9	111.7
2013		111.1	104.7	113.6	109.7	110.6
2014		109.9	105.1	109.3	110.7	109.4
2015		108.2	105.0	105.6	110.4	107.5
平均每年增长	**Yearly Average Growth Rates**					
“一五”时期	**The First Five-Year Plan Period**	**15.8**	**5.9**	**37.7**	**16.9**	
“二五”时期	**The Second Five-Year Plan Period**	**2.0**	**-3.7**	**2.5**	**8.4**	
1963--1965年	**Readjust Period**	**14.2**	**16.1**	**23.4**	**0.3**	
“三五”时期	**The Third Five-Year Plan Period**	**7.1**	**0.1**	**11.7**	**5.4**	
“四五”时期	**The Fourth Five-Year Plan Period**	**5.0**	**4.0**	**5.3**	**5.0**	
“五五”时期	**The Fifth Five-Year Plan Period**	**6.0**	**-0.7**	**6.5**	**10.1**	
“六五”时期	**The Sixth Five-Year Plan Period**	**10.7**	**7.9**	**10.4**	**12.9**	
“七五”时期	**The Seventh Five-Year Plan Period**	**9.6**	**-1.3**	**7.9**	**15.9**	
“八五”时期	**The Eighth Five-Year Plan Period**	**13.8**	**8.5**	**17.8**	**10.7**	**12.3**
“九五”时期	**The Ninth Five-Year Plan Period**	**13.6**	**4.6**	**16.8**	**10.9**	**12.3**
“十五”时期	**The Tenth Five-Year Plan Period**	**13.5**	**4.3**	**15.2**	**13.0**	**11.8**
“十一五”时期	**The Eleventh Five-Year Plan Period**	**15.0**	**6.5**	**14.8**	**15.8**	**13.9**
“十二五”时期	**The Twelve Five-Year Plan Period**	**11.0**	**5.5**	**10.6**	**11.7**	**10.4**

3-3 主要年份生产总值指数（1952年=100）

Indices of Gross Domestic Product in Representative Years(1952= 100)

(本表按可比价格计算) (Data in the table are calculated at constant prices)

年份 Year	生产总值 Gross Domestic Product	第一产业 Primary Industry	第二产业 Secondary Industry	第三产业 Tertiary Industry
1952	100.0	100.0	100.0	100.0
1965	341.6	173.3	1048.3	329.2
1970	481.6	174.3	1821.0	428.6
1975	614.2	211.9	2362.5	547.9
1978	678.7	231.3	2560.8	643.8
1980	821.4	204.2	3237.2	885.2
1983	988.4	222.5	3846.2	1154.4
1984	1213.6	278.2	4748.8	1388.7
1985	1366.8	299.1	5310.6	1632.4
1986	1523.1	322.3	5756.7	1928.9
1987	1730.0	324.9	6280.6	2441.6
1988	1926.3	263.7	7256.6	2801.2
1989	2054.8	271.6	7583.1	3104.6
1990	2162.5	279.7	7772.7	3403.6
1991	2374.4	331.7	8441.2	3696.3
1992	2744.8	362.9	9969.1	4250.7
1993	3400.8	408.2	14225.9	4607.8
1994	3751.1	401.8	15733.8	5216.0
1995	4126.2	419.9	17637.6	5664.6
1996	4741.0	448.5	20953.5	6327.4
1997	5423.7	489.3	24452.7	7112.0
1998	6145.1	521.1	28731.9	7737.9
1999	6894.8	507.6	33242.8	8519.4
2000	7791.1	525.4	38262.5	9499.1
2001	8811.7	538.5	44116.7	10696.0
2002	9983.7	555.2	50734.2	12086.5
2003	11331.5	265.2	59612.7	13440.2
2004	12861.3	603.1	69091.1	15053.0
2005	14661.9	648.3	77589.3	17506.6
2006	16714.6	694.3	88219.0	20115.1
2007	19322.1	725.5	102069.4	23414.0
2008	22471.6	780.6	118808.8	27371.0
2009	25730.0	829.8	134016.3	31832.5
2010	29460.8	887.0	154386.8	36448.2
2011	33438.0	946.5	173685.2	41879.0
2012	37517.5	1003.3	194527.4	47281.3
2013	41681.9	1050.4	220983.1	51867.6
2014	45808.4	1104.0	241534.5	57417.5
2015	49580.4	1158.8	255076.2	63393.7

3-4 主要年份生产总值构成

Composition of Gross Domestic Product in Representative Years

(本表按当年价格计算)
单位:%

(Data in the table are calculated at current prices)
(%)

年份	Year	生产总值 Gross Domestic Product	第一产业 Primary Industry	第二产业 Secondary Industry	第三产业 Tertiary Industry
1952		100	47.18	26.11	26.71
1965		100	20.53	56.58	22.89
1970		100	17.62	61.71	20.67
1975		100	19.41	59.21	21.38
1978		100	19.05	57.55	23.40
1980		100	14.94	59.03	26.03
1985		100	15.21	53.54	31.25
1986		100	14.58	51.47	33.95
1987		100	13.39	47.02	39.59
1988		100	11.56	46.95	41.49
1989		100	11.68	44.72	43.60
1990		100	11.96	43.04	45.00
1991		100	12.61	41.91	45.48
1992		100	11.39	41.99	46.62
1993		100	9.84	48.30	41.86
1994		100	10.93	44.26	44.81
1995		100	12.53	40.97	46.50
1996		100	11.53	39.72	48.75
1997		100	10.50	40.50	49.00
1998		100	9.87	41.14	48.99
1999		100	7.89	42.15	49.96
2000		100	6.91	42.89	50.20
2001		100	6.24	42.58	51.18
2002		100	5.78	42.77	51.45
2003		100	5.36	43.03	51.61
2004		100	5.46	43.26	51.28
2005		100	5.02	41.14	53.84
2006		100	4.58	41.95	53.47
2007		100	4.44	42.12	53.44
2008		100	4.46	42.34	53.20
2009		100	4.05	42.01	53.94
2010		100	4.32	41.86	53.82
2011		100	4.47	40.91	54.62
2012		100	4.45	40.53	55.02
2013		100	4.07	40.59	55.34
2014		100	3.91	39.96	56.13
2015		100	3.80	36.65	59.55
"一五"时期	**The First Five-Year Plan Period**	**100**	**32.88**	**43.92**	**23.20**
"二五"时期	**The Second Five-Year Period**	**100**	**18.08**	**58.63**	**23.29**
1963--1965年	**Readjust Period**	**100**	**19.36**	**55.38**	**25.26**
"三五"时期	**The Third Five-Year Plan Period**	**100**	**18.60**	**57.33**	**24.07**
"四五"时期	**The Fourth Five-Year Plan Period**	**100**	**20.46**	**59.59**	**19.95**
"五五"时期	**The Fifth Five-Year Plan Period**	**100**	**18.41**	**57.69**	**23.90**
"六五"时期	**The Sixth Five-Year Plan Period**	**100**	**16.03**	**55.01**	**28.96**
"七五"时期	**The Seventh Five-Year Plan Period**	**100**	**12.42**	**46.11**	**41.47**
"八五"时期	**The Eighth Five-Year Plan Period**	**100**	**11.44**	**43.52**	**45.04**
"九五"时期	**The Ninth Five-Year Plan Period**	**100**	**9.09**	**41.45**	**49.46**
"十五"时期	**The Tenth Five-Year Plan Period**	**100**	**5.49**	**42.47**	**52.04**
"十一五"时期	**The Eleventh Five-Year Plan Period**	**100**	**4.34**	**42.04**	**53.62**
"十二五"时期	**The Twelve Five-Year Plan Period**	**100**	**4.10**	**39.55**	**56.35**

3-5 主要年份分行业增加值

The Value added by Industry in Representative Years

单位：亿元 (100 million yuan)

年 份 Year	地区生产总值 Gross Domestic Product	农、林、牧、渔业 Farming Forestry Animal Husbandry Fishery	工业 Industry	建筑业 Construction	批发和零售业 Wholesale and Retail Trades
1992	164.85	18.78	61.33	7.89	18.16
1993	229.56	22.58	98.88	12.00	22.63
1994	289.82	31.68	110.52	17.75	27.83
1995	330.35	41.40	112.50	22.83	33.20
1996	406.95	46.94	132.52	29.11	44.51
1997	488.82	51.33	161.97	36.00	59.31
1998	525.85	51.91	175.00	41.32	64.93
1999	577.29	45.53	194.00	49.35	70.27
2000	646.13	44.65	218.44	58.69	65.87
2001	734.86	45.87	246.90	66.00	78.38
2002	826.68	47.77	280.20	73.38	91.57
2003	946.66	50.72	324.88	82.50	106.82
2004	1102.39	60.21	383.46	93.46	125.12
2005	1313.93	66.01	420.00	120.50	147.20
2006	1538.94	70.44	494.22	151.43	166.72
2007	1856.63	82.51	594.95	186.99	195.51
2008	2318.14	103.45	721.40	260.18	242.91
2009	2724.88	110.38	816.92	327.83	298.29
2010	3242.86	140.06	954.38	403.15	352.37
2011	3869.84	173.14	1098.51	484.70	439.75
2012	4394.47	195.59	1228.05	553.04	512.96
2013	4924.97	217.76	1376.74	642.26	575.72
2014	5492.64	233.61	1488.02	728.74	633.65
2015	5801.20	241.69	1376.72	770.29	667.99

注：1999年（含）之前，批发和零售业与住宿和餐饮业无法分类，故1999年（含）之前批发和零售业数据为批发和零售业与住宿和餐饮业合计数。

3-5 续表 continued

单位：亿元 (100 million yuan)

年 份 Year	交通运输、仓储和邮政业 Transportation Storage Post and Telecommunications	住宿和餐饮业 Accommodation and Catering Trade	金融业 Financial Intermediation	房地产业 Real Estate	其他服务业 Others Services
1992	15.21		16.28	1.58	25.62
1993	18.01		20.59	1.97	32.90
1994	22.02		31.19	3.76	45.07
1995	24.60		35.20	4.90	55.72
1996	32.73		40.15	7.42	73.57
1997	43.02		37.50	8.74	90.95
1998	48.64		32.95	11.95	99.15
1999	55.35		30.37	14.42	118.00
2000	43.01	18.46	33.00	16.96	147.05
2001	45.50	21.97	36.21	21.38	172.65
2002	48.25	25.27	43.48	26.90	189.86
2003	51.37	29.41	50.76	32.42	217.78
2004	55.10	35.89	61.49	39.05	248.61
2005	66.30	50.44	75.00	52.48	316.00
2006	74.08	52.23	96.50	62.32	371.00
2007	84.21	70.09	128.50	75.26	438.61
2008	99.16	85.65	160.84	92.97	551.58
2009	112.02	93.82	197.87	128.18	639.57
2010	135.70	102.80	236.36	186.42	731.62
2011	165.18	118.02	294.44	235.20	860.90
2012	192.46	129.58	359.63	260.53	962.63
2013	215.11	135.58	429.51	292.41	1039.88
2014	235.58	144.15	534.00	326.10	1168.79
2015	260.33	159.14	658.90	398.34	1267.80

3-6 主要年份分行业增加值指数（上年=100）

Indices of the Value added by Industry in Representative Years（preceding year = 100）

(本表按可比价格计算) (Data in the table are calculated at constant prices)

年 份 Year	地区生产总值 Gross Domestic Product	农、林、牧、渔业 Farming Forestry Animal Husbandry Fishery	工业 Industry	建筑业 Construction	批发和零售业 Wholesale and Retail Trades
1992	115.6	109.4	118.1	118.2	130.7
1993	123.9	112.5	143.7	135.6	108.0
1994	110.3	98.4	106.8	141.3	103.1
1995	110.0	104.5	108.1	136.6	109.6
1996	114.9	106.8	117.1	126.8	116.0
1997	114.4	109.1	116.4	117.8	124.0
1998	113.3	106.5	116.1	123.4	110.7
1999	112.2	97.4	114.0	122.8	106.4
2000	113.0	103.5	113.8	120.1	111.4
2001	113.1	102.5	116.3	111.8	110.5
2002	113.3	103.1	116.4	109.3	115.3
2003	113.5	101.8	115.7	125.0	110.8
2004	113.5	106.7	115.5	117.3	109.1
2005	114.0	107.5	110.3	120.0	112.7
2006	114.0	107.1	112.3	118.7	112.5
2007	115.6	104.5	114.9	118.4	112.9
2008	116.3	107.6	115.7	118.9	115.0
2009	114.5	106.3	110.1	121.2	121.8
2010	114.5	106.9	114.3	117.6	115.0
2011	113.5	106.7	112.8	111.7	119.5
2012	112.2	106.0	112.7	110.3	114.0
2013	111.1	104.8	114.0	113.9	110.4
2014	109.9	105.1	108.4	110.9	109.3
2015	108.2	105.1	104.8	107.4	105.6

注：1999年（含）之前，批发和零售业与住宿和餐饮业无法分类，故1999年（含）之前批发和零售业数据为批发和零售业与住宿和餐饮业合计数。

3-6 续表 continued

(本表按可比价格计算) (Data in the table are calculated at constant prices)

年 份 Year	交通运输、仓储和邮政业 Transportation Storage Post and Telecommunications	住宿和餐饮业 Accommodation and Catering Trade	金融业 Financial Intermediation	房地产业 Real Estate	其他服务业 Others Services
1992	111.3		107.6	119.5	112.2
1993	102.7		109.7	107.4	111.4
1994	102.5		126.9	160.7	114.8
1995	102.6		103.7	119.7	113.6
1996	115.1		98.7	130.8	114.2
1997	122.4		87.0	109.6	115.1
1998	114.4		88.8	138.3	110.3
1999	111.9		90.6	118.6	117.0
2000	111.7	111.7	107.7	116.6	111.7
2001	111.6	114.2	103.6	123.5	114.2
2002	106.1	116.5	104.6	106.0	116.5
2003	113.6	111.6	107.4	108.8	111.6
2004	115.6	112.9	107.1	110.3	112.9
2005	113.2	136.1	109.3	112.9	117.7
2006	112.3	116.6	107.3	117.5	117.7
2007	110.3	117.3	126.7	119.7	116.3
2008	108.4	111.6	113.6	107.6	122.5
2009	111.0	106.6	123.7	130.8	112.5
2010	119.4	106.6	116.1	128.1	111.9
2011	115.7	108.5	117.9	113.5	112.9
2012	112.6	105.4	124.8	108.8	110.4
2013	108.2	100.7	119.0	111.9	106.1
2014	106.2	102.0	121.1	107.7	110.2
2015	111.3	109.2	119.3	107.9	109.7

3-7 主要年份三次产业贡献率

Three Industry Contribution Rate in Representative Years

年 份 Year	生产总值 Gross Domestic Product	第一产业 Primary Industry	第二产业 Secondary Industry	第三产业 Tertiary Industry
2000	100	1.8	66.9	31.3
2001	100	1.3	50.4	48.3
2002	100	1.5	49.4	49.1
2003	100	0.8	57.7	41.5
2004	100	2.5	54.1	43.4
2005	100	2.6	41.3	56.1
2006	100	2.5	40.2	57.3
2007	100	1.4	41.4	57.2
2008	100	2.0	41.4	56.6
2009	100	1.7	36.5	61.8
2010	100	1.7	42.5	55.8
2011	100	2.1	38.5	59.4
2012	100	2.0	40.7	57.3
2013	100	1.5	50.3	48.2
2014	100	1.7	39.3	59.0
2015	100	1.9	28.4	69.7

3-8 主要年份三次产业拉动率

Three Industries Pulling Rate in Representative Years

年 份 Year	生产总值 Gross Domestic Product	第一产业 Primary Industry	第二产业 Secondary Industry	第三产业 Tertiary Industry
2000	13.0	0.2	8.7	4.1
2001	13.1	0.2	6.6	6.3
2002	13.3	0.2	6.6	6.5
2003	13.5	0.1	7.8	5.6
2004	13.5	0.3	7.3	5.9
2005	14.0	0.4	5.8	7.8
2006	14.0	0.4	5.7	7.9
2007	15.6	0.2	6.4	9.0
2008	16.3	0.3	6.8	9.2
2009	14.5	0.2	5.3	9.0
2010	14.5	0.3	6.2	8.0
2011	13.5	0.3	5.2	8.0
2012	12.2	0.2	5.0	7.0
2013	11.1	0.2	5.6	5.3
2014	9.9	0.2	3.9	5.8
2015	8.2	0.2	2.3	5.7

3-9 分行业增加值

Value added by Industry

单位：亿元 (100 million yuan)

指 标	Item	增加值 Value Added		指数（上年=100） Index	
		2014	2015	2014	2015
地区生产总值	**Gross Domestic Product**	**5492.64**	**5801.20**	**109.9**	**108.2**
农、林、牧、渔业	Farming Forestry Animal Husbandry Fishery	233.61	241.69	105.1	105.1
工业	Industry	1488.02	1376.72	108.4	104.8
建筑业	Construction	728.74	770.29	110.9	107.4
批发和零售业	Wholesale and Retail Trades	633.65	667.99	109.3	105.6
交通运输、仓储及邮政业	Transportation,Storage,Post and Telecommunications	235.58	260.33	106.2	111.3
住宿和餐饮业	Accommodation and Catering Trade	144.15	159.14	102.0	109.2
金融业	Financial Intermediation	534.00	658.90	121.1	119.3
房地产业	Real Estate	326.10	398.34	107.7	107.9
其他服务业	Others Services	1168.79	1267.80	110.2	109.7
第一产业	Primary Industry	214.55	220.20	105.1	105.0
第二产业	Secondary Industry	2194.78	2126.29	109.3	105.6
第三产业	Tertiary Industry	3083.31	3454.71	110.7	110.4

3-10 主要年份各区县生产总值

Gross Domestic Product by Region in Representative Years

单位：亿元　　　　　　　　　　　　　　　　　　　　　　　　　　　　(100 million yuan)

指　标	Item	生产总值 Gross Domestic Product	第一产业 Primary Industry	第二产业 Secondary Industry	第三产业 Tertiary Industry	人均生产总值（元） Per Capita GDP (yuan)
新城区	Xincheng					
2000		77.84	0.02	37.84	39.98	16587
2001		90.84	0.02	48.23	42.59	19301
2002		100.43	0.02	52.02	48.39	21199
2003		110.78	0.02	53.70	57.06	23139
2004		129.62	0.01	63.53	66.08	26813
2005		144.81	0.01	67.85	76.95	23475
2006		167.94	0.01	79.19	88.74	26623
2007		198.47	—	84.74	113.73	31312
2008		244.22	—	97.39	146.83	38969
2009		278.99	—	111.55	167.44	45217
2010		314.61	—	132.51	182.10	52470
2011		363.56	—	150.45	213.11	61495
2012		394.87	—	171.74	223.13	66544
2013		429.07	—	177.99	251.08	72064
2014		467.08	—	186.67	280.41	78172
2015		494.00	—	178.21	315.79	82203
碑林区	Beilin		—			
2000		76.12	0.00	12.19	63.93	12700
2001		85.27	0.01	14.08	71.18	13702
2002		97.60	0.01	16.14	81.45	15022
2003		113.70	—	18.30	95.40	16767
2004		129.23	—	20.98	108.25	18591
2005		145.99	—	27.01	118.98	17856
2006		169.00	—	33.03	135.97	20095
2007		201.04	—	39.29	161.75	25919
2008		250.17	—	50.32	199.85	36003
2009		308.44	—	61.14	247.30	46146
2010		369.07	—	85.98	283.09	58323
2011		443.80	—	109.77	334.03	71876
2012		513.25	—	129.50	383.75	82816
2013		544.66	—	105.91	438.75	87629
2014		617.90	—	120.03	497.87	99158
2015		677.74	—	134.23	543.51	108188
莲湖区	Lianhu					
2000		77.61	0.18	37.30	40.13	13551
2001		88.74	0.15	43.05	45.54	15435
2002		100.95	0.19	47.73	53.03	**17481**
2003		118.06	0.19	55.86	62.01	**20179**
2004		143.03	0.19	69.61	73.23	**24057**
2005		164.50	0.19	79.68	84.63	**22789**
2006		191.20	0.18	91.35	99.67	**26004**
2007		230.76	0.19	109.90	120.67	**31115**
2008		293.13	—	140.60	152.53	**39367**
2009		339.20	—	158.43	180.77	**45218**
2010		367.87	—	164.60	203.27	**51207**
2011		421.50	—	182.01	239.49	**62459**
2012		451.09	—	180.23	270.86	**68300**
2013		501.94	—	194.35	307.59	**74876**
2014		539.53	—	193.90	345.63	**76468**
2015		573.60	—	183.47	390.13	80840

3-10 续表1 continued 1

单位：亿元 （100 million yuan）

指 标	Item	生产总值 Gross Domestic Product	第一产业 Primary Industry	第二产业 Secondary Industry	第三产业 Tertiary Industry	人均生产总值（元） Per Capita GDP （yuan）
灞桥区	**Baqiao**					
2000		27.55	2.73	13.52	11.30	6415
2001		29.64	2.71	15.09	11.84	6855
2002		33.42	2.94	16.95	13.53	7666
2003		39.98	3.14	21.17	15.67	9045
2004		46.30	3.99	24.28	18.03	10326
2005		60.10	4.61	32.52	22.97	11357
2006		72.87	5.28	39.52	28.07	13509
2007		88.77	6.29	47.79	34.69	16291
2008		112.61	7.91	59.38	45.32	20367
2009		144.95	8.79	80.52	55.64	25213
2010		168.37	11.50	89.53	67.34	28269
2011		204.58	14.41	106.11	84.06	34171
2012		238.80	16.08	118.25	104.47	39694
2013		288.05	16.86	140.10	131.09	47612
2014		309.73	18.14	141.61	149.98	50926
2015		312.87	18.74	124.25	169.88	51203
未央区	**Weiyang**					
2000		62.54	2.20	35.05	25.29	16635
2001		70.44	2.19	38.97	29.28	18406
2002		77.92	2.00	41.90	34.02	20046
2003		93.83	1.90	51.75	40.18	23668
2004		109.52	1.90	61.03	46.59	27059
2005		146.90	1.82	76.99	68.09	21737
2006		176.28	1.89	91.48	82.91	25228
2007		217.19	1.74	112.88	102.57	30015
2008		281.85	2.16	148.18	131.51	37547
2009		332.93	2.42	172.39	158.12	42956
2010		397.43	2.48	211.37	183.58	49894
2011		459.54	2.31	232.12	225.11	56782
2012		509.58	2.24	251.68	255.66	62679
2013		607.40	1.41	310.80	295.19	73619
2014		703.14	1.06	371.00	331.08	85686
2015		720.22	1.34	357.72	361.16	87126

3-10 续表2 continued 2

单位：亿元 （100 million yuan）

指　标	Item	生产总值 Gross Domestic Product	第一产业 Primary Industry	第二产业 Secondary Industry	第三产业 Tertiary Industry	人均生产总值（元）Per Capita GDP（yuan）
雁塔区	**Yanta**					
2000		109.82	1.46	45.95	62.41	20535
2001		125.83	1.65	53.63	70.55	21960
2002		141.42	1.68	58.23	81.51	23613
2003		162.88	1.66	65.82	95.40	25470
2004		191.45	1.48	77.20	112.77	28254
2005		231.02	1.57	92.69	136.76	22310
2006		278.52	1.68	116.06	160.78	25543
2007		339.96	1.75	140.03	198.18	30633
2008		432.87	2.12	174.13	256.62	38666
2009		498.58	2.19	180.68	315.71	44134
2010		636.46	2.13	211.23	423.10	54948
2011		765.99	2.61	256.40	506.98	64788
2012		848.00	2.34	282.69	562.97	71447
2013		988.20	1.93	346.45	639.82	82979
2014		1114.46	1.62	389.82	723.02	93245
2015		1165.11	0.14	365.07	799.90	96810
阎良区	**Yanliang**					
2000		22.01	3.68	11.49	6.84	9358
2001		23.32	4.04	12.00	7.28	9807
2002		25.81	4.26	13.42	8.13	10813
2003		27.98	4.56	14.22	9.20	11668
2004		33.86	5.40	18.08	10.38	14032
2005		41.64	6.31	21.87	13.46	17150
2006		49.30	7.03	26.26	16.01	19960
2007		58.51	8.31	31.34	18.86	23311
2008		70.90	10.34	37.94	22.62	27782
2009		82.32	11.29	43.50	27.53	31637
2010		99.38	14.26	51.16	33.96	36712
2011		116.37	17.61	58.94	39.82	41650
2012		137.64	19.70	74.31	43.63	48947
2013		164.88	20.37	94.18	50.33	58220
2014		184.25	22.21	105.61	56.43	64717
2015		188.72	22.37	102.72	63.63	65791

3-10 续表3 continued 3

单位：亿元 （100 million yuan）

指 标	Item	生产总值 Gross Domestic Product	第一产业 Primary Industry	第二产业 Secondary Industry	第三产业 Tertiary Industry	人均生产总值（元） Per Capita GDP（yuan）
临潼区	**Lintong**					
2000		25.00	8.34	7.08	9.58	3710
2001		27.84	8.79	8.32	10.73	4133
2002		33.80	9.30	12.78	11.72	4622
2003		40.22	9.71	17.75	12.76	6016
2004		51.45	11.73	25.31	14.41	7705
2005		60.72	12.52	28.97	19.23	9223
2006		70.35	12.64	35.25	22.46	10625
2007		84.25	15.18	42.60	26.47	12585
2008		104.92	19.74	52.36	32.82	15522
2009		113.01	20.72	54.88	37.41	16556
2010		149.08	25.58	79.79	43.71	22214
2011		181.54	28.27	102.03	51.24	27594
2012		208.07	29.63	120.48	57.96	31426
2013		221.58	29.89	124.06	67.63	33255
2014		221.78	31.16	116.26	74.36	33109
2015		193.10	30.27	81.20	81.63	28653
长安区	**Chang'an**					
2000		31.06	6.75	15.28	9.03	3487
2001		36.56	7.92	17.78	10.86	4075
2002		43.13	8.18	21.14	13.81	4789
2003		52.22	8.79	24.76	18.67	5746
2004		64.45	10.94	30.04	23.47	7006
2005		73.16	12.21	33.74	27.21	7513
2006		86.45	13.13	41.51	31.81	8650
2007		112.91	14.28	60.61	38.02	11174
2008		148.69	17.59	81.55	49.55	14623
2009		225.70	19.20	110.60	95.90	21980
2010		261.53	24.50	130.69	106.34	24708
2011		299.20	28.97	141.93	128.30	27533
2012		328.79	30.06	152.36	146.37	30088
2013		366.82	31.76	157.81	177.25	33413
2014		445.43	33.67	217.23	194.53	40380
2015		513.88	36.53	261.90	215.45	46208

3-10 续表4 continued 4

单位：亿元 （100 million yuan）

指 标	Item	生产总值 Gross Domestic Product	第一产业 Primary Industry	第二产业 Secondary Industry	第三产业 Tertiary Industry	人均生产总值（元） Per Capita GDP（yuan）
高陵区	Gaoling					
2000		10.38	3.35	4.69	2.34	4477
2001		11.33	3.66	5.10	2.57	4853
2002		12.94	3.70	6.16	3.08	5533
2003		15.26	3.92	7.63	3.71	6520
2004		18.49	4.61	9.15	4.73	7927
2005		31.42	5.65	19.49	6.28	13174
2006		41.17	5.13	28.90	7.14	18021
2007		60.28	6.85	44.54	8.89	25012
2008		88.53	8.87	67.12	12.54	31828
2009		107.76	9.20	82.45	16.11	36265
2010		138.46	12.12	106.03	20.31	43168
2011		184.25	16.93	140.71	26.61	55099
2012		238.69	20.33	184.37	33.99	70891
2013		283.23	22.12	213.60	47.51	83524
2014		298.27	25.96	219.67	52.64	87431
2015		297.19	27.70	215.02	54.47	86154
蓝田县	Lantian					
2000		16.61	4.63	4.95	7.03	2639
2001		18.04	5.06	5.49	7.49	2868
2002		19.93	5.33	6.05	8.55	3170
2003		22.52	5.74	6.75	10.03	3568
2004		26.13	6.91	7.56	11.66	4101
2005		29.54	7.59	9.07	12.88	5829
2006		33.44	8.21	11.23	14.00	6559
2007		39.59	9.71	13.34	16.54	7678
2008		49.68	12.17	16.83	20.68	9554
2009		57.32	13.03	20.50	23.79	10931
2010		67.53	16.64	23.84	27.05	12768
2011		78.97	20.49	26.39	32.09	15325
2012		92.83	24.45	31.81	36.57	17931
2013		107.81	24.45	39.99	43.37	20566
2014		109.57	25.90	35.33	48.34	20996
2015		112.10	26.00	32.89	53.21	21388

3-10 续表5 continued 5

单位：亿元 （100 million yuan）

指 标	Item	生产总值 Gross Domestic Product	第一产业 Primary Industry	第二产业 Secondary Industry	第三产业 Tertiary Industry	人均生产总值（元） Per Capita GDP （yuan）
周至县	**Zhouzhi**					
2000		16.00	5.11	3.56	7.33	2516
2001		18.26	5.51	5.00	7.75	2707
2002		19.36	5.68	5.22	8.46	2943
2003		20.20	5.52	5.50	9.18	3275
2004		21.52	5.60	5.82	10.10	3776
2005		24.25	6.52	6.97	10.76	4146
2006		27.56	7.16	8.42	11.98	5126
2007		32.51	8.50	9.59	14.42	5989
2008		40.07	10.65	11.22	18.20	7327
2009		44.90	11.11	12.15	21.64	8127
2010		54.37	15.27	14.30	24.80	9758
2011		66.14	20.30	15.91	29.93	11719
2012		78.34	25.39	19.40	33.55	13795
2013		89.98	26.34	23.44	40.20	15347
2014		98.84	27.62	26.09	45.13	16932
2015		104.33	29.54	25.01	49.78	18041
户 县	**Huxian**					
2000		26.89	5.25	14.10	7.54	4789
2001		30.69	5.64	16.53	8.52	5450
2002		34.34	5.60	19.18	9.56	6089
2003		38.17	5.90	21.45	10.82	6736
2004		44.74	7.45	24.74	12.55	7803
2005		51.03	8.03	28.73	14.27	9099
2006		59.56	8.40	34.67	16.49	10901
2007		70.19	9.72	40.90	19.57	12708
2008		83.77	11.90	46.88	24.99	15034
2009		93.62	12.44	52.32	28.86	16623
2010		104.44	15.59	56.50	32.35	18580
2011		120.00	21.24	60.43	38.33	21525
2012		132.67	25.37	64.26	43.04	23702
2013		146.32	25.32	70.15	50.85	26031
2014		155.92	27.20	71.56	57.16	27616
2015		155.41	27.57	64.60	63.24	27353

3-11 主要年份各区县生产总值指数（上年＝100）

Indices of Gross Domestic Product by Region (preceding year = 100)

(本表按可比价格计算) (Data in the table are calculated at constant prices)

指标	Item	生产总值 Gross Domestic Product	第一产业 Primary Industry	第二产业 Secondary Industry	第三产业 Tertiary Industry	人均生产总值 Per Capita GDP
新城区	**Xincheng**					
2000		117.9	99.1	124.8	113.4	117.9
2001		115.7	50.0	121.0	110.7	115.4
2002		111.4	100.0	110.0	112.8	110.7
2003		110.9	100.0	110.0	111.8	109.7
2004		113.2	100.0	115.4	111.0	112.1
2005		108.4	100.0	109.2	107.6	107.1
2006		112.2	100.0	109.5	114.6	109.7
2007		114.0	—	100.8	125.1	113.5
2008		114.1	—	106.0	119.6	115.4
2009		113.6	—	111.6	115.0	115.4
2010		113.7	—	121.8	108.9	117.0
2011		113.3	—	112.1	114.3	114.9
2012		111.0	—	108.7	112.9	110.6
2013		109.2	—	108.0	110.1	108.8
2014		109.0	—	108.5	109.4	108.6
2015		106.4	—	97.8	112.6	105.8
碑林区	**Beilin**					
2000		124.5	77.1	124.4	124.6	120.8
2001		112.5	100.0	119.0	111.3	108.3
2002		114.1	100.0	114.5	114.0	109.3
2003		112.8	—	113.1	112.7	108.1
2004		112.3	—	111.0	112.5	109.6
2005		111.4	—	117.5	110.1	108.7
2006		112.9	—	116.0	112.2	109.8
2007		115.0	—	112.5	115.6	124.7
2008		115.6	—	113.3	116.1	129.0
2009		115.2	—	112.9	115.7	119.8
2010		114.1	—	116.6	113.5	120.5
2011		114.6	—	123.0	112.0	117.4
2012		113.8	—	113.7	113.8	113.4
2013		110.8	—	112.8	110.4	110.5
2014		110.8	—	110.2	111.0	110.5
2015		109.9	—	113.7	109.1	109.4
莲湖区	**Lianhu**					
2000		130.0	110.0	134.0	129.0	129.7
2001		115.8	94.4	116.1	115.6	115.4
2002		116.0	105.9	116.2	115.8	**115.5**
2003		116.0	100.0	118.3	114.0	**114.5**
2004		117.3	90.1	122.2	112.6	**115.4**
2005		111.1	89.9	108.9	113.4	**91.5**
2006		112.4	84.2	107.5	117.0	**110.4**
2007		115.4	106.3	113.3	117.3	**116.8**
2008		116.9	—	118.8	115.5	**119.1**
2009		113.8	—	110.6	116.6	**114.4**
2010		114.0	—	117.8	111.0	**115.2**
2011		112.3	—	112.0	112.5	**112.6**
2012		111.7	—	107.7	114.8	**111.4**
2013		111.1	—	111.1	111.0	**110.9**
2014		109.0	—	107.6	110.0	**108.7**
2015		107.7	—	100.3	112.9	107.1

3-11 续表1 continued 1

(本表按可比价格计算) (Data in the table are calculated at constant prices)

指 标	Item	生产总值 Gross Domestic Product	第一产业 Primary Industry	第二产业 Secondary Industry	第三产业 Tertiary Industry	人均生产总值 Per Capita GDP
灞桥区	**Baqiao**					
2000		109.8	100.6	112.5	111.3	109.3
2001		109.6	101.9	108.0	125.5	109.0
2002		109.8	105.7	116.7	112.5	109.0
2003		113.1	104.0	120.2	113.2	111.4
2004		109.1	108.8	114.3	109.7	102.6
2005		113.2	109.7	113.6	111.5	105.0
2006		115.1	112.4	116.9	110.5	109.9
2007		116.0	107.0	117.2	112.9	113.3
2008		117.6	108.1	116.9	114.4	116.2
2009		115.0	106.6	113.2	118.9	111.9
2010		115.4	107.3	112.9	119.9	111.2
2011		116.1	108.2	115.6	118.3	113.8
2012		114.0	106.5	107.7	124.0	113.4
2013		114.9	105.4	118.3	110.8	114.3
2014		111.1	105.1	111.2	111.8	110.5
2015		108.8	104.6	105.5	113.1	108.0
未央区	**Weiyang**					
2000		114.8	97.1	114.6	116.8	121.3
2001		113.8	94.1	114.5	114.6	110.6
2002		113.8	91.3	113.5	115.7	108.9
2003		117.9	95.2	120.9	115.2	118.1
2004		115.2	90.1	116.0	115.2	114.3
2005		118.3	89.4	119.0	118.4	115.3
2006		115.3	92.3	111.3	120.5	116.1
2007		118.0	93.8	116.7	119.9	119.0
2008		118.9	105.4	121.4	116.6	125.1
2009		115.5	104.1	114.4	116.7	114.4
2010		115.1	96.8	115.6	114.8	116.2
2011		113.0	90.0	110.1	116.5	113.8
2012		109.6	91.7	106.6	113.0	110.4
2013		111.9	91.5	113.0	110.9	118.7
2014		110.1	93.9	110.0	110.3	115.2
2015		107.0	103.5	105.0	109.0	106.2

3-11 续表2 continued 2

(本表按可比价格计算) (Data in the table are calculated at constant prices)

指 标	Item	生产总值 Gross Domestic Product	第一产业 Primary Industry	第二产业 Secondary Industry	第三产业 Tertiary Industry	人均生产总值 Per Capita GDP
雁塔区	Yanta					
2000		113.0	100.1	110.0	116.9	106.1
2001		113.8	95.9	113.5	114.4	106.2
2002		115.2	102.1	114.0	116.4	110.2
2003		114.0	99.3	115.0	113.5	106.8
2004		115.7	89.0	118.0	114.4	109.2
2005		116.1	106.8	117.0	115.6	110.1
2006		117.0	102.2	117.8	116.7	111.1
2007		118.2	101.0	114.2	121.2	116.2
2008		118.1	100.6	114.0	120.9	117.0
2009		114.4	100.9	112.3	115.8	113.4
2010		113.5	95.4	115.5	112.4	110.7
2011		113.7	95.9	112.1	114.6	111.4
2012		111.5	90.4	109.6	112.5	111.1
2013		110.1	94.5	113.3	108.3	109.7
2014		110.7	95.1	110.7	110.7	110.3
2015		107.8	53.3	103.0	110.5	107.1
阎良区	Yanliang					
2000		109.0	105.6	107.5	114.2	107.4
2001		109.5	105.7	111.0	109.0	108.3
2002		111.0	104.4	112.2	112.5	110.6
2003		109.6	106.9	110.0	110.1	109.1
2004		116.0	106.3	123.7	107.3	115.3
2005		112.6	107.6	110.8	118.6	111.2
2006		113.2	108.8	112.3	116.5	111.3
2007		113.0	107.8	112.8	115.5	111.2
2008		112.9	107.3	113.8	113.7	111.0
2009		112.9	106.6	112.4	116.3	110.7
2010		115.3	107.6	118.0	113.8	110.8
2011		113.5	108.0	116.5	111.5	110.0
2012		112.3	106.4	114.9	110.9	111.6
2013		111.5	105.2	114.8	108.9	110.7
2014		109.9	105.5	110.6	110.4	109.3
2015		105.7	104.7	101.7	112.4	104.9

3-11 续表3 continued 3

(本表按可比价格计算) (Data in the table are calculated at constant prices)

指 标	Item	生产总值 Gross Domestic Product	第一产业 Primary Industry	第二产业 Secondary Industry	第三产业 Tertiary Industry	人均生产总值 Per Capita GDP
临潼区	**Lintong**					
2000		109.6	104.8	114.3	107.7	105.8
2001		110.7	104.6	117.8	110.9	111.4
2002		121.8	104.8	156.2	108.9	111.8
2003		124.6	100.1	139.9	110.3	130.2
2004		120.5	105.1	133.4	111.8	128.1
2005		112.7	103.5	119.1	108.3	114.7
2006		113.0	105.2	113.8	116.8	121.6
2007		112.7	105.6	114.0	114.9	111.5
2008		114.6	109.4	116.1	115.3	113.6
2009		113.5	106.3	119.1	110.3	112.4
2010		113.6	106.9	119.0	108.4	115.5
2011		112.9	104.2	116.5	111.4	115.2
2012		111.8	105.1	113.2	112.8	111.1
2013		111.5	104.8	115.8	107.1	110.9
2014		105.0	105.0	101.9	109.1	83.9
2015		105.6	107.0	103.1	108.2	105.0
长安区	**Chang'an**					
2000		114.8	105.4	116.2	119.0	113.8
2001		117.1	116.5	116.3	119.1	116.3
2002		118.6	102.1	118.6	129.6	118.1
2003		119.3	103.6	116.3	133.3	118.3
2004		117.4	112.1	115.2	123.2	116.0
2005		113.8	107.3	114.6	115.1	107.5
2006		115.0	107.6	117.6	115.0	112.0
2007		114.4	107.2	116.4	115.7	113.2
2008		117.5	108.1	121.2	116.4	116.8
2009		114.8	106.7	118.4	113.1	113.7
2010		114.7	107.5	119.0	112.1	111.2
2011		113.2	107.2	113.1	114.6	110.3
2012		114.3	106.1	112.7	117.8	113.6
2013		111.2	104.8	115.4	107.8	110.7
2014		111.3	105.1	114.6	108.9	110.8
2015		114.3	105.7	119.6	109.9	113.3

3-11 续表4 continued 4

(本表按可比价格计算) (Data in the table are calculated at constant prices)

指 标	Item	生产总值 Gross Domestic Product	第一产业 Primary Industry	第二产业 Secondary Industry	第三产业 Tertiary Industry	人均生产总值 Per Capita GDP
高陵区	Gaoling					
2000		114.1	108.9	117.2	117.2	112.9
2001		113.3	109.3	115.4	114.9	112.5
2002		114.7	101.1	122.9	116.9	114.5
2003		115.4	105.9	119.6	117.7	115.3
2004		117.1	100.4	123.1	121.8	117.5
2005		123.6	105.6	134.7	115.2	120.9
2006		127.6	104.8	138.8	113.3	133.2
2007		135.1	106.6	145.3	120.4	128.1
2008		135.6	108.1	142.0	126.7	117.5
2009		126.8	106.5	128.7	131.1	118.7
2010		124.2	107.7	125.9	124.8	115.1
2011		119.4	108.1	119.7	124.4	114.5
2012		118.3	106.4	117.9	126.7	117.5
2013		117.8	105.9	119.7	110.2	117.0
2014		112.0	105.7	113.4	107.3	111.3
2015		102.7	104.3	102.5	103.1	101.5
蓝田县	Lantian					
2000		110.5	105.1	113.2	112.6	109.5
2001		111.1	105.8	113.9	112.5	110.6
2002		109.3	103.9	111.5	111.0	109.3
2003		110.8	106.1	110.0	114.0	110.5
2004		112.0	109.3	110.0	114.8	110.9
2005		110.1	105.6	112.5	110.9	109.2
2006		119.5	133.1	123.0	110.6	118.5
2007		112.1	104.6	113.4	115.4	110.8
2008		113.1	107.8	116.8	113.2	112.9
2009		112.1	106.0	116.1	112.1	111.2
2010		112.5	106.8	116.5	111.4	111.5
2011		111.9	107.8	114.0	112.7	114.9
2012		111.6	106.3	113.5	113.1	111.1
2013		112.0	108.0	115.0	111.0	111.0
2014		108.8	105.1	109.9	109.5	110.0
2015		106.3	104.1	103.3	110.1	105.9

3-11 续表5 continued 5

(本表按可比价格计算) (Data in the table are calculated at constant prices)

指 标	Item	生产总值 Gross Domestic Product	第一产业 Primary Industry	第二产业 Secondary Industry	第三产业 Tertiary Industry	人均生产总值 Per Capita GDP
周至县	**Zhouzhi**					
2000		109.7	104.5	109.8	110.6	108.6
2001		108.5	102.0	119.5	107.7	107.8
2002		105.5	102.4	104.3	108.2	105.4
2003		105.1	97.2	111.2	107.0	104.9
2004		109.3	106.0	116.3	107.3	108.5
2005		110.9	111.6	112.6	109.4	109.6
2006		111.3	111.0	112.8	110.4	109.8
2007		111.5	104.1	109.8	117.0	110.4
2008		112.3	108.6	110.6	115.4	111.5
2009		111.4	106.5	107.6	116.1	110.3
2010		109.6	108.0	106.0	112.4	108.7
2011		112.0	108.3	111.5	114.5	110.6
2012		111.7	106.8	114.7	113.0	111.0
2013		109.2	105.6	113.5	108.7	108.6
2014		108.8	105.6	109.7	109.8	109.6
2015		109.3	105.6	111.2	110.1	108.5
户 县	**Huxian**					
2000		106.9	101.0	111.0	102.9	107.2
2001		115.1	112.4	119.1	109.5	114.8
2002		114.6	99.3	120.7	113.0	114.4
2003		111.3	104.4	112.8	112.3	110.8
2004		113.0	104.0	114.9	114.3	111.7
2005		111.8	103.8	112.8	113.8	111.3
2006		112.6	107.1	112.6	115.8	111.5
2007		112.1	102.1	113.0	115.5	110.9
2008		110.8	104.3	108.6	117.8	109.8
2009		111.9	106.7	109.5	118.4	110.7
2010		112.0	107.3	113.3	111.7	112.2
2011		110.6	108.2	110.0	112.7	111.5
2012		109.5	106.5	109.0	111.6	109.1
2013		108.2	104.7	108.6	109.2	107.8
2014		107.8	105.0	106.8	110.3	107.3
2015		107.3	104.6	105.9	110.4	106.7

3-12 主要年份非公有制经济增加值

The Added Value of Non-public-owned Economic in Representative Years

年 份 Year	非公有制经济增加值（亿元） the Added Value of Non-public-owned Economic (100 million yuan)	第一产业 Primary Industry	第二产业 Secondary Industry	第三产业 Tertiary Industry
2005	568.45	20.86	232.66	314.93
2006	684.66	26.27	279.06	379.33
2007	854.26	25.25	365.24	463.77
2008	1103.96	36.42	468.58	598.96
2009	1327.87	36.32	535.02	756.53
2010	1611.71	42.66	636.73	932.32
2011	1956.41	52.93	761.31	1142.17
2012	2258.95	59.79	831.93	1367.23
2013	2569.20	53.72	970.24	1545.24
2014	2892.90	57.40	1079.59	1755.91
2015	3060.38	58.09	1060.92	1941.37

3-12 续表 continued

年 份 Year	非公有制经济增加值占GDP比重(%) the Added Value of Non-public-owned Economic Percentage to GDP(%)	第一产业 Primary Industry	第二产业 Secondary Industry	第三产业 Tertiary Industry
2005	43.3	31.6	43.1	44.5
2006	44.5	37.3	43.2	46.0
2007	46.0	30.6	46.7	46.7
2008	47.6	35.2	47.7	48.6
2009	48.7	32.9	46.7	51.5
2010	49.7	30.5	46.9	53.4
2011	50.6	30.6	48.1	54.0
2012	51.4	30.6	46.7	56.6
2013	52.2	26.8	48.5	56.7
2014	52.7	26.8	49.2	56.9
2015	52.8	26.4	49.9	56.2

注：2009年—2012年数据根据第三次经济普查GDP修订结果相应进行了调整。
2013年、2014年数据根据GDP最终核实数据及三次产业划分的变化相应进行了调整。

主要统计指标解释

生产总值（GDP） 是按市场价格计算的一个地区（或国家）所有常住单位在一定时期内生产活动的最终成果。生产总值有三种表现形态，即价值形态、收入形态和产品形态。从价值形态看，它是所有常住单位在一定时期内生产的全部货物和服务价值超过同期中间投入的全部非固定资产货物和服务价值的差额，即所有常住单位的增加值之和；从收入形态看，它是所有常住单位在一定时期内创造并分配给常住单位和非常住单位的初次收入分配之和；从产品形态看，它是所有常住单位在一定时期内最终使用的货物和服务价值与货物和服务净出口价值之和。在实际核算中，生产总值有三种计算方法，即生产法、收入法和支出法。三种方法分别从不同的方面反映生产总值及其构成。

三次产业 指根据社会生产活动历史发展的顺序对产业结构的划分。目前我国的三次产业划分是：

第一产业是指农、林、牧、渔业（不含农、林、牧、渔服务业）。

第二产业是指采矿业（不含开采辅助活动），制造业（不含金属制品、机械和设备修理业），电力、热力、燃气及水生产和供应业，建筑业。

第三产业即服务业，是指除第一产业、第二产业以外的其他行业。

劳动者报酬 指劳动者因从事生产活动所获得的全部报酬。包括劳动者获得的各种形式的工资、奖金和津贴，既包括货币形式的，也包括实物形式的，还包括劳动者所享受的公费医疗和医药卫生费、上下班交通补贴、单位支付的社会保险费、住房公积金等。

生产税净额 指生产税减生产补贴后的余额。生产税指政府对生产单位从事生产、销售和经营活动以及因从事生产活动使用某些生产要素（如固定资产、土地、劳动力）所征收的各种税、附加费和规费。生产补贴与生产税相反，指政府对生产单位的单方面转移支出，因此视为负生产税，包括政策亏损补贴、价格补贴等。

固定资产折旧 指一定时期内为弥补固定资产损耗按照规定的固定资产折旧率提取的固定资产折旧，或按国民经济核算统一规定的折旧率虚拟计算的固定资产折旧。它反映了固定资产年当期生产中的转移价值。各类企业和企业化管理的事业单位的固定资产折旧是指实际计提的折旧费；不计提折旧的政府机关、非企业化管理的事业单位和居民住房的固定资产折旧是按照统一规定的折旧率和固定资产原值计算的虚拟折旧。原则上，固定资产折旧应按固定资产当期的重置价值计算，但是目前我国尚不具备对全社会固定资产进行重估价的基础，所以暂时只能采用上述办法。

营业盈余 指常住单位创造的增加值扣除劳动者报酬、生产税净额和固定资产折旧后的余额。它相当于企业的营业利润加上生产补贴，但要扣除从利润中开支的工资和福利等。

三次产业贡献率 各产业不变价增加值增量与不变价GDP增量之比。

三次产业拉动率 GDP增长速度与各产业贡献率之乘积。

非公有制经济 非公有制经济是指国民经济中除国有经济和集体经济以外的部分，对其中的混合制经济要依据实收资本之间的比例，按经济成分对各主要经济总量进行划分。

Explanatory Notes on Main Statistical Indicators

Gross Domestic Product (GDP) refers to the final products at market prices produced by all resident units in a country (or a region) during a certain period of time. Gross domestic product is expressed in three different perspectives, namely value, income, and products respectively. GDP in its value perspective refers to the total value of all goods and services produced by all resident units during a certain period of time, minus the total value of input of goods and services of the nature of non-fixed assets; in other words, it is the sum of the value-added of all resident units. GDP from the perspective of income includes the primary income created by all resident units and distributed to resident and non-resident units. GDP from the perspective of products refers to the value of all goods and services for final demand by all resident units plus the net exports of goods and services during a given period of time. In the practice of national accounting, gross domestic product is calculated from three approaches, namely production approach, income approach and expenditure approach, which reflect gross domestic product and its composition from different angles.

For a region, it is called as Gross Regional Product(GRP) or regional GDP.

Three Strata of Industry Classification of economic activities into three strata of industry is a common practice in the world, although the grouping varies to some extent from country to country. In China economic activities are categorized into the following three strata of industry:

Primary industry refers to agriculture, forestry, animal husbandry and fishery and services in support of these industries.

Secondary industry refers to mining and quarrying, manufacturing, production and supply of electricity, water and gas, and construction.

Tertiary industry refers to all other economic activities not included in the primary or secondary industries.

Compensation of Employees refers to the total payment of various forms to employees for the productive activities they are engaged in. It includes wages, bonuses and allowances, which the employees earn in cash or in kind. It also includes the free medical services provided to the employees and the medicine expenses, transport

Net Taxes on Production refers to taxes on production less subsidies on production. The taxes on production refers to the various taxes, extra charges and fees levied on the production units on their production, sale and business activities as well as on the use of some factors of production, such as fixed assets, land and labour in the production activities they are engaged in. In contrast to taxes on production, subsidies on production refer to the unilateral government transfer to the production units and are therefore regarded as negative taxes on production. They include subsidies on the loss due to implementation of government policies, price subsidies, etc.

Depreciation of Fixed Assets refers to the depreciation of fixed assets in a given period, drawn in accordance with the stipulated depreciation rate for the purpose of compensating the wear-and-tear loss of the fixed assets or the depreciation of fixed assets imputed in accordance with the stipulated unified depreciation rate in the national economic accounting system. It reflects the value of transfer of the fixed assets in the production of the current period. The depreciation of fixed assets in various enterprises and institutions managed as enterprises refers to the depreciation expenses actually drawn. In government agencies and institutions not managed as enterprises which do not draw the depreciation expenses, as well as for the houses of residents, the depreciation of fixed assets is the imputed depreciation, which is calculated in accordance with the stipulated unified depreciation rate. In principle, the depreciation of fixed assets should be calculated on the basis of the re-purchased value of the fixed assets. However, currently the conditions in China do not facilitate the revaluation of all the fixed assets. Therefore, only the above-mentioned methods can be adopted at present.

Operating Surplus refers to the balance of the value added created by the resident units after deducting the labourers remuneration, net taxes on production and the depreciation of fixed assets. It is equivalent to the business profit of the enterprises plus subsidies to production, but the wages and welfare expenses paid from the profits should be deducted.

Three Industry Contribution Rate The ratio of all industries incremental value added to GDP increment at constant prices.

Three Industries Pulling Rate The product of GDP growth rate and the contribution rate of each industry.

Non–public Economy It refers to the part of in addition to state-owned economy and collective economy in the national economy,On which the mixed-economy should be divided according to the major economic components of total economic output based on the proportion in paid-in capital.

4 人口、从业人员与职工工资

POPULATION,EMPLOYMENT AND WAGES

资料整理：王义龙　张　叶　严孟飞
Data management：Wang Yilong Zhang Ye Yan Mengfei
数据审核：冯军魁
Data audit：Feng Junkui

第四部分　人口、从业人员与职工工资

一、简要说明

本章资料包括主要年份人口、分区县户籍和常住人口及变动、从业人员及劳动报酬等。户籍人口数为公安年报数，1991年以前年份市区数未包括临潼、长安。主要数据由西安市统计局人口就业处提供。

二、主要指标

年末户籍人口（万人）	815.66	比上年增长	0.045%
人口自然增长率（‰）	4.64	与上年	持平
常住人口（万人）	870.56	比上年增长	0.9%
男女性别比（以女性为100）	105.49	比上年下降	0.02%
户籍人口密度（人/平方公里）	808	比上年增加	1人/平方公里
城镇非私营单位在岗职工年平均工资（元）	63193	比上年增长	11.9%

4　POPULATION,EMPLOYMENT AND WAGES

Ⅰ.Brief Introduction

This chapter consists of the data about registered population and permanent resident population consequent years, population of all the districts and counties and the correspondent changes, the employed and their wages. The registered population data are from the annual report of the Xi'an Bureau of Public Security, with Lintong, Chang'an not included before 1991. The population data is provided primarily by Population & Employment Office of the Xi'an Bureau of Statistics.

Ⅱ.Major Indicators

		Increase over Preceding Year
Total registered Population of Year-end(10 000 persons)	815.66	0.045%
Natural Growth Rate(‰)	4.64	essentially on a par with last year's
Permanent Population(10 000 persons)	870.56	0.9%
Sex Ratio (Female=100)	105.49	-0.02%
Density of Population (person/sq.km)	808	1
Aunual Average Wage of Staff and Workers in Urban Non-privite Enterprises(yuan)	63193	11.9%

4-1 主要年份人口数、人口密度和人口发展情况

Population, Population Density and Population Development in Representative Years

单位：万人　　　　(10 000 persons)

年份 Year	总人口 Total population	市区 Urban Area	女性人口 Number of Female	城填人口 Urban Population	人口密度（人／平方公里） Density of Population (person/sq.km)	总人口指数（上年为100）Total Population Index (100 for preceding year) 全市 Whole City	市区 Urban Area
1952	252.92	92.42	118.81	57.61	254	102.6	103.1
1965	400.05	179.88	190.72	136.39	401	102.5	103.4
1970	435.12	188.12	210.47	139.12	436	101.9	101.4
1978	498.10	210.15	241.82	159.98	499	101.7	102.7
1980	511.91	221.19	249.26	172.85	513	101.4	102.6
1985	553.11	245.76	268.40	201.90	554	101.6	102.2
1986	563.97	251.80	273.30	205.92	565	102.0	102.5
1987	574.46	257.69	278.12	210.25	575	101.9	102.3
1988	585.85	264.94	283.68	216.99	587	102.0	102.8
1989	597.36	270.80	289.44	222.54	598	102.0	102.2
1990	608.89	275.69	295.29	226.98	610	101.9	101.8
1991	615.48	419.29	298.13	230.85	617	101.1	152.1
1992	623.20	429.54	301.92	236.45	624	101.3	102.4
1993	630.91	435.41	305.30	240.85	632	101.2	101.4
1994	639.45	442.30	309.17	248.35	641	101.4	101.6
1995	648.21	448.65	313.46	255.71	645	101.4	101.4
1996	654.87	454.68	316.60	261.28	653	101.0	101.3
1997	662.06	461.17	320.18	267.52	663	101.1	101.4
1998	668.22	466.31	323.20	271.75	669	100.9	101.1
1999	674.50	463.56	326.12	276.14	676	100.9	99.4
2000	688.01	483.10	332.83	285.79	689	102.0	104.2
2001	694.84	489.88	336.04	292.62	696	101.0	101.4
2002	702.59	497.38	339.51	300.05	704	101.1	101.5
2003	716.58	510.26	346.26	312.88	718	102.0	102.6
2004	725.01	516.30	350.85	318.50	717	101.2	101.2
2005	741.73	533.21	359.71	333.14	734	102.3	103.3
2006	753.11	540.97	365.74	343.78	745	101.5	101.5
2007	764.25	549.19	371.84	353.85	756	101.5	101.5
2008	772.30	554.73	376.76	363.87	764	101.1	101.0
2009	781.67	561.58	382.39	370.66	773	101.2	101.2
2010	782.73	562.65	383.93	374.64	774	100.1	100.2
2011	791.83	568.77	389.31	391.31	783	101.2	101.1
2012	795.98	572.76	392.04	398.40	788	100.5	100.7
2013	806.93	580.60	398.15	409.82	799	101.4	101.4
2014	815.29	587.16	402.83	418.16	807	101.0	101.1
2015	815.66	588.43	403.43	545.95	808	100.0	100.2

注：人口部分均为公安年报数据，系户籍人口。1991年以前年份，市区数未包括临潼、长安。行政区划面积自2012年发生变更，调整了2012年和2013年户籍人口密度。2015年公安局户籍改革，城乡划分标准分为城填户籍人口与农村人口。

4-2 主要年份人口自然变动情况

Natural Population Movements in Representative Years

单位：万人　　(10 000 persons)

年份 Year	出生 Birth		死亡 Death		自然增长率 (‰) Natural Growth Rate (‰)	迁入人口 Immigrant population	迁出人口 Emigrant population
	人数 Population	出生率 (‰) Birth Rate (‰)	人数 Population	死亡率 (‰) Death Rate (‰)			
1985	8.95	16.30	3.01	5.48	10.82	11.60	8.74
1986	10.14	18.15	2.78	4.97	13.18	11.79	8.39
1987	9.76	17.14	2.83	4.97	12.17	12.58	9.26
1988	9.42	16.24	2.89	4.98	11.26	13.54	8.97
1989	11.78	19.92	3.04	5.13	14.79	12.73	10.15
1990	12.40	20.55	3.45	5.72	14.83	11.82	9.86
1991	8.73	14.25	3.26	5.33	8.92	8.98	6.09
1992	8.98	14.49	3.39	5.48	9.01	13.94	9.54
1993	9.25	14.75	3.37	5.38	9.37	11.50	8.33
1994	8.08	12.71	3.16	4.97	7.74	13.40	8.59
1995	7.69	11.95	3.21	4.98	6.97	14.41	8.85
1996	7.26	11.15	3.41	5.24	5.91	11.94	8.88
1997	6.84	10.38	3.12	4.75	5.63	12.58	8.62
1998	6.40	9.62	3.10	4.66	4.96	10.89	8.36
1999	6.19	9.22	3.88	5.78	3.44	12.58	9.23
2000	8.90	13.07	4.06	5.96	7.11	17.12	9.23
2001	5.11	7.39	2.89	4.19	3.20	15.16	10.83
2002	5.34	7.64	3.08	4.41	3.23	13.90	9.41
2003	6.02	8.48	3.32	4.68	3.80	20.60	9.15
2004	6.63	9.19	4.23	5.87	3.32	15.56	10.19
2005	7.67	9.58	4.13	5.16	4.42	22.61	9.46
2006	8.13	9.98	4.45	5.46	4.52	17.23	11.75
2007	8.27	10.00	4.53	5.48	4.52	19.90	14.01
2008	8.47	10.15	4.65	5.57	4.58	18.49	15.04
2009	8.47	10.08	4.73	5.63	4.45	16.84	13.14
2010	8.23	9.73	4.51	5.34	4.39	14.09	13.50
2011	8.25	9.71	4.57	5.38	4.33	14.21	11.74
2012	8.64	10.13	4.75	5.57	4.56	12.55	13.10
2013	8.20	9.57	4.60	5.37	4.20	10.83	8.60
2014	8.70	10.11	4.71	5.47	4.64	9.10	7.61
2015	8.80	10.15	4.78	5.51	4.64	8.08	11.61

注：2004年以前为公安年报数据。迁入人口和迁出人口为公安年报数据。2010年出生、死亡、自然增长率根据第六次人口普查数据推算得出。2005-2009、2011-2015年出生、死亡、自然增长率为人口变动抽样调查数据。

4-3 人口年龄构成和抚养比

Population Age Composition and Dependency Ratio

单位：% (%)

年 份 Year	各年龄段人口比重 Proportion of Population of All Ages 0-14岁 0-14 year old	15-64岁 15-64 year old	65岁及以上 65 year old and above	总抚养比 Total dependency ratio	少年儿童 children	老年人口 Elderly population
1990	25.71	69.08	5.21	44.76	37.21	7.55
2000	22.27	71.26	6.47	40.33	31.25	9.08
2010	12.89	78.65	8.46	27.15	16.39	10.76
2011	12.57	78.33	9.10	27.66	16.04	11.62
2012	12.54	78.02	9.44	28.17	16.07	12.10
2013	12.46	77.88	9.66	28.40	16.00	12.40
2014	12.52	77.46	10.02	29.10	16.16	12.94
2015	12.56	76.94	10.50	29.98	16.33	13.65

注：1990、2000、2010年数据根据人口普查数据计算得出，2011-2015年数据根据人口变动抽样调查数据推算出。
抚养比指0-14岁、65岁及以上人口占15-64岁人口的比重。

4-4 全市及各区县人口数和户数（2015年）

Population and Households by Region（2015）

单位：万人 (10 000 persons)

区 县	Region	总户数（万户） Number of Households (10 000 households)	总人口 Total Population	城填人口 Urban Population	按性别划分Grouped by Sex 男 Male	女 Female	迁入人口(人) Immigrant population (person)	迁出人口(人) Emigrant population (person)
全 市	**Total**	**253.13**	**815.66**	**545.95**	**412.23**	**403.43**	**80805**	**116114**
新城区	Xincheng	17.23	50.46	50.46	25.57	24.89	3723	3715
碑林区	Beilin	21.44	69.86	69.86	35.41	34.45	10985	19210
莲湖区	Lianhu	23.05	65.86	65.86	33.07	32.79	5489	5815
灞桥区	Baqiao	18.03	53.89	53.63	26.51	27.38	4804	3915
未央区	Weiyang	19.58	59.96	59.96	29.8	30.16	7689	6263
雁塔区	Yanta	27.64	84.49	84.49	42.15	42.34	17037	20609
阎良区	Yanliang	8.01	26.27	12.22	13.19	13.08	1269	1351
临潼区	Lintong	20.77	71.11	24.02	35.99	35.12	3434	10060
长安区	Chang'an	31.92	106.53	45.77	53.05	53.48	9346	11411
高陵区	Gaoling	10.25	32.96	21.81	16.38	16.58	2962	3771
蓝田县	Lantian	19.1	65.2	18.97	33.8	31.4	4794	10426
周至县	Zhouzhi	17.83	68.33	16.71	36.03	32.3	5145	12967
户 县	Huxian	18.28	60.74	22.19	31.28	29.46	4128	6601

注：本表均为公安年报数据。公安2015户籍改革，取消农业与非农业性质划分，按照统计用城乡划分标准统计了城镇户籍人口。

4-5 全市及各区县常住人口数和人口变动情况（2015年）

Permanent Population and Population Changes by Region（2015）

区 县	Region	常住人口（万人）Permanent Population (10 000 persons)	城镇 Urban	出生率（‰）Birth Rate (‰)	死亡率（‰）Death Rate (‰)	自然增长率（‰）Natural Growth Rate (‰)
全 市	**Total**	**870.56**	**635.68**	**10.15**	**5.51**	**4.64**
新城区	Xincheng	60.33	60.33	6.94	3.41	3.53
碑林区	Beilin	62.89	62.89	7.65	3.93	3.72
莲湖区	Lianhu	71.23	71.23	7.3	3.85	3.45
灞桥区	Baqiao	61.39	57.83	10.26	5.53	4.73
未央区	Weiyang	83.05	79.7	10.74	5.52	5.22
雁塔区	Yanta	120.96	120.96	9.57	4.73	4.84
阎良区	Yanliang	28.84	16.36	9.73	5.61	4.12
临潼区	Lintong	67.62	23.2	10.83	5.74	5.09
长安区	Chang'an	111.83	64.38	11.89	7.04	4.85
高陵区	Gaoling	34.77	22.21	10.88	5.81	5.07
蓝田县	Lantian	52.53	15.36	12.18	7.2	4.98
周至县	Zhouzhi	58.09	17.9	12.91	7.38	5.53
户 县	Huxian	57.03	23.33	10.99	6.13	4.86

注：本表数据均为人口变动抽样调查数据。

4-6 主要年份常住人口数

Permanent Population in Representative Years

单位：万人 (10 000 persons)

年 份 Year	年末常住人口 Permanent population (year-end)	城镇 Urban	农村 Rural
2000	741.14	450.36	290.78
2005	806.81	510.55	296.26
2006	822.52	530.94	291.58
2007	830.54	548.99	281.55
2008	837.52	565.16	272.36
2009	843.46	581.4	262.06
2010	847.41	584.71	262.7
2011	851.34	596.79	254.55
2012	855.29	611.62	243.67
2013	858.81	618.77	240.04
2014	862.75	626.44	236.31
2015	870.56	635.68	234.88

注：2000年常住人口为普查数据。2010年常住人口为年末常住人口数，根据第六次人口普查数据推算得出。2005-2009、2011-2015年常住人口为人口变动抽样调查数据。

4-7 主要年份社会从业人数

Number of Social Laborers in Representative Years

单位：万人 (10 000 persons)

年 份 Year	合计 Total	一、按城乡分 Grouped by Urban area and Rural area					二、按三次产业分 Grouped by Industry		
		1.城镇 Urban	国有经济 State-owned Enterprises	集体经济 Collective Enterprises	其他经济 Others	2.乡村 Village	第一产业 Primary Industry	第二产业 Secondary Industry	第三产业 Tertiary Industry
1985	**296.80**	129.07	96.80	29.07	3.20	167.73	135.89	98.61	62.30
1986	**299.45**	132.82	101.28	28.43	3.11	166.63	127.46	100.61	71.38
1987	**312.16**	138.56	104.58	30.72	3.26	173.60	130.36	107.75	74.05
1988	**327.76**	142.24	106.46	30.73	5.05	185.52	138.87	108.12	80.77
1989	**332.65**	145.65	108.80	30.44	6.41	187.00	142.21	106.40	84.04
1990	**343.06**	147.93	110.95	29.78	7.20	195.13	149.64	106.74	86.68
1991	**347.65**	149.48	111.87	29.80	7.81	198.17	152.24	108.19	87.22
1992	**357.51**	151.67	113.19	29.97	8.51	205.84	154.75	110.22	92.54
1993	**363.70**	155.72	112.98	29.77	12.97	207.98	154.02	114.02	95.66
1994	**364.56**	154.88	113.39	27.97	13.52	209.68	153.51	108.53	102.52
1995	**372.60**	158.80	113.79	25.58	19.43	213.80	153.39	109.67	109.54
1996	**379.29**	164.54	113.29	24.82	26.43	214.75	153.43	109.17	116.69
1997	**385.14**	169.52	112.44	23.52	33.56	215.62	153.23	109.46	122.45
1998	**393.95**	177.20	106.06	21.50	49.64	216.75	153.00	110.45	130.50
1999	**400.43**	180.27	105.08	20.50	54.69	220.16	154.64	110.58	135.21
2000	**389.10**	176.45	103.46	18.40	54.59	212.65	147.03	107.26	134.81
2001	**389.30**	177.94	100.47	17.10	60.37	211.36	145.09	108.96	135.25
2002	**397.16**	181.85	100.54	16.90	64.41	215.31	143.04	111.62	142.50
2003	**404.92**	183.23	94.51	16.78	71.94	221.69	146.67	109.09	149.16
2004	**409.57**	187.53	93.43	15.41	78.69	222.04	141.81	111.70	156.06
2005	**415.83**	192.53	93.27	14.47	84.79	223.30	136.31	114.20	165.32
2006	**422.15**	196.16	84.46	14.41	97.29	225.99	135.10	116.09	170.96
2007	**436.36**	214.27	90.58	11.88	111.81	222.09	133.33	125.06	177.97
2008	**448.05**	224.20	90.17	10.60	123.43	223.85	127.87	130.23	189.95
2009	**462.52**	239.39	90.83	7.63	140.93	223.13	122.13	131.57	208.82
2010	**477.58**	252.54	94.01	5.48	153.05	225.04	117.27	145.40	214.91
2011	**495.99**	265.43	91.62	5.33	168.48	230.56	121.05	151.33	223.61
2012	**514.57**	287.65	95.33	5.10	187.22	226.92	114.92	162.35	237.30
2013	**530.71**	308.04	86.06	7.29	214.69	222.67	110.45	151.50	268.76
2014	**532.92**	316.59	84.83	6.67	225.09	216.33	105.02	151.85	276.05
2015	**528.06**	327.68	84.52	5.29	237.87	200.38	107.68	129.51	290.87

注：第一产业从业人员中包括城镇农林牧渔及服务业企业人员。

4-8 按国民经济行业分从业人数（2015年）

单位：万人

行　业	Sector	合计 Total
总计	**Total**	528.06
（一）农、林、牧、渔业	Agriculture ,Forestry,Animal Husbandry and Fishery	107.68
（二）采矿业	Mining	0.06
（三）制造业	Manufacturing	72.44
（四）电力、燃气及水的生产供应业	Production and Distribution of Electricity,Gas and Water	4.95
（五）建筑业	Construction	52.06
（六）批发和零售业	Wholesale and Retail Trades	86.14
（七）交通运输、仓储和邮政业	Traffic,Transport,Storage and Post	27.86
（八）住宿和餐饮业	Hotels and Catering Services	32.17
（九）信息传输、软件和信息技术服务业	Information Transmission,Software and Information Technology Services	14.78
（十）金融业	Financial Intermediation	8.71
（十一）房地产业	Real Estate	8.49
（十二）租赁和商务服务业	Leasing and Business Services	19.62
（十三）科学研究和技术服务业	Scientific Research and Technical Services	15.50
（十四）水利、环境和公共设施管理业	Management of Water Conservancy, Environment and Public Facilities	2.61
（十五）居民服务、修理和其他服务业	Services to Households, Repairs and Other Services	22.63
（十六）教育	Education	22.09
（十七）卫生和社会工作	Health and Social Work	14.85
（十八）文化、体育和娱乐业	Culture, Sports and Entertainment	3.38
（十九）公共管理、社会保障和社会组织	Public Administration, Social Security and Social Organizations	12.04
（二十）国际组织	International Organizations	

Number of Employed Persons Grouped by Industry of the National Economy（2015）

(10 000 persons)

国有经济 State-owned Enterprises	集体经济 Collective Enterprises	城镇其他经济 Urban Other Enterprises	城镇私营经济及个体劳动者 Urban Private Enterprises and Individual Labors	乡村从业人员 Rural Employed Persons
84.52	5.29	108.64	129.23	200.38
0.21		0.01	2.36	105.10
		0.01	0.05	
16.07	0.21	29.23	8.02	18.91
2.82	0.03	2.05	0.05	
3.59	3.32	21.04	4.13	19.98
1.31	0.18	10.60	61.90	12.15
10.33	0.02	5.10	2.13	10.28
0.57	0.01	5.36	18.15	8.08
0.09		7.54	6.34	0.81
1.52	0.21	6.10	0.10	0.78
1.37	0.06	5.72	1.34	0.00
1.13	0.90	6.45	7.27	3.87
9.26	0.08	3.87	1.78	0.51
1.47	0.01	0.98	0.15	
0.40	0.09	0.71	13.85	7.58
15.28	0.04	1.76	0.03	4.98
6.72	0.13	0.98	0.45	6.57
1.15		1.10	1.13	
11.23		0.03		0.78

4-9 全部单位从业人员情况（2015年）

单位：人

分 组	Classify	单位从业人员 Employed Persons	女性 Female
总计	**Total**	**1984561**	**717288**
一、按机构类型分组	**Grouped by Organization Type**		
#企业	Enterprises	1581380	528490
事业	Public institutions	276554	144382
机关	Government units	104452	32692
二、按国民经济行业分组	**Grouped by Economic Sector**		
（一）农业	Agriculture ,Forestry,Animal Husbandry and Fishery	2113	638
（二）采矿业	Mining	81	24
（三）制造业	Manufacturing	454564	150374
（四）电力、燃气及水的生产供应业	Production and Distribution of Electricity,Gas and Water	48961	14593
（五）建筑业	Construction	279676	43916
（六）批发和零售业	Wholesale and Retail Trades	120879	63425
（七）交通运输、仓储和邮政业	Traffic,Transport,Storage and Post	155017	44086
（八）住宿和餐饮业	Hotels and Catering Services	59452	36334
（九）信息传输、软件和信息技术服务业	Information Transmission,Software and Information Technology Services	76335	30043
（十）金融业	Financial Intermediation	78303	43583
（十一）房地产业	Real Estate	71475	28324
（十二） 租赁和商务服务业	Leasing and Business Services	84733	15065
（十三）科学研究和技术服务业	Scientific Research and Technical Services	132113	40428
（十四）水利、环境和公共设施管理业	Management of Water Conservancy, Environment and Public Facilities	24721	10424
（十五）居民服务、修理和其他服务业	Services to Households, Repairs and Other Services	11939	5361
（十六）教育	Education	170846	93864
（十七）卫生和社会工作	Health and Social Work	78252	50807
（十八）文化、体育和娱乐业	Culture, Sports and Entertainment	22481	10541
（十九）公共管理、社会保障和社会组织	Public Administration, Social Security and Social Organizations	112620	35458
（二十）国际组织	International Organizations		

Basic Facts on All Employees（2015）

(persons)

		单位从业人员		
在岗职工合计 Total Fully Employed Staff and Workers	其他从业人员 Other Employed Persons	平均人数 Average Employment	在岗职工 Staff and Workers	其他从业人员 Other Employed Persons
1818638	**165923**	**2074653**	**1903116**	**171537**
1447203	134177	1647554	1507007	140547
259261	17293	303642	286979	16663
90372	14080	100180	86220	13960
1923	190	2115	1925	190
81		301	301	
443681	10883	491176	479250	11926
47882	1079	50362	49196	1166
200214	79462	279702	198572	81130
118251	2628	122242	119662	2580
150202	4815	159396	154403	4993
53891	5561	59794	53981	5813
76046	289	79893	79590	303
59655	18648	74736	53289	21447
70216	1259	71033	69501	1532
83095	1638	92290	90638	1652
128323	3790	146147	142372	3775
22309	2412	24705	22284	2421
10688	1251	11689	10412	1277
159790	11056	181122	170592	10530
73212	5040	82515	77490	5025
21054	1427	22871	21461	1410
98125	14495	122564	108197	14367

4-10 国有单位从业人员情况（2015年）

单位：人

分 组	Classify	单位从业人员 Employed Persons	女性 Female
总计	**Total**	**845235**	**327608**
一、按机构类型分组	**Grouped by Organization Type**		
#企业	Enterprises	466673	152237
事业	Public institutions	272863	142040
机关	Government units	104452	32692
二、按国民经济行业分组	**Grouped by Economic Sector**		
（一）农业	Agriculture ,Forestry,Animal Husbandry and Fishery	2056	615
（二）采矿业	Mining		
（三）制造业	Manufacturing	160650	54033
（四）电力、燃气及水的生产供应业	Production and Distribution of Electricity,Gas and Water	28152	8196
（五）建筑业	Construction	35924	6166
（六）批发和零售业	Wholesale and Retail Trades	13123	7324
（七）交通运输、仓储和邮政业	Traffic,Transport,Storage and Post	103325	26556
（八）住宿和餐饮业	Hotels and Catering Services	5734	3191
（九）信息传输、软件和信息技术服务业	Information Transmission,Software and Information Technology Services	941	267
（十）金融业	Financial Intermediation	15167	7379
（十一）房地产业	Real Estate	13720	5499
（十二）租赁和商务服务业	Leasing and Business Services	11258	4991
（十三）科学研究和技术服务业	Scientific Research and Technical Services	92644	29948
（十四）水利、环境和公共设施管理业	Management of Water Conservancy, Environment and Public Facilities	14730	5891
（十五）居民服务、修理和其他服务业	Services to Households, Repairs and Other Services	4024	1076
（十六）教育	Education	152805	83046
（十七）卫生和社会工作	Health and Social Work	67182	43059
（十八）文化、体育和娱乐业	Culture, Sports and Entertainment	11503	5061
（十九）公共管理、社会保障和社会组织	Public Administration, Social Security and Social Organizations	112297	35310
（二十）国际组织	International Organizations		

Basic Facts on Employees in State-owned Units（2015）

(persons)

在岗职工合计 Total Fully Employed Staff and Workers	其他从业人员 Other Employed Persons	单位从业人员平均人数 Average Employment	在岗职工 Staff and Workers	其他从业人员 Other Employed Persons
798788	**46447**	**919845**	**872985**	**46860**
451276	15397	518461	501902	16559
255899	16964	293802	277467	16335
90372	14080	110351	96391	13960
1866	190	2057	1867	190
156401	3704	187508	183520	3988
27665	525	33690	33163	527
32550	3374	35083	30989	4094
12821	302	13078	12777	301
101014	2836	109187	106301	2886
5107	627	5808	5162	646
935	6	927	904	23
14994	173	13396	13142	254
13322	398	13662	13298	364
10771	487	11162	10685	477
90005	2639	106876	104220	2656
12807	1923	14546	12696	1850
3942	82	3846	3757	89
143646	9141	163293	154645	8648
62339	4843	71588	66792	4796
10801	702	11913	11209	704
97802	14495	122225	107858	14367

4-11 城镇集体单位从业人员情况（2015年）

单位：人

分 组	Classify	单位从业人员 Employed Persons	女性 Female
总计	**Total**	**52922**	**8102**
一、按机构类型分组	**Grouped by Organization Type**		
#企业	Enterprises	52046	7580
事业	Public institutions	859	512
机关	Government units		
二、按国民经济行业分组	**Grouped by Economic Sector**		
（一）农业	Agriculture ,Forestry,Animal Husbandry and Fishery		
（二）采矿业	Mining		
（三）制造业	Manufacturing	2121	756
（四）电力、燃气及水的生产供应业	Production and Distribution of Electricity,Gas and Water	276	56
（五）建筑业	Construction	33177	2994
（六）批发和零售业	Wholesale and Retail Trades	1799	640
（七）交通运输、仓储和邮政业	Traffic,Transport,Storage and Post	183	58
（八）住宿和餐饮业	Hotels and Catering Services	121	69
（九）信息传输、软件和信息技术服务业	Information Transmission,Software and Information Technology Services	18	9
（十）金融业	Financial Intermediation	2128	1021
（十一）房地产业	Real Estate	605	219
（十二）租赁和商务服务业	Leasing and Business Services	8992	674
（十三）科学研究和技术服务业	Scientific Research and Technical Services	793	282
（十四）水利、环境和公共设施管理业	Management of Water Conservancy, Environment and Public Facilities	144	64
（十五）居民服务、修理和其他服务业	Services to Households, Repairs and Other Services	859	322
（十六）教育	Education	434	143
（十七）卫生和社会工作	Health and Social Work	1270	795
（十八）文化、体育和娱乐业	Culture, Sports and Entertainment	2	
（十九）公共管理、社会保障和社会组织	Public Administration, Social Security and Social Organizations		
（二十）国际组织	International Organizations		

Basic Facts on Employees in Urban Collective-owned Units（2015）

(persons)

		单位从业人员		
在岗职工合计 Total Fully Employed Staff and Workers	其他从业人员 Other Employed Persons	平均人数 Average Employment	在岗职工 Staff and Workers	其他从业人员 Other Employed Persons
51363	**1559**	**52223**	**50420**	**1803**
50489	1557	51350	49549	1801
859		856	856	
1967	154	2157	1982	175
276		277	236	41
32496	681	32566	31692	874
1492	307	1802	1488	314
179	4	178	174	4
121		123	123	
18		20	20	
2012	116	2078	1961	117
553	52	579	548	31
8977	15	8941	8926	15
767	26	812	786	26
144		136	136	
657	202	900	696	204
434		430	430	
1268	2	1222	1220	2
2		2	2	

4-12 其他经济类型单位从业人员情况（2015年）

单位：人

分　组	Classify	单位从业人员 Employed Persons	女性 Female
总计	Total	1086404	381578
一、按机构类型分组	Grouped by Organization Type		
#企业	Enterprises	1062661	368673
事业	Public institutions	2832	1830
机关	Government units		
二、按国民经济行业分组	Grouped by Economic Sector		
（一）农业	Agriculture ,Forestry,Animal Husbandry and Fishery	57	23
（二）采矿业	Mining	81	24
（三）制造业	Manufacturing	292338	95585
（四）电力、燃气及水的生产供应业	Production and Distribution of Electricity,Gas and Water	20495	6341
（五）建筑业	Construction	210575	34756
（六）批发和零售业	Wholesale and Retail Trades	105957	55461
（七）交通运输、仓储和邮政业	Traffic,Transport,Storage and Post	50984	17472
（八）住宿和餐饮业	Hotels and Catering Services	53597	33074
（九）信息传输、软件和信息技术服务业	Information Transmission,Software and Information Technology Services	75376	29767
（十）金融业	Financial Intermediation	61008	35183
（十一）房地产业	Real Estate	57150	22606
（十二）租赁和商务服务业	Leasing and Business Services	64483	9400
（十三）科学研究和技术服务业	Scientific Research and Technical Services	38676	10198
（十四）水利、环境和公共设施管理业	Management of Water Conservancy, Environment and Public Facilities	9847	4469
（十五）居民服务、修理和其他服务业	Services to Households, Repairs and Other Services	7056	3963
（十六）教育	Education	17625	10675
（十七）卫生和社会工作	Health and Social Work	9800	6953
（十八）文化、体育和娱乐业	Culture, Sports and Entertainment	10976	5480
（十九）公共管理、社会保障和社会组织	Public Administration, Social Security and Social Organizations	323	148
（二十）国际组织	International Organizations		

Basic Facts on Employees in Other Units（2015）

(persons)

在岗职工合计 Total Fully Employed Staff and Workers	其他从业人员 Other Employed Persons	单位从业人员平均人数 Average Employment	在岗职工 Staff and Workers	其他从业人员 Other Employed Persons
968487	**117917**	**1101585**	**978711**	**122874**
945438	117223	1077743	955556	122187
2503	329	2827	2499	328
57		58	58	
81		301	301	
285313	7025	301511	293748	7763
19941	554	15395	14797	598
135168	75407	212053	135891	76162
103938	2019	107362	105397	1965
49009	1975	50031	47928	2103
48663	4934	53863	48696	5167
75093	283	78946	78666	280
42649	18359	59262	38186	21076
56341	809	56792	55655	1137
63347	1136	72187	71027	1160
37551	1125	38459	37366	1093
9358	489	10023	9452	571
6089	967	6943	5959	984
15710	1915	17399	15517	1882
9605	195	9705	9478	227
10251	725	10956	10250	706
323		339	339	

4-13 城镇非私营单位分行业从业人员平均工资

单位：人

分 组	Classify	2010
总计	**Grouped by Economic Sector**	**37870**
（一）农业	Agriculture ,Forestry,Animal Husbandry and Fishery	21436
（二）采矿业	Mining	32154
（三）制造业	Manufacturing	26663
（四）电力、燃气及水的生产供应业	Production and Distribution of Electricity,Gas and Water	39508
（五）建筑业	Construction	26875
（六）批发和零售业	Wholesale and Retail Trades	25103
（七）交通运输、仓储和邮政业	Traffic,Transport,Storage and Post	41737
（八）住宿和餐饮业	Hotels and Catering Services	19647
（九）信息传输、软件和信息技术服务业	Information Transmission,Software and Information Technology Services	45904
（十）金融业	Financial Intermediation	63952
（十一）房地产业	Real Estate	45273
（十二）租赁和商务服务业	Leasing and Business Services	30267
（十三）科学研究和技术服务业	Scientific Research and Technical Services	55456
（十四）水利、环境和公共设施管理业	Management of Water Conservancy, Environment and Public Facilities	25322
（十五）居民服务、修理和其他服务业	Services to Households, Repairs and Other Services	26443
（十六）教育	Education	53084
（十七）卫生和社会工作	Health and Social Work	44035
（十八）文化、体育和娱乐业	Culture, Sports and Entertainment	31925
（十九）公共管理、社会保障和社会组织	Public Administration, Social Security and Social Organizations	39964
（二十）国际组织	International Organizations	

Average Wages of Urban Non-private Employees by Industry

(persons)

2011	2012	2013	2014	2015
41679	**44533**	**49350**	**54573**	**60557**
23567	31846	36658	42881	43426
38551	33489	40605	42116	46645
34698	38957	44321	49482	56686
47705	55409	59955	61252	65887
29773	35828	39507	48275	52783
27996	34382	37362	40915	46203
48231	48760	54147	59189	62816
22925	26637	29497	30914	33746
51135	63328	67495	100550	109448
72195	75652	97140	104433	106807
34626	37567	44832	48120	52423
31549	34291	42109	46828	52637
64448	68274	69951	69958	72731
26009	29938	38429	43033	45356
23993	25103	32066	32478	37019
54442	54581	59143	58451	63761
48836	56764	61602	59892	61623
34717	40833	50201	57239	61561
42163	47691	49893	47000	51681

4-14 主要年份单位从业人员数及工资总额

Number of Employees and Remuneration in Representative Years

年 份 year	单位从业人员（万人） Number of Employed Persons (10 000 persons)	从业人员工资总额（万元） Remuneration of Employed Persons (10 000 yuan)	城镇非私营单位从业人员年平均工资（元） Aunual Average Wage of Employees in Urban Non-privite Units(yuan)	国有单位从业人员年平均工资（元） Aunual Average Wage of Employees in State Owned units(yuan)	城镇集体单位从业人员年平均工资（元） Aunual Average Wage of Employees in Urban Collective units(yuan)	其他经济类型单位从业人员年平均工资（元） Aunual Average Wage of Employees in Other units (yuan)
1978	67.19	4.71	713	705	609	
1980	91.76	7.31	859	849	699	
1985	127.04	14.17	1148	1215	923	1409
1986	132.78	16.87	1311	1388	1048	1659
1987	135.48	19.13	1446	1544	1107	1583
1988	137.56	22.81	1702	1842	1216	2065
1989	139.86	25.64	1873	2010	1385	2188
1990	141.55	29.48	2133	2290	1545	2044
1991	142.86	26.88	2276	2435	1657	2966
1992	144.51	30.80	2545	2758	1709	3504
1993	146.03	43.25	2999	3274	1910	3551
1994	142.37	58.87	4172	4588	2337	5243
1995	141.17	67.23	4763	5168	2837	5863
1996	140.60	75.64	5407	5858	3216	6225
1997	138.89	80.83	5785	6204	3437	7487
1998	138.78	82.85	6900	7445	3964	6942
1999	115.88	90.13	7764	8238	4374	8217
2000	112.45	103.80	9179	9742	5178	9451
2001	113.93	123.12	10786	11570	5431	10781
2002	115.77	138.88	12138	12877	6230	12543
2003	116.68	155.95	13504	14217	6892	14215
2004	118.15	184.63	15473	15994	7428	17030
2005	123.66	215.67	17728	18420	7612	19066
2006	125.10	250.87	20475	21392	8494	21859
2007	129.40	319.23	25012	25696	9768	27400
2008	130.85	379.29	29749	30246	10834	33344
2009	135.64	450.48	34032	34611	11940	37307
2010	140.38	520.88	37870	38122	12505	40721
2011	154.33	658.73	41679	45217	23241	37643
2012	165.59	770.86	44533	47493	29988	41218
2013	198.42	1031.46	49350	52782	34591	47462
2014	199.41	1151.53	54573	54138	41006	55766
2015	198.46	1255.75	60557	60301	43291	61590

4-15 全部单位从业人员工资总额（2015年）

Total Wages of All Employees of All Units（2015）

单位：万元　　　　(10 000yuan)

分 组	Classify	单位从业人员工资总额 Total Wages of Employment	在岗职工工资总额 Total Wages of Employed Staff and Workers
总计	**Total**	**12557522**	**12020122**
一、按机构类型分组	**Grouped by Organization Type**		
#企业	Enterprises	10005205	9537662
事业	Public institutions	1806796	1760733
机关	Government units	624632	601692
二、按国民经济行业分组	**Grouped by Economic Sector**		
（一）农业	Agriculture ,Forestry,Animal Husbandry and Fishery	9185	9025
（二）采矿业	Mining	1404	1404
（三）制造业	Manufacturing	2784276	2734144
（四）电力、燃气及水的生产供应业	Production and Distribution of Electricity, Gas and Water	331821	328231
（五）建筑业	Construction	1476360	1163974
（六）批发和零售业	Wholesale and Retail Trades	564793	558416
（七）交通运输、仓储和邮政业	Traffic,Transport,Storage and Post	1001262	985758
（八）住宿和餐饮业	Hotels and Catering Services	201781	194689
（九）信息传输、软件和信息技术服务业	Information Transmission,Software and Information Technology Services	874413	872997
（十）金融业	Financial Intermediation	798236	764769
（十一）房地产业	Real Estate	372379	368069
（十二）租赁和商务服务业	Leasing and Business Services	485791	482145
（十三）科学研究和技术服务业	Scientific Research and Technical Services	1062948	1045257
（十四）水利、环境和公共设施管理业	Management of Water Conservancy, Environment and Public Facilities	112053	107096
（十五）居民服务、修理和其他服务业	Services to Households, Repairs and Other Services	43271	39923
（十六）教育	Education	1154848	1125467
（十七）卫生和社会工作	Health and Social Work	508486	492433
（十八）文化、体育和娱乐业	Culture, Sports and Entertainment	140795	136527
（十九）公共管理、社会保障和社会组织	Public Administration, Social Security and Social Organizations	633420	609798
（二十）国际组织	International Organizations		

4-15 续表 continued

单位：万元 (10 000 yuan)

分 组	Classify	其他从业人员劳动报酬 Remuneration of Other Employed Persons	城镇非私营单位从业人员平均工资（元） Aunual Average Wage of Employees in UrbanNon-privite Units(yuan)
总计	**Total**	**537400**	**60557**
一、按机构类型分组	**Grouped by Organization Type**		
#企业	Enterprises	467543	60728
事业	Public institutions	46063	59504
机关	Government units	22940	62351
二、按国民经济行业分组	**Grouped by Economic Sector**		
（一）农业	Agriculture ,Forestry,Animal Husbandry and Fishery	160	43426
（二）采矿业	Mining		46645
（三）制造业	Manufacturing	50132	56686
（四）电力、燃气及水的生产供应业	Production and Distribution of Electricity, Gas and Water	3590	65887
（五）建筑业	Construction	312386	52783
（六）批发和零售业	Wholesale and Retail Trades	6377	46203
（七）交通运输、仓储和邮政业	Traffic,Transport,Storage and Post	15504	62816
（八）住宿和餐饮业	Hotels and Catering Services	7092	33746
（九）信息传输、软件和信息技术服务业	Information Transmission,Software and Information Technology Services	1416	109448
（十）金融业	Financial Intermediation	33467	106807
（十一）房地产业	Real Estate	4310	52423
（十二）租赁和商务服务业	Leasing and Business Services	3646	52637
（十三）科学研究和技术服务业	Scientific Research and Technical Services	17691	72731
（十四）水利、环境和公共设施管理业	Management of Water Conservancy, Environment and Public Facilities	4957	45356
（十五）居民服务、修理和其他服务业	Services to Households, Repairs and Other Services	3348	37019
（十六）教育	Education	29381	63761
（十七）卫生和社会工作	Health and Social Work	16053	61623
（十八）文化、体育和娱乐业	Culture, Sports and Entertainment	4268	61561
（十九）公共管理、社会保障和社会组织	Public Administration, Social Security and Social Organizations	23622	51681
（二十）国际组织	International Organizations		

4-16 国有单位从业人员工资总额（2015年）

Total Wages of State-owned Units Employees（2015）

单位：万元　　　　(10 000yuan)

分　组	Classify	单　位 从业人员 工资总额 Total Wages of Employment	在岗职工 工资总额 Total Wages of Employed Staff and Workers
总计	**Total**	**5546791**	**5422918**
一、按机构类型分组	**Grouped by Organization Type**		
#企业	Enterprises	3132153	3076026
事业	Public institutions	1821866	1777078
机关	Government units	584632	561692
二、按国民经济行业分组	**Grouped by Economic Sector**		
（一）农业	Agriculture ,Forestry,Animal Husbandry and Fishery	9046	8886
（二）采矿业	Mining		
（三）制造业	Manufacturing	1075256	1062772
（四）电力、燃气及水的生产供应业	Production and Distribution of Electricity, Gas and Water	206810	205209
（五）建筑业	Construction	156585	140593
（六）批发和零售业	Wholesale and Retail Trades	66510	65833
（七）交通运输、仓储和邮政业	Traffic,Transport,Storage and Post	720489	712361
（八）住宿和餐饮业	Hotels and Catering Services	18778	17494
（九）信息传输、软件和信息技术服务业	Information Transmission,Software and Information Technology Services	4774	4684
（十）金融业	Financial Intermediation	175528	173584
（十一）房地产业	Real Estate	68861	68025
（十二）租赁和商务服务业	Leasing and Business Services	48651	47624
（十三）科学研究和技术服务业	Scientific Research and Technical Services	695350	683734
（十四）水利、环境和公共设施管理业	Management of Water Conservancy, Environment and Public Facilities	63263	59919
（十五）居民服务、修理和其他服务业	Services to Households, Repairs and Other Services	14524	14216
（十六）教育	Education	1072155	1048236
（十七）卫生和社会工作	Health and Social Work	443294	428187
（十八）文化、体育和娱乐业	Culture, Sports and Entertainment	76323	74589
（十九）公共管理、社会保障和社会组织	Public Administration, Social Security and Social Organizations	630594	606972
（二十）国际组织	International Organizations		

4-16 续表 continued

单位：万元 (10 000yuan)

分 组	Classify	其他从业人员工资总额 Remuneration of Other Employed Persons	城镇非私营单位从业人员平均工资（元） Aunual Average Wage of Employees in UrbanNon-privite Units(yuan)
总计	**Total**	**123873**	**60301**
一、按机构类型分组	**Grouped by Organization Type**		
#企业	Enterprises	56127	60413
事业	Public institutions	44788	62010
机关	Government units	22940	52979
二、按国民经济行业分组	**Grouped by Economic Sector**		
（一）农业	Agriculture ,Forestry,Animal Husbandry and Fishery	160	43977
（二）采矿业	Mining		
（三）制造业	Manufacturing	12484	57345
（四）电力、燃气及水的生产供应业	Production and Distribution of Electricity, Gas and Water	1601	61386
（五）建筑业	Construction	15992	44633
（六）批发和零售业	Wholesale and Retail Trades	677	50856
（七）交通运输、仓储和邮政业	Traffic,Transport,Storage and Post	8128	65987
（八）住宿和餐饮业	Hotels and Catering Services	1284	32331
（九）信息传输、软件和信息技术服务业	Information Transmission,Software and Information Technology Services	90	51499
（十）金融业	Financial Intermediation	1944	131030
（十一）房地产业	Real Estate	836	50403
（十二） 租赁和商务服务业	Leasing and Business Services	1027	43586
（十三）科学研究和技术服务业	Scientific Research and Technical Services	11616	65061
（十四）水利、环境和公共设施管理业	Management of Water Conservancy, Environment and Public Facilities	3344	43492
（十五）居民服务、修理和其他服务业	Services to Households, Repairs and Other Services	308	37764
（十六）教育	Education	23919	65658
（十七）卫生和社会工作	Health and Social Work	15107	61923
（十八）文化、体育和娱乐业	Culture, Sports and Entertainment	1734	64067
（十九）公共管理、社会保障和社会组织	Public Administration, Social Security and Social Organizations	23622	51593
（二十）国际组织	International Organizations		

4-17 城镇集体单位从业人员工资总额（2015年）

Total Wages of Urban Collective-owned Units Employees（2015）

单位：万元 （10 000yuan）

分 组	Classify	单 位 从业人员 工资总额 Total Wages of Employment	在岗职工 工资总额 Total Wages of Employed Staff and Workers
总计	**Total**	**226076**	**220226**
一、按机构类型分组	**Grouped by Organization Type**		
#企业	Enterprises	222072	216227
事业	Public institutions	3957	3957
机关	Government units		
二、按国民经济行业分组	**Grouped by Economic Sector**		
（一）农、林、牧、渔业	Agriculture ,Forestry,Animal Husbandry and Fishery		
（二）采矿业	Mining		
（三）制造业	Manufacturing	5841	5269
（四）电力、燃气及水的生产供应业	Production and Distribution of Electricity, Gas and Water	2248	1871
（五）建筑业	Construction	146721	143979
（六）批发和零售业	Wholesale and Retail Trades	5208	4439
（七）交通运输、仓储和邮政业	Traffic,Transport,Storage and Post	571	553
（八）住宿和餐饮业	Hotels and Catering Services	458	458
（九）信息传输、软件和信息技术服务业	Information Transmission,Software and Information Technology Services	76	76
（十）金融业	Financial Intermediation	17023	16396
（十一）房地产业	Real Estate	2310	2235
（十二）租赁和商务服务业	Leasing and Business Services	28192	28163
（十三）科学研究和技术服务业	Scientific Research and Technical Services	5983	5749
（十四）水利、环境和公共设施管理业	Management of Water Conservancy, Environment and Public Facilities	335	335
（十五）居民服务、修理和其他服务业	Services to Households, Repairs and Other Services	3851	3450
（十六）教育	Education	2680	2680
（十七）卫生和社会工作	Health and Social Work	4569	4563
（十八）文化、体育和娱乐业	Culture, Sports and Entertainment	10	10
（十九）公共管理、社会保障和社会组织	Public Administration, Social Security and Social Organizations		
（二十）国际组织	International Organizations		

4-17 续表 continued

单位：万元 (10 000 yuan)

分　组	Classify	其他从业人员工资总额 Remuneration of Other Employed Persons	城镇非私营单位从业人员平均工资（元） Aunual Average Wage of Employees in UrbanNon-privite Units(yuan)
总计	**Total**	**5850**	**43291**
一、按机构类型分组	**Grouped by Organization Type**		
#企业	Enterprises	5845	43247
事业	Public Institutions		46227
机关	Government Units		
二、按国民经济行业分组	**Grouped by Economic Sector**		
（一）农、林、牧、渔业	Agriculture ,Forestry,Animal Husbandry and Fishery		
（二）采矿业	Mining		
（三）制造业	Manufacturing	572	27078
（四）电力、燃气及水的生产供应业	Production and Distribution of Electricity, Gas and Water	377	81141
（五）建筑业	Construction	2742	45054
（六）批发和零售业	Wholesale and Retail Trades	769	28905
（七）交通运输、仓储和邮政业	Traffic,Transport,Storage and Post	18	32073
（八）住宿和餐饮业	Hotels and Catering Services		37260
（九）信息传输、软件和信息技术服务业	Information Transmission,Software and Information Technology Services		37800
（十）金融业	Financial Intermediation	627	81925
（十一）房地产业	Real Estate	75	39893
（十二） 租赁和商务服务业	Leasing and Business Services	29	31531
（十三）科学研究和技术服务业	Scientific Research and Technical Services	234	73676
（十四）水利、环境和公共设施管理业	Management of Water Conservancy, Environment and Public Facilities		24640
（十五）居民服务、修理和其他服务业	Services to Households, Repairs and Other Services	401	42791
（十六）教育	Education		62321
（十七）卫生和社会工作	Health and Social Work	6	37386
（十八）文化、体育和娱乐业	Culture, Sports and Entertainment		52000
（十九）公共管理、社会保障和社会组织	Public Administration, Social Security and Social Organizations		
（二十）国际组织	International Organizations		

4-18 其他经济类型单位从业人员工资总额（2015年）

Total Wages of Other Units Employees（2015）

单位：万元 （10 000yuan）

分 组	Classify	单 位 从业人员 工资总额 Total Wages of Employment	在岗职工 工资总额 Total Wages of Employed Staff and Workers
总计	**Total**	**6784659**	**6376980**
一、按机构类型分组	**Grouped by Organization Type**		
#企业	Enterprises	6650980	6245409
事业	Public Institutions	20973	19698
机关	Government Units		
二、按国民经济行业分组	**Grouped by Economic Sector**		
（一）农、林、牧、渔业	Agriculture ,Forestry,Animal Husbandry and Fishery	139	139
（二）采矿业	Mining	1404	1404
（三）制造业	Manufacturing	1703178	1666102
（四）电力、燃气及水的生产供应业	Production and Distribution of Electricity, Gas and Water	122763	121151
（五）建筑业	Construction	1173054	879402
（六）批发和零售业	Wholesale and Retail Trades	493074	488143
（七）交通运输、仓储和邮政业	Traffic,Transport,Storage and Post	280202	272844
（八）住宿和餐饮业	Hotels and Catering Services	182545	176737
（九）信息传输、软件和信息技术服务业	Information Transmission,Software and Information Technology Services	869564	868238
（十）金融业	Financial Intermediation	605685	574789
（十一）房地产业	Real Estate	301208	297809
（十二）租赁和商务服务业	Leasing and Business Services	408948	406358
（十三）科学研究和技术服务业	Scientific Research and Technical Services	361616	355775
（十四）水利、环境和公共设施管理业	Management of Water Conservancy, Environment and Public Facilities	48456	46843
（十五）居民服务、修理和其他服务业	Services to Households, Repairs and Other Services	24897	22258
（十六）教育	Education	80014	74551
（十七）卫生和社会工作	Health and Social Work	60623	59683
（十八）文化、体育和娱乐业	Culture, Sports and Entertainment	64463	61928
（十九）公共管理、社会保障和社会组织	Public Administration, Social Security and Social Organizations	2826	2826
（二十）国际组织	International Organizations		

4-18 续表 continued

单位：万元 (10 000 yuan)

分 组	Classify	其他从业人员工资总额 Remuneration of Other Employed Persons	城镇非私营单位从业人员平均工资（元） Aunual Average Wage of Employees in UrbanNon-privite Units(yuan)
总计	**Total**	**407679**	**61590**
一、按机构类型分组	**Grouped by Organization Type**		
#企业	Enterprises	405571	61712
事业	Public Institutions	1275	74187
机关	Government Units		
二、按国民经济行业分组	**Grouped by Economic Sector**		
（一）农、林、牧、渔业	Agriculture ,Forestry,Animal Husbandry and Fishery		23983
（二）采矿业	Mining		46645
（三）制造业	Manufacturing	37076	56488
（四）电力、燃气及水的生产供应业	Production and Distribution of Electricity, Gas and Water	1612	79742
（五）建筑业	Construction	293652	55319
（六）批发和零售业	Wholesale and Retail Trades	4931	45926
（七）交通运输、仓储和邮政业	Traffic,Transport,Storage and Post	7358	56006
（八）住宿和餐饮业	Hotels and Catering Services	5808	33891
（九）信息传输、软件和信息技术服务业	Information Transmission,Software and Information Technology Services	1326	110147
（十）金融业	Financial Intermediation	30896	102205
（十一）房地产业	Real Estate	3399	53037
（十二） 租赁和商务服务业	Leasing and Business Services	2590	56651
（十三）科学研究和技术服务业	Scientific Research and Technical Services	5841	94026
（十四）水利、环境和公共设施管理业	Management of Water Conservancy, Environment and Public Facilities	1613	48345
（十五）居民服务、修理和其他服务业	Services to Households, Repairs and Other Services	2639	35858
（十六）教育	Education	5463	45988
（十七）卫生和社会工作	Health and Social Work	940	62466
（十八）文化、体育和娱乐业	Culture, Sports and Entertainment	2535	58838
（十九）公共管理、社会保障和社会组织	Public Administration, Social Security and Social Organizations		83375
（二十）国际组织	International Organizations		

4–19 主要年份城镇登记失业人数及失业率

Registered Unemployed Persons and Unemployment Rate in Urban Area in Representative Years

年 份 year	城镇登记失业人员数（万人） Real Number of Registered Unemployed Persons (10 000 persons)	城镇登记失业率（%） Registered Unemployment in Urban Area (%)
2002		3.7
2003		4.5
2004	8.29	4.3
2005	8.45	4.3
2006	8.74	4.3
2007	8.77	4.3
2008	9.40	4.2
2009	10.02	4.3
2010	10.46	4.2
2011	10.37	3.9
2012	9.60	3.5
2013	10.13	3.4
2014	10.84	3.4
2015	10.74	3.4

主要统计指标解释

人口数 指一定时点、一定地区范围内的有生命的个人的总和。年度统计的年末人口数，指每年12月31日24时的人口数。

常住人口 指实际经常居住在某地区一定时间（半年以上，含半年）的人口。常住人口包括户口在本辖区人也在本辖区居住的人，户口在本辖区之外但在户口登记地半年以上的人，户口待定（无户口和口袋户口）的人，户口在本辖区但离开本辖区半年以下的人。

城镇人口和乡村人口 城镇人口是指居住在城镇范围内的全部常住人口；乡村人口是除上述人口以外的全部人口。

出生率（又称粗出生率） 指在一定时期内（通常为一年）平均每千人所出生的人数的比率，一般用千分率表示。其计算公式为：

出生率＝年出生人数／年平均人数×1000‰

式中：出生人数指活产婴儿，即胎儿脱离母体时（不管怀孕月数），有过呼吸或其他生命现象。年平均人数指年初、年底人口数的平均数，也可用年中人口数代替。

死亡率（又称粗死亡率） 指在一定时期内（通常为一年）一定地区的死亡人数与同期内平均人数（或期中人数）之比，一般用千分率表示。本资料中的死亡率指年死亡率，其计算公式为：

死亡率＝年死亡人数／年平均人数×1000‰

人口自然增长率 指在一定时期内（通常为一年）人口自然增加数（出生人数减死亡人数）与该时期内平均人数（或期中人数）之比，一般用千分率表示。计算公式为：

人口自然增长率＝（本年出生人数—本年死亡人数）／年平均人数×1000‰。

从业人员 指在16周岁及以上，从事一定社会劳动并取得劳动报酬或经营收入的人员。这一指标反映了一定时期内全部劳动力资源的实际利用情况，是研究我国基本国情国力的重要指标。

单位从业人员 指在各级国家机关、政党机关、社会团体及企业、事业单位中工作，取得工资或其他形式的劳动报酬的全部人员。包括在岗职工、再就业的离退休人员、民办教师以及在各单位中工作的外方人员和港澳台方人员、兼职人员、借用的外单位人员和第二职业者。不包括离开本单位仍保留劳动关系的职工。各单位的就业人员反映了各单位实际参加生产或工作的全部劳动力。

城镇私营和个体就业人员 城镇私营就业人员指在工商管理部门注册登记，其经营地址设在县城关镇（含城关镇）以上的私营企业就业人员；包括私营企业投资者和雇工。城镇个体就业人员指在工商管理部门注册登记，并持有城镇户口或在城镇长期居住，经批准从事个体工商经营的就业人员；包括个体经营者和在个体工商户劳动的家庭帮工和雇工。

国有单位 指资产归国家所有的经济组织。包括按《中华人民共和国企业法人登记管理条例》规定登记注册的非公司制的经济组织，以及中央、地方各级国家机关、事业单位和社会团体。

集体单位 指生产资料归集体所有，并按《中华人民共和国企业法人登记管理条例》规定登记注册的经济组织。

其他单位 包括股份合作单位、联营单位、有限责任公司、股份有限公司、港澳台商投资单位以及外商投资单位等其他登记注册类型单位。

在岗职工 指在本单位工作并由单位支付工资的人员，以及有工作岗位，但由于学习、病伤产假等原因暂未工作，仍由单位支付工资的人员。

职工工资总额 指各单位在一定时期内直接支付给本单位全部职工的劳动报酬总额。工资总额的计算原则应以直接支付给职工的全部劳动报酬为根据。各单位支付给职工的劳动报酬以及其他根据有关规定支付的工资，不论是计入成本的还是不计入成本的，不论是按国家规定列入计征奖金税项目的，还是未列入计征奖金税项目的，不论是以货币形式支付的还是以实物形式支付的，均包括在工资总额内。

职工平均工资 指企业、事业、机关单位的职工在一定时期内平均每人所得的货币工资额。它表明一定时期职工工资收入的高低程度，是反映职工工资水平的主要指标。计算公式为：

职工平均工资＝报告期实际支付的全部职工工资总额/报告期全部职工平均人数

城镇登记失业人员 指有非农业户口，在一定的劳动年龄内，有劳动能力，无业而要求就业，并在当地就业服务机构进行求职登记的人员。

城镇登记失业率 指城镇登记失业人数同城镇从业人数与城镇从业人数与城镇登记失业人数之和的比。计算公式为：

$$\text{城镇登记失业率}=\frac{\text{城镇登记失业人数}}{\text{（城镇单位就业人员-使用的农村劳动力-聘用的离退休人员-聘用的港澳台及外方人员）+不在岗职工+城镇私营业主+城镇个体户主+城镇私营企业及个体就业人员+城镇登记失业人数}}\times 100\%$$

Explanatory Notes on Main Statistical Indicators

The annual statistics on total population is taken at midnight, the 31st of December, not including residents in Taiwan province, Hong Kong SAR and Macao SAR and Chinese national residing abroad.

Permanent population refers to the population of actual habitual residence in a certain area six months or over six months. Permanent popul ation include the accounts in this area which are also living in this area, accounts outside this area but with more than half a year of household registration, accounts to be determined including people without accounts or pockets of accounts, and accounts in the area but leaving this area less than six months.

Urban Population and Rural Population Urban population refers to all people residing in cities and towns, while rural population refers to population other than urban population.

Birth Rate (or Crude Birth Rate) refers to the ratio of the number of births to the average population (or mid-period population) during a certain period of time (usually one year), expressed in ‰. Birth rate in the chapter refers to annual birth rate. The following formula is used:

$$\text{Birth Rate} = \frac{\text{Number of Births}}{\text{Annual Average Population}} \times 1000‰$$

Number of births in the formula refers to live births, i.e. when a baby has breathed or showed any vital phenomena regardless of the length of pregnancy.

Annual average population is the average of the number of population at the beginning of the year and that at the end of the year. Sometimes it is substituted by the mid-year population.

Death Rate (or Crude Death Rate) refers to the ratio of the number of deaths to the average population (or mid-period population) during a certain period of time (usually one year), expressed in ‰. Death rate in the chapter refers to annual death rate. The following formula is used:

$$\text{DeathRate} = \frac{\text{Number of Deaths}}{\text{Annual Average Population}} \times 1000‰$$

Natural Growth Rate of Population refers to the ratio of natural increase in population (number of births minus number of deaths) in a certain period of time (usually one year) to the average population (or mid-period population) of the same period, expressed in ‰. The following formula is applied:

Natural Growth Rate of Population =(Number of Births-Number of Deaths)/Annual Average Population× 1000‰

Employed Persons refer to the ones aged 16 and over who are engaged in gainful employment and thus receive remuneration payment or earn business income. This indicator reflects the actual utilization of total labour force during a certain period of time and is often used for the research on China's economic situation and national power.

Persons Employed in Various Units refer to all the persons working in government agencies of various levels, political and party organizations, social organizations, enterprises and institutions, and receiving wages or other forms of payment. They include fully-employed staff and workers, re-employed retirees, teachers in the schools run by the local people, foreigners and Chinese compatriots from Hong Kong, Macao, and Taiwan working in various units, part-time employees, employees of other units working temporarily at current posts, and employees holding the second job, but do not include persons who have left their working units while keeping their labour contract (employment relation) unchanged. This indicator reflects the total number of laborers actually engaged in production or other operations in various units.

Persons Employed in Private Enterprises and Self- Employed Individuals in Urban Areas Persons employed in private enterprises refer to the persons employed in the private enterprises which have been registered at the departments of industrial and commercial administration for which the business operation are situated at a county town (i.e. a town where the county government is located), or at urban areas with administrative hierarchy higher than a county town. The self-employed individuals in urban areas refer to persons who hold the certificates of residence in urban areas or have resided in the urban areas for a long time and have been registered at the departments of industrial and commercial administration and approved to be engaged in individual industrial or commercial business, including self-employed persons as well as helpers and hired labourers who work in individual households.

State-owned Units refer to economic units whose assets are owned by the state, including non-corporation units registered according to Regulation of the People's Republic of China on the Registration of Enterprises and

Corporations, state organs, institutions and social organizations at the central-level and local levels.

Collective-owned Units refer to economic units registered according to Regulation of the People's Republic of China on the Registration of Enterprises and Corporations where the means of production are collectively owned.

Units of Other Types of Ownership refer to units registered with other types of ownership, including cooperative units, joint ownership units, limited liability corporations, share holding corporations, units funded by entrepreneurs from Hong Kong, Macao, and Taiwan, and foreign- funded units.

Employed Staff and Workers refer to persons who work in, and receive wages from their working units, including persons who have their work posts but are temporarily absent from work for reasons of study or on sick, injury or maternal leave and still receive wages from their working units.

Total Wage Bill refers to the total remuneration payment to employed persons in various units during a certain period of time. The calculation of total wage bill is based on the total remuneration payment to employed persons . Therefore, all the wages and salaries and other payments to employed persons are included in the total wage bill regardless of sources, reckoning the cost of production or not, category, listing as items of premium taxation or not, and forms, paying in cash or in kind.

Average Wage refers to the average wage in money terms per person during a certain period of time for employed persons in enterprises, institutions, and government agencies, which reflects the general level of wage income during a certain period of time and is calculated as follows:

$$\text{AverageWage}=\frac{\text{TotalWage Billof Employed Personsat Reference Time}}{\text{Average Number of Persons Employedat Reference Time}}$$

Registered Unemployed Persons in Urban Areas refer to the persons with non-agricultural household registration at certain working ages (16 years old to retirement age), who are capable of working, unemployed and willing to work, and have been registered at the local employment service agencies to apply for a job.

Registered Unemployment Rate in Urban Areas refers to the ratio of the number of the registered unemployed persons to the sum of the number of persons employed in various units (minus the employed rural labour force, re-employed retirees, and Hong Kong, Macao, Taiwan or foreign employees), laid-off staff and workers in urban units, owners of private enterprises in urban areas, owners of self-employed individuals in urban areas, employees of private enterprises in urban areas, employee of self-employed individuals in urban areas, and the registered unemployed persons in urban areas. The formula is as follows:

$$\text{Registered Unemployment rate in urban areas}=\frac{\text{numberof registered urban unemployed persons}}{\begin{array}{c}\text{number of persons employed in}\\ \text{urbanunits-employed rurallabour force}\\ \text{re-employed retirees - HongKong,}\\ \text{Macao,Taiwan or foreign employees}\\ \text{+ laid-off staff and workers+owners of}\\ \text{urban private Enterprises+ owners of}\\ \text{urbanself-employed Individuals + employees}\\ \text{ofurbanprivate Enterprises+employees of}\\ \text{urbanself- employed Individuals+ registered}\\ \text{unemployed persons in urbanareas}\end{array}}\times 100\%$$

5 固定资产投资

INVESTMENT IN FIXED ASSETS

资料整理：席锋旭　康　敏
Data management：Xi Fengxu　Kang Min
数据审核：黄小丹
Data audit：Huang Xiaodan

第五部分　固定资产投资

一、简要说明

本章资料主要包括全社会固定资产投资、项目投资、房地产开发投资和农户投资以及分区县情况，由西安市统计局固定资产投资处提供。

二、主要指标

全社会固定资产投资（亿元）	5165.98	比上年下降	12.5%
#国有经济单位	1826.62	比上年下降	4.7%
集体经济单位	158.14	比上年下降	22.2%
#固定资产投资	5086.93	比上年下降	12.7%
#房地产开发	1831.67	比上年增长	4.0%
全市新增固定资产（亿元）	2049.71	比上年下降	17.2%
全市竣工住宅面积（万平方米）	826.05	比上年下降	43.5%

5　INVESTMENT IN FIXED ASSETS

Ⅰ.Brief Introduction

This chapter consists of primarily the data on fixed asset investment, Project investment real estate development investment, and farmer Investment provided by Fixed Asset Investment Division of the Xi'an Bureau of Statistics.

Ⅱ.Major Indicators

		Increase over Preceding Year
Investment Fulfilled In Fixed Assets(100 mil. Yuan)	5165.98	-12.5%
State-owned Enterprises	1826.62	-4.7%
Collective-owned Enterprises	158.14	-22.2%
Project Investment	5086.93	-12.7%
Real Estate Development	1831.67	4.0%
Investment Fulfilled Newly Increased FixedAssets(100 mil. yuan)	2049.71	-17.2%
Total Floor Space of Building Completed(10 000 sq.m)	826.05	-43.5%

5-1 主要年份按类别分全社会固定资产投资

Total Investment in Fixed Assets in the Whole Country by Classifications and in Representative Years

单位：亿元 (100 million yuan)

年 份 Year	全社会固定资产投资合计 Total Investment in Fixed Assets in the Whole Country	固定资产投资 Fixed Assets Investment	房地产开发投资 Real Estate Investment	农户投资 Farmer Investment
1979	4.08	3.01		1.07
1980	6.12	4.48		1.64
1981	5.59	4.56		1.03
1982	9.49	8.02		1.47
1983	10.46	9.17		1.29
1984	12.89	10.69		2.20
1985	18.44	14.44		4.00
1986	22.15	18.54		3.61
1987	27.05	23.15		3.90
1988	29.14	24.43		4.71
1989	28.30	23.85		4.45
1990	26.39	23.10	0.91	3.29
1991	30.76	25.55	2.01	5.21
1992	38.48	32.85	3.32	5.63
1993	75.06	66.65	7.39	8.41
1994	85.57	73.47	12.02	12.10
1995	103.42	88.50	21.65	14.92
1996	114.38	96.98	24.66	17.40
1997	116.90	95.17	24.68	21.73
1998	154.80	138.68	38.21	16.12
1999	197.31	172.64	44.30	24.67
2000	232.37	203.01	51.85	29.36
2001	287.72	256.95	67.42	30.77
2002	338.15	307.24	79.37	30.91
2003	478.10	445.74	124.82	32.36
2004	646.69	612.03	169.67	34.66
2005	835.10	776.33	225.23	58.77
2006	1066.62	971.84	285.76	94.78
2007	1435.33	1340.59	387.33	94.74
2008	1906.36	1786.60	540.26	119.76
2009	2500.13	2367.58	696.34	132.55
2010	3250.56	3104.92	842.34	145.64
2011	3346.26	3207.97	996.81	138.29
2012	4243.43	4107.54	1281.90	135.89
2013	5134.56	4982.25	1595.64	152.31
2014	5903.98	5682.42	1761.88	221.56
2015	5165.98	5086.93	1831.67	79.05

注：2015年国家取消了城乡投资分组，表中"农户投资"2014年以前为原先的农村投资。

5-2 主要年份按经济类型分全社会固定资产投资

Total Investment in Fixed Assets in the Whole Country by Registion Stares in Representative Years

单位：亿元 (100 million yuan)

年 份 Year	合计 Total	国有经济 State-owned	集体经济 Collective-owned	个体经济 Self-employed Individual	其他经济 Others
1985	18.44	13.96	1.36	3.12	
1986	22.15	18.05	0.97	3.13	
1987	27.05	22.18	1.50	3.37	
1988	29.14	23.72	1.86	3.56	
1989	28.30	23.22	1.46	3.62	
1990	26.39	22.21	1.44	2.74	
1991	30.76	24.42	2.26	4.08	
1992	38.48	32.04	1.45	4.99	
1993	75.06	59.66	3.03	6.55	5.82
1994	85.57	64.71	4.14	10.09	6.63
1995	103.42	69.08	9.78	11.13	13.43
1996	114.38	80.66	8.73	12.50	12.49
1997	116.90	77.46	10.21	15.11	14.12
1998	154.80	113.07	7.89	10.59	23.25
1999	197.31	136.50	13.62	16.22	30.97
2000	232.37	159.60	14.65	24.40	33.72
2001	287.72	175.58	14.67	38.57	58.90
2002	338.15	200.06	13.70	44.68	79.71
2003	478.10	264.83	22.33	73.43	117.51
2004	646.69	329.14	40.06	48.95	228.54
2005	835.10	373.70	59.23	79.04	323.13
2006	1066.62	401.14	110.68	107.33	447.47
2007	1435.33	476.78	207.08	183.09	568.38
2008	1906.36	694.89	246.89	50.43	914.15
2009	2500.13	932.91	289.91	97.86	1179.45
2010	3250.56	1348.76	326.44	54.73	1520.63
2011	3346.26	1204.80	258.15	74.64	1808.67
2012	4243.43	1661.22	194.71	82.72	2304.78
2013	5134.56	1770.84	219.88	84.43	3059.41
2014	5903.98	1916.31	203.35	83.28	3701.04
2015	5165.98	1826.62	158.14	80.47	3100.75

注：集体经济：包括城镇集体和农村集体。
个体经济：包括私营个体投资及城镇工矿区私人建房和农村私人建房。

5-3 主要年份按产业分全市固定资产投资

Total Investment in Fixed Assets in the Whole City by Three Strata of Industry in Representative Years

单位：亿元　　　(100 million yuan)

年份 Year	全市固定资产投资合计 Total Investment in Fixed Assets in The Whole City	第一产业 Primary Industry	第二产业 Secondary Industry	工业 Industry	第三产业 Tertisry Industry
1979	3.01	0.06	1.24	1.20	1.71
1980	4.48	0.06	2.09	1.99	2.33
1981	4.56	0.11	2.10	1.83	2.35
1982	8.02	0.04	4.07	3.63	3.91
1983	9.17	0.11	4.97	4.41	4.09
1984	10.69	0.19	4.56	3.99	5.94
1985	14.44	0.18	7.22	6.45	7.04
1986	18.54	0.16	8.98	8.37	9.40
1987	23.15	0.19	11.81	11.26	11.15
1988	24.43	0.15	11.95	11.20	12.33
1989	23.85	0.13	11.94	11.50	11.78
1990	23.10	0.25	11.03	10.59	11.82
1991	25.55	0.27	12.48	11.95	12.80
1992	32.85	0.10	15.60	14.73	17.15
1993	66.65	0.07	24.50	22.44	42.08
1994	73.47	0.03	27.04	25.85	46.40
1995	88.50	0.14	28.80	27.71	59.56
1996	96.98	0.13	25.96	24.24	70.89
1997	95.17	0.24	23.65	21.66	71.28
1998	138.68	0.48	35.33	29.86	102.87
1999	172.64	0.94	39.88	36.40	131.82
2000	203.01	0.76	57.21	54.37	145.04
2001	256.95	0.86	63.31	61.28	192.78
2002	307.24	4.29	74.34	68.45	228.61
2003	445.74	3.34	83.25	78.41	359.15
2004	612.03	3.38	97.69	95.67	510.96
2005	776.33	5.26	144.25	140.44	626.82
2006	971.84	10.04	213.43	206.48	748.37
2007	1340.59	10.20	297.53	286.61	1032.86
2008	1786.60	23.75	369.74	356.12	1393.11
2009	2367.58	24.46	458.44	442.70	1884.68
2010	3104.92	39.83	556.10	498.62	2508.99
2011	3207.97	43.10	474.73	390.30	2690.14
2012	4165.99	99.34	671.92	578.17	3394.73
2013	5055.23	73.15	983.09	868.57	3998.99
2014	5824.53	75.15	1261.70	1205.53	4487.68
2015	5086.93	99.78	1158.30	1135.87	3828.85

5-4　主要年份按资金来源及建设性质分全市固定资产投资

单位：万元

指标	Item	1995	2000	2001	2002	2003	2004
一. 投资总额(万元)	**Total Investment (10 000 yuan)**	**884994**	**2030122**	**2569496**	**3072442**	**4457381**	**6120324**
（一）按资金来源分	Grouped by Funds Source						
1. 国家预算内投资	State Budgetary Funds	69185	160982	256403	355960	365263	436496
2. 国内贷款	Domestic Loans	216565	432282	672379	666146	1219234	1565246
3. 债券	Bonds	873	32460	6753	766	3278	
4. 利用外资	Utilization of Foreign Funds	80792	31622	54907	15192	47509	47401
5. 自筹资金	Self-raising Funds	385047	875352	1121502	1392915	1733132	2629720
6. 其他资金	Others	132532	497424	457552	641463	1088965	1441461
（二）按构成分	Grouped by Composition of Funds						
1. 建筑安装工程	Construction and Installation Projects	527220	1404184	1698777	2119151	3067309	4127677
2. 设备、工器具购置	Purchasing of Equipment and Instruments	233730	382495	452602	552251	577240	708988
3. 其它费用	Others	124044	243443	418117	401040	812832	1283659
（三）按建设性质分	Grouped by Type of Construction						
#新建	New Construction	210926	533058	723957	874392	1294032	1874116
扩建	Expansion	180210	542510	581138	868603	1102914	1169537
改建	Reconstruction	157457	263657	344879	343184	447944	670229
二. 房屋施工面积（万平方米）	**Floor Space Under Construction (10 000sq.m)**	**1070.58**	**1702.58**	**1767.13**	**2396.89**	**2716.18**	**3177.36**

Total Investment in Fixed Assets in the Whole City by Sources of Funds and Type of Construction in Representative Years

(10 000 yuan)

2005	2006	2007	2008	2009	2010	2011	2012	2013	2014	2015
7763283	**9718418**	**13405920**	**17865977**	**23675759**	**31049184**	**32079666**	**41659924**	**50552171**	**58245332**	**50869319**
728885	677145	670592	1555809	2562756	1649563	1480412	1851860	1439721	1622413	2250911
1257175	1631689	1619218	2162957	3301919	4288663	3546561	4023452	4146647	5592450	4510474
								11356		
40583	165390	183422	261325	144124	126802	89047	135147	182153	789982	2067810
4001700	5538393	8565573	12771844	15776565	18279153	19400468	28680236	36446760	41430249	33936574
1734940	1705801	2367115	1114042	1890395	6705003	7563178	6969229	8325534	8810238	8103551
5086664	6486233	9165668	12864657	16337466	21690205	25553161	34268466	41672647	44701184	41024301
1021079	1409589	1858720	2024631	2619783	3094336	1911180	3311375	4861642	8847403	4990590
1655540	1822596	2381532	2976689	4718510	6264643	4615325	4080083	4017882	4696745	4854428
2907551	3511432	5123975	6356716	8567540	14292899	16077747	21651399	26063028	29798357	26685245
1208430	1101740	994841	2118013	3054929	2649749	1956527	1685922	1232264	1102377	1017226
782953	1099304	1548130	1921664	2738799	2620997	2155112	2810903	3183300	2605272	1439734
4030.38	**4589.39**	**5759.28**	**6570.94**	**9571.25**	**11166.19**	**12353.11**	**14093.91**	**14749.84**	**16249.30**	**16325.63**

5-5 主要年份全市新增固定资产投资及房屋竣工面积

Value of Newly Added Fixed Assets and Floor Spaces Completed of Municipal Units in Representative Years

年 份 Year	新增固定资产（亿元） Newly Increased Fixed Assets (10 000 mil.yuan)	房屋竣工面积（万平方米） Floor Space of Buildings Completed (10 000sq.m)	住宅 Residential Buildings
1978	4.96	99.10	40.76
1980	4.64	164.87	100.15
1985	8.62	222.42	129.07
1986	13.40	272.95	155.91
1987	16.72	241.48	119.21
1988	16.82	211.83	102.43
1989	16.58	178.45	87.77
1990	20.30	211.88	111.05
1991	17.86	185.34	95.84
1992	22.33	204.75	112.66
1993	41.70	257.90	144.88
1994	55.37	282.91	184.49
1995	62.58	357.67	252.84
1996	60.04	332.18	249.52
1997	62.88	374.46	286.54
1998	80.23	382.80	275.63
1999	118.92	681.04	550.83
2000	150.16	714.83	544.95
2001	167.77	692.56	502.26
2002	198.97	773.28	486.13
2003	279.44	917.96	578.06
2005	261.95	776.59	498.33
2004	409.72	1131.41	598.61
2006	453.01	1199.45	583.10
2007	667.97	1672.16	929.50
2008	725.17	1113.31	693.42
2009	1013.44	1529.13	822.62
2010	1193.05	775.16	521.08
2011	1297.35	1231.91	861.44
2012	1765.05	1626.25	1189.04
2013	1875.00	1118.69	840.02
2014	2476.12	1856.70	1462.86
2015	2049.71	1109.00	826.05

5-6 全市固定资产投资（2015年）

Total Investment in Fixed Assets in the Whole City（2015）

单位：万元 (10 000 yuan)

指 标	Item	合计 Total	房地产开发投资 Real Estate Investment
一、本年完成投资（万元）	**Investment Completed This Year(10 000 yuan)**	**50869319**	**18316688**
#住宅	Residential Buildings	13561968	13121540
（一）按登记注册类型分	**Grouped by Registion Status**		
内资	Domestic Funded Enterprises	46174819	17198835
国有	State-owned Enterprises	17309407	708048
集体	Collective-owned Enterprises	1283869	117375
股份合作	Cooperative Enterprises	294622	150797
联营	Joint Ownership Enterprises	71530	
国有联营	State Joint Ownership Enterprises	68638	
集体联营	Collective Joint Ownership Enterprises	2892	
国有与集体联营	Joint State-collective Ownership Enterprises		
其他联营	Other Joint Ownership Enterprises		
有限责任公司	Limited Liability Corporations	15191674	10202378
国有独资公司	State-funded Corporations	888161	687468
其他有限责任公司	Other Limited Liability Corporations	14303513	9514910
股份有限公司	Stock Limited Corporation	1087591	211017
私营	Private Enterprises	9123009	5783820
私营独资	Private -funded Enterprises	1327174	5435
私营合伙	Private Limited Liability Corporations	268092	
私营有限责任公司	Private Limited Liability Corporations	7352340	5681111
私营股份有限公司	Private Share Holding Corporations	175403	97274
其他	Other	1813117	25400
港澳台商投资	Enterprises Funded by Hong Kong, Macao and Taiwan	715875	597818
与港澳台合资经营	Joint-venture Enterprises	149360	79203
与港澳台合作经营	Cooperative Enterprises	30838	30838
港澳台独资	Wholly Funded from Hong Kong,Macao and Taiwan	520777	487777
港澳台投资股份有限公司	Share-holding Corporations Ltd.	1500	
其他港澳台投资	Investment From Hongkong,Macao,Taiwan	13400	

5-6 续表1 continude 1

单位：万元 (10 000 yuan)

指 标	Item	合计 Total	房地产开发投资 Real Estate Investment
外商投资	Foreign Owned Enterprises	3964465	520035
中外合资经营	Joint-venture Enterprises	918927	163698
中外合作经营	Cooperation Enterprises	39065	38081
外资企业	Foreign Funded Enterprises	2402363	304530
外商投资股份有限公司	Share-holding Corporations Ltd. With Foreign Funds	529110	13726
其他外商投资	Foreign Investment	75000	
（二）按隶属关系分	**Grouped by Jurisdiction of Management**		
中央	Central	3018509	536003
省属	Provincial	2784364	542207
市属	Municipal	45066446	17238478
（三）按建设性质分	**Grouped by Type of Construction**		
#新建	New Construction	26685245	
扩建	Expansion	1017226	
改建和技术改造	Reconstruction	1439734	
（四）按构成分	**Grouped by Composition**		
1. 建筑工程	Construction Projects	36626783	13330886
2. 安装工程	Installment Projects	4397518	2063478
3. 设备、工器具购置	Purchasing of Equipment and Instruments	4990590	177240
4. 其他费用	Others	4854428	2745084

5-6 续表2 continude 2

单位：万元 (10 000 yuan)

指 标	Item	合计 Total	房地产开发投资 Real Estate Investment
二、构成(%)	**Proportion (%)**		
（一）按登记注册类型分组	**Grouped by Status**		
#国有经济	State-owned	35.9	7.6
集体经济	Collective-owned	3.1	1.5
（二）按隶属关系分组	**Grouped by Jurisdiction of Management**		
中央	Central	5.9	2.9
省属	Provincial	5.5	3
市属	Municipal	88.6	94.1
（三）按建设性质分	**Grouped by Type of Construction**		
#新建	New Construction	52.5	
扩建	Expansion	2.0	
改建和技术改造	Reconstruotion	2.8	
（四）按构成分	**Grouped by Composition of Funds**		
1. 建筑工程	Construction Projects	72	72.8
2. 安装工程	Installation Projects	8.6	11.3
3. 设备、工器具购置	Purchasing of the Equipment and Instruments	9.8	1
4. 其他	Others	9.5	15
三、本年新增固定资产（万元）	**Newly Increase in Fixed Assets(10 000 yuan)**	**20497124**	**3359124**
四、房屋面积（万平方米）	**Floor Space (10 000 sq.m)**		
本年施工房屋面积	Floor Space of Buildings Under Construction This Year	16325.63	13392.94
#住宅	Residential Buildings	10399.83	9777.23
本年竣工房屋面积	Floor Space of Buildings Completed This Year	1109.00	976.64
#住宅	Residential Buildings	826.05	766.58
五、竣工房屋价值（万元）	**Value of the Building Completed (10 000 yuan)**	**3018629**	**3018629**
#住宅	Residential Buildings	2366641	2366641

5-7 按国民经济行业分全市固定资产投资（2015年）

Investment in Fixed Assets in the Whole City by Industry（2015）

单位：万元 (10 000 yuan)

行 业	Sector	固定资产投资 Grouped by Sector	工业改建和技术改造 Industrial Reconstruction and Technical Transformation
本年完成固定资产投资（万元）	**Grouped by Sector (10 000 yuan)**	**50869319**	**407220**
（一）农、林、牧、渔业	Agriculture,Forestry,Animal Husbandry and Fishery	1172948	
（二）采矿业	Mining	6527	
（三）制造业	Manufacturing	10125957	263217
农副食品加工业	Processing of Food from Agricultural Products	40990	4428
食品制造业	Manufacture of Foods	190787	5070
酒、饮料和精制茶制造业	Wine, soft drinks and refined tea industry	106403	2320
烟草制品业	Tobacco Processing	16188	
纺织业	Textile Industry	40803	
纺织服装、服饰业	Textile, apparel industry	55093	
皮革、毛皮、羽毛及其制品和制鞋业	Leather, Fur, Feather (eiderdown) and Their Products Industry	1451	
木材加工和木、竹、藤、棕、草制品业	Timber Processing,Bamboo,Cane, Palm Fiber and Straw Products	11655	
家具制造业	Furniture Manufacturing	88620	
造纸及纸制品业	Papermaking and Paper products	15601	
印刷和记录媒介复制业	Printing,Record Medium Reproduction	62050	1791
文教、工美、体育和娱乐用品制造业	Culture, education, Craft art, sports and entertainment goods manufacturing industry	15100	
石油加工、炼焦和核燃料加工业	Petroleum Refining, Ccoke Making and Nuclear Fuel Processing Industry	3267	
化学原料和化学制品制造业	Raw Chemical Materials and Chemical Products	100845	500
医药制造业	Medical and Pharmaceutical Products	240728	2258
化学纤维制造业	Chemical Fiber	11368	
橡胶和塑料制品业	Rubber and plastic products industry	82099	
非金属矿物制品业	Nonmetal Mineral Products	151483	3500
黑色金属冶炼和压延加工业	Smelting and Pressing of Ferrous Metals	77818	
有色金属冶炼和压延加工业	Smelting and Pressing of Nonferrou Metals	249071	5284
金属制品业	Metal Products	259215	4600

5-7 续表 continude

单位：万元 (10 000 yuan)

行 业	Sector	固定资产投资 Grouped by Sector	工业改建和技术改造 Industrial Reconstruction and Technical Transformation
通用设备制造业	General Equipment Manufacturing Industry	783147	26994
专用设备制造业	Special Purpose Equipment	688829	4078
汽车制造业	Automotive Manufacturing	1277695	11866
铁路、船舶、航空航天和其他运输设备制造业	Railroad, Marine, Aerospace and other Transportation Equipment Manufacturing	2386172	2873
电气机械和器材制造业	Electric Equipment and Machinery	594298	38716
计算机、通信和其他电子设备制造业	Communication Equipment, Computer and Other Electronic Equipment Manufacturing Industry	2389891	145189
仪器仪表制造业	Instrument Manufacturing Industry	148838	3750
其他制造业	Other Manufacturing	22952	
废弃资源综合利用	Comprehensive Utilization of waste Resources	8200	
金属制品、机械和设备修理业	Metal Products, Machinery and Equipment Repair Industry	5300	
（四）电力、燃气及水的生产供应业	Production & Supply of Electricity,Gas & Water	1233019	144003
（五）建筑业	Construction	224358	
（六）批发和零售业	Wholesale and Retail Trades	1447691	
（七）交通运输、仓储和邮政业	Transport, Storage and Post	3628355	
（八）住宿和餐饮业	Hotels and Catering Services	375333	
（九）信息传输、软件和信息技术服务业	Information Transmission,Computer Service and Software	1082127	
（十）金融业	Financial Intermediation	69705	
（十一）房地产业	Real Estate	23516991	
（十二） 租赁和商务服务业	Leasing and Business Services	450814	
（十三）科学研究和技术服务业	Scientific Research,Technical Service and Geologic Prospecting	336163	
（十四）水利、环境和公共设施管理业	Management of Water Conservancy, Environment and Public Facilities	4848076	
（十五）居民服务、修理和其他服务业	Services to Households, repairs and other services	123465	
（十六）教育	Education	887191	
（十七）卫生和社会工作	Health and social work	744274	
（十八）文化、体育和娱乐业	Culture, Sports and Entertainment	364678	
（十九）公共管理、社会保障和社会组织	Public administration, social security and social organizations	231647	
（二十）国际组织	International Organizations		

5-8 按国民经济行业分民间投资（2015年）

Private Investment of Municipal Units by Industry（2015）

行 业	Sector	投资额（万元）Investment (10000 yuan)	占民间投资比重（%）Rate(%)
民间投资总计	**Total**	**25848762**	**100**
（一）农、林、牧、渔业	Agriculture, Forestry, Animal Husbandry and Fishery	929687	3.6
（二）采矿业	Mining	6527	
（三）制造业	Manufacturing	4315284	16.7
（四）电力、燃气及水的生产供应业	Generation and Supply of Electricity, Production and Supply of Gas and Water	143099	0.6
（五）建筑业	Construction	119746	0.5
（六）批发和零售业	Wholesale and Retail Trades	1267382	4.9
（七）交通运输、仓储和邮政业	Transportation, Storage and Post	561058	2.2
（八）住宿和餐饮业	Hotels and Catering Services	209498	0.8
（九）信息传输、软件和信息技术服务业	Information Transmission, Computer Service and Software	612115	2.4
（十）金融业	Financial Intermediation	22056	0.1
（十一）房地产业	Real Estate	15457027	59.8
（十二） 租赁和商务服务业	Leasing and Business Services	300313	1.2
（十三）科学研究和技术服务业	Scientific Research and Technical Service	124754	0.5
（十四）水利、环境和公共设施管理业	Management of Water Conservancy, Environment and Public Facilities	1062282	4.1
（十五）居民服务、修理和其他服务业	Services to Households, repairs and other services	78593	0.3
（十六）教育	Education	91324	0.4
（十七）卫生和社会工作	Health and social work	446532	1.7
（十八）文化、体育和娱乐业	Culture, Sports and Entertainment	72077	0.3
（十九）公共管理、社会保障和社会组织	Public administration, social security and social organizations	29408	0.1
（二十）国际组织	International Organizations		

5-9 按国民经济行业分基础设施投资（2015年）

Investment for Basic Infrastructure of Municipal Units by Industry （2015）

指 标	Item	投资额（万元）Investment (10000 yuan)	占基础设施投资比重（%）Rate(%)
基础设施投资总计	**Total Investment of Infrastructure**	**10104576**	**100**
一、交通运输、仓储和邮政业	**Traffic, Transport, Storage and Post**	**3628355**	**35.9**
铁路运输业	Railway transport industry	674451	6.7
道路运输业	The road transport industry	2207632	21.8
水上运输业	Water transportation		
航空运输业	The air transport industry	24972	0.2
管道运输业	Pipeline transportation		
装卸搬运和运输代理服务业	Handling and transport industry	111230	1.1
仓储业	Warehousing industry	610070	6.0
邮政业	The postal service		
二、信息传输、软件和信息技术服务业	**Information Transmission,Software and Information Technology Services**	**1082127**	**10.7**
三、电网建设	**Grid Construction**	**546018**	**5.4**
四、水利、环境和公共设施管理业	**Management of Water Conservancy, Environment and Public Facilities**	**4848076**	**48.0**
水利管理业	Water resources management industry	471023	4.7
生态保护和环境治理业	Ecological protection and environmental control industries	90854	0.9
公共设施管理业	Public facilities management industry	4286199	42.4

5-10 全市固定资产投资资金来源（2015年）

Source of Funds for Total Fixed Assets Investment of Whole City （2015）

单位：万元 （10 000 yuan)

指 标	Item	固定资产投资 Fixed Assets Investment	房地产开发投资 Real Estate Investment
一、本年资金来源合计	**Total of Sources of Funds This Year**	**63030269**	**27659506**
1. 上年末结余资金	Balance of Last Year	9508628	6597283
2. 本年资金来源小计	Subtotal Funds This Year	53521641	21062223
(1) 国家预算资金	State Budgetary Funds	2368273	
(2) 国内贷款	Domestic Loans	4745650	2884192
(3) 债券	Bonds		
(4) 利用外资	Utilization of Foreign Funds	2175625	63200
(5) 自筹资金	Self-raising Funds	35706024	10289457
(6) 其他资金来源	Others	8526069	7825374
二、本年各项应付款合计	**Total Sums of Money to be Paid This Year**	**5888945**	**5414298**

5-11 全市按行业分施工项目（2015年）

Construction Project Grouped by Industry in the Whole City（2015）

行 业	Sector	本年新增固定资产（万元）Increased Fixed Assets This Year (10 000 yuan)	施工项目个数（个）Number of Constructing Projects (unit)
总计	**Total**	**20497124**	**2037**
（一）农、林、牧、渔业	Agriculture, Forestry, Animal Husbandry and Fishery	792097	222
（二）采矿业	Mining	5000	2
（三）制造业	Manufacturing	5714956	404
（四）电力、燃气及水的生产供应业	Generation and Supply of Electricity,Production and Supply of Gas and Water	811182	92
（五）建筑业	Construction	93081	12
（六）批发和零售业	Wholesale and Retail Trades	1142071	107
（七）交通运输、仓储和邮政业	Transportation, Storage and Post	1573009	116
（八）住宿和餐饮业	Hotels and Catering Services	184860	42
（九）信息传输、软件和信息技术服务业	Information Transmission, Computer Service and Software	123902	38
（十）金融业	Financial Intermediation	24541	8
（十一）房地产业	Real Estate	5825067	239
（十二） 租赁和商务服务业	Leasing and Business Services	148838	30
（十三）科学研究和技术服务业	Scientific Research and Technical Service	101429	27
（十四）水利、环境和公共设施管理业	Management of Water Conservancy, Environment and Public Facilities	2897838	458
（十五）居民服务、修理和其他服务业	Services to Households, repairs and other services	76353	16
（十六）教育	Education	412901	103
（十七）卫生和社会工作	Health and social work	237802	46
（十八）文化、体育和娱乐业	Culture, Sports and Entertainment	224095	47
（十九）公共管理、社会保障和社会组织	Public administration, social security and social organizations	108102	28
（二十）国际组织	International Organizations		

5-11 续表 continude

行 业	Sector	本年新开工 Newly Started This Year	本年投产项目个数（个） Projects put into Use (unit)
总计	**Total**	**1332**	**1243**
（一）农、林、牧、渔业	Agriculture, Forestry, Animal Husbandry and Fishery	193	187
（二）采矿业	Mining	2	1
（三）制造业	Manufacturing	208	203
（四）电力、燃气及水的生产供应业	Generation and Supply of Electricity,Production and Supply of Gas and Water	63	57
（五）建筑业	Construction	11	10
（六）批发和零售业	Wholesale and Retail Trades	72	79
（七）交通运输、仓储和邮政业	Transportation, Storage and Post	71	69
（八）住宿和餐饮业	Hotels and Catering Services	32	31
（九）信息传输、软件和信息技术服务业	Information Transmission, Computer Service and Software	22	14
（十）金融业	Financial Intermediation	1	6
（十一）房地产业	Real Estate	103	120
（十二） 租赁和商务服务业	Leasing and Business Services	17	20
（十三）科学研究和技术服务业	Scientific Research and Technical Service	12	9
（十四）水利、环境和公共设施管理业	Management of Water Conservancy, Environment and Public Facilities	353	280
（十五）居民服务、修理和其他服务业	Services to Households, repairs and other services	13	8
（十六）教育	Education	69	58
（十七）卫生和社会工作	Health and social work	36	33
（十八）文化、体育和娱乐业	Culture, Sports and Entertainment	34	36
（十九）公共管理、社会保障和社会组织	Public administration, social security and social organizations	20	22
（二十）国际组织	International Organizations		

5-12 全市固定资产投资效果（2015年）

Achievements of Total Assets Investment of Whole City （2015）

指 标	Item	固定资产投资 Fixed Assets Investment	房地产开发投资 Real Estate Investment
一、建设项目投产率（%）	**Rate of Projects Put Into use(%)**	**61.0**	
施工项目个数（个）	Number of Constructing Projects (unit)	2037	
本年投产项目个数（个）	Number of Projects Put into Use (unit)	1243	
二、固定资产交付使用率（%）	**Rate of Fixed Assets Put into Use(%)**	**40.3**	**18.3**
本年新增固定资产（亿元）	Newly Increased Fixed Assets This Year(100 million yuan)	2049.71	335.91
本年完成投资（亿元）	Investment Completed This Year (100 million yuan)	5086.93	1831.67
三、建设周期（年）	**Construction Period (year)**	**3.9**	**6.0**
计划总投资（亿元）	Total Planned Investment(100 million yuan)	19795.3	10959.01
本年完成投资（亿元）	Investment Completed This Year (100 million yuan)	5086.93	1831.67
四、房屋建筑面积竣工率（%）	**Completion Rate of Buildings (%)**	**6.8**	**7.3**
本年施工房屋面积（万平方米）	Floor Space of the Constructing Buildings This Year (10 000 sq.m)	16325.6	13392.9
本年竣工房屋面积（万平方米）	Floor Space of the Buildings Completed This Year (10 000 sq.m)	1109.0	976.6

5-13 固定资产投资新增生产能力或效益（2015年）

Newly Increased Production Capacity or Project Efficiency through Investment（2015）

能源名称	Name	累计新增生产能力或效益 Cumulative Newly Increased Production Capacity or Project Efficiency
粗钢（万吨/年）	Crude Steel (10 000 tons/year)	937.2
太阳能发电（万千瓦）	Solar Energy (10 000 kw)	1000
其他发电（万千瓦）	Others (10 000 kw)	
输电线路长度（11万伏及以上）（公里）	Length of Transmission Lines (above 110 000 VA) (km)	512.1
水泥（万吨/年）	Cement (10 000 tons/year)	219
平板玻璃（万重量箱/年）	Plate Glass (10 000 Weight-boxs/year)	
氮肥（吨/年）	Nitrogen Fertilizers (ton/year)	5000
磷肥（吨/年）	Phosphate Fertilizer (ton/year)	
钾肥（吨/年）	Potash Fertilizer (ton/year)	
化学农药原药（吨/年）	Chemical Pesticide (ton/year)	
塑料树脂及共聚物（吨/年）	Plastic Resin and Copolymer (ton/year)	6995
合成橡胶（吨/年）	Synthetic Rubber (ton/year)	
轿车制造（辆/年）	Car Manufacturing (car/year)	
化学纤维（吨/年）	Chemical Fiber (ton/year)	
棉纺锭（锭）	Cotton Spirit（Spindle）	
毛纺锭（锭）	Wool Spinning（Spindle）	
啤酒（万吨/年）	Beer (10 000 tons/year)	
白酒（万吨/年）	White Spirit (10 000 tons/year)	
其他酒（万吨/年）	Other Alcohols (10 000 tons/year)	
新建铁路里程（公里）	Newly Railway (km)	
复线里程（公里）	Double-Tracking Length (km)	
高速铁路里程（公里）	Length of High-speed Railway (km)	
新建公路（公里）	Newly Highways (km)	78.23
#高速公路（公里）	Expressway (km)	2.5
一级公路（公里）	First Class (km)	2.75
二级公路（公里）	Second Class (km)	72.98
改建公路（公里）	Reconstructed Highways (km)	70.8
新建独立公路桥梁（延长米）	New-built Separate Highway Bridge (extended meters)	2204
新建独立公路隧道（延长米）	New-built Separate Highway Tunnel (extended meters)	
新（扩）建客、货运站（个）	New (expanded) Passenger and Freight Stations（unit）	4
新（扩）建客、货运站（平方米）	New (expanded) Passenger and Freight Stations（sq.m）	14929
城市自来水供水能力（万吨/日）	Tap Water Supply Capacity in City(10 000 tons/day)	
城市污水处理能力（万吨/日）	Waste Water Treated Capacity in City(10 000 tons/day)	2.96

5-14 全市按国民经济行业分房屋建筑面积（2015年）

单位：平方米

行 业	Sector	本年施工房屋面积 Floor Space of Buildings Under Construction This Year	住宅 Residential Residence
总 计	**Total**	**163256262**	**103998301**
（一）农、林、牧、渔业	Agriculture, Forestry, Animal Husbandry and Fishery	20300	2500
（二）采矿业	Mining	23160	
（三）制造业	Manufacturing	8615828	320
（四）电力、燃气及水的生产供应业	Generation and Supply of Electricity, Production and Supply of Gas and Water	127302	600
（五）建筑业	Construction	168700	
（六）批发和零售业	Wholesale and Retail Trades	1359363	
（七）交通运输、仓储和邮政业	Transportation, Storage and Post	935757	
（八）住宿和餐饮业	Hotels and Catering Services	49680	
（九）信息传输、软件和信息技术服务业	Information Transmission, Computer Service and Software	217101	
（十）金融业	Financial Intermediation	193006	
（十一）房地产业	Real Estate	146152055	102852584
（十二） 租赁和商务服务业	Leasing and Business Services	229530	
（十三）科学研究和技术服务业	Scientific Research and Technical Service	220075	
（十四）水利、环境和公共设施管理业	Management of Water Conservancy, Environment and Public Facilities	449123	49280
（十五）居民服务、修理和其他服务业	Services to Households, repairs and other services	145800	
（十六）教育	Education	2742837	1088217
（十七）卫生和社会工作	Health and social work	1388647	4800
（十八）文化、体育和娱乐业	Culture, Sports and Entertainment	134146	
（十九）公共管理、社会保障和社会组织	Public administration, social security and social organizations	83852	
（二十）国际组织	International Organizations		

Floors Space of Buildings Construction of Municipal Units by Industry（2015）

(sq.m)

本年竣工房屋面积 Floor Space of Buildings Completed This Year	住宅 Residential Residence	本年竣工房屋价值（万元） Value of Buildings Completed (10 000 yuan)	住宅 Residential Residence
11090009	**8260509**	**3018629**	**2366641**
18700	2500		
386713			
130000			
26047			
10100800	7947929	3018629	2366641
84942	47280		
327546	258000		
4800	4800		
10461			

5-15 主要年份市属固定资产投资

Investment In Fixed Assets of Municipal Units in Representative Years

单位：万元 (10 000 yuan)

指标	Item	1995	2000	2001	2002	2003	2004	2005	2006	2007
一、投资总额	**Total Investment**	**432451**	**1263023**	**1539717**	**1848833**	**2978747**	**4355271**	**5788693**	**7835681**	**10555849**
#房地产开发投资	Real Estate Investment	171291	473787	566557	702233	1114809	1492693	2062940	2641871	3515719
按经济类型分	Grouped by Type of Enterprises									
国有经济	State-owned Enterprises	258545	890546	894700	1006245	1586057	1884624	2198836	2591184	2972840
集体经济	Collective-owned Enterprises	5720	52893	62895	63877	142849	257226	258327	363909	1366567
其他经济	Others	168186	319584	582122	778711	1249841	2213421	3331530	4880588	6216442
二、新增固定资产	**Newly Increased Fixed Assets**	**273324**	**953173**	**1159980**	**1295389**	**1812099**	**1962795**	**3011104**	**3495179**	**5279938**
三、房屋竣工面积	**Floor Space of the Building**	**202.52**	**509.48**	**535.98**	**537.44**	**631.89**	**606.23**	**767.70**	**914.80**	**1343.88**
（万平方米）	**Completed(10 000sq.m)**									
#住宅	Residential Buildings	143.30	373.51	396.01	331.45	387.82	388.79	436.43	432.43	734.05

5-15 续表1 continude 1

单位：万元 (10 000 yuan)

指标	Item	2008	2009	2010	2011	2012	2013	2014	2015
一、投资总额	**Total Investment**	**14648360**	**19063075**	**25474854**	**26820029**	**35875223**	**44187825**	**50533650**	**45066446**
#房地产开发投资	Real Estate Investment	4938202	6575526	8020893	9001953	11655613	14410956	16107323	17238478
按经济类型分	Grouped by Type of Enterprises								
国有经济	State-owned Enterprises	4480627	6527566	9306901	8750285	12264895	12847731	12835067	13496036
集体经济	Collective-owned Enterprises	1646111	1614290	2253851	1897980	1932578	2148977	1927394	1493122
其他经济	Others	8521622	10921219	13914102	16171764	21677750	29191117	35771189	30077288
二、新增固定资产	**Newly Increased Fixed Assets**	**6488364**	**8380033**	**10423906**	**10663882**	**15376910**	**16019776**	**21603094**	**17837619**
三、房屋竣工面积	**Floor Space of the Building**	**987.05**	**1359.46**	**668.49**	**1002.82**	**1450.29**	**975.03**	**1591.28**	**902.22**
（万平方米）	**Completed(10 000sq.m)**								
#住宅	Residential Buildings	602.69	727.41	448.46	531.38	1069.61	760.87	1262.20	640.60

5-16 市属固定资产投资（2015年）

Investment in Fixed Assets of Municipal Units （2015）

单位：万元　　　　　　　　　　　　　　　　　　　　　　　　　　　　(10 000 yuan)

指　标	Item	固定资产投资 Fixed Assets Investment	房地产开发投资 Real Estate Investment
一、本年完成投资	**Investment Completed This Year**	**45066446**	**17238478**
#住宅	Residential Buildings	12536341	12281562
（一）按登记注册类型分	**Grouped by Registion Status**		
内资	Domestic Funded Enterprises	40421663	16120625
国有	State-owned Enterprises	12737629	650255
集体	Collective-owned Enterprises	1283869	117375
股份合作	Cooperative Enterprises	206361	67146
联营	Joint Ownership Enterprises	71530	
国有联营	State Joint Ownership Enterprises	68638	
集体联营	Collective Joint Ownership Enterprises	2892	
国有与集体联营	Joint State-collective Ownership Enterprises		
其他联营	Other Joint Ownership Enterprises		
有限责任公司	Limited Liability Corporations	14138234	9267239
国有独资公司	State-funded Corporations	689769	502137
其他有限责任公司	Other Limited Liability Corporations	13448465	8765102
股份有限公司	Stock Limited Corporation	1076950	209390
私营	Private Enterprises	9123009	5783820
私营独资	Private -funded Enterprises	1327174	5435
私营合伙	Private Limited Liability Corporations	268092	
私营有限责任公司	Private Limited Liability Corporations	7352340	5681111
私营股份有限公司	Private Share Holding Corporations	175403	97274
其他	Other	1784081	25400
港澳台商投资	Enterprises Funded by Hong Kong, Macao and Taiwan	695525	597818
与港澳台合资经营	Joint-venture Enterprises	129010	79203
与港澳台合作经营	Cooperative Enterprises	30838	30838
港澳台独资	Wholly Funded from Hong Kong,Macao and Taiwan	520777	487777
港澳台投资股份有限公司	Share-holding Corporations Ltd.	1500	
其他港澳台投资	Investment From Hongkong,Macao,Taiwan	13400	
外商投资	Foreign Owned Enterprises	3935098	520035
中外合资经营	Joint-venture Enterprises	890544	163698
中外合作经营	Cooperation Enterprises	38081	38081
外资企业	Foreign Funded Enterprises	2402363	304530

5-16 续表 continude

单位：万元 (10 000 yuan)

指 标	Item	固定资产投资 Fixed Assets Investment	房地产开发投资 Real Estate Investment
外商投资股份有限公司	Share-holding Corporations Ltd. With Foreign Funds	529110	13726
其他外商投资	Foreign Investment	75000	
（二）按建设性质分	**Grouped by Type of Construction**		
#新建	New Construction	23204993	
扩建	Expansion	887152	
改建和技术改造	Reconstruction	1170800	
（三）按构成分	**Grouped by Composition**		
建筑工程	Construction Projects	32961626	12571424
安装工程	Installment Projects	3639811	1937124
设备、工器具购置	Purchasing of Equipment and Instruments	3912578	168825
其他费用	Others	4552431	2561105
二、本年完成投资额构成(%)	**the Constitution of Compeleted Investment this year (%)**		
（一）按登记注册类型分组	**Grouped by Status**		
# 国有经济	State-owned	29.9	6.7
集体经济	Collective-owned	3.3	1.1
（二）按建设性质分	**Grouped by Type of Construction**		
# 新建	New Construction	51.5	
扩建	Expansion	2	
改建和技术改造	Reconstruction	2.6	
（三）按构成分	**Grouped by Composition of Funds**		
建筑工程	Construction Projects	73.1	72.9
安装工程	Installation Projects	8.1	11.2
设备、工器具购置	Purchasing of the Equipment and Instruments	8.7	1
其他	Others	10.1	14.9
三、本年新增固定资产	**Newly Increase in Fixed Assets**	**17837619**	**3097241**
四、房屋面积（万平方米）	**Floor Space (10 000 sq.m)**		
本年施工房屋面积	Floor Space of Buildings Under Construction This Year	14883.81	12374.31
#住宅	Residential Buildings	9454.07	9007.77
本年竣工房屋面积	Floor Space of Buildings Completed This Year	902.22	806.55
#住宅	Residential Buildings	640.6	615.69
五、竣工房屋价值	**Value of the Building Completed**	**2758217**	**2758217**
#住宅	Residential Buildings	2134627	2134627

5-17 按国民经济行业分市属固定资产投资（2015年）

Investment in Fixed Assets of Municipal Units by Industry（2015）

单位：万元 (10 000 yuan)

行 业	Sector	2015
本年完成固定资产投资	**Grouped by Sector**	**45066446**
（一）农、林、牧、渔业	Agriculture,Forestry,Animal Husbandry and Fishery	1154379
（二）采矿业	Mining	6527
（三）制造业	Manufacturing	8439399
农副食品加工业	Processing of Food from Agricultural Products	40990
食品制造业	Manufacture of Foods	141887
酒、饮料和精制茶制造业	Wine, soft drinks and refined tea industry	106403
烟草制品业	Tobacco Processing	16188
纺织业	Textile Industry	40803
纺织服装、服饰业	Textile, apparel industry	55093
皮革、毛皮、羽毛及其制品和制鞋业	Leather, Fur, Feather (eiderdown) and Their Products Industry	
木材加工和木、竹、藤、棕、草制品业	Timber Processing,Bamboo,Cane,Palm Fiber and Straw Products	11655
家具制造业	Furniture Manufacturing	88620
造纸及纸制品业	Papermaking and Paper products	15601
印刷和记录媒介复制业	Printing,Record Medium Reproduction	37951
文教、工美、体育和娱乐用品制造业	Culture, education, Craft art, sports and entertainment goods manufacturing industry	15100
石油加工、炼焦和核燃料加工业	Petroleum Refining, Ccoke Making and Nuclear Fuel Processing Industry	3267
化学原料和化学制品制造业	Raw Chemical Materials and Chemical Products	100845
医药制造业	Medical and Pharmaceutical Products	212345
化学纤维制造业	Chemical Fiber	11368
橡胶和塑料制品业	Rubber and plastic products industry	82099
非金属矿物制品业	Nonmetal Mineral Products	115483
黑色金属冶炼和压延加工业	Smelting and Pressing of Ferrous Metals	77818
有色金属冶炼和压延加工业	Smelting and Pressing of Nonferrou Metals	249071
金属制品业	Metal Products	245974

5-17 续表 continude

单位：万元 (10 000 yuan)

行 业	Sector	2015
通用设备制造业	General Equipment Manufacturing Industry	633265
专用设备制造业	Special Purpose Equipment	682629
汽车制造业	Automotive Manufacturing	1217245
铁路、船舶、航空航天和其他运输设备制造业	Railroad, Marine, Aerospace and other Transportation Equipment Manufacturing	1266303
电气机械和器材制造业	Electric Equipment and Machinery	560081
计算机、通信和其他电子设备制造业	Communication Equipment, Computer and Other Electronic Equipment Manufacturing Industry	2310808
仪器仪表制造业	Instrument Manufacturing Industry	72255
其他制造业	Other Manufacturing	22952
废弃资源综合利用	Comprehensive Utilization of waste Resources	
金属制品、机械和设备修理业	Metal Products, Machinery and Equipment Repair Industry	5300
（四）电力、燃气及水的生产供应业	Production & Supply of Electricity,Gas & Water	755521
（五）建筑业	Construction	177790
（六）批发和零售业	Wholesale and Retail Trades	1441817
（七）交通运输、仓储和邮政业	Transport, Storage and Post	2664187
（八）住宿和餐饮业	Hotels and Catering Services	353751
（九）信息传输、软件和信息技术服务业	Information Transmission,Computer Service and Software	941548
（十）金融业	Financial Intermediation	54573
（十一）房地产业	Real Estate	21976365
（十二） 租赁和商务服务业	Leasing and Business Services	409295
（十三）科学研究和技术服务业	Scientific Research,Technical Service and Geologic Prospecting	234510
（十四）水利、环境和公共设施管理业	Management of Water Conservancy, Environment and Public Facilities	4606623
（十五）居民服务、修理和其他服务业	Services to Households, repairs and other services	123465
（十六）教育	Education	561411
（十七）卫生和社会工作	Health and social work	659282
（十八）文化、体育和娱乐业	Culture, Sports and Entertainment	309874
（十九）公共管理、社会保障和社会组织	Public administration, social security and social organizations	196129
（二十）国际组织	International Organizations	

5-18 按资金来源及建设性质分市属固定资产投资（2015年）

Investment in Fixed Assets of Municipal Units by Sources of Funds and Type of Construction（2015）

单位：万元 (10 000 yuan)

指 标	Item	2015
投资总额	**Total Investment**	**45066446**
一、按资金来源分	**Grouped by Funds Sources**	
1. 国家预算内资金	State Budgetary Funds	1497937
2. 国内贷款	Domestic Loans	4775378
3. 债券	Bonds	
4. 利用外资	Utilization of Foreign Funds	1675116
5. 自筹资金	Self-raising Funds	28376561
6. 其他资金	Others	8741454
二、按建设性质分	**Grouped by Type of Construction**	
#新建	New Construction	23204993
扩建	Expansion	887152
改建	Reconstruction	1170800
三、按构成分	**Grouped by Composition of Funds**	
1. 建筑工程	Construction Project	32961626
2. 安装工程	Installation Projects	3639811
3. 设备、工器具购置	Purchasing of Equipment and Instruments	3912578
4. 其他费用	Others	4552431
四、房屋施工面积（万平方米）	**Floor Space of Buildings Under Construction (10 000 sq.m)**	**14884**

5-19 分区县、开发区全社会固定资产投资额（2015年）

Investment Fulfilled in Fixed Assets by Region and Development Zone （2015）

单位：亿元 （100 million yuan）

区县、开发区	Region	全社会固定资产投资 Fixed Assets Investment	固定资产投资 Urban Area	房地产开发投资 Real Estate Investment	农户投资 Farmer Investment
区县	**Region**	**5165.98**	**5086.93**	**1831.67**	**79.05**
新城区	Xincheng	289.25	289.25	60.90	
碑林区	Beilin	199.98	199.98	115.73	
莲湖区	Lianhu	283.10	283.10	191.48	
灞桥区	Baqiao	505.92	500.12	256.50	5.80
未央区	Weiyang	927.05	924.62	520.01	2.43
雁塔区	Yanta	812.15	810.00	462.01	2.15
阎良区	Yanliang	287.21	283.80	14.61	3.41
临潼区	Lintong	186.31	174.56	23.14	11.75
长安区	Chang'an	726.53	709.46	124.52	17.07
高陵区	Gaoling	432.08	429.12	31.71	2.96
蓝田县	Lantian	196.68	185.18	6.22	11.50
周至县	Zhouzhi	168.95	156.72	10.28	12.23
户　县	Huxian	150.77	141.01	14.57	9.76
开发区	**Development Zones**	**2780.27**	**2780.27**	**1058.34**	
高新区	GaoXin	734.14	734.14	139.04	
经开区	JingKai	625.61	625.61	251.65	
曲江新区	Qujiang	360.21	360.21	223.63	
浐灞生态区	Chanba Eco-District	423.58	423.58	278.48	
航空基地	Aviation Industry Base	103.85	103.85	6.28	
航天基地	Aerospace Base	115.41	115.41	51.76	
国际港务区	International Trade&Logistic Park	157.51	157.51	29.65	
沣东新城	FengDongXinCheng	259.96	259.96	77.85	

5-20 分区县工业投资（2015年）

Industrial Investment by Region（2015）

单位：万元 (10 000 yuan)

区县	Region	投资额 Investment	改建和技术改造 Reconstruction and Technical Transformation
全　市	**Total**	**11358676**	**407220**
新城区	Xincheng	348171	
碑林区	Beilin	396573	
莲湖区	Lianhu	158605	6101
灞桥区	Baqiao	208019	4330
未央区	Weiyang	950025	62249
雁塔区	Yanta	559378	131422
阎良区	Yanliang	2197922	
临潼区	Lintong	347962	10470
长安区	Chang'an	3004859	183107
高陵区	Gaoling	1951366	1653
蓝田县	Lantian	375204	4600
周至县	Zhouzhi	246633	
户　县	Huxian	613959	3288

5-21 分区县、开发区新增固定资产及房屋施工、竣工面积（2015年）

区县、开发区	Region	本年新增固定资产（亿元） Increased Fixed Assets (100 million yuan)	房屋施工面积（万平方米） Floor Space of Buildings Under Construction (10 000sq.m)	住宅 Residenctial Buildings
区县	**Region**	**2014.03**	**16325.63**	**10399.83**
新城区	Xincheng	187.83	641.40	449.52
碑林区	Beilin	82.41	1185.40	875.28
莲湖区	Lianhu	45.88	1293.43	1082.13
灞桥区	Baqiao	167.06	1562.85	997.63
未央区	Weiyang	255.53	3933.04	2531.33
雁塔区	Yanta	153.24	3681.57	2484.46
阎良区	Yanliang	172.00	194.26	122.15
临潼区	Lintong	148.32	375.49	101.42
长安区	Chang'an	248.96	1687.48	1012.51
高陵区	Gaoling	272.95	1179.78	423.76
蓝田县	Lantian	155.40	73.33	66.50
周至县	Zhouzhi	84.80	198.38	107.99
户　县	Huxian	39.65	319.22	145.15
开发区	**Development Zones**	**777.56**	**7296.76**	**4226.06**
高新区	GaoXin	173.05	1332.45	662.93
经开区	JingKai	222.39	1363.26	723.55
曲江新区	Qujiang	123.93	1552.14	1114.32
浐灞生态区	Chanba Eco-District	53.59	1267.08	802.06
航空基地	Aviation Industry Base	0.60	74.28	37.25
航天基地	Aerospace Base	86.93	848.87	454.80
国际港务区	International Trade&Logistic Park	90.55	228.52	84.70
沣东新城	FengDong Xincheng	26.52	630.16	346.45

Newly Added Fixed Assets and Floor Space of Constructing and Completed Buildings by Region and Development Zone（2015）

本年房屋竣工面积（万平方米）Floor Space of Buildings Completed(10 000 sq.m)	住宅 Residenctial Buildings	本年房屋竣工价值（亿元）Value of Buildings Completed (100 million yuan)	住宅 Residenctial Buildings	本年商品房销售面积（万平方米）Floor Space of Houses Sales this year (sq.m) Houses(10 000sq.m)	本年商品房销售额（亿元）Sales Income of Commercial Houses this year(100 million yuan)
1109.00	**826.05**	**301.86**	**236.66**	**1763.68**	**1146.79**
75.71	65.33	25.18	20.69	46.03	30.06
147.09	94.08	40.40	26.04	98.69	64.09
103.33	88.64	22.93	18.66	109.01	69.97
80.61	64.64	33.74	27.65	267.59	163.55
273.43	210.94	59.72	47.80	450.73	272.76
258.61	199.09	82.70	61.69	554.07	428.23
10.88	8.44	3.24	2.62	31.62	13.32
60.70	8.76	0.96	0.96	9.51	4.48
37.71	35.55	17.45	16.68	123.04	72.37
8.26	7.10	2.66	2.31	40.44	15.79
16.52	14.86	8.00	6.80	11.13	3.72
0.57	0.55	0.17	0.16	8.51	2.66
35.58	28.07	4.71	4.60	13.31	5.79
451.16	**327.74**	**156.05**	**118.12**	**962.83**	**674.45**
56.20	43.18	20.61	15.55	136.89	124.69
127.13	96.08	32.01	24.52	198.43	116.69
94.77	65.11	41.42	27.92	255.05	200.13
76.79	49.22	27.87	19.80	213.10	138.32
				8.13	2.91
42.90	38.73	18.96	17.60	51.03	24.66
21.93	17.68	12.87	10.51	35.05	28.42
31.44	17.74	2.31	2.22	65.15	38.63

5-22 主要年份房地产开发投资主要指标

单位：万平方米

指 标	Item	1997	1998	1999	2000	2001
本年完成投资额（亿元）	Investment Completed This Year(100 million yuan)	24.68	38.21	44.30	51.85	67.42
本年房屋施工面积	Floor Space of Buildings Under Construction This Year	451.47	678.87	793.46	763.18	743.78
#住宅	Residential Buildings	331.16	552.37	649.53	619.85	580.43
本年房屋竣工面积	Floor Space of Buildings Completed This Year	135.62	156.17	377.79	321.10	316.24
#住宅	Residential Buildings	120.33	133.33	352.28	295.55	269.61
本年房屋竣工价值（亿元）	Value of Floor Space of Buildings Completed(100million yuan)	11.96	14.36	38.22	26.94	37.20
#住宅	Residential Buildings	9.63	11.00	33.02	22.97	28.62
商品房销售面积	Floor Space of Commercialized Buildings sold	78.45	117.11	296.97	212.92	225.35
#住宅	Residential Buildings	72.69	108.61	284.95	200.77	192.20
商品房销售额（亿元）	Total Sales of Commercialized Buildings(100 million yuan)	12.81	17.74	35.19	32.52	47.22
#住宅	Residential Buildings	11.39	15.46	32.35	29.46	35.53
本年批准预售面积	Approved Pre-sale Area of This Year	26.35	252.02	30.25	253.03	67.44
#住宅	Residential Buildings	23.27	246.77	27.34	253.03	65.20
待售面积	Area for Sale	58.71	32.52	62.38	36.41	50.82
#住宅	Residential Buildings	50.26	22.81	52.32	24.02	34.18
房屋出租面积	Rental Housing Area	25.69	1.04	1.88	1.17	9.19
#住宅	Residential Buildings	22.87	0.01	0.15	0.02	0.10
本年新增固定资产（亿元）	Newly Increased Fixed Assets This Year(100 million yuan)	14.36	19.93	43.10	38.38	50.77

Main Indicators of Investment in Real Estate Development in Representative Years

(10 000 sq.m)

2002	2003	2004	2005	2006	2007	2008	2009	2010	2011	2012	2013	2014	2015
79.37	124.82	169.67	225.23	285.76	387.33	540.26	696.34	842.34	996.81	1281.90	1595.64	1761.88	1831.67
1172.58	1343.12	1633.68	2174.29	2383.56	2915.95	3632.87	5708.63	6697.39	8247.69	9947.89	10454.27	12422.10	13392.94
964.68	943.61	1204.01	1783.36	1890.27	2376.82	3079.13	4901.59	5777.71	7108.27	8294.92	8461.71	9727.60	9777.23
329.71	339.67	380.84	361.62	399.64	483.30	443.96	542.81	463.65	631.03	1063.70	795.35	1533.70	976.64
290.30	289.56	308.06	316.52	342.15	422.47	412.46	453.49	412.44	564.59	903.82	663.20	1307.64	766.58
36.93	54.73	73.75	80.58	82.02	101.13	106.50	168.08	145.62	213.29	310.57	279.63	442.74	301.86
30.46	44.01	55.58	68.11	65.80	77.13	96.02	137.42	128.69	185.31	260.04	222.64	368.25	236.66
252.90	252.74	305.47	497.34	621.50	833.92	760.72	1256.02	1587.81	1778.02	1538.91	1662.75	1707.71	1763.68
237.04	230.28	279.90	476.39	584.06	782.91	715.76	1202.12	1523.24	1674.85	1383.84	1522.50	1525.95	1584.08
51.35	54.29	81.35	171.29	206.15	281.79	296.44	488.55	707.00	1091.31	1017.74	1112.87	1100.71	1146.79
45.46	44.25	71.27	158.03	179.47	251.74	268.92	450.71	661.27	973.71	858.53	976.19	928.74	985.35
61.02	52.35	17.60	300.07	428.20	491.07	569.22	1125.44	1510.20	3105.76	2627.73	1787.89	842.98	751.15
55.73	49.12	159.10	287.13	408.11	457.54	541.20	1095.17	1452.20	2826.79	2340.69	1597.82	727.31	583.55
57.14	63.85	108.52	123.59	112.49	45.42	55.40	40.68	34.32	59.76	102.58	74.59	187.13	296.50
44.70	52.34	72.76	99.17	85.89	38.62	35.40	28.73	26.23	45.41	83.78	61.24	143.21	185.96
15.75	10.56	11.18	17.32	8.53	10.84	34.94	38.23	28.60	8.01	15.16	15.57	7.15	19.64
1.13	5.43	5.78	4.09	3.74	5.36	4.53	6.55	0.70	3.25	4.03	0.73	0.07	1.47
48.43	62.13	83.36	92.78	100.22	143.17	124.02	195.71	168.20	25.53	358.03	334.41	531.44	335.91

5-23 分区县、开发区房地产开发主要指标（2015年）

单位：万元

区县、开发区	Region	企业（单位）个数（个） Number of Enterprises (Unit)	本年完成投资 Investment Completed This Yea	本年新增固定资产 Increased Fixed Assets This Year
区县	**Region**	859	18316688	3359124
新城区	Xincheng	36	609005	272953
碑林区	Beilin	91	1157252	467633
莲湖区	Lianhu	80	1914808	278840
灞桥区	Baqiao	86	2564955	454757
未央区	Weiyang	153	5200122	637534
雁塔区	Yanta	199	4620068	853205
阎良区	Yanliang	35	146085	32447
临潼区	Lintong	9	231416	10000
长安区	Chang'an	77	1245180	179732
高陵区	Gaoling	31	317140	34266
蓝田县	Lantian	13	62165	80048
周至县	Zhouzhi	20	102805	8558
户　县	Huxian	29	145687	49151
开发区	**Development Zones**	336	10583443	1622919
高新区	GaoXin	68	1390424	213323
经开区	JingKai	57	2516515	320148
曲江新区	Qujiang	77	2236348	432517
浐灞生态区	Chanba Eco-District	64	2784813	310326
航空基地	Aviation Industry Base	8	62751	
航天基地	Aerospace Base	27	517612	194886
国际港务区	International Trade&Logistic Park	12	296464	128668
沣东新城	FengDongXinCheng	23	778516	23051

Main Indicators of Real Estate Development by Region and Development Zone (2015)

(10 000 yuan)

房屋施工面积（平方米）Floor Space of Buildings Under Constmction(sq.m)	住宅 Residenctial Buildings	房屋竣工面积（平方米）Floor Space of Buildings Completed(sq.m)	住宅 Residenctial Buildings	竣工房屋价值 Value of Buildings Completed	住宅 Residenctial Buildings
133929413	97772274	9766426	7665795	3018629	2366641
5697894	4307228	757078	653264	251807	206896
10703079	8104275	1464035	940762	404022	260437
12579670	10563321	775257	628391	229346	186633
13794158	9976329	806135	646385	337384	276529
32507062	21737964	2457410	1962644	597269	478031
35200520	24535591	2586057	1990895	826953	616858
1847324	1221487	108790	84352	32447	26218
1084669	883072	33000	33000	9570	9570
13002246	10125107	377077	355472	174465	166779
4407191	3756246	82568	70955	26569	23089
710784	663041	163780	148629	80048	68006
1379129	1079920	5668	5487	1698	1644
1015687	818693	149571	145559	47051	45951
64078664	42230606	4381574	3277408	1560472	1181229
12737941	6629273	562003	431936	206195	155630
12359761	7235467	1271323	960784	320067	245204
15397644	11143248	947716	651108	414158	279158
10248305	8020635	767857	492162	278714	197973
742785	372496				
5892178	4548009	428989	387255	189619	175965
2285176	846982	219281	176790	128668	105127
4414874	3434496	184405	177373	23051	22172

5-24 房地产开发投资主要指标（2015年）

Main Indicators of Investment in Real Estate Development（2015）

单位：万元 (10 000 yuan)

指标	Item	全市合计 Total	国有 State-owned	市区 Urban	市属 Municipal
一、企业（单位）个数（个）	**Number of Enterprises(unit)**	859	52	740	801
二、本年完成投资	**Investment Completed This Year**	18316688	1395516	18006031	17238478
按工程用途分	Grouped by Function				
住宅	Residential Buildings	13121540	1080304	12909925	12281562
#别墅、高档公寓	Villas and Top-Grade Apartments	2019555	177084	1573250	1773711
办公楼	Office Buildings	1439780	67147	1419568	1353466
商业营业用房	Houses for Business Use	2477129	125237	2367396	2408785
其他	Others	1298451	122828	1288930	1194665
三、本年新增固定资产	**Increased Fixed Assets This Year**	3359124	166121	3227453	3097241
四、房屋施工面积（平方米）	**Floor Space of Buildings Under Construction (sq.m)**	133929413	10069099	130823813	123743115
#住宅	Residential Buildings	97772274	7671200	95210620	90077692
五、本年房屋竣工面积（平方米）	**Floor Space of Buildings Completed (sq.m)**	9766426	414723	9447407	8065528
#住宅	Residential Buildings	7665795	378972	7366120	6156863
六、本年房屋竣工价值	**Value of Buildings Completed**	3018629	157694	2889832	2758217
#住宅	Residential Buildings	2366641	141811	2251040	2134627
七、本年商品房屋销售面积（平方米）	**Floor Space of Commercialized Buildings Sold(sq.m)**	17636762	695699	17307360	16032610
本年商品房销售额	Sales Income of Commercialized Buildings	11467912	539145	11092603	10413426

5-25 商品房销售情况（2015年）

Sales of Commercial Houses（2015）

指 标	Item	全市合计 Total	国有 State-owned	市区 Urban	市属 Municipal
商品房销售面积（平方米）	**Floor Space of Commercialized Buildings Sold(sq.m)**	**17636762**	**695699**	**17307360**	**16032610**
现房销售面积（平方米）	**Floor Space of Completed Apartment Sales**	**2426633**	**45353**	**2384402**	**2346799**
期房销售面积（平方米）	**Floor Space of Forward Delivery Housing Sales**	**15210129**	**650346**	**14543339**	**13685811**
住宅	Residential Buildings	15840754	628400	15528742	14392569
#别墅、高档公寓	Villas and High-grade Apartments	276556	84077	275572	264484
办公楼	Office Buildings	503019	42158	503019	428407
商业营业用房	Houses for Business Use	870281	9341	854391	829986
其他	Others	422708	15800	421208	381648
本年商品房销售额（万元）	**Real estate sales this year(Wan Yuan)**	**11467912**	**539145**	**11092603**	**10413426**
现房销售额（万元）	**Floor Space of Completed Apartment Sales**	**1621439**	**24778**	**1390132**	**1571026**
期房销售额（万元）	**Floor Space of Forward Delivery Housing Sales**	**9846473**	**514367**	**9602471**	**8842400**
住宅	Residential Buildings	9853452	440994	9486488	8965553
#别墅高档公寓	Villas and High-grade Apartments	260983	59219	258281	250981
办公楼	Office Buildings	490403	70751	490403	391801
商业营业用房	Houses for Business Use	910344	19918	903499	864438
其他	Others	213713	7482	212213	191634
待售面积（平方米）	**Area for Sale(Sqm)**	**2964998**	**227114**	**2693052**	**2897351**
#待售一年以上（一—三年）	Being Idle for One Year	1004090	46032	964065	982852
待售三年以上（含三年）	Being Idle for Three Year	51869	6591	49601	45278
住宅	Residence	1859571	212465	1617652	1804194
#别墅高档公寓	Villas and High-grade Apartments	5294			5294
办公楼	Office Buildings	39586		39586	39586
商业营业用房	Houses for Business Use	678203	9592	650221	670742
其他	Others	387638	5057	385593	382829
房屋出租面积（平方米）	**Rental area(Sqm)**	**196395**		**190908**	**196395**
住宅	Residential Buildings	14652		14652	14652
办公楼	Office Buildings	37215		37215	37215
商业营业用房	Houses for Business Use	144362		138875	144362
其他	Others	166		166	166

5-26 房地产开发投资资金来源（2015年）

Source of Funds for Investment in Real Estate Development（2015）

单位：万元 (10 000 yuan)

指 标	Item	全市合计 Total	国有 State-owned	市区 Urban	市属 Municipal
一. 本年资金来源合计	**Total**	**27659506**	**2055677**	**26423609**	**25623952**
1. 上年末结余资金	Balance of Last Year	6597283	457836	5895041	6067644
2. 本年资金来源小计	Total Funds This Year	21062223	1597841	20528568	19556308
(1) 国内贷款	Domestic Loans	2884192	172000	2627750	2557282
#银行贷款	Bank Loan	2266677	172000	2029790	2057977
非银行金融机构贷款	Loans from financial Institutions except Bank	617515		617515	499305
(2) 利用外资	Utilization of Foreign Funds	63200		62400	63200
#外商直接投资	Foreign Direct Investment	63200		61400	63200
(3) 自筹资金	Self-raising Funds	10289457	855854	10258125	9883403
#自有资金	Funds at the disposal of Enterprises	4180976	438037	4075304	3926741
(4) 其他资金	Others	7825374	569987	7580293	7052423
#定金及预收款	Earnest Money and Advance payment	4008180	285790	3896165	3698374
个人按揭贷款	Personal Mortgage loan	2401615	100572	2261344	2221705
二. 本年各项应付款合计	**Total Sums of Money to be Paid This Year**	**5414298**	**434649**	**5193625**	**5074257**
#工程款	Project Fund	3177658	244516	3030985	3006025

5-27 房地产开发经营情况（2015年）

Running of Real Estate Development（2015）

单位：万元 (10 000 yuan)

指标	Item	全市合计 Total	国有 State-owned	市区 Urban	市属 Municipal
一、资产负债情况	Assets and Liabilities				
1. 资产总计	Total Assets	690116906	54393966	678984022	636820756
2. 负债总计	Total Liabilities	580007827	38300811	570236952	535544711
3. 所有者权益合计	Total Creditor's Equity	110231217	16093155	108869208	101398183
#实收资本	Held Capital	77746589	7416532	76368671	72901240
二、损益及分配情况	Profit or Loss and the Distribution				
1. 主营业务收入	Revenue from Principal Business	104237733	7200295	102465389	92548362
土地转让收入	Revenue of Land Transferred	83581	5600	75546	78581
商品房屋销售收入	Revenue of Commercial Houses Sold	98527251	4298797	96790890	88723474
房屋出租收入	Revenue of Houses Leased	801766	121356	796021	781763
其他收入	Other Revenue	4825135	2774542	4802932	2964544
2. 主营业务成本	Cost of Principal Business	78949644	5790605	77573577	71184157
3. 主营业务税金及附加	Taxes and Other Charges on Principal Business	7247665	523033	7134823	6546696
4. 其他业务利润	Other Business Profit	201483	307	201483	185481
5. 销售费用	Sales Expenditures	4227603	158137	4174322	3870568
6. 管理费用	Management Cost	4710368	360971	4606745	4368059
#税金	Tax	330752	19415	328385	305796
7. 财务费用	Fiscal Expenditure	1556751	94281	1532920	1512886
#利息支出	Interest Exchange	1274308	28681	1268357	1213639
8. 营业利润	Operating Profit	8713094	2630337	8587636	6307551
投资收益	Investment Revenue	667051	315137	666629	633596
营业外收入	Non-business Revenue	518329	54376	517414	492236
营业外支出	Non-business Expenditures	294250	25160	284338	271791
9. 利润总额	Total Profit	8937144	2659553	8810683	6527967
10. 应付职工薪酬	Salary Payable	3699547	675000	3613655	3358245
三、全部从业人员年平均人数	Average Number of Employed Persons	47583	9835	45888	44698
四、本年应付工资总额	Total Wages This Year	313858	59962	307166	287820

主要统计指标解释

全社会固定资产投资 是以货币形式表现的在一定时期内全社会建造和购置固定资产的工作量以及与此有关的费用的总称。该指标是反映固定资产投资规模、结构和发展速度的综合性指标，又是观察工程进度和考核投资效果的重要依据。全社会固定资产投资按登记注册类型可分为国有、集体、联营、股份制、私营和个体、港澳台商、外商、其他等。

城镇固定资产投资 指城镇各种登记注册类型的企业、事业、行政单位及个体户进行的计划总投资500万元及500万元以上的建设项目投资和房地产开发投资。县城及以上区域内发生的投资，县及县以上各级政府及主管部门直接领导、管理的建设项目和企业事业单位的投资均为城镇固定资产投资。

房地产开发投资 指各种登记注册类型的房地产开发公司、商品房建设公司及其他房地产开发法人单位和附属于其他法人单位实际从事房地产开发或经营活动的单位统一开发的包括统代建、拆迁还建的住宅、厂房、仓库、饭店、宾馆、度假村、写字楼、办公楼等房屋建筑物和配套的服务设施，土地开发工程（如道路、给水、排水、供电、供热、通讯、平整场地等基础设施工程）的投资；不包括单纯的土地交易活动。

农村投资 包括在农村区域范围内进行固定资产投资活动的企业、事业、行政单位及农户投资。

固定资产投资的资金来源 根据固定资产投资的资金来源不同，分为国家预算资金、国内贷款、利用外资、自筹资金和其他资金。

（1）国家预算资金：包括一般预算、政府性基金预算、国有资本经营预算和社保基金预算等资金。

（2）国内贷款：指报告期固定资产投资单位向银行及非银行金融机构借入的用于固定资产投资的各种国内借款，包括银行利用自有资金及吸收的存款发放的贷款、上级主管部门拨入的国内贷款、国家专项贷款、地方财政专项资金安排的贷款、国内储备贷款、周转贷款等。

（3）利用外资：指报告期收到的用于固定资产建造和购置的境外资金（包括设备、材料、技术在内）。包括对外借款（外国政府、国际金融组织贷款、出口信贷、外国银行商业贷款、对外发行债券和股票）、外商直接投资及外商其他投资。不包括我国自有外汇资金（国家外汇、地方外汇、留成外汇、调剂外汇和中国银行自有资金发行的外汇贷款等）。计算利用外资时，需要折算成人民币，折算中所使用的外汇汇率按现汇计算，即按使用外汇时的汇率计算。

（4）自筹资金：指固定资产投资单位报告期收到的，由各地区、各部门及企、事业单位筹集用于固定资产投资的预算外资金，包括中央各部门、各级地方和企、事业单位的自筹资金。

（5）其他资金：指在报告期收到的除以上各种资金之外其他用于固定资产投资的资金，包括企业或金融机构通过发行各种债券筹集到的资金、社会集资、个人资金、无偿捐赠的资金及其他单位拨人的资金等。

固定资产投资按国民经济行业分 根据现有企业、事业、行政单位和建设项目建成投产后的主要产品种类或主要用途及社会经济活动性质来确定国民经济行业。一般情况下，一个建设项目或一个企业、事业单位只能属于一种国民经济行业。

固定资产投资按隶属关系分 是按建设单位或企业、事业、行政单位的主管上级机关确定的。

（1）中央：是指中共中央、人大常委会和国务院各部、委、局、总公司以及直属机构直接领导的建设项目和企业、事业、行政单位。这些单位的固定资产投资计划由国务院各部门直接编制和下达，建设中所需物资、主要设备以及建设中的问题都由中央有关部门安排和解决。

（2）地方：是由省（自治区、直辖市）、地区（州、盟、省辖市）、县（旗、县级市）三级政府及业务主管部门直接领导和管理的建设项目、企业、事业、行政单位。地方项目还包括不隶属以上各级政府及主管部门的建设项目和企业、事业单位，如外商投资企业和无主管部门的企业等。

固定资产投资按建设性质分 根据整个建设项目情况来确定。建设项目的性质一般分为新建、扩建、改建和技术改造、单纯建造生活设施、迁建、恢复、单纯购置。房地产开发单位、农户投资不划分建设性质。

（1）新建：一般指从无到有开始建设的企业、事业和行政单位或建设项目。有的单位原有基础很小，经过建设后新增的固定资产价值超过该企、事业、行政单位原有固定资产价值（原值）三倍以上的也应作为新建。

（2）扩建：指在厂内或其他地点，为扩大原有产品的生产能力（或效益）或增加新的产品生产能力，而增建主要的生产车间（或主要工程）、分厂、独立的生产线。行政、事业单位在原单位增建业务用房（如学校增建教学用房、医院增建门诊部、病房等）也作为扩建。

现有企、事业单位为扩大原有主要产品生产能力或增加新的产品生产能力，增建一个或几个主要生产车间（或主要工程）、分厂，同时进行一些更新改造工程的，也应作为扩建。

（3）改建和技术改造：指现有企业、事业单位，对原有设施进行技术改造或更新（包括相应配套的辅助性生产、生活福利设施）的建设项目。现有企业、事业单位为适应市场变化的需要，而改变企业的主要产品种类（如军工企业转产民用品等）的建设项目，应作为改建。原有产品生产作业线由于各工序（车间）之间能力不平衡，为填平补齐充分发挥原有生产能力而增建不增加本企业主要产品设计能力的车间，也应作为改建。技术改造是指企业、事业单位在现有基础上，用先进的技术代替落后的技术，用先进的工艺和装备代替落后的工艺和装备，以改变企业落后的技术经济面貌，实现以内涵为主的扩大再生产，达到提高产品质量、促进产品更新换代、节约能源、降低消耗、扩大生产规模、全面提高社会经济效益的目的。技术改造具体包括以下内容：机器设备和工具的更新改造；生产工艺改革、节约能源和原材料的改造；厂房建筑和公共设施的改造；劳动条件和生产环境的改造等。

固定资产投资按构成分 固定资产投资活动按其工作内容和实现方式分为建筑安装工程，设备工具器具购置和其他费用三个部分。

（1）建筑安装工程（建筑安装工作量）：指各种房屋、建筑物的建造工程和各种设备、装置的安装工程。包括各种房屋建造工程；各种用途设备基础和各种工业窑炉的砌筑工程及金属结构工程；为施工而进行的各种准备工作和临时工程以及完工后的清理工作等；铁路、道路的铺设，矿井的开凿及石油管道的架设等；水利工程；防空地下建筑等特殊工程；列人房屋丁程预算内的暖气、卫生、通风、照明、煤气等设备的价值及装设油饰工程；列入建筑工程预算内的各种管道（蒸汽、压缩空气、石油、给排水等管道）、电力、电讯电缆导线等的敷设工程；以及各种机械设备的安装下程；为测定安装工程质量，对设备进行的试运工作；房地产开发单位进行的商品房屋开发建设工程、土地开发工程。

在建筑安装工程中，不包括被安装设备本身的价值。

（2）设备工具器具购置：指建设单位或企、事业单位购置或自制的，达到固定资产标准的设备、工具、器具的价值。新建单位及扩建单位的新建车间，按照设计或计划要求购置或自制的全部设备、工具、器具，不论是否达到固定资产标准均计入“设备工具器具购置”中。

（3）其他费用：指在固定资产建造和购置过程中发生的，除上述几项内容以外的各种应分摊计人固定资产的费用。

施工项目 指报告期内所有施工的建设项目个数，包括本年新开工的项目和以前年度开工在本年继续施工的建设项目。凡是报告期内施过工的建设项目，不论施工时间长短，均作为施工项目统计。施工项目个数可以反映一定时期固定资产投资的实际规模，与同期全部建成投产项目个数相比，可以从建设速度的角度反映固定资产投资的效果。

全部建成投产项目 指报告期内按设计文件规定的全部生产能力（或效益）建成投产，经验收合格交付使用的建设项目。

新增生产能力（或工程效益） 指通过固定资产投资活动而增加的设计能力（或工程效益）。主要指标包括建设规模、本年施工规模、自开始建设累计新增生产能力（或工程效益）、本年新增生产能力（或工程效益）等。

建设规模 指建设项目或工程设计文件中规定的全部设计能力（或工程效益）。包括已经建成投产和尚未建成投产的工程的生产能力（或工程效益）。

本年施工规模 指报告期内施工的单项工程的设计能力（或工程效益），即全部建设规模中在本年正式施工的部分。

自开始建设累计新增生产能力（或工程效益） 指自开始建设至本年底止建成投产的全部单项工程累计的新增生产能力（或工程效益）。

本年新增生产能力（或工程效益） 指在本年度内按照新增生产能力（或工程效益）的计算条件和标准，实际建成投入生产或交付使用的生产能力（或工程效益）。

施工房屋面积 指报告期内施工的全部房屋（包括地下室、半地下室以及配套房屋）建筑面积。包括本期新开工的面积和上期开工跨入本期继续施工的房屋面积，以及上期已停建在本期恢复施工的房屋面积。本期竣工和本期施工后又停缓建的房屋，其建筑面积仍计入本期房屋施工面积中。

竣工房屋面积 指在报告期内房屋建筑按照设计要求已经全部完工，达到住人和使用条件，经验收鉴定合格（或达到竣工验收标准），可正式移交使用单位的各栋房屋建筑面积的总和。

新增固定资产 指报告期内交付使用的固定资产价值。包括本年内建成投入生产或交付使用的工程投资和达到固定资产标准的设备、工具、器具的投资及有关应摊入的费用。该指标是表示固定资产投资成果的价值指标，也是反映建设进度，计算固定资产投资效果的重要指标。

项目建成投产率 指一定时期内全部建成投产项目个数与同期施工项目个数的比率。该指标是从建设单位建设速度的角度反映投资效果的指标。

固定资产交付使用率 指一定时期新增固定资产与同期完成投资额的比率。该指标是反映固定资产动用速度，衡量建设过程中宏观投资效果的综合指标。由于新增固定资产是较长时期内形成的结果，而投资额则是当年完成的，因此，该指标一般适宜于反映较长时期内固定资产的动用情况。

商品房销售面积 指报告期内出售商品房屋的合同总面积（即双方签署的正式买卖合同中所确定的建筑面积）。由现房销售建筑面积和期房销售建筑面积两部分组成。

商品房销售额 指报告期内出售商品房屋的合同总价款（即双方签署的正式买卖合同中所确定的合同总价）。该指标与商品房销售面积同口径，由现房销售额和期房销售额两部分组成。

经济适用房 指根据经济适用房计划安排建设的政策性住宅。经济是指房屋建筑造价和销售价格低于一般商品住宅；适用是指适合中低收入家庭购买使用。经济适用房主要是由地方政府统一下达投资计划，房地产公司开发，对外销售；用地一般采用行政划拨或招标投标方式，免收土地出让金；对各种经批准的收费减半征收，开发利润不超过3%；销售价格实行政府指导价。该指标可以分析房地产投资结构，反映中低收入家庭商品住宅的供求平衡情况。

Explanatory Notes on Main Statistical Indicators

Total Investment in Fixed Assets in the Whole Country refers to the volume of activities in construction and purchases of fixed assets of the whole country and related fees, expressed in monetary terms during the reference period. It is a comprehensive indicator which shows the size, structure and growth of the investment in fixed assets, providing a basis for observing the progress of construction projects and evaluating results of investment. Total investment in fixed assets in the whole country includes, by type of ownership, the investment by State-owned units, collective-owned units, joint ownership units, share-holding units, private units individuals as well as investments by entrepreneurs from Hong Kong, Macao and Taiwan, foreign investors and others.

Urban Investment in Fixed Assets refers to construction projects involving a total planned investment of 5000 000 yuan and over by enterprises of various types of ownership, institutions, administrative units and individuals in urban areas, investment in real estate development. In other words, all investments that take place in county towns and urban areas, investment in construction projects under the direct leadership and management of government agencies at and above county levels and investments by enterprises and institutions at and above county levels are covered in urban investment in fixed assets.

Investment in Real Estate Development refers to investment by real estate development companies, commercialized buildings construction companies and other real estate development units of various types of ownership in the construction of buildings, such as residential buildings, factory buildings, warehouses, hotels, guesthouses, holiday villages, office buildings, and the complementary service facilities and land development projects, such as roads, water supply, water drainage, power supply, heating supply, telecommunications, land leveling and other infrastructural projects. It does not include activities in pure land transactions.

Investment in Rural Areas refers to investment in fixed assets by enterprises, institutions, administrative units and households in rural areas.

Sources of Funds for Investment in Fixed Assets are categorized as funds from the State budget, domestic loans, foreign investment, self-raised funds, and others, depending on the sources of investment.

(1) Fund from the State budget consists of budgetary appropriation and loans from the State budget. More specifically, it includes, from the budget of the central government, capital construction fund (operation fund and non-operational fund), special expenses, loans from repayment, discount fund, expenses on innovation and trial production of new products, expenses on urban construction, expenses on temporary construction from business departments, development fund for less developed areas, as well as local budgetary fund transferred from the central budget.

(2) Domestic loans refer to loans of various forms borrowed by investing units from banks and non-bank financial institutions during the reference period for the purpose of investment in fixed assets, including loans issued by banks from their self-owned funds and deposit, loans appropriated by higher authorities, special loans by government, loans arranged by local government from special funds, domestic reserve loan, and working loan.

(3) Foreign investment refers to overseas funds received during the reference period for the construction and purchase of investment in fixed assets (covering equipment, materials and technology), including foreign borrowings (loans from foreign governments and international financial institutions, export credit, commercial loans from foreign banks, issue of bonds and stocks overseas), foreign direct investment and other foreign investments. Excluded from this category is capital in foreign exchanges owned by China (foreign exchanges owned by the central and local governments, foreign exchanges retained by enterprises, foreign exchanges by enterprises through the regulating mechanism, loans in foreign exchanges issued by the Bank of China with its own fund, etc). In calculating the utilization of foreign capital, foreign currencies are converted into Chinese Renminbi applying the current exchange rate when the foreign capitals are actually used.

(4) Self-raised funds refer to extra-budgetary funds for investment in fixed assets received during the reference period by investing units from central government ministries, local governments, enterprises and institutions, including their self-raised funds.

(5) Others refer to funds for investment in fixed assets received from sources other than those listed above, including capital raised through issuing bonds by

enterprises or financial institutions, funds raised from individuals and through donations, and funds transferred from other units.

Investment in Fixed Assets by Sector The classification of construction projects by sector is determined by enterprises, institutions, administrative units and the major products or the purpose of the projects of existing enterprises, institutional and administrative units when they are put into production or use, and by the nature of their social economic activities. In general, one project or one enterprise or institution can only be classified into one sector.

Investment in Fixed Assets by Jurisdiction of Management refers to the classification of investment by the competent authorities under which investment is made by construction units, enterprises, institutions or administrative units.

(1) Central investment refers to the investment in projects or by enterprises, institutions or administrative units which are under the direct leadership and management of the State Council and of the national commissions, ministries, agencies and State-owned large corporations. Various ministries and departments of the State Council prepare and implement plans for investment in fixed assets by those departments, and arrange and ensure the supply of materials and key equipment required for the projects.

(2) Local investment refers to the investment in projects or by enterprises, institutions or administrative units which are under the direct leadership and management of departments under the provincial, prefecture and county governments. Also included are projects by foreign-invested enterprises and enterprises without competent managing authorities.

Investment in Fixed Assets by Type of Construction Construction projects in general can be classified, by the type of construction, into new construction, expansion, reconstruction and technical transformation, purely construction of living facilities, moving, restoration and purely purchasing. However, investment by type of construction is not applied to investment by real-estate development units and investment by rural households.

(1) New construction in general refers to construction projects, which start from scratch, of enterprises, institutions, administrative agencies. In case the size of the existing unit is quite small, and the value of newly added fixed assets is more than three times of the original value, the expansion will be considered as new construction.

(2) Expansion refers to construction of new major production workshop, branch factory or independent production line within a factory or in other locations, for the purpose of increasing the production capacity (or improving efficiency) or adding new production capacity. Newly constructed accommodation for the operation of institutions and administrative organizations (such as newly constructed buildings for teaching in schools, buildings for clinics or wards in hospitals, etc.) are also classified as expansion.

Also included in expansion are investments by existing enterprises or institutions in building major production line(s) or branch factory(ies) along with some work on innovation, for the purpose of expanding the production capacity of original products or producing new products.

(3) Reconstruction and technical transformation refers to construction projects by existing enterprises or institutions in innovation or technical transformation of the old facilities (including auxiliary production equipment and welfare facilities). Also considered as reconstruction is the construction of new workshops by the existing enterprises or institutions to change the variety of products to meet the market demand (such as the production of civil products by defence industries), or to bring the designed production capacity into full play through a more balanced production process on production lines. Technical transformation refers to replacement of old technology or equipment by new technology or equipment, in order to expand the reproduction through improvement of technology contents in production, to improve product quality, to promote new products to save energy,to reduce consumption, to expand the production scale and to improve overall social-economic efficiency. Contents of technical transformation include: updating of machinery, equipment and tools; reforming production process by using energy or materials saving technology; construction of factory workshops and transformation of public facilities; improvement of working conditions and environment, etc.

Investment in Fixed Assets by Structure By their

contents and the mode of implementation, investment activities are classified into 3 categories, i.e. construction and installation, purchase of equipment and instrument, and other expenses.

(1) Construction and installation (work volume of construction and installation) refers to the construction of houses and buildings and the installation of various kinds of equipment and instruments. They include construction of houses; equipment foundations, industrial kilns and stoves, and metal structure work; preparation works and temporary works for project construction, and clearing up works post project construction; pavement of railways and roads, drilling of mines and putting up of oil pipes; construction of water conservancy; construction of underground air-raid shelters and construction of other special projects; value of equipment for heating, sanitation, ventilation, lighting, gas, painting, etc. that are covered by the budget of housing projects; laying out of various pipelines (for steam, compressed air, petroleum, tap water and sewage) and wiring and cabling for electric power and for communications; installation of various machinery and equipment; testing operation for pre- testing the quality of installation projects, and land and other development work conducted by real estate developers for commercialized housing.

The value of equipment installed is itself not included in the value of construction and installation projects.

(2) Purchase of equipment and instruments refers to the total value of equipment, tools, and instruments purchased or self-produced which come up to the cut-off point for fixed assets by the construction units or investing enterprises or institutions. Equipment, tools and instruments purchased or self-produced for new workshops by newly established or expanded units are categorized as "purchase of equipment and instruments" no matter whether they come up to the cut-off point for fixed assets.

(3) Other expenses refer to expenses arising during the construction or purchase of fixed assets other than those mentioned above.

Projects under Construction refer to number of all projects with construction activities newly started in current year or left-over from the previous year in the reference period. All projects that have construction activities undertaken during the reference period are reported as projects under construction irrespective of the length of construction work. The number of projects under construction can reflect the actual size of investment in fixed assets during a given period, and when compared with the number of projects completed and put into use during the same period, it demonstrates the results of investment in fixed assets from the angle of the speed of the construction.

Projects Completed and Put into Use refer to projects have been completed in accordance with the design documents, resulting in forming production capacity (efficiency) and have been checked and accepted after relevant tests, and have been formally delivered for use.

Newly Increased Production Capacity (or Project Efficiency) refers to the increase in design capacity (or project efficiency) through investment in fixed assets. The main indicators include: construction scale, scale of projects under construction in current year, the accumulated newly increased production capacity (project efficiency) since the start of the projects and the newly increased production capacity (project efficiency) of current year.

Construction Scale refers to the total designed production capacity (project efficiency) of the construction projects in accordance with the design document, including those have been put into operation and those that have not been completed.

Scale of Projects under Construction in Current Year refers to the designed production capacity (project efficiency) of a single project under construction in the reference period, i.e. the part of the total scale of project which is officially under construction in current year.

The Accumulated Newly Increased Production Capacity (project efficiency) since the Start of the Projects refers to the accumulated newly increased production capacity of all the single projects which have been put into use from the beginning of the projects till the end of current year.

The Newly Increased Production Capacity (project efficiency) of Current Year refers to the production capacity (project efficiency) that has been completed and put into operation in current year according to the calculation conditions and standards on newly increased production capacity (project efficiency).

Floor Space of Buildings under Construction refers to the total floor space of all the buildings (including basement, semi-basement and auxiliary buildings), including the effective area and the area occupied by the structure. This indicator is one of the important indicators in physical terms to reflect the scale and accomplishment of the construction industry and also an important basis for monitoring the progress, Calculating the cost, analyzing the efficiency and studying the supply of building materials in relation to the construction projects.

Floor Space Completed refers to the floor space of all buildings completed in the reference period, which have been appraised and accepted (or come up to the designed standards) and have been transferred to owner units.

Newly Increased Fixed Assets refer to the value of fixed that has been put into use, including investment in projects that have been completed and put into operation in current year and the investment in equipment, tools and appliance that meet the standard of fixed assets and fees that should be apportioned. This is an indicator that demonstrates the results of investment in fixed assets in monetary terms, and an important indicator to reflect the speed of construction and to calculate the efficiency of investment.

Rate of Construction Projects Completed and Put into Use refers to the ratio of the number of construction projects completed and put into use in a certain period of time to the number of projects under construction in the same period. This reflects the investment efficiency from the perspective of the speed of projects construction.

Rate of Projects of Fixed Assets Completed and Put into Operation refers to the ratio of the newly increased fixed assets to the total investment made in the same period. This is a comprehensive indicator reflecting the speed of the employment of fixed assets and the investment efficiency at the macro-level. As the newly increase fixed assets is the result of a long period while the investment is completed in the current year, this indicator is expected to be used to reflect the employment of fixed assets over a long period of time.

6 财　政

GOVERNMENT FINANCE

资料整理：刘　婷
Data management:Liu Ting
数据审核：陈　英
Data audit:Chen Ying

第六部分　财政

一、简要说明

本章资料主要包括地方财政收入、支出总额构成及分区县情况，由西安市统计局综合处根据西安市财政局提供资料整理。

二、主要指标

财政总收入（亿元）	1114.98	比上年增长	9.3%
一般公共预算收入（亿元）	650.99	比上年增长	16.3%
一般公共预算支出（亿元）	917.24	比上年增长	12.9%

6　GOVERNMENT FINANCE

Ⅰ.Brief Introduction

This chapter consists of primarily data on regional revenue, expenditure of the municipal government, regional revenue and expenditure of the districts and the counties. The data are provided by the Xi'an Bureau of Finance and are compiled by Integration division of the Xi'an Bureau of Statistics.

Ⅱ.Major Indicators

		Increase over Preceding Year
Total Government Revenue(100 mil. Yuan)	1114.98	9.3%
General Pubilc Budgetary Revenue(100 mil. Yuan)	650.99	16.3%
Ordinary Budgetary Expenditures(100 mil. Yuan)	917.24	12.9%

6-1 主要年份地方财政一般预算收入及支出

General Revenue Local Government Revenue and Expenditure in Representative Years

单位：亿元　　　　(100 million yuan)

年份 Year	财政收入 Fiscal Revenue	地方财政一般预算收入 General Budgetary Revenue of Local Government	地方财政一般预算支出 General Budgetary Expenditure of Local Government	收支差额 Balance of Payments	财政收入比上年增长（%） Fiscal Revenue Increased over the Previous Year (%)	地方财政一般预算收入比上年增长(%) Local Fiscal General Budget Revenue Growth over the Previous Year(%)	地方财政一般预算支出比上年增长（%） Local Fiscal General Budget Expenditures Growth over the Previous Year(%)
2000	61.57	46.80	52.00	-5.20		14.4	
2001	75.79	51.45	57.30	-5.85	23.1	9.9	10.2
2002	99.84	54.50	63.80	-9.30	31.7	16.9	11.3
2003	120.64	72.90	76.60	-3.70	20.8	33.8	20.1
2004	133.52	75.30	87.30	-12.00	10.7	3.3	14.0
2005	163.87	72.92	97.61	-24.69	22.7	15.8	11.8
2006	195.96	85.89	119.22	-33.33	19.6	18.6	21.9
2007	260.70	112.92	161.25	-48.33	33.0	31.5	35.3
2008	324.49	145.61	226.99	-81.38	24.5	28.9	40.8
2009	400.29	181.40	276.85	-95.45	23.4	24.6	22.0
2010	510.69	241.86	371.62	-129.76	27.6	33.3	34.2
2011	649.88	318.55	494.58	-176.03	27.3	31.7	33.1
2012	753.07	396.96	597.49	-200.53	15.9	24.6	20.8
2013	902.76	501.98	729.81	-227.83	19.9	26.5	22.1
2014	1019.69	583.79	819.54	-235.75	13.0	16.3	12.3
2015	1114.98	650.99	917.24	-266.25	9.3	16.3	12.9

注：本表数据来源于市财政局。

6-2 财政收入（2015年）

Government Revenue（2015）

单位：万元 （10 000 yuan）

指　标	Item	2015
财政总收入	**Total Government Revenue**	**11149760**
#一般公共预算收入	**General Pubilc Budgetary Revenue**	**6509853**
一、税收收入	**Total Tax Revenue**	**4086911**
1. 国内增值税	Value-added Tax	299034
2. 改征增值税	Levying VAT	269355
3. 营业税	Business Tax	1116087
4. 企业所得税	Corporate Income Tax	408813
5. 企业所得税退税	Return for Corporate Income Tax	
6. 个人所得税	Individual Income Tax	171602
7. 资源税	Resource Tax	287
8. 城市维护建设税	City Maintenance and Construction Tax	308080
9. 房产税	House Property Tax	170789
10. 印花税	Stamp Tax	102816
11. 城镇土地使用税	Urban Land Use Tax	80344
12. 土地增值税	Land Appreciation Tax	319901
13. 车船税	Tax on the Use of Vehicles and Ships	76613
14. 耕地占用税	Farm Land Occupatian Tax	305160
15. 契税	Deed Tax	458030
二、非税收入	**Total Non-tax Revenue**	**2422942**
1. 专项收入	Special Program Receipts	314462
2. 行政性收费收入	Charge of Adminnistrative and Institutional Units	500193
3. 罚没收入	Penalty Receipts	124687
4. 国有资本经营收入	State-owned Assets Profit	580854
5. 国有资源（资产）有偿使用收入	Revenue for the use of State-owned Assets (Resources)	882837
6. 其他收入	Other Revenue	19909
政府性基金收入	**Governmental Fund Revenue**	**2998455**

注：本表数据来源于市财政局。

6-3 财政支出（2015年）

Government Expenditures（2015）

单位：万元 （10 000 yuan）

指 标	Item	2015
一、政府性基金支出	**Governmental Fund Revenue Expenditure**	**2840038**
二、一般公共预算收入	**General Pubilc Budgetary Revenue**	**9172400**
1.一般公共服务支出	Expenditure for General Public Services	567604
2.国防支出	Expenditure for National Defense	4555
3.公共安全支出	Expenditure for Public Security	461862
4.教育支出	Expenditure for Education	1183865
5.科学技术支出	Expenditure for Science and Technology	254413
6.文化体育与传媒支出	Expenditure for Cultural, Sports and Media	221059
7.社会保障和就业支出	Expenditure for Social Safety Net and Employment Effort	949925
8.医疗卫生与计划生育支出	Expenditure for Medical 、 Health Care and Brith Control Planning	698540
9.节能环保支出	Expenditure for Energy Saving	346696
10.城乡社区支出	Expenditure for Urban and Rural Community Aaffairs	2329622
11.农林水支出	Expenditure for Agriculture, Forestry and Water Conservancy	566231
12.交通运输支出	Expenditure for Transportation	404711
13.资源勘探信息等支出	Expenditure for Exploration of the Power of Information	373098
14.商业服务业等支出	Expenditure for Business Services	133388
15.金融支出	Expenditure for Finance	6083
16.国土海洋气象等支出	Expenditure for Land and Marine Meteorology	33793
17.住房保障支出	Expenditure for Housing Secnrity	573422
18.粮油物资储备支出	Expenditure for Grain and Oil Stockpiles	18870
19.国债还本付息支出	Expenditure for National Debt and Interest	19476
20.其它支出	Other Expenditure	25187

注：本表数据来源于市财政局。

6-4 各区县、开发区财政收入（2015年）

单位：万元

区县、开发区	Region	一般公共预算收入 General Public Budgetary Revenue	税收收入 Tax Revenue	增值税 Value Added Tax	营业税 Business Revenue	企业所得税 Corporate Income Tax
合计	**Total**	**6509853**	**4086911**	**568389**	**1116087**	**408813**
市本级合计	**Sum of city level**	**973781**	**443934**	**81377**	**11673**	**67106**
区、县合计	**Region**	**3407654**	**2299551**	**299826**	**772374**	**204305**
新城区	Xincheng	370669	193114	21134	62135	39107
碑林区	Beilin	453335	312416	66333	83044	49851
莲湖区	Lianhu	491623	274350	53045	91085	27976
雁塔区	Yanta	501690	401831	56410	155027	40590
灞桥区	Baqiao	254221	203003	12280	71790	6851
未央区	Weiyang	378000	288338	30616	115031	17254
阎良区	Yanliang	128342	91750	9891	13075	2781
临潼区	Lintong	137407	102669	10565	21782	3225
长安区	Chang'an	377767	236981	15471	92951	9728
高陵区	Gaoling	141334	90833	9229	27107	2725
蓝田县	Lantian	42564	26717	1936	10442	606
周至县	Zhouzhi	39260	20015	2328	8408	395
户　县	Huxian	91442	57534	10588	20497	3216
开发区合计	**Sum of Development Zones**	**2128418**	**1343426**	**187186**	**332040**	**137402**
高新区	GaoXin	1035785	610819	127044	126303	75106
经开区	JingKai	426905	244136	45920	64777	22365
曲江新区	Qujiang	411710	318132	7398	93601	33008
浐灞生态区	Chanba Eco-District	155245	100002	2027	28017	3450
航天基地	Aerospace Base	48305	31444	2240	10316	2511
航空基地	Aviation Industry Base	10269	8335	1018	2079	462
国际港务区	International Trade&Logistic Park	40199	30558	1539	6947	500

注：本表数据来源于市财政局。

Goverment revenue by Region and Development Zone（2015）

（10 000 yuan）

一般公共预算收入 General Public Budgetary Revenue					
税收收入 Tax Revenue					
个人所得税 Individual Income Tax	资源税 Resource Tax	城市维护建设税 City Maintenance and Construction Tax	耕地占用税 Farm Land Occupation Tax	契税 Deed Tax	其他各项税收收入 Other Tax Revenue
171602	**287**	**308080**	**305160**	**458030**	**750463**
39655		**62612**		**86095**	**95416**
78390	**285**	**149020**	**283160**	**174524**	**337667**
8070	2	13901	800	14556	33409
21797		23616		15927	51848
9786	1	23762		21561	47134
16734		27498	16372	34038	55162
2903		11195	62854	8227	26903
6154	1	19240	27331	20655	52056
4096		4089	22063	25765	9990
1762	2	5636	48294	2709	8694
3866	13	8377	62804	17504	26267
1854		5338	22955	8023	13602
217	180	1254	7258	1396	3428
240	29	858	4605	1200	1952
911	57	4256	7824	2963	7222
53557	**2**	**96448**	**22000**	**197411**	**317380**
41467		56181	22000	44446	118272
6641	2	22246		32315	49870
2811		10742		68811	101761
534		3583		36976	25415
1210		1771		5919	7477
223		849		718	2986
671		1076		8226	11599

6-4 续表1

单位：万元

区县、开发区	Region	一般公共预算收入 General Public Budgetary Revenue		
		非税收入 Non-tax Revenue	专项收入 Special Program Receipts	行政事业性收费收入 Charge of Adiministrative and Institutional Units
合计	**Total**	**2422942**	**314462**	**500193**
市本级合计	**Sum of city level**	**529847**	**119936**	**212741**
区、县合计	**Region**	**1108103**	**100502**	**229034**
新城区	Xincheng	177555	7908	5723
碑林区	Beilin	140919	13689	9557
莲湖区	Lianhu	217273	14256	23181
雁塔区	Yanta	99859	15059	14495
灞桥区	Baqiao	51218	9050	3583
未央区	Weiyang	89662	10730	14537
阎良区	Yanliang	36592	2457	32188
临潼区	Lintong	34738	3535	2590
长安区	Chang'an	140786	4599	62689
高陵区	Gaoling	50501	7015	34147
蓝田县	Lantian	15847	1552	5700
周至县	Zhouzhi	19245	2725	10371
户　县	Huxian	33908	7927	10273
开发区合计	**Sum of Development Zones**	**784992**	**94024**	**58418**
高新区	GaoXin	424966	32546	35941
经开区	JingKai	182769	13453	12786
曲江新区	Qujiang	93578	28599	3381
浐灞生态区	Chanba Eco-District	55243	10476	3779
航天基地	Aerospace Base	16861	6882	457
航空基地	Aviation Industry Base	1934	484	1363
国际港务区	International Trade&Logistic Park	9641	1584	711

continued 1

(10 000 yuan)

罚没收入 Penalty Receipts	国有资本经营收入 State-owned Assets Profit	国有资源(资产)有偿使用收入 The Revenues of the Compensation for the Use of State-owned Resoures(Assants)	其他收入 Other Income	政府性基金收入 Governmental Funds Revenue
124687	**580854**	**882837**	**19909**	**2998455**
62904	**2422**	**119937**	**11907**	**801098**
54098	**6090**	**713534**	**4845**	**560426**
4717		159207		216
2679		114967	27	
3427		176409		126606
1563		65727	3015	
1081		37397	107	93458
5587		58808		1037
1087	90	770		4915
4175	6000	18438		30016
12437		61061		163055
5012		4327		38215
2292		6230	73	10058
4249		1900		13151
5792		8293	1623	79699
7685	**572342**	**49366**	**3157**	**1636931**
3703	337800	14976		317409
1614	142000	12916		485386
1141	45157	15300		196739
606	34316	6066		350671
430	5900	49	3143	203721
60		13	14	35028
131	7169	46		47977

6-5 各区县、开发区财政支出（2015年）

单位：万元

区县、开发区	Region	一般公共一般预算支出 General Public Budgetary Expenditures	一般公共服务支出 General Public Services	国防支出 Expenditure for National Defense	公共安全支出 Expenditure for Public Safety
合计	**Total**	**9172400**	**567604**	**4555**	**461862**
市本级合计	**Sum of city level**	**2941855**	**172322**	**2064**	**209811**
区、县合计	**Region**	**4383403**	**293071**	**2456**	**230230**
新城区	Xincheng	341540	14645	140	23638
碑林区	Beilin	321992	33439	269	27018
莲湖区	Lianhu	410484	23565	336	21286
雁塔区	Yanta	347450	18764	235	25232
灞桥区	Baqiao	295407	26548	165	14479
未央区	Weiyang	282397	18877	232	29397
阎良区	Yanliang	220632	12643		8882
临潼区	Lintong	392195	18616		12891
长安区	Chang'an	534331	43843	339	23521
高陵区	Gaoling	255372	25335	144	11382
蓝田县	Lantian	301002	15569	344	11722
周至县	Zhouzhi	341695	18356	157	10164
户　县	Huxian	338906	22871	95	10618
开发区合计	**Sum of Development Zones**	**1847142**	**102211**	**35**	**21821**
高新区	GaoXin	975688	30822	35	7711
经开区	JingKai	292896	22351		5761
曲江新区	Qujiang	325290	24867		1185
浐灞生态区	Chanba Eco-District	138841	8317		4155
航天基地	Aerospace Base	54031	6405		3009
航空基地	Aviation Industry Base	17842	5876		
国际港务区	International Trade&Logistic Park	42554	3573		

注：本表数据来源于市财政局。

Expenditure by Region and Development Zone（2015）

（10 000 yuan）

一般公共预算收入 General Public Budgetary Revenue					
教育支出 Expenditure for Education	科学技术支出 Expenditure for Science and Technology	文化体育与传媒支出 Expenditure for Culture,Sport and Media	社会保障和就业支出 Expenditure for Social Safety Net and Employment Effort	医疗卫生与计划生育支出 Medical 、 Health and Family Planning Expenditure	节能环保支出 Expenditure for Energy Saving and Environment Protection
1183865	**254413**	**221059**	**949925**	**698540**	**346696**
220030	**44397**	**77513**	**370393**	**260492**	**93859**
893879	**28492**	**40052**	**576965**	**435670**	**65123**
60231	2128	498	43673	11521	86
53841	5256	1405	55134	17509	1029
75839	2381	711	54027	18704	1590
65291	3397	1360	41489	28872	584
60794	1625	2554	34414	24087	22725
59636	2216	5622	29591	20422	3221
38563	1672	1525	22385	23650	2303
77610	1895	3156	50151	42526	5249
123169	3042	4950	82448	71368	2639
44090	2235	3207	23496	47529	2552
64263	435	4980	50645	45694	3588
91316	569	5337	41702	43078	7546
79236	1641	4747	47810	40710	12011
69956	**181524**	**103494**	**2567**	**2378**	**187714**
24673	165129	4884	1691	248	169332
10900	9929		512		9199
14532		96317		130	1500
11606	129				1888
5995	6167	578	364	2000	3701
1150	120	15			94
1100	50	1700			2000

6-5 续表1

单位：万元

区县、开发区	Region	一般公共预算收入 General Public Budgetary Revenue			
		城乡社区支出 Expenditure for Urban and Rural Community Affairs	农林水支出 Expenditure for Agriculture, Foresty and Water Conservancy	交通运输支出 Expenditure for Industry,Commerce and Banking	资源勘探电力信息等支出 Expenditure for Exploration of the Power of Information
合计	**Total**	**2329622**	**566231**	**404711**	**373098**
市本级合计	**Sum of city level**	**474288**	**99208**	**345150**	**148684**
区、县合计	**Region**	**1042893**	**448178**	**58556**	**57930**
新城区	Xincheng	175337	140	1005	345
碑林区	Beilin	119411	76	462	436
莲湖区	Lianhu	183146	43	538	16647
雁塔区	Yanta	134883	3108	936	563
灞桥区	Baqiao	48423	23034	5931	15573
未央区	Weiyang	87497	8241	2054	306
阎良区	Yanliang	64488	27532	2763	8852
临潼区	Lintong	61923	78197	2643	3336
长安区	Chang'an	90114	44512	16358	482
高陵区	Gaoling	19849	39381	7536	3707
蓝田县	Lantian	16783	72563	3691	482
周至县	Zhouzhi	15659	90163	4020	2298
户　县	Huxian	25380	61188	10619	4903
开发区合计	**Sum of Development Zones**	**812441**	**18845**	**1005**	**166484**
高新区	GaoXin	396352	824		131790
经开区	JingKai	191315	257	55	24293
曲江新区	Qujiang	140300	8102		662
浐灞生态区	Chanba Eco-District	66615	3642		39
航天基地	Aerospace Base	14425	3020	750	5814
航空基地	Aviation Industry Base	3430	3000	200	1936
国际港务区	International Trade&Logistic Park	4			1950

continued 1

（10 000 yuan）

商业服务业等支出 Expenditure for Business Services:	金融支出 Expenditure for Finance	国土海洋气象等支出 Land and Marine Meteorological and Other Expenses	住房保障支出 Expenditure for Housing Support	粮油物资储备支出 Expenditure for Grain and Oil Stockpiles
133388	**6083**	**33793**	**573422**	**18870**
70162	**4748**	**4607**	**298183**	**14830**
16733	**1197**	**26795**	**153261**	**4040**
708	695	589	6113	4
3302	46	726	1358	15
1249	218	730	9409	6
790		1710	19846	3
717		2275	11889	108
276		1672	12934	10
321	185	1372	1458	710
2111		1435	28972	272
1594		4791	20488	619
612	7	6377	16991	533
930	35	1165	7003	590
2057	5	1934	5519	414
2066	6	2019	11281	756
46493	**138**	**2391**	**121978**	
6702	77	738	34289	
686		45	16423	
2666	61		34645	
11719		1409	27892	
154		199	1350	
152			1319	
24414			6060	

6-5 续表2 continued 2

单位：万元 （10 000 yuan）

区县、开发区	Region	公共财政支出 Public expenditure 国债还本付息支出 Expenditure for National Debt and Interst	其他支出 Other Expenditure	政府性基金支出 Governmental Fund Revenue Expenditure
合计	**Total**	**19476**	**25187**	**2840038**
市本级合计	**Sum of city level**	**17605**	**13509**	**671152**
区、县合计	**Region**	**1845**	**6037**	**600395**
新城区	Xincheng	44		31611
碑林区	Beilin	59	1201	2373
莲湖区	Lianhu	23	36	111808
雁塔区	Yanta	1	386	20518
灞桥区	Baqiao	16	50	73878
未央区	Weiyang	183	10	8557
阎良区	Yanliang	168	1160	10349
临潼区	Lintong	292	920	41112
长安区	Chang'an	54		168981
高陵区	Gaoling	108	301	47602
蓝田县	Lantian	150	370	12824
周至县	Zhouzhi	504	897	20613
户　县	Huxian	243	706	50169
开发区合计	**Sum of Development Zones**	**26**	**5641**	**1568491**
高新区	GaoXin		391	292054
经开区	JingKai		1170	480641
曲江新区	Qujiang	23	300	191950
浐灞生态区	Chanba Eco-District		1430	317228
航天基地	Aerospace Base		100	188695
航空基地	Aviation Industry Base		550	36551
国际港务区	International Trade&Logistic Park	3	1700	61372

主要统计指标解释

财政收入 指国家财政参与社会产品分配所取得的收入，是实现国家职能的财力保证。主要包括：

（1）税收收入：包括增值税、消费税、营业税、企业所得税、企业所得税退税、个人所得税、资源税、城市维护建设税、房产税、印花税、城镇土地使用税、土地增值税、车船税、船舶吨税、车辆购置税、关税、耕地占用税、契税、烟叶税等。

（2）非税收入：包括专项收入、行政事业性收费、罚没收入、国有资本经营收入、国有资源（资产）有偿使用收入和其他收入。

财政支出 指国家财政将筹集起来的资金进行分配使用，以满足经济建设和各项事业的需要。主要包括：

（1）一般公共服务支出：指政府提供基本公共管理与服务的支出，包括人大事务、政协事务、政府办公厅（室）及相关机构事务、发展与改革事务、统计信息事务、财政事务、税收事务、审计事务、海关事务、人力资源事务、纪检监察事务、商贸事务、知识产权事务、工商行政管理事务、质量技术监督与检验检疫事务、民族事务、宗教事务、港澳台侨事务、档案事务、民主党派及工商联事务、群众团体事务、共产党事务等。

（2）外交支出：指政府外交事务支出，包括外交管理事务、驻外机构、对外援助、国际组织、对外合作与交流、对外宣传、边界勘界联检等方面的支出。

（3）国防支出：指政府用于国防方面的支出，包括用于现役部队、国防科研事业、专项工程、国防动员等方面的支出。

（4）公共安全支出：指政府维护社会公共安全方面的支出，包括武装警察、公安、国家安全、检察、法院、司法、监狱、劳教、国家保密、缉私警察等。

（5）教育支出：指政府教育事务支出，包括教育管理、学前教育、普通教育、职业教育、成人教育、广播电视教育、留学教育、特殊教育、进修及培训、教育费附加安排的支出等。

（6）科学技术支出：指用于科学技术方面的支出，包括科学技术管理事务、基础研究、应用研究、技术研究与开发、科技条件与服务、社会科学、科学技术普及、科技交流与合作、科技重大专项等。

（7）文化体育与传媒支出：指政府在文化、文物、体育、广播影视、新闻出版等方面的支出。

（8）社会保障和就业支出：指政府在社会保障与就业方面的支出，包括人力资源和社会保障管理事务、民政管理事务、财政对社会保险基金的补助、补充全国社会保障基金、行政事业单位离退休、企业改革补助、就业补助、抚恤、退役安置、社会福利、残疾人事业、城市居民最低生活保障、其他城市生活救助、自然灾害生活救助、红十字事业、农村最低生活保障、其他农村生活救助、补充道路交通事故社会救助基金等。

（9）医疗卫生和计划生育支出：指政府医疗卫生方面的支出，包括医疗卫生管理事务、公立医院、基层医疗卫生机构、公共卫生、医疗保障、中医药、食品和药品监督管理、人口与计划生育事务等。

（10）节能环保支出：指政府节能环保支出，包括环境保护管理事务、环境监测与监察、污染治理、自然生态保护、天然林保护工程、退耕还林、风沙荒漠治理、退牧还草、已垦草原退耕、能源节约利用、污染减排、可再生能源和资源综合利用等支出。

（11）城乡社区支出：指政府城乡社区事务支出，包括城乡社区管理事务、城乡社区规划与管理、城乡社区公共设施、城乡社区环境卫生、建设市场管理与监督等。

（12）农林水支出：指政府用于农林水事务支出，包括农业、林业、水利、南水北调、扶贫、农业综合开发、农业综合改革、促进金融支农等。

（13）交通运输支出：指政府交通运输和邮政业方面的支出，包括公路水路运输、铁路运输、民用航空运输、石油价格改革对交通运输的补贴、邮政业、车辆购置税等。

（14）资源勘探电力信息支出：指政府用于资源勘探、制造业、建筑业、电力信息等方面的支出，包括资源勘探开发、制造业、建筑业、电力监管、工业和信息产业监管、安全生产监管、国有资产监管、支持中小企业发展和管理等。

（15）商业服务业支出：指政府用于商业服务业方面的支出，包括商业流通事务、旅游业管理与服务、涉外发展服务等。

（16）金融支出：指政府用于金融方面的支出，包括金融部门行政、金融部门监管、金融发展、金融调控等。

（17）援助其他地区支出：指用于援助方政府安排并管理的对其他地区各类援助、捐赠等资金支出。

（18）国土海洋气象支出：指政府用于国土资源、海洋、测绘、地震、气象等公益服务事业方面的支出。

（19）住房保障支出：指政府用于住房方面的支出，包括保障性安居工程、住房改革、城乡社区住宅等。

（20）粮油物资储备支出：指政府用于粮油物资储备方面的支出，包括粮油事务、物资事务、能源储备、粮油储备、重要商品储备等。

（21）国债还本付息支出：指国债还本、付息、发行等方面的支出。

（22）其他支出：指不能划分到上述功能科目的其它政府支出。

中央财政收入和地方财政收入 指按现行分税制财政体制划分的中央本级收入和地方本级收入。属于中央财政的收入包括关税，进口货物增值税和消费税，出口货物退增值税和消费税，消费税，铁道部门、各银行总行、各保险公司总公司等集中交纳的营业税和城市维护建设税，增值税75%部分，纳入共享范围的企业所得税60%部分，未纳入共享范围的中央企业所得税、中央企业上交的利润，个人所得税60%部分，车辆购置税，船舶吨税，证券交易印花税97%部分，海洋石油资源税，中央非税收入等。属于地方财政的收入包括营业税（不含铁道部门、各银行总行、各保险公司总公司集中交纳的营业税），地方企业上交利润，城市维护建设税（不含铁道部门、各银行总行、各保险公司总公司集中交纳的部分），房产税，城镇土地使用税，土地增值税，车船税，耕地占用税，契税，烟叶税，印花税，增值税25%部分，纳入共享范围的企业所得税40%部分，个人所得税40%部分，证券交易印花税3%部分，海洋石油资源税以外的其他资源税，地方非税收入等。

中央财政支出和地方财政支出 指根据政府在经济和社会活动中的不同职责，划分中央和地方政府的责权，按照政府的责权划分确定的支出。中央财政支出包括一般公共服务，外交支出，国防支出，公共安全支出，以及中央政府调整国民经济结构、协调地区发展、实施宏观调控的支出等。地方财政支出包括一般公共服务，公共安全支出，地方统筹的各项社会事业支出等。

Explanatory Notes on Main Statistical Indicators

Government Revenue refers to income for the government finance through participating in the distribution of social products. It is the financial guarantee to ensure government functioning. The contents of government revenue include the following main items:

(1)Tax revenue, including business tax, corporate income tax, corporate income tax refund ,individual income tax, resource tax, city maintenance and construct tax, house property tax, stamp tax, urban land use tax, land appreciation tax, tax on vehicles and boat operation, ship tonnage tax, vehicle purchase tax, tariffs, farm land occupation tax, deed tax, and tobacco leaf tax, etc.

(2) Non-tax revenue, including special program receipts, charge of administrative and institutional units, penalty receipts ,state-owned capital operating income,State-owned resources (assets) compensation for the use of incomeand others non-tax receipts.

Government Expenditure refers to the distribution and use of the funds which the government finance has raised, so as to meet the needs of economic construction and various causes. It includes the following main items:

(1) Expenditure for general public services: It refers to the spending on the basic public management and services which provided by governments, including the expense on affairs of People' s Congress, affairs of People' s Political Consultative Conference, affairs of government general office and relative institutions, affairs of development and reform, affairs of statistics, affairs of finance, affairs of taxation, affairs of audit, affairs of customs, affairs of human resources and social security, affairs of discipline inspection and supervision, affairs of population and family planning, affairs of commerce and trade, affairs of intellectual property, affairs of administration for industry and commerce, affairs of land and resources, affairs of oceanic administration, affairs of surveying and mapping, affairs of earthquake, ethnic affairs, religious affairs, affairs of Hong Kong, Macao, Taiwan, and Overseas Chinese, affairs of archives administration, affairs of Chinese Communist Party, affairs of democratic parties and federation of industry and commerce, affairs of mass organization, and affairs of lottery, etc.

(2) Expenditure for foreign affairs: It refers to the spending of government on foreign affairs, including the expense on administration of foreign affairs, missions overseas, external assistance, international organizations, foreign cooperation and communication, surveying and joint inspection on borderline, etc.

(3) Expenditure for national defense: It refers to the spending of government on national defense, including the expense on active force, scientific research on national defense, special projects, mobilization of national defense, etc.

(4) Expenditure for public security: It refers to the spending of government on maintaining social and public security, including the expense on armed police force, public security, state security, prosecution, courts, justice, prison, labor education and rehabilitation, protection of state secrecy, anti-smuggling police, etc.

(5) Expenditure for education: It refers to the spending of government on education, including the expense on the administration of education, pre-primary education, regular vocational school education, adult education,radio and television education, student abroad education, special education, education and training,education surtax arrangementsspending, etc.

(6) Expenditure for science and technology: It refers to the spending of government on science and technology (S&T), including the expense on the administration of S&T, basic research, applied research, research and development, conditions and services of S&T, popularization of social science, science and technology, exchanges and cooperation of S&T, etc.

(7) Expenditure for culture, sport and media: It refers to the spending of government on culture, cultural heritage, sports, radio, film, television, press and publication, etc.

(8) Expenditure for social safety net and employment effort: It refers to the spending of government on social safety net and employment, including the expense on administration of social safety net and employment, civil affairs, budgetary subsidy on the social insurance funds, subsidy on National Social Security Fund, retirees of administrative units and institutions, subsidy on enterprise reform, subsidy on

employment effort, pension, placement of ex-serviceman, social welfare, the handicapped undertakings, the system of cost of living allowances for urban residents, other urban social relief, rural social relief, living relief of natural disasters, affairs of Red Cross Society, etc.

(9) Expenditure for medical health care and birth control planning: It refers to gov ernment spending on health care, including health management services, public hospitals, primary health care institutions, public health, health care, the pharmaceutical, food and drug supervision and manangement, population and family planning affairs.

(10) Expenditure for energy saving: It refers to the government energy-saving and environmental protection expenditures, including environmental management services, environmental monitoring and surveillance, pollution control, ecological protection, natural forest protection project, forest, desert sand control, pasture, grassland of cultivated farmland, energy conservation and utilization expenditure pollution reduction, renewable energy and comprehensive utilization of resources, etc.

(11) Expenditure for urban and rural community affairs: It refers to the spending of government on urban and rural community affairs, including the expense on administration of urban and rural community, planning and management of urban and rural community, public facilities of urban and rural community, housing of urban and rural community, sanitation of urban and rural community, management and supervision on the construction market, etc.

(12) Expenditure for agriculture, forestry and water conservancy: It refers to the spending of government on agriculture, forestry and water conservancy, including the expense on agriculture, forestry, water conservancy, South-to-North Water Diversion Project, poverty alleviation, agricultural comprehensive development, comprehensive agricultural reform, promoting financial support for agriculture, etc.

(13) Expenditure for transportation: It refers to the spending of government on transportation and postal services, including the expense on road transport, sea transport, rail transport, civil aviation transportation, oil price reform subsidies for transportation, postal services, vehicle purchase tax, etc.

(14) Expenditure for exploration of the power of information: It refers to the spending on exploration, manufacturing, construction, electricity and other aspects of information, including resource exploration and development, manufacturing, construction, electricity regulation, industry and information industry regulation, safety supervision, the state-owned assets supervision and support of small and medium enterprise development and management, etc.

(15) Expenditure for business services: It refers to government spending on commercial aspects of services, including commercial distribution business, tourism management and services, foreign development services, etc.

(16) Expenditure for financial: It refers to government spending on financial aspects, including administrative of financial sector, financial sector supervision, financial development, financial control, etc.

(17) Expenditure for assistance to other parts: It refers to the various types of assistance to other regions, financial donations, donors, government expenditure and management arrangements, etc.

(18) Expenditure for Land and Marine Meteorology: It refers to government spending on land resources, marine, mapping, seismic, weather and other aspects of public service undertakings, etc.

(19) Expenditure for housing security: It refers to government spending on housing, including affordable housing projects, housing reform, urban and rural communities housing, etc.

(20) Expenditure for Grain and Oil stockpiles: It refers to government spending on supplies of grain and oil reserves, including grain and oil services, supplies services, energy reserves, grain and oil reserves, reserves of other important commodities, etc.

(21) Expenditure for Treasury debt service: It refers to the national debt principal, interest expenses, and other aspects of the issue, etc.

(22) Other expenditure:It refers to other government spending cannot be divided into the above functions subjects.

Revenue of the Central Government and Revenue of the Local Governments refers to the revenue collected by the Central Government and that by the local governments as defined by the decentralized taxation system. In accordance with this system, the revenue of the Central Government includes tariff, VAT and consumption tax from imports, VAT and consumption tax rebate for exports, consumption tax, business tax and city maintenance and construct tax from the Ministry of Railways, head offices of banks, head offices of insurance company, which arc handed over to the government in a centralized way, 75% of the value added tax, 60% the share part of the corporate income tax, unshared part of corporate income tax of the central enterprises, profit handed in by the central enterprises, 60% of individual income tax, vehicle purchase tax, ship tonnage tax, 97% of stamp tax on securities transactions, resource tax on the offshore petroleum resources. The revenue of the local governments includes business tax (excluding the part of the Ministry of Railways, head offices of banks, head offices of insurance company, which are handed over to the government in a centralized way), profit handed in by the local enterprises, city maintenance and construct tax (excluding the part of the Ministry of Railways, head offices of banks, head offices of insurance company, which are handed over to the government in a centralized way), house property tax, urban land use tax, land appreciation tax, tax on vehicles and boat operation, farm land occupation tax, deed tax, and tobacco leaf tax, stamp tax, 25% of the value added tax, 40% the share part of the corporate income tax, 40% of individual income tax, 3% of stamp tax on securities transactions, resource tax other than the tax on offshore petroleum resources, local non-tax revenue, etc.

Expenditure of the Central Government and Expenditure of the Local Governments according to the different functions of the Central Government and local governments in economic and social activities, the rights of affairs administration are demarcated between those of the Central Government and those of local governments; and the classification of the expenditure between the Central Government and local governments are made on the basis of the classification of the rights of affairs administration between them. The expenditure of the Central Government includes the expenditure for general public services, expenditure for foreign affairs, expenditure for public security, and the expenditure of the Central Government for adjusting the national economic structure; coordinating the development among different regions; and exercising macroeconomic regulation. The expenditure of the local governments includes mainly the expenditure for general public services, expenditure for public security, and expenditures for social development which are planned by local governments, etc.

7 物价指数

PRICE INDICES

资料整理：周　文　王　晶　王　茹
Data management:Zhou Wen Wang Jing Wang Ru
数据审核：刘　青　祝立新　党　军　雷麦鸽
Data audit：Liu Qing Zhu Lixin Dang Jun Lei Maige

第七部分　物价指数

一、简要说明

本章资料主要包括居民消费、商品零售、工业生产者出厂、工业生产者购进、房地产销售以及固定资产投资等价格指数，由国家统计局西安调查队提供。

二、主要指标

商品零售价格总指数（上年=100）	99.7	比上年下降	1.0个百分点
居民消费价格总指数（上年=100）	100.7	比上年下降	0.7个百分点

7　PRICE INDICES

Ⅰ.Brief Introduction

This chapter consists of primarily data on consumer price indices, retail price indices, producer price indices for industrial products,purchasing price indices for industrial products,real estate selling, fixed asset investment,provided by Fixed Asset NBS Survey Office in Xi'an.

Ⅱ.Major Indicators

		Increase over Preceding Year
Retail Price Index(the price preceding year=100)	99.7	-1.0 percentage points
Consumer Price Index(the price preceding year=100)	100.7	-0.7 percentage points

7-1 主要年份各种价格指数

Price Indices in Representative Years

(以上年价格为100) (the price of preceding year= 100)

年 份 Year	居民消费价格指数 Consumer Price Index	商品零售价格指数 Retail Price Index	工业生产者出厂价格指数 Producer Price Indiees (PPI) for Industrial Producers	工业生产者购进价格指数 Industrial Purchasing Indices （IPI） for Industrial Producers	固定资产投资价格指数 Price Index for Investment in Fixed Assets
1980	108.7	109.3			
1981	102.4	102.7			
1982	100.9	101.0			
1983	102.6	102.0			
1984	104.7	104.8			
1985	109.7	109.3			
1986	108.5	107.4			
1987	110.6	111.4			
1988	122.8	123.2			
1989	118.3	117.8			
1990	102.5	100.9			
1991	109.4	108.3			
1992	112.2	112.4			
1993	117.2	112.8	102.5	104.3	
1994	128.5	126.2	132.2	115.0	
1995	117.0	114.6	110.8	113.1	
1996	110.9	107.9	100.7	103.8	
1997	106.0	101.5	98.6	102.5	
1998	97.9	95.5	94.4	97.5	
1999	96.8	97.4	97.5	96.9	100.8
2000	100.2	98.7	99.4	102.4	102.1
2001	99.9	98.9	99.3	101.0	101.3
2002	98.6	98.5	98.2	98.4	101.2
2003	100.5	100.0	101.5	105.3	102.4
2004	102.3	101.9	102.7	110.4	103.3
2005	100.3	99.7	103.9	109.6	102.4
2006	101.6	101.5	103.2	106.1	102.0
2007	104.7	103.7	101.9	106.2	103.5
2008	106.0	105.4	103.7	108.5	110.5
2009	99.7	99.5	99.9	100.7	97.9
2010	103.5	102.7	102.3	106.3	103.8
2011	105.6	104.4	102.5	108.8	105.4
2012	102.8	102.3	100.5	97.2	101.9
2013	102.7	101.7	99.5	97.2	100.8
2014	101.4	100.7	99.5	99.5	100.8
2015	100.7	99.7	98.5	94.5	97.9

注：本表数据来源国家统计局西安调查队。

7–2 居民消费价格指数（2015年）

Residents Consumer Price Indices（2015）

(以上年价格为100) (the price of preceding year=100)

指 标	Item	2015
居民价格消费总指数	**Consumer Price Index**	**100.7**
非食品价格指数	Non-foodstuff Price Index	100.8
服务项目价格指数	Price Index of Service	101.0
工业品价格指数	Ex-factory Price Indices of Industrial Products	100.7
扣除食品烟酒和能源价格指数	Price Index with Food,Tobacco,Liquor and Energy Excluded	101.1
扣除鲜菜鲜果总指数	Price Index with Fresh Vegetables and Fruits Excluded	101.1
消费品价格指数	Price Index of Consumer Goods	100.6
一、食品	**Food**	**100.5**
1. 粮食	Grain	104.5
2. 淀粉及制品	Starches and Processed Products	93.7
3. 干豆类及豆制品	Beans and Bean Products	103.7
4. 油脂	Oil or Fat	96.4
5. 肉禽及其制品	Meat,Poultry and Processed Products	105.3
6. 蛋	Eggs	94.6
7. 水产品	Aquatic Products	100.6
8. 菜	Vegetables	96.4
9. 调味品	Flavouring	106.6
10. 糖	Carbohydrate	101.7
11. 茶及饮料	Tea and Beverages	103.0
12. 干鲜瓜果	Dried and Fresh Melons and Fruits	93.6
13. 糕点饼干面包	Cake,Biscuit and Bread	101.5
14. 液体乳及乳制品	Milk and Its Product	100.0
15. 在外用膳食品	Dining Out	101.0
16. 其他食品	Other Food	98.3
二、烟酒	**Tobacco and Liquor**	**102.6**
1. 烟草	Tobacco	103.3
2. 酒	Liquor	101.3
三、衣着	**Clothing**	**103.3**
1. 服装	Garments	101.3
2. 衣着材料	Clothing Material	100.0
3. 鞋袜帽	Footgear and Hats	109.6
4. 衣着加工服务费	Clothing Manufacturing Services	104.0

注：本表数据来源国家统计局西安调查队。

7-2 续表 continued

(以上年价格为100) (the price of preceding year= 100)

指 标	Item	2015
四、家庭设备用品及维修服务	**Household facilities,Articles and Services**	**99.7**
1. 耐用消费品	Durable Consumer Goods	97.6
2. 室内装饰品	Interior Decorations	99.6
3. 床上用品	Bed Articles	97.8
4. 家庭日用杂品	Daily Use Household Articles	101.9
5. 家庭服务及加工维修服务	Household Service and Maintenance Renovation	101.6
五、医疗保健和个人用品	**Health Care and Personal Articles**	**102.2**
1. 医疗保健	Health Care	103.0
(1)医疗器具及用品	Medical Instrument Articles	105.2
(2)中药材及中成药	Traditional Chinese Medicine	100.9
(3)西药	Western Medicine	107.3
(4)保健器具及用品	Health Care Appliances and Articles	103.3
(5)医疗保健服务	Health Care Services	100.0
2. 个人用品及服务	Personal Articles and Services	100.5
六、交通和通信	**Transportation and Communication**	**98.8**
1. 交通	Transportation	98.8
(1)交通工具	Transportation Facility	94.7
(2)车用燃料及零配件	Fuels and Parts	83.8
(3)车辆使用及维修费	Fees for Vehicles Use and Maintenance	104.6
(4)市区公共交通费	Incity Traffic Fare	110.9
(5)城市间交通费	Intercity Traffic Fare	96.5
2. 通信	Communication	98.8
(1)通信工具	Telecommunication Facility	93.2
(2)通信服务	Telecommunication Service	99.2
七、娱乐教育文化用品及服务	**Recreation,Education and Culture Articles**	**101.3**
1. 文娱用耐用消费品及服务	Durable Consumer Goods for Cultural and Recreational Use and Services	98.4
2. 教育	Education	103.9
3. 文化娱乐用品	Cultural and Recreational Articles	101.7
4. 旅游	Touring	93.2
八、居住	**Residence**	**99.7**
1. 建房及装修材料	Building and Building Decoration Materials	98.9
2. 住房租金	Rental Housing	98.0
3. 自有住房	Private Housing	100.1
4. 水、电、燃料	Water, Electricity and Fuels	99.9

7-3 商品零售价格指数（2015年）

Retail Price Indices（2015）

(以上年价格为100)　　(the price of preceding year= 100)

指　标	Item	2015
商品零售价格总指数	**Retail Price Indices**	**99.7**
一、食品	**Food**	**100.6**
1. 粮食	Grain	104.1
2. 淀粉及制品	Starches and Processed Products	93.7
3. 干豆类及豆制品	Beans and Bean Products	103.7
4. 油脂	Oil or Fat	96.4
5. 肉禽及其制品	Meat,Poultry and Processed Products	105.6
6. 蛋	Eggs	94.4
7. 水产品	Aquatic Products	100.9
8. 菜	Vegetables	96.4
9. 调味品	Flavouring	105.5
10. 糖	Carbohydrate	101.4
11. 干鲜瓜果	Dried and Fresh Melons and Fruits	93.6
12. 糕点饼干面包	Cake,Biscuit and Bread	101.2
13. 液体乳及乳制品	Milk and Its Product	100.0
14. 在外用膳食品	Dining Out	101.2
15. 其他食品	Other Food and Manufacturing Services	98.3
二、饮料、烟酒	**Beverages,Tobacco and Liquor**	**103.5**
1. 茶及饮料	Tea and Beverages	105.1
2. 烟草	Tobacco	102.9
3. 酒	Liquor	101.3
三、服装、鞋帽	**Garments,Shoes and Hats**	**103.4**
1. 服装	Garments	101.2
2. 鞋袜帽	Footgear and Hats	110.0
3. 其他	Others	96.3
四、纺织品	**Textiles**	**98.5**
1. 衣着材料	Cotton Cloth	100.0
2. 床上用品	Blend Cloth	97.8
五、家用电器及音像器材	**Household Appliances,Music and Video Equipment**	**95.9**
1. 家庭设备	Household facility	96.2
2. 文娱用耐用消费品	Durable Consumer Goods on Cultural and Recreational Use	94.2
3. 专业音像器材	Music and Video Equipment	99.2

注：本表数据来源国家统计局西安调查队。

7-3 续表 continued

(以上年价格为100) (the price of preceding year= 100)

指　标	Item	2015
六、文化办公用品	**Cultural and Office Appliances**	**103.2**
七、日用品	**Articles for Daily Use**	**100.7**
1. 日用百货	General Merchandise for Daily Use	98.7
2. 日用杂品	Miscellaneous for Daily Use	103.8
3. 洗涤用品	Daily Use Articles For Washing	104.1
4. 其他日用品	Other Daily Articles	98.3
八、体育娱乐用品	**Sports and Recreation Articles**	**101.5**
1. 体育用品	Sports Goods	101.2
2. 娱乐用品	Receration Goods	101.7
九、交通、通信用品	**Transportation and Communication Goods**	**95.6**
1. 交通运输机械	Transportation Machinery	95.6
2. 通信器材	Communication Machinery	95.8
十、家具	**Furniture**	**99.7**
十一、化妆品	**Cosmetics**	**101.0**
十二、金银珠宝	**Gold,Silver and Jewelry**	**86.3**
十三、中西药品及医疗保健用品	**Traditional Chinese and Western Medicines And Health Care Articles**	**104.6**
1. 医疗器具及用品	Medical Apparatus and Article	105.2
2. 中药材及中成药	Traditional Chinese Medicinal Materials and Medicines	100.7
3. 西药	Western Medicine	106.7
4. 保健器具及用品	Health Care Apparatus and Article	103.1
十四、书报杂志及电子出版物	**Books,Newspapers,Magazines and Electronic Publications**	**102.1**
1. 教材及参考书	Teaching Materials and Reference Books	99.7
2. 书报杂志	Books, Newspapers and Magazines	104.2
3. 电子音像制品	Electronic Audio-video Products	105.6
十五、燃料	**Fuel**	**90.8**
1、煤炭及制品	Coal and Its Products	94.9
2、石油及制品	Oil and Its Products	90.4
十六、建筑材料及五金电料	**Building Materials and Hardware**	**97.5**
1. 建筑装潢材料	Building Decoration Materials	97.1
2. 五金电料	Hardware	99.2

7-4 主要年份工业生产者出厂价格指数

(上年价格=100)

类 别	Classify	1997	1998	1999	2000	2001
工业生产者出厂价格指数	**Producer Price Index**	**98.6**	**94.4**	**97.5**	**99.4**	**99.3**
按轻重工业分	Grouped by Light Industry and Heavy Industry					
轻工业	Light Industry	98.2	91.1	95.9	97.8	99.6
以农产品为原料	Using Farm Products as Raw Materials	99.2	89.5	95.2	99.2	99.0
以非农产品为原料	Using Non-farm Products as Raw Materials	96.8	93.4	97.0	95.5	100.6
重工业	Heavy Industry	99.0	97.3	98.9	100.8	99.2
采掘	Mining & Quarrying		104.1	101.5	97.5	94.8
原料	Raw Materials	101.0	100.7	102.3	107.7	101.1
加工	Processing	97.9	95.6	98.0	98.4	98.5
按生产生活资料分	by means of production and livelihood					
生产资料	Means of Production	99.6	96.6	98.3	100.5	99.1
采掘	Mining & Quarrying		104.1	101.5	97.5	94.8
原料	Raw Materials	100.9	100.6	100.2	106.4	101.1
加工	Processing	98.9	94.7	97.6	98.7	98.5
生活资料	Consumer Goods	97.0	91.4	96.5	97.3	99.9
食品	Food	108.2	97.8	95.8	94.4	99.6
衣着	Clothing	93.0	83.9	95.2	101.6	99.4
一般日用品	Articles for Daily Use	91.6	95.1	97.6	96.9	101.9
耐用消费品	Durable Consumer Goods	99.7	95.4	98.0	95.9	97.0
按工业部门分	Grouped by Industrial Sector					
1. 冶金工业	Metallurgical Industry	99.2	97.5	91.2	98.2	97.2
2. 电力工业	Power Industry	111.3	111.2	109.3	109.6	102.4
3. 煤炭及炼焦工业	Coal and Coking Industry	98.9	98.5	96.3	100.5	110.3
4. 石油工业	Petroleum Industry			107.1	134.2	96.6
5. 化学工业	Chemical Industry	91.8	92.9	96.6	96.7	100.5
6. 机械工业	Machine Manufacturing Industry	98.8	94.6	98.1	98.0	98.3
7. 建筑材料工业	Building Materials Industry	98.2	99.3	96.7	98.5	100.6
8. 森林工业	Timber Industry	107.6	104.5	97.9	98.9	98.1
9. 食品工业	Food Industry	106.8	95.3	95.5	94.3	99.8
10. 纺织工业	Textiles Industry	94.3	82.6	93.7	103.4	97.5
11. 缝纫工业	Tailoring Industry	100.1	97.3	99.1	103.5	100.0
12. 皮革工业	Leather Industry	91.2	96.8	98.0	99.2	101.0
13. 造纸工业	Paper Industry			95.3	96.7	102.3
14. 文教艺术用品工业	Cultural,Educational & Handicrafts Articles			96.7	96.4	101.1
15. 其它工业	Other Industry	109.5	109.2	98.9	104.8	107.1

注：本表数据来源国家统计局西安调查队。

Producer Price Indices (PPI) for Industrial Producers in Representative Years

(the price of preceding year= 100)

2002	2003	2004	2005	2006	2007	2008	2009	2010	2011	2012	2013	2014	2015
98.2	**101.5**	**102.7**	**103.9**	**103.2**	**101.9**	**103.7**	**99.9**	**102.3**	**102.5**	**100.5**	**99.5**	**99.5**	**98.5**
98.4	101.3	103.4	99.9	100.2	101.8	103.7	100.6	102.5	107.0	100.4	100.7	100.9	100.3
98.4	104.5	108.7	97.3	100.1	103.3	106.0	98.9	104.0	109.3	100.3	101.0	100.8	99.1
98.6	99.9	100.8	101.2	100.2	100.8	102.1	101.8	101.4	100.9	100.5	99.9	101.3	103.3
98.2	101.6	101.9	107.9	105.5	101.9	103.8	99.3	102.2	101.6	100.5	99.2	99.2	98.2
101.3	103.4	140.5	107.9	100.6	111.6	122.3	90.0	150.2	102.6	101.8	100.6	100.6	99.8
101.3	111.2	109.0	114.2	111.8	104.9	110.8	99.5	108.9	111.2	108.6	95.1	97.6	90.4
97.7	100.1	100.6	106.7	104.2	101.2	101.9	99.4	100.8	100.1	99.2	99.9	99.5	99.3
98.0	101.8	102.7	105.3	104.2	101.3	103.4	99.3	102.2	101.9	100.3	99.2	99.5	98.3
101.3	103.4	140.5	107.9	100.6	111.6	122.3	90.0	150.2	102.6	101.8	100.6	100.6	99.8
101.0	108.1	106.6	111.3	111.6	104.8	110.2	99.7	109.0	111.3	108.7	95.2	97.7	90.5
97.4	100.9	102.0	104.3	103.0	100.6	102.0	99.3	101.0	100.3	98.9	99.9	99.7	99.6
99.1	100.5	102.5	100.4	100.4	103.5	104.7	101.4	102.5	104.5	100.8	100.4	99.7	99.4
101.2	101.0	103.6	100.3	100.4	105.3	106.6	100.3	103.3	109.5	101.6	100.9	101.2	100.1
100.8	99.4	102.7	102.0	103.3	104.6	105.1	102.7	101.2	111.9	99.4	100.4	99.1	96.0
97.9	101.2	101.2	101.3	100.8	100.1	102.7	102.6	101.2	101.5	101.5	99.1	101.3	102.1
98.1	97.2	98.3	99.1	99.4	100.7	100.7	103.9	101.9	99.5	99.0	100.9	95.9	95.6
98.7	103.8	107.1	103.9	106.5	103.2	104.8	92.0	105.8	116.3	100.7	97.5	97.5	96.5
100.0	103.2	104.1	110.6	107.9	105.5	110.0	109.0	101.2	104.7	111.2	100.6	99.4	98.9
106.7	136.8	131.4	97.1	95.4	106.8	104.8	101.7	110.6	109.3	101.5	100.0	100.0	100.0
100.7	118.6	110.5	121.7	117.6	104.8	115.6	96.7	114.2	108.4	108.2	89.7	97.2	81.0
99.2	100.2	100.8	103.2	100.8	101.1	104.1	102.6	100.8	104.2	100.3	99.6	100.9	100.6
97.6	99.8	100.6	104.9	103.4	101.0	101.7	99.9	100.9	99.5	99.0	100.0	99.4	99.5
99.6	99.7	100.0	98.6	98.9	98.9	101.8	101.9	99.9	100.6	99.6	99.3	99.1	99.5
98.9	100.1	100.2	101.6	101.6	101.1	101.1	101.1	101.7	105.2	103.2	103.4	101.6	91.7
101.1	102.8	107.5	98.3	99.0	106.1	109.3	98.3	104.3	110.1	101.7	101.0	101.3	99.8
94.9	117.3	119.1	89.9	102.4	98.4	99.7	97.5	108.9	107.2	88.7	103.9	99.3	96.0
101.1	100.2	103.6	100.8	103.5	104.6	105.1	102.6	101.3	113.4	99.4	100.4	99.0	93.4
101.8	98.7	99.6	101.2	100.0	99.0	99.6	99.7	99.6	98.0	99.9	99.9	100.0	118.9
95.0	96.9	100.2	101.2	100.0	100.1	104.5	98.4	100.4	103.4	99.2	98.4	98.1	98.1
103.4	97.5	96.5	98.1	100.1	99.1	99.2	102.2	99.9	100.7	106.0	97.5	100.0	102.6
99.4	103.3	105.0	103.4	105.7	111.4	104.3	99.7	100.5	104.3	101.2	99.6	100.0	100.0

7-5 主要年份工业生产者购进价格指数

Industrial Purchasing Indices (IPI) for Industrial Producers in Representative Years

(上年价格=100) (the price of preceding year= 100)

指 标	Item	2000	2001	2002	2003	2004	2005	2006	2007
工业生产者购进价格指数	**Industrial Producer Price Index**	**102.4**	**101.0**	**98.4**	**105.3**	**110.4**	**109.6**	**106.1**	**106.2**
(一)燃料、动力类	Fuel and Power	105.0	101.8	100.9	105.7	109.4	123.5	112.6	107.0
(二)黑色金属材料类	Ferrous Metals	102.7	102.1	98.5	107.4	117.4	107.6	99.2	104.8
#钢材	Steel	103.4	102.4	97.9	106.0	114.8	107.5	98.5	104.9
(三)有色金属材料和电线类	Non-ferrous Metals and Electric Wires	105.2	95.5	96.8	105.8	114.1	107.8	116.5	110.7
(四)化工原料类	Raw Chemical Materials	104.6	102.5	97.9	102.4	106.3	106.1	101.6	105.6
(五)木材及纸浆类	Timber and Paper Pulp	101.2	102.8	99.4	101.2	100.3	108.2	111.7	105.9
(六)建筑材料及非金属矿类	Building Materials and Non-metal ores	100.3	99.7	98.6	99.6	110.4	99.3	100.7	104.0
(七)其它工业原材料及半成品类	Other Industrial Raw Materials and Semi-Products	98.8	100.8	98.9	102.5	111.2	106.1	104.3	108.8
(八)农副产品类	Agricultural Products	100.4	102.8	98.2	113.7	112.7	100.9	107.2	107.2
(九)纺织原料类	Textile Materials	98.0	96.8	90.6	103.4	103.9	97.6	101.5	100.5

注：本表数据来源国家统计局西安调查队。

7-5 续表 continued

(上年价格=100) (the price of preceding year= 100)

指 标	Item	2008	2009	2010	2011	2012	2013	2014	2015
工业生产者购进价格指数	**Industrial Producer Price Index**	**108.5**	**100.7**	**106.3**	**108.8**	**97.2**	**97.2**	**99.5**	**94.5**
(一)燃料、动力类	Fuel and Power	109.8	105.1	108.6	113.5	102.3	96.8	98.2	95.3
(二)黑色金属材料类	Ferrous Metals	111.3	99.2	103.1	102.9	93.4	98.0	97.9	91.6
#钢材	Steel	111.7	98.7	103.5	102.9	93.3	98.0	97.9	91.5
(三)有色金属材料和电线类	Non-ferrous Metals and Electric Wires	99.1	93.9	113.6	118.9	93.0	94.5	96.6	96.3
(四)化工原料类	Raw Chemical Materials	111.4	95.0	103.9	108.1	87.7	90.8	104.6	91.3
(五)木材及纸浆类	Timber and Paper Pulp	106.5	102.6	101.1	105.4	100.9	99.2	100.7	101.0
(六)建筑材料及非金属矿类	Building Materials and Non-metal ores	104.8	106.8	102.1	102.9	97.4	102.2	101.1	98.1
(七)其它工业原材料及半成品类	Other Industrial Raw Materials and Semi-Products	110.6	101.4	108.1	109.4	100.3	98.9	100.9	99.1
(八)农副产品类	Agricultural Products	108.9	99.6	106.5	107.4	103.4	100.5	98.8	92.8
(九)纺织原料类	Textile Materials	99.8	97.6	104.6	107.0	89.1	97.6	99.3	89.7

7-6 住宅销售价格指数（2015年）

Selling Price Indices of Residential Buildings（2015）

(上年价格=100)　　(the price of preceding year= 100)

指　标	Item	2015
新建住宅	**Newly built residential buildings**	**96.2**
一、保障性住房	guaranteed house	
二、新建商品住宅	New commodity residential house	95.8
（一）90平方米及以下	90 square meters and less	95.7
（二）90-144平方米	90-144 square metre	96.5
（三）144平方米以上	144 square meters and more	94.5
二手住宅	**used/second hand residential buildings**	**93.3**
一、90平方米及以下	90 square meters and the following	94.0
二、90-144平方米	90-144 square metre	92.9
三、144平方米以上	144 square meters and more	93.4

注：本表数据来源国家统计局西安调查队。

7-7 主要年份固定资产投资价格指数

Price Indices for Investment in Fixcd Assets in Representative Years

(上年价格=100)　　(the price of preceding year= 100)

指　标	Item	2000	2004	2005	2006	2007	2008	2009	2010	2011	2012	2013	2014	2015
固定资产投资价格指数	**Price Indices for Investment in Fixed Assets**	**102.1**	**103.3**	**102.4**	**102.0**	**103.5**	**110.5**	**97.9**	**103.8**	**105.4**	**101.9**	**100.8**	**100.8**	**97.9**
一、建筑安装工程	**Construction and Installation Engineering**	**103.9**	**104.6**	**102.3**	**102.6**	**104.9**	**114.9**	**97.1**	**105.5**	**107.2**	**102.6**	**101.0**	**100.8**	**97.0**
1. 材料费	Material Costs	104.4	105.1	101.4	101.1	104.3	117.6	94.1	105.2	106.3	99.0	97.5	98.1	93.3
钢材	Steel	109.0	108.6	101.4	97.0	104.5	127.2	86.7	106.4	107.9	94.7	92.9	93.7	84.6
木材	Wood	103.6	102.2	101.9	101.9	102.5	106.9	101.8	105.0	104.5	104.9	104.5	105.2	107.6
水泥	Cement	101.5	101.8	100.1	101.1	102.7	107.8	109.4	103.8	100.9	100.3	101.4	100.4	97.3
地方材料	Local Materials	101.6	102.4	101.4	102.6	103.5	108.5	103.8	104.7	105.8	102.0	102.4	102.0	100.4
化工材料	Chemical Materials	107.1	104.8	104.6	113.6	113.0	110.0	95.5	104.5	105.4	104.2	102.5	100.9	95.6
电料	Electrical Materials and Sppliances	100.6	101.3	100.9	107.5	110.4	110.1	102.6	104.1	104.1	101.5	100.9	99.9	97.8
其他材料	Other Materials	103.4	101.9	101.7	103.2	107.4	108.5	101.6	102.7	104.5	102.7	101.6	100.7	100.4
2. 人工费	Labor Costs	103.6	105.2	106.9	108.3	109.1	114.5	110.6	111.9	114.0	112.9	109.7	108.8	105.7
3. 机械使用费	Mechanical Service Costs	103.9	102.8	102.5	104.5	104.5	106.5	99.3	103.3	106.7	104.8	104.0	102.2	100.8
二、设备、工器具购置	**Purchase of Equipment and Instruments**	97.9	100.5	104.5	100.8	100.7	101.0	98.6	100.0	100.6	99.1	99.5	99.9	99.1
三、其他费用	**Others**	**100.0**	**100.6**	**100.5**	**100.5**	**100.6**	**101.9**	**100.9**	**100.8**	**102.8**	**102.7**	**101.9**	**101.8**	**100.4**

注：本表数据来源国家统计局西安调查队。

主 要 统 计 指 标 解 释

居民消费价格指数 是反映一定时期内城乡居民所购买的生活消费品和服务项目价格变动趋势和程度的相对数，是对城市居民消费价格指数和农村居民消费价格指数进行综合汇总计算的结果。通过该指数可以观察和分析消费品的零售价格和服务项目价格变动对城乡居民实际生活费支出的影响程度。

商品零售价格指数 是反映一定时期内城乡商品零售价格变动趋势和程度的相对数。商品零售价格的变动与国家的财政收入、市场供需的平衡、消费与积累的比例关系有关。因此，该指数可以从一个侧面对上述经济活动进行观察和分析。

工业生产者价格指数 是反映工业产品价格变化趋势和变动幅度的统计指标，是工业企业的产品价格在不同的时间和空间条件下平均变动的相对数。工业生产者价格包括工业品第一次出售时的出厂价格和企业作为中间投入的原材料、燃料、动力购进价格，简称工业生产者出厂价格和工业生产者购进价格。工业生产者价格指数是进行国民经济核算和经济管理的主要依据。

固定资产投资价格指数 是反映一定时期内固定资产投资品和取费项目价格的变动趋势和变动幅度的相对数。固定资产投资额是由建筑安装工程投资完成额、设备工器具购置投资完成额和其他费用投资完成额三部分组成的。编制固定资产投资价格指数应首先分别编制上述三部分投资的价格指数，然后采用加权算术平均法求出固定资产投资价格总指数。

该指数可以准确地反映固定资产投资中涉及的各类投资品和取费项目价格变动趋势和变动幅度，消除按现价计算的固定资产投资指标中的价格变动因素，真实地反映固定资产投资的规模、速度、结构和效益，为国家科学地制定、检查固定资产投资计划和进行国民经济核算提供科学的、可靠的依据。

Explanatory Notes on Main Statistical Indicators

Consumer Price Indices reflect the trend and degree of changes in prices of consumer goods and services purchased by urban and rural households during a given period. They are obtained by combining Consumer Price Indices of Urban Household and Consumer Price Indices of Rural Household. The Indices enable the observation and analysis of the degree of impact of the changes in the prices of retailed goods and services on the actual living expenses of urban and rural residents.

Retail Price Indices reflect the trend and degree of change in retail prices of commodities during a given period. The change in retail prices of commodities is related to government revenue, the equilibrium of market supply and demand, and the ratio of consumption to accumulation. Therefore, the retail price indices are useful from an oblique perspective for observing and analyzing the changes of the above economic activities.

Industrial Producer Price Index refelct the trend and degree of changes of industrial product price, which is the relative number of average change prices of industrial enterprises products under different condition of time and space. Including the first time of sale prices of industrial products and the price of raw materials, fuel and power as intermediate inputs, be called for short of PPI and IPI.

Industrial producer price Index is an important basis for national accounts and economic manegement.

Price Indices for Investment in Fixed Assets reflect the trend and degree of changes in prices of investment goods and projects in fixed assets during a given period. The investment in fixed assets consists of three components, namely the investment in construction and installation, the investment in purchases of equipment and instrument, and the investment in other items. Price indices for investment in fixed assets are calculated as the weighted arithmetic mean of the price indices for the three components of investment in fixed assets.

Removing the factor of price change in the aggregates of investment at current prices, this indicator shows the changes in the prices of commodities and fees involved in the investment of fixed assets, and can be used to observe the actual size, growth, structure, and efficiency of investment in fixed assets and provides reliable and scientific data for government planning and further improving the current national accounting .

8 人民生活

PEOPLE´S LIVELIHOOD

资料整理：安海军　赵兰莉　严孟飞
Data management：An Haijun　Zhao Lanli　Yan Mengfei
数据审核：冯军魁
Data audit：Feng Junkui

第八部分　人民生活

一、简要说明

本章资料反映我市城乡常住居民生活现状及变化情况，2015年数据为实施城乡住户调查一体化改革后的全市居民生活主要数据，由西安市统计局人口就业处提供。

二、主要指标

全体居民人均可支配收入（元）	27845	比上年增长	8.77%
城镇常住居民人均可支配收入（元）	33188	比上年增长	8.05%
城镇常住居民人均消费支出（元）	22415	比上年增长	7.28%
农村常住居民人均可支配收入（元）	14072	比上年增长	9.10%
农村常住居民人均消费支出（元）	9518	比上年增长	9.30%

8 PEOPLE'S LIVELIHOOD

Ⅰ.Brief Introduction

The data in this chapter reflected the city's urban and rural residents living situation and changes in circumstances,Data reflected the implementation of the city's residents in 2015 integrated household survey reformed life.The data is provided by Population and Employment office of the Xi'an Bureau of Statistics.

Ⅱ.Major Indicators

		Increase over Preceding Year
per capita disposable income of all residents(yuan)	27845	8.77%
per capita disposable income of Urban residents (yuan)	33188	8.05%
Per capita consumption expenditure of urban residents (yuan)	22415	7.28%
Per capita disposable income of Rural residents (yuan)	14072	9.10%
Per capita consumption expenditure of Rural residents(yuan)	9518	9.30%

8-1 主要年份城乡居民人均收入及恩格尔系数

Per Capita Annual Income and Engel's Coefficient of Urban and Rural Households in Representative Years

年 份 Year	城镇居民家庭人均可支配收入 Per Capita Annual Disposable Income of Urban Households		农村居民家庭人均纯收入 Per Capita Annual Net Income of Rural Households		城镇居民家庭恩格尔系数（%） Engel's Coefficient of Urban Households （%）	农村居民家庭恩格尔系数（%） Engel's Coefficient of Rural Households （%）
	绝对数(元) Absoulte number (yuan)	指数 1980年=100 Index year of 1980=100	绝对数(元) Absoulte number (yuan)	指数 1978年=100 Index year of 1978=100		
1978			140			
1979						
1980	414	100.0	190	135.7	53.3	53.3
1981	446	107.7	207	147.9	52.9	53.7
1982	479	115.6	254	181.4	55.1	56.7
1983	509	122.9	245	175.0	55.1	58.4
1984	540	130.3	299	213.6	54.9	51.7
1985	719	173.5	351	250.7	49.5	48.5
1986	911	219.8	390	278.6	49.9	47.9
1987	1034	249.7	434	310.0	50.6	50.3
1988	1142	275.6	482	344.3	44.9	47.5
1989	1344	324.3	530	378.6	51.7	48.2
1990	1518	366.5	610	435.7	53.1	49.5
1991	1619	390.9	707	505.0	51.6	46.7
1992	1992	481.0	783	559.3	52.5	50.9
1993	2661	642.5	870	621.4	46.4	46.0
1994	3517	849.1	1078	770.0	45.2	50.1
1995	4153	1002.5	1353	966.4	44.7	50.3
1996	5023	1212.6	1586	1132.9	42.6	49.9
1997	5344	1290.1	1846	1318.6	40.7	49.2
1998	5670	1368.7	2052	1465.7	39.8	42.4
1999	5999	1448.3	2203	1573.6	36.3	39.1
2000	6364	1536.5	2344	1674.3	36.5	36.6
2001	6705	1618.8	2490	1778.6	34.8	33.9
2002	7184	1734.3	2641	1886.4	34.4	31.1
2003	7748	1870.7	2838	2027.1	34.8	37.6
2004	8544	2062.8	3143	2245.0	36.1	35.7
2005	9628	2324.5	3460	2471.4	37.0	36.3
2006	10905	2632.9	3808	2720.0	34.4	36.8
2007	12662	3057.0	4399	3142.1	36.6	38.2
2008	15207	3671.4	5212	3722.9	36.4	37.0
2009	18963	4578.2	6275	4482.3	32.4	35.8
2010	22244	5370.4	7750	5535.7	31.3	32.5
2011	25981	6272.6	9788	6991.4	31.3	31.9
2012	29982	7238.5	11442	8172.9	32.5	33.8
2013	33100	7991.3	12930	9235.7	32.5	33.0
2014	36100	8718.5	14462	10334.7	32.3	34.2
2015	39007	9422.0	15778	11270.0	32.7	32.2

注：2014年实施城乡住户一体化调查后，统计口径发生变化，新老口径存在差异。本表为老口径数据。

8-2 主要年份城乡居民人民币储蓄存款

Savings Deposit of Urban and Rural Households in Representative Years

单位：亿元 (100 million yuan)

年 份 Year	年末余额 Balance at Ycar-end	指数（上年＝100） Index(preccding year=100)
1978	3.72	
1979	4.85	130.4
1980	5.48	113.0
1981	6.36	116.1
1982	7.76	122.0
1983	10.02	129.1
1984	14.70	146.7
1985	16.70	113.6
1986	23.10	138.3
1987	32.13	139.1
1988	32.51	101.2
1989	45.78	140.8
1990	62.23	135.9
1991	78.64	126.4
1992	96.09	122.2
1993	124.61	129.7
1994	174.19	139.8
1995	230.63	132.4
1996	394.02	170.8
1997	358.78	91.1
1998	499.68	139.3
1999	586.40	117.4
2000	675.83	115.3
2001	800.86	118.5
2002	988.04	123.4
2003	1210.56	122.5
2004	1432.86	118.4
2005	1716.76	119.8
2006	1950.53	113.6
2007	2002.38	102.7
2008	2513.70	125.5
2009	3084.20	122.7
2010	3641.09	118.1
2011	4155.65	114.1
2012	4787.03	115.2
2013	5357.05	111.9
2014	5698.15	106.4
2015	6571.18	105.8

注：本表数据来源于人民银行西安营管部。

8-3 各区县城乡居民人均收入

Per Capita Income of Urban and Rural Households by Region

区 县	Region	城镇居民人均可支配收入 Per Capita Disposable Income of Urban Households			农村居民人均纯收入 Per Capita net Income of Rural Households		
		绝对数（元） Absoulte number(yuan)		2015年比2014年增长% Growth of 2015 than 2014 (%)	绝对数（元） Absoulte number(yuan)		2015年比2014年增长% Growth of 2015 than 2014 (%)
		2014	2015		2014	2015	
全 市	**Total**	**36100**	**39007**	**8.05**	**14462**	**15778**	**9.10**
新城区	Xincheng	37029	40014	8.06			
碑林区	Beilin	37765	40804	8.04			
莲湖区	Lianhu	37757	40802	8.07			
灞桥区	Baqiao	35147	38011	8.15	16982	18521	9.06
未央区	Weiyang	36462	39397	8.05	18364	20024	9.04
雁塔区	Yanta	38345	41428	8.04			
阎良区	Yanliang	37503	40533	8.08	17007	18572	9.20
临潼区	Lintong	29804	32197	8.03	13595	14838	9.14
长安区	Chang'an	32377	35048	8.25	14206	15502	9.12
高陵区	Gaoling	28581	30842	7.91	13615	14863	9.17
蓝田县	Lantian	23907	25834	8.06	9911	10835	9.32
周至县	Zhouzhi	24445	26427	8.11	9961	10897	9.40
户 县	Huxian	27026	29153	7.87	12218	13310	8.94

注：2014年实施城乡住户一体化调查后，统计口径发生变化，新老口径存在差异。本表为老口径数据。

8-4 全市居民家庭基本情况

Basic Conditions of All Households

指标名称	Item	2014	2015
调查户数（户）	Number of Households Surveyed (household)	2378	2382
调查户人口（人）	Residents Surveyed(person)		
平均每户常住人口	Average Household Size	3.0	3.1
平均每户劳动力人数	Average Number of Employed Persons	2.3	2.3
平均每劳动力负担人口	Average Number of Persons Supported by a Laborer	1.4	1.3
人均可支配收入（元）	Annual Per Capita Disposable Income(yuan）	25599.2	27844.9
工资性收入	Wages Income	15976.7	17210.8
经营净收入	Household Business Income	2533.7	2667.8
财产净收入	Property Income	1988.5	2220.1
转移净收入	Transfer Income	5100.3	5746.2
人均消费支出（元）	Annual Per Capita Consumption Expenditure (yuan)	17394.3	18810.2
食品烟酒	Food,Tobacco and Alcohol	5098.7	5528.3
衣着	Clothing	1539.2	1607.8
居住	Residence	3214.6	3491.1
生活用品及服务	Living Articles and Services	1248.8	1373.8
交通通信	Transport and Communication Services	2374.8	2434.7
教育文化娱乐	Recreation, Education and Culture Services	2133.0	2325.8
医疗保健	Medical and Health Care Services	1366.5	1562.3
其他用品和服务	Other Commodities and Services	418.7	486.4

8-5 全市居民家庭人均可支配收入

Per Capita Annual Disposable Income of All Households

单位：元 (yuan)

指标名称	Item	2014	2015
可支配收入	Disposable income	25599.2	27844.9
一、工资性收入	Wage income	15976.7	17210.8
（一）工资	Wage	15141.4	16147.8
（二）实物福利	Benefits in kind	108.2	81.8
（三）其他	Others	727.1	981.2
二、经营净收入	Net Income from Business	2533.7	2667.8
（一）第一产业经营净收入	Net Income from Primary Industry Business	513.3	528.8
（二）第二产业经营净收入	Net Income from Secondary Industry Business	197.6	156.1
（三）第三产业经营净收入	Net Income from Tertiary Industry Business	1822.8	1982.9
三、财产净收入	Net Income from Properties	1988.5	2220.1
#利息净收入	Net interest	98.8	40.4
红利收入	Bonus	138.7	182.9
转让承包土地经营权租金净收入	Net Rental from Transfer of Contracted Land Management Rights	25.4	49.3
出租房屋财产性收入	The Property Income by Renting House	814.9	986.5
出租机械、专利、版权等资产的收入	The Income by Renting Assets like Mechanical, Patents, Copyright ect.	32.4	19.6
四、转移净收入	Net Income from Transfer	5100.3	5746.2
（一）转移性收入	Net Income from Transfer	6257.0	7016.7
（二）转移性支出	Transfer Expenditure	1156.7	1270.5

8-6 全市居民家庭年人均消费支出

Per Capita Living Expenditure of All Households

单位：元 (yuan)

指标名称	Item	2014	2015
消费支出	**Total Living Expenditure**	**17394.3**	**18810.2**
一、食品烟酒	**Food,Tobacco and Alcohol**	**5098.7**	**5528.3**
1.食品	food	3311.2	3390.0
2.烟酒	Alcohol and tobacco	465.0	541.7
3.饮料	Drink	108.4	153.4
4.饮食服务	Catering Services	1214.1	1443.2
二、衣着	**Clothing**	**1539.2**	**1607.8**
衣类	Garments	1190.2	1203.4
鞋类	Footwear	349.0	404.4
三、居住	**Residence**	**3214.6**	**3491.1**
#租赁房房租	Rental Housing Rent	268.3	332.8
住房维修及管理	Housing Repair and Management	287.1	386.5
水电燃料及其他	Water,Electric Power Fuel and Others	927.7	886.2
四、生活用品及服务	**Living Articles and Services**	**1248.8**	**1373.8**
家具及室内装饰品	Furniture and External Decorations	204.5	279.9
家用器具	Household Appliances	331.3	285.3
家用纺织品	Household textile	119.8	114.4
家庭日用杂品	Household Articles of Daily Use	346.8	352.5
个人用品	Personal Items	213.7	283.3
家庭服务	Household Services	32.7	58.4
五、交通通信	**Transportation and Communications**	**2374.8**	**2434.7**
交通	Transportation	1580.9	1596.8
通信	Communications	793.9	837.9
六、教育文化娱乐	**Recreation, Education and Culture Services**	**2133.0**	**2325.8**
教育	Education	1090.7	1091.7
文化娱乐	Recreation	1042.3	1234.1
七、医疗保健	**Medicine and Medical Services**	**1366.5**	**1562.3**
医疗器具及药品	Medical Instruments and Medicines	533.9	635.5
医疗服务	Medical Services	832.6	926.8
八、其他用品和服务	**Others**	**418.7**	**486.4**

8-7 全市居民家庭人均购买主要商品数量

Per Capita Annual Purchases of Major Commodities of All Households

单位：千克 (kg)

指标名称	Item	2014	2015
面粉	Flour	22.9	20.5
大米	Rice	17.7	18.1
薯类	Potato	10.3	13.3
豆类	Beans	8.4	9.7
食用植物油	Edible vegetable oil	11.1	11.4
鲜菜	Fresh vegetables	80.3	87.3
猪肉	Pork	9.5	10.4
牛肉	Beef	1.5	1.5
羊肉	Lamb	0.4	0.7
鸡	Chicken	2.0	2.4
鱼类	Fish	2.7	3.2
虾类	Shrimp	0.5	0.6
鲜蛋	Eggs	7.8	9.8
鲜奶	Milk	11.8	14.9
酸奶	Yogurt	4.0	4.8
奶粉	Milk	0.8	0.9
鲜瓜果	Fresh fruit	47.4	55.6
糕点	Cake	4.1	5.2
茶叶	Tea	0.3	0.5
卷烟（盒）	Cigarettes (box)	23.0	28.2
啤酒	Beer	3.7	4.4
白酒	Liquor	0.8	1.1
果酒	Wine	0.3	0.4
鞋(双)	Footwear (pair)	2.7	3.0
水（吨）	Water (tons)	19.9	25.0
电（度）	Electricity （kwh）	540.7	665.9
煤炭	Coal	47.1	51.7
管道天燃气（立方米）	Gas pipeline (cu.m)	49.7	65.0
罐装液化石油气	Bottled liquefied petroleum gas	4.4	3.4

8-8 全市居民家庭每百户年末耐用品拥有情况（2015年）

Ownership of Major Durable Consumer Goods Every 100 Households（2015）

指标名称	Item	2014	2015
家用汽车（辆）	Automobile (unit)	25.7	28.8
摩托车（辆）	Motorcycles (unit)	22.2	18.9
助力车（台）	Strength-aid Cycle (unit)	38.5	38.1
洗衣机（台）	washing machine (unit)	97.4	97.6
电冰箱（柜）	Refrigerator (unit)	91.2	91.7
微波炉（台）	Microwave Oven (unit)	46.5	49.2
彩色电视机（台）	Color TV Set (unit)	116.9	115.0
#接入有线电视（台）	Cable TV Set(unit)	76.0	76.1
空调（台）	Air conditioning(unit)	120.1	126.4
热水器（台）	Water heaters(unit)	79.8	81.5
#太阳能热水器（台）	Solar water heaters (unit)	37.5	37.1
消毒碗柜（台）	Sterilizing Cupboard (unit)	4.8	5.1
洗碗机（台）	Dishwasher (unit)	1.0	1.3
排油烟机（台）	Exhauster (unit)	65.9	69.1
固定电话（线）	Ordinary Telephone (unit)	52.1	45.9
移动电话（部）	Mobile phones (unit)	233.9	234.2
#接入互联网（部）	Access to the Internet(unit)	84.3	99.0
计算机（台）	Computer (a)	64.4	68.8
#接入互联网（台）	Access to the Internet(unit)	52.2	54.9
摄像机（台）	Pickup Camera (unit)	7.2	7.6
照相机（台）	Camera (unit)	38.0	39.5
中高档乐器（架）	High-end Instruments (unit)	3.2	3.3
健身器材（台）	Setting-up Apparatus (unit)	3.0	4.8
组合音响（套）	Music Center (unit)	6.6	6.5

8-9 城镇常住居民家庭基本情况

Basic Conditions of Urban Resident Households

指标名称	Item	2014	2015
调查户数（户）	Number of Households Surveyed (household)	1752	1696
调查户人口（人）	Residents Surveyed(person)		
平均每户常住人口	Average Household Size	2.7	2.8
平均每户劳动力人数	Average Number of Employed Persons	2.2	2.2
平均每劳动力负担人口	Average Number of Persons Supported by a Laborer	1.3	1.3
人均可支配收入（元）	Annual Per Capita Disposable Income(yuan)	30714.7	33187.6
工资性收入	Wages Income	19754.7	21095.9
经营净收入	Household Business Income	2095.8	2200.8
财产净收入	Property Income	2646.9	2913.1
转移净收入	Transfer Income	6217.3	6975.8
人均消费支出（元）	Annual Per Capita Consumption Expenditure (yuan)	20892.8	22414.8
食品烟酒	Food,Tobacco and Alcohol	6102.5	6632.5
衣着	Clothing	1898.2	1968.6
居住	Residence	3738.2	3985.8
生活用品及服务	Living Articles and Services	1507.2	1663.0
交通通信	Transport and Communication Services	2957.5	2983.8
教育文化娱乐	Recreation, Education and Culture Services	2632.2	2796.8
医疗保健	Medical and Health Care Services	1528.7	1774.2
其他用品和服务	Other Commodities and Services	528.3	610.1

8-10 按收入五等份分组的城镇常住居民人均可支配收入（2015年）

Per capita Annual Disposable Income of Urban Households by Income Percentile（2015）

单位：元 （yuan）

指标名称	Item	总平均 Total	低收入户 Low income households	中低收入户 Lower Middle income households
可支配收入	Disposable income	33187.6	16407.8	25876.9
一、工资性收入	Wage income	21095.9	12705.3	15591.5
（一）工资	Wage	19658.9	12414.4	14783.9
（二）实物福利	Benefits in kind	111.9	49.6	143.7
（三）其他	Others	1325.1	241.3	663.9
二、经营净收入	Net Income from Business	2200.8	984.4	1555.2
（一）第一产业经营净收入	Net Income from Primary Industry Business	84.9	97.9	170.7
（二）第二产业经营净收入	Net Income from Secondary Industry Business	137.8	281.4	54.2
（三）第三产业经营净收入	Net Income from Tertiary Industry Business	1978.1	605.1	1330.3
三、财产净收入	Net Income from Properties	2915.1	1177.9	3613.5
#利息净收入	Net interest	53.7	-76.6	-18.0
红利收入	Bonus	239.9	135.5	546.0
出租房屋财产性收入	The Property Income by Renting House	1297.9	436.5	2106.4
出租机械、专利、版权等资产的收入	The Income by Renting Assets like Mechanical, Patents, Copyright ect.Patents, Copyright ect.	25.6	11.6	1.8
四、转移净收入	Net Income from Transfer	6975.8	1540.2	5116.7
（一）转移性收入	Net Income from Transfer	8659.2	2490.4	6417.2
（二）转移性支出	Transfer Expenditure	1683.4	950.2	1300.5

8-10 续表 continued

指标名称	Item	中等收入户 Middle income households	中高收入户 Upper Middle income households	高收入户 High income households
可支配收入	Disposable income	32701.6	40560.3	60301.9
一、工资性收入	Wage income	21105.8	26065.0	35367.2
（一）工资	Wage	19823.1	23912.0	31997.8
（二）实物福利	Benefits in kind	68.0	88.8	242.1
（三）其他	Others	1214.7	2064.2	3127.3
二、经营净收入	Net Income from Business	1471.9	1370.0	6702.8
（一）第一产业经营净收入	Net Income from Primary Industry Business	0.6	131.9	
（二）第二产业经营净收入	Net Income from Secondary Industry Business	-17.9	9.0	368.9
（三）第三产业经营净收入	Net Income from Tertiary Industry Business	1489.2	1229.1	6333.9
三、财产净收入	Net Income from Properties	3443.2	2131.2	4827.2
#利息净收入	Net interest	12.0	131.5	307.0
红利收入	Bonus	260.5	59.7	166.0
出租房屋财产性收入	The Property Income by Renting House	1955.9	270.2	1871.4
出租机械、专利、版权等资产的收入	The Income by Renting Assets like Mechanical, Patents, Copyright ect.Patents, Copyright ect.	3.3	-0.8	135.2
四、转移净收入	Net Income from Transfer	6680.7	10994.1	13404.7
（一）转移性收入	Net Income from Transfer	8298.5	13011.7	16398.0
（二）转移性支出	Transfer Expenditure	1617.8	2017.6	2993.3

8-11 城镇常住居民人均消费支出

Per Capita Living Expenditure of Urban Households

单位：元 (yuan)

指标名称	Item	2014	2015
消费支出	**Total Living Expenditure**	20892.9	22414.8
一、食品烟酒	**Food,Tobacco and Alcohol**	6102.5	6632.5
1.食品	food	3881.2	3973.0
2.烟酒	Alcohol and tobacco	531.9	606.9
3.饮料	Drink	133.4	189.9
4.饮食服务	Catering Services	1556.0	1862.7
二、衣着	**Clothing**	1898.3	1968.6
衣类	Garments	1469.4	1472.1
鞋类	Footwear	428.9	496.5
三、居住	**Residence**	3738.2	3985.8
#租赁房房租	Rental Housing Rent	326.8	418.2
住房维修及管理	Housing Repair and Management	304.3	414.9
水电燃料及其他	Water,Electric Power Fuel and Others	1114.0	1060.4
四、生活用品及服务	**Living Articles and Services**	1507.2	1663.0
家具及室内装饰品	Furniture and External Decorations	244.3	341.3
家用器具	Household Appliances	403.5	337.5
家用纺织品	Household textile	137.9	132.3
家庭日用杂品	Household Articles of Daily Use	402.7	416.4
个人用品	Personal Items	278.1	361.5
家庭服务	Household Services	40.7	74.0
五、交通通信	**Transportation and Communications**	2957.5	2983.8
交通	Transportation	1993.1	1981.0
通信	Communications	964.4	1002.8
六、教育文化娱乐	**Recreation, Education and Culture Services**	2632.2	2796.8
教育	Education	1253.6	1216.5
文化娱乐	Recreation	1378.6	1580.3
#健身器材	Fitness Equipment	7.9	12.9
体育及户外用品	Sports and outdoor products	17.9	16.5
体育健身活动	Sports fitness activity	45.1	32.2
七、医疗保健	**Medicine and Medical Services**	1528.7	1774.2
医疗器具及药品	Medical Instruments and Medicines	632.6	749.8
医疗服务	Medical Services	896.1	1024.4
八、其他用品和服务	**Others**	528.3	610.1

8-12 城镇常住居民家庭人均购买主要商品数量

Per Capita Annual Purchases of Major Commodities of Urban Households

单位：千克 (kg)

指标名称	Item	2014	2015
面粉	Flour	23.8	22.9
大米	Rice	20.1	20.0
薯类	Potato	11.9	15.0
豆类	Beans	9.1	10.7
食用植物油	Edible vegetable oil	11.1	11.5
鲜菜	Fresh vegetables	89.3	96.1
猪肉	Pork	10.5	11.3
牛肉	Beef	2.0	1.9
羊肉	Lamb	0.5	0.9
鸡	Chicken	2.5	3.0
鱼类	Fish	3.4	4.1
虾类	Shrimp	0.7	0.8
鲜蛋	Eggs	8.8	10.7
鲜奶	Milk	15.3	17.5
酸奶	Yogurt	4.6	5.8
奶粉	Milk	0.6	0.9
鲜瓜果	Fresh fruit	55.1	63.6
糕点	Cake	4.8	5.9
茶叶	Tea	0.4	0.5
卷烟（盒）	Cigarettes (box)	21.3	27.3
啤酒	Beer	3.8	4.7
白酒	Liquor	0.9	1.2
果酒	Wine	0.3	0.5
鞋(双)	Footwear (pair)	2.9	3.2
水（吨）	Water (tons)	25.2	31.6
电（度）	Electricity （kwh）	608.2	748.6
煤炭	Coal	33.4	41.2
管道天燃气（立方米）	Gas pipeline (cu.m)	68.7	88.9
罐装液化石油气	Bottled liquefied petroleum gas	4.1	3.3

8-13 城镇常住居民家庭每百户耐用品拥有情况

Ownership of Major Durable Consumer Goods Every 100 Urban Households

指标名称	Item	2014	2015
家用汽车（辆）	Automobile (unit)	27.9	31.5
摩托车（辆）	Motorcycles (unit)	11.8	9.4
助力车（台）	Strength-aid Cycle (unit)	30.9	29.4
洗衣机（台）	washing machine (unit)	97.6	97.8
电冰箱（柜）	Refrigerator (unit)	95.4	95.7
微波炉（台）	Microwave Oven (unit)	55.9	58.9
彩色电视机（台）	Color TV Set (unit)	113.9	113.3
空调（台）	Air conditioning(unit)	136.9	143.8
热水器（台）	Water heaters(unit)	85.4	87.0
#太阳能热水器（台）	Solar water heaters (unit)	34.2	32.2
消毒碗柜（台）	Sterilizing Cupboard (unit)	6.1	6.6
洗碗机（台）	Dishwasher (unit)	1.2	1.4
排油烟机（台）	Exhauster (unit)	79.8	82.1
固定电话（线）	Ordinary Telephone (unit)	56.3	51.8
移动电话（部）	Mobile phones (unit)	224.0	225.8
计算机（台）	Computer (a)	75.0	79.3
摄像机（台）	Pickup Camera (unit)	9.3	9.8
照相机（台）	Camera (unit)	47.4	49.2
中高档乐器（架）	High-end Instruments (unit)	3.9	4.2
健身器材（台）	Setting-up Apparatus (unit)	3.6	5.7
组合音响（套）	Music Center (unit)	6.4	6.4

8-14 城镇常住居民家庭居住情况

Housing Conditions of Urban Households

指标名称	Item	2014	2015
调查户数（户）	**Number of Households Surveyed (household)**	**1752**	**1696**
平均每户居住人口（人）	**Average Number of Resident Population (person)**	**2.9**	**2.8**
人均现住房建筑面积（平方米/人）	**The Average Floor Area Per Person (sq.m / person)**	**32.1**	**32.1**
一、按居住空间样式分（%）	**by Living space style（%）**	**100.0**	**100.0**
单栋楼房	Single building Room	6.7	4.1
单栋平房	Single-storey House	4.8	1.5
单元房	Apartment	81.0	87.5
筒子楼或连片平房	Tube-shaped Apartment or Lace Single-storey Houses	7.4	6.8
其他	Other	0.1	0.1
二、按主要建筑材料分（%）	**by main construction materials（%）**	**100.0**	**100.0**
钢筋混凝土	Reinforced concrete soil	25.2	29.1
砖混材料	Brick and concrete material	74.2	70.4
砖瓦砖土	Tile and brick earth	0.5	0.3
其他	Others	0.1	0.2
三、按房屋来源分（%）	**by Source of Housing（%）**	**100.0**	**100.0**
租赁住房	Rental housing	11.4	12.1
自建住房	Self-establish Housing	12.7	5.7
购买商品房	Commercial Residential Housing	31.7	34.9
购买房改住房	Private Housing through Housing Reform	34.9	37.3
购买保障性住房	Indemnificatory Housing	2.3	2.9
拆迁安置房	Resettlement Housing	4.2	4.0
继承或获赠住房	Inheriting and Donation Housing	0.5	0.9
其他	Others	2.3	2.2
四、住房外道路为硬化路面的户比重（%）	**proportion of households which outer road is Hardened road（%）**	**99.1**	**99.8**
五、按住宅有管道供水情况分（%）	**By Piped Water Supply Condition（%）**	**100.0**	**100.0**
管道供水入户	Pipe water into People's Homes	98.4	98.6
管道供水至公共取水点	Pipe water to Public Watering Points	0.9	1.1
没有管道设施	No Pipeline Facilities	0.7	0.3
六、按住户主要饮水来源情况分（%）	**By Source of main Drinking Water（%）**	**100.0**	**100.0**
经过净化处理的自来水	Purified Tap Water	88.5	91.9
受保护的井水和泉水	Protected Wells and Springs	8.4	5.3
不受保护的井水和泉水	Unprotected Wells and Springs	1.3	1.2
江河湖泊水	Rivers and Lakes Water	0.3	0.3
其他饮用水来源	Others	1.5	1.3
七、按住宅内厕所类型分（%）	**By Household Lavatory Type (%)**	**100.0**	**100.0**
水冲式卫生厕所	Sanitary Water Closet	92.1	98.3
水冲式非卫生厕所	Insanitary Water Closet	0.7	0.7
卫生旱厕	Sanitary Latrine	2.9	0.2
普通旱厕	Latrine	3.9	0.6
无厕所	No Lavatory	0.4	0.2
八、按主要炊用能源状况分（%）	**By Cooking Fuel Condition（%）**	**100.0**	**100.0**
天然气、煤气、液化石油气	Pipeline Natural Gas，Pipeline Gas，Pipeline Liquified Petroleum Gas	75.0	78.0
煤炭	Coal	3.1	1.0
电	Electricity	20.3	20.2
沼气	Methane	0.2	
其他	Others	1.4	0.8

8-15 农村常住居民家庭基本情况

Basic Conditions of rural Resident Households

指标名称	Item	2014	2015
调查户数（户）	Number of Households Surveyed (household)	626	686
调查户人口（人）	Residents Surveyed(person)		
平均每户常住人口	Average Household Size	3.5	3.6
平均每户劳动力人数	Average Number of Employed Persons	2.5	2.6
平均每劳动力负担人口	Average Number of Persons Supported by a Laborer	1.4	1.4
人均可支配收入（元）	Annual Per Capita Disposable Income(yuan)	12898.1	14071.7
工资性收入	Wages Income	6596.3	7195.2
经营净收入	Household Business Income	3621.1	3871.5
财产净收入	Property Income	353.6	428.6
转移净收入	Transfer Income	2327.1	2576.4
人均消费支出（元）	Annual Per Capita Consumption Expenditure (yuan)	8707.6	9517.7
食品烟酒	Food,Tobacco and Alcohol	2606.5	2681.7
衣着	Clothing	647.6	677.6
居住	Residence	1914.6	2215.7
生活用品及服务	Living Articles and Services	607.4	628.4
交通通信	Transport and Communication Services	927.8	1019.3
教育文化娱乐	Recreation, Education and Culture Services	893.7	1111.4
医疗保健	Medical and Health Care Services	963.6	1016.1
其他用品和服务	Other Commodities and Services	146.4	167.5

8-16 按收入五等份分组的农村常住居民家庭人均可支配收入（2015年）

Per capita Annual Disposable Income of Rural Households by Income Percentile (2015)

单位：元 (yuan)

指标名称	Item	总平均 Total	低收入户 Low income households	中低收入户 Lower Middle income households
可支配收入	Disposable income	14071.7	6539.5	9976.2
一、工资性收入	Wage income	7195.2	3731.4	5253.3
（一）工资	Wage	7096.6	3677.0	5184.1
（二）实物福利	Benefits in kind	4.0	0.9	2.1
（三）其他	Others	94.6	53.5	67.1
二、经营净收入	Net Income from Business	3871.5	1916.9	1497.8
（一）第一产业经营净收入	Net Income from Primary Industry Business	1673.0	1124.3	1178.0
（二）第二产业经营净收入	Net Income from Secondary Industry Business	203.2	4.1	3.1
（三）第三产业经营净收入	Net Income from Tertiary Industry Business	1995.3	788.5	316.7
三、财产净收入	Net Income from Properties	428.6	50.3	603.3
#利息净收入	Net interest	6.1	-145.2	24.6
红利收入	Bonus	35.9	12.4	10.2
转让承包土地经营权租金净收入	Net Rental from Transfer of Contracted Land Management Rights	161.1	62.6	152.9
出租房屋财产性收入	The Property Income by Renting House	183.6	95.4	366.8
出租机械、专利、版权等资产的收入	The Income by Renting Assets like Mechanical, Patents, Copyright ect.Patents, Copyright ect.	4.2	-0.4	-7.2
四、转移净收入	Net Income from Transfer	2576.4	840.9	2621.8
（一）转移性收入	Net Income from Transfer	2782.3	925.0	2820.3
（二）转移性支出	Transfer Expenditure	205.9	84.1	198.5

8-16 续表 continued

指标名称	Item	中等收入户 Middle income households	中高收入户 Upper Middle income households	高收入户 High income households
可支配收入	Disposable income	13300.4	17252.4	25902.0
一、工资性收入	Wage income	7897.2	7352.5	12878.0
（一）工资	Wage	7845.6	7263.6	12623.8
（二）实物福利	Benefits in kind	2.4	7.1	8.8
（三）其他	Others	49.2	81.8	245.4
二、经营净收入	Net Income from Business	2856.4	6390.5	7523.8
（一）第一产业经营净收入	Net Income from Primary Industry Business	1417.6	2908.5	1904.9
（二）第二产业经营净收入	Net Income from Secondary Industry Business	24.4	3.1	1108.1
（三）第三产业经营净收入	Net Income from Tertiary Industry Business	1414.4	3478.9	4510.8
三、财产净收入	Net Income from Properties	203.7	668.5	729.5
#利息净收入	Net interest	7.2	57.0	126.4
红利收入	Bonus	18.8	120.6	23.8
转让承包土地经营权租金净收入	Net Rental from Transfer of Contracted Land Management Rights	68.8	184.9	380.2
出租房屋财产性收入	The Property Income by Renting House	82.7	284.5	103.2
出租机械、专利、版权等资产的收入	The Income by Renting Assets like Mechanical, Patents, Copyright ect.Patents, Copyright ect.	-0.2	-4.7	37.6
四、转移净收入	Net Income from Transfer	2343.1	2840.9	4770.7
（一）转移性收入	Net Income from Transfer	2470.6	3064.0	5216.3
（二）转移性支出	Transfer Expenditure	127.5	223.1	445.6

8-17 农村常住居民家庭人均消费支出

Per Capita Living Expenditure of Rual Households by Income Percentile

单位：元 (yuan)

指标名称	Item	2014	2015
消费支出	**Total Living Expenditure**	8707.6	9517.7
一、食品烟酒	**Food,Tobacco and Alcohol**	2606.5	2681.7
1.食品	food	1896.1	1887
2.烟酒	Alcohol and tobacco	298.9	373.7
3.饮料	Drink	46.3	59.5
4.饮食服务	Catering Services	365.2	361.5
二、衣着	**Clothing**	647.6	677.6
衣类	Garments	496.8	510.7
鞋类	Footwear	150.8	166.9
三、居住	**Residence**	1914.6	2215.7
#租赁房房租	Rental Housing Rent	122.9	112.6
住房维修及管理	Housing Repair and Management	244.2	313.6
水电燃料及其他	Water,Electric Power Fuel and Others	465.2	436.9
四、生活用品及服务	**Living Articles and Services**	607.4	628.4
家具及室内装饰品	Furniture and External Decorations	105.8	121.6
家用器具	Household Appliances	152.2	150.8
家用纺织品	Household textile	74.6	68.2
家庭日用杂品	Household Articles of Daily Use	208.3	187.8
个人用品	Personal Items	53.6	81.7
家庭服务	Household Services	12.9	18.3
五、交通通信	**Transportation and Communications**	927.8	1019.3
交通	Transportation	557.1	606.4
通信	Communications	370.7	412.9
六、教育文化娱乐	**Recreation, Education and Culture Services**	893.7	1111.4
教育	Education	686.4	769.9
文化娱乐	Recreation	207.3	341.5
七、医疗保健	**Medicine and Medical Services**	963.6	1016.1
医疗器具及药品	Medical Instruments and Medicines	288.7	340.7
医疗服务	Medical Services	674.9	675.4
八、其他用品和服务	**Others**	146.4	167.5

8-18 农村常住居民家庭人均购买主要商品数量

Per Capita Annual Purchases of Major Commodities of Rural Households by Income Percentile

单位：千克 (kg)

指标名称	Item	2014	2015
面粉	Flour	20.8	14.5
大米	Rice	11.7	13.3
薯类	Potato	6.3	8.8
豆类	Beans	6.4	7.2
食用植物油	Edible vegetable oil	11.0	11.2
鲜菜	Fresh vegetables	57.7	64.6
猪肉	Pork	6.8	8.1
牛肉	Beef	0.2	0.4
羊肉	Lamb	0.1	0.3
鸡	Chicken	0.6	0.7
鱼类	Fish	0.8	0.8
虾类	Shrimp	0.1	0.1
鲜蛋	Eggs	5.3	7.5
鲜奶	Milk	3.3	8.2
酸奶	Yogurt	2.2	2.3
奶粉	Milk	1.1	0.8
鲜瓜果	Fresh fruit	28.3	35.1
糕点	Cake	2.3	3.1
茶叶	Tea	0.2	0.6
卷烟（盒）	Cigarettes (box)	27.1	30.7
啤酒	Beer	3.4	3.8
白酒	Liquor	0.7	0.8
果酒	Wine	0.4	0.3
鞋(双)	Footwear (pair)	2.2	2.5
水（吨）	Water (tons)	6.9	8.0
电（度）	Electricity（kwh）	373.0	452.9
煤炭	Coal	81.0	78.5
管道天燃气（立方米）	Gas pipeline (cu.m)	2.5	3.3
罐装液化石油气	Bottled liquefied petroleum gas	5.2	3.8

8-19 农村常住居民家庭平均每百户耐用品拥有情况

Ownership of Major Durable Consumer Goods Every 100 Rural Households

指标名称	Item	2014	2015
家用汽车（辆）	Automobile (unit)	19.5	21.3
摩托车（辆）	Motorcycles (unit)	51.6	45.7
助力车（台）	Strength-aid Cycle (unit)	59.8	62.5
洗衣机（台）	washing machine (unit)	96.8	97.0
电冰箱（柜）	Refrigerator (unit)	79.3	80.6
微波炉（台）	Microwave Oven (unit)	20.2	21.9
彩色电视机（台）	Color TV Set (unit)	125.3	119.8
空调（台）	Air conditioning(unit)	73.2	77.4
热水器（台）	Water heaters(unit)	64.2	66.0
#太阳能热水器（台）	Solar water heaters (unit)	46.8	50.8
消毒碗柜（台）	Sterilizing Cupboard (unit)	1.4	1.0
洗碗机（台）	Dishwasher (unit)	0.3	0.9
排油烟机（台）	Exhauster (unit)	26.9	32.4
固定电话（线）	Ordinary Telephone (unit)	40.4	29.2
移动电话（部）	Mobile phones (unit)	261.6	257.7
计算机（台）	Computer (a)	34.6	39.1
#接入互联网（台）	Access to the Internet(unit)	24.9	30.8
摄像机（台）	Pickup Camera (unit)	1.4	1.3
照相机（台）	Camera (unit)	11.5	12.0
中高档乐器（架）	High-end Instruments (unit)	1.4	0.9
健身器材（台）	Setting-up Apparatus (unit)	1.1	2.1
组合音响（套）	Music Center (unit)	7.1	6.8

8-20 农村常住居民家庭居住情况

Housing Conditions of Urban Households

指标名称	Item	2014	2015
调查户数（户）	**Number of Households Surveyed (household)**	626	686
平均每户居住人口（人）	**Average Number of Resident Population (person)**	3.5	3.6
人均现住房建筑面积（平方米/人）	**The Average Floor Area Per Person (sq.m / person)**	48.8	50.7
一、按居住空间样式分（%）	**by Living space style（%）**	100.0	100.0
单栋楼房	Single building Room	42.5	43.0
单栋平房	Single-storey House	44.1	41.4
单元房	Apartment	11.8	11.4
筒子楼或连片平房	Tube-shaped Apartment or Lace Single-storey Houses	0.3	2.8
其他	Other	1.3	1.4
二、按主要建筑材料分（%）	**by main construction materials（%）**	100.0	100.0
钢筋混凝土	Reinforced concrete soil	21.8	19.0
砖混材料	Brick and concrete material	67.9	73.9
砖瓦砖土	Tile and brick earth	8.8	5.9
竹草土坯	Bamboo grass mud	1.3	0.9
其他	Others	0.2	0.3
三、按房屋来源分（%）	**by Source of Housing（%）**	100.0	100.0
租赁住房	Rental housing	4.1	2.3
自建住房	Self-establish Housing	84.4	86.5
购买商品房	Commercial Residential Housing	2.7	4.0
购买房改住房	Private Housing through Housing Reform	1.1	0.9
购买保障性住房	Indemnificatory Housing	1.4	1.1
拆迁安置房	Resettlement Housing	6.0	5.0
继承或获赠住房	Inheriting and Donation Housing		0.1
其他	Others	0.3	0.1
四、住房外道路为硬化路面的户比重（%）	**proportion of households which outer road is Hardened road（%）**	94.3	94.4
五、按住宅有管道供水情况分（%）	**By Piped Water Supply Condition （%）**	100.0	100.0
管道供水入户	Pipe water into People's Homes	90.2	92.0
管道供水至公共取水点	Pipe water to Public Watering Points	0.5	0.8
没有管道设施	No Pipeline Facilities	9.3	7.2
六、按住户主要饮水来源情况分（%）	**By Source of main Drinking Water （%）**	100.0	100.0
经过净化处理的自来水	Purified Tap Water	66.9	63.3
受保护的井水和泉水	Protected Wells and Springs	21.5	26.6
不受保护的井水和泉水	Unprotected Wells and Springs	11.0	8.1
江河湖泊水	Rivers and Lakes Water	0.6	0.8
其他饮用水来源	Others		1.2
七、按住宅内厕所类型分（%）	**By Household Lavatory Type (%)**	100.0	100.0
水冲式卫生厕所	Sanitary Water Closet	39.8	38.8
水冲式非卫生厕所	Insanitary Water Closet	5.9	4.5
卫生旱厕	Sanitary Latrine	18.1	19.4
普通旱厕	Latrine	35.1	36.3
无厕所	No Lavatory	1.1	1.0
八、按主要炊用能源状况分（%）	**By Cooking Fuel Condition （%）**	100.0	100.0
天然气、煤气、液化石油气	Pipeline Natural Gas，Pipeline Gas，Pipeline Liquified Petroleum Gas	33.4	31.3
煤炭	Coal	3.8	7.5
电	Electricity	34.4	35.0
沼气	Methane	0.3	0.4
其他	Others	28.1	25.8

主要统计指标解释

住户 指居住在一个住宅内，共同分享生活开支或收入的一群人。居住在同一房间内、不共同分享生活开支的人群，每个人都视为一个住户。住家保姆、住家家庭帮工视为单独的住户。

常住居民 指住户成员中，经常在家居住、或者调查期内居住时间超过一半的人员，以及本住户供养的学生。常住居民是住户收支的调查对象。

整、半劳动力 整劳动力是指男子18周岁到50周岁，女子18周岁到45周岁；半劳动力是指男子16周岁到17周岁，51周岁到60周岁；女子16周岁到17周岁，46周岁到55周岁，同时具有劳动能力的人。虽然在劳动年龄之内，但已丧失劳动能力的人，不应算为劳动力；超过劳动年龄，但能经常参加劳动，计入半劳动力数内。常住人口中的职工，若这些职工为劳动力，就包括在本户的整半劳动力中。

居民人均可支配收入 指调查期内居民家庭成员人均获得的、可用于最终消费支出和储蓄的总和，即居民可以用来自由支配的收入，既包括现金收入，也包括实物收入。全体居民可支配收入可以体现各地区城乡一体的居民收入及生活水平变化情况。按照收入的来源，可支配收入包含四项，分别为：工资性收入、经营净收入、财产净收入、转移净收入。

工资性收入 指就业人员通过各种途径得到的全部劳动报酬和各种福利，包括受雇于单位或个人、从事各种自由职业、兼职和零星劳动得到的全部劳动报酬和福利。

经营净收入 指住户或住户成员从事生产经营活动所获得的净收入，是全部经营收入中扣除经营费用、生产性固定资产折旧和生产税净额（生产税减去生产补贴）之后得到的净收入。计算公式为：

经营净收入 = 经营收入 – 经营费用 – 生产性固定资产折旧 – 生产税净额（生产税–生产补贴）

财产净收入 指住户或住户成员将其所拥有的金融资产和自然资源交由其他机构单位、住户或个人支配而获得的回报并扣除相关的费用之后得到的净收入。计算公式为：

财产净收入 = 财产性收入 – 财产性支出

转移净收入 指国家、单位、社会团体对住户的各种经常性转移支付和住户之间的经常性收入转移。包括政府、非行政事业单位、社会团体对居民转移的养老金或退休金、社会救济和补助、政策性生活补贴、救灾款、经常性捐赠和赔偿以及报销医疗费等；住户之间的赡养收入、经常性捐赠和赔偿以及农村地区（村委会）在外（含国外）工作的本住户非常住成员寄回带回的收入等。计算公式为：

转移净收入–转移性收入–转移性支出

居民收入五等份分组 指将所有调查户按人均收入水平从低到高顺序排列，平均分为五个等份，处于最高20%的收入群体为高收入组，依此类推依次为中高收入组、中等收入组、中低收入组、低收入组。

居民人均生活消费支出 指住户用于满足家庭日常生活消费需要的全部支出，包括用于消费品的支出和用于服务性消费的支出。根据用途不同，消费支出可划分为食品烟酒、衣着、居住、生活用品及服务、交通通信、教育文化娱乐、医疗保健、其他用品及服务八大类。

城镇居民人均可支配收入（老口径） 指城镇家庭总收入扣除交纳的个人所得税和个人交纳的各项社会保障支出之后，按照城镇居民家庭人口平均的收入水平。其中家庭总收入是指该家庭中生活在一起的所有家庭人员从各种渠道得到的所有收入之和。计算公式为：

可支配收入= 家庭总收入– 交纳个人所得税–个人交纳的社会保障支出–记账补贴

农村居民人均纯收入（老口径） 指农村住户当年从各个来源得到的家庭总收入扣除有关费用性支出后，最终归农村居民所有的收入总和，按照农村住户人口平均的纯收入水平。计算公式为：

纯收入 = 总收入–家庭经营费用支出–税费支出–生产性固定资产折旧–赠送农村内部亲友

Explanatory Notes on Main Statistical Indicators

Households refer to persons living and sharing economically together in one house. When people don't share living expenses, every single person are deemed to be one household. Live-in Nanny and family helpers are deemed to be one household.

Usual Resident Population refers to persons staying at home regularly or for over half of time in survey period and students provided by the household. Usual resident population is the respondent of household living expenses.

Full/Semi Labour Force Full labour force refers to persons capable of work, aged 18-50 for males and 18-45 for females. Semi labour force refers to persons capable of work, aged 16-17 and 51-60 for males and 16-17 and 46-55 for females. Persons at their working ages but not capable of work are not to be included as labour force. Persons not at working ages but participating regularly in work are included in semi labour force. For staff and workers who are usual residents, are included as full or semi labour force of the household if they are in the labour force.

Disposable Income of Residents refers to the actual income at the disposal of members of the households which can be used for final consumption and savings in survey period, residents can use that at their disposal. It includes cash income and physical income. This income demonstrates the situation about incomes of both rural and urban residents and living standard in various regions. According to the source of income, disposable income include wage income, net business income, net property income and net transferability income.

Wages Income refers to the work reward and all benefits received in various ways by the members of rural households,include the work reward and all benefits received from employed by other units or individuals,liberal professions, part-time job and sporadic labor.

Net Business Income refers to the net income received by households engaged in manufacturing & managing activities.This equals to total business income minus operating costs, depreciation for productive plant assets and net product tax(production taxes minus production subsidies).The following formula is used:

Net business income=business income-operating costs-depreciation for productive plant assets- net product tax(production taxes-production subsidies)

Net Property Income refers to the income received as returns by owners of financial assets or nature sources by providing nature sources to other institutional units,households and individuals. The following formula is used:

Net property income = property income - property expenditure

Net Transferability Income refers to various current transfers of nation, units and social organizations pay to households and recurring revenue transfer between households. This income includes pension transferred from government, the non administrative institutions and social organizations to households, social assistance, policy living allowance, disaster relief funds, regular donation and compensation, recoverable medical cost; alimony income, regular donation and compensation, income from the ones who are not resident in rural areas between the households.The following formula is used:

Net transferability income = transfer income - transfer expenditure

Five Equal Groups of Resident Income According to income per head, all investigative households are arranged from low to high. Divided five groups equally, the maximum 20% of the income groups is high-income groups, and so on, there are middle and upper-income groups, middle-income groups, medium-low-income groups and low-income groups.

Consumption Expenditure of Households refers to total expenditure of households for consumption in daily life, including expenditure on the eight categories of food; clothing; housing; household appliances and services; health care and medical services; transport and communications; recreation, education and cultural services; and miscellaneous goods and services.

The per capita disposable income(the old range) This equals to total income minus income tax, personal contribution to social security and subsidy for keeping diaries in being a sample household. The following formula is used:

Disposable income = total household income - income tax - personal contribution to social security - subsidy for keeping diaries for a sampled household

The Average Per Capita Net Income of Rural Residents(the old range) refers to the total income of rural households from all sources minus all corresponding expenses. The formula for calculation is as follows:

Net income = total income - household operation expenses - taxes and fees paid - taxes and fees depreciation of fixed assets for production - gifts to non-rural relatives.

9 城市公用事业

URBAN PUBLIC UTILITIES

资料整理：郝　静
Data management：Hao Jing
数据审核：王金桂
Data audit：Wang Jingui

第九部分　城市公用事业

一、简要说明

本章资料主要包括城市供水、供燃气、供热、公共交通、市政设施、市政设施水平、城市规模及用地状况、园林绿地、环境卫生等情况，由西安市统计局服务业和社会科技处根据西安市建委、市交通局及地铁办提供的数据整理。

二、主要指标

人均公园绿地面积（平方米）	11.47	比上年同口径增长	2.2%
人均城市道路面积（平方米）	18.26	比上年同口径增长	1.4%
用水普及率（%）	100	比上年同口径增加	持平
燃气普及率（%）	98.79	比上年同口径提高	0.08个百分点

9　URBAN PUBLIC UTILITIES

Ⅰ.Brief Introduction

Data in this chapter reflects basic condition of urban public utilities of Xi'an City. Data on public utilities primarily consist of urban water supply, gas sales, urban heating, public transportation, municipal facilities, level of municipal construction, scale of the city, condition of land utilization, parks, greenbelt and environmental sanitation. Data in this chapter is compiled by Tertiary Industry and Social Science & Technology Division of Xi'an Bureau of Statistics according to the data provided by Committee of Urban Construction of Xi'an, Xi'an Burean of Transportation and Xi'an Metro office.

Ⅱ.Major Indicators

		Increase over Preceding Year
Per Capita Public Green Areas (sq.m)	11.47	2.2%
Per Captia Area of Roads (sq.m)	18.26	1.4%
Water-Consuming Popularization (%)	100	essentially on a par with last year's
Gas-Consuming Popularization (%)	98.79	0.08 percentage points

9-1 城市供水

Urban Water Supply

指 标	Item	2010	2011	2012	2013	2014	2015
年末水厂个数（个）	Number of Water Factory at Year-end (units)	9	15	15	15	16	22
供水综合生产能力（万立方米/日）	Total Volume of Water Supply (10 000 cu.m/day)	197.40	197.40	200.33	195.52	196.50	211.50
# 地下水	Groundwater	55.80	54.80	57.04	51.35	51.33	62.86
年末供水管道总长度（公里）	Length of Water Supply Pipelines at Year-end (kms)	2416	2721	3207.73	3385.33	3499.97	4371.05
全年供水总量（万立方米）	Total Annual Volume of Water Supply (10 000 cu.m)	41089	38934	45791.8	51372.07	53798.99	56055.25
#全年售水量	Annual Volume of Water Sales	35099	33139	39734.9	44701.26	46755.71	49499.10
#生产运营用水	For Productive Use	6267	5484	5334.28	6272.62	15680.53	16146.29
居民家庭用水	For Residential Use	20944	19945	24703.7	26138.73	28497.40	30742.79
用水人口（万人）	Population with Access to Tap Water (10 000 persons)	410.90	394.10	406.32	444.35	452.57	463.05

注：本表数据来源于市建委和市水务局。

9-2 城市供燃气

Gas Supply in Urban Area

指 标	Item	2010	2011	2012	2013	2014	2015
一、天然气	**Natural Gas**						
管道长度（公里）	Total Length of Gas Pipelines (km)	4488	4500	5075.19	6163.39	6892.25	7465.73
供气总量（万立方米）	Total Gas Supply(10 000 cu.m)	109052	120330	142263	153488.90	186259.15	196826.38
#销售气量	Volume of Gas Sales	104055	114955	136531	147592.97	179536.78	189066.21
#家庭用量	Residential Households	20989	22868	27760.6	36671.17	59057.38	65952.81
用气人口（万人）	Population with Access to Gas (10 000 persons)	333	356	371.54	410.56	425.72	437.96
二、液化石油气	**Liquefied Petroleum Gas**						
供气总量（吨）	Total Gas Supply (tons)	11469	5920	4529.7	6047.90	5299.70	5030.30
#销售气量	Volume of Gas Sales	11441	5891	4482	5986.20	5244.00	4950.00
#家庭用量	Residential Households	7376	4352	4254	4945.00	4281.00	4064.00
用气人口（万人）	Population with Access to Gas (10 000 persons)	31.20	28.60	27.44	27.92	21.00	19.50

注：本表数据来源于市建委。

9-3 城市供热

Heating in Urban Area

指 标	Item	2010	2011	2012	2013	2014	2015
供热能力	Heating Capacity						
蒸气（吨/小时）	Steam (tons/hour)	2235	2075	3073	4283	2893	3013
热水（兆瓦）	Hot Water (megawatts)	3531	4570	5401.9	12691.1	13967.0	17191.9
供热总量(万吉焦)	Volume Supplied (10 000 gigajoules)						
蒸气	Steam	1674	1421	1616.98	1667.88	1743.87	1671.14
热水	Hot Water	2570	2901	2443.57	2990.38	3726.89	4241.30
管道长度（公里）	Length of Pipelines (km)						
蒸气	Steam	180	167	187.07	204.33	231.04	235.24
热水	Hot Water	361	500	516.18	608.12	663.20	819.17
供热面积（万平方米）	Heated Area (10 000sq.m)	6094	6524	8512.84	10980.27	13492.55	16690.65
#住宅	Residential Buildings	5009	5226	7328.16	9874.54	11828.59	14730.49

注：本表数据来源于市建委。

9-4 城市公共交通

Urban Public Traffic

指 标	Item	2010	2011	2012	2013	2014	2015
运营车辆（辆）	Operating Vehicles (units)	7107	7462	7695	8128	7769	7781
标准运营车辆（标台）	Standard Vehicles (units)	8139	8598	8925.6	9371	9050	9061
公交客运总量（万人次）	Total of Bus Passenger(10 000 person-times)	162400	175234	175241	174051	170960	161032
公交客运收入（万元）	Bus Passenger Transport Income (10 000 yuan)	129397	141505	135505	146417	140914	137492
出租汽车数（辆）	Number of Taxis (units)	12786	13839	14139	14139	14159	14459
地铁运营线路长度（公里）	Length of Subway Lines in Operation(km)			19.87	44.68	50.94	50.94
地铁客运量（万人次）	Total of Subway Passenger(10 000 person-times)			5911.64	12189.61	29953.07	34209.35

注：本表数据来源于市交通局和地铁办。

9–5 市政设施

Municipal Facilities

指　标	Item	2010	2011	2012	2013	2014	2015
一、道路长度（公里）	**Length of Roads (km)**	**2662**	**2755**	**3119.3**	**3387.43**	**3461.18**	**3570.58**
二、道路面积（万平方米）	**Area of Roads (10 000 sq.m)**	**5965**	**6259**	**7126.56**	**7931.80**	**8144.22**	**8457.14**
三、人行道面积（万平方米）	**Area of Sidewalks (10 000 sq.m)**	**1834**	**1867**	**2105.31**	**2259.29**	**2310.46**	**2381.20**
四、桥梁数（座）	**Number of Bridges (units)**	**347**	**402**	**422**	**432**	**437**	**448**
#立交桥	Overpasses	71	91	97	97	105	106
五、路灯盏数（盏）	**Number of Street Lights (units)**	**291754**	**311991**	**329881**	**333393**	**337991**	**343465**
六、排水管道长度（公里）	**Length of Drainage Pipelines (km)**	**3765**	**4043**	**4435.92**	**4629.70**	**4839.49**	**4984.94**
七、污水年排放量（万立方米）	**Annual Discharge Volume of Sewage (10 000 cu.m)**	**34706**	**36673**	**40302.7**	**46186**	**51673**	**62092**
八、污水处理厂处理能力（万立方米/日）	**Daily Disposal Capacity of Sewage (10 000 cu.m/day)**	**106.5**	**111.6**	**128.1**	**153.1**	**153.1**	**200.6**
九、污水年处理量（万立方米）	**Yearly Disposal Capacity of Sewage Disposal Plant (10 000 cu.m)**	**25088**	**31512**	**35463**	**41898**	**47907**	**57034**

注：本表数据来源于市建委。

9–6 城市设施水平

Urban Municipal Facilities

指　标	Item	2010	2011	2012	2013	2014	2015
一、人均日生活用水量（升）	**Per Capita Daily Consumption of Tap Water For Residential Use (liters)**	**186.2**	**185.2**	**220.96**	**225.78**	**178.45**	**187.79**
二、用水普及率(%)	**Water-Consuming Popularization (%)**	**98.8**	**100**	**100**	**100**	**100**	**100**
三、每万人拥有公共交通车辆（标台）	**Number of Public Transport Vehicles Per 10 000 Population (units)**	**13.9**	**14.4**	**14.6**	**15.1**	**14.4**	**14.3**
四、燃气普及率(%)	**Gas-Consuming Popularization (%)**	**97**	**97.5**	**98.19**	**98.68**	**98.71**	**98.79**
五、人均城市道路面积（平方米）	**Per Captia Area of Roads (sq.m)**	**15.4**	**15.9**	**17.54**	**17.85**	**18.00**	**18.26**
六、建成区排水管道密度（公里/平方公里）	**Density of Drainage Pipelines in Developed Areas (km/sq.km)**	**9.5**	**9.7**	**9.83**	**9.17**	**9.27**	**9.09**
七、污水处理率(%)	**Rate of Sewerage Disposal (%)**	**84**	**85.9**	**89.51**	**90.72**	**92.71**	**91.85**
八、园林绿化	**Afforestation and Parks and Gardens**						
人均公园绿地面积（平方米）	Per Capita Public Green Areas (sq.m)	9.1	9.9	10.22	10.70	11.22	11.47
建城区绿地率（%）	Rate of Green Areas in Developed Areas (%)	29.2	30.9	31.20	32.32	32.60	34.03
九、生活垃圾无害化处理率(%)	**Rate of No Harm Disposal of Garbage (%)**	**93.9**	**93.7**	**94.93**	**93.95**	**93.48**	**98.09**

注：本表数据来源于市建委。
每万人拥有公共交通车辆计算数据口径调整，故与2009年前数据不可比。
住建部对2015年全国城建统计年报数据进行了核准，并根据国务院及住建部有关统计工作的要求对全国部分数据进行了调整。

9-7　城市规模及用地情况

City Scale and Land Use

单位：平方公里　　(sq.km)

指　标	Item	2010	2011	2012	2013	2014	2015
建成区面积	Area of the Constructed Regions	395	415	451.38	504.68	521.91	548.60
城市建设用地	Land use for Construction	336	349	376.39	489.03	507.66	536.10

注：本表数据来源于市建委。

9-8　城市园林绿化

Urban Parks,Gardens and Green Areas in Cities

指　标	Item	2010	2011	2012	2013	2014	2015
一、公园个数（个）	**Number of Parks (units)**	**68**	**66**	**72**	**81**	**85**	**91**
二、公园面积（公顷）	**Area of Parks (hectares)**	**1335**	**1478**	**1529**	**2406**	**2483.83**	**2599.83**
三、绿地面积（公顷）	**Total Area of Parks,Gardens and Green Areas (hectares)**	**12140**	**13680**	**15196**	**17751**	**18914.05**	**20582.44**
#公园绿地面积	Public Green Areas	3526	3898	4154	4756	5075.85	5310.58
四、年末绿化覆盖面积（公顷）	**Coverage Space of Green Areas at year-end (hectares)**	**15646**	**17325**	**19017**	**21865**	**23216.65**	**25639.88**
五、建成区绿化覆盖率（%）	**Coverage of Green Areas in Developed Areas (%)**	**37.50**	**38.96**	**39.53**	**40.29**	**40.76**	**42.04**

注：本表数据来源于市建委。

9-9 城市环境卫生

Urban Environment Sanitation

指 标	Item	2010	2011	2012	2013	2014	2015
清扫面积（万平方米）	Area Under Cleaning Program (10 000 sq.m)	6290	6411	6952	8725	10110	9842
清运生活垃圾（万吨）	Volume of Residential Garbage Disposal (10 000 tons)	237	265	287.32	290.76	359.37	359.16
清运粪便（万吨）	Volume of Excrement and Urine Disposal (10 000 tons)	3	4	2.99	2.96	2.90	3.15
公共厕所（座）	Number of Public Lavatories (units)	1257	1493	1594	1770	2151	2239
市容环卫专用车辆设备总数（辆）	Special Vehicles of Environmental Sanitation (units)	1042	1200	1279	1639	1990	2050

注：本表数据来源于市建委。

9-10 市区及县供水（2015年）

Urban Water Supply（2015）

指 标	Item	西安 Xi'an	市区 City	蓝田 Lantian	周至 ZhouZhi	户县 Huxian
年末水厂个数（个）	Number of Water Factory at Year-end (units)	22	18	1	1	2
供水综合生产能力（万立方米/日）	Total Volume of Water Supply (10 000 cu.m/day)	211.50	201.40	2.80	1.80	5.50
#地下水	Groundwater	62.86	57.41	2.00	1.20	2.25
年末供水管道总长度（公里）	Length of Water Supply Pipelines at Year-end (km)	4371.05	4095.65	124.92	56.00	94.48
全年供水总量（万立方米）	Total Annual Volume of Water Supply (10 000 cu.m)	56055.25	53237.00	621.16	538.09	1659.00
#销售水量	Volume of Water Sales	49499.10	46839.85	595.16	483.09	1581.00
#生产运营用水	For Productive Use	16146.29	15599.52	137.15	12.10	397.52
居民家庭用水	For Residential Use	30742.79	29138.38	393.60	399.00	811.81
用水人口（万人）	Population with Access to Tap Water (10 000 persons)	463.05	423.86	15.28	7.20	16.71

注：本表数据来源于市建委及市水务局。

9-11 市区及县供燃气（2015年）

Gas Supply in Urban Area（2015）

指 标	Item	西安 Xi'an	市区 Urban	蓝田 Lantian	周至 ZhouZhi	户县 Huxian
一、天然气	**Natural Gas**					
管道长度（公里）	Total Length of Gas Pipelines (km)	7465.73	7262.53	72.20	42.00	89.00
供气总量（万立方米）	Total Gas Supply(10 000 cu.m)	196826.38	193039.28	1302.10	650.00	1835.00
#销售气量	Volume of Gas Sales	189066.21	185281.21	1300.00	650.00	1835.00
#家庭用量	Residential Households	65952.81	63052.81	760.00	630.00	1510.00
用气人口（万人）	Population with Access to Gas (10 000 persons)	437.96	421.86	5.27	1.23	9.60
二、液化石油气	**Liquefied Petroleum Gas**					
供气总量（吨）	Total Gas Supply (tons)	5030.30	1974.60	802.20	1150.50	1103.00
#销售气量	Volume of Gas Sales	4950.00	1945.00	802.00	1150.00	1053.00
#家庭用量	Residential Households	4064.00	1198.00	663.00	1150.00	1053.00
用气人口（万人）	Population with Access to Gas (10 000 persons)	19.50	2.00	5.00	5.50	7.00

注：本表数据来源于市建委。

9-12 市区及县供热（2015年）

Heating in Urban Area（2015）

指 标	Item	西安 Xi'an	市区 Urban	蓝田 Lantian	周至 ZhouZhi	户县 Huxian
供热能力	Heating Capacity					
蒸气（吨/小时）	Steam (tons/hour)	3013.00	2583.00			430.00
热水（兆瓦）	Hot Water (megawatts)	17191.90	17191.90			
供热总量(万吉焦)	Volume Supplied(10 000 gigajoules)					
蒸气	Steam	1671.14	1626.14			45.00
热水	Hot Water	4241.30	4241.30			
管道长度（公里）	Length of Pipelines (km)					
蒸气	Steam	235.24	213.54			21.70
热水	Hot Water	819.17	819.17			
供热面积（万平方米）	Heated Area (10 000sq.m)	16690.65	16625.65			65.00
#住宅	Residential Buildings	14730.49	14665.49			65.00

注：本表数据来源于市建委。

9-13 市区及县市政设施（2015年）

Municipal Facilities in Urban Area（2015）

指 标	Item	西安 Xi'an	市区 Urban	蓝田 Lantian	周至 ZhouZhi	户县 Huxian
一、道路长度（公里）	**Length of Roads (km)**	**3570.58**	**3323.39**	**75.60**	**43.43**	**128.16**
二、道路面积（万平方米）	**Area of Roads (10 000 sq.m)**	**8457.14**	**7747.30**	**136.18**	**84.30**	**489.36**
三、人行道面积（万平方米）	**Area of Sidewalks (10 000 sq.m)**	**2381.20**	**2184.63**	**58.96**	**33.80**	**103.81**
四、桥梁数（座）	**Number of Bridges (units)**	**448**	**427**	**11**	**3**	**7**
#立交桥	Crossroads	106	103			3
五、路灯盏数（盏）	**Number of Street Lights (units)**	**343465**	**327729**	**1576**	**4917**	**9243**
六、排水管道长度（公里）	**Length of Drainage Pipelines (km)**	**4984.94**	**4687.84**	**86.86**	**47.46**	**162.78**
七、污水年排放量（万立方米）	**Annual Discharge Volume of Sewage (10 000 cu.m)**	**62092**	**59956**	**472**	**409**	**1255**
八、污水处理厂处理能力（万立方米/日）	**Daily Disposal Capacity of Sewage (10 000 cu.m/day)**	**200.6**	**195.0**	**1.5**	**1.1**	**3.0**
九、污水年处理量（万立方米）	**Yearly Disposal Capacity of Sewage Disposal Plant (10 000 cu.m)**	**57034**	**55377**	**366**	**317**	**974**

注：本表数据来源于市建委。

9-14 市区及县市政设施水平（2015年）

Urban Municipal Facilities in Urban Area（2015）

指 标	Item	西安 Xi'an	市区 City	蓝田 Lantian	周至 ZhouZhi	户县 Huxian
一、人均日生活用水量（升）	**Per Capita Daily Consumption of Tap Water For Residential Use (liters)**	**187.79**	**192.50**	**81.55**	**178.67**	**169.25**
二、用水普及率(%)	**Water-Consuming Popularization (%)**	**100**	**100**	**100**	**100**	**100**
三、每万人拥有公共交通车辆（标台）	**Number of Public Transport Vehicles Per 10 000 Population (units)**	**14.3**				
四、燃气普及率（%）	**Gas-Consuming Popularization (%)**	**98.79**	**100**	**67.21**	**93.47**	**99.34**
五、人均城市道路面积（平方米）	**Per Captia Area of Roads (sq.m)**	**18.26**	**18.28**	**8.91**	**11.71**	**29.29**
六、建成区排水管道密度（公里/平方公里）	**Density of Drainage Pipelines (km/sq.km)**	**9.09**	**9.36**	**7.23**	**4.75**	**6.26**
七、污水处理率(%)	**Rate of Sewerage Disposal (%)**	**91.85**	**92.36**	**77.54**	**77.51**	**77.61**
八、园林绿化	**Afforestation and Parks and Gardens**					
人均公园绿地面积（平方米）	Per Capita Public Green Areas (sq.m)	11.47	11.74	4.34	15.00	9.71
建城区绿地率（%）	Rate of Green Areas in Developed Areas(%)	34.03	34.28	29.56	21.40	36.01
九、生活垃圾无害化处理率(%)	**Rate of No Harm Disposal of Garbage (%)**	**98.09**	**100**		**100**	**100**

注：本表数据来源于市建委。

主要统计指标解释

建成区面积 城市行政区内实际已成片开发建设、市政公用设施和公共设施基本具备的区域。对核心城市，它包括集中连片的部分以及分散的若干个已经成片建设起来，市政公用设施和公共设施基本具备的地区；对一城多镇来说，它包括由几个连片开发建设起来的，市政公用设施和公共设施基本具备的地区组成。因此建成区范围，一般是指建成区外轮廓线所能包括的地区，也就是这个城市实际建设用地所达到的范围。

供水综合生产能力 指按供水设施取水、净化、送水、出厂输水干管等环节设计能力计算的综合生产能力。包括在原设计能力的基础上，经挖、革、改增加的生产能力。计算时，以四个环节中最薄弱的环节为主确定能力。

供水管道长度 指从送水泵至用户水表之间所有管道的长度。不包括新安装尚未使用、水厂内以及用户建筑物内的管道。在同一条街道埋设两条或两条以上管道时，应按每条管道的长度计算。

供水总量 指报告期供水企业（单位）供出的全部水量。包括有效供水量和漏损水量。

用水普及率 指报告期末城区内用水人口与总人口的比率。计算公式:

$$用水普及率 = \frac{用水人口（含暂住人口）}{人口+暂住人口} \times 100\%$$

供气管道长度 指报告期末从气源厂压缩机的出口或门站出口至各类用户引入管之间的全部已经通气投入使用的管道长度。不包括煤气生产厂、输配站、液化气储存站、灌瓶站、储配站、气化站、混气站、供应站等厂（站）内的管道。

供气总量 指报告期燃气企业（单位）向用户供应的燃气数量。包括销售量和损失量。

燃气普及率 指报告期末城区内使用燃气的人口与总人口的比率。计算公式：

$$燃气普及率 = \frac{用气人口（含暂住人口）}{人口+暂住人口} \times 100\%$$

供热能力 指供热企业（单位）向城市热用户输送热能的设计能力。不是热电厂的生产能力。

供热总量 指在报告期供热企业（单位）向城市热用户输送全部蒸汽和热水的总热量。

供热管道长度 指从各类热源到热用户建筑物接入口之间的全部蒸汽和热水的管道长度。不包括各类热源厂内部的管道长度。

供热面积 指供热企业（单位）向城市各类房屋建筑物、构筑物及其附属设施供热的全部建筑面积。

道路长度 指道路长度和与道路相通的桥梁、隧道的长度，按车行道中心线计算。

道路面积 指道路实际铺装面积和与道路相通的广场、桥梁、隧道的铺装面积（统计时，将人行道面积单独统计）。

人行道面积按道路两侧面积相加计算，包括步行街和广场，不含人车混行的道路。

排水管道长度 指所有排水总管、干管、支管、检查井及连接井进出口等长度之和。计算时按单管计算，即在同一条街道上如有两条或两条以上并排的排水管道时，应按每条排水管道的长度相加计算。

绿化覆盖面积 指城市中的乔木、灌木、草坪等所有植被的垂直投影面积。包括公园绿地、防护绿地、生产绿地、附属绿地、其他绿地的绿化种植覆盖面积、屋顶绿化覆盖面积以及零散树木的覆盖面积，不含各类绿地中的水域面积以及没有被植被覆盖的面积（硬化道路、无屋顶绿化的建筑物等）。乔木树冠下重迭的灌木和草本植物不重复计算。

人均城市道路面积 指报告期末城区内平均每人拥有的城市道路面积。计算公式：

$$人均城市道路面积= \frac{城区道路面积}{城区人口+城区暂住人口}$$

建成区排水管道密度 指报告期末建成区排水管道分布的疏密程度，计算公式：

$$排水管道密度 = \frac{排水管道长度}{建成区面积}$$

污水处理率 指报告期内污水处理总量与污水排放总量的比率。计算公式：

$$污水处理率 = \frac{污水处理总量}{污水排放总量} \times 100\%$$

人均公园绿地面积 指报告期末城区内平均每人拥有的公园绿地面积。计算公式：

$$人均公园绿地面积 = \frac{城区公园绿地面积}{城区人口+城区暂住人口}$$

建成区绿地率 指报告期末建成区内绿地面积与建成区面积的比率。计算公式：

$$建成区绿地率 = \frac{建成区绿地面积}{建成区面积} \times 100\%$$

Explanatory Notes on Main Statistical Indicators

Area of the Constructed Regions refers to developed and built city administrative area where basic municipal utilities and public facilities complete constructed. To core city, it includes part of contiguous centralized and a number of decentralized part where basic municipal utilities and public facilities complete constructed. To a multi-city town, it consists of several contiguous developed and build area where municipal utilities and public facilities with basic composition. Therefore, the range of built-up area, generally refers to the built-up areas in the contour line, which is the actual construction site of the city achieved range.

Production Capacity of Water Supply refers to the designed overall production capacity of water facilities, covering the four segments of water collection, purification, conveyance, and out flow through trunk pipelines. Increased capacity through transformation and innovation projects is included as well. The capacity is determined mainly on the weakest of the above-mentioned four segments.

Length of Water Supply Pipelines at Year–end refers to the total length of all the pipelines between the water pumps and the user water meters, excluding pipelines newly installed but not used yet, pipeline in the water factory, and pipeline in the user's buildings.

Volume of Water Supply refers to the total volume of water supplied by water-works(units) during the reference period, including both the effective water supply and loss during the water supply.

Coverage Rate of Urban Population with Access to Tap Water refers to the ratio of the urban population with access to tap water to the total urban population . The formula is :

$$\text{Coverage of urban population with access to tap water} = \frac{\text{population with access to tap water}}{\text{population}} \times 100\%$$

Length of Gas Pipeline refers to the total length of pipelines in use between the outlet of the compressor of gas-work of outlet gas stations and the leading pipe of users , excluding pipelines within gasworks , delivery stations ,LPG storage stations ,refilling stations, gas-mixing stations and supply stations.

Volume of Gas Supply refers to the total volume of gas provided to users by gas-producing enterprises (units) in a year ,including the volume sold and the volume lost .

Coverage Rate of Urban Population with Access to Gas refers to the ratio of the urban population with access to gas to the total urban population at the end of the reference period. The formula is :

$$\text{Coverage rate of urban population with access to gas} = \frac{\text{population with access to gas}}{\text{population}} \times 100\%$$

City Heating capacity in Urban Areas refers to the designed capacity of heating enterprises (units) in supplying heating energy to urban users during the reference period .

City Quantity of Heat Supplied in Urban Areas refers to the total quantity of heat from steam and hot water urban users by heating enterprises (units) during the reference period .

City Length of Urban Heating Pipelines refers to the total length of steam or hot water pipelines for sources of heat to the leading pipelines of the building of the users ,excluding internal pipelines in heat generating enterprises

Heated Area refers to the total structure area of heat supplied to urban constructions, structures and ancillary facilities by heating enterprises (units) during the reference period .

Length of Paved Roads refers to the length of roads with paved surface including bridges and tunnels connected with roads. Length of the roads is measured by the central lines .

Area of Paved Roads refers to the actual pavement area of roads and the actual pavement area of squares, bridges and tunnels connecting to the roads (the area of sidewalk pavements is calculated separately).

The area of sidewalk pavements is the sum of area of roads on sides of road, including pedestrian streets and squares, excluding roads for both pedestrians and vehicles .

Length of exhaust pipelines refers to the total length of all main drain piles ,trunk pipes ,branch pipes

,access manholes ,and connector well entrances and exits ,and so on . The whole length is calculated as of single pipes. Namely ,if there are two or more drain pipes parallel on a street ,the length of every pipe shall be summed .

Total area of green land refers to vertical projection area of all vegetation including trees, shrubs, lawns. Including parks, protective green space, production green space, green subsidiaries, green plants covering area, covering an area other green spaces, green roofs and covering area of scattered trees, excluding kinds of water area in kinds of green area and the area not covered by vegetation(hardened road, building of no green roof). shrubs and herbaceous plants overlap under the canopy of trees do not double counting.

Per Capita Area of Paved Roads refers to the area of urban roads per capita at the end of the reporting period. The formula is :

$$\text{Per capita area of paved roads} = \frac{\text{Area of urban roads}}{\text{Urban population+temporary resident population}}$$

Density of Drainage Pipelines refers to density of drainage pipelines in developed areas at the end of the reporting period .The formula is :

$$\text{Density of drainage pipelines} = \frac{\text{Length of drainage pipelines}}{\text{Ares of developed areas}}$$

Rate of Sewerage Disposal refers to the ratio of waste water disposed with the total discharge of waste water in the reporting period .The formula is:

$$\text{Rate of Sewerage Disposal} = \frac{\text{Waste Water Disposed}}{\text{Total Discharge of Waste Water}} \times 100\%$$

Per Capita Area of Public Green refers to the area of public green areas per capita at end of the reporting period .The formula is :

$$\text{Per capita area of public green} = \frac{\text{Area of public green areas}}{\text{Urban population+temporary resident population}}$$

Coverage of Green Areas in Developed Areas refers to the ratio of green areas in built-up areas with the area of developed areas at the end of reporting period . The formula is:

$$\text{Coverage of green land in developed areas} = \frac{\text{Area of green land in developed aresa}}{\text{Area of developed areas}} \times 100\%$$

10 环境保护

ENVIRONMENT PROTECTION

资料整理：李　炜
Data management：Li Wei
数据审核：陈　英
Data audit：Chen Ying

第十部分　环境保护

一、简要说明

本章资料反映环境保护、工业污染排放及处理利用情况、危险废物集中处置情况、生活及其他污染情况和工业污染治理项目建设情况，由西安市统计局综合处根据西安市环保局提供的数据资料整理。

二、主要指标

工业用水重复利用率（%）	74.04	比上年提高	5.16个百分点
工业固体废物综合利用率（%）	90.82	比上年下降	1.61个百分点
全年环境空气达到二级以上天数（天）	251	比上年增加	40天

10 ENVIRONMENT PROTECTION

Ⅰ.Brief Introduction

This chapter contain information that reflect environment protection, discharge and treatment of industrial pollutant, centralized treatment of dangerous wastes, domestic pollution and other pollution, construction of projects of industrial pollution treatment. Data in this chapter is compiled by General Division of the Xi'an Bureau of Statistics according to the reported data from Environment Protection Administration department of the municipal government.

Ⅱ.Major Indicators

		Increase over Preceding Year
Percentage of Industrial Water Recycled (%)	74.04	5.16 percentage points
Percentage of Industrial Solid Waste Utilized (%)	98.82	−1.61 percentage points
Days of Air Quality up to the secondarylevels（day）	251	40

10-1 城市环境保护（2015年）

Urban Environmental Protection（2015）

指　标	Item	2015
一、饮用水环境	**Potable Water Environment**	
全市饮用水水质达标率(%)	Compliance Rate of the City's Potable Water Quality (%)	100
二、大气环境	**Atmospheric Environment**	
1、可吸入颗粒物浓度年平均值(毫克/立方米)	Annual Average Concentration of Particulate Matters(mg/cu.m)	0.125
二氧化硫浓度年平均值	Annual Average Concentration of Sulphur Dioxide	0.024
二氧化氮浓度年平均值	Annual Average Concentration of Nitrogen Dioxide	0.044
2、全年环境空气质量达标天数(天)	Days of Air Quality up to the Standards(days)	251
全年环境空气质量达标率(%)	Annual compliance rate of Ambient Air Quality(%)	69.10
三、声环境	**Voice**	
1、功能区噪声平均值(dB(A))	Average Noise Value of Functional Districts(dB(A))	
0类区	Class 0	53.0
1类区	Class 1	59.4
2类区	Class 2	57.1
3类区	Class 3	63.0
4类区	Class 4	70.1
2、道路交通噪声平均值(dB(A))	Average Noise Value of Road Traffic(dB(A))	68.3
3、区域噪声平均值(dB(A))	Average Noise Value of Region(dB(A))	54.7
四、环境污染治理	**Environmental pollution treatment**	
当年完成环保验收项目环境保护投资（亿元）	Year Completed Investment in Environmental Protection Projects of Environmental acceptance(100 million yuan)	25.00

注：本表数据来源于市环保局。

10-2 主要年份工业"三废"排放及处理利用情况

指　标	Item	2000	2006
一、工业废水排放量（万吨）	**Volume of Waste Water Discharge (10 000 tons)**	9145	16389
工业废水处理量（万吨）	Volume of Industrial Wastewater Disposal (10 000 tons)		
废水治理设施数（套）	Number of Facilities for Treatment of Waste Water (sets)		
二、工业废气排放量（亿立方米）	**Total Volume of Industrial Waste Gas Emission (100 million cu.m)**	275.97	642.51
废气治理设施数（套）	Number of Facilities for Treatment of Waste Gas(sets)		466
三、工业固体废物产生量（万吨）	**Volume of Industrial Solid Wastes Produced (10 000 tons)**	107	161
工业固体废物处置量（万吨）	Volume of Industrial Solid Wastes Treated (10 000 tons)	20	5
工业固体废物综合利用量（万吨）	Volume of Industrial Solid Waste Utilized (10 000 tons) in a Comprehensive Way	63	143
工业固体废物综合利用率（%）	Percentage of Volume of Industrial Solid Waste Utilized in a Comprehensive Way(%)	58.88	89.07
四、工业锅炉（台/蒸吨）	**Industrial Boilers (units/tons)**		

注：本表数据来源于市环保局。

2010年全国统一进行了污染源普查动态更新调查工作，"十二五"的环境统计体系与污染源普查体系相衔接，与"十一五"环境统计口径不同。

Discharge and Treatrment of Waste Gas, Water & Solid Wastes in Repersentative Years

2010	2011	2012	2013	2014	2015
13840	**13148**	**10223.73**	**8972.97**	**6339.85**	**5203.56**
10673.52	12632.38	9089.04	6798.71	5818.27	4783.60
267	314	312	295	305	315
791.56	**1018.46**	**1043.31**	**844.11**	**901.23**	**1108.48**
816	745	649	661	740	801
267.29	**279**	**259.14**	**255.78**	**252.66**	**238.53**
3.56	6	9.24	9.68	17.54	20.95
262	271	248.58	244.08	233.52	216.64
98.05	97.3	95.92	95.43	92.43	90.82
		503/8785	**576/13466**	**520/14177**	**501/18278**

10-3 工业污染排放及处理利用情况（2015年）

Discharge and Treatment of Industrial Pollution（2015）

指　标	Item	2015
一、被调查企业基本情况	**Basic condition of Enterprises investigated**	
1. 企业数（个）	Number of Enterprises (units)	495
2. 工业总产值（亿元）（当年价格）	Gross Industry Output Value (100 millian yuan)	2184.01
3. 工业锅炉数（台/蒸吨）	Industrial Boilers (units/tons)	501/18278
4. 工业炉窑数（座）	Number of Industrial Grates (items)	222
二、工业废水	**Industrial Waste Water**	
1. 工业用水总量（万吨）	Total Volume of Industrial Water (10 000 tons)	38657.28
新鲜水量	Volume of Fresh Water	10036.98
重复用水量	Volume of Water Recycled	28620.30
2. 工业用水重复利用率（%）	Percentage of Industrial Water Recycled (%)	74.04
3. 废水治理设施数（套）	Number of Facilities for Treatment of Waste Water (sets)	315
4. 废水治理设施处理能力（万吨/日）	Disposal Capacity of Facilities for Treatment of Waste Water (10 000 tons/day)	23.78
5. 废水治理设施运行费用（万元）	Operating Expense of Facilities for Treatment of Waste Water (10 000 yuan)	27527
6. 工业废水排放量（万吨）	Volume of Industrial Waste Water Discharged (10 000 tons)	5203.56
三、工业废气	**Industrial Waste Gas**	
1. 煤炭消费量（万吨）	Total Coal Consumption (10 000 tons)	781.71
2. 燃料油消费量（不含车船用）（万吨）	Fuel Oil Consumption (10 000 tons)	0.24
3. 天然气消费量（亿立方米）	Natural Gas Consumption (100 millian cu.m)	2.56
4. 工业废气排放总量（亿立方米）	Total Volume of Industrial Waste Gas Emission (100 millian cu.m)	1108.48
5. 废气治理设施数（套）	Number of Facilities for Treatment of Waste Gas (sets)	801
6. 废气治理设施处理能力（万立方米/时）	Disposal Capacity of Facilities for Treatment of Waste Gas (10 000 cu.m./h)	3994.51
7. 废气治理设施设备运行费用（万元）	Operating Expense of Facilities for Treatment of Waste gas(10 000 yuan)	60542.80
8. 二氧化硫去除量（吨）	Volume of Sulphur Dioxide Removed (tons)	138257.96
9. 二氧化硫排放量（吨）	Volume of Sulphur Dioxide Emission (tons)	38691.36
10. 氮氧化物生产量（吨）	Production of nitrogen oxides(tons)	44497.34
11. 氮氧化物排放量（吨）	Nitrogen oxide emissions(tons)	22364.26
12. 烟（粉）尘生产量（吨）	Tobacco (powder) dust production(tons)	1474034.34
13. 烟（粉）尘排放量（吨）	The smoke (powder) dust emissions(tons)	16443.53
四、工业固体废物	**Industrial Solid Waste**	
1. 工业固体废物产生量（万吨）	Volume of Industrial Solid Waste Produced (10 000tons)	238.53
2. 工业固体废物综合利用量（万吨）	Volume of Industrial Solid Waste Utilized (10 000tons)	216.64
3. 工业固体废物综合利用率（%）	Percentage of Industrial Solid Waste Utilized (%)	90.82
4. 工业固体废物贮存量（万吨）	Volume of Industrial Solid Waste Accumulated (10 000tons)	0.95
5. 工业固体废物处置量（万吨）	Volume of Industrial Solid Waste Treated (10 000tons)	20.95
6. 工业固体废物倾倒丢弃量（吨）	Volume of Industrial Solid Waste Discharged (tons)	

注：本表数据来源于市环保局。

10-4 城市污水处理情况（2015年）

Urban Sewage Treatment（2015）

指　标	Item	2015
一、污水处理厂数（座）	**Number of Sewage Treatment Works(units)**	**36**
污水处理厂处理能力（万吨/日）	Daily Disposal Capacity of Sewage(10 000 tons/day)	200.28
二、污水处理	**Sewgae Disposal**	
污水实际处理量（万吨）	Volume of Sewgae Disposal(10 000 tons)	56868.88
生活污水处理量	Volume of Domestic Sewgae Disposal	55429.37
工业污水处理量	Volume of Industrial Sewage Disposal	1439.51
三、再生水（万吨）	**Recycled water (10 000 tons)**	
生产量	Production	934.77
利用量	Utilization	812.06
四、化学需氧量去除量（吨）	**Volume of COD Removed (tons)**	**192471.92**
五、氨氮去除量（吨）	**Volume of Ammonia and Nitrogen Removed(tons)**	**18455.09**
六、总磷去除量（吨）	**Volume of Total Phosphorus Removed(tons)**	**2507.92**
七、污泥生产量（万吨）	**Volume of Sludge Produced(10 000 tons)**	**52.76**
八、污泥处置量（万吨）	**Volume of Sludge Disposal(10 000 tons)**	**52.76**
九、污泥倾倒丢弃量（吨）	**Dumping sludge discards (tons)**	
十、本年运行费用（万元）	**Operating Expense(10 000 yuan)**	**55123.94**

注：本表数据来源于市环保局。

10-5 危险废物（医疗废物）集中处理情况(2015年)

Condition of Collected Dangerous Wastes Treated (2015)

指 标	Item	2015
一、危险废物集中处理（置）厂数（个）	**Number of Colleted Dangerous Wastes Treated Plants(items)**	**2**
二、医疗废物集中处理（置）厂数（个）	**The number of Manufacturing Plants of Medical waste treatment (units)**	**1**
三、危险废物设计处置能力（吨/日）	**Design hazardous waste disposal capacity (tons / day)**	**443.00**
四、实际处置危险废物量（吨）	**The actual amount of hazardous waste disposal (tons)**	**60219.79**
五、危险废物综合利用量（吨）	**Volume of Dangerous Wastes Utilized in a Comprehensive Way (tons)**	
六、焚烧残渣流向（千克）	**Flow Direction of Residuum after Burning (kg)**	
1. 焚烧残渣量	Volume of Residuum after Burning	429074.10
2. 焚烧残渣安全填进处理量	Secure landfill disposal incineration residues	429074.10
3. 焚烧飞灰生产量	Fly ash production	74372.84
4. 焚烧飞灰安全填进处理量	Fly ash landfill disposal safety	74372.84
七、当年运行费用（万元）	**Operating Expenses in Current year(10 000 yuan)**	**6229.51**

注：本表数据来源于市环保局。

10-6 生活及其他污染情况(2015年)

Domestic Pollution and Other Conditions (2015)

指 标	Item	2015
一、基本情况	**Basic Condition**	
1. 生活天然气消费量（万立方米）	Volume of Living natural gas consumption (10 000 cu.m)	196826.38
2. 生活用水总量（万吨）	Volume of Living water (10 000 tons)	68948.20
二、污染排放情况	**Discharge of Pollutant**	
1. 城镇生活污水排放量（万吨）	Volume of Urban Domestic Sewage Discharged(10 000 tons)	59347.99
2. 生活污水处理量（万吨）	Volume of Domestic Sewgae Disposal(10 000 tons)	55480.59
3. 生活CDD生产量（吨）	Volume of Life CDD production (tons)	164344.13
4. 生活CDD排放量（吨）	Volume of Life CDD emissions (tons)	53426.71
5. 生活氨氮生产量（吨）	Volume of Ammonia and Nitrogen in Urban Domestic Sewage Produced (tons)	20634.30
6. 生活氨氮排放量（吨）	Volume of Ammonia and Nitrogen in Urban Domestic Sewage Discharged (tons)	9225.95
7. 二氧化硫排放量（吨）	Volume of Domestic and Other Sulphur Dioxide Emission (tons)	53585.98
8. 氮氮化物排放量（吨）	Volume of Ammonia and Nitrogen in Urban Domestic Sewage Discharged (tons)	16713.44
9. 烟尘排放量（吨）	Volume of Soot Emission (tons)	15563.02

注：本表数据来源于市环保局。

10-7 工业污染治理项目建设情况（2015年）

Condition of Anti-Industrial-Pollution Projects（2015）

指　标	Item	2015
一、工业企业数（个）	**Number of Industrial Enterprises (units)**	**23**
二、老工业污染源项目治理本年施工总数（个）	**The total number of construction projects of Old industrial pollution sources control this year(units)**	**28**
#工业废水治理项目	Treatment of Waste Water	8
工业废气治理项目	Treatment of Waste Gas	15
工业固体废物治理项目	Treatmen of Solid Wastes	
三、老工业污染源项目治理本年竣工总数（个）	**The Total Number of Old Industrial Pollution Control Projects Completed this year(units)**	**23**
#工业废水治理项目	Treatment of Waste Water	5
工业废气治理项目	Treatment of Waste Gas	14
工业固体废物治理项目	Treatmen of Solid Wastes	
四、老工业污染源治理项目本年完成投资（万元）	**Investment completed in Old industrial pollution control projects this Year(10 000 yuan)**	**64845.49**
#废水治理项目	Treatment of Waste Water	3238.63
废气治理项目	Treatment of Waste Gas	21437.47
固体废物治理项目	Treatmen of Solid Wastes	
五、老工业污染源治理项目本年投资来源（万元）	**Source of Investment in Old industrial pollution control projects this Year(10 000 yuan)**	64845.49
#排污费补助	Pollution Charges Subsidies	300.00
政府其他补助	Other Government Subsidies	5933.65
企业自筹	Self-raising Funds	58611.84
#银行贷款	Lonans	11169.00
六、“三同时”项目竣工验收数（个）	**number of "Three simultaneous"project completion and acceptance (a)**	**3**
七、“三同时”竣工验收项目实际环保投资（万元）	**"Three simultaneous" actual environmental investment completed and accepted (10 000 yuan)**	**874**
八、“三同时”项目废水治理新增处理能力（万吨/日）	**"Three simultaneous"Add processing capacity of wastewater treatment (10 000 tons / day)**	**0.1**
九、“三同时”项目废气治理新增处理能力（万立方米/时）	**"Three simultaneous"Add processing capacity of Exhaust treatment (10 000 cu.m/h)**	

注：本表数据来源于市环保局。

“三同时”指建设项目中防治污染的措施，必须与主体工程同时设计，同时施工，同时投产使用。

10-8 各区县、开发区环境保护基本情况（2015年）

区县、开发区	Region	本年完成环保验收项目环保投资额（万元）Investment Completed in accepted Environmental projects this year (10 000 yuan)	工业二氧化硫排放量（吨）Volume of Industrial Sulphur Dioxide Discharged (tons)
全　市	**Total**	**249971.5**	**38691.36**
新城区	Xincheng	3055.4	82.30
碑林区	Beilin	3616.0	1767.73
莲湖区	Lianhu	1837.4	1304.46
灞桥区	Baqiao	8571.1	7283.30
未央区	Weiyang	7638.1	687.48
雁塔区	Yanta	1907.4	2763.86
阎良区	Yanliang	2374.6	2166.40
临潼区	Lintong	1121.5	1083.10
长安区	Chang'an	14825.9	3045.62
高陵区	Gaoling	2690.6	864.47
蓝田县	Lantian	613.0	532.48
周至县	Zhouzhi	12.0	245.19
户　县	Huxian	12378.0	6987.76
高新开发区	Gaoxinkaifaqu	23753.5	1176.05
经济开发区	Jingjikaifaqu	17657.0	2638.08
航天基地	Hangtianjidi	660.0	614.00
沣东新城	Fendongxincheng	3092.0	5449.08

注：本表数据来源于市环保局。

环境统计中污水处理厂个数包含部分大学园区及部分大型小区的污水处理厂。

Condition of Environment Protection by Regions（2015）

工业化学需氧量排放量（吨）Volume of COD Removed (tons)	垃圾处理站数（座）Number of Rubbish Disposal Works (units)	污水处理厂数（个）Number of Sewage Treatment Works (units)
24296.30	**3**	**36**
284.42		
3.38		
700.06		2
644.07	1	3
2596.04		5
281.85		3
440.45	1	1
1943.45		3
1335.96		8
181.38	1	1
78.36		3
108.50		1
5155.73		3
2557.39		1
3571.62		1
841.54		0
3577.10		1

主要统计指标解释

工业用水 指工矿企业在生产过程中用于制造、加工、冷却、空调、净化、洗涤等方面的用水，按新水取用量计，不包括企业内部的重复利用水量。

工业废水排放量 指经过企业厂区所有排放口排到企业外部的工业废水量。包括生产废水、外排的直接冷却水、超标排放的矿井地下水和与工业废水混排的厂区生活污水，不包括外排的间接冷却水（清污不分流的间接冷却水应计算在内）。

直接排入海的 指经企业位于海边的排放口，直接排入海的废水量。直接排放指废水经过工厂的排污口直接排入海，而未经过城市下水道或其他中间体，也不受其他水体的影响。

工业废水排放达标量 指报告期内废水中各项污染物指标都达到国家或地方排放标准的外排工业废水量，包括未经处理外排达标的，经废水处理设施处理后达标排放的，以及经污水处理厂处理后达标排放的。

生活污水排放量 指城镇居民每年排放的生活污水。用人均系数法测算。测算公式为：

$$\text{生活污水排放量} = \text{城镇生活污水排放系数} \times \text{市镇非农业人口} \times 365$$

生活污水中化学需氧量（COD）排放量 指城镇居民每年排放的生活污水中的COD的量。用人均系数法测算。测算公式为：

$$\text{城镇生活污水中COD产生系数} = \text{城镇牛活污水中COD排放量} \times \text{市镇非农业人口} \times 365$$

化学需氧量（COD） 指用化学氧化剂氧化水中有机污染物时所需的氧量。COD值越高，表示水中有机污染物污染越重。

工业废气排放量 指报告期内企业厂区内燃料燃烧和生产工艺过程中产生的各种排入大气的含有污染物的气体的总量，以标准状态（273K，101325Pa）计算。测算公式为：

$$\text{工业废气排放量} = \text{燃料燃烧过程中废气排放量} + \text{生产工艺过程中废气排放量}$$

生活及其他SO_2排放量 以生活及其他煤炭消费量和其含硫量为基础，根据以下公式计算：

$$\text{生活及其他}SO_2\text{排放量} = \text{生活及其他煤炭消费量} \times \text{含硫量} \times 0.8 \times 2$$

工业SO_2排放量 指报告期内企业在燃料燃烧和生产工艺过程中排入大气的SO_2总量，计算公式为：

$$\text{工业}SO_2\text{排放量} = \text{燃料燃烧过程中}SO_2\text{排放量} + \text{生产工艺过程中}SO_2\text{排放量}$$

工业烟尘排放量 指企业厂区内燃料燃烧过程中产生的烟气中夹带的颗粒物排放量。

生活及其他烟尘排放量 指除工业生产活动以外的所有社会、经济活动及公共设施的经营活动中燃烧所排放的烟尘纯重量。以生活及其他煤炭消费量为基础进行测算。

工业粉尘排放量 指企业在生产工艺过程中排放的能在空气中悬浮一定时间的固体颗粒物排放量。如钢铁企业的耐火材料粉尘、焦化企业的筛焦系统粉尘、烧结机的粉尘、石灰窑的粉尘、建材企业的水泥粉尘等。不包括电厂排入大气的烟尘。

工业固体废物产生量 指报告期内企业在生产过程中产生的固体状、半固体状和高浓度液体状废弃物的总量，包括危险废物、冶炼废渣、粉煤灰、炉渣、煤矸石、尾矿、放射性废物和其他废物等；不包括矿山开采的剥离废石和掘进废石（煤矸石和呈酸性或碱性的废石除外）。酸性或碱性废石指采掘的废石其流经水、雨淋水的pH值小于4或pH值大于10.5者。

危险废物 指列入国家危险废物名录或根据国家规定的危险废物鉴别标准和鉴别方法认定的，具有爆炸性、易燃性、易氧化性、毒性、腐蚀性、易传染疾病等危险特性之一的废物。

工业固体废物综合利用量 指报告期内企业通过回收、加工、循环、交换等方式，从固体废物中提取或者使其转化为可以利用的资源、能源和其他原材料的固体废物量（包括当年利用往年的工业固体废物贮存量），如用作农业肥料、生产建筑材料、筑路等。综合利用量由原产生固体废物的单位统计。

工业固体废物综合利用率 指工业固体废物综合利用量占丁业固体废物产生量（包括综合利用往年贮存量）的百分率。计算公式为：

$$\text{工业固体废物综合利用率}=\frac{\text{工业固体废物综合利用量}}{\text{工业固体废物产生量}+\text{综合利用往年贮存量}}\times 100\%$$

工业固体废物贮存量 指报告期内企业以综合利用或处置为目的，将固体废物暂时贮存或堆存在专设的贮存设施或专设的集中堆存场所内的数量。专设的固体废物贮存场所或贮存设施必须有防扩散、防流失、防渗漏、防止污染大气、水体的措施。

工业固体废物处置量 指报告期内企业将固体废物焚烧或者最终置于符合环境保护规定要求的场所，并不再回取的工业固体废物量（包括当年处置往年的工业固体废物贮存量）。处置方式有填埋（其中危险废物应安全填埋）、焚烧、专业贮存场（库）封场处理、深层灌注、回填矿井及海洋处置（经海洋管理部门同意投海处置）等。

工业固体废物排放量 指报告期内企业将所产生的固体废物排到固体废物污染防治设施、场所以外的数量，不包括矿山开采的剥离废石和掘进废石（煤矸石和呈酸性或碱性的废石除外）。

“三废”综合利用产品产值 指报告期内利用“三废”作为主要原料生产的产品价值（现行价）；已经销售或准备销售的应计算产品价值，留作生产自用的不应计算产品价值。

生活垃圾清运量 指报告期内收集和运送到各生活垃圾处理厂（场）和生活垃圾最终消纳点的生活垃圾数量。生活垃圾指城市日常生活或为城市日常生活提供服务的活动中产生的固体废物以及法律行政规定的视为城市生活垃圾的固体废物。包括：居民生活垃圾、商业垃圾、集市贸易市场垃圾、街道清扫垃圾、公共场所垃圾和机关、学校、厂矿等单位的生活垃圾。

生活垃圾无害化处理率 指报告期生活垃圾无害化处理量与生活垃圾产生量的比率。在统计上，由于生活垃圾产生量不易取得，可用清运量代替。计算公式为：

$$\text{生活垃圾无害化处理率}=\frac{\text{生活垃圾无害化处理量}}{\text{生活垃圾产生量}}\times 100\%$$

Explanatory Notes on Main Statistical Indicators

Water Use by Industry refers to new withdrawals of water, excluding reuse of water within enterprises.

Waste Water Discharged by Industry refers to the volume of waste water discharged by industrial enterprises through all their outlets, including waste water from production process, directly cooled water, groundwater from mining wells which does not meet discharge standards and sewage from households mixed with waste water produced by industrial activities, but excluding indirectly cooled water discharged (It should be included if the discharge is not separated from waste water).

Waste Water Directly Discharged into Sea refers to the volume of waste water directly discharged into sea through outlets of enterprises situated by sea without going through municipal sewerage networks or any other intermediates or being affected by any other water bodies.

Industrial Waste Water Meeting Discharge Standards refers to volume of industrial waste water discharge which, with or without treatment, reaches national or local standards with regard to all pollutants.

Urban Non-industrial Waste Water Discharge refers to annual discharge of non-industrial waste water by urban households. It is estimated by per capita coefficient using the formula:

$$\text{Urban non-industrial waste water discharge} = \text{urban non-industrial waste water discharge coefficient} \times \text{urban non-alagricultur population} \times 365$$

Volume of Chemical Oxygen Demand (COD) Generated by Urban Non-industrial Waster Water refers to chemical oxygen demand generated through the annual discharge of non-industrial waste water by urban households. It is estimated as:

$$\text{Volume of chemical oxygen demand (cod) generated by urban non-industrial waster water} = \text{Coefficient of COD generated through urban non-industrial waste water} \times \text{urban non-agricultura population} \times 365$$

Chemical Oxygen Demand (COD) refers to the amount of oxygen required when chemical oxidants are used to oxidize organic pollutants in water. A higher value of COD corresponds to more serious pollution by organic pollutants.

Industrial Waste Air Emission refers to the discharge into atmosphere of waste air containing pollutants generated from fuel burning and production processes in enterprises within a given period of time. It is calculated at standard status (273K, 101325Pa) as:

$$\text{Industrial waste air emission} = \text{tnoissimehrough fuel burning} + \text{tnoissimehrough production process}$$

SO_2 Emission through Non-industrial and Other Activities is calculated on the basis of consumption of coal by households and other activities and the sulphur content of coal with the following formula:

$$SO_2 \text{ emission through non-industrial and other activities} = \text{of coalby households andother activities} \times \text{sulphur content} \times 0.8 \times 2$$

SO_2 Emission through Industrial Activities refers to volume of sulphur dioxide emission from fuel burning and production process by enterprises during a given period of time. It is calculated as:

$$SO_2 \text{ emission through industrial activities} = SO_2 \text{emIssIon from fuel burning} + SO_2 \text{ emission from production process}$$

Industrial Soot Emission refers to the volume of soot in smoke emitted in the process of fuel burning in the premises of enterprises.

Soot Emission by Consumption and Others refers to the net volume of soot emitted by fuel burning from all social and economic activities and operations of public facilities other than industrial activities. It is calculated on the basis of coal consumption by households and others.

Industrial Dust Emission refers to volume of dust emitted by production process of enterprises and suspended in the air for a given period of time, including dust from refractory material of iron and steel works, dust from coke-screening systems and sintering machines of coke plants, dust from lime kilns and dust from cement production in building material enterprises, but excluding soot and dust emitted from power plants.

Industrial Solid Wastes Produced refers to total volume of solid, semi-solid and high concentration liquid residues produced by industrial enterprises from production process in a given period of time, including hazardous wastes, slag, coal ash, gangue, tailings, radioactive residues and other wastes, but excluding stones stripped or dug out in mining - gangue and acid or alkaline stones not included (a stone is acid or alkaline according to the pH value of the water being below 4 or above 10.5 when the stone is in, or soaked by water).

Hazardous Wastes refers to those included in the national hazardous wastes catalogue or specified as any one of the following properties in the national hazardous wastes identification standards: explosive, ignitable, oxidizable, toxic, corrosive or liable to cause infectious diseases or lead to other dangers.

Industrial Solid Wastes Utilized refers to volume of solid wastes from which useful materials can be extracted or which can be converted into usable resources, energy or other materials by means of reclamation, processing, recycling and exchange (including utilizing in the year the stocks of industrial solid wastes of the previous year). Examples of such utilizations include fertilizers, building materials and road materials. The information shall be collected by the producing units of the wastes.

Rate of Utilization of Industrial Solid Wastes refers to the percentage of industrial solid wastes utilized over industrial solid wastes produced (including stocks of the previous years). It is calculated as:

$$\text{Rate of utilization of industrial solid wastes} = \frac{\text{volume of industrial solid wastes utilized}}{\text{industrial solid wastesproduced+ stock of previous years}} \times 100\%$$

Stock of Industrial Solid Wastes refers to the volume of solid wastes placed in special facilities or special sites for purposes of utilization or disposal. The sites or facilities should take measures against dispersion, loss, seepage, and air and water contamination.

Industrial Solid Wastes Disposed refers to the quantity of industrial solid wastes which are burnt or placed ultimately in the sites meeting the requirements for environmental protection and not salvaged or recycled (including disposition in the year of those wastes of previous years). The disposition includes landfill (Safe landfills should be conducted for hazardous wastes), incineration, containment spaces, deep underground disposal, backfill in mining pits and disposal at sea.

Industrial Solid Wastes Discharged refers to the volume of industrial solid wastes discharged by producing enterprises to disposal facilities or to other sites. The wastes exclude stones stripped or dug from mining (gangue and acid or alkaline waste stones not included).

Output Value of Products Made from Waste Gas, Waste Water and Solid Wastes refers to the current value of products with waste gas, waste water and solid wastes as main materials of production. Products sold and ready to sell shall be included while those produced for own use shall not be included.

Consumption Wastes Transported refers to volume of consumption wastes collected and transported to disposal factories or sites. Consumption wastes are solid wastes produced from urban households or from service activities for urban households, and solid wastes regarded by laws and regulations as urban consumption wastes, including those from households, commercial activities, markets, cleaning of streets, public sites, offices, schools, factories, mining units and other sources.

Ratio of Consumption Wastes Treated refers to consumption wastes treated over that produced. In practical statistics, as it is difficult to estimate, the volume of consumption wastes produced is replaced with that transported. It is calculated as:

$$\text{Ratio of consumption wastes treated} = \frac{\text{consumption wastes treated}}{\text{consumption wastes produced}} \times 100\%$$

11 农　业

AGRICULTURE

资料整理：张喜兰　马秋娟　薛　丰
Data management：Zhang Xilan　Ma Qiujuan　Xue Feng
数据审核：王明珠
Data audit：Wang Mingzhu

第十一部分　农业

一、简要说明

本章资料主要包括农村基本情况、农业生产条件与生产情况、耕地、农林牧渔及服务业产值、主要农产品产量以及各区县农业生产和农村经济效益主要指标，由西安市统计局农村处提供。

二、主要指标

年末耕地面积（万亩）	356.89	比上年下降	1.1%
农林牧渔及服务业总产值（亿元）	380.76	比上年增长	5.1%
农作物播种面积（万亩）	675.59	比上年下降	1.3%
粮食产量（万吨）	180.86	比上年增长	3.0%

11 AGRICULTURE

Ⅰ.Brief Introduction

Data in this chapter reflects basic condition of agriculture production of Xi'an city. It is primarily consist of basic condition of rural area, condition of agriculture production, plow land, production value of farming, forestry, animal husbandry and fishery, gross yield of primary produce and primary indicators of agriculture production and rural area economic performance. The data are provided and compiled by Rural Area Division of the Xi'an Bureau of Statistics.

Ⅱ.Major Indicators

		Increase over Preceding Year
Cultivated Area Year-end(10 000 mu)	356.89	-1.1%
Gross Output Value of Farming, Forestry, Animal Husbandry, Fishery and Service(100 mil. Yuan)	380.76	5.1%
Sown Area of Crops(10 000 mu)	675.59	-1.3%
Grain Output(10 000 tons)	180.86	3.0%

11-1 主要年份农村基层组织、乡村户数、人口及劳动力情况

Grassroots Organizations in Rural Areas, Rural Households, Population and Labor Force in Representative Years

指 标	Item	2000	2005	2006	2007	2008	2009
一、乡村户数（万户）	**Rural Households(10000 households)**	**98.77**	**101.5**	**102.35**	**100.85**	**101.02**	**101**
二、农村人口和从业人员情况	**Condition of Rural Population and Employment**						
1.乡村劳动力资源总数（万人）	Total Rural Labor Force (10000 persons)	240.76	255.93	257.66	254.06	256.17	255
2.乡村从业人员数（万人）	Number of Rural Workers (10000 persons)	212.65	223.3	225.99	222.09	223.85	223.13
#女性	Female	99.07	103.22	103.87	101.83	103.11	102.76
#农业	Agricultural	146.07	137.69	135.64	131.96	126.46	121.78
三、自来水受益村数（个）	**The Number of Tap Water Villages (unit)**	**1527**	**1756**	**1794**	**1881**	**1934**	**2058**
四、通汽车村数	**The Number of Villages with Bus Service**	**2785**	**2952**	**2923**	**2973**	**2996**	**2989**
五、通电话村数	**The Number of Villages with Telephone Service**	**2885**	**3101**	**3113**	**3129**	**3086**	**3071**

11-1 续表 continued

指 标	Item	2010	2011	2012	2013	2014	2015
一、乡村户数（万户）	**Rural Households(10000 households)**	**01.43**	**102.59**	**101.92**	**101.37**	**99.26**	**92.77**
二、农村人口和从业人员情况	**Condition of Rural Population and Employment**						
1.乡村劳动力资源总数（万人）	Total Rural Labor Force (10000 persons)	256.36	260.97	259.06	257.96	252.4	230.21
2.乡村从业人员数（万人）	Number of Rural Workers (10000 persons)	225.04	230.56	226.92	222.67	216.33	200.38
#女性	Female	03.25	109.61	107.63	106.7	104.03	96.46
#农业	Agricultural	16.58	116.15	113.29	108.48	110.3	105.1
三、自来水受益村数（个）	**The Number of Tap Water Villages (unit)**	**2184**	**2400**	**2545**	**2650**	**2765**	**2718**
四、通汽车村数	**The Number of Villages with Bus Service**	**2989**	**2978**	**2936**	**2927**	**2186**	**2209**
五、通电话村数	**The Number of Villages with Telephone Service**	**3052**	**3033**	**2974**	**2966**	**2536**	**2593**

11-2 各区县乡村从业人员数（2015年）

Number of Rural Employees by Region（2015）

单位：万人　　(10 000 persons)

区　县	Region	乡村劳动力资源总数 Total rural labor force	乡村从业人员数合计 Total number of employees in rural areas	女性从业人员 Female employees	农林牧渔业 Forestry Animal Husbandry and Fishery
合　计	**Total**	**230.21**	**200.38**	**96.46**	**105.10**
新城区	Xingcheng				
碑林区	Beilin				
莲湖区	Lianhu				
灞桥区	Baqiao	18.56	14.50	6.21	5.09
未央区	Weiyang	8.49	5.32	2.40	1.54
雁塔区	Yanta				
阎良区	Yanliang	10.79	9.56	4.49	5.77
临潼区	Lintong	36.54	32.04	15.22	19.03
长安区	Chang'an	37.55	36.41	15.73	22.87
高陵区	Gaoling	8.65	7.08	3.38	2.36
蓝田县	Lantian	36.05	34.60	22.07	14.39
周至县	Zhouzhi	40.20	32.34	13.64	18.13
户　县	Huxian	33.38	28.53	13.32	15.92

11–3 主要年份耕地面积

Area of Cultivated Land in Representative Years

单位：万亩 (10 000 mu)

年 份 Year	年末实有耕地面积 Cultivated Area Year-end	水田 Paddy Field	水浇地 Irrigable Land
1970	554.09	18.20	297.05
1975	538.35	20.34	349.13
1978	530.96	16.70	370.46
1980	526.29	17.45	372.96
1985	508.88	17.63	328.10
1990	495.32	17.97	311.91
1991	492.09	17.03	309.17
1992	485.30	16.44	298.19
1993	479.04	14.36	304.49
1994	471.44	13.98	299.58
1995	463.97	17.04	278.01
1996	451.50	14.21	283.76
1997	456.62	11.90	290.49
1998	455.15	11.18	282.23
1999	450.74	11.31	281.96
2000	443.37	10.26	284.04
2001	431.69	9.00	274.73
2002	424.46	7.98	275.96
2003	413.84	6.65	263.75
2004	404.87	6.59	254.04
2005	400.17	5.55	254.04
2006	395.79	5.33	263.75
2007	391.77	4.80	255.95
2008	390.77	4.64	255.36
2009	387.89	4.39	260.71
2010	383.32	4.03	257.43
2011	377.10	3.80	253.46
2012	369.91	3.32	248.97
2013	366.23	5.33	263.75
2014	360.73	2.42	237.26
2015	356.89	2.37	228.14

11-4 各区县耕地面积（2015年）

单位：亩

区 县	Region	年末实有耕地面积 Cultivated Area Year-end	水田 Paddy Field	旱地 Dry Land	水浇地 Irrigable Land
合 计	**Total**	**3568922**	**23742**	**3545180**	**2281371**
新城区	Xincheng				
碑林区	Beilin				
莲湖区	Lianhu				
灞桥区	Baqiao	130628		130628	81664
未央区	Weiyang	12499		12499	12499
雁塔区	Yanta				
阎良区	Yanliang	232172		232172	222958
临潼区	Lintong	693697		693697	527121
长安区	Chang'an	621422	21840	599582	303400
高陵区	Gaoling	226143		226143	226143
蓝田县	Lantian	595194	412	594782	46074
周至县	Zhouzhi	494348	860	493488	361352
户 县	Huxian	562819	630	562189	500160

Area of Cultivated Land by Region（2015）

(mu)

当年增加的耕地面积		当年减少的耕地面积			
Area of Newly Increased Cultivated Land	新开荒地面积 Area of Newly Reclamation of Wasteland	Decrease in Cultivated Area in the Year	国家基建占地 Capital Construction	退耕改果、茶、桑面积 Area for Change into Fruit, Tea and Mulberry	退耕造林面积 Area for Change into Woods
4719	**810**	**45127**	**19964**	**20186**	**324**
99		8089	2473	5611	
		3202	1903		
		6511	6511		
		2304	1545	206	
		3784	2659	1125	
1365		5458	2671	693	104
		742	742		
		806			
3255	810	14031	1260	12551	220
		200	200		

11-5 主要年份农业机械拥有量（年末数）

指标	Item	2006	2007	2008
农用机械总动力（千瓦）	Total Power of Agricultural Machinery(kw)	2277584	2348856	2712616
大中型拖拉机（台）	Large and Medium Tractors(unit)	8963	10431	11092
小型拖拉机（台）	Mini-tractors(unit)	23437	21555	19036
大中型拖拉机配套农具（台）	Number of Large and Medium Tractor Towing Farm Machinery(unit)	18724	23487	25125
小型拖拉机配套农具（台）	Mini-Tractor Towing Farm Machinery (unit)	30439	28780	26984
农用排灌柴油机（台）	Agricultural Diesel Engines(unit)	3547	2709	2670
农用排灌电动机（台）	Agricultural Motors(unit)	76614	84416	85349
农用水泵（台）	Agricultural Water Pump(unit)	73039	80722	80462
节水灌溉类机械（套）	Equipment in Water-saving Irrigation(set)	2656	1991	1728
联合收割机（台）	Combine Harvesters(unit)	5026	5294	5390
自走式机动割晒机（台）	Self-propelled Motorized Swather(unit)	1342	4918	2174
机动脱粒机（台）	Motorized Huller (unit)	5806	11585	23781
农用运输车（辆）	Agricultucal Transporter(unit)	50395	49576	54860

Possession of Agricultural Machinery in Representative Years（Number of year-end）

2009	2010	2011	2012	2013	2014	2015
2616053	2677334	2890247	2983979	3108354	3203302	3253733
11479	14675	12585	12987	12927	9946	9652
18406	14194	13008	11471	8971	7538	8447
26575	29215	36209	32166	32662	31451	32602
29039	24393	29624	27869	25853	21806	21518
2691	3309	2639	2891	2509	2409	2409
83243	79462	87461	87056	86216	85244	84975
80174	77367	75426	80982	80575	79849	79695
1799	1710	1733	2106	2218	2562	2517
6155	6718	7854	8502	9114	7815	8144
1220	208	187				
11960	13231	13407	14493	14700	14749	14504
50671	51665	51838	51850	51710	51410	51365

11-6 各区县农业机械拥有量（2015年）

指标	Item	西安市 Xi' an	灞桥区 Baqiao	未央区 Weiyang
农用机械总动力（千瓦）	Total Power of Agricultural Machinery(kw)	3253733	183011	46397
大中型拖拉机（台）	Large and Medium Tractors(unit)	9652	110	117
小型拖拉机（台）	Mini-tractors(unit)	8447	68	
大中型拖拉机配套农具（台）	Number of Large and Medium Tractor Towing Farm Machinery(unit)	32602	318	387
小型拖拉机配套农具（台）	Mini-Tractor Towing Farm Machinery (unit)	21518	132	
农用排灌柴油机（台）	Agricultural Diesel Engines(unit)	2409		
农用排灌电动机（台）	Agricultural Motors(unit)	84975	3188	984
农用水泵（台）	Agricultural Water Pump(unit)	79695	2927	791
节水灌溉类机械（套）	Equipment in Water-saving Irrigation(set)	2517	55	106
联合收割机（台）	Combine Harvesters(unit)	8144	86	30
自走式机动割晒机（台）	Self-propelled Motorized Swather(unit)			
机动脱粒机（台）	Motorized Huller (unit)	14504	50	7
农用运输车（辆）	Agricultucal Transporter(unit)	51365	3681	467

Possession of Agricultural Machinery by Region（2015）

雁塔区 Yanta	阎良区 Yanliang	临潼区 Lintong	长安区 Chang'an	高陵区 Gaoling	蓝田县 Lantian	周至县 Zhouzhi	户 县 Huxian
92155	188099	612966	553869	290920	309088	479107	498121
35	860	1395	1594	1399	1114	1358	1670
8	266	151	1014	155	854	4319	1612
70	2149	7795	5078	5700	2341	2092	6672
30	585	3783	1806	705	4098	7155	3224
		73	1309		682	289	56
520	5932	16974	22411	3760	3147	15324	12735
500	5776	16460	16823	3760	2486	17437	12735
	463	142	1267		63	272	149
16	714	1947	1419	582	366	344	2640
	1247	4948	982	545	1919	2431	2375
725	2244	14007	7782	5868	4476	8337	3778

11-7 主要年份农业机械化、化肥、水利、水电情况

指标	Item	2000	2005	2006
一、农业机械化水平（万亩）	**Statistics on Agricultural Machinery (10 000 mu)**			
当年机械耕地面积（实际）	Area Ploughed by Tractors	366.81	360.68	354.05
当年机械播种面积（作业）	Seeded Area by Tractors	482.74	485.62	519
当年机械收获面积（作业）	Harvest Area by Tractors	272.83	271.77	280.88
二、农用化肥施用量（吨）	**Use of Agricultural Fertilizers and Insecticides(ton)**			
1. 按实物量计算合计	Practicality Consumption	697243	749802	759882
氮肥	Nitrogenous Fertilizer	392366	411161	413514
磷肥	Phosphate Fertilizer	155480	161444	164781
钾肥	Potash Fertilizer	31841	34114	31414
复合肥	Compound Fertilizer	78620	115458	121124
2. 按折纯法计算合计	Standard Consumption	196343	211790	216093
氮肥	Nitrogenous Fertilizer	102982	107645	110137
磷肥	Phosphate Fertilizer	18658	19368	19772
钾肥	Potash Fertilizer	15921	17055	15709
复合肥	Compound Fertilizer	39313	57009	59731
三、农用塑料薄膜使用量（公斤）	**Plastic Sheet for Agricultural Use(kg)**	**1622198**	**1855383**	**1931527**
四、农用柴油使用量（吨）	**Diesel Oil for Agricultural Use (ton)**	**52706**	**50832**	**49686**
五、农药使用量（公斤）	**Pesticide (kg)**	**1559333**	**1427879**	**1471672**
六、农村水利化情况（万亩）	**Irrigation and Water Conservancy (10 000 mu)**			
有效灌溉面积	Effective Irrigation Area	335.97	280.1	276.58
旱涝保收面积	Stable-Harvesting Arable Land	294.06	255.37	253.66
机电排灌面积	Electrical Irrigation Area	249.11	223.74	214.03
七、农村电气化情况	**Rural electrization**			
乡村及村以下办水电站（个）	Hydropower Station in Rural Areas(unit)	67	79	79
装机容量（千瓦）	Installed Power Generation Capacity(kw)	7236	13775	14252
发电量（万千瓦小时）	Generating Capacity (10 000 kwh)	1137.95	2239	2253
已配套机电井（眼）	Electricity Powered Well(unit)	50289	46505	46112

Agricultural Machinery,Chemical Fertilizers,Water Conservancy, Hydropower in Representative Years

2007	2008	2009	2010	2011	2012	2013	2014	2015
361.62	404.42	413.7	367.32	427.03	425.4	425.21	549.07	533.21
521.36	539.81	544.86	548.28	507.55	529.99	523.15	509.58	492.9
296.06	313.11	342.82	403.5	413.93	428.28	443.57	466.21	474.1
762401	767980	776319	781072	785885	807900	794361	820315	810849
408847	413397	414481	397975	398395	414339	401140	412544	408396
160932	157145	153825	152943	151005	151967	152565	156662	157601
34284	34149	33069	37715	38195	43356	39630	42504	46284
124784	132481	142137	158062	163797	198238	201026	208605	198568
220251	225949	230299	235532	239497	243281	239701	251217	246284
109484	112000	112275	108868	110412	113662	109497	116055	108833
19311	18855	18457	18315	18026	18061	18023	18505	18584
17141	17077	16534	17997	18095	21267	18973	20110	21986
62398	66247	71042	78811	81764	90291	93208	96547	96881
2096169	**2122310**	**2141969**	**2450496**	**2533372**	**2683201**	**2678745**	**2657870**	**2770750**
50137	**51097**	**51346**	**61917**	**61637**	**57451**	**62563**	**74935**	**59360**
1444867	**1465819**	**1325459**	**1243105**	**1242773**	**1252490**	**1210060**	**1220638**	**1174883**
276.28	274.48	273.17	281.28	262.32	267.84	240.22	248.34	244.72
247.99	249.31	247.6	234.15	214.62	211.31	196.96	189.69	188.50
210.51	211.01	213.42	224.6	200.36	198.66	229.29	230.58	239.63
76	76	75	44	44	46	46	48	48
24827	24827	25047	22325	22325	78848	80433	80633	80423
10085	10477	10678	7268	7268	26447	19613	25526.08	
45783	47032	46790	44310	40345	33959			

11-8 各区县农业机械化、化肥、水利、水电情况（2015年）

指标	Item	西安市 Xi'an	灞桥区 Baqiao	未央区 Weiyang
一、农业机械化水平（万亩）	**Statistics on Agricultural Machinery (10 000 mu)**			
当年机械耕地面积（实际）	Area Ploughed by Tractors	5332095	181005	17715
当年机械播种面积（作业）	Seeded Area by Tractors	4929045	166005	3495
当年机械收获面积（作业）	Harvest Area by Tractors	4740975	156015	3300
二、农用化肥施用量（吨）	**Use of Agricultural Fertilizers and Insecticides(ton)**			
1. 按实物量计算合计	Practicality Consumption	810849	20851	4014
氮肥	Nitrogenous Fertilizer	408396	8172	2415
磷肥	Phosphate Fertilizer	157601	1444	395
钾肥	Potash Fertilizer	46284	2283	11
复合肥	Compound Fertilizer	198568	8952	1193
2.按折纯法计算合计	Standard Consumption	246284	7798	1418
氮肥	Nitrogenous Fertilizer	108833	3518	885
磷肥	Phosphate Fertilizer	18584	176	36
钾肥	Potash Fertilizer	21986	951	5
复合肥	Compound Fertilizer	96881	3153	492
三、农用塑料薄膜使用量（公斤）	**Plastic Sheet for Agricultural Use(kg)**	2770750	184520	16000
四、农用柴油使用量（吨）	**Diesel Oil for Agricultural Use (ton)**	59360	547	695
五、农药使用量（公斤）	**Pesticide (kg)**	1174883	27491	4801
六、农村水利化情况（万亩）	**Irrigation and Water Conservancy (10 000 mu)**			
有效灌溉面积	Effective Irrigation Area	244.72	10.84	1.50
旱涝保收面积	Stable-Harvesting Arable Land	188.50		2.10
机电排灌面积	Electrical Irrigation Area	239.63	8.52	2.05
七、农村电气化情况	**Rural electrization**			
乡村及村以下办水电站（个）	Hydropower Station in Rural Areas(unit)	48		
装机容量（千瓦）	Installed Power Generation Capacity(kw)	80423		
发电量（万千瓦小时）	Generating Capacity (10 000 kwh)			
已配套机电井（眼）	Electricity Powered Well(unit)			

Agricultural Machinery,Chemical Fertilizers,Water Conservancy,

Hydropower by Region （2015）

雁塔区 Yanta	阎良区 Yanliang	临潼区 Lintong	长安区 Chang'an	高陵区 Gaoling	蓝田县 Lantian	周至县 Zhouzhi	户　县 Huxian
	274080	980010	1099380	352095	574815	988005	864990
	230775	901095	1032195	357000	630000	743490	864990
	313470	920010	1014990	407910	478005	582285	864990
	69654	151465	117902	59804	122477	149251	115431
	31683	80522	66505	25332	64853	62533	66381
	14315	44525	22405	15238	25764	16002	17513
	6022	2856	8047	2734	8310	9112	6909
	17634	23562	20945	16500	23550	61604	24628
	25050	39813	27318	15752	46208	48221	34706
	12085	21259	9868	4306	28245	10943	17724
	1638	5343	2673	1829	2885	1920	2084
	2937	1428	4020	1367	3620	4556	3102
	8390	11783	10757	8250	11458	30802	11796
	1154510	225230	187000	40430	261200	98860	603000
	2998	15257	12388	3328	10002	3365	10780
	192304	319156	128693	198519	74290	165833	63796
	21.69	53.74	31.17	20.26	11.24	48.65	45.63
	22.55	46.50	20.31	20.50		28.76	47.78
	21.94	49.77	27.48	20.74	21.78	45.40	41.95
			7		6	28	7
			5475		14400	55928	4620

11-9 主要年份农林牧渔及服务业总产值及指数

Gross Output Value of Farming,Forestry,Animal Husbandry,Fishery, Service and Related Indices in Representative Years

单位：万元 (10 000 yuan)

年 份 Year	农林牧渔及服务总产值（现价） Gross Output Value (At current prices)	农业 Farming	林业 Forestry	牧业 Animal Husbandry	渔业 Fishery	农林牧渔服务业 Service of Farming, Forestry, Animal Husbandry and Fishery	指数（上年=100）（可比价） Indices(preceding year= 100) (At cinstant prices)
1970	40617	35965	713	3896	43		111.2
1975	55322	47378	1509	6403	32		93.9
1978	65423	56519	1444	7427	33		104.7
1980	65322	54004	1177	10106	35		85
1985	134933	105888	2559	26186	300		106.4
1990	262073	191088	3134	65840	2011		102.5
1991	295620	208324	3362	81070	2864		108.6
1992	321155	219160	4225	94045	3725		108.6
1993	387068	261959	5031	115810	4268		112.8
1994	565056	359609	7819	192140	5488		102.4
1995	754597	513348	7185	228598	5466		106.8
1996	786003	552726	7573	219214	6490		102.1
1997	836201	585973	9226	233623	7379		110.3
1998	853279	625465	8146	212045	7623		107.5
1999	739905	530029	8883	194552	6441		100.7
2000	743712	514845	8482	212612	7773		104.3
2001	767511	527160	8427	223861	8063		102.8
2002	797444	539978	11378	238761	7327		103
2003	837857	551398	10550	269610	6299		101.5
2004	967946	580798	12773	314517	6728	53130	108.4
2005	1065437	657262	13086	329856	7340	57893	107.7
2006	1141484	686748	15188	346626	7017	85905	107.2
2007	1341450	798163	15845	410213	9051	108178	105.3
2008	1682725	956549	19031	564095	11084	131966	107.8
2009	1787032	1061756	22663	546191	11830	144592	106.5
2010	2270994	1438934	26787	629376	12830	163067	107.4
2011	2726608	1729295	34453	754593	14856	193411	106.6
2012	3083562	1933149	62291	820392	19877	247853	106
2013	3428905	2173363	80199	863902	22773	288668	104.9
2014	3672101	2363649	86889	879515	24030	318018	105.1
2015	3807573	2444234	97776	887325	19519	358719	105.1

11-10 主要年份农林牧渔及服务业总产值指数

Related Indices of Gross Output Value of Farming,Forestry,Animal Husbandry,Fishery and Service in Representative Years

年 份 Year	农林牧渔及服务业总产值指数（上年=100）（可比价） Indices(preceding year= 100) (At constant prices)	农业 Farming	林业 Forestry	牧业 Animal Husbandry	渔业 Fishery	农林牧渔服务业 Service of Farming, Forestry, Animal Husbandry and Fishery
2005	107.7	108.0	98.7	107.3	112.6	107.9
2006	107.2	106.0	102.5	109.3	104.5	109.4
2007	105.3	106.4	101.3	102.4	106.3	108.7
2008	107.8	107.9	112.2	106.0	100.5	113.7
2009	106.5	105.4	121.3	106.8	107.4	110.2
2010	107.4	108.7	115.2	104.3	92.7	108.9
2011	106.6	108.2	105.7	102.9	102.1	107.7
2012	106.0	105.6	143.0	104.8	113.4	108.5
2013	104.9	104.3	131.3	104.0	110.1	105.9
2014	105.1	105.8	105.7	103.2	106.0	105.9
2015	105.1	106.7	113.8	100.2	71.2	106.2

11-11 主要年份农林牧渔及服务业总产值构成

Gross Output Value and Its Composition of Farming, Forestry, Animal Husbandry,Fishery and Service at Current Price in Representative Years

年 份 Year	农林牧渔及服务业总产值(%) Service of Farming, Forestry, Animal Husbandry and Fishery(%)	农业 Farming	林业 Forestry	牧业 Animal Husbandry	渔业 Fishery	农林牧渔服务业 Service of Farming, Forestry, Animal Husbandry and Fishery
2005	100	61.7	1.2	31.0	0.7	5.4
2006	100	60.9	1.3	31.5	0.6	5.7
2007	100	59.5	1.2	30.6	0.7	8.0
2008	100	56.9	1.1	33.5	0.7	7.8
2009	100	59.4	1.3	30.5	0.7	8.1
2010	100	63.3	1.2	27.7	0.6	7.2
2011	100	63.4	1.3	27.7	0.5	7.1
2012	100	62.7	2.0	26.6	0.7	8.0
2013	100	63.4	2.3	25.2	0.7	8.4
2014	100	64.4	2.4	24.0	0.7	8.5
2015	100	64.2	2.6	23.3	0.5	9.4

11-12 各区县农林牧渔及服务业总产值（2015年）

Gross Output Value of Farming, Forestry, Animal Husbandry, Fishery and Service by Region（2015）

单位：万元 （10 000 yuan）

区 县	Region	农林牧渔及服务业总产值 Gross Output Value	农业 Farming	林业 Forestry	牧业 Animal Husbandry	渔业 Fishery	农林牧渔服务业 Service of Farming, Forestry, Animal Husbandry and Fishery
合 计	**Total**	**3807573**	**2444234**	**97776**	**887325**	**19519**	**358719**
新城区	Xincheng						
碑林区	Beilin						
莲湖区	Lianhu						
灞桥区	Baqiao	307940	235260	1285	39125	1434	30836
未央区	Weiyang	25786	11169	308	11182	411	2716
雁塔区	Yanta	3205			2416		789
阎良区	Yanliang	368854	272577	898	60379	325	34675
临潼区	Lintong	551556	289993	4524	195802	6211	55026
长安区	Chang'an	584120	392921	12778	121381	7094	49946
高陵区	Gaoling	495452	284923	1955	162018	337	46219
蓝田县	Lantian	465601	278999	23258	120984	1924	40436
周至县	Zhouzhi	508904	354957	39511	75580	609	38247
户 县	Huxian	496155	323435	13259	98458	1174	59829

11-13 各区县农林牧渔及服务业总产值指数和构成（2015年）

Gross Output Value and Its Composition of Farming, Forestry, Animal Husbandry,Fishery and Service at Current Price by Region (2015)

单位：% (%)

区 县	Region	农林牧渔及服务业总产值 Gross Output Value	农业 Farming	林业 Forestry	牧业 Animal Husbandry	渔业 Fishery	农林牧渔服务业 Service of Farming, Forestry, Animal Husbandry and Fishery
全市指数	**Total**	**105.1**	**106.7**	**113.8**	**100.2**	**71.2**	**106.2**
新城区	Xincheng						
碑林区	Beilin						
莲湖区	Lianhu						
灞桥区	Baqiao	105.0	108.4	43.6	92.8	46.3	110.1
未央区	Weiyang	104.8	81.6	2987.5	165.6	18.5	140.5
雁塔区	Yanta	53.9			225.2		98.4
阎良区	Yanliang	105.7	105.4	132.2	100.7	100.3	118.5
临潼区	Lintong	104.8	118.0	52.6	97.0	97.5	68.5
长安区	Chang'an	105.0	106.7	210.1	95.5	114.9	99.7
高陵区	Gaoling	105.9	106.4	56.6	103.9	20.6	118.8
蓝田县	Lantian	104.9	105.1	111.8	102.5	41.7	116.3
周至县	Zhouzhi	106.0	107.2	101.7	101.2	65.7	111.6
户 县	Huxian	105.8	104.7	325.8	95.5	78.3	116.5
全市构成	**Total**	100.0	64.2	2.6	23.3	0.5	9.4
新城区	Xincheng						
碑林区	Beilin						
莲湖区	Lianhu						
灞桥区	Baqiao	100.0	76.4	0.4	12.7	0.5	10.0
未央区	Weiyang	100.0	43.3	1.2	43.4	1.6	10.5
雁塔区	Yanta	100.0	0.0		75.4		24.6
阎良区	Yanliang	100.0	73.9	0.2	16.4	0.1	9.4
临潼区	Lintong	100.0	52.6	0.8	35.5	1.1	10.0
长安区	Chang'an	100.0	67.2	2.2	20.8	1.2	8.6
高陵区	Gaoling	100.0	57.5	0.4	32.7	0.1	9.3
蓝田县	Lantian	100.0	59.9	5.0	26.0	0.4	8.7
周至县	Zhouzhi	100.0	69.7	7.8	14.9	0.1	7.5
户 县	Huxian	100.0	65.2	2.7	19.8	0.2	12.1

11-14 主要年份农林牧渔及服务业增加值

Value-Added of Farming, Forestry, Animal Husbandry, Fishery and Service in Representative Years

单位：万元 (10 000 yuan)

年 份 Year	农林牧渔及服务业增加值 Farming,Forestry, Animal Husbandry, Fishery and Service	农业 Farming	林业 Forestry	牧业 Animal Husbandry	渔业 Fishery	农林牧渔服务业 Service of Farming, Forestry, Animal Husbandry and Fishery
1995	413981	329662	4413	76746	3160	
1996						
1997						
1998						
1999						
2000	446481	336777	4323	101353	4028	
2001	458720	342427	4258	108096	3939	
2002	477691	351358	6419	116591	3323	
2003	458378	312849	5473	137236	2820	
2004	582009	393349	6811	164572	2919	14358
2005	660148	444320	6888	169701	3373	35866
2006	704427	465823	8556	177431	3227	49390
2007	825053	538794	8420	210930	4467	62442
2008	1034471	639071	10592	301305	5598	77905
2009	1103793	698043	11958	303594	5913	84285
2010	1400575	935489	14362	349204	6503	95017
2011	1731398	1161249	18807	428169	7679	115494
2012	1955931	1297824	33973	465476	10115	148543
2013	2177588	1459093	43740	490162	11589	173004
2014	2336074	1586842	47388	499021	12229	190594
2015	2416880	1632882	53533	505551	9986	214928

11–15 主要年份农林牧渔及服务业增加值指数

Indices of Value-Added of Farming, Forestry, Animal Husbandry, Fishery and Service in Representative Years

年 份 Year	农林牧渔及服务业增加值指数（上年=100）（可比价） Farming,Forestry,Animal Husbandry,Fishery and Service	农业 Farming	林业 Forestry	牧业 Animal Husbandry	渔业 Fishery	农林牧渔服务业 Service of Farming, Forestry, Animal Husbandry and Fishery
2008	107.6	107.6	112.0	105.8	100.0	114.0
2009	106.3	103.6	114.6	111.2	106.3	108.8
2010	106.9	107.9	108.7	104.3	94.0	108.9
2011	106.7	108.1	106.1	102.8	102.7	108.1
2012	106.0	105.6	142.8	104.8	113.4	108.5
2013	104.8	104.3	131.3	104.0	110.1	105.9
2014	105.2	105.8	104.1	103.2	106.0	105.9
2015	105.1	106.5	114.0	100.5	71.3	106.2

11–16 各区县农林牧渔及服务业增加值（2015年）

Value-Added of Farming, Forestry, Animal Husbandry, Fishery and Service by Region (2015)

单位：万元 (10 000 yuan)

年 份 Year	Region	农林牧渔及服务业增加值 Farming,Forestry, Animal Husbandry, Fishery and Service	农业 Farming	林业 Forestry	牧业 Animal Husbandry	渔业 Fishery	农林牧渔服务业 Service of Farming, Forestry, Animal Husbandry and Fishery
合 计	**Total**	**2416880**	**1632882**	**53533**	**504193**	**9986**	**214928**
新城区	Xincheng						
碑林区	Beilin						
莲湖区	Lianhu						
灞桥区	Baqiao	204717	160197	778	25902	513	17327
未央区	Weiyang	15218	7116	162	6021	147	1772
雁塔区	Yanta	1990			2622		632
阎良区	Yanliang	245258	186695	461	36386	143	21573
临潼区	Lintong	337810	193415	2532	103460	3329	35074
长安区	Chang'an	395357	297916	7213	55989	4095	30144
高陵区	Gaoling	308494	178697	1085	97086	91	31535
蓝田县	Lantian	283835	173790	13523	71995	750	23777
周至县	Zhouzhi	317254	228984	20428	45678	288	21876
户 县	Huxian	306947	206072	7351	61676	630	31218

11-17 各区县农林牧渔及服务业增加值指数（2015年）

Indices of Value-Added of Farming, Forestry, Animal Husbandry, Fishery and Service by Region (2015)

（上年=100）（可比价） (preceding year = 100) (At constant prices)

区县 Region	农林牧渔及服务业增加值指数 Farming,Forestry,Animal Husbandry,Fishery and Service	农业 Farming	林业 Forestry	牧业 Animal Husbandry	渔业 Fishery	农林牧渔服务业 Service of Farming, Forestry, Animal Husbandry and Fishery
合　计　Total	**105.1**	**106.5**	**114.0**	**100.5**	**71.3**	**106.2**
新城区　Xincheng						
碑林区　Beilin						
莲湖区　Lianhu						
灞桥区　Baqiao	105.0	107.8	43.7	93.4	41.3	110.2
未央区　Weiyang	104.8	79.9	12400.0	164.2	16.3	138.5
雁塔区　Yanta	68.5			306.0		120.3
阎良区　Yanliang	105.7	105.2	133.1	101.8	90.1	119.1
临潼区　Lintong	104.8	121.3	46.9	88.6	87.4	73.4
长安区　Chang'an	105.0	104.7	212.6	106.1	103.6	93.1
高陵区　Gaoling	105.9	105.6	56.7	104.4	18.4	118.7
蓝田县　Lantian	104.9	104.5	112.2	103.2	37.2	116.4
周至县　Zhouzhi	106.0	106.7	102.1	102.1	58.8	111.9
户　县　Huxian	105.8	104.8	328.7	96.8	89.4	117.3

11-18 主要年份农作物播种面积

Sown Areas of Farm Crops In Representative Years

单位：万亩　　　　(10 000mu)

年　份 Year	总播种面积 Total Sown Area	粮食 Grain Crops	小麦 Wheat	玉米 Corn	棉花 Cotton	油料 Oil-bearing Crops	蔬菜 Vegetables
1980	835.43	706.35	324.17	273.14	81.23	10.01	24.02
1985	795.41	704.36	378.20	271.14	21.02	8.01	45.03
1990	816.41	731.42	387.20	282.14	15.02	12.00	51.03
1991	820.41	731.37	389.19	283.14	19.01	13.01	47.03
1992	820.65	715.50	384.60	273.60	26.70	16.20	54.60
1993	821.63	713.49	380.40	273.69	17.66	14.84	63.90
1994	821.10	719.00	375.90	272.40	19.70	13.80	59.90
1995	784.74	690.63	370.41	259.55	11.07	18.57	57.59
1996	797.40	709.00	366.30	286.80	7.70	18.80	55.50
1997	755.78	670.83	367.71	248.79	4.50	15.53	59.36
1998	789.99	705.03	370.17	285.45	3.56	14.69	60.95
1999	793.08	709.95	371.94	294.00	2.85	12.74	60.68
2000	784.94	697.55	369.89	283.70	2.48	13.46	64.35
2001	763.16	678.05	359.19	278.57	2.91	11.87	61.77
2002	751.10	655.59	350.64	271.95	2.63	11.40	67.71
2003	737.06	632.55	336.05	261.89	3.38	11.04	69.44
2004	753.83	630.63	311.52	286.50	4.94	9.74	77.55
2005	757.91	642.75	325.10	287.87	5.40	9.51	83.33
2006	769.49	648.00	313.23	307.89	6.09	8.58	87.03
2007	762.38	637.05	306.98	304.13	6.93	7.41	91.07
2008	756.06	630.31	319.39	286.69	6.35	8.59	93.02
2009	757.11	628.69	318.36	285.20	6.45	8.59	94.83
2010	751.74	621.71	317.18	279.93	6.26	8.98	95.71
2011	704.17	573.13	306.39	243.06	5.97	8.83	96.97
2012	701.33	572.50	305.34	242.20	5.00	7.70	97.82
2013	695.53	567.87	298.93	245.64	2.57	7.67	99.89
2014	684.28	551.46	290.53	238.65	0.37	7.01	101.56
2015	675.59	537.69	280.73	235.83	0.33	6.83	103.49

注：2011年农作物播种面积为陕西省统计局依据(国统字办[2011]68号)文件调整数。

11-19 各区县主要农作物播种面积（2015年）

Sown Areas of Major Farm Crops by Region（2015）

单位：万亩　　　　(10 000 mu)

区　县	Region	总播种面积 Total Sown Area	粮食 Grain Crops	小麦 Wheat	玉米 Corn	棉花 Cotton	油料 Oil-bearing Crops	蔬菜 Vegetables	瓜果类 Fruits Class
合　计	**Total**	**675.59**	**537.69**	**280.73**	**235.83**	**0.33**	**6.83**	**103.49**	**22.05**
新城区	Xincheng								
碑林区	Beilin								
莲湖区	Lianhu								
灞桥区	Baqiao	25.54	17.37	10.77	6.17	0.08	0.31	7.36	0.42
未央区	Weiyang	1.82	0.61	0.34	0.27			1.20	0.01
雁塔区	Yanta								
阎良区	Yanliang	46.15	21.41	11.75	9.64	0.03	0.09	17.82	6.77
临潼区	Lintong	123.50	100.25	54.57	41.28		1.03	14.29	7.09
长安区	Chang'an	130.03	100.78	50.74	49.09		1.36	23.33	3.62
高陵区	Gaoling	52.23	40.54	20.59	19.60			11.22	0.46
蓝田县	Lantian	109.40	94.86	49.62	32.87	0.22	2.12	9.55	1.63
周至县	Zhouzhi	87.76	74.77	37.67	35.42	0.00	1.51	9.18	0.14
户　县	Huxian	99.94	87.10	44.68	41.49	0.00	0.41	9.54	1.91

11-20 主要年份农作物产品产量

Yield of Major Farm Crops in Representative Years

单位：万吨

(10 000 ton)

年份 Year	粮食作物 Grain Crops	夏粮 Summer Grain	小麦 Wheat	秋粮 Autumn Grain	稻谷 Rice	玉米 Corn	棉花 Cotton	油料 Oil-bearing Crops	油菜籽 Rapeseeds	蔬菜 Vegetables
1978	132.80	64.20	58.20	68.70	5.10	55.80	2.85	0.09	0.07	45.66
1979	145.70	81.80	74.20	63.90	4.50	53.40	2.63	0.33	0.29	49.11
1980	114.40	56.60	52.20	57.80	4.70	47.70	1.97	0.54	0.50	40.13
1981	116.10	78.70	74.30	37.40	3.40	31.50	1.36	0.76	0.75	34.06
1982	148.90	85.60	82.20	63.30	4.90	55.50	2.88	0.51	0.49	53.71
1983	148.10	81.80	79.60	66.30	4.80	58.50	0.85	0.36	0.34	46.99
1984	157.60	82.40	81.00	75.20	5.00	66.50	1.49	0.46	0.29	75.47
1985	150.10	76.10	74.80	74.00	5.10	65.10	0.49	0.75	0.39	86.44
1986	162.40	91.70	90.10	70.70	4.80	61.80	0.44	1.25	0.82	85.84
1987	171.20	87.00	85.20	84.20	5.00	74.30	0.47	1.57	1.22	95.16
1988	158.00	86.80	84.60	71.10	3.80	61.40	0.42	0.89	0.51	113.50
1989	173.60	93.50	91.20	80.20	4.70	70.40	0.55	1.33	0.94	129.32
1990	172.40	91.70	89.70	80.80	5.50	70.40	0.70	1.35	0.94	119.32
1991	178.80	91.10	89.20	87.70	5.00	77.50	0.97	1.20	0.74	117.41
1992	183.40	101.70	99.60	81.70	4.70	72.30	0.74	1.49	0.87	128.12
1993	190.00	101.10	99.00	88.90	4.90	78.60	0.75	1.40	1.00	145.80
1994	157.40	86.90	84.90	70.50	4.50	61.40	0.65	1.08	0.78	135.26
1995	175.30	99.80	97.40	75.50	3.40	67.80	0.29	2.17	1.90	133.60
1996	187.50	80.10	78.40	107.40	3.40	95.60	0.24	1.83	1.55	138.01
1997	190.50	114.30	112.30	76.30	3.50	69.40	0.17	1.86	1.65	142.11
1998	212.70	104.40	104.00	108.30	3.20	99.10	0.14	1.67	1.36	148.87
1999	204.40	95.50	94.40	108.90	2.90	99.70	0.15	1.30	1.00	153.24
2000	201.90	92.60	91.60	109.30	3.10	100.50	0.14	1.34	0.95	162.14
2001	197.10	98.10	97.20	98.90	2.70	91.30	0.17	1.23	0.90	152.80
2002	192.40	94.50	93.50	97.90	2.10	91.60	0.18	1.22	0.84	169.74
2003	176.30	98.20	96.70	78.20	1.60	72.30	0.22	1.13	0.70	169.67
2004	195.80	97.80	96.00	98.00	1.70	91.60	0.40	1.14	0.84	180.96
2005	205.50	100.00	99.10	105.50	1.60	99.30	0.45	1.16	0.89	195.70
2006	193.50	86.00	85.40	107.40	1.40	101.20	0.48	1.08	0.87	189.30
2007	189.10	77.30	76.70	111.80	1.50	105.60	0.59	0.96	0.77	204.30
2008	214.40	105.90	105.60	108.50	0.90	103.00	0.62	1.15	0.95	221.53
2009	218.20	103.00	102.10	115.20	0.90	109.50	0.63	1.12	0.93	242.41
2010	221.70	106.60	105.80	115.10	0.80	108.90	0.60	1.20	1.00	253.10
2011	182.04	90.54	89.68	91.49	0.67	85.30	0.56	1.17	0.95	261.66
2012	192.55	95.73	94.92	96.82	0.57	89.29	0.47	1.02	0.88	277.80
2013	183.12	83.59	82.77	99.52	0.39	91.83	0.25	1.00	0.87	298.12
2014	175.61	88.05	87.35	87.56	0.25	83.30	0.03	0.98	0.80	316.28
2015	180.86	93.12	92.40	87.74	0.00	84.04	0.03	0.95	0.80	332.79

注：2011年农作物产品产量为陕西省统计局依据(国统字办[2011]70号)文件调整数。

11-21 各区县主要农作物产品产量（2015年）

Yield of Major Farm Crops by Region (2015)

单位：万吨 (10 000 tons)

区 县	Region	粮食作物 Grain Crops	夏粮 Summer Grain	小麦 Wheat	秋粮 Autumn Grain	稻谷 Rice	玉米 Corn
合 计	**Total**	**180.86**	**93.12**	**92.40**	**87.74**		**84.04**
新城区	Xincheng						
碑林区	Beilin						
莲湖区	Lianhu						
灞桥区	Baqiao	5.40	3.23	3.23	2.17		2.07
未央区	Weiyang	0.19	0.10	0.10	0.09		0.09
雁塔区	Yanta						
阎良区	Yanliang	8.82	4.93	4.93	3.89		3.89
临潼区	Lintong	32.87	17.85	17.84	15.02		13.67
长安区	Chang'an	34.59	16.50	16.49	18.09		17.92
高陵区	Gaoling	19.28	9.06	9.06	10.22		10.13
蓝田县	Lantian	26.04	14.01	13.65	12.03		10.26
周至县	Zhouzhi	23.17	11.86	11.68	11.31		11.16
户 县	Huxian	30.50	15.58	15.42	14.92		14.85

11-21 续表 continued

单位：万吨 (10 000 tons)

区 县	Region	棉花 Cotton	油料 Oil-bearing Crops	油菜籽 Rapeseeds	蔬菜 Vegetables	瓜果类 Fruits Class
合 计	**Total**	**0.33**	**0.95**	**0.80**	**332.79**	**54.34**
新城区	Xincheng					
碑林区	Beilin					
莲湖区	Lianhu					
灞桥区	Baqiao	0.08	0.04	0.04	29.59	0.67
未央区	Weiyang				2.67	0.04
雁塔区	Yanta					
阎良区	Yanliang	0.03	0.01	0.01	81.72	24.55
临潼区	Lintong		0.14	0.11	44.62	7.11
长安区	Chang'an		0.24	0.23	58.77	8.36
高陵区	Gaoling		0.00	0.00	46.17	3.29
蓝田县	Lantian	0.22	0.24	0.24	18.32	4.18
周至县	Zhouzhi		0.20	0.11	21.03	0.50
户 县	Huxian		0.08	0.06	29.90	5.64

11-22 主要年份农作物单位面积产量

Yield of Farm Crops Per Unit Area in Representative Years

单位：公斤/亩 (kg/mu)

年份 Year	粮食作物 Grain Crops	夏粮 Summer Grain	小麦 Wheat	秋粮 Autumn Grain	玉米 Corn	棉花 Cotton	油料 Oil-bearing Crops	油菜籽 Rapeseeds	蔬菜 Vegetables
1990	236	232	232	241	249	46	103	101	2349
1991	245	229	229	264	274	51	94	89	2332
1992	256	259	259	253	264	28	92	101	2344
1993	266	260	260	274	287	42	94	107	2282
1994	219	226	226	211	225	33	79	84	2260
1995	254	263	263	243	261	27	117	128	2320
1996	265	214	214	321	333	32	86	100	2489
1997	284	305	306	257	279	38	76	129	2395
1998	302	278	279	328	347	40	114	121	2443
1999	288	253	254	327	339	52	102	106	2526
2000	289	247	248	338	354	55	102	112	2520
2001	291	270	271	314	328	60	104	113	2474
2002	293	266	267	326	337	70	107	115	2507
2003	279	287	288	269	276	67	102	110	2444
2004	310	308	308	313	320	81	117	129	2333
2005	320	304	305	336	345	84	121	132	2349
2006	299	273	273	323	329	80	125	135	2175
2007	297	250	250	341	347	85	129	132	2245
2008	340	330	331	350	359	97	134	137	2382
2009	347	320	321	375	384	97	131	131	2556
2010	357	333	334	381	389	94	130	131	2644
2011	318	293	293	347	351	95	133	134	2698
2012	336	310	311	367	369	94	132	130	2840
2013	322	277	277	374	374	96	130	125	2985
2014	318	301	301	339	349	89	140	130	3114
2015	336	329	329	345	356	89	139	133	3216

注：2011年农作物单产为陕西省统计局依据(国统字办[2011]72号)文件调整数。

11-23 各区县主要农作物单位面积产量（2015年）

The Output of Main Crops Per Unit Area by Region (2015)

单位：公斤/亩 (kg/mu)

区 县	Region	粮食作物 Grain Crops	夏粮 Summer Grain	小麦 Wheat	秋粮 Autumn Grain	玉米 Corn
合 计	**Total**	**336**	**329**	**329**	**345**	**356**
新城区	Xincheng					
碑林区	Beilin					
莲湖区	Lianhu					
灞桥区	Baqiao	311	300	300	330	336
未央区	Weiyang	324	306	306	346	346
雁塔区	Yanta					
阎良区	Yanliang	412	419	419	403	403
临潼区	Lintong	328	327	327	329	331
长安区	Chang'an	343	325	325	362	365
高陵区	Gaoling	475	440	440	512	517
蓝田县	Lantian	275	276	275	272	312
周至县	Zhouzhi	310	308	310	312	315
户 县	Huxian	350	343	345	358	358

11-23 续表 continued

单位：公斤/亩 (kg/mu)

区 县	Region	棉花 Cotton	油料 Oil-bearing Crops	油菜籽 Rapeseeds	蔬菜 Vegetables	瓜果类 Fruits Class
合 计	**Total**	**89**	**139**	**133**	**3216**	**2464**
新城区	Xincheng					
碑林区	Beilin					
莲湖区	Lianhu					
灞桥区	Baqiao	66	131	131	4016	1563
未央区	Weiyang				2230	3288
雁塔区	Yanta					
阎良区	Yanliang	109	126	125	4582	3625
临潼区	Lintong		137	120	3121	1003
长安区	Chang'an		173	178	2519	2307
高陵区	Gaoling				4113	7117
蓝田县	Lantian	95	114	114	1919	2574
周至县	Zhouzhi		133	108	2291	3714
户 县	Huxian		184	189	3142	2960

11-24 设施农业生产情况（2015年）

Agricultural Production Facilities (2015)

指　标	Item	种植面积（亩） planting area (mu)	产量（吨） output(ton)
一、蔬菜	**Vegetables**	**266385**	**1403796**
其中：芹菜	Celery	80099	378582
油菜	Rape	4905	18293
菠菜	Spinach	17870	47767
黄瓜	Cucumber	24442	161943
西红柿	Tomato	15593	60616
辣椒	Chilli	27243	141999
二、瓜果类	**Fruits class**	**104141**	**392421**
其中：草莓	Strawberry	7278	19663
三、花卉苗木	**Flower seedling wood**	**17610**	
四、食用菌	**Edible Fungi**	**1814**	**20634**
五、其他	**Others**	**1015**	
补充资料：　蔬菜大棚个数（个）	Number of Vegetable Greenhouses	**139457**	
蔬菜大棚面积	Area of Vegetable Greenhouses	**237378**	

11-25 主要年份林业生产情况

Statistics on Forestry in Representative Years

指　标	Item	2000	2009	2010	2011	2012	2013	2014	2015
一、营林情况	**Afforestation**								
当年造林面积合计（万亩）	Build Forestry Areas(10 000 mu)	27.47	15.60	16.10	10.42	9.08	12.29	14.70	8.28
迹地更新面积（万亩）	Reforestation Area (10000 mu)								
封山育林面积（万亩）	Hill-closeure for Afforestation Areas (10 000 mu)	18.78	37.40	55.10	41.30	41.90	44.40	42.99	44
零星四旁植树（万株）	Planting(10 000 plants)	731.0	931.0	509.2	536.7	579.2	588.3	621.0	516
育苗面积（万亩）	Raise Seedlings Areas(10 000 mu)	2.05	3.41	11.95	9.93	11.64	17.37	17.73	19.84
#本年新育	New Seedling of Current Year	1.69	1.86	1.75	1.93	1.98	6.10	2.70	1
二、主要林产品产量（吨）	**Main Forestry Product(ton)**								
生漆	Lacquer	11	5	10	4				
核桃	Walnuts	997	4306	7875	13235	15253	18033	16531	24344
板栗	Chinese Chestnut	744	3122	7736	8229	7654	4379	6922	8225
花椒	Pepper	140	689	1420	889	879	319	371	204
三、村及村以下采伐木材（万立方米）	**Timber Harvested at or below** Village Level (10 000 cu.m)	1.62	0.97	3.30	1.39	1.04	0.88		0.07

11-26 各区县林业生产情况（2015年）

Statistics On Forestry by Region (2015)

区 县	Region	当年造林面积（亩）Build Forestry Areasin in The Year(mu)	零星植树（万株）Planting (10 000 plants)	育苗面积（亩）Raise Seedlings Areas(mu)	核桃产量（吨）Output of Walnuts (ton)	板栗产量（吨）Output of Chinese Chestnut (ton)
合 计	**Total**	**82770**	**516**	**198360**	**24344**	**8225**
新城区	Xincheng					
碑林区	Beilin					
莲湖区	Lianhu					
灞桥区	Baqiao	495		3000	2274	99
未央区	Weiyang		30			
雁塔区	Yanta					
阎良区	Yanliang	3000		510	2	
临潼区	Lintong	11955	72		1359	201
长安区	Chang'an	4800	142	14685	2707	130
高陵区	Gaoling	1200	30	3990		
蓝田县	Lantian	26460	80	24825	9800	5000
周至县	Zhouzhi	23865	80	132045	8202	2795
户 县	Huxian	10995	82	19305		

11-27 主要年份果业生产情况

Statistics on Fruits in Representative Years

指标	Item	2000	2005	2011	2012	2013	2014	2015
果园面积合计（万亩）	**Areas of Orchards (10 000 mu)**	**47.86**	**55.55**	**74.27**	**76.83**	**78.06**	**81.23**	**79.21**
苹果园	Apple Orchards	12.15	5.96	1.53	1.44	1.28	1.22	1.24
梨园	Pears Orchards	5.79	3.01	1.66	1.65	1.68	1.61	1.55
葡萄园	Grapes Orchards	1.89	3.02	4.91	5.46	6.70	9.39	9.50
桃园	Peach Orchards	3.47	8.66	6.87	6.78	6.49	6.14	6.09
猕猴桃园	Chinese Goosebeery Orchards	16.83	4.33	36.97	41.36	41.99	42.16	39.62
杏园	Apricot Orchards	0.62	2.50	3.60	3.59	3.52	3.99	3.96
柿子园	Presimmons Orchards	1.96	2.69	2.83	2.91	2.78	2.59	3.05
石榴园	Pomegranate Orchards			3.38	3.61	3.57	3.59	3.59
水果产量（吨）	**Output of Fruits (ton)**	**343551**	**512869**	**911361**	**932054**	**951851**	**996570**	**1052000**
苹果	Apple	89416	53387	34313	28675	25212	26047	31970
梨	Pears	65459	57059	48026	47463	47618	48757	50729
葡萄	Grapes	16647	30951	69003	75516	92380	99889	126625
桃	Peach	27010	89755	137683	125857	122186	125147	131228
猕猴桃	Chinese Goosebeery	96640	137853	357066	386336	395847	410614	425250
杏	Apricot			34340	57772	55330	61145	63726
柿子	Persimmon			31625	41211	41712	43705	39560
石榴	Pomegranate			34340	32329	30642	32793	29840

11-28 各区县果业生产情况（2015年）

Area and Output of Fruits by Region (2015)

区 县	Region	果园面积（万亩） Area of Orchards(10 000 mu)	水果产量（吨） Output of Fruits(ton)
合 计	**Total**	**79.21**	**1052000**
新城区	Xincheng		
碑林区	Beilin		
莲湖区	Lianhu		
灞桥区	Baqiao	7.38	122793
未央区	Weiyang	0.06	637
雁塔区	Yanta	0.05	
阎良区	Yanliang	2.76	68349
临潼区	Lintong	5.32	59915
长安区	Chang'an	5.37	79257
高陵区	Gaoling	3.09	71526
蓝田县	Lantian	7.34	124451
周至县	Zhouzhi	40.34	426920
户 县	Huxian	7.50	98152

11-29 主要年份畜牧业生产情况

Statistics on Livestock Husbandry in Representative Years

指标	Item	2000	2005	2010	2011	2012	2013	2014	2015
一、大牲畜年末总头数（头）	**Large Animals In Stock** at Year-end (head)	**260742**	**322521**	**216043**	**212351**	**211852**	**211791**	**217257**	**199438**
# 役畜	Draught Animals	98130	90717	42243	32877	31866	31510	26760	24412
1. 牛	Cattle	256073	320773	215072	211334	210819	210743	216326	199386
# 能繁殖母畜	Female Animals of Reprductive Ability	136626	176445	144012	142977				
# 当年生仔畜	Newborn Livestock in the Year	69015	72163	40052	36093				
#肉牛	Farm Cattle			65447	62127	60233	60165	64478	65863
#奶牛	Dairy Cattle	48164	96498	118747	117149	119888	120836	126174	109520
2. 马（匹）	Horses	736	559	456	496	533	549	513	52
3. 驴	Donkeys	476	175	67	71	46	52	59	
4. 骡	Mules	3457	1014	448	450	454	447	359	
二、猪年末头数（头）	**Hogs in Stock Year-end (head)**	**1284592**	**1472869**	**943183**	**943987**	**966018**	**965683**	**950124**	**924870**
# 能繁殖的母猪	Female Hogs of Reprductive Ability	93775	123543	106610	101332	103926	103967	99989	94000
三、羊年末只数（只）	**Sheeps and Goats in Stock at Year-end(head)**	**421103**	**532471**	**294539**	**295995**	**284596**	**273747**	**279207**	**283334**
1. 山羊	Goats	397121	520354	288738	288346	278738	267382	271722	273941
# 奶山羊	Milch Goats	266525	358733	246442	245118	234643	222546	224901	208909
2. 绵羊	Sheeps	23982	12117	5801	7649	5858	6365	7485	9393
四、家禽年末存栏（万只）	**Poultry in Stock at Year-end (10 000 heads)**	**1623.81**	**1372.56**	**1034.2**	**1153.76**	**1176.73**	**1172.61**	**1161.16**	**1183.23**
五、年末养蜂箱数（箱）	**Honey (box)**	**20408**	**24287**	**22984**	**17567**	**17161**	**17415**	**20663**	**19536**

11-30 各区县畜牧业生产情况（2015年）

Statistics On Livestock, Animal Husbandry by Region（2015）

区 县	Region	大牲畜年末头数（头）Large Animals In Stock at Year-end (head)	役畜 Draught Animals	牛（头）Cattle (head)	奶牛 Dairy Cattle	马（匹）Horses (head)	驴（头）Donkeys (head)	骡（头）Mutes (head)
合 计	**Total**	**199438**	**24412**	**199386**	**109520**	**52**		
新城区	Xincheng							
碑林区	Beilin							
莲湖区	Lianhu							
灞桥区	Baqiao	6272	6	6251	6178	21		
未央区	Weiyang	2451		2451	1918			
雁塔区	Yanta							
阎良区	Yanliang	18535		18535	17795			
临潼区	Lintong	66180	7619	66180	58561			
长安区	Chang'an	10935	543	10904	4461	31		
高陵区	Gaoling	14692		14692	10420			
蓝田县	Lantian	39204	7717	39204	2975			
周至县	Zhouzhi	32339	8482	32339	2832			
户 县	Huxian	8830	45	8830	4380			

11-30 续表 continued

区 县	Region	猪（头）Swine (head)	能繁殖的母猪 breeding sows	羊（只）Sheep and Goats (head)	山羊 Goats	奶山羊 Milch Goats	家禽（万只）Poultry (10 000 head)	蜂（箱）Honey (box)
合 计	**Total**	**924870**	**94000**	**283334**	**273941**	**208909**	**1183.23**	**19536**
新城区	Xincheng							
碑林区	Beilin							
莲湖区	Lianhu							
灞桥区	Baqiao	45611	5132	10292	10292	10268	39.1	330
未央区	Weiyang	13076	704	1098	798		4.63	
雁塔区	Yanta							
阎良区	Yanliang	37230	4160	53233	53233	53233	61.84	650
临潼区	Lintong	234832	20252	84826	84826	70813	284.5	1598
长安区	Chang'an	117398	10573	17492	14144	4560	298.56	4458
高陵区	Gaoling	50753	6649	21840	17187	14013	147	
蓝田县	Lantian	79515	8217	73823	72873	46952	115	3055
周至县	Zhouzhi	193705	22803	13520	13378	2240	102.6	5027
户 县	Huxian	152750	15510	7210	7210	6830	130	4418

11-31 主要年份畜产品和水产品产量

Output of Livestock Products and Aquatic Products in Representative Years

单位：吨　　　　　　　　　　　　　　　　　　　　　　　　　　　　　　　(ton)

年 份 Year	肉类总产量 Output of Meat	猪 肉 Pork	牛 肉 Beef	羊 肉 Mutton	禽 肉 Poultry
1990	63273	50646	4667	1931	5885
1991	72268	55086	5623	2162	9062
1992	88994	68134	6468	2460	11290
1993	93420	71274	7249	2220	12174
1994	106691	79433	8298	2350	15681
1995	127815	86513	11251	3731	23948
1996	91468	63750	5402	2578	19324
1997	106597	75381	6672	3468	20596
1998	134152	98974	8788	4710	21424
1999	130124	93859	9827	4147	21963
2000	147571	106137	12066	4766	23760
2001	157277	113353	11900	5153	20540
2002	161092	118634	11516	5394	20515
2003	165860	122759	13241	5180	19682
2004	171545	126404	13641	5874	18493
2005	182046	136503	14031	6106	18803
2006	108634	81199	8267	2841	13417
2007	102191	73254	8589	3111	14075
2008	115352	84654	9840	3335	16060
2009	126182	94490	10142	3677	17190
2010	136501	102296	10854	3875	18338
2011	144631	104816	11860	3645	19390
2012	151711	110506	12079	3697	20046
2013	157449	114288	12143	4036	20817
2014	161886	118627	12288	4198	20887
2015	161254	115953	12361	4287	21441

注：2010年起，根据统计制度要求，水产品产量及养殖面积统计数据取自水务部门。

11-31 续表 continued

单位：吨 (ton)

年 份 Year	奶类产量 Output of Milk	牛 奶 Cow Milk	禽 蛋 Poultry Eggs	蜂蜜（公斤） Honey(kg)	水产品 Output of Aquatic Products	养殖面积（万亩） Water Raise Areas (10 000 mu)
1990	82017	50528	55938	1035392	4259	2.55
1991	91006	57700	90558	1022797	4949	2.63
1992	100080	63586	104970	739275	6015	2.8
1993	111070	73897	125244	662049	7132	2.97
1994	145412	99025	146503	547808	7900	3.1
1995	132909	85753	141227	535891	8517	3.21
1996	133372	86103	138044	613290	8910	3.51
1997	150964	98078	156066	713918	10054	3.46
1998	174099	119719	142519	537304	10480	3.4
1999	209144	145191	135981	541613	11061	3.38
2000	245913	176155	138305	460598	11384	3.35
2001	255437	179977	132303	479839	12480	3.17
2002	288009	202826	134336	497530	12017	3.31
2003	336296	245407	128833	537805	9967	2.48
2004	384319	289564	117597	449765	9721	2.46
2005	422229	327961	118115	421052	9370	2.38
2006	471438	374813	97816	414271	11937	1.6
2007	528037	428462	98140	401761	12402	1.38
2008	589697	475681	108515	503031	12487	1.4
2009	618186	498394	116685	528731	13044	1.52
2010	633663	509178	123793	436759	11850	2.24
2011	647978	509777	125639	217632	11800	2.2
2012	666439	513337	129970	213174	14010	2.95
2013	657748	512796	135382	219344	14200	2.19
2014	658016	514587	135191	250464	14218	2.31
2015	637340	485640	145470	243198	14190	2.26

11-32 各区县主要畜产品和水产品产量（2015年）

Output of Major Livestock Products and Aquatic Products by Region (2015)

单位：吨 (ton)

区 县	Region	肉类总产量 Output of Meat	猪 肉 Pork	牛 肉 Beef	羊 肉 Mutton	禽 肉 Poultry
合 计	**Total**	**161254**	**115953**	**12361**	**4287**	**21441**
新城区	Xincheng					
碑林区	Beilin					
莲湖区	Lianhu					
灞桥区	Baqiao	7532	5369	1121	147	871
未央区	Weiyang	2873	2075	720	22	51
雁塔区	Yanta	407	332	32	2	41
阎良区	Yanliang	7514	4793	668	680	1039
临潼区	Lintong	43687	30765	3265	1680	4751
长安区	Chang'an	20973	14184	684	275	5430
高陵区	Gaoling	10102	6977	470	214	2046
蓝田县	Lantian	19856	10382	2942	999	3127
周至县	Zhouzhi	28388	24610	1824	187	1720
户 县	Huxian	19922	16466	635	81	2365

11-32 续表 continued

区 县	Region	奶类产量 Output of Milk	牛 奶 Cow Milk	禽 蛋 Poultry Eggs	蜂蜜（公斤） Honey(kg)	水产品 Output of Aquatic Products	养殖面积（亩） Water Raise Areas (mu)
合 计	**Total**	**637340**	**485640**	**145470**	**243198**	**14190**	**22560**
新城区	Xincheng						
碑林区	Beilin						
莲湖区	Lianhu						
灞桥区	Baqiao	45863	41259	5114	8300	701	1245
未央区	Weiyang	8561	8556	60		1729	3585
雁塔区	Yanta	14	9	78		50	15
阎良区	Yanliang	101007	76262	6560	17820	225	165
临潼区	Lintong	317828	263338	35705	42585	3305	4965
长安区	Chang'an	33627	20433	47390	77562	4950	5640
高陵区	Gaoling	51119	36963	15621		230	180
蓝田县	Lantian	41075	8634	10074	24854	1300	3660
周至县	Zhouzhi	13798	10578	10280	51017	500	2310
户 县	Huxian	24448	19608	14588	21060	1200	795

11-33 农业科技、教育情况（2015年）

Agricultural Science and Technology Education（2015）

指标	Item	2015
农业研究开发机构（个）	Agricultural research and development institutions (unit)	368
农业科技人员（人）	Agricultural scientific and technical personnel(persons)	3535
农业科研成果（个）	Agricultural scientific research achievements (unit)	20
农民技能培训人数（万人）	The number of peasants skills training(10000 persons)	17.6
良种推广面积（万亩）	Thoroughbred promotion area (10000 mu)	
农业信息站（个）	information station of Agricultural (unit)	3104

11-34 主要年份农产品人均占有量

Per Capita Output of Major Farm Products in Representative Years

单位：公斤/人　　　　(kg/ person)

年份 rear	粮食 Grain	棉花 Cotton	油料 Oil-bearing Crops	猪牛羊肉 Pork Beef and Mutton	禽蛋 Poultry Eggs	奶类 Milk	水果 Fruits	蔬菜 Vegetables
1978	266.7	5.7	0.2	5.4	0.9	3.3	6.8	91.7
1979	288.6	5.2	0.6	6.7	1.0	4.0	5.1	97.3
1980	223.5	3.8	1.1	5.9	1.2	4.1	6.9	78.4
1981	222.9	2.6	1.5	6.6	1.7	4.7	5.8	65.4
1982	281.5	5.5	1.0	4.9	2.7	5.6	5.9	101.6
1983	276.6	1.6	0.7	4.9	3.2	6.5	5.0	87.8
1984	289.4	2.7	0.8	4.8	6.2	8.7	4.8	138.6
1985	271.4	0.9	1.4	6.8	5.7	10.2	7.6	156.3
1986	288.0	0.8	2.2	7.8	6.4	12.1	9.6	152.2
1987	298.0	0.8	2.7	7.3	6.8	13.8	10.6	165.6
1988	269.7	0.7	1.5	8.0	8.9	15.6	11.1	193.7
1989	290.7	0.9	2.2	8.4	7.6	13.1	10.2	216.5
1990	298.7	1.2	2.1	9.4	9.2	14.2	11.5	196.0
1991	290.6	1.6	2.0	10.2	14.7	14.8	11.7	190.8
1992	294.3	1.2	2.4	12.4	16.8	16.2	17.3	205.6
1993	301.2	1.2	2.2	12.8	19.9	17.6	25.9	231.1
1994	246.1	1.0	1.7	14.1	22.9	22.7	28.0	211.5
1995	270.4	0.5	3.4	15.7	21.8	20.5	37.5	206.1
1996	286.3	0.4	3.2	11.0	21.1	20.4	43.9	210.8
1997	287.8	0.3	2.8	12.9	23.6	22.8	43.3	214.7
1998	318.3	0.2	2.5	16.8	21.3	26.1	50.0	222.8
1999	303.0	0.2	1.9	16.0	20.2	31.0	52.7	227.2
2000	293.5	0.2	1.9	17.9	20.1	35.7	49.9	235.7
2001	283.7	0.2	1.8	18.8	19.0	36.8	48.8	219.9
2002	273.8	0.3	1.7	19.3	19.1	41.0	53.5	241.6
2003	246.0	0.3	1.6	19.7	18.0	46.9	53.6	236.8
2004	270.1	0.6	1.6	20.1	16.2	53.0	63.9	249.6
2005	277.1	0.6	1.6	21.1	15.9	56.9	69.1	263.8
2006	256.9	0.6	1.4	12.3	13.0	62.6	73.5	251.4
2007	247.4	0.8	1.3	11.1	12.8	69.1	79.2	267.3
2008	256.0	0.7	1.4	11.7	13.0	70.4	85.6	264.5
2009	258.7	0.7	1.3	12.8	13.8	73.3	93.6	287.4
2010	261.8	0.7	1.4	13.8	14.6	74.8	100.1	298.9
2011	213.8	0.7	1.4	14.1	14.8	76.1	107.1	318.9
2012	225.6	0.6	1.2	14.8	15.2	78.1	109.2	325.6
2013	213.2	0.3	1.2	15.2	15.8	76.6	110.8	347.1
2014	204.0	0.0	1.1	15.7	15.7	76.3	115.8	367.5
2015	208.7	0.0	1.1	15.3	16.8	73.5	121.4	384.0

11-35 主要年份农村经济效益指标

Main Indicators of Rural Economic Benefit in Representative Years

年份 Year	每一劳动力创造的 Average Labor Force Production 农林牧渔及服务业总产值（元） Gross Output Value of Farming,Forestry, Animal Husbandry, Fishery and Service (yuan)	粮食（公斤） Grain Crops(kg)	棉花（公斤） Cotton (kg)	油料（公斤） Oil-bearing Crops(kg)	每亩耕地种植业总产值（元） Output of Each Unit of Area Planting(yuan)	每百元物耗生产的总产值（元） Output per 100-Yuan of Material Consumed(yuan)
1978	504.7	1024.6	22.0	0.7	104.3	
1979	549.0	1096.5	19.8	2.3	116.0	
1980	483.1	846.1	14.5	4.0	99.2	
1981	502.8	840.5	9.9	5.5	105.4	
1982	631.5	1058.9	20.5	3.6	139.3	
1983	606.5	1053.2	6.1	2.6	124.1	
1984	850.7	1154.2	10.9	3.4	163.6	
1985	1020.1	1134.6	3.7	5.6	183.1	
1986	1132.2	1236.4	3.4	9.5	204.6	
1987	1280.3	1277.2	3.5	11.7	231.5	
1988	1558.4	1148.0	3.0	6.5	273.2	
1989	1605.3	1231.9	3.9	9.5	295.0	
1990	1766.3	1279.1	5.2	10.0	343.4	233.3
1991	1958.8	1326.6	7.2	8.9	380.4	238.4
1992	2093.7	1360.7	5.5	11.1	451.6	241.8
1993	2528.9	1409.7	5.6	10.4	546.8	240.1
1994	3705.0	1167.8	4.8	8.0	762.8	227.6
1995	4953.0	1300.6	2.2	16.1	1106.5	225.9
1996	5154.8	1391.2	1.8	13.6	1224.2	234.5
1997	5493.0	1413.4	1.3	13.8	1283.3	239.2
1998	5615.9	1578.1	1.0	12.4	1374.3	247.0
1999	4826.5	1516.6	1.1	9.7	1175.9	251.7
2000	5091.5	1498.0	1.0	9.9	1161.1	250.2
2001	5328.5	1462.4	1.3	9.1	1221.1	248.6
2002	5617.4	1427.5	1.3	9.1	1272.0	265.9
2003	5761.2	1308.1	1.6	8.4	1332.4	254.3
2004	6885.4	1452.7	3.0	8.5	1434.6	261.7
2005	7737.9	1524.7	3.3	8.6	1642.3	262.9
2006	8415.5	1435.7	3.6	8.0	1756.9	263.1
2007	10165.6	1403.0	4.4	7.1	2037.3	259.8
2008	13306.4	1695.4	4.9	9.1	2447.9	259.6
2009	14674.3	1791.7	5.1	9.2	2737.9	261.6
2010	19480.7	1901.3	5.1	10.0	3753.4	260.9
2011	23474.6	1567.2	4.9	10.1	4585.8	274.0
2012	27219.4	1699.6	4.2	10.1	5175.7	273.5
2013	31608.7	1688.0	2.3	9.2	5934.5	274.0
2014	33292.2	1605.0	0.3	8.9	6552.4	274.9
2015	36228.8	1720.9	0.3	9.0	7069.8	273.8

主 要 统 计 指 标 解 释

农林牧渔业总产值 指以货币表现的农、林、牧、渔业全部产品和对农林牧渔业生产活动进行的各种支持性服务活动的价值总量，它反映一定时期内农林牧渔业生产总规模和总成果。1957年以前的农林牧渔业总产值中包括了厩肥和农民自给性手工业（如农民自制衣服、鞋、袜，自己从事粮食初步加工等）。1958年及以后，林业中增加了村及村以下竹木采伐产值；牧业中取消了厩肥产值；副业中取消了农民自给性手工业产值，增加了村及村以下办的工业产值；渔业中增加了海洋捕捞水产品产值。1980年及以后，在副业中增加了农民家庭兼营工业商品部分的产值。从1984年起村及村以下工业产值划归工业。从1993年起取消副业，将野生动物的捕猎划入牧业，野生植物采集和农民家庭兼营商品性工业划归农业。从2003年起，执行新的国民经济行业分类标准，农林牧渔业总产值中包括了农林牧渔服务业产值。林业中增加了森林采运业产值。农业中取消了家庭兼营商品性工业产值，将野生林产品的采集划归林业。第一次农业普查以后，由于畜牧业产品年报数据与普查数据之间存在一定的差距，根据农业普查结果对畜牧业年报数据进行了修正，对畜牧业产值进行了相应修正。

农林牧渔业总产值的计算方法通常是按农、林、牧、渔业产品及其副产品的产量分别乘以各自单位产品价格求得；少数生产周期较长，当年没有产品或产品产量不易统计的，则采用间接方法匡算其产值；然后将四业产品产值及农林牧渔服务业产值相加即为农林牧渔业总产值。

粮食产量 指全社会的产量。包括国有经济经营的、集体统一经营的和农民家庭经营的粮食产量，还包括工矿企业办的农场和其他生产单位的产量。粮食除包括稻谷、小麦、玉米、高粱、谷子及其他杂粮外，还包括薯类和豆类。其产量计算方法，豆类按去豆荚后的干豆计算；薯类（包括甘薯和马铃薯，不包括芋头和木薯）1963年以前按每4公斤鲜薯折1公斤粮食计算，从 1964年开始改为按5公斤鲜薯折1公斤粮食计算。城市郊区作为蔬菜的薯类（如马铃薯等）按鲜品计算，并且不作粮食统计。其他粮食一律按脱粒后的原粮计算。1989年以前全国粮食产量数据主要靠全面报表取得，1989年开始使用抽样调查数据。

棉花产量 指全社会的产量。包括春播棉和夏播棉。产量按皮棉计算。不包括木棉。

油料产量 指全部油料作物的生产量。包括花生、油菜籽、芝麻、向日葵籽、胡麻籽（亚麻籽）和其他油料。不包括大豆、木本油料和野生油料。花生以带壳干花生计算。

水产品产量 指人工养殖的水产品和天然生长的水产品的捕捞量。包括海水的鱼类、虾蟹类、贝类和藻类以及内陆水域的鱼类、虾蟹类和贝类，不包括淡水生植物。水产品产量是通过各级水产和统计部门逐级上报取得数据。1995年及以前，贝类中牡蛎按鲜肉计算；蚶、蛤、蛙按5斤鲜品折1斤计算。1996年以后则统一按鲜品计算。

猪、牛、羊肉产量 指当年出栏并已屠宰、除去头蹄下水后带骨肉（即胴体重）的重量。包括全社会范围内的产量。1996年前为各级逐级上报数据。1996年第一次农业普查以后，由于畜牧业产品年报数据与普查数据之间存在一定的差距，根据普查结果对畜牧业年报数据进行了修正。1999年以后，国家统计局在部分地区开展了猪、牛、羊、禽等主要畜禽品种的抽样调查，并用抽样数据作为国家定案数据使用。未开展抽样调查的地区和品种，仍使用各级统计部门逐级上报数据。2007年，根据第二次农业普查结果，对2000-2006年畜牧业年报数据进行了修正。2008年，建立了主要畜禽监测调查制度，猪、牛、羊、禽等主要畜牧业数据均以抽样调查数为法定数据。

期初（末）畜禽存栏头（只）数 指报告期初（末）农村各种合作经济组织和国营农场、农民个人、机关、团体、学校、工矿企业、部队等单位以及城镇居民饲养的大牲畜、猪、羊、家禽等畜禽的存栏数。

常用耕地 是指耕地总资源中专门种植农作物并经常进行耕种、能够正常收获的土地。包括当年实际耕种的熟地；弃耕、休闲不满三年，随时可以复耕的地；开荒利用三年以上的地。不包括临时种植农作物的坡度在25度以上的陡坡地；在河套、湖畔、库区临时开发的成片或零星土地；也不包括已列为国家和省（区、市）退耕计划但临时耕种的土地。

农作物播种面积 指实际播种或移植有农作物的面积。凡是实际种植有农作物的面积，不论种植在耕地上还是种植在非耕地上，均包括在农作物播种面积中。在播种季节基本结束后，因遭灾而重新改种和补种的农作物面积，也包括在内。它是反映我国耕地面积利用情况的一个重要指标。目前，农作物播种面积主要包括粮食、棉花、油料、糖料、麻类、烟叶、蔬菜和瓜类、药材和其他农作物九大类。

有效灌溉面积 指具有一定的水源，地块比较平整，灌溉工程或设备已经配套，在一般年景下，当年能够进行正常灌溉的耕地面积。在一般情况下，有效灌溉面积应等于灌溉工程或设备已经配备，能够进行正常灌溉的水田和水浇地面积之和。它是反映我国耕地抗旱能力的一个重要指标。

农用化肥施用量 指本年内实际用于农业生产的化肥数量，包括氮肥、磷肥、钾肥和复合肥。化肥施用量要求按折纯量计算数量。折纯量是指把氮肥、磷肥、钾肥分别按含氮、含五氧化二磷、含氧化钾的百分之百成份进行折算后的数量。复合肥按其所含主要成分折算。公式为：

折纯量=实物量×某种化肥有效成份含量的百分比

农业机械总动力 指主要用于农、林、牧、渔业的各种动力机械的动力总和。包括耕作机械、排灌机械、收获机械、农用运输机械、植物保护机械、牧业机械、林业机械、渔业机械和其他农业机械【内燃机按引擎马力折成瓦（特）计算、电动机按功率折成瓦（特）计算】。不包括专门用于乡、镇、村、组办工业、基本建设、非农业运输、科学试验和教学等非农业生产方面用的动力机械与作业机械。这个指标的统计数据主要来源于农机部门。

Explanatory Notes on Main Statistical Indicators

Gross Output Value of Agriculture, Forestry, Animal Husbandry and Fishery refers to the total value of products of agriculture, forestry, animal husbandry and fishery, and total value of services in support of agriculture, forestry, animal husbandry and fishery activities. It reflects the total scale and results of agricultural production during a given period. Prior to 1957, China's gross agricultural output value included barnyard manure and handicraft products for self- consumption (clothes, shoes, stockings, and initial grain processing undertaken by peasants). Since 1958, cutting and felling of bamboo and trees by villages and other cooperative organizations under villages have been included in forestry; value of barnyard manure has been excluded from animal husbandry; self consumed handicrafts have not been included from sideline occupations, while the output value of industries run by villages and cooperative organizations under village has been included in sideline occupations; and the output value of fish catches by motor fishing boats has been added to fishery. Since 1980, the value of handicraft products made for sale by individuals in households has been added to sideline occupations. Since 1984, industries run by villages and under villages have been included in the sector of industry. Since 1993, the subdivision of sideline occupations has been cancelled, and the hunting of wild animals has been classified into animal husbandry, and the gathering of wild plants and commodity industry run by rural household have been included in farming. A new industrial classification of economic activities was introduced in 2003. Under the new classification, value of services to agriculture, forestry, animal husbandry and fishery is included in the gross output value of agriculture, value of wood felling and transport is included in forestry, value of industrial output by rural households is not included in agriculture, and the collection of wild forest products is taken from agriculture and included in forestry. The First Agriculture Census of China revealed some discrepancy between the production of animal products from the annual reports and that from the census. According to the result of the First Agriculture census, efforts were made to adjust the output value of animal husbandry to make the figures from the annual reports consistent with the census data.

Gross output value of agrieulture is obtained by multiplying the output of each product or by-product by its price, resulting in the output value of each single item. For a small number of products, annual output of which is not available or difficult to get due to the long production (growing) process involved, the output value is estimated through an indirect approach. The sum of output values of all products of agriculture, forestry, animal husbandry and fishery and services in support to those industries is then equal to the gross output value of agriculture.

Grain Output refers to the total output in the whole country including grains produced by State farms, collective units, rural households, as well as by farms affiliated to industrial and mining enterprises and other production units. Grain includes rice, wheat, corn, sorghum, millet and other miscellaneous grains as well as tubers and beans. Output of beans refers to dry beans without pods. The output of tubers (sweet potatoes and potatoes, not including taros and cassava) are converted into that of grain at the ratio 4:1, i.e. 4 kilograms of fresh tubers were equivalent to 1 kilogram of grain up to 1963. Since 1964 the ratio for conversion has been 5:1. Tubers supplied as vegetables (such as potatoes) in cities and suburbs are calculated as fresh vegetables and their output is not included in the output of grain. Output of all other grains refers to husked grain. Data on grain production before 1989 were obtained through the Comprehensive Statistical Reporting System. Since 1989, data from sample surveys are used.

Cotton Output refers to cotton production in the whole country including cotton planted in spring and in autumn. Output is measured as the weight of ginned cotton. Ceiba is not included.

Output of Oil–bearing Crops refers to the total production of oil-bearing crops of various kinds, including peanuts (dry, in shell), rapeseeds, sesame, sunflower seeds, flax seeds, and other oil-bearing crops. Soybeans, oil-bearing woody plants, and wild oil-bearing crops are not included.

Output of Aquatic Products refers to catches of both artificially cultured and naturally grown aquatic products, including fish, shrimps, crabs and shellfish in sea and inland water as well as seaweed. Freshwater plants are not included. Data on output of aquatic products are reported by aquatic product and statistical agencies level by level. Before 1995, among the shellfish, oyster was counted as fresh meat; 5 kilograms of ark shell, clams and frogs are equivalent to 1 kilogram of fresh aquatic products; they have all been counted as flesh aquatic products since 1996.

Output of Pork, Beef, and Mutton refers to the meat of slaughtered hogs, cattle, sheep and goats with head, feet, and offal taken away. Data refers to the production of the whole country. The First Agricultural Census of China in 1996 revealed some discrepancy between the production of animal products from the annual reports and that from the census. Efforts were made to adjust the output value of animal husbandry to make the figures from the annual reports consistent with the census data. Since 1999, the NBS conducted sample surveys for the major animal husbandry products, such as hogs, cattle, sheep and goats and fowls, and the data from sample surveys are used as national finalized data. Those products, which are not covered by the sample survey, are still reported by statistical agencies level by level. In 2007. the data on animal husbandry from 2000 to 2006 were revised according to the results of the Second Agriculture Census of China. In 2008, A Monitoring and Survey Program was set up on main livestock, the data on the main livestock such as hog, cattle, sheep and poultry became the official data based on the sampling survey.

Number of Livestock or Poultry in Stock at Beginning (or End) of Period refers to the total number of large animals, pigs, sheep, fowls, etc. raised by rural cooperative organizations, State farms, rural individuals, government agencies, schools, industrial and mining enterprises, army, and urban residents at the beginning (or end) of the reference period.

Regularly Cultivated Land refers to farmland among the total land resources which is exclusively used for farming and is under regular cultivation with harvest in normal years. Included are currently cultivated land, land that has been abandoned or put in idle for less than 3 years and could be re-used for cultivation at any time, and new-claimed land that has been put into cultivation for more than 3 years. Excluded under this category are steep slope land over 25 degrees under temporary cultivation, land (large or small plots) that is claimed along river bends, lake sides or banks of reservoirs, as well as land that has been designated under the "Green for Grain" programmes of the state and provincial governments but is still temporarily under cultivation.

Sown Area of Crops refers to area of transplanted with crops regardless of being land sown or in cultivated area or non-cultivated area. Area of land re-sown due to lso included. This is an important indicator that can reflect the utilization condition of the cultivated land in China. At present, the sown area of crops mainly include the following 9 categories of crops: grain, cotton, oil-bearing crops, sugar crops, flax crops, tobacco, vegetables and melons, medicinal materials and other farm crops.natural disasters is also included. This is an important indicator that can reflect the utilization condition of the cultivated land in China. At present, the sown area of crops mainly include the following 9 categories of crops: grain, cotton, oil-bearing crops, sugar crops, flax crops, tobacco, vegetables and melons, medicinal materials and other farm crops.

Irrigated Area refers to area of land that are effectively irrigated, i.e. relatively level land, where there are water sources or complete sets of irrigation facilities to lift and move adequate water for irrigation purpose under normal conditions. Under normal situations, irrigated area is the sum of watered fields and irrigated fields where irrigation systems or equipment have been installed for regular irrigation purpose. This important indicator reflects drought resistance capacity of the cultivated land in China.

Consumption of Chemical Fertilizers in Agriculture refers to the quantity of chemical fertilizers applied in agriculture in the year, including nitrogenous fertilizer, phosphate fertilizer, potash fertilizer, and compound fertilizer. The consumption of chemical fertilizers is calculated in terms of volume of effective components by means of converting the gross weight of the respective fertilizers into weight containing effective component (e.g. nitrogen content in nitrogenous fertilizer, phosphorous pentoxide contents in phosphate fertilizer, and potassium oxide contents in potash fertilizer). Compound fertilizer is converted in regard to its major components. The formula is:

Volume of effective component= physical quantity × effective component of certain chemical fertilizer (%)

Total Power of Agricultural Machinery refers to total mechanical power of machinery used in agriculture, forestry, animal husbandry and fishery, including machinery for ploughing, irrigation and drainage, harvesting, transport, plant protection, animal husbandry, forestry and fishery and other agricultural machineries. (For the power of internal combustion engines, it is converted from its horsepower into watts while for electric motors the output power is converted into watts.) Machinery employed for non-agricultural purposes, such as the machines used in township-run and village-run industry, construction, non-agricultural transport, scientific experiments and teaching, are not included. Data are mainly from agricultural machinery agencies.

12 工 业

INDUSTRY

资料整理：赵　晖　王凤玲　赵　博　陈小兵　李　玫　王　玥
Data management：Zhao Hui Wang Fengling Zhao Bo Chen Xiaobing Li Mei Wang Yue
数据审核：马　琰
Data audit：Ma Yan

第十二部分 工业

一、简要说明

本章资料包括规模以上工业企业单位数、总产值、主要经济指标等，由西安市统计局工业处提供。

二、主要指标

规模以上工业企业单位数（个）	1150	比上年增长	0.4%
规模以上工业增加值（亿元）	1285.08	比上年增长	4.5%

12 INDUSTRY

Ⅰ.Brief Introduction

Data in this chapter includes number of industrial enterprises above designated size and gross product, primary economic. Data in this chapter are provided and compiled by Industry Division of the Xi'an Bureau of Statistics.

Ⅱ.Major Indicators

		Increase over Preceding Year
Number of Industrial Enterprises Above Designated Size(item)	1150	0.4%
Value Added of Industry Above Designated Size(100 million yuan)	1285.08	4.5%

12-1 主要年份全部工业总产值

Gross Output Value of Industry In Representative Years

单位：万元 (10 000 yuan)

年份 Year	全部工业总产值 Gross Industrial Output Value	工业总产值指数（上年=100） Index of Gross Industry Output Value (Preceding Year=100)	国有经济 State-owned Enterprises	集体经济 Collective-owned Enterprises	其他经济类型 Enterprises of Other Ownership
1952	23512	139.6	9917	464	13131
1962	120833	86.8	102103	17599	1131
1965	200416	132.1	183164	17252	
1970	333386	143.5	305303	28083	
1975	385509	106.1	332982	52527	
1978	483262	116.9	405376	77886	
1979	517483	106.6	438850	78633	
1980	531755	101.8	440139	91577	39
1981	524587	98.6	433740	90675	172
1982	549200	107.1	450308	98516	456
1983	603507	112.2	493773	108923	811
1984	674963	112.8	520593	153056	1314
1985	853196	120.4	632702	218893	1601
1986	976326	112.1	706380	267282	2664
1987	1142220	114.2	809186	328701	4341
1988	1429811	116.0	1012268	416217	1326
1989	1653472	106.1	1160877	486754	5814
1990	1771310	107.4	1196777	548605	25928
1991	2002727	110.0	1325242	604495	72990
1992	2300472	112.5	1488541	561369	250562
1993	3045988	121.7	1748145	1071122	226721
1994	3891584	120.6	1960533	1581321	349730
1995	4058952	108.7	2071755	1663536	323661
1996	5338510	133.4	2132140	2836176	370194
1997	5794532	121.8	1915536	2005610	1873386
1998	6738224	117.3	2593405	2077273	2067546
1999	7151528	117.1	2128243	2174220	2849065
2000	6394812	115.3	2749778	2094680	1550354
2001	7361510	116.4	3098431	2380910	1882169
2002	8379363	115.8	3472067	2312923	2594373
2003	9750800	115.1	4149015	1501372	4100413
2004	11853224	118.4	5414952	875412	5562860
2005	13085580	106.3	5916553	674900	6494127
2006	15573516	119.0	7527607	514810	7531099
2007	19798593	122.1	10179303	365329	9253961
2008	23881446	120.6	12479652	441987	10959807
2009	28270652	118.3	14440321	388777	13441554
2010	35628753	126.0	18353877	435206	16839669
2011	40933178	114.9	20654524	377199	19901455
2012	46560824	113.8	24303736	376427	21880661
2013	50426416	108.3	25358096	325004	24743316
2014	56606272	112.3	27352693	332712	28920867
2015	51599121	91.2	25008248	161009	26429864

注：2013年数据为全国第三次经济普查数据。

12-1 续表 continued

单位：万元 (10 000 yuan)

年份 Year	轻工业 Light Industry	重工业 Heavy Industry	大型工业 Large-size Industry Enterprises	中型工业 Medium-size Industry Enterprises	小型工业 Small-size Industry Enterprises
1952	20800	2712			
1962	68221	52618			
1965	98631	101785			
1970	124467	208919			
1975	167285	218224	145262	130592	109655
1978	220480	262782	168397	121813	193052
1979	243043	274440	189877	133759	193847
1980	283475	248280	193092	130053	208610
1981	309199	215388	178130	140810	205639
1982	303249	246031	213015	128597	207668
1983	315785	287722	245053	127164	231290
1984	321678	353285	241842	143165	289956
1985	401748	451448	333820	147488	371888
1986	458270	518056	401037	150644	424609
1987	516776	625452	472958	171698	497572
1988	699593	730210	615946	210089	603776
1989	712743	940729	696368	258414	698690
1990	787857	983453	716421	279098	775791
1991	897676	1105051	888052	303151	844524
1992	967104	1333368			
1993	1121957	1924031	1258137	384255	1403596
1994	1578875	2312709	1479613	390233	2021738
1995	1636219	2432733	1575030	371156	2112766
1996	2347887	2990623	1693985	358913	3285612
1997	2700085	3094447	1675521	274888	3844123
1998	3232681	3505543	1821556	308424	4608244
1999	3488547	3662981	1744637	337795	5069096
2000	3121419	3273393	2320973	328494	3745345
2001	3518054	3843456	2656010	368497	4337003
2002	3935764	4443599	3038828	398834	4941701
2003	4028859	5721941	2662073	2027256	5061471
2004	4211592	7641632	3595150	3237701	5020373
2005	4078417	9007163	4640325	3228553	5216702
2006	4510970	11062546	5970535	3414468	6188513
2007	7331719	12466874	8351303	4171131	7276159
2008	6010865	17870581	10472686	5005676	8403084
2009	6636464	21634188	12309192	6186395	9775065
2010	7841869	27786884	15002737	8537140	12088876
2011	8992547	31940631	16844272	6207660	17881246
2012	10218288	36342536	22563292	6243799	17753733
2013	9297919	41128497	17390620	7271086	25764710
2014	10369659	46236614	24880136	8754767	22971370
2015	10089660	41509461	26485412	8432031	16681678

12-2 主要年份各区县规模以上工业总产值

Gross Output Value of Industry In Representative Years

单位：亿元 (100 million yuan)

区 县	Region	1998	1999	2000	2001	2002	2003	2004	2005	2006	2007
合 计	**Total**	**350.38**	**366.59**	**417.97**	**482.61**	**544.78**	**638.66**	**830.06**	**981.02**	**1187.74**	**1577.05**
新城区	Xincheng	67.19	71.36	78.25	89.87	105.92	137.46	145.61	196.00	135.14	157.18
碑林区	Beilin	20.57	19.48	21.50	23.15	30.32	22.22	15.92	20.13	18.31	19.10
莲湖区	Lianhu	63.24	65.92	75.68	93.78	106.33	124.24	157.67	185.86	200.75	281.57
灞桥区	Baqiao	19.55	19.95	21.35	20.56	22.99	28.80	37.25	42.29	57.11	80.01
未央区	Weiyang	53.31	52.84	61.41	73.63	80.14	93.23	145.63	170.16	220.08	265.93
雁塔区	Yanta	65.00	75.88	94.38	102.58	107.75	113.99	151.61	144.51	167.58	204.70
阎良区	Yanliang	26.54	26.06	27.56	36.22	40.04	40.98	55.86	68.10	75.84	95.29
临潼区	Lintong	8.90	7.55	7.64	9.36	14.14	34.67	53.49	66.91	85.96	114.09
长安区	Chang'an	7.92	7.70	8.70	8.42	9.96	10.81	19.40	26.43	67.19	101.61
高陵区	Gaoling	1.60	1.83	2.58	3.28	3.97	7.09	14.89	16.50	97.94	177.65
蓝田县	Lantian	2.58	2.37	3.81	4.76	5.12	5.00	5.34	5.69	8.35	13.13
周至县	Zhouzhi	1.24	2.41	2.05	1.73	1.51	1.45	2.92	3.16	3.94	5.52
户 县	Huxian	12.75	13.24	13.07	15.27	16.58	18.74	24.48	35.28	49.55	61.28

12-2 续表 continued

单位：亿元 (100 million yuan)

区 县	Region	2008	2009	2010	2011	2012	2013	2014	2015
合 计	**Total**	**2007.85**	**2468.27**	**3130.15**	**3552.21**	**4066.31**	**4436.58**	**4961.12**	**4924.57**
新城区	Xincheng	147.54	195.45	272.13	323.64	307.67	344.30	372.75	398.68
碑林区	Beilin	48.99	58.60	108.14	138.72	18.46	23.48	27.66	29.59
莲湖区	Lianhu	356.90	399.83	458.30	457.96	459.41	419.81	407.16	402.62
灞桥区	Baqiao	123.34	178.82	242.15	280.52	278.37	308.04	300.73	175.89
未央区	Weiyang	327.65	393.22	499.88	510.39	684.55	733.75	858.40	839.29
雁塔区	Yanta	262.32	249.69	286.19	367.97	587.65	624.55	694.34	677.00
阎良区	Yanliang	109.43	128.99	163.55	176.67	219.31	276.71	300.25	321.23
临潼区	Lintong	130.93	165.77	222.01	277.75	341.01	404.45	418.75	263.29
长安区	Chang'an	154.74	277.98	334.89	350.68	354.65	383.41	546.35	720.87
高陵区	Gaoling	256.55	305.94	402.98	516.33	662.99	741.34	854.73	869.60
蓝田县	Lantian	17.62	23.40	31.93	35.87	41.60	49.33	46.22	49.32
周至县	Zhouzhi	6.76	9.03	11.11	15.29	17.08	26.01	29.10	41.25
户 县	Huxian	65.09	81.54	96.89	100.42	93.55	101.40	104.68	135.94

12-3 各区县规模以上工业企业工业总产值（2015年）

单位：亿元

区县、开发区	Regin	单位数（个）Name of Enterprises (unit)	工业总产值 Gross Industrial Output Value	国有经济 State-owned Enterprises	集体经济 Collective-owned Enterprises	其他经济类型 Enterprises of Other Ownership
新城区	Xincheng	14	398.68	233.97		164.71
碑林区	Beilin	13	29.59			29.59
莲湖区	Lianhu	33	402.62	208.10		194.52
灞桥区	Baqiao	85	175.89	29.05	4.88	141.96
未央区	Weiyang	202	839.29	1.77	0.62	836.90
雁塔区	Yanta	249	677.00	98.04		578.96
阎良区	Yanliang	83	321.23	8.75	2.90	309.58
临潼区	Lintong	56	263.29	6.36		256.93
长安区	Chang'an	130	720.87	81.64		639.23
高陵区	Gaoling	133	869.60	7.12		862.48
蓝田县	Lantian	29	49.32	9.97	0.89	38.46
周至县	Zhouzhi	41	41.25		0.72	40.53
户　县	Huxian	82	135.94	13.14	0.68	122.12

Gross Output Value of Industrial Enterprises above Designated Size by Region (2015)

(100 million yuan)

轻工业 Light Industry	重工业 Heavy Industry	大型工业 Large-size Industry Enterprises	中型工业 Medium-size Industry Enterprises	小型工业 Small-size Industry Enterprises
71.70	326.98	382.25	12.17	4.26
14.17	15.42	6.98	15.70	6.91
43.23	359.39	371.86	21.57	9.19
45.96	129.93	50.20	38.38	87.31
273.60	565.69	198.27	151.60	489.42
89.30	587.70	294.21	201.91	180.88
60.34	260.89	161.92	28.70	130.61
152.44	110.85	107.11	73.36	82.82
63.88	656.99	541.40	100.72	78.75
53.04	816.56	456.37	159.54	253.69
20.53	28.79	8.51	9.88	30.93
24.30	16.95		9.21	32.04
53.84	82.10	69.45	20.46	46.03

12-4 主要年份规模以上工业企业主要经济指标（2015年）

单位：亿元

年份 Year	企业单位数（个） Number of Enterprises (unit)	工业总产值（当年价格） Gross Industrial Output Value (At Current Prices)	工业增加值（现价） Industrial added value （at current prices）	从业人员年平均人数（万人） Annual Average Employers (10 000person)
1998	793	350.38	99.20	51.71
1999	770	366.59	106.56	45.64
2000	816	417.97	130.18	43.25
2001	785	482.61	149.06	40.12
2002	771	544.78	170.39	38.48
2003	735	638.66	202.74	36.55
2004	1066	830.06	254.17	38.08
2005	902	981.02	314.01	37.92
2006	904	1187.74	370.11	37.94
2007	937	1577.05	499.96	38.55
2008	1032	2007.85	605.25	40.17
2009	1131	2468.27	700.31	43.42
2010	1126	3130.15	824.09	47.11
2011	891	3552.21	951.58	50.42
2012	970	4066.31	1064.29	49.23
2013	1056	4436.57	1194.88	44.27
2014	1146	4961.12	1304.12	49.53
2015	1150	4924.57	1285.08	50.59

注：2013年数据为全国第三次经济普查数据，根据三经普对2009-2012年规模以上工业增加值数据进行了修订。

Output of Major Industrial Products of Enterprises above Designated Size in Repre sentative Years（2015）

（100 million yuan)

资产总计 Total Assets	负债合计 Total Liabilites	所有者权益合计 Total Owners' Equities	主营业务收入 Cost of Principal Business	利润总额 Total Profits	利税总额 Total Pre-tax Profits
810.56	548.68	261.88	346.84	-1.26	14.82
853.90	577.94	275.96	346.26	8.26	27.30
958.05	622.46	323.72	420.42	16.11	36.29
1054.36	657.88	384.65	451.62	17.97	40.84
1065.76	643.78	412.27	541.64	25.43	51.31
1195.69	733.04	460.97	645.53	33.82	64.99
1333.91	869.30	464.60	812.46	38.57	74.23
1503.85	977.42	508.82	980.97	28.72	67.25
1651.67	1062.11	578.33	1183.51	61.46	110.23
1940.52	1254.01	686.51	1561.25	106.22	168.54
2426.13	1518.86	907.27	1928.05	84.89	168.63
2913.56	1779.38	1130.76	2384.52	177.20	280.68
3592.13	2069.29	1515.65	3011.19	245.37	373.56
3975.38	2295.49	1678.19	3381.27	172.94	312.78
4775.92	2835.55	1926.72	3758.56	167.77	320.57
5127.69	3049.36	2071.72	4171.21	211.26	392.14
6048.34	3607.62	2436.06	4566.20	226.17	401.20
6740.26	3860.55	2926.55	4374.11	206.88	341.40

12-5 各区县规模以上工业企业主要经济指标（2015年）

单位：亿元

区县、开发区	Region	企业单位数（个）Number of Enterprises (unit)	从业人员年平均人数（万人）Annual Average Employers (10 000 persons)	资产合计（亿元）Total Assets (100 mill yuan)
新城区	Xingcheng	14	4.09	515.7
碑林区	Beilin	13	0.58	75.86
莲湖区	Lianhu	33	6.2	880.67
灞桥区	Baqiao	85	2.84	230.33
未央区	Weiyang	202	6.67	682.07
雁塔区	Yanta	249	9.28	1420.29
阎良区	Yanliang	83	3.53	389.28
临潼区	Lintong	56	1.4	279.35
长安区	Chang'an	130	7.8	1267.16
高陵区	Gaoling	133	5.66	774.43
蓝田县	Lantian	29	0.5	62.67
周至县	Zhouzhi	41	0.42	28.57
户　县	Huxian	82	1.61	133.88

Main Economic Indicators of All Industrial Enterprises above Designated Size by Region (2015)

(100 million yuan)

负债合计 Total Liabilites	所有者权益合计 Total Owners' Equities	主营业务收入 Revenue from Principal Business	利润总额 Total Profits	利税总额 Total Pre-tax Profits
307.15	208.55	350.59	9.66	28.54
51.82	24.04	34.52	3.81	5.87
370.82	509.86	363.7	26.33	45.76
145.71	84.62	158.86	11.78	17.69
389.77	292.3	763.76	30.16	48.91
831.11	637.47	682.97	41.84	72.37
276.46	112.82	282.29	8.35	9.23
149.33	129.76	197.64	12.03	18.39
722.09	545.08	678.85	42.43	56.01
496.35	276.88	695.8	10.73	22.13
34.67	28	40.81	3.09	4.18
12.54	16.03	31.61	1.9	2.66
72.73	61.15	92.7	4.75	9.65

12-6 规模以上工业企业主要工业产品产量（2015年）

Output of Major Industrial Products of Enterprises above Designated Size(2015)

产品名称	Name of Products	2015	比上年增长(%) Increase over Preceding Year (%)
自来水生产量(亿立方米)	Tap Water Production (100 million cu.m)	4.45	4.2
大米(万吨)	Rice (10 000 ton)	2.83	-28.5
小麦粉(万吨)	Wheat Flour (10 000 tons)	140.72	0.7
精制食用植物油(万吨)	Edible Vegetable Oil (10 000 ton)	17.13	-20.2
鲜、冷藏肉（万吨）	Fresh/Frozen Meat(10 000 ton)	4.85	9.8
饲料	Mixed Feed(10 000 ton)	120.43	2.4
配合饲料	Compound feed	24.83	-5.3
混合饲料	Mixed feed	94.43	5.1
方便面(万吨)	instant Noodle(10 000 ton)	9.05	6.3
乳制品(万吨)	Dairy Products (10 000 ton)	107.01	-3.6
液体乳(万吨)	Milk	92.63	-5.2
固体及半固体乳制品	Solid and semi-solid dairy products	14.37	8.3
饮料酒(万千升)	Beverage Wine (10 000 kiloliter)	45.86	2.5
白酒（折65度，商品量）	Liquor (as 65 degree, amount of goods)	0.05	-37.5
啤酒	Beer	45.82	2.6
软饮料(万吨)	Soft Beverage (10 000 ton)	269.24	31.3
碳酸饮料类（汽水）（万吨）	Carbonated Beverage	52.11	6.3
果汁和蔬菜汁饮料	Juice and Fruit Beverage	70.15	9.7
包装饮用水类	Canned Drinking Water	71.37	45.9
纱(万吨)	Yarn (10 000 ton)	3.52	67.4
1. 棉纱	Cotton Yarn	1.78	137.1
2. 棉混纺纱	Blend Fabric	0.40	235.5
3. 化学纤维纱	Pure Chemical-Fibre Yarn	1.33	8.4
布(亿米)	Cloth (100 million m)	1.04	58.8
1. 棉布	Cotton Cloth	0.31	62.4
2. 棉混纺布	Blend Fabric	0.19	304.7
3. 化学纤维布	Pure Chemical-Fibre Cloth	0.54	29.7
服装（万件）	Garment (10 000 units)	0.09	13.6
梭织服装	Shuttle-Woven Garment	0.09	13.6
鞋(万双)	shoes(10000 pairs)	0.03	43.1
皮革鞋靴（万双）	Leather Shoes (10 000 pairs)	0.03	43.1
人造板（万立方米）	Artificial Board (10 000 cu.m)	41.12	-16.9
纤维板	Fibre Board	41.12	-16.9
家具（万件）	Furniture (10 000unit)	22.45	-17.5
木质家具	Wooden Furniture	10.51	-20.4
金属家具	Metal furniture	3.43	-25.2

12-6 续表1 continued1

产品名称	Name of Products	2015	比上年增长(%) Increase over Preceding Year (%)
软体家具	Soft Furniture (inc.: Sofa ,Mattress etc.)	8.16	-11.4
机制纸及纸板(外购原纸加工除外)(万吨)	Machine Made Paper(not including processing of procured base paper)(10 000 ton)	12.22	8.7
纸制品(万吨)	Paper-Made Products (10 000 ton)	11.99	10.4
瓦楞纸箱	Corrugated Paper	8.47	6.7
单色印刷(万令)	Monochrom Printed products(10 000 reams)	103.22	-36.4
多色印刷品(万对开色令)	Colored Printed products(10 000 reams)	952.42	-6.9
化学农药原药(折有效成分100%)(万吨)	Chemical Pesticide(100% effective content)(10 000 ton)	0.33	-58.2
涂料(万吨)	Construction Paint(10 000 ton)	1.25	-3.1
合成洗涤剂(万吨)	Synthetic Detergents (10 000 ton)	9.07	-21.7
合成洗衣粉(万吨)	Washing Power	1.87	-29.2
液体洗涤剂	Liquid detergent	5.63	-19.6
化学原料药(万吨)	Chemical Medicine (10 000 ton)	0.02	-11.4
中成药(万吨)	Traditional Chinese Medicine (10 000 ton)	0.37	-24.9
化学纤维(万吨)	Chemical Fiber	2.25	-23.3
人造纤维(纤维素纤维)(万吨)	Man-made Fiber	2.25	-7.8
塑料制品(万吨)	Plastic Product (10 000 ton)	13.81	-8.1
水泥(万吨)	Cement (10 000 ton)	330.73	-19.8
硅酸盐水泥熟料(万吨)	Portland Cement Clinker (10 000 ton)	120.20	-18.4
水泥混凝土电杆(万根)	Cement Pole(10 000 unit)	2.12	-37.6
商品混凝土(万立方米)	Ready-mixed Concrete (10 000 cu.m)	2941.19	6.1
沥青和改性沥青防水卷材(万平方米)	Asphalt and Modified Bitumen Membrane(10 000 sq.m)	2577.24	2.4
钢化玻璃(万平方米)	Toughened Glass(10 000 sq.m)	272.96	76.3
日用玻璃制品(万吨)	Glassware(10 000 ton)	0.50	-35.6
钢材(万吨)	Rolled-steel Final Products (10 000 ton)	37.03	-10.0
盘条(线材)	Wire Rod	13.71	-14.5
其他钢材	Other steel	23.33	-7.1
铁合金(万吨)	Ferroalloy (10 000 ton)	0.29	-71.6
铝材(万吨)	Aluminum Material (10 000 ton)	4.64	15.3
黄金(千克)	Gold (kg)	290.00	10.7
单晶硅(万千克)	Monocrystalline Silicon (10 000kg)	341.21	7.2
工业锅炉(蒸发量吨)	industrial Boiler steam(ton)	1740.00	-29.3
发动机(万千瓦)	Engine (10 000 kw)	213.60	-35.4
汽车发动机(万千瓦)	Motor Engine(10 000 kw)	213.60	-35.4
金属切削机床(万台)	Metal-cutting Machines (10 000 unit)	0.51	-16.7
泵(万台)	Pump (Liquid pump)(10 000 unit)	0.76	-78.8

12-6 续表2 continued2

产品名称	Name of Products	2015	比上年增长(%) Increase over Preceding Year (%)
风机（万台）	Fan(10 000 unit)	0.98	66.5
气体压缩机（万台）	Gas Compressor(10 000 unit)	29.17	-28.9
阀门（万吨）	Valves (10 000 ton)	0.07	-0.2
铸铁件（万吨）	iron Castings (10 000 ton)	0.95	-8.2
铸钢件（万吨）	Steel Castings (10 000 ton)	2.86	-2.6
锻件（万吨）	Forgings (10 000 ton)	0.60	19.9
矿山专用设备（万吨）	Mining Equipment (10 000 ton)	3.38	256.0
炼油、化工生产专用设备（万吨）	Oil Refining and Chemical industry Machine(10 000 ton)	0.37	-28.1
金属冶炼设备（吨）	Metal Smelting Equipments(ton)	3171.50	-51.9
金属轧制设备（吨）	Metal-rolling Machine(ton)	2034.50	18.5
印刷专用设备（吨）	Printing Equipment(ton)	145.00	-13.2
环境污染防治设备(台/套)	Special Equipment for Environment Protection	133.00	0.8
大气污染防治设备	Equipment for Preventing Atmospheric Pollution	133.00	8.1
铁路货车（辆）	Freight(unit)	738.00	-69.2
汽车（万辆）	Motor Vehicle(10 000unit)	34.14	-8.9
基本型乘用车（轿车）（万辆）	Basic Passenger Vehicles (10 000Cars)	24.01	-10.1
1升<排量≤1.6升	1.0L- 1.6L Gas Displacement(1.6L included)	23.74	-10.9
1.6升<排量≤2.0升	1.6L-2.0L Gas Displacement(2.0L included)	0.15	109.6
客车	Passenger Vehicles	0.34	184.0
大型客车（车长>10）	Buses	0.06	3.7
轻型客车（车长<7）	Large(40seats and above)	0.28	356.8
载货汽车	Trucks	8.31	-22.0
改装汽车（万辆）	Refit Trucks (10 000 ton)unit)	0.98	-32.4
电动机（万千瓦）	Electric motor(Ten thousand kilowatts)	725.67	-14.3
直流电动机	DC motors	53.32	0.7
交流电动机	Alternating Current Motor(10 000kw)	671.02	-15.3
变压器（万千伏安）	Transformer(10 000KVA)	13583.25	-8.1
高压开关板（万面）	High-voltage Switch Panel(10 000 unit)	1.90	-22.7
低压开关板（万面）	Low-voltage Switch Panel(10 000 unit)	2.20	-17.7
电力电缆(万千米)	Electric Power Cables(10 000 km)	2.59	40.6
通信及电子网络用电缆(万对千米)	Communication Cables(10 000 pair km)	2.95	-4.0
光缆(光纤通讯电缆)（万芯千米）	Cable (Optical Communication Cable) (10 000 Core.km)	697.94	35.8
绝缘制品(吨)	Insulating Products(ton)	9308.20	1.1
电子元件（亿只）	Electronic Components(100 million units)	2.23	-10.0
工业自动化调节仪表与控制系统（万台、套）	Automatization meter and system (10 000 unit)	5.14	-46.5
电工仪器仪表（万台）	Electrical instrumentation (10 000 sets)	88.84	89.0

12-6 续表3 continued 3

产品名称	Name of Products	2015	比上年增长(%) Increase over Preceding Year (%)
分析仪器及装置（万台、套）	Analysis instruments and Apparatus(10 000 sets)	3.07	1.5
化学试剂（万吨）	Chemicals Reagents(10000 ton)	27.49	-19.8
水泥混凝土排水管（千米）	Cement concrete drain (kilometers)	1501.60	53.0
十种有色金属（万吨）	Ten kinds of nonferrous metals (10 000tonnes)	10.39	55.0
锌	Zinc	7.57	77.8
镍	Nickel	2.82	15.3
起重机（吨）	Crane (tons)	240.00	-77.7
减速机（台）	Reducer (a)	2825.00	-53.1
石油钻井设备（台/套）	Oil drilling equipment (units / sets)	1040.00	-64.4
模具（万套）	Molds (10 000sets)	2.36	-14.2
机械化农业及园艺机具（万台）	Mechanization of agriculture and horticulture machinery (10 000a)	2.03	1.2
电动自行车（万辆）	Electric bicycle (10 000cars)	62.77	5.0
互感器（台）	Transformers (a)	5515.00	14.4
电力电容器（万千乏）	Power capacitors (10 000kW)	2345.29	15.2
高压开关设备（11万伏以上）（万台）	High Voltage Switchgear (above 110,000 volts) (10 000a)	1.43	-10.0
安全、自动化监控设备（万台/套）	Security, automated monitoring equipment (10 000units / sets)	1.57	-0.4
灯具及照明装置（万套/台/个）	Lamps and lighting equipment (10 000sets /a)	4.14	14.3
移动通信手持机（手机）（万台）	Mobile handset (phone) (10 000a)	9.13	-68.6
半导体分立器件（亿/只）	Discrete semiconductor devices (100million units)	27.88	-35.2
光电子器件（亿只/片）	Optoelectronic devices (100million units)	14.81	98.6
工业仪表（万台/个）	Industrial Instrumentation (10 000a)	2.66	24.3
环境监测专用仪器仪表（台）	Special instrumentation for environmental monitoring (a)	94.30	-0.6
汽车仪器仪表（万台）	Automotive instrument (10 000Tai)	6.73	12.9
原油加工量（万吨）	Crude Oil Processing (10 000 ton)	28.16	-81.0
汽油（万吨）	Petrol(10 000 ton)	8.16	-75.7
柴油（万吨）	Diesel(l0 000 ton)	7.38	-81.7
燃料油（万吨）	Fuel Oil(10 000 ton)		
液化石油气（万吨）	Liquefied Petroleum Gas (10 000 ton)	1.61	-78.0
石油焦（万吨）	Petroleum Coke (10 000 ton)		
石油沥青（万吨）	Petroleum Pitch (10 000 ton)	8.22	-80.8
发电量（亿千瓦小时）	Power generation(One hundred million kilowatt-hours)	158.68	-11.6
火力发电量（亿千瓦小时）	Thermal power generation(One hundred million kilowatt-hours	136.53	-15.2
水力发电量（亿千瓦小时）	Hydropower(One hundred million kilowatt-hours)	20.12	24.4
风力发电量（亿千瓦小时）	Wind power generation(One hundred million kilowatt-hours)	2.02	-13.8

12-7 规模以上工业企业分行业工业增加值(2015年)

Value Added of Industrial Enterprises above Designated Size by Sector (2015)

单位:亿元 (100 million yuan)

行业	Sector	2015
总计	**Total**	**1285.08**
按工业行业大类分	**Grouped by Sector**	
煤炭开采和洗选业	Mining and Washing of Coal	
石油和天然气开采业	Extraction of Petroleum and Natural Gas	
黑色金属矿采选业	Mining and Processing of Ferrous Metal Ores	
有色金属矿采选业	Mining and Processing of Non-ferrous Metal Ores	
非金属矿采选业	Mining and Processing of Nonmetal Ores	
开采辅助活动	Mining Auxiliary Activities	20.57
其他采矿业	Mining of Other Ores	
农副食品加工业	Processing of Food from Agricultural Porducts	34.22
食品制造业	Manufacture of Foods	35.01
酒、饮料和精制茶制造业	Manufacture of Alcohol,Beverages and Tea	34.63
烟草制品业	Manufacture of Tobacco	0.87
纺织业	Manufacture of Textile	7.36
纺织服装、服饰业	Textile, Garments industry	1.78
皮革、毛皮、羽毛及其制品和制鞋业	Manufacture of Leather, Fur, Feather and Related Products	0.98
木材加工和木、竹、藤、棕、草制品业	Processing of Timber, Manufacture of Wood,Plam and Straw Products	4.53
家具制造业	Manufacture of Furniture	2.57
造纸及纸制品业	Manufacture of Paper and Paper Products	2.28
印刷和记录媒介复制	Printing,Reproduction of Recording Media	23.56
文教、工美、体育和娱乐用品制造业	Manufacture of Articles For Cultural,Educational and Sports Activities	12.37
石油加工业、炼焦和核燃料加工业	Processing of Petroleum, Cokeing,Processing of Nuclear and Nuclear Fuel	8.74
化学原料及化学制品制造业	Manufacture of Raw Chemical Materials and Chemical Products	66.37
医药制造业	Manufacture of Medicines	68.28
化学纤维制造业	Manufacture of Chemical Fibers	3.70
橡胶和塑料制品业	Manufacture of Rubber and Plastics	16.83
非金属矿物制品业	Manufacture of Non-metallic Mineral Products	30.33
黑色金属冶炼和压延加工业	Smelting and Pressing of Ferrous Metals	6.70
有色金属冶炼和压延加工业	Smelting and Pressing of Non-ferrous Metals	40.37
金属制品业	Manufacture of Metal Products	24.85
通用设备制造业	Manufacture of General Purpose Machinery	33.65
专用设备制造业	Manufacture of Special Equipment	71.45
汽车制造业	Manufacture of Motor Vehicle	164.74
铁路、船舶、航空航天和其他运输设备制造业	Railways, Shipbuilding,Aerospace and Other Transportation Equipment Manufacturing Industry	134.10
电气机械和器材制造业	Manufacture of Electric Equipment and Machinery	129.60
计算机、通讯和其他电子设备制造业	Manufacture of Communication Equipment, Computers and other Electronic Equipment	150.86
仪器仪表制造业	Manufacture of Measuring Instruments and Machinery	33.91
其他制造业	Manufacture of Other Manufacturing	1.63
废弃资源综合利用业	Recycling and Disposal of Waste	
金属制品、机械和设备修理业	Metal Products,Machinery and Equipment Repair Industry	0.63
电力、热力的生产和供应业	Production and Supply of Electric Power and Heat Power	95.42
燃气生产和供应业	Gas Mining and Supplying Industry	16.69
水的生产和供应业	Production and Supply of Water	5.52

12-8 主要年份规模以上工业企业经济效益指标（2015年）

Indicators of Economic Benefit of Industrial Enterprises above Designated Size in Representative Years（2015）

年　份 Year	总资产贡献率 (%) Ratio of Total Assets to Industrial Output Value (%)	资产负债率 (%) Assets-Liability Ratio (%)	流动资产周转次数 (次/年) Rate of Annual Turnover Working Capitals (times/year)	成本费用利润率 (%) Ratio of Profits to Cost (%)	全员劳动生产率 (元/人·年) Overall Labor Productivity (yuan/person·ear)	产品销售率 (%) Proportion of Industrial Products Sold (%)
1998		67.7	0.9	-266.1	19185	95.3
1999		67.7	0.9	2.5	22878	95.9
2000		65.0	1.0	4.2	29496	97.1
2001	5.8	62.4	0.9	4.1	38267	96.7
2002	6.2	60.4	1.1	5.1	46940	96.7
2003	7.0	61.3	1.1	5.7	58801	96.3
2004	6.9	65.2	1.2	5.0	66752	97.9
2005	8.4	65.0	1.3	3.1	82815	97.5
2006	7.8	64.3	1.4	5.5	97561	98.2
2007	10.2	64.6	1.6	7.3	129706	96.8
2008	8.6	62.6	1.5	4.6	150641	96.1
2009	11.3	61.1	1.7	8.1	161289	97.6
2010	12.2	57.6	1.7	8.8	188483	97.1
2011	8.6	57.7	1.5	5.2	194105	97.4
2012	7.7	59.4	1.5	4.5	230032	96.7
2013	8.5	59.5	1.5	5.2	264324	95.7
2014	7.4	59.7	1.4	5.2	275288	94.9
2015	5.7	57.3	1.3	4.8	268182	94.5

12-9 规模以上工业企业主要经济指标（2015年）

单位：万元

分组	Classify	企业单位数（个）Number of Enterprises (unit)	亏损企业（个）Loss Making Enterprises	工业总产值（当年价格）Gross Industrial Output Value (At Current Prices)
总计	**Total**	**1150**	**240**	**49245721**
#市区	Urban	998	214	47435220
#亏损企业	Deficit Enterprises	240	240	9109313
按隶属关系分	**Grouped by Jurisdiction of Management**			
中央企业	Central Enterprises	85	15	12019310
省属企业	Provincial Enterprises	68	22	8092686
市属企业	Municipal Enterprises	997	203	29133725
按登记注册类型分组	**Grouped by Registion Status**			
内资企业	Domestic Investment Enterprises	1033	212	40261709
国有	State-owned Enterprises	41	5	6979067
集体	Collective-owned Enterprises	8		106881
股份合作	Share-holding Corperative	7	2	18970
联营	Joint Ownership Enterprises			
国有联营	State Joint Ownership Enterprises			
集体联营	Collective Joint Ownership Enterprises			
国有与集体联营	Joint State-collective Ownership Enterprises			
其他联营	Other Joint Ownership Enterprises			
有限责任公司	Limited Liability Corporations	573	129	24183793
国有独资公司	State Sole Funded Enterprises	38	12	3846652
其他有限责任公司	Other Limited Liability Corporation	535	117	20337141
股份有限公司	Share-holding Corperation Ltd.	94	18	3353649
私营	Private Enterprises	309	58	5615584
私营独资	Private-funded Enterprises	10	1	102351
私营合伙	Private Partnership Enterprises	2		3593
私营有限责任公司	Private Limited Liability Corporations	277	53	5204839
私营股份有限公司	Private Share Holding Corporations	20	4	304800
其他	Other Domestic Funded Enterprises	1		3766
港澳台商投资	Enterprises with Funds from Hong Kong,Macao and Taiwan	27	4	2733793
外商投资	Foreign Funded Enterprises	90	24	6250219
按轻重工业分	**Grouped by Light Industry and Heavy Industry**			
轻工业	Light Industry	313	65	9663363
重工业	Heavy Industry	837	175	39582358

Main Economic Indicators of All Industrial Enterprises above Designated Size (2015)

(10 000yuan)

工业销售产值（当年价） Value of Industry Products Sales (At Current Prices)	出口交货值 Export Delivery Value	从业人员年平均人数（人） Annual Average Employers (person)	资产总计 Total Assets	流动资产合计 Total Working Capitals	固定资产合计 Total Fixed Assets	固定资产原价 Origing Value of Fixed Assets	累计折旧 Accumulative Total Depreciation
46541465	**4647152**	**505895**	**67402622**	**34104930**	**21056202**	**32223684**	**12234373**
44822605	4616340	480954	65216238	32988023	20202953	30990120	11647837
8785159	261938	97575	11464399	6390810	2252747	3589952	1389684
11746321	493485	173874	23453772	11257817	7870123	12249984	4763751
7783113	227306	76097	11495986	6221232	2056081	3201582	1299607
27012031	3926361	255924	32452865	16625881	11129999	16772118	6171014
38470059	2466065	428450	54585740	29824650	14336370	23057786	9560845
6782684	178339	99129	13696187	6984627	4036700	5560406	1823014
103706		1142	79405	53300	21613	30289	15133
19373		748	40098	30643	5327	12030	7198
23161778	1185759	253362	30609325	17079030	8168366	13454646	5677242
3724070	298334	69994	10872550	4771246	4107334	6962860	2952346
19437709	887424	183368	19736775	12307784	4061032	6491785	2724896
3033498	527944	37423	6950732	3651874	1383225	2634395	1348549
5365284	574024	36517	3206883	2023624	719631	1364037	689233
98838		679	39964	18573	12083	57221	46717
3482		165	3888	3042	847	1785	939
4961457	573790	33550	2906661	1860625	680693	1237567	597370
301506	234	2123	256370	141385	26009	67463	44206
3736		129	3110	1552	1508	1984	476
2467843	147301	36009	2347234	929546	779548	1077761	370748
5603563	2033786	41436	10469649	3350733	5940284	8088138	2302780
9200480	706421	81197	7315632	4147325	2269206	3970626	1934812
37340984	3940731	424698	60086990	29957604	18786997	28253059	10299561

12-9 续表1

单位：万元

分组	Classify	负债合计 Total Liabilites	流动负债合计 Total Working Liabilities	非流动负债 Non-Working Liabilities
总计	**Total**	**38605518**	**28969015**	**5846068**
#市区	Urban	37442284	28048542	5699024
#亏损企业	Deficit Enterprises	7661623	6272074	921177
按隶属关系分	**Grouped by Jurisdiction of Management**			
中央企业	Central Enterprises	13967181	8888759	2769215
省属企业	Provincial Enterprises	6144667	5110788	600187
市属企业	Municipal Enterprises	18493671	14969468	2476665
按登记注册类型分组	**Grouped by Registion Status**			
内资企业	Domestic Investment Enterprises	31263782	23246613	5013859
国有	State-owned Enterprises	7474102	5683777	2071291
集体	Collective-owned Enterprises	49487	48238	1150
股份合作	Share-holding Corperative	17106	15103	2002
联营	Joint Ownership Enterprises			
国有联营	State Joint Ownership Enterprises			
集体联营	Collective Joint Ownership Enterprises			
国有与集体联营	Joint State-collective Ownership Enterprises			
其他联营	Other Joint Ownership Enterprises			
有限责任公司	Limited Liability Corporations	19248745	13922918	2230247
国有独资公司	State Sole Funded Enterprises	6625125	3252047	789833
其他有限责任公司	Other Limited Liability Corporation	12623620	10670871	1440414
股份有限公司	Share-holding Corperation Ltd.	2650948	2071923	468665
私营	Private Enterprises	1820719	1501979	240504
私营独资	Private-funded Enterprises	16650	5654	638
私营合伙	Private Partnership Enterprises	2792	1105	1687
私营有限责任公司	Private Limited Liability Corporations	1733962	1436285	231349
私营股份有限公司	Private Share Holding Corporations	67316	58935	6830
其他	Other Domestic Funded Enterprises	2676	2676	
港澳台商投资	Enterprises with Funds from Hong Kong,Macao and Taiwan	1535872	1302689	171201
外商投资	Foreign Funded Enterprises	5805865	4419713	661008
按轻重工业分	**Grouped by Light Industry and Heavy Industry**			
轻工业	Light Industry	4227948	3426234	683661
重工业	Heavy Industry	34377570	25542781	5162407

continued1

(10 000yuan)

所有者权益合计 Total Owners' Equities	实收资本 Total Capital Hold	营业收入 Total Revenue	主营业务收入 Revenue from Principal Business	营业成本 Total Cost	主营业务成本 Cost of Principal Business	营业税金及附加 Taxs and Other Changes	主营业务税金及附加 Taxes and Other Charges on Principal Business
29265509	**12258142**	**44880060**	**43741064**	**38402779**	**37015651**	**257467**	**242896**
28242359	11825777	43270387	42140869	37121707	35742175	246846	232374
4273283	2558427	6938397	6779433	6354908	6243710	21562	20172
9486543	3291658	12011875	11600043	10391408	9584299	74404	72437
5839064	1704256	6875198	6604690	5995982	5795154	23621	23445
13939902	7262228	25992987	25536331	22015390	21636198	159441	147015
23790364	8615941	36764818	35798238	31828251	30564820	184609	170388
6704557	1302288	6665032	6278895	5661864	4977552	44148	42842
29918	8716	103191	86817	93871	81299	401	401
22992	14537	18658	18208	14769	14538	183	183
11358016	5227947	21955391	21464505	19220729	18743472	102850	92469
4247425	1427879	4292974	4183071	3566762	3479505	38027	29830
7110591	3800068	17662417	17281433	15653967	15263967	64824	62639
4300300	1327527	2980766	2947010	2394613	2376861	16777	14384
1374148	734726	5038044	4999067	4439033	4367725	20239	20099
23314	13443	95976	95317	85027	84696	285	285
1097	1002	3482	3482	2930	2930	19	19
1160683	616713	4651226	4617986	4112991	4044570	16969	16834
189054	103568	287360	282283	238085	235529	2966	2961
434	200	3736	3736	3372	3372	12	12
811361	219739	2572601	2520630	2302002	2259712	49375	49373
4663784	3422463	5542641	5422195	4272525	4191119	23483	23135
3081888	1429713	8391375	8293003	6671429	6607818	53748	50742
26183621	10828429	36488685	35448061	31731350	30407833	203719	192155

12-9 续表2

单位：万元

分 组	Classify	销售费用 Expenses for Sales	管理费用 Expenses for Management	财务费用 Financial cost
总计	**Total**	**1578066**	**2608410**	**511790**
#市区	Urban	1474647	2493959	490743
#亏损企业	Deficit Enterprises	284339	449539	96220
按隶属关系分	**Grouped by Jurisdiction of Management**			
中央企业	Central Enterprises	216627	786928	215095
省属企业	Provincial Enterprises	354389	409346	42326
市属企业	Municipal Enterprises	1007051	1412137	254368
按登记注册类型分组	**Grouped by Registion Status**			
内资企业	Domestic Investment Enterprises	1142395	2085007	378122
国有	State-owned Enterprises	157218	491816	74487
集体	Collective-owned Enterprises	2370	1971	272
股份合作	Share-holding Corperative	879	2608	321
联营	Joint Ownership Enterprises			
国有联营	State Joint Ownership Enterprises			
集体联营	Collective Joint Ownership Enterprises			
国有与集体联营	Joint State-collective Ownership Enterprises			
其他联营	Other Joint Ownership Enterprises			
有限责任公司	Limited Liability Corporations	663622	1174185	233443
国有独资公司	State Sole Funded Enterprises	94909	339917	104425
其他有限责任公司	Other Limited Liability Corporation	568713	834268	129018
股份有限公司	Share-holding Corperation Ltd.	156288	228355	33751
私营	Private Enterprises	161995	185974	35698
私营独资	Private-funded Enterprises	1408	4202	630
私营合伙	Private Partnership Enterprises	190	239	13
私营有限责任公司	Private Limited Liability Corporations	146713	161305	32291
私营股份有限公司	Private Share Holding Corporations	13683	20229	2764
其他	Other Domestic Funded Enterprises	23	97	149
港澳台商投资	Enterprises with Funds from Hong Kong,Macao and Taiwan	61531	71080	14383
外商投资	Foreign Funded Enterprises	374140	452323	119285
按轻重工业分	**Grouped by Light Industry and Heavy Industry**			
轻工业	Light Industry	769354	447193	64607
重工业	Heavy Industry	808712	2161218	447182

continued2

(10 000yuan)

营业利润 Operating Profit	利润总额 Total Profits	亏损企业亏损额 Total Loss of Deficit Enterprises	利税总额 Total Pre-tax Profits	应付职工薪酬 Salary Payable	本年应交增值税 Value Added Tax Payable
1715144	**2068829**	**233551**	**3413991**	**3430422**	**1087695**
1630813	1976229	219325	3256052	3298154	1032978
-294705	-233551	233551	-107613	539447	104376
569744	621290	47870	1084039	1284170	388345
28911	95603	48173	321025	557780	201801
1116489	1351937	137508	2008927	1588472	497549
1347060	1589925	191995	2652345	2812638	877810
352205	372226	20016	629668	628770	213294
4248	5257		7212	3723	1555
275	288	342	1476	2314	1005
675712	834452	133333	1448058	1712836	510756
203399	244065	20707	514842	594270	232750
472312	590387	112626	933216	1118566	278005
160469	211803	19908	306565	238571	77986
154069	165817	18396	259172	226110	73116
2582	2640	88	3282	2885	357
91	91		280	514	171
142370	153315	17637	239386	209011	69102
9026	9771	672	16223	13700	3486
83	83		195	314	100
80748	88489	1532	167520	173691	29656
287335	390415	40024	594126	444093	180229
339169	380218	36102	723900	561168	289934
1375975	1688611	197449	2690091	2869254	797761

12-9 续表3

单位：万元

分　组	Classify	企业单位数（个）Number of Enterprises (unit)	亏损企业（个）Loss Making Enterprises	工业总产值（当年价格）Gross Industrial Output Value (At Current Prices)
按企业规模分	**Grouped by Size of Enterprises**			
大型企业	Large-size	61	10	26485412
中型企业	Medium-size	164	37	8432031
小型企业	Small-size	925	193	14328278
按经济组织类型分组	**Grouped by Economic Type of Orgnization**			
独资企业	Appropratorship	104	16	10893945
合作、合伙企业	Partnership	12	2	33811
股份有限公司	Corporaton	117	23	3994467
有限责任公司	Limited Liability Company	917	199	34323499
按控股情况分	**Grouped by Cast strand**			
国有控股	State owned shares	246	57	24676418
集体控股	Collective shares	29	2	1133603
私人控股	Private holdings	727	147	15878715
港澳台控股	Hong Kong and Macao Holdings	20	4	932174
外商投资	Foreign Investment	62	16	5445125
其他	Others	66	14	1179685
按工业行业大类分	**Grouped by Sector**			
煤炭开采和洗选业	Mining and Washing of Coal			
石油和天然气开采业	Extraction of Petroleum and Natural Gas			
黑色金属矿采选业	Mining and Processing of Ferrous Metal Ores			
有色金属矿采选业	Mining and Processing of Non-ferrous Metal Ores			
非金属矿采选业	Mining and Processing of Nonmetal Ores			
开采辅助活动	Mining Auxiliary Activities	4	1	556199
其他采矿业	Mining of other Ores			
农副食品加工业	Processing of Food from Agricultural Porducts	48	11	1972615
食品制造业	Manufacture of Foods	40	4	1484457
酒、饮料和精制茶制造业	Manufacture of Alcohol,Beverages and Tea	18	5	1012208
烟草制品业	Manufacture of Tobacco	1		10473
纺织业	Manufacture of Textile	13	3	208214
纺织服装、服饰业	Textile, apparel industry	4		99309
皮革、毛皮、羽毛及其制品和制鞋业	Manufacture of Leather, Fur, Feather and Related Products, and Shoes	3		56603
木材加工和木、竹、藤、	Processing of Timber, Manufacture of Wood,Plam	5	2	133470

continued3

(10 000yuan)

工业销售产值（当年价）Value of Industry Products Sales (At Current Prices)	出口交货值 Export Delivery Value	从业人员年平均人数（人）Annual Average Employers (person)	资产总计 Total Assets	流动资产合计 Total Working Capitals	固定资产合计 Total Fixed Assets	固定资产原价 Origing Value of Fixed Assets	累计折旧 Accumulative Total Depreciation
25414861	2791549	310415	43260532	20502900	15905562	23782218	8505502
7588166	641134	96301	12809841	6471725	2580401	4250127	1787765
13538438	1214469	99179	11332249	7130305	2570240	4191340	1941106
10314358	2108251	122356	21275460	8632387	9104659	12291860	3525680
33637	995	1197	56769	40002	11212	16801	9201
3515210	630548	41554	7673963	3987844	1632427	3186675	1656179
32678260	1907358	340788	38396430	21444697	10307905	16728349	7043313
23862347	1141329	306154	42460910	22315870	11523938	17981534	7032679
1076382	368224	8107	1400040	771484	534598	1263001	742670
14775954	975982	138435	12356115	7237150	2949061	4664573	2045400
869471	100945	4971	417287	173044	120997	217524	100853
4848395	1990179	33964	9241992	2617027	5628409	7620355	2121083
1108915	70493	14264	1526279	990355	299201	476698	191688
552133		6164	696966	449492	149525	339025	189499
1937975	1700	7950	852789	567347	196471	542246	354224
1412679	4949	13074	698993	350152	243418	452898	219432
1020592	101469	7358	1033143	442414	438621	873173	436763
10617		226	25064	11749	3669	7015	3346
181893	11034	8126	383821	150156	184893	230653	53069
92395		1678	176423	142307	6849	10050	3780
56622		1003	54188	31733	4691	7902	3265
111541		780	162030	67303	55278	69000	36776

12-9 续表4

单位：万元

分 组	Classify	负债合计 Total Liabilites	流动负债合计 Total Working Liabilities	非流动负债 Non-Working Liabilities
按企业规模分	**Grouped by Size of Enterprises**			
大型企业	Large-size	25738701	18680283	3720526
中型企业	Medium-size	6423678	4978656	1399857
小型企业	Small-size	6443139	5310076	725685
按经济组织类型分组	**Grouped by Economic Type of Orgnization**			
独资企业	Appropratorship	11724899	8762523	2517900
合作、合伙企业	Partnership	27066	22295	4312
股份有限公司	Corporaton	3015093	2383227	495102
有限责任公司	Limited Liability Company	23838460	17800970	2828755
按控股情况分	**Grouped by Cast strand**			
国有控股	State owned shares	24939142	17975276	4216318
集体控股	Collective shares	636410	603807	30184
私人控股	Private holdings	6898171	5752629	888987
港澳台控股	Hong Kong and Macao Holdings	239565	162440	15143
外商投资	Foreign Investment	5135480	3813309	606772
其他	Others	756751	661554	88665
按工业行业大类分	**Grouped by Sector**			
煤炭开采和洗选业	Mining and Washing of Coal			
石油和天然气开采业	Extraction of Petroleum and Natural Gas			
黑色金属矿采选业	Mining and Processing of Ferrous Metal Ores			
有色金属矿采选业	Mining and Processing of Non-ferrous Metal Ores			
非金属矿采选业	Mining and Processing of Nonmetal Ores			
开采辅助活动	Mining Auxiliary Activities	208300	207373	927
其他采矿业	Mining of other Ores			
农副食品加工业	Processing of Food from Agricultural Porducts	669514	632407	30471
食品制造业	Manufacture of Foods	264950	245054	16044
酒、饮料和精制茶制造业	Manufacture of Alcohol,Beverages and Tea	631413	591875	28846
烟草制品业	Manufacture of Tobacco	13301	13301	
纺织业	Manufacture of Textile	256241	147402	108839
纺织服装、服饰业	Textile, apparel industry	121580	81192	13000
皮革、毛皮、羽毛及其制品和制鞋业	Manufacture of Leather, Fur, Feather and Related Products, and Shoes	22279	17311	4873
木材加工和木、竹、藤、	Processing of Timber, Manufacture of Wood,Plam	103375	63867	39508

continued4

(10 000yuan)

所有者权益合计 Total Owners' Equities	实收资本 Total Capital Hold	营业收入 Total Revenue	主营业务收入 Revenue from Principal Business	营业成本 Total Cost	主营业务成本 Cost of Principal Business	营业税金及附加 Taxs and Other Changes	主营业务税金及附加 Taxes and Other Charges on Principal Business
18004303	6958025	24377363	23932188	20996769	20010198	163494	153873
6386171	2288352	7494677	6962322	6108177	5867038	40856	37038
4875035	3011765	13008020	12846553	11297833	11138415	53117	51985
10033032	4077074	10229557	9793720	8547579	7824451	54828	53521
29703	18647	32832	32382	27128	26897	216	216
4659385	1474584	3420304	3379031	2758149	2736654	20508	18051
14543388	6687837	31197367	30535932	27069923	26427648	181915	171109
18009465	6176534	23241140	22380090	20313928	19178239	129268	119356
763630	277103	935331	908426	774772	748339	3466	3466
5438653	2124277	13991158	13824081	12009153	11846189	100811	96541
177721	157801	871944	865408	792324	787588	1214	1214
4106512	3049708	4751325	4702247	3626115	3594872	18355	18011
769528	472720	1089162	1060813	886488	860423	4353	4310
488666	264989	366847	360986	280900	278196	5534	5478
183275	108400	1617322	1598872	1494876	1488343	1782	1774
434042	179674	1288161	1262330	1036908	1012904	5409	5408
401730	183799	888335	869276	666173	656467	15728	15669
11763	11515	11582	11339	7094	7009	104	104
127579	45093	180570	173349	158444	152490	1210	1210
54842	21900	79227	77581	64144	62323	2530	326
31909	21680	62436	61906	55456	55009	473	473
58655	15790	90280	90249	85993	85993	224	224

12-9 续表5

单位：万元

分组	Classify	销售费用 Expenses for Sales	管理费用 Expenses for Management	财务费用 Financial cost
按企业规模分	**Grouped by Size of Enterprises**			
大型企业	Large-size	757135	1476091	346742
中型企业	Medium-size	387942	523276	78276
小型企业	Small-size	432990	609044	86771
按经济组织类型分组	**Grouped by Economic Type of Orgnization**			
独资企业	Appropratorship	301265	791494	172773
合作、合伙企业	Partnership	1385	3384	568
股份有限公司	Corporaton	178241	261892	49643
有限责任公司	Limited Liability Company	1097176	1551640	288805
按控股情况分	**Grouped by Cast strand**			
国有控股	State owned shares	521985	1459545	279004
集体控股	Collective shares	54655	55873	6269
私人控股	Private holdings	546115	603050	100317
港澳台控股	Hong Kong and Macao Holdings	31758	17575	3982
外商投资	Foreign Investment	349503	399469	117009
其他	Others	74050	72898	5209
按工业行业大类分	**Grouped by Sector**			
煤炭开采和洗选业	Mining and Washing of Coal			
石油和天然气开采业	Extraction of Petroleum and Natural Gas			
黑色金属矿采选业	Mining and Processing of Ferrous Metal Ores			
有色金属矿采选业	Mining and Processing of Non-ferrous Metal Ores			
非金属矿采选业	Mining and Processing of Nonmetal Ores			
开采辅助活动	Mining Auxiliary Activities	3689	29870	-1378
其他采矿业	Mining of other Ores			
农副食品加工业	Processing of Food from Agricultural Porducts	49140	43520	12838
食品制造业	Manufacture of Foods	128317	42267	-608
酒、饮料和精制茶制造业	Manufacture of Alcohol,Beverages and Tea	100249	41022	8591
烟草制品业	Manufacture of Tobacco	195	2253	-23
纺织业	Manufacture of Textile	3512	12214	766
纺织服装、服饰业	Textile, apparel industry	4363	5165	2636
皮革、毛皮、羽毛及其制品和制鞋业	Manufacture of Leather, Fur, Feather and Related Products, and Shoes	1448	1955	130
木材加工和木、竹、藤、	Processing of Timber, Manufacture of Wood,Plam	1096	3216	2665

continued5

(10 000yuan)

营业利润 Operating Profit	利润总额 Total Profits	亏损企业亏损额 Total Loss of Deficit Enterprises	利税总额 Total Pre-tax Profits	应付职工薪酬 Salary Payable	本年应交增值税 Value Added Tax Payable
943686	1160292	56818	1985441	2109332	661655
336600	417372	94320	672667	713461	214439
434858	491165	82413	755883	607629	211601
459734	566873	35848	875043	852530	253342
527	631	342	2208	3906	1361
161188	227663	21686	341199	265386	93028
1093694	1273662	175675	2195541	2308600	739964
793733	967185	142328	1734253	2167376	637800
71876	75494	1476	103685	51234	24726
557705	619814	44822	956993	728033	236368
27614	27688	1532	37961	37434	9059
222645	323675	29780	501522	361386	159491
41572	54973	13613	79577	84959	20252
40238	45034	2411	85012	99599	34444
-2951	6211	9713	22483	39134	14491
61115	62737	5116	105616	82467	37470
57668	70233	5555	127121	45310	41160
1958	1977		2881	2883	801
3232	9034	643	15334	33422	5090
357	2894		7394	5136	1970
3088	3067		3434	6505	-106
-2966	-1412	1732	2572	3007	3760

12-9 续表6

单位：万元

分 组	Classify	企业单位数（个） Number of Enterprises (unit)	亏损企业（个） Loss Making Enterprises	工业总产值（当年价格） Gross Industrial Output Value (At Current Prices)
棕、草制品业	and Straw Products			
家具制造业	Manufacture of Furniture	11	1	74476
造纸及纸制品业	Manufacture of Paper and Paper Products	23	6	224125
印刷和记录媒介复制	Printing,Reproduction of Recording Media	22	4	633107
文教、工美、体育和娱乐用品制造业	Manufacture of Articles For Cultural,Educational and Sports Activities	8	1	702231
石油加工业、炼焦和核燃料加工业	Processing of Petroleum, Cokeing,Processing of Nuclear and Nuclear Fuel	7	4	231212
化学原料及化学制品制造业	Manufacture of Raw Chemical Materials and Chemical Products	73	12	2107895
医药制造业	Manufacture of Medicines	53	14	1959005
化学纤维制造业	Manufacture of Chemical Fibers	4	3	120229
橡胶和塑料制品业	Manufacture of Rubber and Plastics	26	1	684750
非金属矿物制品业	Manufacture of Non-metallic Mineral Products	97	27	1356901
黑色金属冶炼和压延加工业	Smelting and Pressing of Ferrous Metals	14	1	345685
有色金属冶炼和压延加工业	Smelting and Pressing of Non-ferrous Metals	38	10	2148347
金属制品业	Manufacture of Metal Products	54	12	1282071
通用设备制造业	Manufacture of General Purpose Machinery	80	17	1772623
专用设备制造业	Manufacture of Special Equipment	109	31	2464156
汽车制造业	Manufacture of Motor Vehicle	50	15	8468555
铁路、船舶、航空航天和其他运输设备制造业	Railways,Shipbuilding,Aerospace and Other Transportation Equipment Manufacturing Industry	59	3	4664353
电气机械和器材制造业	Manufacture of Electric Equipment and Machinery	123	19	5522131
计算机、通讯和其他电子设备制造业	Manufacture of Communication Equipment, Computers and other Electronic Equipment	72	13	4539493
仪器仪表制造业	Manufacture of Measuring Instruments and Machinery	52	11	1389106
其他制造业	Manufacture of Other Manufacturing	6	3	45430
废弃资源综合利用业	Recycling and Disposal of Waste			
金属制品、机械和设备修理业	Metal Products,Machinery and Equipment Repair Industry	4	1	12897
电力、热力的生产和供应业	Production and Supply of Electric Power and Heat Power	14	3	2331849
燃气生产和供应业	Gas Mining and Supplying Industry	10	1	525609
水的生产和供应业	Production and Supply of Water	5	1	105939

continued6

(10 000yuan)

工业销售产值（当年价）Value of Industry Products Sales (At Current Prices)	出口交货值 Export Delivery Value	从业人员年平均人数（人）Annual Average Employers (person)	资产总计 Total Assets	流动资产合计 Total Working Capitals	固定资产合计 Total Fixed Assets	固定资产原价 Origing Value of Fixed Assets	累计折旧 Accumulative Total Depreciation
66631		1423	74572	52365	18085	24176	10278
222457		2730	123468	68245	39023	54238	18412
630451	902	6835	575661	275559	225189	440949	230009
701444	566419	723	217654	212610	3886	9361	5476
232842		4954	167480	46395	80999	119410	38436
1981466	476248	21738	2690558	1396837	961831	1918825	971431
1763793	11077	16590	1674430	1046916	399033	517856	248479
117180		632	169208	66614	98422	143974	51331
593516	3773	15400	1168506	757224	227580	325543	124064
1295255	1653	11381	1042983	622303	261774	539271	325356
330967	3521	1946	171772	101309	62822	95985	33779
1957754	128950	11273	2873343	1173934	424692	680792	281927
1243537	12985	23282	2056922	1181026	570585	913449	375337
1783048	146457	26019	3980506	2854604	568085	934526	460584
2275444	208330	29364	4960786	2754776	1018450	1492458	575842
7930021	218391	80958	7674934	4358824	1810578	2741418	1020337
4402575	692042	65727	8305606	4470553	1340275	2221723	1031802
5235725	148221	44561	6896530	4877212	1182587	1922432	759900
4046431	1844581	43041	9188495	2899281	5046413	6762783	1705363
1349170	64297	17026	2018473	1283770	409341	666453	264307
43098	155	825	56978	41195	7863	14312	6449
12702		374	28758	23863	2275	3885	1610
2321628		25014	6067253	870299	4621272	6524972	2119476
521945		4500	883163	349271	256146	347843	98727
105939		3220	251169	107292	135579	275090	175509

12-9 续表7

单位：万元

分 组	Classify	负债合计 Total Liabilites	流动负债合计 Total Working Liabilities	非流动负债 Non-Working Liabilities
棕、草制品业	and Straw Products			
家具制造业	Manufacture of Furniture	40697	35661	2555
造纸及纸制品业	Manufacture of Paper and Paper Products	60113	52502	2068
印刷和记录媒介复制	Printing,Reproduction of Recording Media	186358	155498	16681
文教、工美、体育和娱乐用品制造业	Manufacture of Articles For Cultural,Educational and Sports Activities	209089	185168	13
石油加工业、炼焦和核燃料加工业	Processing of Petroleum, Cokeing,Processing of Nuclear and Nuclear Fuel	104996	84841	20155
化学原料及化学制品制造业	Manufacture of Raw Chemical Materials and Chemical Products	1379696	1059600	311076
医药制造业	Manufacture of Medicines	850270	732583	100540
化学纤维制造业	Manufacture of Chemical Fibers	98695	42437	56258
橡胶和塑料制品业	Manufacture of Rubber and Plastics	904756	643226	251373
非金属矿物制品业	Manufacture of Non-metallic Mineral Products	646027	573763	28995
黑色金属冶炼和压延加工业	Smelting and Pressing of Ferrous Metals	80270	72634	4965
有色金属冶炼和压延加工业	Smelting and Pressing of Non-ferrous Metals	911920	745302	153444
金属制品业	Manufacture of Metal Products	1271633	989668	278846
通用设备制造业	Manufacture of General Purpose Machinery	2163251	1948951	184390
专用设备制造业	Manufacture of Special Equipment	2135255	1852096	248061
汽车制造业	Manufacture of Motor Vehicle	4612482	3902824	300712
铁路、船舶、航空航天和其他运输设备制造业	Railways,Shipbuilding,Aerospace and Other Transportation Equipment Manufacturing Industry	4887414	3690895	1117351
电气机械和器材制造业	Manufacture of Electric Equipment and Machinery	3485928	2942536	493833
计算机、通讯和其他电子设备制造业	Manufacture of Communication Equipment, Computers and other Electronic Equipment	5500912	4125483	633839
仪器仪表制造业	Manufacture of Measuring Instruments and Machinery	1024490	863240	480614
其他制造业	Manufacture of Other Manufacturing	28955	25852	3102
废弃资源综合利用业	Recycling and Disposal of Waste			
金属制品、机械和设备修理业	Metal Products,Machinery and Equipment Repair Industry	18788	18788	
电力、热力的生产和供应业	Production and Supply of Electric Power and Heat Power	5007355	1590964	844199
燃气生产和供应业	Gas Mining and Supplying Industry	551351	522063	29289
水的生产和供应业	Production and Supply of Water	153863	112661	41203

continued7

(10 000yuan)

所有者权益合计 Total Owners' Equities	实收资本 Total Capital Hold	营业收入 Total Revenue	主营业务收入 Revenue from Principal Business	营业成本 Total Cost	主营业务成本 Cost of Principal Business	营业税金及附加 Taxs and Other Changes	主营业务税金及附加 Taxes and Other Charges on Principal Business
33875	15050	68077	67843	50363	50219	1772	1772
63355	30954	218238	217467	201303	198043	381	380
389302	209520	610505	605765	505176	502325	3403	3344
8564	5930	594630	594620	589895	589893	233	233
62484	46528	172885	170630	158225	156630	1037	980
1310863	564133	1896274	1853375	1629024	1588514	5873	5865
819422	255055	1664190	1658121	942372	941930	11926	11887
70513	55900	117030	117003	96061	96061	441	441
262695	143977	657229	624977	552434	529499	3192	3010
396954	276999	1244483	1219894	1114175	1050607	4989	4986
91502	37089	330195	325337	292214	291791	1725	1715
1961423	623839	2058456	1924609	1869738	1753264	2935	2932
785288	402625	1140001	1126052	977539	969286	5633	4944
1815778	435979	1656811	1645280	1382615	1372587	15055	9624
2825531	984847	2234381	2205920	1777452	1761283	11594	11467
3055702	842922	6963249	6775573	6378154	6252460	59868	59816
3418172	1143768	4427779	4148052	3973957	3818121	15424	14419
3410600	1019094	4845254	4739497	4057258	3972738	34262	33770
4170037	2936023	4292269	4271071	3618210	3607737	9485	8336
993981	357856	1247005	1241535	1002498	440513	5445	4760
28023	15120	45936	45581	37203	37042	371	371
9970	4655	23081	23063	17229	17229	118	118
1059898	710608	3107739	3048760	2777586	2730246	24732	22923
331812	240048	565401	481477	458497	401495	3797	3764
97306	46786	114202	103675	93614	87404	783	375

12-9 续表8

单位：万元

分 组	Classify	销售费用 Expenses for Sales	管理费用 Expenses for Management	财务费用 Financial cost
棕、草制品业	and Straw Products			
家具制造业	Manufacture of Furniture	7649	2805	506
造纸及纸制品业	Manufacture of Paper and Paper Products	3928	5841	1706
印刷和记录媒介复制	Printing,Reproduction of Recording Media	15401	51785	342
文教、工美、体育和娱乐用品制造业	Manufacture of Articles For Cultural,Educational and Sports Activities	583	1495	-69
石油加工业、炼焦和核燃料加工业	Processing of Petroleum, Cokeing,Processing of Nuclear and Nuclear Fuel	5655	12624	1772
化学原料及化学制品制造业	Manufacture of Raw Chemical Materials and Chemical Products	56124	134384	25535
医药制造业	Manufacture of Medicines	394636	155944	19804
化学纤维制造业	Manufacture of Chemical Fibers	800	5285	2601
橡胶和塑料制品业	Manufacture of Rubber and Plastics	23881	32307	12239
非金属矿物制品业	Manufacture of Non-metallic Mineral Products	28605	45703	7488
黑色金属冶炼和压延加工业	Smelting and Pressing of Ferrous Metals	4486	11472	1515
有色金属冶炼和压延加工业	Smelting and Pressing of Non-ferrous Metals	15857	61497	11700
金属制品业	Manufacture of Metal Products	21879	102250	19295
通用设备制造业	Manufacture of General Purpose Machinery	49801	173612	10826
专用设备制造业	Manufacture of Special Equipment	106275	190829	21740
汽车制造业	Manufacture of Motor Vehicle	158925	297182	21425
铁路、船舶、航空航天和其他运输设备制造业	Railways,Shipbuilding,Aerospace and Other Transportation Equipment Manufacturing Industry	64678	266722	43774
电气机械和器材制造业	Manufacture of Electric Equipment and Machinery	202713	320511	24621
计算机、通讯和其他电子设备制造业	Manufacture of Communication Equipment, Computers and other Electronic Equipment	46367	367026	102772
仪器仪表制造业	Manufacture of Measuring Instruments and Machinery	31730	120715	4896
其他制造业	Manufacture of Other Manufacturing	1773	3739	966
废弃资源综合利用业	Recycling and Disposal of Waste			
金属制品、机械和设备修理业	Metal Products,Machinery and Equipment Repair Industry	1665	3236	63
电力、热力的生产和供应业	Production and Supply of Electric Power and Heat Power	4906	19767	148179
燃气生产和供应业	Gas Mining and Supplying Industry	33204	27735	2277
水的生产和供应业	Production and Supply of Water	4540	12463	201

continued8

(10 000yuan)

营业利润 Operating Profit	利润总额 Total Profits	亏损企业亏损额 Total Loss of Deficit Enterprises	利税总额 Total Pre-tax Profits	应付职工薪酬 Salary Payable	本年应交增值税 Value Added Tax Payable
4911	4688	28	8922	5173	2462
4547	5853	674	8955	11070	2721
32991	33521	291	59632	74742	22708
2493	2602	166	3515	3285	679
-6244	-6108	8095	2036	16932	7106
87809	105250	7130	137826	152397	26703
131622	129612	4090	286656	158225	145117
10750	11013	2552	9664	6794	-1790
32885	34998	113	53894	39476	15705
39581	40766	4410	68894	56423	23139
18256	17778	192	25012	14394	5509
89862	106093	6387	136429	71252	27400
13770	32718	12370	57666	160994	19316
108866	120015	9558	175590	209260	40520
124362	153424	28897	225257	258453	60240
26912	78086	35552	243528	434990	105574
168601	190960	23659	272324	521484	65940
268458	297906	15887	456035	321041	123867
122905	226366	33883	264366	317291	28514
85346	72926	6354	103653	88442	25282
1804	2209	478	4515	4270	1935
609	822	216	1943	2767	1003
133897	158260	6668	366532	108522	183541
45598	45486	463	61611	46351	12328
2810	3811	271	7692	28933	3097

12-10 规模以上国有及国有控股工业企业主要经济指标（2015年）

单位：万元

分 组	Classify	企业单位数（个）Number of Enterprises (unit)	亏损企业 Loss Making Enterprises	工业总产值（当年价格）Gross Industrial Output Value (At Current Prices)
总计	**Total**	**246**	**57**	**24676418**
#市区	Urban	236	53	24233879
#亏损企业	Deficit Enterprises	57	57	6034288
按隶属关系分	**Grouped by Jurisdiction of Management**			
中央企业	Central Enterprises	84	15	12012909
省属企业	Provincial Enterprises	48	18	7080700
市属企业	Municipal Enterprises	114	24	5582809
按轻重工业分	**Grouped by Light Industry and Heavy Industry**			
轻工业	Light Industry	38	14	983804
重工业	Heavy Industry	208	43	23692614
按企业规模分	Grouped by Size of Enterprises			
大型企业	Large-size	41	7	17712305
中型企业	Medium-size	75	20	3976109
小型企业	Small-size	130	30	2988004
按工业行业大类分	**Grouped by Sector**			
煤炭开采和洗选业	Mining and Washing of Coal			
石油和天然气开采业	Extraction of Petroleum and Natural Gas			
黑色金属矿采选业	Mining and Processing of Ferrous Metal Ores			
有色金属矿采选业	Mining and Processing of Non-ferrous Metal Ores			
非金属矿采选业	Mining and Processing of Nonmetal Ores			
开采辅助活动	Mining Auxiliary Activities	2		517783
其他采矿业	Mining of Other Ores			
农副食品加工业	Processing of Food from Agricultural Porducts	4	3	37234
食品制造业	Manufacture of Foods	5	1	156112
酒、饮料和精制茶制造业	Manufacture of Alcohol,Beverages and Tea	1		108200
烟草制品业	Manufacture of Tobacco	1		10473
纺织业	Manufacture of Textile	4	1	77640
纺织服装、服饰业	Textile, apparel industry			
皮革、毛皮、羽毛及其制品和制鞋业	Leather fur feathers and its products and footwear	1		51289
木材加工和木、竹、藤、棕、草制品业	Processing of Timber, Manufacture of Wood,Plato and Straw Products			

Economic Indicators of all State-owned and State-holding Share Industrial Enterprises above Designated Size (2015)

(10 000yuan)

工业销售产值（当年价）Value of Industry Products Sales (At Current Prices)	出口交货值 Export Delivery Value	从业人员年平均人数（人）Annual Average Employers (person)	资产总计 Total Assets	流动资产合计 Total Working Capitals	固定资产合计 Total Fixed Assets	固定资产原价 Origing Value of Fixed Assets	累计折旧 Accumulative Total Depreciation
23862347	**1141329**	**306154**	**42460910**	**22315870**	**11523938**	**17981534**	**7032679**
23423419	1141329	297899	41650371	21992347	11119013	17271737	6642186
5945210	217434	66053	8375581	4613420	1509836	2444181	931479
11739920	493485	173804	23440742	11246814	7869953	12249409	4763347
6870867	205886	68374	10540471	5617491	1865613	2951155	1153227
5251560	441958	63976	8479697	5451565	1788372	2780970	1116105
1137006	14365	21613	1479332	707507	619865	1108806	549325
22725341	1126964	284541	40981578	21608363	10904073	16872728	6483354
17434995	697765	237395	31304022	16662421	9450059	14547104	5556002
3524152	303951	51059	8224953	3695992	1484692	2571329	1146978
2903200	139613	17700	2931935	1957457	589187	863101	329699
513717		5308	603585	392369	119650	289400	169749
36098	1700	1157	69253	46558	19781	39549	19768
154177		1742	58725	37797	19166	40786	21620
256644		1376	128480	60002	19631	54963	35726
10617		226	25064	11749	3669	7015	3346
76910	7335	6941	306769	103083	171869	209999	44670
51224		848	46239	23971	4571	7660	3089

12-10 续表1

单位：万元

分 组	Classify	负债合计 Total Liabilites	流动负债合计 Total Working Liabilities	非流动负债 Non-Working Liabilities
总计	**Total**	**24939142**	**17975276**	**4216318**
#市区	Urban	24440970	17653842	4108962
#亏损企业	Deficit Enterprises	5720753	4662083	643286
按隶属关系分	**Grouped by Jurisdiction of Management**			
中央企业	Central Enterprises	13960345	8881923	2769215
省属企业	Provincial Enterprises	5600208	4682418	502893
市属企业	Municipal Enterprises	5378589	4410935	944210
按轻重工业分	**Grouped by Light Industry and Heavy Industry**			
轻工业	Light Industry	775667	605569	169091
重工业	Heavy Industry	24163475	17369707	4047227
按企业规模分	Grouped by Size of Enterprises			
大型企业	Large-size	19010472	13376375	3010912
中型企业	Medium-size	3976382	2925042	1043153
小型企业	Small-size	1952288	1673859	162253
按工业行业大类分	**Grouped by Sector**			
煤炭开采和洗选业	Mining and Washing of Coal			
石油和天然气开采业	Extraction of Petroleum and Natural Gas			
黑色金属矿采选业	Mining and Processing of Ferrous Metal Ores			
有色金属矿采选业	Mining and Processing of Non-ferrous Metal Ores			
非金属矿采选业	Mining and Processing of Nonmetal Ores			
开采辅助活动	Mining Auxiliary Activities	182248	181320	930
其他采矿业	Mining of Other Ores			
农副食品加工业	Processing of Food from Agricultural Porducts	87504	87504	
食品制造业	Manufacture of Foods	20558	20556	2
酒、饮料和精制茶制造业	Manufacture of Alcohol,Beverages and Tea	55504	54348	1156
烟草制品业	Manufacture of Tobacco	13301	13301	
纺织业	Manufacture of Textile	218053	112009	106044
纺织服装、服饰业	Textile, apparel industry			
皮革、毛皮、羽毛及其制品和制鞋业	Leather fur feathers and its products and footwear	20888	16014	4873
木材加工和木、竹、藤、棕、草制品业	Processing of Timber, Manufacture of Wood,Plato and Straw Products			

continued1

(10 000yuan)

所有者权益合计 Total Owners' Equities	实收资本 Total Capital Hold	营业收入 Total Revenue	主营业务收入 Revenue from Principal Business	营业成本 Total Cost	主营业务成本 Cost of Principal Business	营业税金及附加 Taxs and Other Changes	主营业务税金及附加 Taxes and Other Charges on Principal Business
18009465	**6176534**	**23241140**	**22380090**	**20313928**	**19178239**	**129268**	**119356**
17697098	6051942	22804807	21946499	19953294	18820006	127018	117105
3142563	1655530	4625771	4514208	4294643	4223396	10166	10070
9480350	3288658	12005473	11593648	10386430	9579321	74378	72411
5428007	1557127	5938300	5673884	5416982	5220443	18055	17878
3101108	1330749	5297367	5112558	4510516	4378475	36835	29067
703665	425264	1168580	1136713	944702	920620	15748	15335
17305800	5751270	22072560	21243377	19369226	18257619	113520	104021
12776022	3929070	16500490	16138484	14381097	13457044	101817	94518
4248581	1446981	3881802	3410223	3391226	3192674	16809	14410
984862	800483	2858848	2831383	2541605	2528521	10642	10428
421336	251806	326074	321541	250174	248364	4455	4401
-18251	11253	30811	30234	27366	27004	106	106
38167	24191	161639	153092	133674	125611	579	579
72976	28790	256644	256457	196343	196182	9815	9815
11763	11515	11582	11339	7094	7009	104	104
88716	17746	86186	78965	79449	73504	390	390
25351	15000	54189	53660	47799	47352	438	438

12-10 续表2

单位：万元

分组	Classify	销售费用 Expenses for Sales	管理费用 Expenses for Management	财务费用 Financial cost
总计	**Total**	**521985**	**1459545**	**279004**
#市区	Urban	516612	1420315	269505
#亏损企业	Deficit Enterprises	124939	311523	61512
按隶属关系分	**Grouped by Jurisdiction of Management**			
中央企业	Central Enterprises	216417	786038	215109
省属企业	Provincial Enterprises	155807	344029	28002
市属企业	Municipal Enterprises	149761	329478	35893
按轻重工业分	**Grouped by Light Industry and Heavy Industry**			
轻工业	Light Industry	43751	85117	-93
重工业	Heavy Industry	478234	1374428	279097
按企业规模分	Grouped by Size of Enterprises			
大型企业	Large-size	383800	1077460	218851
中型企业	Medium-size	92247	258320	36181
小型企业	Small-size	45938	123765	23972
按工业行业大类分	**Grouped by Sector**			
煤炭开采和洗选业	Mining and Washing of Coal			
石油和天然气开采业	Extraction of Petroleum and Natural Gas			
黑色金属矿采选业	Mining and Processing of Ferrous Metal Ores			
有色金属矿采选业	Mining and Processing of Non-ferrous Metal Ores			
非金属矿采选业	Mining and Processing of Nonmetal Ores			
开采辅助活动	Mining Auxiliary Activities	1177	27442	-1618
其他采矿业	Mining of Other Ores			
农副食品加工业	Processing of Food from Agricultural Porducts	2645	2576	645
食品制造业	Manufacture of Foods	8080	6434	-18
酒、饮料和精制茶制造业	Manufacture of Alcohol,Beverages and Tea	12543	3377	-2340
烟草制品业	Manufacture of Tobacco	195	2253	-23
纺织业	Manufacture of Textile	1391	9451	338
纺织服装、服饰业	Textile, apparel industry			
皮革、毛皮、羽毛及其制品和制鞋业	Leather fur feathers and its products and footwear	1333	1540	127
木材加工和木、竹、藤、棕、草制品业	Processing of Timber, Manufacture of Wood,Plato and Straw Products			

continued2

(10 000yuan)

营业利润 Operating Profit	利润总额 Total Profits	亏损企业亏损额 Total Loss of Deficit Enterprises	利税总额 Total Pre-tax Profits	应付职工薪酬 Salary Payable	本年应交增值税 Value Added Tax Payable
793733	**967185**	**142328**	**1734253**	**2167376**	**637800**
761291	930001	139934	1675810	2106128	618791
-195679	-142328	142328	-65655	380390	66508
569593	620946	47870	1083466	1283623	388143
-45006	25186	46413	149009	442635	105768
269146	321053	48045	501778	441118	143889
82027	90093	9959	152435	158235	46594
711706	877092	132369	1581818	2009141	591206
631904	733419	42313	1321882	1624454	486646
79621	131704	73090	252675	390918	104162
82208	102062	26925	159696	152004	46992
37289	41817		79329	91735	33053
-1889	-1481	2792	-699	4226	676
12883	13101	722	18623	10449	4944
37936	37973		59294	9446	11506
1958	1977		2881	2883	801
-4489	1419	600	3066	29583	1257
3067	3046		3186	6006	-298

12-10 续表3

单位：万元

分组	Classify	企业单位数（个） Number of Enterprises (unit)	亏损企业 Loss Making Enterprises	工业总产值（当年价格） Gross Industrial Output Value (At Current Prices)
家具制造业	Manufacture of Furniture			
造纸及纸制品业	Manufacture of Paper and Paper Products			
印刷和记录媒介复制	Printing,Reproduction of Recording Media	3	1	205166
文教、工美、体育和娱乐用品制造业	Manufacture of Articles For Cultural,Educational and Sports Activities			
石油加工业、炼焦和业核燃料加工	Processing of Petroleum, Cokeing,Processing of Nuclear and Nuclear Fuel			
化学原料及化学制品制造业	Manufacture of Raw Chemical Materials and Chemical Products	16	4	684927
医药制造业	Manufacture of Medicines	3	1	24432
化学纤维制造业	Manufacture of Chemical Fibers	2	1	93315
橡胶和塑料制品业	Manufacture of Rubber and Plastics	3		345857
非金属矿物制品业	Manufacture of Non-metallic Mineral Products	9	1	178777
黑色金属冶炼和压延加工业	Smelting and Pressing of Ferrous Metals	1		173301
有色金属冶炼和压延加工业	Smelting and Pressing of Non-ferrous Metals	17	4	877236
金属制品业	Manufacture of Metal Products	13	2	958475
通用设备制造业	Manufacture of General Purpose Machinery	17	2	1246719
专用设备制造业	Manufacture of Special Equipment	26	6	1171763
汽车制造业	Manufacture of Motor Vehicle	18	8	6337752
铁路、船舶、航空航天和其他运输设备制造业	Railways,Shipbuilding,Aerospace and Other Transportation Equipment Manufacturing Industry	31	3	3990822
电气机械和器材制造业	Manufacture of Electric Equipment and Machinery	20	7	3137569
计算机、通讯和其他电子设备制造业	Manufacture of Communication Equipment, Computers and other Electronic Equipment	17	5	737032
仪器仪表制造业	Manufacture of Measuring Instruments and Machinery	12	4	838872
其他制造业	Manufacture of Other Manufacturing	2	1	19785
废弃资源综合利用业	Recycling and Disposal of Waste			
金属制品、机械和设备修理业	Metal Products,Machinery and Equipment Repair Industry	1		2891
电力、热力的生产和供应业	Production and Supply of Electric Power and Heat Power	8	1	2225364
燃气生产和供应业	Gas Mining and Supplying Industry	4		361693
水的生产和供应业	Production and Supply of Water	5	1	105939

continued3

(10 000yuan)

工业销售产值（当年价）Value of Industry Products Sales (At Current Prices)	出口交货值 Export Delivery Value	从业人员年平均人数（人）Annual Average Employers (person)	资产总计 Total Assets	流动资产合计 Total Working Capitals	固定资产合计 Total Fixed Assets	固定资产原价 Origing Value of Fixed Assets	累计折旧 Accumulative Total Depreciation
213853		2723	301807	145907	149492	298063	159803
621945	83713	13790	981817	505143	320167	547248	235589
27565		1045	80449	36805	23207	30400	7194
95041		330	64024	39823	22999	70707	47709
347239	2778	12877	982997	653053	157454	203809	71834
172621	1653	1752	202402	130645	37160	50041	16522
162511	1876	344	72221	47522	20215	33448	13848
779484	23149	4758	1949547	725211	195346	285254	112889
927245	12307	19127	1715064	1020416	474389	786736	334396
1285807	67212	18451	3331074	2403557	460431	767025	382466
1033755	119421	16045	3261108	1744860	582953	939223	371649
6005879	170858	46403	5469472	3389567	1080142	1771763	698941
3802418	518349	62444	7867616	4169723	1263727	2085980	966703
3065323	93631	29422	5047506	3644723	852291	1390050	538814
690443	26877	16943	1927578	1145448	346566	600962	233093
816267	10315	10749	1317880	820587	294822	507728	213335
20030	155	291	14251	11297	2443	4137	1694
2891		55	3166	3092	73	164	90
2225364		24108	5710306	637724	4527915	6398036	2078371
361340		3679	671341	257946	218230	286298	74262
105939		3220	251169	107292	135579	275090	175509

12-10 续表4

单位：万元

分 组	Classify	负债合计 Total Liabilites	流动负债合计 Total Working Liabilities	非流动负债 Non-Working Liabilities
家具制造业	Manufacture of Furniture			
造纸及纸制品业	Manufacture of Paper and Paper Products			
印刷和记录媒介复制	Printing,Reproduction of Recording Media	34595	34557	31
文教、工美、体育和娱乐用品制造业	Manufacture of Articles For Cultural,Educational and Sports Activities			
石油加工业、炼焦和业核燃料加工	Processing of Petroleum, Cokeing,Processing of Nuclear and Nuclear Fuel			
化学原料及化学制品制造业	Manufacture of Raw Chemical Materials and Chemical Products	573425	480054	88999
医药制造业	Manufacture of Medicines	51235	51080	155
化学纤维制造业	Manufacture of Chemical Fibers	12934	12449	485
橡胶和塑料制品业	Manufacture of Rubber and Plastics	823029	578472	243558
非金属矿物制品业	Manufacture of Non-metallic Mineral Products	108327	100217	803
黑色金属冶炼和压延加工业	Smelting and Pressing of Ferrous Metals	44080	36975	4433
有色金属冶炼和压延加工业	Smelting and Pressing of Non-ferrous Metals	485268	379425	96077
金属制品业	Manufacture of Metal Products	1126995	858842	268153
通用设备制造业	Manufacture of General Purpose Machinery	1851406	1703253	147842
专用设备制造业	Manufacture of Special Equipment	1415493	1269692	128948
汽车制造业	Manufacture of Motor Vehicle	3223081	2665711	154041
铁路、船舶、航空航天和其他运输设备制造业	Railways,Shipbuilding,Aerospace and Other Transportation Equipment Manufacturing Industry	4681375	3497826	1104401
电气机械和器材制造业	Manufacture of Electric Equipment and Machinery	2439082	2142660	295978
计算机、通讯和其他电子设备制造业	Manufacture of Communication Equipment, Computers and other Electronic Equipment	1485381	1144803	338281
仪器仪表制造业	Manufacture of Measuring Instruments and Machinery	665116	571967	445198
其他制造业	Manufacture of Other Manufacturing	6143	6140	2
废弃资源综合利用业	Recycling and Disposal of Waste			
金属制品、机械和设备修理业	Metal Products,Machinery and Equipment Repair Industry	2388	2388	
电力、热力的生产和供应业	Production and Supply of Electric Power and Heat Power	4720402	1418251	730058
燃气生产和供应业	Gas Mining and Supplying Industry	437468	422801	14667
水的生产和供应业	Production and Supply of Water	153863	112661	41203

continued4

(10 000yuan)

所有者权益合计 Total Owners' Equities	实收资本 Total Capital Hold	营业收入 Total Revenue	主营业务收入 Revenue from Principal Business	营业成本 Total Cost	主营业务成本 Cost of Principal Business	营业税金及附加 Taxs and Other Changes	主营业务税金及附加 Taxes and Other Charges on Principal Business
267212	155362	219273	217399	168473	166995	2189	2185
408392	181771	641280	619145	538286	516429	3220	3220
29214	14377	27640	27565	18080	18064	233	233
51090	50800	95043	95043	78268	78268	434	434
159968	83388	358629	347309	300112	296237	2121	1939
94075	74246	172702	172246	161540	161397	485	485
28140	21615	158731	154142	148002	147829	341	330
1464279	492452	874764	744573	779311	664321	1968	1968
588069	286696	844221	832028	718087	711219	3729	3070
1479668	257530	1179354	1170504	979325	970378	11687	6300
1845616	670535	1033787	1024015	862379	858519	6083	5962
2251654	711259	4970897	4835077	4638114	4555825	10348	10315
3186221	1056371	3821069	3542516	3452577	3298333	13594	12589
2608424	486953	2761696	2669696	2247636	2177772	24362	24277
924652	206999	805738	798700	677057	672303	2933	2933
652764	184317	788820	786617	668846	110215	2108	1475
8108	4000	23082	22947	19916	19916	100	100
777	200	2891	2885	1902	1902	34	34
989905	654596	2990375	2947788	2673956	2639189	23302	22005
233873	175980	429821	360932	346548	300698	3327	3294
97306	46786	114202	103675	93614	87404	783	375

12-10 续表5

单位：万元

分 组	Classify	销售费用 Expenses for Sales	管理费用 Expenses for Management	财务费用 Financial cost
家具制造业	Manufacture of Furniture			
造纸及纸制品业	Manufacture of Paper and Paper Products			
印刷和记录媒介复制	Printing,Reproduction of Recording Media	4332	30599	-1419
文教、工美、体育和娱乐用品制造业	Manufacture of Articles For Cultural,Educational and Sports Activities			
石油加工业、炼焦和业核燃料加工	Processing of Petroleum, Cokeing,Processing of Nuclear and Nuclear Fuel			
化学原料及化学制品制造业	Manufacture of Raw Chemical Materials and Chemical Products	19123	73214	11018
医药制造业	Manufacture of Medicines	3563	5007	-3
化学纤维制造业	Manufacture of Chemical Fibers	423	3179	-93
橡胶和塑料制品业	Manufacture of Rubber and Plastics	11028	16509	8788
非金属矿物制品业	Manufacture of Non-metallic Mineral Products	829	6045	1358
黑色金属冶炼和压延加工业	Smelting and Pressing of Ferrous Metals	2346	4249	930
有色金属冶炼和压延加工业	Smelting and Pressing of Non-ferrous Metals	5941	42067	2636
金属制品业	Manufacture of Metal Products	14502	84163	16528
通用设备制造业	Manufacture of General Purpose Machinery	31257	141756	7372
专用设备制造业	Manufacture of Special Equipment	46237	100647	4878
汽车制造业	Manufacture of Motor Vehicle	118182	222316	11176
铁路、船舶、航空航天和其他运输设备制造业	Railways,Shipbuilding,Aerospace and Other Transportation Equipment Manufacturing Industry	51454	240540	42253
电气机械和器材制造业	Manufacture of Electric Equipment and Machinery	132435	216020	11699
计算机、通讯和其他电子设备制造业	Manufacture of Communication Equipment, Computers and other Electronic Equipment	18265	86585	18933
仪器仪表制造业	Manufacture of Measuring Instruments and Machinery	5364	82775	3130
其他制造业	Manufacture of Other Manufacturing	392	595	122
废弃资源综合利用业	Recycling and Disposal of Waste			
金属制品、机械和设备修理业	Metal Products,Machinery and Equipment Repair Industry	115	384	30
电力、热力的生产和供应业	Production and Supply of Electric Power and Heat Power	215	14453	145274
燃气生产和供应业	Gas Mining and Supplying Industry	24078	22906	-2918
水的生产和供应业	Production and Supply of Water	4540	12463	201

continued5

(10 000yuan)

营业利润 Operating Profit	利润总额 Total Profits	亏损企业亏损额 Total Loss of Deficit Enterprises	利税总额 Total Pre-tax Profits	应付职工薪酬 Salary Payable	本年应交增值税 Value Added Tax Payable
15950	16078	187	33371	46361	15104
10796	25012	3314	43837	102363	15605
766	714	802	3022	5034	2074
12819	12873	691	18072	4292	4765
19903	21379		32921	27105	9422
2063	2352	438	5179	9801	2343
2334	1621		3579	5942	1617
36127	45666	3670	66128	40984	18494
7969	26425	7951	42058	140357	11905
92424	102954	4183	145707	175067	31066
19149	44575	19479	80428	161613	29769
-54648	-11510	34576	75175	275187	76337
127978	148713	23659	214296	488246	51990
199949	214696	6272	337256	224938	98199
877	5705	27840	18343	99883	9706
29724	12602	2781	23563	29476	8853
1864	1995	60	2869	1824	774
426	433		748	577	281
135018	150759	2040	357563	102635	183502
42680	42480		56766	42430	10958
2810	3811	271	7692	28933	3097

12-11 规模以上外商及港澳台商投资工业企业主要经济指标（2015年）

单位：万元

分 组	Classify	企业单位数（个） Number of Enterprises (unit)	亏损企业 Loss Making Enterprises	工业总产值（当年价格） Gross Industrial Output Value (At Current Prices)
总计	**Total**	**117**	**28**	**8984012**
#市区	Urban Area	109	26	8769766
#亏损企业	Deficit Enterprises	28	28	952090
按隶属关系分	**Grouped by Jurisdiction of Management**			
中央企业	Central Enterprises	4	1	137303
省属企业	Provincial Enterprises	8	1	767874
市属企业	Municipal Enterprises	105	26	8078835
按登记注册类型分组	**Grouped by Type of Registration**			
港澳台商投资	Enterprises with Funds from Hong Kong, Macao &Taiwan	27	4	2733793
与港澳台商合资经营	Cooperative Enterprises	15	2	2428342
与港澳台商合作经营	Joint-venture Enterprises			
港澳台商独资	Enterprises with Sole Investment	10	1	253118
港澳台商投资股份有限公司	Share-holding Corporations Ltd. With their Investment	2	1	52333
其他港澳台投资	Other			
外商投资	Foreign Funded Enterprises	90	24	6250219
中外合资经营	Joint-venture Enterprises	52	15	2506525
中外合作经营	Cooperation Enterprises	1		4521
外资企业	Foreign Funded Enterprises	35	9	3452528
外商投资股份有限公司	Share-holding Corporations Ltd. With Foreign Funds	1		283684
其他外商投资	Other	1		2961
按轻重工业分	**Grouped by Light Industry and Heavy Industry**			
轻工业	Light Industry	37	10	2691524
重工业	Heavy Industry	80	18	6292488
按企业规模分	**Grouped by Size of Enterprises**			
大型企业	Large-size	12	2	6030258
中型企业	Medium-size	25	5	1146305
小型企业	Small-size	80	21	1807449
按工业行业大类分	**Grouped by Sector**			
煤炭开采和洗选业	Mining and Washing of Coal			
石油和天然气开采业	Extraction of Petroleum and Natural Gas			
黑色金属矿采选业	Mining and Processing of Ferrous Metal Ores			
有色金属矿采选业	Mining and Processing of Non-ferrous Metal Ores			
非金属矿采选业	Mining and Processing of Nonmetal Ores			
开采辅助活动	Mining Auxiliary Activities			
其他采矿业	Mining of Other Ores			

Economic Indicators of Foreign Fund Industrial Enterprises above Designated Size (2015)

(10 000 yuan)

工业销售产值（当年价） Value of Industry Products Sales (At Current Prices)	出口交货值 Export Delivery Value	从业人员年平均人数（人） Annual Average Employers (person)	资产总计 Total Assets	流动资产合计 Total Working Capitals	固定资产合计 Total Fixed Assets	固定资产原价 Origing Value of Fixed Assets	累计折旧 Accumulative Total Depreciation
8071406	**2181086**	**77445**	**12816883**	**4280280**	**6719833**	**9165899**	**2673528**
7865110	2179204	76033	12629266	4189931	6644652	9003303	2576872
923378	34245	11430	853709	335847	380380	548170	176541
139029	12989	1038	143577	87957	30696	88664	58741
711547	1032	5318	674040	446391	128607	144967	95873
7220830	2167065	71089	11999266	3745932	6560530	8932268	2518914
2467843	147301	36009	2347234	929546	779548	1077761	370748
2159526	53386	31985	2065464	805548	687803	922065	306797
254947	93013	3034	171913	74357	80613	133330	52717
53370	902	990	109857	49641	11132	22367	11234
5603563	2033785	41436	10469649	3350734	5940285	8088138	2302780
2395498	94423	21891	2814979	1699493	771043	1114072	461904
4425	995	129	5876	3787	1002	1002	588
3074183	1836899	18372	7287992	1501531	4953650	6510614	1588099
126836	101469	1018	357004	144943	212061	462450	252189
2621		26	3797	979	2528		
2441326	140788	18182	2375209	1182061	899886	1453315	658533
5630080	2040298	59263	10441674	3098219	5819947	7712584	2014995
5312298	1737392	54818	9846611	2635336	5752885	7751411	2162057
1098828	234479	13104	1425942	853396	434398	672896	262083
1660280	209215	9523	1544330	791548	532550	741592	249388

12-11 续表1

单位：万元

分　组	Classify	负债合计 Total Liabilites	流动负债合计 Total Working Liabilities	非流动负债 Non-Working Liabilities
总计	**Total**	**7341736**	**5722402**	**832209**
#市区	Urban Area	7250882	5638611	825151
#亏损企业	Deficit Enterprises	532173	406624	114881
按隶属关系分	**Grouped by Jurisdiction of Management**			
中央企业	Central Enterprises	30304	28892	1412
省属企业	Provincial Enterprises	399915	302097	83657
市属企业	Municipal Enterprises	6911517	5391413	747140
按登记注册类型分组	**Grouped by Type of Registration**			
港澳台商投资	Enterprises with Funds from Hong Kong, Macao &Taiwan	1535872	1302689	171201
与港澳台商合资经营	Cooperative Enterprises	1369691	1174084	158757
与港澳台商合作经营	Joint-venture Enterprises			
港澳台商独资	Enterprises with Sole Investment	104347	91595	12444
港澳台商投资股份有限公司	Share-holding Corporations Ltd. With their Investment	61834	37010	
其他港澳台投资	Other			
外商投资	Foreign Funded Enterprises	5805864	4419713	661008
中外合资经营	Joint-venture Enterprises	1486062	1267683	208402
中外合作经营	Cooperation Enterprises	2655	2432	222
外资企业	Foreign Funded Enterprises	4080313	2933259	432376
外商投资股份有限公司	Share-holding Corporations Ltd. With Foreign Funds	234997	215360	19607
其他外商投资	Other	1839	979	400
按轻重工业分	**Grouped by Light Industry and Heavy Industry**			
轻工业	Light Industry	1350642	1101098	224382
重工业	Heavy Industry	5991094	4621304	607827
按企业规模分	**Grouped by Size of Enterprises**			
大型企业	Large-size	5819671	4596574	508390
中型企业	Medium-size	699364	535638	149564
小型企业	Small-size	822701	590190	174255
按工业行业大类分	**Grouped by Sector**			
煤炭开采和洗选业	Mining and Washing of Coal			
石油和天然气开采业	Extraction of Petroleum and Natural Gas			
黑色金属矿采选业	Mining and Processing of Ferrous Metal Ores			
有色金属矿采选业	Mining and Processing of Non-ferrous Metal Ores			
非金属矿采选业	Mining and Processing of Nonmetal Ores			
开采辅助活动	Mining Auxiliary Activities			
其他采矿业	Mining of Other Ores			

continued 1

(10 000 yuan)

所有者权益合计 Total Owners' Equities	实收资本 Total Capital Hold	营业收入 Total Revenue	主营业务收入 Revenue from Principal Business	营业成本 Total Cost	主营业务收入 Cost of Principal Business	营业税金及附加 Taxs and Other Changes	主营业务税金及附加 Taxes and Other Charges on Principal Business
5475145	**3642201**	**8115242**	**7942825**	**6574528**	**6450831**	**72857**	**72508**
5378383	3585825	7940484	7770705	6427162	6303716	71717	71368
321536	413980	716396	709007	603406	599414	2668	2611
113273	96194	138342	138314	114781	114776	840	840
274125	78908	762026	756795	448932	445114	4463	4463
5087747	3467099	7214874	7047716	6010815	5890941	67554	67205
811361	219739	2572601	2520630	2302002	2259712	49375	49373
695772	116798	2280240	2233769	2067832	2029327	48351	48349
67565	63922	251322	246041	202660	198875	729	729
48024	39019	41039	40820	31510	31510	295	295
4663784	3422463	5542641	5422195	4272526	4191119	23482	23135
1328917	726380	2310509	2219671	1668371	1610280	13744	13457
3222	1108	4425	4425	3808	3808	2	2
3207679	2688705	3114036	3086649	2504158	2482029	9265	9264
122008	4470	111140	108919	93941	92754	471	413
1959	1800	2531	2531	2248	2248		
1024566	434038	2246545	2213196	1625505	1603261	14494	14207
4450579	3208163	5868697	5729629	4949023	4847570	58363	58301
4026940	2628359	5254714	5116937	4170931	4070637	60209	60093
726578	431081	1061063	1036937	817353	801408	8374	8147
721627	582761	1799465	1788951	1586244	1578786	4274	4268

12-11 续表2

单位：万元

分 组	Classify	销售费用 Expenses for Sales	管理费用 Expenses for Management	财务费用 Financial cost
总计	**Total**	**435671**	**523403**	**133668**
#市区	Urban Area	434001	516132	131875
#亏损企业	Deficit Enterprises	78730	58506	12455
按隶属关系分	**Grouped by Jurisdiction of Management**			
中央企业	Central Enterprises	1815	8218	-551
省属企业	Provincial Enterprises	172168	55025	11360
市属企业	Municipal Enterprises	261688	460160	122859
按登记注册类型分组	**Grouped by Type of Registration**			
港澳台商投资	Enterprises with Funds from Hong Kong, Macao &Taiwan	61531	71080	14383
与港澳台商合资经营	Cooperative Enterprises	31089	58493	10564
与港澳台商合作经营	Joint-venture Enterprises			
港澳台商独资	Enterprises with Sole Investment	28073	9704	1843
港澳台商投资股份有限公司	Share-holding Corporations Ltd. With their Investment	2369	2883	1976
其他港澳台投资	Other			
外商投资	Foreign Funded Enterprises	374140	452323	119285
中外合资经营	Joint-venture Enterprises	255752	157658	12506
中外合作经营	Cooperation Enterprises	165	310	1
外资企业	Foreign Funded Enterprises	112195	283801	95542
外商投资股份有限公司	Share-holding Corporations Ltd. With Foreign Funds	5900	10425	11153
其他外商投资	Other	128	130	84
按轻重工业分	**Grouped by Light Industry and Heavy Industry**			
轻工业	Light Industry	337491	122622	25708
重工业	Heavy Industry	98180	400781	107960
按企业规模分	**Grouped by Size of Enterprises**			
大型企业	Large-size	351108	362706	107441
中型企业	Medium-size	47351	80701	11234
小型企业	Small-size	37212	79996	14993
按工业行业大类分	**Grouped by Sector**			
煤炭开采和洗选业	Mining and Washing of Coal			
石油和天然气开采业	Extraction of Petroleum and Natural Gas			
黑色金属矿采选业	Mining and Processing of Ferrous Metal Ores			
有色金属矿采选业	Mining and Processing of Non-ferrous Metal Ores			
非金属矿采选业	Mining and Processing of Nonmetal Ores			
开采辅助活动	Mining Auxiliary Activities			
其他采矿业	Mining of Other Ores			

continued 2

(10 000 yuan)

营业利润 Operating Profit	利润总额 Total Profits	亏损企业亏损额 Total Loss of Deficit Enterprises	利税总额 Total Pre-tax Profits	应付职工薪酬 Salary Payable	本年应交增值税 Value Added Tax Payable
368084	**478904**	**41556**	**761646**	**617784**	**209885**
351700	462085	40397	736110	608771	202307
-40777	-41556	41556	-27737	72752	11151
12733	13385	1805	18232	14496	4007
69566	65189	923	159002	103653	89351
285785	400330	38828	584412	499635	116527
80748	88489	1532	167520	173691	29656
68935	75968	420	145799	145772	21480
9369	9582	6	16263	22710	5952
2444	2939	1106	5458	5209	2224
287336	390415	40024	594126	444093	180229
206678	209928	24286	362299	240981	138627
139	139		228	668	86
91330	177168	15738	218617	194442	32184
-10751	3150		12954	7906	9332
-61	29		29	96	
120506	136630	9525	292571	189262	141447
247578	342274	32031	469075	428522	68438
192674	293333	8558	517741	421021	164199
99198	105296	17167	141081	106774	27411
76212	80275	15831	102824	89989	18275

12-11 续表3

单位：万元

分组	Classify	企业单位数（个）Number of Enterprises (unit)	亏损企业 Loss Making Enterprises	工业总产值（当年价格）Gross Industrial Output Value (At Current Prices)
农副食品加工业	Processing of Food from Agricultural Porducts	2		13585
食品制造业	Manufacture of Foods	5	1	771179
酒、饮料和精制茶制造业	Manufacture of Alcohol,Beverages and Tea	9	4	793559
烟草制品业	Manufacture of Tobacco			
纺织业	Manufacture of Textile	1	1	5845
纺织服装、服饰业	Textile, apparel industry			
皮革、毛皮、羽毛及其制品和制鞋业	Leather fur feathers and its products and footwear			
木材加工和木、竹、藤、棕、草制品业	Processing of Timber,Manufacture of Wood,Plam and Straw Products			
家具制造业	Manufacture of Furniture			
造纸及纸制品业	Manufacture of Paper and Paper Products	2	1	61761
印刷和记录媒介复制	Printing,Reproduction of Recording Media	1		51309
文教、工美、体育和娱乐用品制造业	Manufacture of Articles For Cultural,Educational and Sports Activities	2		32330
石油加工业、炼焦和核燃料加工业	Processing of Petroleum, Cokeing,Processing of Nuclear and Nuclear Fuel	2	2	211230
化学原料及化学制品制造业	Manufacture of Raw Chemical Materials and Chemical Products	10	1	166062
医药制造业	Manufacture of Medicines	5	1	714251
化学纤维制造业	Manufacture of Chemical Fibers	2	1	112323
橡胶和塑料制品业	Manufacture of Rubber and Plastics	3		18603
非金属矿物制品业	Manufacture of Non-metallic Mineral Products	4	2	121252
黑色金属冶炼和压延加工业	Smelting and Pressing of Ferrous Metals	2		13542
有色金属冶炼和压延加工业	Smelting and Pressing of Non-ferrous Metals	5	2	117735
金属制品业	Manufacture of Metal Products	3	1	27457
通用设备制造业	Manufacture of General Purpose Machinery	4	1	101391
专用设备制造业	Manufacture of Special Equipment	8	1	396842
汽车制造业	Manufacture of Motor Vehicle	7	2	1857377
铁路、船舶、航空航天和其他运输设备制造业	Railways,Shipbuilding,Aerospace and Other Transportation Equipment Manufacturing Industry	8		178435
电气机械和器材制造业	Manufacture of Electric Equipment and Machinery	15	4	808940
计算机、通讯和其他电子设备制造业	Manufacture of Communication Equipment, Computers and other Electronic Equipment	9	1	2045676
仪器仪表制造业	Manufacture of Measuring Instruments and Machinery	4	1	77303
其他制造业	Manufacture of Other Manufacturing	1	1	3301
废弃资源综合利用业	Recycling and Disposal of Waste			
金属制品、机械和设备修理业	Metal Products,Machinery and Equipment Repair Industry	2		7736
电力、热力的生产和供应业	Production and Supply of Electric Power and Heat Power			
燃气生产和供应业	Gas Mining and Supplying Industry	1		274988
水的生产和供应业	Production and Supply of Water			

continued 3

(10 000 yuan)

工业销售产值（当年价） Value of Industry Products Sales (At Current Prices)	出口交货值 Export Delivery Value	从业人员年平均人数（人） Annual Average Employers (person)	资产总计 Total Assets	流动资产合计 Total Working Capitals	固定资产合计 Total Fixed Assets	固定资产原价 Origing Value of Fixed Assets	累计折旧 Accumulative Total Depreciation
13585		546	14268	11892	1658	5637	3979
735880		4103	354435	178109	103632	171722	72417
655514	101469	5064	860902	352728	409528	799903	392092
3148		95	10424	3888	1337	2011	674
60738		290	29674	8371	11591	15732	4142
52346	902	929	58666	25303	10539	21207	10668
32330	32330	210	8130	5993	1275	2342	1067
211230		4675	139389	21798	78244	114783	36539
161367	57935	525	276739	83257	162330	191846	32353
665572	2547	5553	609383	402760	155287	159826	99912
109283		398	146812	60202	84497	131368	49972
14695	995	381	30160	16483	10120	22260	12728
113713		748	122392	43437	74939	107299	47629
14420	580	168	7464	5765	1699	4183	2485
94020	66929	420	61358	39018	15714	17642	11221
27401	604	639	51521	12196	34786	48193	13407
82678	15853	1249	122899	87595	25060	59561	37187
396744	62948	2656	312561	206446	72659	115796	45966
1658058	48275	31407	1950468	780847	697479	882459	260328
162582	31389	1300	278306	252902	22140	24784	13449
682300	2578	3745	607676	315207	164732	245963	82671
1760521	1720452	8386	6086733	1002297	4395031	5761270	1366639
76959	35300	1111	162008	135846	23898	38339	15888
3598		116	5281	2793	1996	3568	1573
7736		262	21267	18911	329	1250	920
274988		2469	487967	206236	159333	216955	57622

12-11 续表4

单位：万元

分组	Classify	负债合计 Total Liabilites	流动负债合计 Total Working Liabilities	非流动负债 Non-Working Liabilities
农副食品加工业	Processing of Food from Agricultural Porducts	6349	6349	
食品制造业	Manufacture of Foods	120922	119613	1309
酒、饮料和精制茶制造业	Manufacture of Alcohol,Beverages and Tea	549149	511694	26763
烟草制品业	Manufacture of Tobacco			
纺织业	Manufacture of Textile	3791	3791	
纺织服装、服饰业	Textile, apparel industry			
皮革、毛皮、羽毛及其制品和制鞋业	Leather fur feathers and its products and footwear			
木材加工和木、竹、藤、棕、草制品业	Processing of Timber,Manufacture of Wood,Plam and Straw Products			
家具制造业	Manufacture of Furniture			
造纸及纸制品业	Manufacture of Paper and Paper Products	14040	13394	646
印刷和记录媒介复制	Printing,Reproduction of Recording Media	26834	12672	
文教、工美、体育和娱乐用品制造业	Manufacture of Articles For Cultural,Educational and Sports Activities	5609	5301	
石油加工业、炼焦和核燃料加工业	Processing of Petroleum, Cokeing,Processing of Nuclear and Nuclear Fuel	86961	66927	20035
化学原料及化学制品制造业	Manufacture of Raw Chemical Materials and Chemical Products	180871	97296	83116
医药制造业	Manufacture of Medicines	350050	281259	68791
化学纤维制造业	Manufacture of Chemical Fibers	92920	37147	55773
橡胶和塑料制品业	Manufacture of Rubber and Plastics	13994	13254	740
非金属矿物制品业	Manufacture of Non-metallic Mineral Products	80419	77684	2497
黑色金属冶炼和压延加工业	Smelting and Pressing of Ferrous Metals	3016	3016	
有色金属冶炼和压延加工业	Smelting and Pressing of Non-ferrous Metals	30423	13076	7603
金属制品业	Manufacture of Metal Products	29941	29941	
通用设备制造业	Manufacture of General Purpose Machinery	23125	23119	6
专用设备制造业	Manufacture of Special Equipment	98757	83696	15061
汽车制造业	Manufacture of Motor Vehicle	1289968	1154866	135102
铁路、船舶、航空航天和其他运输设备制造业	Railways,Shipbuilding,Aerospace and Other Transportation Equipment Manufacturing Industry	126046	94478	31567
电气机械和器材制造业	Manufacture of Electric Equipment and Machinery	346479	208201	101434
计算机、通讯和其他电子设备制造业	Manufacture of Communication Equipment, Computers and other Electronic Equipment	3439697	2464000	261020
仪器仪表制造业	Manufacture of Measuring Instruments and Machinery	61514	54614	6900
其他制造业	Manufacture of Other Manufacturing	2535	2532	2
废弃资源综合利用业	Recycling and Disposal of Waste			
金属制品、机械和设备修理业	Metal Products,Machinery and Equipment Repair Industry	12818	12818	
电力、热力的生产和供应业	Production and Supply of Electric Power and Heat Power			
燃气生产和供应业	Gas Mining and Supplying Industry	345508	331664	13844
水的生产和供应业	Production and Supply of Water			

continued 4

(10 000 yuan)

所有者权益合计 Total Owners' Equities	实收资本 Total Capital Hold	营业收入 Total Revenue	主营业务收入 Revenue from Principal Business	营业成本 Total Cost	主营业务收入 Cost of Principal Business	营业税金及附加 Taxs and Other Changes	主营业务税金及附加 Taxes and Other Charges on Principal Business
7919	1892	15297	14799	12088	11809	124	124
233513	78908	646274	633971	531548	519493	2544	2543
311753	141758	538055	519303	407007	397509	5568	5509
6634	6529	2085	2085	1772	1772		
15634	5540	60079	59507	56760	56677	69	69
31833	7500	40015	39796	30534	30534	295	295
2521	845	32330	32330	31675	31675		
52428	39841	151407	149617	141007	139562	837	780
95869	93670	165543	165100	140852	140633	805	803
259333	78871	719079	718308	396571	396271	4589	4589
53892	26900	109312	109285	88912	88912	434	434
16166	11788	11685	11646	8892	8864	83	83
41972	26255	109084	106708	99236	99236	525	525
4448	3836	16216	15954	14068	13818	56	56
30935	27395	109264	109197	100423	100380	115	115
21581	19567	35499	35468	28642	28642	194	194
99774	51313	107412	107053	94350	94299	230	230
213804	64890	384505	377867	294181	290267	1821	1819
660495	116196	1772082	1720889	1565740	1523273	48368	48367
152260	46985	162026	161734	110677	110621	986	986
261197	260285	709243	705781	642985	637185	1211	984
2647036	2398225	1776495	1771598	1429353	1427930	479	479
100493	27957	79247	78370	50325	50287	676	676
2746	1800	3733	3598	3327	3327	27	27
8450	3455	18171	18159	13807	13807	77	77
142459	100000	341104	274702	279796	234048	2744	2744

12-11 续表5

单位：万元

分 组	Classify	销售费用 Expenses for Sales	管理费用 Expenses for Management	财务费用 Financial cost
农副食品加工业	Processing of Food from Agricultural Porducts	188	1390	-99
食品制造业	Manufacture of Foods	77599	13873	-2863
酒、饮料和精制茶制造业	Manufacture of Alcohol,Beverages and Tea	67761	31179	10549
烟草制品业	Manufacture of Tobacco			
纺织业	Manufacture of Textile	30	339	-8
纺织服装、服饰业	Textile, apparel industry			
皮革、毛皮、羽毛及其制品和制鞋业	Leather fur feathers and its products and footwear			
木材加工和木、竹、藤、棕、草制品业	Processing of Timber,Manufacture of Wood,Plam and Straw Products			
家具制造业	Manufacture of Furniture			
造纸及纸制品业	Manufacture of Paper and Paper Products	911	1199	301
印刷和记录媒介复制	Printing,Reproduction of Recording Media	2252	2249	1095
文教、工美、体育和娱乐用品制造业	Manufacture of Articles For Cultural,Educational and Sports Activities	90	373	8
石油加工业、炼焦和核燃料加工业	Processing of Petroleum, Cokeing,Processing of Nuclear and Nuclear Fuel	5257	11035	1378
化学原料及化学制品制造业	Manufacture of Raw Chemical Materials and Chemical Products	4610	7148	7218
医药制造业	Manufacture of Medicines	183434	55819	13122
化学纤维制造业	Manufacture of Chemical Fibers	630	4164	2440
橡胶和塑料制品业	Manufacture of Rubber and Plastics	489	987	220
非金属矿物制品业	Manufacture of Non-metallic Mineral Products	350	4470	2649
黑色金属冶炼和压延加工业	Smelting and Pressing of Ferrous Metals	411	986	43
有色金属冶炼和压延加工业	Smelting and Pressing of Non-ferrous Metals	2196	4387	1041
金属制品业	Manufacture of Metal Products	1211	3618	828
通用设备制造业	Manufacture of General Purpose Machinery	4102	7311	-325
专用设备制造业	Manufacture of Special Equipment	8359	25068	1880
汽车制造业	Manufacture of Motor Vehicle	32175	65006	10359
铁路、船舶、航空航天和其他运输设备制造业	Railways,Shipbuilding,Aerospace and Other Transportation Equipment Manufacturing Industry	4405	12884	3992
电气机械和器材制造业	Manufacture of Electric Equipment and Machinery	14689	30805	1649
计算机、通讯和其他电子设备制造业	Manufacture of Communication Equipment, Computers and other Electronic Equipment	3274	213566	82392
仪器仪表制造业	Manufacture of Measuring Instruments and Machinery	5917	5926	-625
其他制造业	Manufacture of Other Manufacturing	180	206	7
废弃资源综合利用业	Recycling and Disposal of Waste			
金属制品、机械和设备修理业	Metal Products,Machinery and Equipment Repair Industry	1523	2220	-18
电力、热力的生产和供应业	Production and Supply of Electric Power and Heat Power			
燃气生产和供应业	Gas Mining and Supplying Industry	13628	17195	-3565
水的生产和供应业	Production and Supply of Water			

continued 5

(10 000 yuan)

营业利润 Operating Profit	利润总额 Total Profits	亏损企业亏损额 Total Loss of Deficit Enterprises	利税总额 Total Pre-tax Profits	应付职工薪酬 Salary Payable	本年应交增值税 Value Added Tax Payable
2711	2712		3679	1731	843
24595	25640	2061	49355	36156	21171
16056	28521	5520	61712	31473	27623
-48	-6	6	-6	392	
310	1041	62	1917	1679	808
4028	4045		6564	4870	2224
183	219		629	1059	409
-7922	-7893	7893	-482	15238	6574
4930	5074	1753	7903	6639	2024
64382	59890	119	153727	98467	89248
11652	11867	1698	10413	5128	-1888
1014	1089		1777	1867	605
2756	3096	645	7456	3898	3835
652	685		1166	990	425
515	1269	2247	2491	3246	1106
983	1046	802	2011	5195	770
1700	1691	1768	2806	9074	885
55508	55894	921	62706	23626	4991
54753	62225	7017	133201	142207	22609
27221	27615		36232	17822	7632
18405	25443	7728	30516	40437	3862
28057	112082	750	113631	119543	1070
17019	17086	506	20718	11294	2956
-59	-60	60	133	378	166
399	604		1311	1799	630
38284	38029		50080	33576	9307

12-12 规模以上大中型工业企业主要经济指标（2015年）

单位：万元

分组	Classify	企业单位数（个）Number of Enterprises (unit)	亏损企业 Loss Making Enterprises	工业总产值（当年价格）Gross Industrial Output Value (At Current Prices)
总计	**Total**	**225**	**47**	**34917443**
#市区	Urban	212	43	34196978
#亏损企业	Deficit Enterprises	47	47	7401392
按隶属关系分	**Grouped by Jurisdiction of Management**			
中央企业	Central Enterprises	45	9	10760798
省属企业	Provincial Enterprises	34	11	7701311
市属企业	Municipal Enterprises	146	27	16455334
按登记注册类型分组	**Grouped by Registion Status**			
内资企业	Domestic Investment Enterprises	188	40	27740880
国有	State-owned Enterprises	27	4	6743052
集体	Collective-owned Enterprises			
股份合作	Share-holding Corperative			
联营	Joint Ownership Enterprises			
国有联营	State Joint Ownership Enterprises			
集体联营	Collective Joint Ownership Enterprises			
国有与集体联营	Joint State-collective Ownership Enterprises			
其他联营	Other Joint Ownership Enterprises			
有限责任公司	Limited Liability Corporations	107	28	16636444
国有独资公司	State Sole Funded Enterprises	24	8	3616408
其他有限责任公司	Other Limited Liability Corporation	83	20	13020036
股份有限公司	Share-holding Corperation Ltd.	38	3	2551478
私营	Private Enterprises	16	5	1809906
私营独资	Private-funded Enterprises			
私营合伙	Private Partnership Enterprises			
私营有限责任公司	Private Limited Liability Corporations	15	5	1673789
私营股份有限公司	Private Share Holding Corporations	1		136117
其他	Other Domestic Funded Enterprises			
港澳台商投资	Enterprises with Funds from Hong Kong,Macao and Taiwan	6		1975536
外商投资	Foreign Funded Enterprises	31	7	5201027
按轻重工业分	**Grouped by Light Industry and Heavy Industry**			
轻工业	Light Industry	57	13	4851811
重工业	Heavy Industry	168	34	30065632
按企业规模分	**Grouped by Size of Enterprises**			
大型企业	Large-size	61	10	34917443

Economic Indicators of Large and Medium-sized Industrial Enterprises above Designated Size (2015)

(10 000 yuan)

工业销售产值（当年价） Value of Industry Products Sales (At Current Prices)	出口交货值 Export Delivery Value	从业人员年平均人数（人） Annual Average Employers (person)	资产总计 Total Assets	流动资产合计 Total Working Capitals	固定资产合计 Total Fixed Assets	固定资产原价 Origing Value of Fixed Assets	累计折旧 Accumulative Total Depreciation
33003027	**3432683**	**406716**	**56070373**	**26974624**	**18485963**	**28032345**	**10293267**
32314166	3432683	394951	54961105	26508650	17952115	27168966	9858265
7175887	202044	77799	8858247	4918290	1677916	2805072	1138299
10501012	476603	168431	22413701	10520356	7689092	11929343	4607152
7425288	205965	71293	10942453	5858896	1966346	3075587	1246219
15076727	2750115	166992	22714219	10595372	8830525	13027415	4439896
26591901	1460813	338794	44797820	23485892	12298681	19608038	7869127
6562994	176463	96642	13451261	6837270	3967404	5445660	1771965
15994553	813742	202627	24801600	13265640	6884498	11395920	4711600
3494943	298179	67853	10679239	4647472	4072537	6877336	2901619
12499610	515563	134774	14122361	8618168	2811961	4518584	1809981
2279821	470085	29639	5620618	2824540	1186399	2386512	1260914
1754533	523	9886	924341	558442	260380	379946	124648
1619271	523	9523	905400	551195	253368	371131	122846
135262		363	18941	7247	7012	8815	1802
1783907	104412	33641	2028786	785029	705240	950592	313253
4627219	1867459	34281	9243767	2703703	5482042	7473715	2110887
4640940	118175	51627	4684092	2662461	1488217	2541491	1218928
28362087	3314508	355089	51386281	24312163	16997746	25490854	9074339
33003027	3432683	406716	56070373	26974624	18485963	28032345	10293267

12-12 续表1

单位：万元

分组	Classify	负债合计 Total Liabilites	流动负债合计 Total Working Liabilities	非流动负债 Non-Working Liabilities
总计	**Total**	**32162380**	**23658939**	**5120383**
#市区	Urban	31498956	23177469	5007812
#亏损企业	Deficit Enterprises	6046868	4993285	711787
按隶属关系分	**Grouped by Jurisdiction of Management**			
中央企业	Central Enterprises	13329372	8305468	2736696
省属企业	Provincial Enterprises	5747735	4811764	577932
市属企业	Municipal Enterprises	13085273	10541707	1805755
按登记注册类型分组	**Grouped by Registion Status**			
内资企业	Domestic Investment Enterprises	25643344	18526727	4462429
国有	State-owned Enterprises	7331944	5562490	2053092
集体	Collective-owned Enterprises			
股份合作	Share-holding Corperative			
联营	Joint Ownership Enterprises			
国有联营	State Joint Ownership Enterprises			
集体联营	Collective Joint Ownership Enterprises			
国有与集体联营	Joint State-collective Ownership Enterprises			
其他联营	Other Joint Ownership Enterprises			
有限责任公司	Limited Liability Corporations	15642505	10846012	1878005
国有独资公司	State Sole Funded Enterprises	6495744	3147222	765578
其他有限责任公司	Other Limited Liability Corporation	9146761	7698790	1112427
股份有限公司	Share-holding Corperation Ltd.	2078538	1653870	420013
私营	Private Enterprises	590357	464355	111319
私营独资	Private-funded Enterprises			
私营合伙	Private Partnership Enterprises			
私营有限责任公司	Private Limited Liability Corporations	589057	463055	111319
私营股份有限公司	Private Share Holding Corporations	1300	1300	
其他	Other Domestic Funded Enterprises			
港澳台商投资	Enterprises with Funds from Hong Kong,Macao and Taiwan	1368563	1202717	151684
外商投资	Foreign Funded Enterprises	5150473	3929496	506270
按轻重工业分	**Grouped by Light Industry and Heavy Industry**			
轻工业	Light Industry	2701250	2137581	544838
重工业	Heavy Industry	29461130	21521358	4575545
按企业规模分	**Grouped by Size of Enterprises**			
大型企业	Large-size	32162380	23658939	5120383

continued 1

(10 000 yuan)

所有者权益合计 Total Owners' Equities	实收资本 Total Capital Hold	营业收入 Total Revenue	主营业务收入 Revenue from Principal Business	营业成本 Total Cost	主营业务成本 Cost of Principal Business	营业税金及附加 Taxs and Other Changes	主营业务税金及附加 Taxes and Other Charges on Principal Business
24390474	**9246377**	**31872040**	**30894510**	**27104946**	**25877236**	**204350**	**190911**
23944630	9102593	31194156	30223973	26532105	25307546	201080	187684
3293851	1626852	5417526	5302452	4975754	4903668	14304	12997
9084329	2936785	10778971	10378216	9282465	8478322	70254	68394
5677199	1541990	6498347	6234649	5675408	5480435	21240	21094
9628946	4767602	14594722	14281645	12147073	11918479	112856	101423
19636956	6186937	25556264	24740636	22116663	21005191	135767	122672
6601789	1250595	6452647	6071879	5481089	4798229	42030	40734
9159095	3797535	15018586	14611000	13145917	12729853	74891	65467
4183495	1364354	4051592	3942659	3348930	3262270	37248	29081
4975600	2433181	10966994	10668341	9796987	9467583	37643	36386
3542089	982970	2259419	2237207	1842506	1833497	12636	10261
333983	155837	1825612	1820550	1647151	1643612	6210	6210
316343	145837	1698497	1693435	1541332	1537793	3992	3992
17640	10000	127115	127115	105819	105819	2218	2218
660224	76976	1872257	1821581	1638984	1597774	48904	48904
4093294	2982464	4443520	4332293	3349299	3274271	19679	19336
1982842	771890	4182015	4114134	3073248	3024677	36373	33481
22407632	8474487	27690025	26780376	24031698	22852559	167977	157430
24390474	9246377	31872040	30894510	27104946	25877236	204350	190911

12-12 续表2

单位：万元

分　组	Classify	销售费用 Expenses for Sales	管理费用 Expenses for Management	财务费用 Financial cost
总计	**Total**	**1145076**	**1999367**	**425018**
#市区	Urban	1120986	1953845	411039
#亏损企业	Deficit Enterprises	210554	337955	61755
按隶属关系分	**Grouped by Jurisdiction of Management**			
中央企业	Central Enterprises	204886	745982	210564
省属企业	Provincial Enterprises	342678	376410	33151
市属企业	Municipal Enterprises	597512	876975	181303
按登记注册类型分组	**Grouped by Registion Status**			
内资企业	Domestic Investment Enterprises	746617	1555960	306344
国有	State-owned Enterprises	152945	475324	73262
集体	Collective-owned Enterprises			
股份合作	Share-holding Corperative			
联营	Joint Ownership Enterprises			
国有联营	State Joint Ownership Enterprises			
集体联营	Collective Joint Ownership Enterprises			
国有与集体联营	Joint State-collective Ownership Enterprises			
其他联营	Other Joint Ownership Enterprises			
有限责任公司	Limited Liability Corporations	425906	868679	186616
国有独资公司	State Sole Funded Enterprises	90396	328958	103416
其他有限责任公司	Other Limited Liability Corporation	335510	539721	83200
股份有限公司	Share-holding Corperation Ltd.	113615	163712	31593
私营	Private Enterprises	54151	48245	14873
私营独资	Private-funded Enterprises			
私营合伙	Private Partnership Enterprises			
私营有限责任公司	Private Limited Liability Corporations	46028	38831	14381
私营股份有限公司	Private Share Holding Corporations	8123	9414	492
其他	Other Domestic Funded Enterprises			
港澳台商投资	Enterprises with Funds from Hong Kong,Macao and Taiwan	54901	58300	12500
外商投资	Foreign Funded Enterprises	343558	385107	106175
按轻重工业分	**Grouped by Light Industry and Heavy Industry**			
轻工业	Light Industry	556695	266620	38839
重工业	Heavy Industry	588381	1732747	386179
按企业规模分	**Grouped by Size of Enterprises**			
大型企业	Large-size	1145076	1999367	425018

continued 2

(10 000 yuan)

营业利润 Operating Profit	利润总额 Total Profits	亏损企业亏损额 Total Loss of Deficit Enterprises	利税总额 Total Pre-tax Profits	应付职工薪酬 Salary Payable	本年应交增值税 Value Added Tax Payable
1280286	**1577664**	**151138**	**2658108**	**2822793**	**876094**
1252730	1544053	143382	2600748	2747082	855615
-203179	-151138	151138	-46111	433892	90724
530849	580600	42244	1018377	1231945	367522
28401	89169	39456	303774	526431	193365
721036	907895	69438	1335957	1064417	315207
988414	1179035	125414	1999286	2294998	684484
343772	363941	19865	614656	606382	208686
468032	595338	89898	1062803	1415758	392573
197732	237754	17813	503119	579929	228117
270299	357585	72085	559683	835829	164456
130687	172923	6574	243547	184104	57988
45923	46833	9077	78280	88754	25237
44874	45784	9077	75013	84168	25237
1049	1049		3267	4586	
63023	70309		145708	150489	26495
228850	328320	25725	513114	377305	165115
210145	242240	18813	500475	397364	221862
1070141	1335424	132325	2157633	2425429	654232
1280286	1577664	151138	2658108	2822793	876094

12-12 续表3

单位：万元

分 组	Classify	企业单位数（个） Number of Enterprises (unit)	亏损企业 Loss Making Enterprises	工业总产值（当年价格） Gross Industrial Output Value (At Current Prices)
中型企业	Medium-size	164	37	8432031
小型企业	Small-size			
微型企业	Microenterprise			
按经济组织类型分组	**Grouped by Economic Type of Orgnization**			
独资企业	Appropratorship	42	7	9857585
合作、合伙企业	Partnership			
股份有限公司	Corporaton	41	3	3022588
有限责任公司	Limited Liability Company	142	37	22037270
按控股情况分	**Grouped by Cast strand**			
国有控股	State owned shares	116	27	21688414
集体控股	Collective shares	8		892114
私人控股	Private holdings	62	13	6820328
港澳台控股	Hong Kong and Macao Holdings	3		195604
外商投资	Foreign Investment	25	6	4724913
其他	Others	11	1	596070
按工业行业大类分	**Grouped by Sector**			
煤炭开采和洗选业	Mining and Washing of Coal			
石油和天然气开采业	Extraction of Petroleum and Natural Gas			
黑色金属矿采选业	Mining and Processing of Ferrous Metal Ores			
有色金属矿采选业	Mining and Processing of Non-ferrous Metal Ores			
非金属矿采选业	Mining and Processing of Nonmetal Ores			
开采辅助活动	Mining Auxiliary Activities	2		533553
其他采矿业	Mining of other Ores			
农副食品加工业	Processing of Food from Agricultural Porducts	6	4	774327
食品制造业	Manufacture of Foods	10	2	958004
酒、饮料和精制茶制造业	Manufacture of Alcohol,Beverages and Tea	6	1	794105
烟草制品业	Manufacture of Tobacco			
纺织业	Manufacture of Textile	3	1	68899
纺织服装、服饰业	Textile, apparel industry	1		54698
皮革、毛皮、羽毛及其制品和制鞋业	Manufacture of Leather, Fur, Feather and Related Products, and Shoes	1		51289
木材加工和木、竹、藤、棕、草制品业	Processing of Timber, Manufacture of Wood,Plam and Straw Products	1	1	101686
家具制造业	Manufacture of Furniture	1		11694

continued 3

(10 000 yuan)

工业销售产值（当年价）Value of Industry Products Sales (At Current Prices)	出口交货值 Export Delivery Value	从业人员年平均人数（人）Annual Average Employers (person)	资产总计 Total Assets	流动资产合计 Total Working Capitals	固定资产合计 Total Fixed Assets	固定资产原价 Origing Value of Fixed Assets	累计折旧 Accumulative Total Depreciation
7588166	641134	96301	12809841	6471725	2580401	4250127	1787765
9363070	1939997	114503	20276316	8191830	8646448	11674819	3346382
2594265	572455	31949	6055229	3002033	1416011	2878983	1525574
21045692	920231	260264	29738828	15780761	8423504	13478543	5421311
20959146	1001716	288454	39528975	20358412	10934750	17118433	6702980
847435	368224	5468	1158386	621648	464440	1169849	706853
6246984	111397	72017	6031747	3192053	1625846	2249743	742128
203779	58094	2938	166446	72867	63156	119254	56098
4185479	1852611	29509	8374835	2200818	5247119	7153041	2012685
560204	40641	8330	809984	528826	150652	222025	72523
529955		5880	656176	428911	131719	313247	181528
756645	1700	3685	580628	438992	86495	165663	79168
927301		8977	465483	250956	148806	254876	108855
806564	101469	5875	849415	367871	377411	791371	416070
67666	6381	6781	296825	93768	171411	207474	42603
50621		1250	105650	88450	3235	5515	2279
51224		848	46239	23971	4571	7660	3089
83505		495	151484	59734	52755	65259	35477
12203		352	16610	11907	4430	11935	7505

12-12 续表4

单位：万元

分组	Classify	负债合计 Total Liabilites	流动负债合计 Total Working Liabilities	非流动负债 Non-Working Liabilities
中型企业	Medium-size	6423678	4978656	1399857
小型企业	Small-size			
微型企业	Microenterprise			
按经济组织类型分组	**Grouped by Economic Type of Orgnization**			
独资企业	Appropratorship	11103162	8323876	2348247
合作、合伙企业	Partnership			
股份有限公司	Corporaton	2341669	1883202	439620
有限责任公司	Limited Liability Company	18717549	13451861	2332516
按控股情况分	**Grouped by Cast strand**			
国有控股	State owned shares	22986854	16301417	4054065
集体控股	Collective shares	510483	483756	26727
私人控股	Private holdings	3589140	3027109	539216
港澳台控股	Hong Kong and Macao Holdings	93346	77741	1443
外商投资	Foreign Investment	4623937	3451461	457769
其他	Others	358620	317455	41163
按工业行业大类分	**Grouped by Sector**			
煤炭开采和洗选业	Mining and Washing of Coal			
石油和天然气开采业	Extraction of Petroleum and Natural Gas			
黑色金属矿采选业	Mining and Processing of Ferrous Metal Ores			
有色金属矿采选业	Mining and Processing of Non-ferrous Metal Ores			
非金属矿采选业	Mining and Processing of Nonmetal Ores			
开采辅助活动	Mining Auxiliary Activities	185749	184822	926
其他采矿业	Mining of other Ores			
农副食品加工业	Processing of Food from Agricultural Porducts	530412	505300	25112
食品制造业	Manufacture of Foods	154283	147662	6621
酒、饮料和精制茶制造业	Manufacture of Alcohol,Beverages and Tea	492366	464417	27919
烟草制品业	Manufacture of Tobacco			
纺织业	Manufacture of Textile	212420	106795	105625
纺织服装、服饰业	Textile, apparel industry	89380	76380	13000
皮革、毛皮、羽毛及其制品和制鞋业	Manufacture of Leather, Fur, Feather and Related Products, and Shoes	20888	16014	4873
木材加工和木、竹、藤、棕、草制品业	Processing of Timber, Manufacture of Wood,Plam and Straw Products	97012	59904	37108
家具制造业	Manufacture of Furniture	13285	13285	

continued 4

(10 000 yuan)

所有者权益合计 Total Owners' Equities	实收资本 Total Capital Hold	营业收入 Total Revenue	主营业务收入 Revenue from Principal Business	营业成本 Total Cost	主营业务成本 Cost of Principal Business	营业税金及附加 Taxs and Other Changes	主营业务税金及附加 Taxes and Other Charges on Principal Business
6386171	2288352	7494677	6962322	6108177	5867038	40856	37038
9655625	3837259	9152146	8741432	7602490	6895979	50840	49545
3713570	1004940	2537689	2513036	2072800	2062604	15619	13186
11021279	4404178	20182205	19640042	17429656	16918653	137891	128180
17024603	5376051	20382292	19548707	17772323	16649718	118627	108928
647903	228419	707795	698164	576295	567218	2312	2312
2442606	563792	6099210	6035823	5242300	5197525	64821	61424
73100	51222	190912	185505	141924	138139	867	867
3750899	2769373	3944786	3903727	2949903	2924801	15948	15605
451363	257520	547045	522584	422201	399835	1775	1775
470427	253188	344282	338842	261354	259250	5049	4994
50216	40877	522531	521586	496181	495820	735	735
311201	102979	810951	785908	617440	594190	4140	4140
357049	102779	691629	673305	515360	506596	15334	15275
84405	14556	76986	69765	72080	66135	348	348
16270	7500	53511	53379	41811	41287	2447	245
25351	15000	54189	53660	47799	47352	438	438
54472	12500	63376	63345	61258	61258	173	173
3325	2200	11545	11545	9856	9856	37	37

12-12 续表5

单位：万元

分组	Classify	销售费用 Expenses for Sales	管理费用 Expenses for Management	财务费用 Financial cost
中型企业	Medium-size	387942	523276	78276
小型企业	Small-size			
微型企业	Microenterprise			
按经济组织类型分组	**Grouped by Economic Type of Orgnization**			
独资企业	Appropratorship	277709	736901	157741
合作、合伙企业	Partnership			
股份有限公司	Corporaton	129890	185799	44333
有限责任公司	Limited Liability Company	737477	1076667	222944
按控股情况分	**Grouped by Cast strand**			
国有控股	State owned shares	476047	1335780	255032
集体控股	Collective shares	47975	46419	5475
私人控股	Private holdings	222978	221838	54548
港澳台控股	Hong Kong and Macao Holdings	26793	8680	2377
外商投资	Foreign Investment	325259	351589	104174
其他	Others	46024	35061	3412
按工业行业大类分	**Grouped by Sector**			
煤炭开采和洗选业	Mining and Washing of Coal			
石油和天然气开采业	Extraction of Petroleum and Natural Gas			
黑色金属矿采选业	Mining and Processing of Ferrous Metal Ores			
有色金属矿采选业	Mining and Processing of Non-ferrous Metal Ores			
非金属矿采选业	Mining and Processing of Nonmetal Ores			
开采辅助活动	Mining Auxiliary Activities	922	29065	-1723
其他采矿业	Mining of other Ores			
农副食品加工业	Processing of Food from Agricultural Porducts	23687	8455	8100
食品制造业	Manufacture of Foods	112530	28838	-2536
酒、饮料和精制茶制造业	Manufacture of Alcohol,Beverages and Tea	78219	29230	7246
烟草制品业	Manufacture of Tobacco			
纺织业	Manufacture of Textile	793	8436	343
纺织服装、服饰业	Textile, apparel industry	3841	4268	2514
皮革、毛皮、羽毛及其制品和制鞋业	Manufacture of Leather, Fur, Feather and Related Products, and Shoes	1333	1540	127
木材加工和木、竹、藤、棕、草制品业	Processing of Timber, Manufacture of Wood,Plam and Straw Products	614	1999	2628
家具制造业	Manufacture of Furniture		1107	

continued 5

(10 000 yuan)

营业利润 Operating Profit	利润总额 Total Profits	亏损企业亏损额 Total Loss of Deficit Enterprises	利税总额 Total Pre-tax Profits	应付职工薪酬 Salary Payable	本年应交增值税 Value Added Tax Payable
336600	417372	94320	672667	713461	214439
426006	530851	28395	829677	790584	247986
125014	181168	6574	266332	201466	69544
729266	865645	116169	1562099	1830743	558564
711524	865123	115404	1574557	2015372	590808
60987	63318		85044	38596	19415
279646	312249	15498	473764	384525	96695
10692	10772		18256	17005	6617
181085	280844	19629	448634	321637	151862
36352	45358	607	57833	45658	10697
41581	46240	-1	85249	97125	33957
-12934	-6469	8147	-2559	14515	3176
47202	48189	3952	82715	57486	30386
47345	61273	2834	115705	36773	39099
-4677	670	600	2057	28407	1039
-1402	1137		4975	3617	1391
3067	3046		3186	6006	-298
-3273	-1729	1729	2029	1996	3585
545	334		683	1037	312

12-12 续表6

单位：万元

分组	Classify	企业单位数（个） Number of Enterprises (unit)	亏损企业 Loss Making Enterprises	工业总产值（当年价格） Gross Industrial Output Value (At Current Prices)
造纸及纸制品业	Manufacture of Paper and Paper Products	1	1	6003
印刷和记录媒介复制	Printing,Reproduction of Recording Media	7	1	386719
文教、工美、体育和娱乐用品制造业	Manufacture of Articles For Cultural,Educational and Sports Activities			
石油加工业、炼焦和核燃料加工业	Processing of Petroleum, Cokeing,Processing of Nuclear and Nuclear Fuel	1	1	184502
化学原料及化学制品制造业	Manufacture of Raw Chemical Materials and Chemical Products	11	2	1145763
医药制造业	Manufacture of Medicines	13		1367821
化学纤维制造业	Manufacture of Chemical Fibers			
橡胶和塑料制品业	Manufacture of Rubber and Plastics	3		393027
非金属矿物制品业	Manufacture of Non-metallic Mineral Products	5		223793
黑色金属冶炼和压延加工业	Smelting and Pressing of Ferrous Metals	1	1	6600
有色金属冶炼和压延加工业	Smelting and Pressing of Non-ferrous Metals	8	2	1547722
金属制品业	Manufacture of Metal Products	7	2	857589
通用设备制造业	Manufacture of General Purpose Machinery	10	3	1155849
专用设备制造业	Manufacture of Special Equipment	22	4	1526102
汽车制造业	Manufacture of Motor Vehicle	18	6	8148193
铁路、船舶、航空航天和其他运输设备制造业	Railways,Shipbuilding,Aerospace and Other Transportation Equipment Manufacturing Industry	20	3	3913079
电气机械和器材制造业	Manufacture of Electric Equipment and Machinery	21	4	2869794
计算机、通讯和其他电子设备制造业	Manufacture of Communication Equipment, Computers and other Electronic Equipment	27	7	4177044
仪器仪表制造业	Manufacture of Measuring Instruments and Machinery	8	1	1025694
其他制造业	Manufacture of Other Manufacturing			
废弃资源综合利用业	Recycling and Disposal of Waste			
金属制品、机械和设备修理业	Metal Products,Machinery and Equipment Repair Industry			
电力、热力的生产和供应业	Production and Supply of Electric Power and Heat Power	5		2159312
燃气生产和供应业	Gas Mining and Supplying Industry	5		385750
水的生产和供应业	Production and Supply of Water	1		88832

continued 6

(10 000 yuan)

工业销售产值（当年价）Value of Industry Products Sales (At Current Prices)	出口交货值 Export Delivery Value	从业人员年平均人数（人）Annual Average Employers (person)	资产总计 Total Assets	流动资产合计 Total Working Capitals	固定资产合计 Total Fixed Assets	固定资产原价 Origing Value of Fixed Assets	累计折旧 Accumulative Total Depreciation
6003		318	8306	5629	900	900	23
393667	902	4983	436993	221589	174347	350251	187137
184502		4640	131922	17770	75690	109934	34244
1067703	374091	17201	1853504	921574	716099	1608983	893515
1230477	2547	11405	1097672	709145	254734	310011	164190
379292	2778	13125	1002121	652303	178747	243857	84565
199562		1977	203612	110342	76715	123243	60254
5825		316	14665	6998	6655	7671	1016
1389868	39268	7828	2446144	894595	336429	501526	176376
848060	12011	18457	1591091	954393	434278	733292	319395
1197510	79929	19424	3289060	2382621	443287	734867	365431
1392810	99208	19852	3826466	2040181	763506	1201624	452808
7619834	217321	77711	7234429	4084247	1715645	2579366	938952
3725167	497533	61520	7676203	4075653	1177739	1990565	944054
2738602	140550	34806	5386922	3680036	1029839	1645052	615373
3705281	1814871	37004	8695447	2550821	4982408	6666101	1666658
999545	42124	11683	1451799	892166	343088	566665	223794
2159312		23608	5574239	607135	4471130	6309511	2046631
385491		4081	799423	315015	229900	310484	86778
88832		2634	181845	87851	93994	215442	155499

12-12 续表7

单位：万元

分　组	Classify	负债合计 Total Liabilites	流动负债合计 Total Working Liabilities	非流动负债 Non-Working Liabilities
造纸及纸制品业	Manufacture of Paper and Paper Products	5345	5345	
印刷和记录媒介复制	Printing,Reproduction of Recording Media	118388	92160	12059
文教、工美、体育和娱乐用品制造业	Manufacture of Articles For Cultural,Educational and Sports Activities			
石油加工业、炼焦和核燃料加工业	Processing of Petroleum, Cokeing,Processing of Nuclear and Nuclear Fuel	85513	65478	20035
化学原料及化学制品制造业	Manufacture of Raw Chemical Materials and Chemical Products	886773	680118	205410
医药制造业	Manufacture of Medicines	513756	427188	81936
化学纤维制造业	Manufacture of Chemical Fibers			
橡胶和塑料制品业	Manufacture of Rubber and Plastics	822024	575466	246558
非金属矿物制品业	Manufacture of Non-metallic Mineral Products	115770	110906	2336
黑色金属冶炼和压延加工业	Smelting and Pressing of Ferrous Metals	12068	12068	
有色金属冶炼和压延加工业	Smelting and Pressing of Non-ferrous Metals	632307	514933	117352
金属制品业	Manufacture of Metal Products	1048270	781978	266292
通用设备制造业	Manufacture of General Purpose Machinery	1797952	1667926	130026
专用设备制造业	Manufacture of Special Equipment	1643591	1436743	193241
汽车制造业	Manufacture of Motor Vehicle	4367090	3758375	279693
铁路、船舶、航空航天和其他运输设备制造业	Railways,Shipbuilding,Aerospace and Other Transportation Equipment Manufacturing Industry	4612364	3466025	1078157
电气机械和器材制造业	Manufacture of Electric Equipment and Machinery	2537259	2081658	452100
计算机、通讯和其他电子设备制造业	Manufacture of Communication Equipment, Computers and other Electronic Equipment	5233695	3904938	611782
仪器仪表制造业	Manufacture of Measuring Instruments and Machinery	732087	634284	440751
其他制造业	Manufacture of Other Manufacturing			
废弃资源综合利用业	Recycling and Disposal of Waste			
金属制品、机械和设备修理业	Metal Products,Machinery and Equipment Repair Industry			
电力、热力的生产和供应业	Production and Supply of Electric Power and Heat Power	4574623	1300167	702364
燃气生产和供应业	Gas Mining and Supplying Industry	516020	490532	25489
水的生产和供应业	Production and Supply of Water	111690	78072	33618

continued 7

(10 000 yuan)

所有者权益合计 Total Owners' Equities	实收资本 Total Capital Hold	营业收入 Total Revenue	主营业务收入 Revenue from Principal Business	营业成本 Total Cost	主营业务成本 Cost of Principal Business	营业税金及附加 Taxs and Other Changes	主营业务税金及附加 Taxes and Other Charges on Principal Business
2962	3000	6003	6003	5584	5584	3	3
318606	176298	378378	375883	311687	309998	2741	2736
46409	33000	124426	122889	114120	112676	781	724
966731	328257	990837	973070	834637	816598	3104	3104
583916	143093	1231025	1229797	683433	683091	8670	8670
180097	91857	391876	380757	323040	319279	2125	1943
87842	28800	210720	194402	175020	161133	2015	2015
2597	3000	5353	5348	4424	4424	12	12
1813837	469800	1507752	1375623	1373345	1258224	1692	1689
542821	249436	759401	747377	650239	643371	2168	1509
1491107	245696	1093685	1085966	899663	892234	11671	6242
2182874	727948	1383397	1362861	1056239	1043105	8163	8044
2867338	730926	6686236	6505923	6157941	6038642	58501	58468
3063838	967605	3744981	3467761	3410307	3256966	13359	12354
2849663	603373	2383406	2283961	1828329	1748397	23109	22832
3944235	2786587	3955586	3937861	3352093	3344549	7588	6439
719712	220946	891725	890840	723906	165534	2656	2121
999615	637596	2940570	2901615	2631938	2597725	23150	21914
283403	208580	458637	386406	364056	318205	3421	3387
70155	39000	99046	88832	81806	75757	720	320

12-12 续表8

单位：万元

分　组	Classify	销售费用 Expenses for Sales	管理费用 Expenses for Management	财务费用 Financial cost
造纸及纸制品业	Manufacture of Paper and Paper Products	75	206	185
印刷和记录媒介复制	Printing,Reproduction of Recording Media	8041	35508	673
文教、工美、体育和娱乐用品制造业	Manufacture of Articles For Cultural,Educational and Sports Activities			
石油加工业、炼焦和核燃料加工业	Processing of Petroleum, Cokeing,Processing of Nuclear and Nuclear Fuel	5102	9633	1333
化学原料及化学制品制造业	Manufacture of Raw Chemical Materials and Chemical Products	31060	93325	13184
医药制造业	Manufacture of Medicines	302716	112634	14167
化学纤维制造业	Manufacture of Chemical Fibers			
橡胶和塑料制品业	Manufacture of Rubber and Plastics	15637	17946	9439
非金属矿物制品业	Manufacture of Non-metallic Mineral Products	10955	7164	1424
黑色金属冶炼和压延加工业	Smelting and Pressing of Ferrous Metals	67	1026	70
有色金属冶炼和压延加工业	Smelting and Pressing of Non-ferrous Metals	6015	38739	5315
金属制品业	Manufacture of Metal Products	12851	77317	14092
通用设备制造业	Manufacture of General Purpose Machinery	33135	140646	7479
专用设备制造业	Manufacture of Special Equipment	76307	131867	17644
汽车制造业	Manufacture of Motor Vehicle	147283	270384	19299
铁路、船舶、航空航天和其他运输设备制造业	Railways,Shipbuilding,Aerospace and Other Transportation Equipment Manufacturing Industry	49534	229518	39842
电气机械和器材制造业	Manufacture of Electric Equipment and Machinery	142273	253624	18363
计算机、通讯和其他电子设备制造业	Manufacture of Communication Equipment, Computers and other Electronic Equipment	34339	333272	100135
仪器仪表制造业	Manufacture of Measuring Instruments and Machinery	14972	87192	2066
其他制造业	Manufacture of Other Manufacturing			
废弃资源综合利用业	Recycling and Disposal of Waste			
金属制品、机械和设备修理业	Metal Products,Machinery and Equipment Repair Industry			
电力、热力的生产和供应业	Production and Supply of Electric Power and Heat Power	215	11920	141976
燃气生产和供应业	Gas Mining and Supplying Industry	28705	24492	1855
水的生产和供应业	Production and Supply of Water	3855	10016	-222

continued 8

(10 000 yuan)

营业利润 Operating Profit	利润总额 Total Profits	亏损企业亏损额 Total Loss of Deficit Enterprises	利税总额 Total Pre-tax Profits	应付职工薪酬 Salary Payable	本年应交增值税 Value Added Tax Payable
-50	-7	7	23	1107	27
20972	21281	34	43296	63673	19274
-6543	-6496	6496	398	14957	6113
55076	70296	452	89876	120635	16475
109019	105690		233402	133274	119042
23464	24976		38566	29405	11465
15088	15295		25736	10731	8426
-243	-192	192	-181	1250	
77075	88365	1509	110745	48450	20689
3647	21294	7951	33074	133144	9612
85852	95952	2545	137625	174144	30002
97011	122815	19110	170252	197184	39275
11670	58711	30578	214214	414930	97002
131808	151618	23659	220387	482409	55410
191759	216486	8906	335464	253009	95868
103531	202896	31189	231691	276295	21207
64443	47607	1249	66273	52397	16009
133214	142638		349290	98552	183502
42959	42883		57713	44312	11409
3082	2865		6224	25973	2640

12-13 规模以上高技术产业工业企业主要经济指标（2015年）

单位：万元

行 业	Sector	企业单位数（个） Number of Enterprises (unit)	亏损企业 Loss Making Enterprises
总计	**Total**	**237**	**48**
一、医药制造业	**Pharmaceutical Manufacturing**	**53**	**14**
（一）化学药品制造	Chemical manufacturing	19	6
化学药品原料药制造	Chemical raw materials Medicine manufacturing	4	1
化学药品制剂制造	Chemical preparations manufacturing	15	5
（二）中药饮片加工	Chinese medicine Pieces processing	1	
（三）中成药生产	Chinese medicine production	22	5
（四）兽用药品制造	Veterinary pharmaceutical manufacturing	2	1
（五）生物药品制造	Biopharmaceutical manufacturing	6	2
（六）卫生材料及医药用品制造	Sanitary materials and medical supplies manufacturing	3	
二、航空航天器制造业	**Aerospace & aviation industry**	**40**	**3**
（一）飞机制造	Aircraft Manufacturing	12	1
（二）航天器制造	Spacecraft Manufacturing	4	
（三）航空、航天相关设备制造	Aviation and aerospace-related equipment manufacturing	20	1
（四）其他航空航天器制造	Other aerospace manufacturing	2	
（五）航空航天器修理	Aerospace vehicle repair	2	1
三、电子及通讯设备制造业	**Electronic and communication equipment manufacturing**	**80**	**16**
（一）电子工业专用设备制造	Electronic equipment manufacturing	5	1
（二）光纤、光缆制造	Optical fiber, cable manufacturing	2	
（三）锂离子电池制造	Lithium-ion battery manufacturing	3	2
（四）通信设备制造	Communications equipment manufacturing	16	4
通信系统设备制造	Communications system equipment	14	4
通信终端设备制造	Communication Terminal Equipment	2	
（五）广播电视设备制造	Broadcasting and TV Equipment	3	1
广播电视节目制作及发射设备制造	Radio and television program production and transmission equipment		
广播电视接收设备及器材制造	Radio and television reception apparatus and equipment manufacturing	1	
应用电视设备及其他广播电视设备制造	Application television equipment and other radio and television equipment manufacturing	2	1
（六）雷达及配套设备制造	Radar and ancillary equipment manufacturers	3	1
（七）视听设备制造	Audiovisual equipment manufacturing	1	
电视机制造	TV manufacturing	1	
音响设备制造	Audio Equipment manufacturing		
影视录放设备制造	Video recording equipment manufacturing		
（八）电子器件制造	Electronic device manufacturing	21	4
电子真空器件制造	Electronic vacuum device manufacturing		
半导体分立器件制造	Discrete semiconductor device manufacturing	8	1
集成电路制造	Semiconductor Manufacturing	6	1
光电子器件及其他电子器件制造	Optoelectronic devices and other electronic device manufacturing	7	2
（九）电子元件制造	Electronics Manufacturing	19	2
电子元件及组件制造	Electronic components and component manufacturing	17	2
印刷电路板制造	Printed circuit board manufacturing	2	
（十）其他电子设备制造	Other electronic equipment manufacturing	7	1

Economic Indicators of High Technology Industry

Industrial Enterprises above Designated Size (2015)

(10 000 yuan)

工业总产值（当年价格）Gross Industrial Output Value (At Current Prices)	工业销售产值（当年价）Value of Industry Products Sales (At Current Prices)	出口交货值 Export Delivery Value	从业人员年平均人数（人）Annual Average Employers (person)	资产总计 Total Assets	流动资产合计 Total Working Capitals	固定资产合计 Total Fixed Assets	固定资产原价 Origing Value of Fixed Assets	累计折旧 Accumulative Total Depreciation
12693884	**11712339**	**2978055**	**138491**	**21569789**	**9668136**	**7701789**	**11280084**	**3849941**
1959005	**1763793**	**11077**	**16590**	**1674430**	**1046916**	**399033**	**517856**	**248479**
1081270	963756	2521	8681	863849	554296	216847	244711	126638
26173	21848		722	45564	28773	12297	17818	6075
1055097	941908	2521	7959	818285	525523	204550	226893	120563
8530	8530	8530	11	446	445	1	1	1
540902	497136	26	4938	450334	288244	86699	110878	42590
29079	28755		889	103477	85028	16275	6717	2872
278877	245413		1688	244374	112514	75323	149885	74563
20347	20203		383	11950	6389	3888	5664	1815
3956870	**3749299**	**691716**	**56973**	**7363688**	**3782667**	**1238532**	**2029122**	**928572**
2910914	2778192	533044	44556	5613518	2906625	827917	1359186	576730
397632	397520	1850	6672	1038979	494061	221929	311721	164756
585262	510563	156822	5135	621565	311630	175303	349972	183804
54390	54547		483	72272	57488	11340	5196	2278
8672	8477		127	17354	12863	2043	3047	1004
4728319	**4195185**	**1849809**	**44995**	**9527509**	**3088609**	**5186996**	**6929012**	**1731646**
26873	25085	51	603	62784	50858	8219	10793	3211
97874	75674		570	51090	41582	7739	24538	16799
73465	58118	5177	1028	242302	107280	125842	133221	7379
1113104	1095130	18448	10598	624941	442333	147862	190596	55872
315563	312170	18448	9004	441978	263934	143848	185684	54975
797541	782960		1594	182963	178399	4014	4912	897
15936	15800	7337	336	32398	26911	3210	6043	2833
4155	4155		98	13985	12788	698	1947	1249
11781	11645	7337	238	18413	14123	2512	4096	1584
421945	318668	18811	8263	1022979	674886	233664	339865	111632
3810	3770		83	4425	585	3841	4254	414
3810	3770		83	4425	585	3841	4254	414
2448670	2118315	1735344	12767	6635359	1303593	4536826	6015610	1436641
268443	238894	113389	2415	302550	159907	80847	139966	59519
2001158	1706756	1619742	8688	6254008	1102918	4429959	5840909	1367272
179069	172665	2213	1664	78801	40768	26020	34735	9850
492895	446734	64593	10056	790942	392101	114030	196310	93878
427224	381186	7401	9106	731109	370492	78579	143569	76587
65671	65548	57192	950	59833	21609	35451	52741	17291
33747	37891	48	691	60289	48480	5763	7782	2987

12-13 续表1

单位：万元

行 业	Sector	负债合计 Total Liabilites	流动负债合计 Total Working Liabilities
总计	**Total**	**12404244**	**9505258**
一、医药制造业	**Pharmaceutical Manufacturing**	**850270**	**732583**
（一）化学药品制造	Chemical manufacturing	438355	355124
化学药品原料药制造	Chemical raw materials Medicine manufacturing	21206	20753
化学药品制剂制造	Chemical preparations manufacturing	417149	334371
（二）中药饮片加工	Chinese medicine Pieces processing	359	359
（三）中成药生产	Chinese medicine production	297914	276516
（四）兽用药品制造	Veterinary pharmaceutical manufacturing	30463	30213
（五）生物药品制造	Biopharmaceutical manufacturing	78117	66309
（六）卫生材料及医药用品制造	Sanitary materials and medical supplies manufacturing	5062	4062
二、航空航天器制造业	**Aerospace & aviation industry**	**4388786**	**3253029**
（一）飞机制造	Aircraft Manufacturing	3460667	2624682
（二）航天器制造	Spacecraft Manufacturing	509615	317546
（三）航空、航天相关设备制造	Aviation and aerospace-related equipment manufacturing	381348	287460
（四）其他航空航天器制造	Other aerospace manufacturing	26738	12923
（五）航空航天器修理	Aerospace vehicle repair	10418	10418
三、电子及通讯设备制造业	**Electronic and communication equipment manufacturing**	**5725965**	**4275875**
（一）电子工业专用设备制造	Electronic equipment manufacturing	33555	32364
（二）光纤、光缆制造	Optical fiber, cable manufacturing	28047	28047
（三）锂离子电池制造	Lithium-ion battery manufacturing	170663	96693
（四）通信设备制造	Communications equipment manufacturing	446470	361333
通信系统设备制造	Communications system equipment	304454	223420
通信终端设备制造	Communication Terminal Equipment	142016	137913
（五）广播电视设备制造	Broadcasting and TV Equipment	25395	25005
广播电视节目制作及发射设备制造	Radio and television program production and transmission equipment		
广播电视接收设备及器材制造	Radio and television reception apparatus and equipment manufacturing	11483	11093
应用电视设备及其他广播电视设备制造	Application television equipment and other radio and television equipment manufacturing	13912	13912
（六）雷达及配套设备制造	Radar and ancillary equipment manufacturers	721745	640950
（七）视听设备制造	Audiovisual equipment manufacturing	907	907
电视机制造	TV manufacturing	907	907
音响设备制造	Audio Equipment manufacturing		
影视录放设备制造	Video recording equipment manufacturing		
（八）电子器件制造	Electronic device manufacturing	3688813	2657624
电子真空器件制造	Electronic vacuum device manufacturing		
半导体分立器件制造	Discrete semiconductor device manufacturing	163124	119543
集成电路制造	Semiconductor Manufacturing	3504539	2518295
光电子器件及其他电子器件制造	Optoelectronic devices and other electronic device manufacturing	21150	19786
（九）电子元件制造	Electronics Manufacturing	588322	414961
电子元件及组件制造	Electronic components and component manufacturing	551496	378590
印刷电路板制造	Printed circuit board manufacturing	36826	36371
（十）其他电子设备制造	Other electronic equipment manufacturing	22048	17991

continued 1

(10 000 yuan)

非流动负债 Non-Working Liabilities	所有者权益合计 Total Owners' Equities	实收资本 Total Capital Hold	营业收入 Total Revenue	主营业务收入 Revenue from Principal Business	营业成本 Total Cost	主营业务成本 Cost of Principal Business	营业税金及附加 Taxs and Other Changes	主营业务税金及附加 Taxes and Other Charges on Principal Business
2378404	**9643247**	**4782770**	**11621653**	**11307743**	**9595455**	**8869275**	**39612**	**36531**
100540	**819422**	**255055**	**1664190**	**1658121**	**942372**	**941930**	**11926**	**11887**
71586	420756	126786	990093	989097	568279	567979	6389	6389
283	24358	18000	21269	21069	11777	11777	205	205
71303	396398	108786	968824	968028	556502	556202	6184	6184
	87	500	8530	8530	8360	8260	3	3
21003	152420	70243	451494	451323	238319	238299	3813	3774
250	73014	5200	28755	28755	15719	15719	463	463
6701	166257	50146	168423	163521	97757	97735	1180	1180
1000	6888	2180	16895	16895	13938	13938	78	78
1057328	**2974881**	**916311**	**3732331**	**3459284**	**3419053**	**3272874**	**11855**	**10881**
835985	2152851	731717	2708272	2691924	2565031	2428027	8353	7740
124605	529364	36987	452625	197366	373050	364718	2015	1677
93888	240216	132967	512004	510586	461584	460741	954	931
2850	45514	10640	51009	50994	12890	12890	500	500
	6936	4000	8421	8414	6498	6498	33	33
708500	**4284000**	**3042748**	**4428162**	**4403443**	**3734356**	**3720727**	**10008**	**8625**
1191	29229	15600	24447	23106	17019	16586	158	152
	23044	23825	63731	61465	52471	49723	228	228
73969	71639	72900	57924	57924	51424	51424	236	8
82840	178443	149189	1268569	1260579	1158927	1157130	1569	1569
78737	137497	116189	314899	306908	211826	210029	835	835
4103	40946	33000	953670	953670	947101	947101	734	734
390	7003	8000	15969	15794	12671	12640	48	48
390	2501	2000	4155	4155	3245	3245	43	43
	4502	6000	11814	11639	9426	9395	5	5
80795	301234	61335	385871	384144	337544	336483	1950	801
	3519	3000	3988	3988	3062	3062		
	3519	3000	3988	3988	3062	3062		
305436	2946546	2593014	2102377	2101038	1694478	1694353	3137	3137
33692	139425	54959	227247	226915	199599	199475	394	394
271565	2749471	2498148	1710666	1709987	1360778	1360777	236	236
179	57650	39907	164464	164136	134101	134101	2507	2507
159871	685102	89525	469763	460700	381548	374536	2477	2477
159416	662094	58721	400785	394155	321746	316069	2389	2389
455	23008	30804	68978	66545	59802	58467	88	88
4008	38241	26360	35523	34705	25212	24790	205	205

12-13 续表2

单位：万元

行 业	Sector	销售费用 Expenses for Sales	管理费用 Expenses for Management
总计	**Total**	**532858**	**885647**
一、医药制造业	**Pharmaceutical Manufacturing**	**394636**	**155944**
（一）化学药品制造	Chemical manufacturing	218448	93619
化学药品原料药制造	Chemical raw materials Medicine manufacturing	2531	3956
化学药品制剂制造	Chemical preparations manufacturing	215917	89663
（二）中药饮片加工	Chinese medicine Pieces processing	49	34
（三）中成药生产	Chinese medicine production	138856	45978
（四）兽用药品制造	Veterinary pharmaceutical manufacturing	1676	1088
（五）生物药品制造	Biopharmaceutical manufacturing	34665	14049
（六）卫生材料及医药用品制造	Sanitary materials and medical supplies manufacturing	942	1176
二、航空航天器制造业	**Aerospace & aviation industry**	**45839**	**206155**
（一）飞机制造	Aircraft Manufacturing	35877	130958
（二）航天器制造	Spacecraft Manufacturing	2847	38703
（三）航空、航天相关设备制造	Aviation and aerospace-related equipment manufacturing	5385	30357
（四）其他航空航天器制造	Other aerospace manufacturing	1494	4615
（五）航空航天器修理	Aerospace vehicle repair	236	1522
三、电子及通讯设备制造业	**Electronic and communication equipment manufacturing**	**52940**	**380805**
（一）电子工业专用设备制造	Electronic equipment manufacturing	2157	3635
（二）光纤、光缆制造	Optical fiber, cable manufacturing	2827	3270
（三）锂离子电池制造	Lithium-ion battery manufacturing	2462	9601
（四）通信设备制造	Communications equipment manufacturing	8432	36700
通信系统设备制造	Communications system equipment	8353	33812
通信终端设备制造	Communication Terminal Equipment	79	2888
（五）广播电视设备制造	Broadcasting and TV Equipment	1563	1661
广播电视节目制作及发射设备制造	Radio and television program production and transmission equipment		
广播电视接收设备及器材制造	Radio and television reception apparatus and equipment manufacturing	264	386
应用电视设备及其他广播电视设备制造	Application television equipment and other radio and television equipment manufacturing	1299	1275
（六）雷达及配套设备制造	Radar and ancillary equipment manufacturers	3781	29950
（七）视听设备制造	Audiovisual equipment manufacturing	830	32
电视机制造	TV manufacturing	830	32
音响设备制造	Audio Equipment manufacturing		
影视录放设备制造	Video recording equipment manufacturing		
（八）电子器件制造	Electronic device manufacturing	14750	247175
电子真空器件制造	Electronic vacuum device manufacturing		
半导体分立器件制造	Discrete semiconductor device manufacturing	4109	12431
集成电路制造	Semiconductor Manufacturing	1896	220699
光电子器件及其他电子器件制造	Optoelectronic devices and other electronic device manufacturing	8745	14045
（九）电子元件制造	Electronics Manufacturing	14096	43448
电子元件及组件制造	Electronic components and component manufacturing	12644	41939
印刷电路板制造	Printed circuit board manufacturing	1452	1509
（十）其他电子设备制造	Other electronic equipment manufacturing	2042	5333

continued 2

(10 000 yuan)

财务费用 Financial cost	营业利润 Operating Profit	利润总额 Total Profits	亏损企业亏损额 Total Loss of Deficit Enterprises	利税总额 Total Pre-tax Profits	应付职工薪酬 Salary Payable	本年应交增值税 Value Added Tax Payable
174854	**496267**	**612008**	**69467**	**894609**	**1049815**	**242993**
19804	**131622**	**129612**	**4090**	**286656**	**158225**	**145117**
14692	87687	83498	1241	194571	114194	104683
736	2064	2189	12	4217	3221	1823
13956	85623	81309	1229	190354	110973	102860
75	9	9		13	69	1
4480	19998	21643	1712	56972	27718	31516
228	9582	9726	51	10709	3712	520
207	13707	13988	1086	22855	11218	7687
122	639	748		1536	1314	710
38554	**113559**	**132951**	**17891**	**184365**	**448983**	**39559**
30134	59600	73834	10287	109222	315945	27034
1795	41005	44701		52589	82727	5873
6521	3041	4119	7388	7041	44240	1969
67	9978	10169		15057	5133	4388
37	-65	128	216	456	938	295
105193	**118837**	**227888**	**37440**	**268588**	**332761**	**30694**
130	1120	1110	192	2534	3748	1267
646	4224	4195		6131	4827	1708
1836	-8022	-2157	3365	-1938	9089	-16
3089	52611	59836	23707	71864	59828	10459
2848	49983	57143	23707	59625	49426	1647
241	2628	2693		12239	10402	8812
286	-638	-510	1282	-122	1616	339
149	69	172		488	424	273
137	-707	-682	1282	-610	1192	66
348	16219	17439	3522	20543	47784	1154
9	56	481		481	113	
9	56	481		481	113	
87591	33620	125625	3289	131064	142926	2301
2227	8406	11776	203	13090	15099	920
84576	20935	109347	2997	110559	117637	975
788	4279	4502	89	7415	10190	406
10898	17455	19075	2080	33213	57974	11662
9587	12640	14261	2080	28190	50539	11542
1311	4815	4814		5023	7435	120
360	2192	2794	3	4818	4856	1820

12-13 续表3

单位：万元

行 业	Sector	企业单位数（个） Number of Enterprises (unit)	亏损企业 Loss Making Enterprises
四、计算机及办公设备制造业	**Computer and office equipment manufacturing**	**2**	
（一）计算机整机制造	Computer machine manufacturing		
（二）计算机零部件制造	Computer parts manufacturing		
（三）计算机外围设备制造	Computer peripheral equipment manufacturing	1	
（四）其他计算机制造	Other computer manufacturing	1	
（五）办公设备制造	Office Equipment manufacturing		
复印和胶印设备制造	Photocopying and offset printing equipment manufacturing		
计算器及货币专用设备制造	Calculator and money and special equipment manufacturing		
五、医疗设备及仪器仪表制造业	**Medical equipment and instrumentation manufacturing**	**59**	**13**
（一）医疗仪器设备及器械制造	Medical equipment and device manufacturing	7	2
医疗诊断、监护及治疗设备制造	Medical diagnosis, monitoring and treatment equipment manufacturing	2	1
口腔科用设备及器具制造	Stomatology manufacture equipment and appliances		
医疗实验室及医用消毒设备和器具制造	Medical laboratory and medical sterilization equipment and equipment manufacturing		
医疗、外科及兽医用器械制造	Medical, surgical and veterinary instruments manufacturing		
机械治疗及病房护理设备制造	Mechanical treatment and ward care equipment manufacturing	1	1
假肢、人工器官及植（介）入器械制造	Prostheses, artificial organs and implantable(interventional) device manufacturing	1	
其他治疗设备及器械制造	Other treatment equipment and equipment manufacturing	3	
（二）仪器仪表制造	Instruments manufacturing	52	11
工业自动控制系统装置制造	Manufacture of industrial automation control system devices manufacturing	12	4
电工仪器仪表制造	Electrical Instruments manufacturing	5	2
绘图、计算及测量仪器制造	Drawings, calculation and measurement equipment manufacturing	1	
实验分析仪器制造	Experimental analysis equipment manufacturing	1	
试验机制造	Testing Machine Manufacturing		
供应用仪表及其他通用仪器制造	Supply of manufacturing devices and other general instrument Manufacturing	6	1
环境检测专用仪器仪表制造	Environmental testing special Instruments Manufacturing	3	
运输设备及生产用计数仪表制造	Transport equipment and manufacturing with the counting instrument manufacturing		
导航、气象及海洋专用仪器制造	Navigation, meteorological and oceanographic special equipment manufacturing	1	
农林牧渔专用仪器仪表制造	Agriculture, forestry, animal husbandry and fishery special Instruments manufacturing	1	
地质勘探和地震专用仪器制造	Geological exploration and seismic special equipment manufacturing	8	3
教学专用仪器制造	Teaching special equipment manufacturing		
核子及核辐射测量仪器制造	Nucleon and nuclear radiation measuring instruments manufacturing	2	
电子测量仪器制造	Electronic Measuring Instruments Manufacturing	1	
其他专用仪器制造	Other special equipment manufacturing	3	
光学仪器制造	Optical Instruments Manufacturing	3	
其他仪器仪表制造业	Other instrumentation manufacturing	5	1
六、信息化学品制造业	**Information chemicals manufacturing**	3	2
（一）信息化学品制造	Information Chemical Manufacturing	3	2

continued 3

(10 000 yuan)

工业总产值（当年价格）Gross Industrial Output Value (At Current Prices)	工业销售产值（当年价）Value of Industry Products Sales (At Current Prices)	出口交货值 Export Delivery Value	从业人员年平均人数（人）Annual Average Employers (person)	资产总计 Total Assets	流动资产合计 Total Working Capitals	固定资产合计 Total Fixed Assets	固定资产原价 Origing Value of Fixed Assets	累计折旧 Accumulative Total Depreciation
9388	**10124**		**247**	**17162**	**10392**	**1218**	**2323**	**1105**
6313	7049		187	14577	9998	827	1706	879
3075	3075		60	2585	394	391	617	226
1426737	**1386121**	**64335**	**17787**	**2088638**	**1336257**	**421395**	**683577**	**269378**
37631	36952	38	761	70165	52487	12054	17123	5070
9588	10248	38	238	35682	24149	6666	8640	1976
2432	2353		145	5706	3742	1514	2901	1386
5973	4906		71	4793	1910	2820	3227	407
19638	19445		307	23984	22686	1054	2355	1301
1389106	1349169	64297	17026	2018473	1283770	409341	666454	264308
261011	258370	3491	1701	235711	106579	59412	85449	24951
17990	19972	1204	656	66055	43581	1178	3554	2377
8277	9106	959	208	25431	13917	1472	2534	1061
3147	5013		122	7239	6980	239	599	360
43476	39142		909	46467	36749	4995	7282	3047
121218	121215	31809	900	91150	83386	7567	16851	10433
6584	6584		120	11522	10904	584	1379	795
20369	22209		109	11118	7879	2986	3236	1065
42891	44131	4447	1307	189212	144753	34898	44895	11853
34768	37738	17	802	73496	44216	4376	10560	6116
3458	2955		119	4949	4145	696	1613	923
52421	46068	12038	546	100625	57250	6737	14296	11322
732091	695824	10332	8816	1100626	686894	272544	457308	184764
41405	40842		711	54872	36537	11657	16898	5241
613565	607817	361118	1899	898362	403295	454615	1118194	670761
613565	607817	361118	1899	898362	403295	454615	1118194	670761

12-13 续表4

单位：万元

行业	Sector	负债合计 Total Liabilites	流动负债合计 Total Working Liabilities
四、计算机及办公设备制造业	**Computer and office equipment manufacturing**	**7212**	**6712**
（一）计算机整机制造	Computer machine manufacturing		
（二）计算机零部件制造	Computer parts manufacturing		
（三）计算机外围设备制造	Computer peripheral equipment manufacturing	6086	5586
（四）其他计算机制造	Other computer manufacturing	1126	1126
（五）办公设备制造	Office Equipment manufacturing		
复印和胶印设备制造	Photocopying and offset printing equipment manufacturing		
计算器及货币专用设备制造	Calculator and money and special equipment manufacturing		
五、医疗设备及仪器仪表制造业	**Medical equipment and instrumentation manufacturing**	**1059949**	**883729**
（一）医疗仪器设备及器械制造	Medical equipment and device manufacturing	35458	20488
医疗诊断、监护及治疗设备制造	Medical diagnosis, monitoring and treatment equipment manufacturing	23047	9332
口腔科用设备及器具制造	Stomatology manufacture equipment and appliances		
医疗实验室及医用消毒设备和器具制造	Medical laboratory and medical sterilization equipment and equipment manufacturing		
医疗、外科及兽医用器械制造	Medical, surgical and veterinary instruments manufacturing		
机械治疗及病房护理设备制造	Mechanical treatment and ward care equipment manufacturing	967	467
假肢、人工器官及植（介）入器械制造	Prostheses, artificial organs and implantable(interventional) device manufacturing	2102	1847
其他治疗设备及器械制造	Other treatment equipment and equipment manufacturing	9342	8842
（二）仪器仪表制造	Instruments manufacturing	1024491	863241
工业自动控制系统装置制造	Manufacture of industrial automation control system devices manufacturing	167912	152074
电工仪器仪表制造	Electrical Instruments manufacturing	27729	26154
绘图、计算及测量仪器制造	Drawings, calculation and measurement equipment manufacturing	11712	11712
实验分析仪器制造	Experimental analysis equipment manufacturing	5611	5611
试验机制造	Testing Machine Manufacturing		
供应用仪表及其他通用仪器制造	Supply of manufacturing devices and other general instrument Manufacturing	20868	20448
环境检测专用仪器仪表制造	Environmental testing special Instruments Manufacturing	25761	25406
运输设备及生产用计数仪表制造	Transport equipment and manufacturing with the counting instrument manufacturing		
导航、气象及海洋专用仪器制造	Navigation, meteorological and oceanographic special equipment manufacturing	6251	6251
农林牧渔专用仪器仪表制造	Agriculture, forestry, animal husbandry and fishery special Instruments manufacturing	2723	2723
地质勘探和地震专用仪器制造	Geological exploration and seismic special equipment manufacturing	104982	94942
教学专用仪器制造	Teaching special equipment manufacturing		
核子及核辐射测量仪器制造	Nucleon and nuclear radiation measuring instruments manufacturing	39346	39152
电子测量仪器制造	Electronic Measuring Instruments Manufacturing	1400	1400
其他专用仪器制造	Other special equipment manufacturing	57652	14061
光学仪器制造	Optical Instruments Manufacturing	529539	442867
其他仪器仪表制造业	Other instrumentation manufacturing	23005	20440
六、信息化学品制造业	**Information chemicals manufacturing**	372062	353330
（一）信息化学品制造	Information Chemical Manufacturing	372062	353330

continued 4

(10 000 yuan)

非流动负债 Non-Working Liabilities	所有者权益合计 Total Owners' Equities	实收资本 Total Capital Hold	营业收入 Total Revenue	主营业务收入 Revenue from Principal Business	营业成本 Total Cost	主营业务成本 Cost of Principal Business	营业税金及附加 Taxs and Other Changes	主营业务税金及附加 Taxes and Other Charges on Principal Business
500	**9951**	**5600**	**10209**	**10124**	**4769**	**4743**	**99**	**99**
500	8492	4600	7081	7049	2857	2856	78	78
	1459	1000	3128	3075	1912	1887	21	21
495585	**1028692**	**372611**	**1284962**	**1279325**	**1022131**	**460046**	**5646**	**4961**
14970	34709	14754	37959	37791	19633	19532	200	200
13715	12635	9334	11881	11795	7398	7339	55	55
500	4740	1000	2354	2354	1256	1256	26	26
255	2691	1020	4197	4197	2668	2668	5	5
500	14643	3400	19527	19445	8311	8269	114	114
480615	993983	357857	1247003	1241534	1002498	440514	5446	4761
6433	67799	100356	179326	178988	137908	137741	821	821
1275	38325	12350	21541	21536	18985	18985	214	214
	13719	5900	9106	7663	5992	5270	37	29
	1628	7800	5013	5013	3993	3993	34	34
420	25599	16800	39142	39142	27706	27706	280	280
355	65389	13267	121917	121213	92419	92419	1041	997
	5271	1303	10400	10400	7678	7678	150	150
	8396	2000	22209	22209	19585	19585	13	13
10040	84230	46992	46650	44629	31726	28924	530	432
194	34150	8811	38646	38646	26691	26691	564	29
	3549	600	3193	2955	1754	1687	28	28
22867	42973	16070	44387	44387	26394	26394	579	579
439021	571087	116377	663060	662966	567235	9074	940	940
10	31868	9231	42413	41787	34432	34367	215	215
15951	526301	190445	501799	497446	472774	468955	78	78
15951	526301	190445	501799	497446	472774	468955	78	78

12-13 续表5

单位：万元

行 业	Sector	销售费用 Expenses for Sales	管理费用 Expenses for Management
四、计算机及办公设备制造业	**Computer and office equipment manufacturing**	**874**	**2727**
（一）计算机整机制造	Computer machine manufacturing		
（二）计算机零部件制造	Computer parts manufacturing		
（三）计算机外围设备制造	Computer peripheral equipment manufacturing	381	2120
（四）其他计算机制造	Other computer manufacturing	493	607
（五）办公设备制造	Office Equipment manufacturing		
复印和胶印设备制造	Photocopying and offset printing equipment manufacturing		
计算器及货币专用设备制造	Calculator and money and special equipment manufacturing		
五、医疗设备及仪器仪表制造业	**Medical equipment and instrumentation manufacturing**	**36458**	**126478**
（一）医疗仪器设备及器械制造	Medical equipment and device manufacturing	4728	5763
医疗诊断、监护及治疗设备制造	Medical diagnosis, monitoring and treatment equipment manufacturing	1535	3006
口腔科用设备及器具制造	Stomatology manufacture equipment and appliances		
医疗实验室及医用消毒设备和器具制造	Medical laboratory and medical sterilization equipment and equipment manufacturing		
医疗、外科及兽医用器械制造	Medical, surgical and veterinary instruments manufacturing		
机械治疗及病房护理设备制造	Mechanical treatment and ward care equipment manufacturing	436	740
假肢、人工器官及植（介）入器械制造	Prostheses, artificial organs and implantable(interventional) device manufacturing	474	988
其他治疗设备及器械制造	Other treatment equipment and equipment manufacturing	2283	1029
（二）仪器仪表制造	Instruments manufacturing	31730	120715
工业自动控制系统装置制造	Manufacture of industrial automation control system devices manufacturing	7532	9649
电工仪器仪表制造	Electrical Instruments manufacturing	625	1912
绘图、计算及测量仪器制造	Drawings, calculation and measurement equipment manufacturing	1330	1211
实验分析仪器制造	Experimental analysis equipment manufacturing	288	577
试验机制造	Testing Machine Manufacturing		
供应用仪表及其他通用仪器制造	Supply of manufacturing devices and other general instrument Manufacturing	3519	5221
环境检测专用仪器仪表制造	Environmental testing special Instruments Manufacturing	6240	6612
运输设备及生产用计数仪表制造	Transport equipment and manufacturing with the counting instrument manufacturing		
导航、气象及海洋专用仪器制造	Navigation, meteorological and oceanographic special equipment manufacturing	40	680
农林牧渔专用仪器仪表制造	Agriculture, forestry, animal husbandry and fishery special Instruments manufacturing	448	736
地质勘探和地震专用仪器制造	Geological exploration and seismic special equipment manufacturing	2692	8279
教学专用仪器制造	Teaching special equipment manufacturing		
核子及核辐射测量仪器制造	Nucleon and nuclear radiation measuring instruments manufacturing	1778	6101
电子测量仪器制造	Electronic Measuring Instruments Manufacturing	330	827
其他专用仪器制造	Other special equipment manufacturing	2058	4955
光学仪器制造	Optical Instruments Manufacturing	2249	70742
其他仪器仪表制造业	Other instrumentation manufacturing	2601	3213
六、信息化学品制造业	**Information chemicals manufacturing**	2111	13538
（一）信息化学品制造	Information Chemical Manufacturing	2111	13538

continued 5

(10 000 yuan)

财务费用 Financial cost	营业利润 Operating Profit	利润总额 Total Profits	亏损企业亏损额 Total Loss of Deficit Enterprises	利税总额 Total Pre-tax Profits	应付职工薪酬 Salary Payable	本年应交增值税 Value Added Tax Payable
191	**1390**	**1627**		**2505**	**2195**	**780**
192	1293	1531		2262	1985	653
-1	97	96		243	210	127
5915	**91963**	**79917**	**7185**	**112145**	**92671**	**26584**
1020	6617	6989	831	8490	4228	1302
867	-979	-664	705	-380	1712	229
47	-151	-126	126	110	654	210
37	26	58		66	320	4
69	7721	7721		8694	1542	859
4895	85346	72928	6354	103655	88443	25282
670	22572	23509	2224	30724	25612	6393
98	-372	-234	1068	152	2570	172
-84	620	807		1151	1103	307
-22	-62	59		318	778	225
187	1976	2301	209	4605	4420	2025
-1183	16820	17663		22546	9756	3842
39	1796	1801		2178	1420	227
108	1320	1397		1430	398	20
820	2296	2722	2698	5064	11600	1812
488	7666	7830		11437	4682	3044
49	205	244		501	645	230
829	9573	10560		12771	3800	1632
2562	18708	1313		6555	15154	4302
334	2228	2956	155	4223	6505	1051
5197	38896	40013	2861	40350	14980	259
5197	38896	40013	2861	40350	14980	259

12-14 规模以上工业企业主要经济效益指标（2015年）

行 业	Sector	总资产贡献率（%） Ratio of Total Assets to Industrial Output Value (%)	资产负债率（%） Assets-Liability Ratio (%)
总计	**Total**	**5.7**	**57.3**
按工业行业大类分	**Grouped by Sector**		
煤炭开采和洗选业	Mining and Washing of Coal		
石油和天然气开采业	Extraction of Petroleum and Natural Gas		
黑色金属矿采选业	Mining and Processing of Ferrous Metal Ores		
有色金属矿采选业	Mining and Processing of Non-ferrous Metal Ores		
非金属矿采选业	Mining and Processing of Nonmetal Ores		
开采辅助活动	Mining Auxiliary Activities	12.1	29.9
其他采矿业	Mining of Other Ores		
农副食品加工业	Processing of Food from Agricultural Porducts	4.0	78.5
食品制造业	Manufacture of Foods	14.9	37.9
酒、饮料和精制茶制造业	Manufacture of Alcohol,Beverages and Tea	13.5	61.1
烟草制品业	Manufacture of Tobacco	11.4	53.1
纺织业	Manufacture of Textile	4.2	66.8
纺织服装、服饰业	Textile, Garments industry	5.3	68.9
皮革、毛皮、羽毛及其制品和制鞋业	Manufacture of Leather, Fur, Feather and Related Products	6.8	41.1
木材加工和木、竹、藤、棕、草制品业	Processing of Timber, Manufacture of Wood,Plam and Straw Products	3.2	63.8
家具制造业	Manufacture of Furniture	12.5	54.6
造纸及纸制品业	Manufacture of Paper and Paper Products	8.2	48.7
印刷和记录媒介复制	Printing,Reproduction of Recording Media	10.4	32.4
文教、工美、体育和娱乐用品制造业	Manufacture of Articles For Cultural,Educational and Sports Activities	1.8	96.1

Main Indicators of Economic Benefit of Industrial Enterprises above Designated Size (2015)

流动资产周转率（次） Rate of Annual Turnover Working Capitals (times)	成本费用利润率（%） Ratio of Profits to Cost (%)	工业产品销售率（%） Proportion of Industrial Products Sold (%)	产值利税率（%） Ratio of Output Value to Profits and Tax (%)	每百元固定资产实现利税（元） Profit and Tax per 100 yuan of Fixed Assets (yuan)	每百元销售收入实现利税（元） Profit and Tax per 100 yuan of Sales Revenue (yuan)
1.3	**4.8**	**94.5**	**6.9**	**16.2**	**7.8**
0.8	14.4	99.3	15.3	56.9	23.5
2.9	0.4	98.2	1.1	11.4	1.4
3.7	5.2	95.2	7.1	43.4	8.4
2.0	8.6	100.8	12.6	29.0	14.6
1.0	20.8	101.4	27.5	78.5	25.4
1.2	5.2	87.4	7.4	8.3	8.8
0.6	3.8	93.0	7.4	108.0	9.5
2.0	5.2	100.0	6.1	73.2	5.5
1.3	-1.5	83.6	1.9	4.7	2.9
1.3	7.6	89.5	12.0	49.3	13.2
3.2	2.8	99.3	4.0	22.9	4.1
2.2	5.9	99.6	9.4	26.5	9.8
2.8	0.4	99.9	0.5	90.4	0.6

12-14 续表1

行　业	Sector	总资产贡献率（%） Ratio of Total Assets to Industrial Output Value (%)	资产负债率（%） Assets-Liability Ratio (%)
石油加工业、炼焦和核燃料加工业	Processing of Petroleum, Cokeing,Processing of Nuclear and Nuclear Fuel	2.2	62.7
化学原料及化学制品制造业	Manufacture of Raw Chemical Materials and Chemical Products	6.0	51.3
医药制造业	Manufacture of Medicines	17.6	50.8
化学纤维制造业	Manufacture of Chemical Fibers	7.0	58.3
橡胶和塑料制品业	Manufacture of Rubber and Plastics	5.5	77.4
非金属矿物制品业	Manufacture of Non-metallic Mineral Products	7.2	61.9
黑色金属冶炼和压延加工业	Smelting and Pressing of Ferrous Metals	15.5	46.7
有色金属冶炼和压延加工业	Smelting and Pressing of Non-ferrous Metals	5.0	31.7
金属制品业	Manufacture of Metal Products	3.7	61.8
通用设备制造业	Manufacture of General Purpose Machinery	4.7	54.4
专用设备制造业	Manufacture of Special Equipment	5.2	43.0
汽车制造业	Manufacture of Motor Vehicle	3.5	60.1
铁路、船舶、航空航天和其他运输设备制造业	Railways, Shipbuilding,Aerospace and Other Transportation Equipment Manufacturing Industry	3.7	58.8
电气机械和器材制造业	Manufacture of Electric Equipment and Machinery	6.9	50.6
计算机、通讯和其他电子设备制造业	Manufacture of Communication Equipment, Computers and other Electronic Equipment	3.1	59.9
仪器仪表制造业	Manufacture of Measuring Instruments and Machinery	5.4	50.8
其他制造业	Manufacture of Other Manufacturing	9.6	50.8
废弃资源综合利用业	Recycling and Disposal of Waste		
金属制品、机械和设备修理业	Metal Products,Machinery and Equipment Repair Industry	6.8	65.3
电力、热力的生产和供应业	Production and Supply of Electric Power and Heat Power	8.5	82.5
燃气生产和供应业	Gas Mining and Supplying Industry	8.0	62.4
水的生产和供应业	Production and Supply of Water	3.4	61.3

continued 1

流动资产周转率（次） Rate of Annual Turnover Working Capitals (times)	成本费用利润率（%） Ratio of Profits to Cost (%)	工业产品销售率（%） Proportion of Industrial Products Sold (%)	产值利税率（%） Ratio of Output Value to Profits and Tax (%)	每百元固定资产实现利税（元） Profit and Tax per 100 yuan of Fixed Assets (yuan)	每百元销售收入实现利税（元） Profit and Tax per 100 yuan of Sales Revenue (yuan)
3.7	-3.4	100.7	0.9	2.5	1.2
1.4	5.7	94.0	6.5	14.3	7.4
1.6	8.6	90.0	14.6	71.8	17.3
1.8	10.5	97.5	8.0	9.8	8.3
0.9	5.6	86.7	7.9	23.7	8.6
2.0	3.4	95.5	5.1	26.3	5.6
3.3	5.7	95.7	7.2	39.8	7.7
1.8	5.4	91.1	6.4	32.1	7.1
1.0	2.9	97.0	4.5	10.1	5.1
0.6	7.4	100.6	9.9	30.9	10.7
0.8	7.3	92.3	9.1	22.1	10.2
1.6	1.1	93.6	2.9	13.5	3.6
1.0	4.4	94.4	5.8	20.3	6.6
1.0	6.5	94.8	8.3	38.6	9.6
1.5	5.5	89.1	5.8	5.2	6.2
1.0	6.3	97.1	7.5	25.3	8.3
1.1	5.1	94.9	9.9	57.4	9.9
1.0	3.7	98.5	15.1	85.4	8.4
3.6	5.4	99.6	15.7	7.9	12.0
1.6	8.7	99.3	11.7	24.1	12.8
1.1	3.4	100.0	7.3	5.7	7.4

12-15 规模以上大中型工业企业主要经济效益指标(2015年)

行　业	Sector	总资产贡献率（%） Ratio of Total Assets to Industrial Output Value (%)	资产负债率（%） Assets-Liability Ratio (%)
总计	**Total**	**5.4**	**57.4**
按国民经济行业分	**Grouped by Sector**		
煤炭开采和洗选业	Mining and Washing of Coal		
石油和天然气开采业	Extraction of Petroleum and Natural Gas		
黑色金属矿采选业	Mining and Processing of Ferrous Metal Ores		
有色金属矿采选业	Mining and Processing of Non-ferrous Metal Ores		
非金属矿采选业	Mining and Processing of Nonmetal Ores		
开采辅助活动	Mining Auxiliary Activities	12.8	28.3
其他采矿业	Mining of other Ores		
农副食品加工业	Processing of Food from Agricultural Porducts	0.9	91.4
食品制造业	Manufacture of Foods	17.3	33.1
酒、饮料和精制茶制造业	Manufacture of Alcohol,Beverages and Tea	15.0	58.0
烟草制品业	Manufacture of Tobacco		
纺织业	Manufacture of Textile	0.9	71.6
纺织服装、服饰业	Textile, apparel industry	6.5	84.6
皮革、毛皮、羽毛及其制品和制鞋业	Leather fur feathers and its products and footwear	7.4	45.2
木材加工和木、竹、藤、棕、草制品业	Processing of Timber,Manufacture of Wood,Plam and Straw Products	3.0	64.0
家具制造业	Manufacture of Furniture	4.1	80.0
造纸及纸制品业	Manufacture of Paper and Paper Products	0.3	64.4
印刷和记录媒介复制业	Printing,Reproduction of Recording Media	10.0	27.1
文教、工美、体育和娱乐用品制造业	Manufacture of Articles For Cultural,Educational and Sports Activities		

The Main Economic Indicators over the Size of Above-scale and Medium-sized Industrial Enterprises (2015)

流动资产周转率（次）Rate of Annual Turnover Working Capitals (times)	成本费用利润率（%）Ratio of Profits to Cost (%)	工业产品销售率（%）Proportion of Industrial Products Sold (%)	产值利税率（%）Ratio of Output Value to Profits and Tax (%)	每百元固定资产实现利税（元）Profit and Tax per 100 yuan of Fixed Assets (yuan)	每百元销售收入实现利税（元）Profit and Tax per 100 yuan of Sales Revenue (yuan)
1.2	**5.1**	**94.5**	**7.6**	**14.4**	**8.6**
0.8	16.0	99.3	16.0	64.7	25.2
1.2	-1.2	97.7	-0.3	-3.0	-0.5
3.2	6.4	96.8	8.6	55.6	10.5
1.9	9.7	101.6	14.6	30.7	17.2
0.8	0.8	98.2	3.0	1.2	2.9
0.6	2.2	92.6	9.1	153.8	9.3
2.3	6.0	99.9	6.2	69.7	5.9
1.1	-2.6	82.1	2.0	3.8	3.2
1.0	3.0	104.4	5.8	15.4	5.9
1.1	-0.1	100.0	0.4	2.5	0.4
1.7	6.0	101.8	11.2	24.8	11.5

12-15 续表1

行 业	Sector	总资产贡献率（%） Ratio of Total Assets to Industrial Output Value (%)	资产负债率（%） Assets-Liability Ratio (%)
石油加工、炼焦和核燃料加工业	Processing of Petroleum, Cokeing,Processing of Nuclear and Nuclear Fuel	1.3	64.8
化学原料和化学制品制造业	Manufacture of Raw Chemical Materials and Chemical Products	5.6	47.8
医药制造业	Manufacture of Medicines	21.5	46.8
化学纤维制造业	Manufacture of Chemical Fibers		
橡胶和塑料制品业	Manufacture of Rubber and Plastics	4.8	82.0
非金属矿物制品业	Manufacture of Non-metallic Mineral Products	13.4	56.9
黑色金属冶炼和压延加工业	Smelting and Pressing of Ferrous Metals	-0.7	82.3
有色金属冶炼和压延加工业	Smelting and Pressing of Non-ferrous Metals	4.7	25.9
金属制品业	Manufacture of Metal Products	3.0	65.9
通用设备制造业	Manufacture of General Purpose Machinery	4.5	54.7
专用设备制造业	Manufacture of Special Equipment	5.1	43.0
汽车制造业	Manufacture of Motor Vehicle	3.2	60.4
铁路、船舶、航空航天和其他运输设备制造业	Railways,Shipbuilding,Aerospace and Other Transportation Equipment Manufacturing Industry	3.3	60.1
电气机械和器材制造业	Manufacture of Electric Equipment and Machinery	6.5	47.1
计算机、通信和其他电子设备制造业	Manufacture of Communication Equipment, Computers and other Electronic Equipment	2.9	60.2
仪器仪表制造业	Manufacture of Measuring Instruments and Machinery	4.7	50.4
其他制造业	Manufacture of Other Manufacturing		
废弃资源综合利用	Recycling and Disposal of Waste		
金属制品、机械和设备修理业	Metal Products,Machinery and Equipment Repair Industry		
电力、热力生产和供应业	Production and Supply of Electric Power and Heat Power	8.8	82.1
燃气生产和供应业	Gas Mining and Supplying Industry	8.4	64.6
水的生产和供应业	Production and Supply of Water	3.6	61.4

continued 1

流动资产周转率（次）Rate of Annual Turnover Working Capitals (times)	成本费用利润率（%）Ratio of Profits to Cost (%)	工业产品销售率（%）Proportion of Industrial Products Sold (%)	产值利税率（%）Ratio of Output Value to Profits and Tax (%)	每百元固定资产实现利税（元）Profit and Tax per 100 yuan of Fixed Assets (yuan)	每百元销售收入实现利税（元）Profit and Tax per 100 yuan of Sales Revenue (yuan)
7.0	-5.0	100.0	0.2	0.5	0.3
1.1	7.2	93.2	7.8	12.6	9.2
1.7	9.5	90.0	17.1	91.6	19.0
0.6	6.8	96.5	9.8	21.6	10.1
1.9	7.9	89.2	11.5	33.5	13.2
0.8	-3.4	88.3	-2.7	-2.7	-3.4
1.7	6.2	89.8	7.2	32.9	8.1
0.8	2.8	98.9	3.9	7.6	4.4
0.5	8.9	103.6	11.9	31.0	12.7
0.7	9.6	91.3	11.2	22.3	12.5
1.6	0.9	93.5	2.6	12.5	3.3
0.9	4.1	95.2	5.6	18.7	6.4
0.7	9.7	95.4	11.7	32.6	14.7
1.6	5.3	88.7	5.5	4.7	5.9
1.0	5.8	97.5	6.5	19.3	7.4
4.8	5.1	100.0	16.2	7.8	12.0
1.5	10.2	99.9	15.0	25.1	14.9
1.1	3.0	100.0	7.0	6.6	7.0

12-16 规模以上工业主要产品生产能力（2015年）

Production Capacity of main Products of Industrial Enterprises above Designated Size（2015）

指 标	Item	2015
原煤	Coal	
卷烟	Cigarettes	
棉纺锭（锭）	Cotton Spindles （unit）	292220
气流纺锭（头）	Air Spindles（unit）	14467
棉布织机（台）	Cotton Loom （unit）	1492
原油加工能力（吨）	Crude Oil Processing Capacity (ton)	2100
农用氮、磷、钾化学肥料总计（折纯）（吨）	Chemical Fertilizers （ton)	80000
初级形态的塑料（吨）	Plastic in Primary Form (ton)	8000
化学纤维（吨）	Chemical Fibre (ton)	25004
硅酸盐水泥熟料（吨）	Portland Cement Clinker (ton)	1500000
水泥（吨）	Cement （ton)	4439524
平板玻璃（重量箱）	Plate Glass (Weight case)	267543
生铁（吨）	Pig Iron (ton)	
钢材（吨）	Rolled Steel (ton)	620200
铁合金（吨）	Ferroalloy (ton)	6000
金属切削机床（台）	Metal-cutting Machine Tools （unit）	8380
汽车（辆）	Motor Vehicles（unit)	573000
其中：基本型乘用车（辆）	Basic Passenger Vehicles（unit)	280000
运动型多用途乘用车（辆）	Sport Utility Vehicle （unit)	20000
交叉型多用途乘用车（辆）	Cross Utility Vehicle （unit)	80000
载货汽车（辆）	Trucks（unit）	190000
微型计算机设备（台）	Micro Computer Equipment （unit）	20000
移动通信手持机（台）	Mobile Handset （unit）	7840900
彩色电视机（台）	Color TV Set （unit）	46576
发电设备容量总计（万千瓦）	Installed Capacity of Power Generation （10 000kw）	367
其中：火电设备容量（万千瓦）	Thermal Power（10 000kw）	287
水电设备容量（万千瓦）	Hydropower（10 000kw）	70
风电设备容量（万千瓦）	Wind Power （10 000kw）	10

主要统计指标解释

工业 指从事自然资源的开采，对采掘品和农产品进行加工和再加工的物质生产部门。具体包括：（1）对自然资源的开采，如采矿、晒盐等（但不包括禽兽捕猎和水产捕捞）；（2）对农副产品的加工、再加工，如粮油加工、食品加工、缫丝、纺织、制革等；（3）对采掘品的加工、再加工，如炼铁、炼钢、化工生产、石油加工、机器制造、木材加工等，以及电力、自来水、煤气的生产和供应等；（4）对工业品的修理、翻新，如机器设备的修理、交通运输工具（如汽车）的修理等。

工业统计调查单位为独立核算法人工业企业。

独立核算法人工业企业指从事工业生产经营活动的单位。独立核算法人工业企业应同时具备以下条件：①依法成立，有自己的名称、组织机构和场所，能够承担民事责任；②独立拥有和使用资产，承担负债，有权与其他单位签订合同；③独立核算盈亏，并能够编制资产负债表。

国有及国有控股企业 指国有企业加上国有控股企业。国有企业（即原全民所有制工业或国营工业）指企业全部资产归国家所有，并按《中华人民共和国企业法人登记管理条例》规定登记注册的非公司制的经济组织。包括国有企业、国有独资公司和国有联营企业。1957年以前的公私合营和私营工业，后均改造为国营工业，1992年改为国有工业，这部分工业的资料不单独分列时，均包括在国有企业内。国有控股企业是对混合所有制经济的企业进行的“国有控股”分类。它是指这些企业的全部资产中国有资产（股份）相对其他所有者中的任何一个所有者占资（股）最多的企业。该分组反映了国有经济控股情况。

本篇涉及的其他企业登记注册类型的解释详见综合篇。

轻工业 指主要提供生活消费品和制作手工工具的工业。按其所使用的原料不同，可分为两大类：（1）以农产品为原料的轻工业，是指直接或间接以农产品为基本原料的轻工业。主要包括食品制造、饮料制造、烟草加工、纺织、缝纫、皮革和毛皮制作、造纸以及印刷等工业；（2）以非农产品为原料的轻工业，是指以工业品为原料的轻工业。主要包括文教体育用品、化学药品制造、合成纤维制造、日用化学制品、日用玻璃制品、日用金属制品、手工工具制造、医疗器械制造、文化和办公用机械制造等工业。

重工业 指为国民经济各部门提供物质技术基础的主要生产资料的工业。按其生产性质和产品用途，可以分为下列三类：（1）采掘（伐）工业，是指对自然资源的开采，包括石油开采、煤炭开采、金属矿开采、非金属矿开采等工业；（2）原材料工业，指向国民经济各部门提供基本材料、动力和燃料的工业。包括金属冶炼及加工、炼焦及焦炭、化学、化工：原料、水泥、人造板以及电力、石油和煤炭加工等工业；（3）加工工业，是指对工业原材料进行再加工制造的工业。包括装备国民经济各部门的机械设备制造工业、金属结构、水泥制品等工业，以及为农业提供的生产资料如化肥、农药等工业。

根据上述划分原则，修理业中以重工业产品为修理作业对象的划为重工业，反之划为轻工业。

工业总产值

（1）定义：

工业总产值是工业企业在一定时期内生产的以货币形式表现的工业最终产品和提供工业性劳务活动的总价值量。它反映一定时间内工业生产的总规模和总水平。

（2）计算原则：

工业生产的原则，即凡是企业在报告期生产的经检验合格的产品，不管是否在报告期销售，均包括在内。

最终产品的原则，即凡是计入工业总产值的产品，必须是本企业生产的经检验合格的，不需要再进行任何加工的最终产品。如果企业有中间产品（半成品）对外销售，则对外销售的中间产品应视为企业的最终产品。

工厂法原则，即工业总产值是以下业企业作为基本计算（核算）单位，即按企业的最终产品计算工业总产值。按这种方法计算的工业总产值，不允许同一产品价值在企业内部重复计算，不能把企业内部各个车间（分厂）生产的成果相加，但允许企业间的重复计算。

（3）内容及计算方法：

1995年全国工业普查对工业总产值（原规定）的内容及计算原则和方法做了某些修订，修订后的工业总产值（新规定）包括三项内容：即本期生产成品价值、对外加工费收入、在制品半成品期末期初差额价值三部分。

本期生产成品价值指企业本期生产，并在报告期内不再进行加工，经检验、包装入库的全部工业成品（半成品）价值合计，包括企业生产的自制设备及提供给本企业在建工程、其他非工业部门和福利部门等单位使用的成品价值。本期生产成品价值为按自备原材料生产的产品的数量乘以本期不含增值税（销项税额）的产品实际销售平均单价计算；会计核算中按成本价格转帐的自制设备和自产自用的成品，按成本价格计算生产成品价值。生产成品价值中不包括用定货者来料加工的成品（半成品）价值。

对外加工费收入指企业在报告期内完成的对外承接的工业品加工（包括用定货者来料加工产品）的加工费收入和对外工业修理作业所取得的加工费收入。对外加工费收入按不含增值税（销项税额）的价格计算，可根据会计“产品销售收入”科目的有关资料取得。

对于本企业对内非工业部门提供的加工修理、设备安装的劳务收入，如果企业会计核算基础较好，能取得这部分资料，而且这部分价值所占比重较大，应包括在对外加工费收入中。

自制半成品在制品期末期初差额价值指企业报告期在制品期末减期初的差额价值，本指标一般可以从会计核算资料中取得。如果会计产品成本核算中不计算半成品、在制品的成本，则总产值中也不包括这部分价值，反之则包括。

（4）工业总产值统计范围变化和计算方法修订情况：

1984年以前工业总产值不包括村办工业，村办工业总产值划归农业。1984年以后工业总产值包括村办工业。

1995年工业普查对工业总产值计算方法做了修订，即从1995年始按新修订（新规定）方法计算工业总产值。新规定与原规定的区别如下：

全价与加工费的计算原则不同：新规定为凡自备原材料，不论其生产繁简程度如何，一律按全价计算工业总产值；凡来料加工，允许按加工费计算工业总产值。原规定则视生产加工的繁简程度不同，规定哪些行业按全价，哪些行业按加工费计算工业总产值。

自制半成品、在产品期末期初差额价值的计算原则不同：新规定要求，凡会计产品成本核算时计算了成本的差额价值，总产值中就应包括，否则可不包括；原规定则按生产周期六个月的界限区分，凡生产周期六个月以上的企业，总产值计算中应包括这部分差额价值，否则可不包括。

计算价格不同：新规定按不含增值税（销项税额）的价格计算；原规定则按含增值税（销项税额）的价格计算。

工业增加值 指工业企业在报告期内以货币表现的工业生产活动的最终成果。

工业增加值有两种计算方法：一是生产法，即工业总产出减去工业中间投入加上应交增值税；二是收入法，即从收入的角度出发，根据生产要素在生产过程中应得到的收入份额计算，具体构成项目有固定资产折旧、劳动者报酬、生产税净额、营业盈余，这种方法也称要素分配法。本年鉴中的工业增加值是以收入法计算的。

生产法工业增加值的计算方法为：

工业增加值＝工业总产出-工业中间投入+应交增值税

（1）工业总产出：指工业企业在一定时期内工业生产活动的总成果。工业总产出包括：成品生产价值，对外加工费收入，自制半成品、在产品期末期初差额价值。1995年后用新规定计算的工业总产值代替。

（2）工业中间投入：指工业企业在工业生产活动中消耗的外购物质产品和对外支付的服务费用。服务费用包括支付给物质生产部门（工业、农业、批发零售贸易业、建筑业、运输邮电业）的服务费用和支付给非物质生产部门（如保险、金融、文化教育、科学研究、医疗卫生、行政管理等）的服务费用。工业中间投入的确定须遵循以下原则：必须从外部购入的，并已计入工业总产出的产品和服务价值；必须是本期投入生产，并一次性消耗掉（包括本期摊销的低值易耗品等）的产品和服务价值。

工业中间投入包括直接材料费用、制造费用中的工业中间投入、管理费用中的工业中间投入、销售费用中的工业中间投入和利息支出五部分。

资产总计 指企业拥有或控制的能以货币计量的经济资源，包括各种财产、债权和其他权利。资产按流动性分为流动资产、长期投资、固定资产、无形资产、递延资产和其他资产。该指标根据企业会计“资产负债表”中“资产总计”项目的期末数增列。

流动资产 指企业可以在一年内或者超过一年的一个生产周期内变现或者耗用的资产，包括现金及各种存款、短期投资，应收及预付款项、存货等。

固定资产原价 指企业在建造、购置、安装、改建、扩建、技术改造某项固定资产时所支出的全部货币总额。它一般包括买价、包装费、运杂费和安装费等。

固定资产净值 指固定资产原价减去历年已提折旧额后的净额。计算公式为：

固定资产净值=固定资产原价-累计折旧

负债合计 指企业所承担的能以货币计量，将以资产或劳务偿付的债务，偿还形式包括货币、资产或提供劳务。负债一般按偿还期长短分为流动负债和长期负债。根据会计“资产负债表”中“负债合计”的年末数填列。

所有者权益合计 指企业投资人对企业净资产的所有权。企业净资产为企业全部资产与企业全部负债的差额，包括实收资本、资本公积、盈余公积、未分配利润等。根据会计“资产负债表”中“所有者权益”项的期末数填列。

主营业务收入 指会计“利润表”中对应指标的本年累计数。未执行2001年《企业会计制度》的企业，用“产品销售收入”的本期累计数代替。

主营业务成本 指会计“利润表”中对应指标的本年累计数。未执行2001年《企业会计制度》的企业，用“产品销售成本”的本期累计数代替。

主营业务税金及附加 指会计“利润表”中对应指标的本年累计数。未执行2001年《企业会计制度》的企业，用“产品销售税金及附加”的本期累计数代替。

利润总额 指企业在生产经营过程中各种收入扣除各种耗费后的盈余，反映企业在报告期内实现的盈亏总额，包括营业利润、补贴收入、投资净收益和营业外收支净额。根据会计“利润表”中的对应指标的本期累计数填列。

本年应交增值税 指企业按税法规定，从事货物销售或提供加工、修理修配劳务等增加货物价值的活动本期应交纳的税金。指企业在报告期应交增值税额。计算公式为：

本年应交增值税=销项税额-（进项税额-进项税额转出）-出口抵减内销产品应纳税额-减免税款+出口退税

本年进项税额 指工业企业在报告期内购入货物或接受应税劳务而支付的、准予从销项税额中抵扣的增值税额。

本年销项税额 指工业企业在报告期内销售货物或提供应税劳务应收取的增值税额。

从业人员平均人数 是指报告期内每天拥有的从业人员人数。其计算公式为：

月平均人数=报告月内每天实有人数之和／报告月日历日数

季平均人数=季内各月平均人数之和／3

年平均人数=年内各月平均人数之和／12

总资产贡献率 反映企业全部资产的获利能力，是企业经营业绩和管理水平的集中体现，是评价和考核企业盈利能力的核心指标。计算公式为：

总资产贡献率（%）=（利润总额+税金总额+利息支出）／平均资产总额×100%

公式中：税金总额为产品销售税金及附加与应交增值税之和；平均资产总额为期初期末资产之和的算术平均值。

资产负债率 该指标既反映企业经营风险的大小，也反映企业利用债权人提供的资金从事经营活动的能力。计算公式为：

资产负债率（%）=负债总额／资产总额×100%

资产与负债均为报告期期末数。

流动资产周转次数 指一定时期内流动资产完成的周转次数，反映投入工业企业流动资金的周转速度。计算公式为：

流动资产周转次数：产品销售收入／全部流动资产平均余额

公式中：全部流动资产平均余额为期初和期末的流动资产之和的算术平均值。

成本费用利润率 反映企业投入的生产成本及费用的经济效益，同时也反映企业降低成本所取得的经济效益。计算公式为：

成本费用利润率（%）=利润总额／成本费用总额×100%

公式中：成本费用总额为产品销售成本、销售费用、管理费用、财务费用之和。

产品销售率 该指标反映工业产品已实现销售的程度，是分析工业产销衔接情况，研究工业产品满足社会需求的指标。计算公式为：

产品销售率（%）=工业销售产值／工业总产值（现价）×100%

Explanatory Notes on Main Statistical Indicators

Industry refers to the material production sector which is engaged in the extraction of natural resources and processing and reprocessing of minerals and agricultural products, including (1) extraction of natural resources, such as mining, salt production (but not including hunting and fishing); (2) processing and reprocessing of farm and sideline produces, such as rice husking, flour milling, wine making, oil pressing, silk reeling, spinning and weaving, and leather making; (3) manufacture of industrial products, such as steel making, iron smelting, chemicals manufacturing, petroleum processing, machine building, timber processing; water and gas production and electricity generation and supply; (4)repairing of industrial products such as the repairing of machinery and means of transport (including cars).

In industrial statistics surveys, the units of enquiry are corporate industrial enterprises with independent accounting systems.

Corporate industrial enterprises with independent accounting systems refer to enterprises engaging in industrial production activities, which meet the following requirements: (1) They are established legally, having their own names, organizations, location and able to take civil liability; (2) They possess and use their assets independently, assume liabilities and are entitled to sign contracts with other units; (3) They are financially independent and compile their own balance sheets.

State-owned and State-holding Enterprises refer to state-owned enterprises plus State-holding enterprises. State-owned enterprises (originally known as State-run enterprises with ownership by the whole society) are non-corporate economic entities registered in accordance with the Regulation of the People's Republic of China on the Management of Registration of Legal Enterprises, where all assets are owned by the State. Included in this category are State-owned enterprises, State-funded corporations and State-owned joint-operation enterprises. Joint State- private industries and private industries, which existed before 1957, were transformed into state-run industries since 1957, and into State-owned industries after 1992. Statistics on those enterprises are included in the State- owned industries instead of being grouped them separately. State-holding enterprises are a sub- classification of enterprises with mixed ownership, referring to enterprises where the percentage of State assets (or shares by the State) is larger than any other single share holder of the same enterprise. This sub- classification illustrates the control of the State over a particular industry.

For explanation of enterprises of other types of registration covered in this chapter, please refer to General Survey.

Light Industry refers to the industry that produces consumer goods and hand tools. It consists of two categories, depending on the materials used:

(1) Industries using farm products as raw materials. These are the branches of light industry which directly or indirectly use farm products as basic raw materials, including the manufacture of food and beverages, tobacco processing, textile, clothing, fur and leather manufacturing, paper making, printing, etc.

(2) Industries using non-farm products as raw materials. These are the branches of light industry which use manufactured goods as raw materials, including the manufacture of cultural, educational articles and sports goods, chemicals, synthetic fibre, chemical products for daily use, glass products for daily use, metal products for daily use, hand tools, medical apparatus and instruments, and the manufacture of cultural and office machinery.

Heavy Industry refers to the industry which produces capital goods, and provides various sectors of the national economy with necessary material and technical basis for production. It consists of the following three branches according to the purpose of production or the use of products:

(1) Mining, quarrying and logging industry, which refers to the industry that extracts natural resources, including extraction of petroleum, coal, metal and non-metal ores.

(2) Raw materials industry refers to the industry that provides various sectors of the national economy with raw materials, fuels and power. It includes smelting and processing of metals, coking and coke chemistry, chemical materials and building materials such as cement, plywood, and power, petroleum refining and coal dressing

(3) Manufacturing industry which refers to the industry that processes raw materials. It includes machine-building industries which equip sectors of the national economy; industries producing metal structure and cement products; and industries producing means of agricultural production, such as chemical fertilizers and pesticides.

In accordance with the above principles of classification, the repairing trades, which are engaged primarily in repairing products of heavy industry, are classified as heavy industry while those which are engaged in repairing products of light industry are classified as light industry.

Gross Industrial Output Value

(1) Definition: Gross industrial output value is the total volume of final industrial products produced and industrial services provided during a given period in monetary terms. It reflects the total achievements and overall scale of industrial production during a given period.

(2) Principles for calculation:

Statistics on industrial production follow the principle that all products produced by the enterprises and accepted through quality check during the reference period are to be included no matter whether they are sold or not during the reference period.

Determination of final products follows the principle that all products that are included in the calculation of gross industrial output value are the final products of the enterprise which have been accepted through quality check and require no further processing. If an enterprise has intermediate (semi-finished) products to sell, these intermediate products are considered as the final products of the enterprise.

Gross industrial output value is calculated following the principle of factory approach, i.e. industrial enterprise is used as the basic accounting unit in calculating the gross industrial output value. By this approach, value of the same product is not to be double-counted, and the output value of different workshops (branch factories) within the enterprise should not be added. However, this approach allows the possibility of double counting between enterprises.

(3) Content and method of calculation: The old definition of gross industrial output value was modified during the 1995 National Industrial Census. The revised (new) definition of gross industrial output value consists of 3 components: value of the finished products during the reference period, income from processing for external parties, and value of change in semi-finished products between the end and the beginning of the reference period.

Value of finished products during the reference period: refers to the value of all finished (semi-finished) industrial products that are produced during the reference period without the need for further processing, checked for acceptance, packed and put into the warehouse of the enterprise, including the value of own-produced equipment and the value of products provided to the projects under construction of the enterprise, and to other non-industrial or welfare units. Value of finished products during the reference period is calculated by the quantity of products produced using own materials multiplied by the average unit prices at which products are sold (excluding value-added tax). Own-produced equipment and products produced for own use are valued at cost prices as in the case of enterprise accounting. Value of finished products does not include the value of finished products (semi-finished products) that are produced using the materials from the clients who place the orders.

Income from external processing: refers to income from contracted external processing of industrial products (including processing of industrial products using materials from the clients), and the income from industrial repairing work provided to other parties. Income from external processing is calculated using information from the item "products sales income" in the enterprise accounting at the prices with value-added tax excluded.

For income from services such as processing, repairing and installation of equipment provided to non- industrial units within the enterprise, if the accounting work of the enterprise is good enough to separate it from other records, and the share of such services is significant, it should also be included in the income from external processing.

Value of change in semi-finished products between the end and the beginning of the reference period: refers to the value of change in semi-finished products between the end and the beginning of the reference period, which generally can be obtained from accounting records of enterprises. If the enterprise accounting excludes the cost of semi-finished products, then it should not be included in the gross industrial output value, and the reverse if otherwise.

(4) Changes in the scope and method of calculation of the gross industrial output value

Prior to 1984, the value of rural industry run by villages was classified into agriculture instead of industry Since 1984, it has been included in the gross industrial output value. Method of calculation for the gross industrial output value was modified in the industriaLcensus in 1995. The difference in the new method as compared with the old one is outlined below:

Principle in using full value vs. processing fee: The new method stipulates that all products produced using own materials are to be calculated with full value in reporting the gross industrial output value irrespective of the complexity of production, and for external processing, it allows calculation using processing fee. In the old method, however, the use of full value or processing fee was determined by the degree of complexity of production in different branches of industries.

Principle in determining the value of change in semi-finished products: The new method requires that value of change in semi-finished products should be included in the gross industrial output value if it is included in the accounting record of the enterprise, otherwise it should not be included. In the old method, it is determined by the type of enterprises in terms of production cycle. If the production cycle is over 6 months, the value of change in semi-finished products is included in the gross industrial output value, otherwise it is not.

Difference in prices: The new method uses prices excluding value-added tax in the calculation of gross industrial output value, while the old method used prices including value-added tax.

Value–added of Industry refers to the final results of industrial production of industrial enterprises in money terms during the reference period.

Industrial value-added can be calculated by two approaches: the production approach, i.e. gross industrial output value minus intermediate input plus value-added tax, and the income approach, i.e. income for various factors used in the course of production, including depreciation of fixed assets, remuneration of labourers, net of production tax, and operating surplus. Value-added of industry in the Yearbook is calculated by the income approach as follows:

Value-added of industry = gross industrial output - industrial intermediate input + value-added tax

(1) Gross industrial output: refers to the total achievements of industrial production activities during a given period. Gross industrial output includes value of finished products, income from external processing, and value of change in semi-finished products between the end and the beginning of the reference period. Since 1995, the gross industrial output value obtained by the new method is used in the calculation.

(2) Industrial intermediate input: refers to purchased goods and paid services consumed during the industrial production of enterprises. Fees paid for services include fees paid for the services provided by material production sectors (industry, agriculture, wholesale and retail trade, construction, transport, post and telecommunications) and by non-material production sectors (insurance, banking, culture, education, scientific research, health and medical care, public administration, etc.). The determination of industrial intermediate input follows the principle that the goods and services must be purchased from outside and included in the gross industrial output, and that the goods and services are inputted into production and consumed (include low-value consumables) during the reference period.

Industrial intermediate input includes 5 components, namely direct consumption of materials, industrial intermediate input in manufacturing cost, industrial intermediate input in management cost, industrial intermediate input in marketing cost and expenditure on interest.

Total Assets refer to all economic resources, in monetary term, these are owned or controlled by enterprises, including properties, creditor's equity and other economic rights of all forms. Classified by the degree of liquidity, total assets include working capitals, long-term investment, fixed assets, intangible assets, deferred assets and other assets. Data on this indicator can be obtained by the year-end figures of total assets in the Assets and Liability Table of accounting records of enterprises.

Working Capital refers to capital that an enterprise can cash or use during one year or one production cycle that may exceed one year, including cash and savings deposits of various forms, short-term investment, money receivable and prepaid money, inventories, etc.

Original Value of Fixed Assets refers to the total value, in monetary terms, that an enterprise spent on fixed assets, through construction, purchase, installation, transformation, expansion or technical upgrading. Generally, it covers cost of purchase, packing, transportation and installation, etc.

Net Value of Fixed Assets refers to the original value of fixed assets minus depreciation over the years, i.e.:

Net value of fixed assets = original value of fixed assets - cumulative depreciation

Total Liabilities refer to payable liabilities of enterprises that have to be repaid in terms of money, assets or labour services. In terms of payment, it can be divided into liquid liabilities and long-term liabilities. Data on this item is obtained from the ending figures on total liabilities from the Assets and Liability Table from the enterprises.

Total Equity refers to the ownership of net assets of enterprise by its investors. Net assets equal total assets minus total liabilities of the enterprise, including the paid-in capital, accumulation of capital and operating surplus and non-distributed profits. Data are obtained from the ending figures on "total equity" from the "balance sheets" .

Revenue from Principal Business refers to the annual accumulation of the corresponding item in the "profit table" of the accountant. For enterprises that do not follow the 2001 Enterprise Accounting Standards, the year-end accumulation of revenue from the sales of products is used as a substitute.

Cost of Principal Business refers to the annual accumulation of the corresponding item in the "profit table" of the accountant. For enterprises that do not follow the 2001 Enterprise Accounting Standards, theyear-end accumulation of cost for the sales of products is used as a substitute.

Tax and Extra Charges from Principal Bosiness refer to the annual accumulation of the corresponding item in the "profit table" of the accountant. For enterprises that do not follow the 2001 Enterprise Accounting Standards, the year-end accumulation of tax and extra charges from the sales of products is used as a substitute.

Total Profits refers to the balance of various incomes minus various spendings in the course of operation, reflecting the total profits and losses of enterprises in reporting period. It includes: operating profits, income from subsidies, net investment income and net income from activities other than operation. Data are obtained from the annual accumulation of the corresponding item in the "profit table" of the accountant.

Value-added Tax Payable in the Current Year refers to the payable tax of enterprises which engaged in selling of goods or providing services that bring added value to the goods, such as processing, repairing, fitting and other activities should be paid according to Tax Law. It refers to the amount of the value-added tax which should be paid by the enterprises during the reference period. The formula is as tollows:

Value-added Tax Payable in the Current Year = tax on sales-(tax on purchase-transferred tax on purchase)- exports deduct tax payable on domestic sales-tax relief+the export tax rebate.

Tax on Purchase in Current Year refers to goods purchased by industrial enterprises or value added tax that should be paid but being granted the right to deduct from the tax on sales.

Tax on Sales in Current Year refers to value added tax on industrial enterprises from sales of goods or taxable services that should be charged value added tax.

Average number of employed persons refers to the number of employee everyday during the reference period, calculated with the following formula:

$$\text{Monthly average Number} = \frac{\text{sum of actual employees everyday in reference month}}{\text{number of calendar dates in reference month}}$$

$$\text{Quarterly average number} = \frac{\text{sum of monthly average number in reference quarter}}{3}$$

$$\text{Annual average number} = \frac{\text{sum of monthly average number in reference year}}{12}$$

Ratio of Profits, Taxes and Interests to Average Assets reflects the profit-making capability of all assets of the enterprise and is a key indicator manifesting the performance and management and evaluating the profit-making potential of the enterprise. It is calculated as

$$\text{Ratio of Profits, Taxes and Interests toAverageAssets(\%)} = \frac{\text{otal profits+ total taxes+ interest payment}}{\text{average assets}} \times 100\%$$

In the above formula, total taxes is the sum of tax and extra charges on the sales of products and value-added tax payable; and average assets is the arithmetic mean of the sum of beginning assets and ending assets.

Ratio of Debts to Assets reflects both the operation risk and the capability of the enterprise in making use of the capital from the creditors. It is calculated as follows:

$$\text{Ratio of Debts toAssets(\%)} = \frac{\text{total debts}}{\text{total assets}} \times 100\%$$

Both assets and debts are figures at the end of the reference period.

Turnover of Working Capital refers to the number of times of turnover of working capital in a given period of time, which reflects the speed of the turnover of working capital of industrial enterprises, and is calculated as follows:

$$\text{Turnover of Working Capital} = \frac{\text{sales revenue of products}}{\text{average balance of total working capital}}$$

In the above formula, average balance of total working capital refers to the arithmetic mean of the sum of working capital at the beginning and at the end of the reference period.

Ratio of Profits to Total Industrial Costs refers to the ratio of profits realized in a given period to the total costs in the same period, which reflects the economic efficiency of input cost and is calculated as follows:

$$\text{Ratio of Profits to Total Industrial Cost (\%)} = \frac{\text{total profits}}{\text{total costs}} \times 100\%$$

Total costs in the above formula are the sum of cost of products sold, marketing cost, management cost and financial cost.

Sales Ratio of Products is an indicator reflecting the actual sale of industrial products, analyzing the production-selling and supply-demand relations. It is calculated as:

$$\text{Sales Ratio of Products (\%)} = \frac{\text{value of industrial sales}}{\text{gross industrial output value (current prices)}} \times 100\%$$

13 能 源

ENERGY

资料整理：张　育　李　婷　雷稳强
Data management：Zhang Yu　Li Ting　Lei Wenqiang
数据审核：丁抗玲
Data audit：Ding Kangling

第十三部分　能源

一、简要说明

本章资料包括规模以上工业能源购销存情况、全市单位GDP能耗、规模以上工业单位增加值能耗、规模以上工业企业用水情况等，由西安市统计局能源处提供。

二、主要指标

规模以上工业综合能源消费量（万吨标准煤）	487.94	比上年下降	14.2%
单位GDP能耗（吨标准煤/万元）	0.470	比上年下降	3.20%
规模以上工业单位增加值能耗（吨标准煤/万元）	0.345	比上年下降	19.48%

13 ENERGY

Ⅰ.Brief Introduction

Data in this chapter reflects energy purchases consumption and inventory of industrial enterprises above designated size,energy consumption per unit of GDP in whole city,energy consumption per unit of industrial value-added above designated size and statistics on water use of industrial enterprises above designated size. data in this chapter are provided and compiled by Energy Division ransportation Division of the Xi'an Bureau of Statistics.

Ⅱ.Major Indicators

		Increase over Preceding Year
Comprehensive Energy Consumption Above Designated Size(10 000 Tons of Standard Coal)	487.94	-14.2%
Energy Consumption of GDP per Unit (Tons of Standard Coal /10 000 yuan)	0.470	-3.20%
Energy Consumption of value added per Unit of Industrial Enterprises Above Designated Size (Tons of Standard Coal/10 000 yuan)	0.345	-19.48%

13-1 全市及各区县单位GDP能耗

Energy Consumption per Unit of GDP by Region

单位：吨标准煤 / 万元 (ton of SCE/10 000 yuan)

地 区	Region	单位GDP能耗 Energy Consumption Per Unit of GDP											
		GDP按2005年价格计算 GDP are calculated at 2005 constant prices						GDP按2010年价格计算 GDP are calculated at 2010 constant prices					
		2005	2006	2007	2008	2009	2010	2010	2011	2012	2013	2014	2015
西安市	**Xi'an**	**0.911**	**0.873**	**0.823**	**0.768**	**0.726**	**0.711**	**0.575**	**0.555**	**0.535**	**0.516**	**0.486**	**0.470**
新城区	Xincheng	0.783	0.751	0.708	0.667	0.629	0.621	0.563	0.544	0.525	0.506	0.479	0.463
碑林区	Beilin	0.640	0.613	0.580	0.547	0.514	0.510	0.438	0.421	0.406	0.392	0.368	0.356
莲湖区	Lianhu	0.766	0.735	0.701	0.646	0.609	0.587	0.521	0.501	0.483	0.466	0.430	0.416
灞桥区	Baqiao	1.194	1.163	1.091	1.023	0.964	0.923	0.663	0.638	0.615	0.592	0.562	0.543
未央区	Weiyang	1.122	1.078	1.019	0.951	0.894	0.882	0.680	0.655	0.632	0.609	0.563	0.539
雁塔区	Yanta	0.884	0.842	0.795	0.749	0.703	0.674	0.512	0.494	0.476	0.459	0.441	0.425
阎良区	Yanliang	0.825	0.778	0.740	0.695	0.656	0.652	0.533	0.515	0.497	0.480	0.444	0.430
临潼区	Lintong	0.940	0.912	0.860	0.790	0.753	0.717	0.676	0.652	0.629	0.607	0.558	0.541
长安区	Chang'an	1.059	0.994	0.939	0.890	0.841	0.824	0.642	0.619	0.596	0.575	0.555	0.532
高陵区	Gaoling	0.892	0.848	0.790	0.747	0.704	0.677	0.487	0.467	0.451	0.435	0.403	0.391
蓝田县	Lantian	1.727	1.673	1.606	1.517	1.444	1.414	1.083	1.047	1.011	0.978	0.924	0.895
周至县	Zhouzhi	1.502	1.465	1.386	1.309	1.237	1.212	0.959	0.928	0.897	0.867	0.801	0.778
户 县	Huxian	1.411	1.367	1.287	1.188	1.123	1.089	0.978	0.940	0.906	0.873	0.844	0.811

13-1 续表 continude

地 区	Region	比上年增长(%) Growth Rates over Preceding Year(%)									
		2006	2007	2008	2009	2010	2011	2012	2013	2014	2015
西安市	**Xi'an**	**-4.15**	**-5.75**	**-6.65**	**-5.56**	**-2.06**	**-3.56**	**-3.51**	**-3.57**	**-5.89**	**-3.20**
新城区	Xincheng	-4.15	-5.67	-5.79	-5.80	-1.15	-3.51	-3.50	-3.50	-5.39	-3.27
碑林区	Beilin	-4.18	-5.44	-5.65	-5.95	-0.91	-3.89	-3.50	-3.50	-6.06	-3.20
莲湖区	Lianhu	-4.07	-4.60	-7.93	-5.65	-3.58	-3.84	-3.60	-3.61	-7.76	-3.14
灞桥区	Baqiao	-2.54	-6.20	-6.24	-5.80	-4.20	-3.81	-3.62	-3.64	-5.20	-3.30
未央区	Weiyang	-3.97	-5.44	-6.63	-6.05	-1.31	-3.60	-3.60	-3.60	-7.60	-4.16
雁塔区	Yanta	-4.71	-5.64	-5.80	-6.08	-4.18	-3.61	-3.61	-3.60	-3.89	-3.58
阎良区	Yanliang	-5.77	-4.80	-6.08	-5.62	-0.61	-3.38	-3.50	-3.50	-7.59	-3.00
临潼区	Lintong	-3.03	-5.73	-8.16	-4.58	-4.81	-3.52	-3.51	-3.51	-8.07	-3.00
长安区	Chang'an	-6.15	-5.53	-5.22	-5.50	-2.08	-3.60	-3.63	-3.63	-3.40	-4.10
高陵区	Gaoling	-4.85	-6.85	-5.50	-5.70	-3.82	-3.93	-3.52	-3.54	-7.32	-3.00
蓝田县	Lantian	-3.13	-4.01	-5.50	-4.84	-2.06	-3.39	-3.40	-3.30	-5.48	-3.17
周至县	Zhouzhi	-2.46	-5.43	-5.51	-5.50	-2.06	-3.30	-3.30	-3.30	-7.63	-2.90
户 县	Huxian	-3.07	-5.85	-7.70	-5.50	-2.99	-3.85	-3.60	-3.62	-3.40	-3.82

注：能源消耗按等价值计算；2013年以前数据，根据第三次经济普查结果进行了调整。

13-2 主要年份全市及各区县规模以上工业企业单位工业增加值能耗

Energy Consumption Per Unit of Industrial Value Added above Designated Size by Region in Representative Years

单位：吨标准煤 / 万元 (ton of SCE/10 000 yuan)

地 区	Region	单位工业增加值能耗 Energy Consumption Per Unit of Industrial Value Added											
		工业增加值按2005年价格计算 VAI are calculated at 2005 constant prices						工业增加值按2010年价格计算 VAI are calculated at 2010 constant prices					
		2005	2006	2007	2008	2009	2010	2010	2011	2012	2013	2014	2015
西安市	**Xi'an**	**1.220**	**1.100**	**1.092**	**0.915**	**0.800**	**0.703**	**0.593**	**0.502**	**0.448**	**0.497**	**0.388**	**0.345**
新城区	Xincheng	0.822	0.798	0.716	0.663	0.420	0.379	0.329	0.361	0.329	0.317	0.259	0.267
碑林区	Beilin	0.876	0.846	0.782	0.763	0.293	0.246	0.115	0.073	0.067	0.451	0.368	0.245
莲湖区	Lianhu	0.861	0.832	0.775	0.639	0.269	0.232	0.226	0.207	0.200	0.164	0.126	0.112
灞桥区	Baqiao	3.029	2.871	2.446	2.078	2.072	2.032	1.447	1.106	1.066	0.915	0.801	0.729
未央区	Weiyang	1.030	1.000	0.876	0.770	1.008	0.936	0.786	0.651	0.637	0.547	0.348	0.252
雁塔区	Yanta	1.358	1.308	1.123	1.000	0.578	0.414	0.359	0.341	0.249	1.104	0.863	0.657
阎良区	Yanliang	0.876	0.849	0.761	0.625	0.354	0.271	0.255	0.209	0.198	0.185	0.047	0.044
临潼区	Lintong	1.031	0.992	0.882	0.715	0.644	0.371	0.203	0.166	0.141	0.132	0.143	0.124
长安区	Chang'an	1.370	1.300	1.208	1.087	0.725	0.698	0.366	0.323	0.183	0.175	0.219	0.258
高陵区	Gaoling	0.966	0.905	0.719	0.693	0.239	0.221	0.223	0.189	0.232	0.190	0.107	0.103
蓝田县	Lantian	2.579	2.515	2.133	2.084	3.670	3.487	2.534	2.087	1.525	1.438	1.031	0.811
周至县	Zhouzhi	1.946	1.900	1.891	1.842	0.364	0.336	0.257	0.237	0.429	0.411	0.372	0.292
户 县	Huxian	7.467	7.168	5.857	4.910	4.514	4.036	3.570	3.135	2.962	2.480	2.287	2.274

注：本表2005—2010年统计范围为主营业务收入500万元及以上的法人工业企业；2010—2015年统计范围为主营业务收入2000万元及以上的法人工业企业；能源消耗按当量值计算。

13-2 续表 continude

单位：吨标准煤 / 万元 (ton of SCE/10 000 yuan)

地 区	Region	比上年增长(%) Growth Rates over Preceding Year(%)									
		2006	2007	2008	2009	2010	2011	2012	2013	2014	2015
西安市	**Xi'an**	**-3.04**	**-12.56**	**-13.43**	**-10.48**	**-12.18**	**-15.44**	**-10.56**	**-17.69**	**-15.21**	**-19.48**
新城区	Xincheng	-2.92	-10.26	-7.38	-2.68	-9.69	9.68	-6.44	-3.52	-2.44	-7.59
碑林区	Beilin	-3.42	-7.59	-2.45	-0.44	-15.89	-36.63	-8.39	-11.40	-16.18	-34.78
莲湖区	Lianhu	-3.47	-6.91	-17.61	0.89	-13.63	-8.19	-8.02	-17.72	-27.16	-17.01
灞桥区	Baqiao	-5.22	-14.79	-15.04	0.29	-1.92	-23.61	-2.90	-13.76	-11.29	-12.07
未央区	Weiyang	-2.91	-10.63	-12.15	-15.20	-7.18	-17.17	3.64	-15.19	-30.83	-28.68
雁塔区	Yanta	-3.68	-14.14	-10.98	-13.98	-28.43	-4.88	-28.97	-21.74	-16.24	-24.05
阎良区	Yanliang	-3.05	-10.42	-17.83	-18.36	-23.44	-18.11	-6.88	-7.36	-36.89	-13.69
临潼区	Lintong	-3.82	-11.06	-18.99	3.05	-42.41	-18.32	-15.27	-10.22	-35.39	-11.01
长安区	Chang'an	-5.11	-4.06	-10.05	-18.68	-3.67	-11.88	-43.40	-28.21	28.64	-19.04
高陵区	Gaoling	-6.32	-20.52	-3.56	-18.90	-7.65	-15.26	-10.91	-18.63	-16.45	-15.77
蓝田县	Lantian	-2.48	-15.18	-2.29	-3.39	-5.00	-17.63	-28.90	-5.75	-25.90	-22.51
周至县	Zhouzhi	-2.38	-0.48	-2.62	-12.27	-7.71	-7.56	-14.72	-12.89	-13.61	-28.18
户 县	Huxian	-4.01	-18.29	-16.17	-18.48	-10.58	-12.19	-5.13	-16.12	-5.64	-16.57

13-3 主要年份全社会用电量

单位：万千瓦时

行 业	Sector	2000	2007
总 计	**Total**	**732373**	**1482896**
#行业用电量合计	Total of Industry of Electricity	599855	1215799
1. 第一产业	Primary Industry	77579	120134
2. 第二产业	Secondary Industry	354245	700026
3. 第三产业	Tertiary Industry	168031	395639
一、农、林、牧、渔、水利业	Agriculture ,Forestry,Animal Husbandry and Fishery	77579	120134
二、工业	Industry	345175	674990
1. 轻工业	Light Industry	152125	187323
2. 重工业	Heavy Industry	193050	487667
三、建筑业	Construction	9070	25036
四、交通运输、仓储及邮政业	Traffic,Transport, Storage and Post	22904	53825
五、信息传输、计算机服务和软件业	Information Transmission,Computer Service and Software		21938
六、商业、住宿和餐饮业	Commercial,Hotels and Catering Services		107343
七、金融、房地产、商务及居民服务业	Finance,Real Estate,Business Affairs and Households Services		67674
八、公共事业及管理组织	Public Utilities and Management Organization		144859
九、城乡居民生活用电	Electricity Consumption of Urban and Rural Residents	132518	267097
1. 乡村	Rural	31281	38395
2. 城市	City	101237	228702

注：本表数据来源于国网陕西省供电公司西安供电公司。

Electricity Consumption of the Whole Society in Representative Years

(10 000 kw. h)

2008	2009	2010	2011	2012	2013	2014	2015
1605089	**1724067**	**1993751**	**2167453**	**2352571**	**2554679**	**2753213**	**2844836**
1293574	1358483	1499903	1590486	1706859	1854696	2002503	2049492
127054	99083	108720	117984	109086	110405	95997	89970
724852	766029	883259	910360	932622	991202	1086105	1088866
441668	493371	507924	562142	665151	753089	820401	870656
127054	99083	108720	117984	109086	110405	95997	89970
696291	724920	838317	859796	875018	920024	998132	997115
182176	167144	177362	183766	175392	170246	165933	165290
514115	557776	660955	676030	699626	749778	832199	831826
28561	41108	44942	50564	57605	71179	87973	91750
56614	62031	58509	66684	69633	78722	88805	90914
26680	29328	30760	33191	37444	39551	42662	46203
111676	122203	148418	166558	199970	228117	253199	277248
81674	102400	116163	131236	150832	165833	180824	185329
165024	177409	154074	164473	207271	240866	254911	270962
311515	365585	493848	576966	645713	699982	750710	795344
63072	99941	142059	169898	197937	216148	235938	553425
248443	265644	351789	407068	447776	483834	514773	241920

13-4 规模以上工业企业能源购进、消费及库存（2015年）

Energy Purchases Consumption and Inventory of Industrial Enterprises above Designated Size (2015)

能源名称	Name	年初库存量 Stock (year-beginning)	购进量 Purchases	其中：购自省外 Wherein: purchased from outside the province
原煤(吨)	Raw Coal (ton)	1023163	8225248	46024
洗精煤(吨)	Washed Coal(ton)	10192	46037	
其他洗煤(吨)	Other Washed Coals(ton)			
煤制品（吨）	Briquettes(ton)	137	2811	503
焦炭(吨)	Coke(ton)	117	1490	
其他焦化产品(吨)	Other Coking Products(ton)			
天然气（气态）（万立方米）	Natural Gas(10 000cu.m)	95	31009	
液化天然气（液态）（吨）	Liquefied Natural Gas (Liquid)(ton)		16	
原油(吨)	Crude Oil(ton)	75737	261089	111588
汽油(吨)	Gasoline(ton)	132	20546	512
煤油(吨)	Kerosene(ton)	36	284	
柴油(吨)	Diesel Oil(ton)	1590	59054	2947
燃料油(吨)	Fuel Oil(ton)	20	1070	238
液化石油气(吨)	LPG(ton)		301	
润滑油（吨）	Lubricating Oil (ton)		93	
溶剂油（吨）	Solvent Oil (ton)	1	368	
其它石油制品(吨)	Other Petroleum Products(ton)	62	1683	
热力(百万千焦)	Heat (1 million kilo-joule)		5533963	
电力(万千瓦时)	Electricity(10 000kwh)		636785	3290
生物质废料用于燃料（吨）	Biomass Waste for Fuel (ton)		536	
其他燃料（吨标准煤）	Other Fuels(ton of SCE)	21	2184	
能源合计(吨标准煤)	Total Energy(ton of SCE)			

13-4 续表 continued

能源名称	Name	消费量 合计 Consumption Total	工业 生产消费 Industrial Production Consume	用于 原材料 as Raw Material	非工业 生产消费 Non-industrial Production Consume	年末库存 Stock (year-end)
原煤(吨)	Raw Coal (ton)	8446904	8432739	2637	14165	812185
洗精煤(吨)	Washed Coal(ton)	56229	56229			
其他洗煤(吨)	Other Washed Coals(ton)					
煤制品（吨）	Briquettes(ton)	2781	2175	503	605	168
焦炭(吨)	Coke(ton)	1508	1500		8	107
其他焦化产品(吨)	Other Coking Products(ton)					
天然气（气态）（万立方米）	Natural Gas(10 000cu.m)	29678	29020	663	658	1979
液化天然气（液态）（吨）	Liquefied Natural Gas (Liquid)(ton)	16	7		9	
原油(吨)	Crude Oil(ton)	281674	281673	14	1	55152
汽油(吨)	Gasoline(ton)	20788	17322	55	3467	34
煤油(吨)	Kerosene(ton)	307	297		11	15
柴油(吨)	Diesel Oil(ton)	59343	57486	2040	1857	765
燃料油(吨)	Fuel Oil(ton)	1078	1078			7
液化石油气(吨)	LPG(ton)	301	299	2	1	
润滑油（吨）	Lubricating Oil (ton)	93	93			1
溶剂油（吨）	Solvent Oil (ton)	368	368	333		2
其它石油制品(吨)	Other Petroleum Products(ton)	1682	1682			63
热力(百万千焦)	Heat (1 million kilo-joule)	6944123	6800326		143797	
电力(万千瓦时)	Electricity(10 000kwh)	723119	712995		10125	
生物质废料用于燃料（吨）	Biomass Waste for Fuel (ton)	7112	7112			
其他燃料（吨标准煤）	Other Fuels(ton of SCE)	2184	2184			1
能源合计(吨标准煤)	Total Energy(ton of SCE)	8015811	7971352		44459	

13–5 规模以上工业企业分行业主要能源品种消费量（2015年）

Major Energy Consumption above Designated Size by Industry（2015）

行 业	Sector	原煤（吨）Raw Coal (ton)	天然气（万立方米）Natural Gas(10 000 cu.m)	原油（吨）Crude Oil (ton)
总 计	**Total**	**8446904**	**29678**	**281674**
煤炭开采和洗选业	Coal Mining and Dressing			
石油和天然气开采业	Petroleum and Natural Gas Extraction			
黑色金属矿采选业	Ferrous Metals Mining and Dressing			
有色金属矿采选业	Nonferrous Metals Mining and Dressing			
非金属矿采选业	Nonmetal Minerals Mining and Dressing			
开采辅助活动	Ancillary activities for mining	350	124	2
其他采矿业	Other Mining Industry			
农副食品加工业	Agricultural Products and Non-stable Food Processing Industry	187199	250	
食品制造业	Food Production	30215	2692	
酒、饮料和精制茶制造业	Wine, soft drinks and refined tea industry	69673	920	
烟草制品业	Tobacco Processing	27		
纺织业	Textile Industry	903	216	
纺织服装、服饰业	Textile, apparel industry		12	
皮革、毛皮、羽毛及其制品和制鞋业	Leather, Fur, Feather (eiderdown) and Their Products Industry			
木材加工和木、竹、藤、棕、草制品业	Timber Processing,Bamboo,Cane,Palm Fiber and Straw Products			
家具制造业	Furniture Manufacturing	2		
造纸及纸制品业	Papermaking and Paper products	8551	64	
印刷和记录媒介复制业	Printing,Record Medium Reproduction	174	469	
文教、工美、体育和娱乐用品制造业	Culture, education, Craft art, sports and entertainment goods manufacturing industry	109		
石油加工、炼焦和核燃料加工业	Petroleum Refining, Ccoke Making and Nuclear Fuel Processing Industry	12375	294	281644
化学原料和化学制品制造业	Raw Chemical Materials and Chemical Products	24176	2210	
医药制造业	Medical and Pharmaceutical Products	12497	1368	
化学纤维制造业	Chemical Fiber			
橡胶和塑料制品业	Rubber and plastic products industry	150728	498	
非金属矿物制品业	Nonmetal Mineral Products	201787	786	
黑色金属冶炼和压延加工业	Smelting and Pressing of Ferrous Metals	7057	353	
有色金属冶炼和压延加工业	Smelting and Pressing of Nonferrou Metals	1460	693	
金属制品业	Metal Products	12756	254	
通用设备制造业	General Equipment Manufacturing Industry	258	712	13
专用设备制造业	Special Purpose Equipment	68	510	
汽车制造业	Automotive Manufacturing	39296	4881	
铁路、船舶、航空航天和其他运输设备制造业	Railroad, marine, aerospace and other transportation equipment manufacturing	17206	195	
电气机械和器材制造业	Electric Equipment and Machinery	109	2219	15
计算机、通信和其他电子设备制造业	Communication Equipment, Computer and Other Electronic Equipment Manufacturing Industry		2428	
仪器仪表制造业	Instrument manufacturing industry		340	
其他制造业	Other manufacturing	211		
废弃资源综合利用	Comprehensive utilization of waste resources			
金属制品、机械和设备修理业	Metal products, machinery and equipment repair industry			
电力、热力生产和供应业	Electric Power, Heating Power Generating and Supplying Industry	7669715	6744	
燃气生产和供应业	Gas Mining and Supplying Industry		182	
水的生产和供应业	Water Processing and Supplying Industry	1	265	

13-5 续表 continued

行 业	Sector	汽油 (吨) Gasoline (ton)	柴油 (吨) Diesel Oil (ton)	热力 (百万千焦) Heat (million kilo joule)	电力 (万千瓦时) Electricity (10 000 kwh)
总 计	**Total**	**20788**	**59343**	**6944123**	**723119**
煤炭开采和洗选业	Coal Mining and Dressing				
石油和天然气开采业	Petroleum and Natural Gas Extraction				
黑色金属矿采选业	Ferrous Metals Mining and Dressing				16
有色金属矿采选业	Nonferrous Metals Mining and Dressing				
非金属矿采选业	Nonmetal Minerals Mining and Dressing				
开采辅助活动	Ancillary activities for mining	125	3498		640
其他采矿业	Other Mining Industry				
农副食品加工业	Agricultural Products and Non-stable Food Processing Industry	1628	1511	1356075	19141
食品制造业	Food Production	811	539	399162	14455
酒、饮料和精制茶制造业	Wine, soft drinks and refined tea industry	576	1803	177841	19426
烟草制品业	Tobacco Processing	24		5668	225
纺织业	Textile Industry	59	6	127105	18936
纺织服装、服饰业	Textile, apparel industry	33	1		613
皮革、毛皮、羽毛及其制品和制鞋业	Leather, Fur, Feather (eiderdown) and Their Products Industry	37		14040	280
木材加工和木、竹、藤、棕、草制品业	Timber Processing,Bamboo,Cane,Palm Fiber and Straw Products	9			5017
家具制造业	Furniture Manufacturing	135	147		875
造纸及纸制品业	Papermaking and Paper products	148	109	39036	3098
印刷和记录媒介复制业	Printing,Record Medium Reproduction	319	171	64871	8071
文教、工美、体育和娱乐用品制造业	Culture, education, Craft art, sports and entertainment goods manufacturing industry	14	5		364
石油加工、炼焦和核燃料加工业	Petroleum Refining, Ccoke Making and Nuclear Fuel Processing Industry	1020	195		6250
化学原料和化学制品制造业	Raw Chemical Materials and Chemical Products	469	435	21920	35752
医药制造业	Medical and Pharmaceutical Products	1029	69	159442	11214
化学纤维制造业	Chemical Fiber	20	10	684821	5338
橡胶和塑料制品业	Rubber and plastic products industry	280	2994	2205	18086
非金属矿物制品业	Nonmetal Mineral Products	1294	31088	1764	34804
黑色金属冶炼和压延加工业	Smelting and Pressing of Ferrous Metals	51	43		6736
有色金属冶炼和压延加工业	Smelting and Pressing of Nonferrou Metals	447	103	963340	53855
金属制品业	Metal Products	480	225	5000	10266
通用设备制造业	General Equipment Manufacturing Industry	921	193	6793	7992
专用设备制造业	Special Purpose Equipment	2140	1015	64508	30361
汽车制造业	Automotive Manufacturing	3214	7589	411217	90769
铁路、船舶、航空航天和其他运输设备制造业	Railroad, marine, aerospace and other transportation equipment manufacturing	537	394	167897	13604
电气机械和器材制造业	Electric Equipment and Machinery	2010	611	1045419	49288
计算机、通信和其他电子设备制造业	Communication Equipment, Computer and Other Electronic Equipment Manufacturing Industry	746	65	134367	122149
仪器仪表制造业	Instrument manufacturing industry	1121	5163	6654	8874
其他制造业	Other manufacturing	111	97		427
废弃资源综合利用	Comprehensive utilization of waste resources				
金属制品、机械和设备修理业	Metal products, machinery and equipment repair industry	69	53		74
电力、热力生产和供应业	Electric Power, Heating Power Generating and Supplying Industry	145	1121	1084978	109433
燃气生产和供应业	Gas Mining and Supplying Industry	471	79		7391
水的生产和供应业	Water Processing and Supplying Industry	296	10		9299

13-6 规模以上工业企业分行业综合能源消费量（2015年）

Comprehensive Energy Consumption by Sector above Designated Size（2015）

单位：吨标准煤 (ton of SCE)

行 业	Scetor	2015	比上年增长(%) Increase over Preceding Year (%)
总 计	**Total**	**4879446**	**-14.2**
煤炭开采和洗选业	Coal Mining and Dressing		
石油和天然气开采业	Petroleum and Natural Gas Extraction		
黑色金属矿采选业	Ferrous Metals Mining and Dressing	19	-83.0
有色金属矿采选业	Nonferrous Metals Mining and Dressing		
非金属矿采选业	Nonmetal Minerals Mining and Dressing		
开采辅助活动	Ancillary activities for mining	8030	-18.3
其他采矿业	Other Mining Industry		
农副食品加工业	Agricultural Products and Non-stable Food Processing Industry	160516	8.3
食品制造业	Food Production	90789	-12.9
酒、饮料和精制茶制造业	Wine, soft drinks and refined tea industry	94839	-26.0
烟草制品业	Tobacco Processing	362	-10.1
纺织业	Textile Industry	29054	61.8
纺织服装、服饰业	Textile, apparel industry	945	-4.6
皮革、毛皮、羽毛及其制品和制鞋业	Leather, Fur, Feather (eiderdown) and Their Products Industry	877	20.4
木材加工和木、竹、藤、棕、草制品业	Timber Processing,Bamboo,Cane,Palm Fiber and Straw Products	9462	-23.6
家具制造业	Furniture Manufacturing	1488	-8.3
造纸及纸制品业	Papermaking and Paper products	12606	-18.2
印刷和记录媒介复制业	Printing,Record Medium Reproduction	18673	-12.1
文教、工美、体育和娱乐用品制造业	Culture, education, Craft art, sports and entertainment goods manufacturing industry	581	-9.1
石油加工、炼焦和核燃料加工业	Petroleum Refining, Ccoke Making and Nuclear Fuel Processing Industry	43835	-81.3
化学原料和化学制品制造业	Raw Chemical Materials and Chemical Products	93100	4.9
医药制造业	Medical and Pharmaceutical Products	47263	1.0
化学纤维制造业	Chemical Fiber	29950	-5.7
橡胶和塑料制品业	Rubber and plastic products industry	47290	-1.4
非金属矿物制品业	Nonmetal Mineral Products	241782	-20.5
黑色金属冶炼和压延加工业	Smelting and Pressing of Ferrous Metals	18377	-53.5
有色金属冶炼和压延加工业	Smelting and Pressing of Nonferrou Metals	112292	24.3
金属制品业	Metal Products	26645	-18.8
通用设备制造业	General Equipment Manufacturing Industry	17906	-3.9
专用设备制造业	Special Purpose Equipment	48385	-15.3
汽车制造业	Automotive Manufacturing	196205	-7.8
铁路、船舶、航空航天和其他运输设备制造业	Railroad, marine, aerospace and other transportation equipment manufacturing	32354	-5.8
电气机械和器材制造业	Electric Equipment and Machinery	128841	3.4
计算机、通信和其他电子设备制造业	Communication Equipment, Computer and Other Electronic Equipment Manufacturing Industry	185450	9.9
仪器仪表制造业	Instrument manufacturing industry	24640	37.1
其他制造业	Other manufacturing	981	-16.2
废弃资源综合利用	Comprehensive utilization of waste resources		
金属制品、机械和设备修理业	Metal products, machinery and equipment repair industry	238	-8.0
电力、热力生产和供应业	Electric Power, Heating Power Generating and Supplying Industry	3130667	-14.1
燃气生产和供应业	Gas Mining and Supplying Industry	12207	0.5
水的生产和供应业	Water Processing and Supplying Industry	12798	-0.4

13-7 规模以上工业企业用水情况（2015年）

Statistics on Water Use of Industrial Enterprises above Designated Size（2015）

指 标	Item	取水量（万立方米） Water Use (10 000 cu.m)	外供水量（万立方米） Outward Water Supply (10 000 cu.m)
合 计	**Total**	**59085**	**49962**
地表淡水	Surface fresh water	38284	
地下淡水	Underground fresh water	10624	1139
自来水	Tap Water	9132	48823
陆地苦咸水	Land lake Salt water	7	
矿井水	Mine Water	2	
雨水	Rain Water		
再生水	Reclaimed Water	1034	
其他水	Other Water	2	
外排水量	Efflux capacity	3780	
重复用水量	Repeated water consumption	7318	

13-8 规模以上工业企业分行业用水情况（2015年）

Volume of Water Use of Industrial Enterprises above Designated Size by Industry（2015）

行 业	Sector	取水量（万立方米）Water Use (10 000 cu.m)
总 计	**Total**	**59085**
煤炭开采和洗选业	Coal Mining and Dressing	
石油和天然气开采业	Petroleum and Natural Gas Extraction	
黑色金属矿采选业	Ferrous Metals Mining and Dressing	7
有色金属矿采选业	Nonferrous Metals Mining and Dressing	
非金属矿采选业	Nonmetal Minerals Mining and Dressing	
开采辅助活动	Ancillary activities for mining	7
其他采矿业	Other Mining Industry	
农副食品加工业	Agricultural Products and Non-stable Food Processing Industry	189
食品制造业	Food Production	375
酒、饮料和精制茶制造业	Wine, soft drinks and refined tea industry	867
烟草制品业	Tobacco Processing	1
纺织业	Textile Industry	93
纺织服装、服饰业	Textile, apparel industry	21
皮革、毛皮、羽毛及其制品和制鞋业	Leather, Fur, Feather (eiderdown) and Their Products Industry	2
木材加工和木、竹、藤、棕、草制品业	Timber Processing,Bamboo,Cane,Palm Fiber and Straw Products	2
家具制造业	Furniture Manufacturing	3
造纸及纸制品业	Papermaking and Paper products	17
印刷和记录媒介复制业	Printing,Record Medium Reproduction	49
文教、工美、体育和娱乐用品制造业	Culture, education, Craft art, sports and entertainment goods manufacturing industry	4
石油加工、炼焦和核燃料加工业	Petroleum Refining, Ccoke Making and Nuclear Fuel Processing Industry	79
化学原料和化学制品制造业	Raw Chemical Materials and Chemical Products	243
医药制造业	Medical and Pharmaceutical Products	296
化学纤维制造业	Chemical Fiber	41
橡胶和塑料制品业	Rubber and plastic products industry	219
非金属矿物制品业	Nonmetal Mineral Products	251
黑色金属冶炼和压延加工业	Smelting and Pressing of Ferrous Metals	7
有色金属冶炼和压延加工业	Smelting and Pressing of Nonferrou Metals	200
金属制品业	Metal Products	65
通用设备制造业	General Equipment Manufacturing Industry	74
专用设备制造业	Special Purpose Equipment	273
汽车制造业	Automotive Manufacturing	741
铁路、船舶、航空航天和其他运输设备制造业	Railroad, marine, aerospace and other transportation equipment manufacturing	121
电气机械和器材制造业	Electric Equipment and Machinery	548
计算机、通信和其他电子设备制造业	Communication Equipment, Computer and Other Electronic Equipment Manufacturing Industry	866
仪器仪表制造业	Instrument manufacturing industry	214
其他制造业	Other manufacturing	8
废弃资源综合利用	Comprehensive utilization of waste resources	
金属制品、机械和设备修理业	Metal products, machinery and equipment repair industry	2
电力、热力生产和供应业	Electric Power, Heating Power Generating and Supplying Industry	2965
燃气生产和供应业	Gas Mining and Supplying Industry	19
水的生产和供应业	Water Processing and Supplying Industry	50216

13-8 续表 continude

行 业	Sector	外供水量（万立方米）Outward Water Supply (10 000 cu.m)
总 计	**Total**	**49962**
煤炭开采和洗选业	Coal Mining and Dressing	
石油和天然气开采业	Petroleum and Natural Gas Extraction	
黑色金属矿采选业	Ferrous Metals Mining and Dressing	
有色金属矿采选业	Nonferrous Metals Mining and Dressing	
非金属矿采选业	Nonmetal Minerals Mining and Dressing	
开采辅助活动	Ancillary activities for mining	
其他采矿业	Other Mining Industry	
农副食品加工业	Agricultural Products and Non-stable Food Processing Industry	
食品制造业	Food Production	
酒、饮料和精制茶制造业	Wine, soft drinks and refined tea industry	
烟草制品业	Tobacco Processing	
纺织业	Textile Industry	
纺织服装、服饰业	Textile, apparel industry	
皮革、毛皮、羽毛及其制品和制鞋业	Leather, Fur, Feather (eiderdown) and Their Products Industry	
木材加工和木、竹、藤、棕、草制品业	Timber Processing,Bamboo,Cane,Palm Fiber and Straw Products	
家具制造业	Furniture Manufacturing	
造纸及纸制品业	Papermaking and Paper products	
印刷和记录媒介复制业	Printing,Record Medium Reproduction	
文教、工美、体育和娱乐用品制造业	Culture, education, Craft art, sports and entertainment goods manufacturing industry	
石油加工、炼焦和核燃料加工业	Petroleum Refining, Ccoke Making and Nuclear Fuel Processing Industry	
化学原料和化学制品制造业	Raw Chemical Materials and Chemical Products	
医药制造业	Medical and Pharmaceutical Products	
化学纤维制造业	Chemical Fiber	
橡胶和塑料制品业	Rubber and plastic products industry	
非金属矿物制品业	Nonmetal Mineral Products	
黑色金属冶炼和压延加工业	Smelting and Pressing of Ferrous Metals	
有色金属冶炼和压延加工业	Smelting and Pressing of Nonferrou Metals	
金属制品业	Metal Products	
通用设备制造业	General Equipment Manufacturing Industry	
专用设备制造业	Special Purpose Equipment	3
汽车制造业	Automotive Manufacturing	
铁路、船舶、航空航天和其他运输设备制造业	Railroad, marine, aerospace and other transportation equipment manufacturing	
电气机械和器材制造业	Electric Equipment and Machinery	
计算机、通信和其他电子设备制造业	Communication Equipment, Computer and Other Electronic Equipment Manufacturing Industry	
仪器仪表制造业	Instrument manufacturing industry	
其他制造业	Other manufacturing	
废弃资源综合利用	Comprehensive utilization of waste resources	
金属制品、机械和设备修理业	Metal products, machinery and equipment repair industry	
电力、热力生产和供应业	Electric Power, Heating Power Generating and Supplying Industry	
燃气生产和供应业	Gas Mining and Supplying Industry	
水的生产和供应业	Water Processing and Supplying Industry	49959

13-9 分区县规模以上工业企业综合能源消费量（2015年）

Comprehensive Energy Consumption above Designated Size by Region（2015）

区 县	Region	综合能源消费量 Comprehensive Energy Consumption	增速（%） Growth Rate (%)
全 市	**Total**	**4879446**	**-14.2**
新城区	Xincheng	280215	-3.2
碑林区	Beilin	26614	-30.3
莲湖区	Lianhu	156286	-16.6
灞桥区	Baqiao	875941	-6.5
未央区	Weiyang	546620	-25.6
雁塔区	Yanta	1274670	-21
阎良区	Yanliang	27064	-11.8
临潼区	Lintong	77408	-10.8
长安区	Chang'an	420583	-0.3
高陵区	Gaoling	201991	-14
蓝田县	Lantian	143219	-17.3
周至县	Zhouzhi	17094	-15
户 县	Huxian	831741	-9.4

主要统计指标解释

能源消费总量 指一定时期内，地区各行业和居民生活消费的各种能源的总和。该指标是观察能源消费水平、构成和增长速度的总量指标。能源消费总量包括原煤和原油及其制品、天然气、电力等，不包括低热值燃料、生物质能和太阳能等的利用。能源消费总量分为终端能源消费量、能源加工转换损失量和能源损失量三部分。

（1）终端能源消费量：指一定时期内，全国生产和生活消费的各种能源在扣除了用于加工转换二次能源消费量和损失量以后的数量。

（2）能源加工转换损失量：指一定时期内，全国投入加工转换的各种能源数量之和与产出各种能源产品之和的差额。该指标是观察能源在加工转换过程中损失量变化的指标。

（3）能源损失量：指一定时期内，能源在输送、分配、储存过程中发生的损失和由客观原因造成的各种损失量，不包括各种气体能源放空、放散量。

工业生产能源消费 指工业企业为进行工业生产活动所消费的能源。

非工业生产能源消费 指在工业企业能源消费中，除“工业生产能源消费”以外的能源消费，即非工业生产用能和工业企业附属的不从事工业生产活动的非独立核算单位用能。

运输工具消费 指在厂区内、外进行交通运输活动的交通运输工具所消费的能源。

能源加工转换投入 能源的加工转换是指为了特定的用途，将一种能源（一般为一次能源），经过一定的工艺，加工或转换成另外一种能源（一般为二次能源）。能源加工转换的投入即能源加工、转换消费。

一次能源 是指自然界中以现成形式存在，不经任何改变或转换的天然能源资源，即从自然界直接取得并不改变其形态和品位的能源。如原煤、原油、天然气、核燃料、植物燃料、风能、水能、太阳能、地热能、海洋能、潮汐能等。

二次能源 是指为了满足生产工艺和生活的特定需要以合理利用能源，将一次能源直接或间接加工转换产生的其它种类和形式的人工能源。如原煤加工产出的洗煤；由煤炭加工转换产出的焦炭，煤气；由原油加工产出的汽油、煤油、柴油、燃料油、液化石油气、炼厂干气等；由煤炭、石油、天然气转换产出的电力。

综合能源消费量 报告期内工业企业在工业生产活动中实际消费的各种能源的总和净值。计算综合能源消费量时，需要先将使用的各种能源折算成标准燃料后再进行计算。

单位生产总值能耗 指一定时期内，一个国家或地区每生产一个单位的生产总值所消耗的能源。计算公式为：

单位生产总值能耗=能源消费总量／生产总值

单位工业增加值能耗 指一定时期内，一个国家或地区每生产一个单位的工业增加值所消耗的能源。计算公式为：

单位工业增加值能耗=工业能源消费量／工业增加值

Explanatory Notes on Main Statistical Indicators

Total Energy Consumption refers to the total consumption of energy of various kinds by the production sectors and the households in the country in a given period of time. It is a comprehensive indicator to show the scale,composition and pace of increase of energy consumption. Total energy consumption includes that of coal,crude oil and their products,natural gas and electricity. However,it does not include the consumption of fuel of low calorific value, bio-energy and solar energy. Total energy consumption can be divided into three parts: end-use energy consumption; loss during the process of energy conversion; and energy loss.

(1) End-use Energy Consumption: It refers to the total energy consumption by the production sectors and the households in the country (region) in a given period of time. It does not include the consumption during the conversion of primary energy into secondary energy and the loss in the process of energy conversion.

(2) Loss During the Process of Energy Conversion: It refers to the total input of various kinds of energy for conversion, minus the total output of various kinds of energy in the country in a given period of time. It is an indicator to show the loss that occurs during the process of energy conversion.

(3) Energy Loss: It refers to the total of the loss of energy during the course of energy transport, distribution and storage and the loss caused by any objective reason in a given period of time. The loss of various kinds of gas due to gas discharges and stocktaking is not included.

Industry Consumption Energy refers to the volume of energy consumed by Industrial enterprises for industrial production activities.

Non–industry Consumption Energy refers to the energy consumed by industrial enterprises except for industrial production activities,means that energy consumed by non-industry production and not independent accounting units which was not engaged in industrial production activities affiliated to industrial enterprises.

Vehicle Energy refers to the energy consumed by vehicles which carried out transport activities in and out of factories.

Energy Processing Conversion Devoted energy processing conversion refers to for specialized application, a source of energy (normally primary energy), after a certain technology, processed or converted to another kind of energy (normally secondary energy). The input of energy conversion processing that is energy processing, and conversion consumption.

Primary Energy Source refers to natural energy resources as found naturally in the form of ready-made,without any change or conversion,as energy obtaineddirectly from natural and not change its shape and grade,such as raw coal, crude oil, natural gas, nuclear fuel, plantfuel, wind energy, water energy, solar energy,geothermalenergy, oceanic energy, tidal energy and so on.

Secondary Energy refers to other types and formsof artificial energy which was processed and conversed from primary energy sources directly or indirectly, in order to meet the specific needs in production process and life to use energy more effectively. Such as washing coalprocessed from raw coal; coke and coal gas processed andtransformed from raw coal; gasoline, kerosene, diesel oil, fuel oil, liquefied petroleum gas, dry gas refinery processed from crude oil; electric power conversed from coal, oil and natural gas.

Comprehensive energy consumption refers to the total and net energy actually consumed in industrial production activities by industrial enterprises in the reference period. When calculated the volume of consumption of comprehensive energy, should converted sorts of energy which was used into standards fuel firstly.

Energy Consumption per Unit of GDP refers to the energy consumption per unit of Gross Domestic Product in a country or the Gross Regional Product in a region in the same reference period. The formula is:

$$\text{Energy Consumption per Unit of GDP} = \frac{\text{Total Energy Consumption}}{\text{Gross Domestic Product}}$$

Energy Consumption per Unit of Industrial Value–added refers to the energy consumption per unit of industrial value-added in a country or region in the same reference period. The formula is:

$$\text{Energy Consumption per Unit of Industrial Value-added} = \frac{\text{Total Energy Consumption}}{\text{Industrial Value-added}}$$

14 建筑业

CONSTRUCTION

资料整理：杨雪峰　鲍　勇
Data management: Yang xuefeng Bao Yong
数据审核：黄小丹
Ydata audit: Huang Xiaodan

第十四部分　建筑业

一、简要说明

本章资料主要包括建筑业基本情况、建筑业施工企业生产情况和财务状况，由西安市统计局固定资产投资处提供。

二、主要指标

企业个数（个）	706	比上年增长	31.0%
建筑业总产值（亿元）	2650.41	比上年增长	2.5%
#国有及国有控股企业	2044.05	比上年增长	3.2%
房屋建筑竣工面积（万平方米）	2712.01	比上年增长	6.9%
房屋建筑面积竣工率(%)	22.6	比上年下降	0.1个百分点

14　CONSTRUCTION

Ⅰ.Brief Introduction

This chapter consists of primarily the data basic situation of the construction industry, production situation and financial situation of the construction enterprises, provided by Fixed Asset Investment Division of the Xi'an Bureau of Statistics.

Ⅱ.Major Indicators

		Increase over Preceding Year
Number of Enterprises(item)	706	31.0%
Total Output Value of Construction(100 mil. yuan)	2650.41	2.5%
State-owned Or State Holding Majority Shares	2044.05	3.2%
Floor Space of Buildings Completed(10 000 sq.m)	2712.01	6.9%
Rate of Floor Space of Buildings Completed(%)	22.6	-0.1 percentage points

14-1 主要年份建筑业总产值

Total Output Value of Construction in Representative Years

单位：亿元 (100mil. yuan)

年份 Year	单位数（个） Number of Enterprises (unit)	建筑业总产值 Total Output Value of Construction	国有及国有控股 State-owned Or State Holding Majority Shares	集体企业 Collective-owned Enterprises
2000	184	105.93	78.87	14.87
2001	205	114.81	91.82	15.47
2002	223	133.47	85.03	15.35
2003	204	177.11	119.99	13.40
2004	244	244.42	201.68	16.59
2005	235	326.65	276.68	19.61
2006	217	416.48	348.20	23.65
2007	279	604.75	432.63	32.67
2008	328	915.12	676.12	460.14
2009	326	1074.55	875.19	47.15
2010	324	1334.00	1034.04	58.39
2011	336	1619.09	1278.33	79.42
2012	396	1874.23	1364.70	96.83
2013	420	2228.41	1702.08	154.87
2014	539	2586.33	1981.24	95.02
2015	706	2650.41	2044.05	69.73

注：1、1996年以后建筑业年报统计范围由往年的县及县以上（含县级建制镇）各种经济类型的建筑企业，改为具有建筑业资质等级三级及三级以上的各种经济类型的建筑施工企业；2002年改为具有建筑业资质等级的各种经济类型的建筑施工企业。

2、本表资料含劳务分包企业。

3、由于统计口径变化，对部分年份建筑业总产值相关数据进行了修订。

14-2 全市建筑施工总承包企业基本情况（2015年）

Basic Situation of Construction General Contracting Business in Whole City（2015）

指　　标	Item	合计 Total	国有及国有控股 State-owned Or State Holding Majority Shares
企业单位数（个）（施工总承包）	Number of Enterprises (unit) (Overall Contractor For Construction)	462	103
#二级以上企业（施工总承包）	First and Second Class Enterprise	399	91
计算劳动生产率的平均人数（人）（施工总承包）	Average Number of Employed Persons in Calculation of Labor Productivity (person) (Overall Contractor For Construction)	559505	390732
#二级以上企业（施工总承包）	First and Second Class Enterprise	536983	376009
建筑业总产值（亿元）（施工总承包）	Total Output Value of Construction(100 million yuan) (Overall Contractor For Construction)	2392.85	1918.48
#二级以上企业（施工总承包）	First and Second Class Enterprise	2315.37	1862.09
全员劳动生产率 按总产值计算(元/人)	Overall Labor Productivity Calculated by Total Output Value(yuan/person)	427672	490997

14-3 施工总承包和专业承包建筑企业生产情况（2015年）

分 组	Classify	签订的合同额（万元）Contract Value (10 000 yuan)	建筑业总产值（万元）Total Output Value of Constrution (10 000 yuan)
总计	**Total**	**66617072**	**26504127**
#国有及国有控股	State-Owned and State Holding Majority Shares	56355790	20440544
一、按登记注册类型分	**Grouped by Registion Status**		
内资	Domestic Investment Enterprises	65319181	25914944
国有企业	State-owned Enterprises	7078159	3322858
集体企业	Collective-owned Enterprises	921889	697255
股份合作企业	Share-holding Corperative Enterprises	8251	8120
联营企业	Joint Ownership Enterprises	17545	7945
国有独资公司	State-owned Company	6285867	2650781
有限责任公司	Limited Liability Corporations	42312201	14435792
股份有限公司	Share-holding Corperation Ltd.	1246469	521075
私营企业	Private Enterprises	7448800	4271118
其他企业	Others		
港澳台商投资企业	Enterprises with Funds from Hong Kong,Macao and Taiwan	328	252
外商投资企业	Enterprises with Foreign Investment	1297563	588931
二、按国民经济行业分	**Grouped by Sector**		
房屋建筑业	Building Engineering Construction	24562148	10180921
土木工程建筑业	Civil Engineering Construction	38358176	13740709
建筑安装业	Installation of Construction	2369204	1566385
建筑装饰和其他建筑业	Architectural decoration and other Construction	1327544	1016112
三、按隶属关系分	**Grouped by Administrative Relationship**		
中央	Central	38039011	11559819
地方	Region	28578061	14944308
四、按企业资质等级分	**Grouped by Class of Enterprises**		
1. 施工总承包	Overall Contractor for Construction	62692818	23928467
#特级	Special Class	12281023	2897759
一级	First Class	45241812	17884517
二级	Second Class	3981048	2371436
2. 专业承包	Special Contractor	3924254	2575660
#一级以上	First Class	3102774	1819009
二级	Second Class	603821	624501

Main Indicators on Overall Constructing Contractors and Professional Contractors by Registration Status（2015）

在外省完成的产值 Output value in other provinces	建筑工程产值 Output Value of Constrution	安装工程产值 Output Value of Installation	其他产值 Others	竣工产值（万元） Completed output value (10 000 yuan)	计算劳动生产率的平均人数（人） Average Number of Employed Persons in Calculation of Labour Productivity(person)
11883102	**23781808**	**2135487**	**586832**	**12371520**	**651272**
11443581	19212871	1007609	220064	9031351	438525
11440311	23194554	2133558	586832	12368576	646174
1287320	3108983	171910	41965	1555600	68006
18216	530202	134887	32166	465937	27680
	8120				236
	7945			3763	536
1328271	2512155	122267	16359	961887	79691
8408212	13173015	931759	331019	6700698	296802
130086	466689	41548	12838	327628	14953
268206	3387445	731187	152485	2353063	158270
	252			215	13
442791	587002	1929		2729	5085
1820142	9381370	626696	172856	5836955	287154
9248767	12852584	595233	292892	5395245	299518
701934	853438	650152	62795	538477	31946
112259	694416	263406	58289	600843	32654
8931744	10917852	510700	131267	4624929	246450
2951358	12863956	1624787	455565	7746591	404822
11420560	22089693	1367539	471235	10937859	559505
2036899	2851045		46714	740696	22708
8537594	16444391	1115817	324309	8697034	422625
388660	2121050	180613	69774	1313033	91650
462542	1692115	767948	115597	1433661	91767
416181	1378227	330840	109942	1213954	65026
7422	205968	413086	5447	154058	21193

14-3 续表

分 组	Classify	期末从业人员数（人）Number of Employment at Year-end (person)	工程技术人员 Technical Personnel	一级建造师 First class construction engineer
总计	**Total**	**596245**	**86524**	**7543**
#国有及国有控股	State-Owned and State Holding Majority Shares	393852	54133	4349
一、按登记注册类型分	**Grouped by Registion Status**			
内资	Domestic Investment Enterprises	591126	86414	7538
国有企业	State-owned Enterprises	50342	10555	690
集体企业	Collective-owned Enterprises	25661	2669	110
股份合作企业	Share-holding Corperative Enterprises	238	33	
联营企业	Joint Ownership Enterprises	540	239	20
国有独资公司	State-owned Company	74993	7976	505
有限责任公司	Limited Liability Corporations	271511	38555	3374
股份有限公司	Share-holding Corperation Ltd.	15213	1788	179
私营企业	Private Enterprises	152628	24599	2660
其他企业	Others			
港澳台商投资企业	Enterprises with Funds from Hong Kong,Macao and Taiwan	12	4	
外商投资企业	Enterprises with Foreign Investment	5107	106	5
二、按国民经济行业分	**Grouped by Sector**			
房屋建筑业	Building Engineering Construction	257229	41409	3407
土木工程建筑业	Civil Engineering Construction	283657	36918	3007
建筑安装业	Installation of Construction	29485	5801	750
建筑装饰和其他建筑业	Architectural decoration and other Construction	25874	2396	379
三、按隶属关系分	**Grouped by Administrative Relationship**			
中央	Central	223742	28974	2536
地方	Region	372503	57550	5007
四、按企业资质等级分	**Grouped by Class of Enterprises**			
1. 施工总承包	Overall Contractor for Construction	516145	78534	6618
#特级	Special Class	16361	5527	924
一级	First Class	393335	54147	4541
二级	Second Class	84844	14446	1065
2. 专业承包	Special Contractor	80100	7990	925
#一级以上	First Class	54359	5272	699
二级	Second Class	22748	2356	157

continued

企业总产值（万元）Gross output value of enterprises (10 000 yuan)	房屋建筑施工面积（平方米）Number of Projects under Constrution (sq.m)	本年新开工 Beginning Projects in this year	房屋建筑竣工面积（平方米）Floor Space of Buildings Completed (sq.m)	房屋竣工价值（万元）Housing completi on value (10 000 yuan)	自有机械设备年末净值（万元）The net value of machinery and equipment owned at the end of the year (10 000 yuan)	自有机械设备年末总台数（台）The total number of machinery and equipment owned owned (stand)	自有机械设备年末总功率（千瓦）Total power of machinery and equipment owned at the end of the year (kw)
27693352	**119791582**	**31237845**	**27120073**	**5231669**	**757960**	**95768**	**3565024**
21599659	89643876	20988501	17068053	3675603	504673	49763	2453825
27104169	119791582	31237845	27120073	5231669	740143	94996	3481764
3356544	19795231	4102646	3538316	793419	69158	9112	343761
697853	4101597	1965189	2124964	357366	21149	5842	52950
8120							
11851	60746	47857	14784	1045	5991	1500	8120
2726280	7547623	457553	786967	130282	69439	10546	453815
15490526	63018056	16625210	13326137	2835642	387206	44851	1704349
521318	1425725	156499	344993	48527	6395	1464	15465
4291677	23842604	7882891	6983912	1065388	180805	21681	903304
252							
588931					17817	772	83260
10216522	107844628	27874694	25759362	5066124	193275	42699	990449
14759730	8646476	2101288	959033	104103	496082	44752	2271205
1608443	3292636	1261863	398316	61242	43576	4598	125520
1108657	7842		3362	200	25027	3719	177850
12670923	27767216	5429104	3175869	827389	372552	33920	1850988
15022429	92024366	25808741	23944204	4404280	385408	61848	1714036
25007817	118919177	30723548	26875156	5206399	677511	87060	3183844
3649757	10636283	3297100	1990804	531556	73516	11012	523645
18185983	97092606	23040198	20648651	3970072	465814	54551	2172853
2392006	10381613	3916496	3831404	641684	125829	18878	435414
2685535	872405	514297	244917	25270	80449	8708	381180
1926037	334354	1815	10937	2160	75664	7214	358593
627696	531368	510279	231777	22914	4750	1469	22320

14-4 施工总承包和专业承包建筑业企业主要指标

指　　标	Item	企业数（个） Number of Enterprises (unit)	总产值（万元） Total Output Value (10 000 yuan)	直接从事生产经营活动的平均人数（人） Directly engaged in the production and business activities of the average number of people (person)
总计	**Total**	**697**	**26504127**	**651272**
#国有及国有控股	State-Owned and State Holding Majority Shares	137	20440544	438525
一、按登记注册类型分	**Grouped by Registion Status**			
内资	Domestic Investment Enterprises	695	25914944	646174
国有企业	State-owned Enterprises	30	3322858	68006
集体企业	Collective-owned Enterprises	40	697255	27680
股份合作企业	Share-holding Corperative Enterprises	1	8120	236
联营企业	Joint Ownership Enterprises	2	7945	536
国有独资公司	State-owned Company	30	2650781	79691
有限责任公司	Limited Liability Corporations	95	14435792	296802
股份有限公司	Share-holding Corperation Ltd.	9	521075	14953
私营企业	Private Enterprises	488	4271118	158270
其他企业	Others			
港澳台商投资企业	Enterprises with Funds from Hong Kong,Macao and Taiwan	1	252	13
外商投资企业	Enterprises with Foreign Investment	1	588931	5085
二、按国民经济行业分	**Grouped by Sector**			
房屋建筑业	Building Engineering Construction	308	10180921	287154
土木工程建筑业	Civil Engineering Construction	183	13740709	299518
建筑安装业	Installation of Construction	93	1566385	31946
建筑装饰和其他建筑业	Architectural decoration and other Construction	113	1016112	32654
三、按隶属关系分	**Grouped by Administrative Relationship**			
中央	Central	50	11559819	246450
地方	Region	647	14944308	404822
四、按企业资质等级分	**Grouped by Class of Enterprises**			
1. 施工总承包	Overall Contractor for Construction	462	23928467	559505
#特级	Special Class	6	2897759	22708
一级	First Class	152	17884517	422625
二级	Second Class	241	2371436	91650
2. 专业承包	Special Contractor	235	2575660	91767
#一级以上	First Class	114	1819009	65026
二级	Second Class	92	624501	21193

The Main Indicators of Over All Contractors and Professional Contractors

建筑业企业期末从业人员数（人）The number of employees in construction enterprises at the end of period (person)	利润总额（万元）Total profit (10000 yuan)	利税总额（万元）Total profits and taxes (10000 yuan)	按总产值计算劳动生产率（万元/人）Productivity by gross output value (10000 yuan/person)	产值利润率（%）Profit rate of output value (%)	产值利税率（%）Profit and tax rate of output value (%)	资产总计（万元）Total assets (10000 yuan)	负债总计（万元）Total liabilities (10000 yuan)	资产负债率（%）Asset liability ratio (%)
596245	**602216**	**1515498**	**40.70**	**2.3**	**5.7**	**32481531**	**23611457**	**72.7**
393852	395635	1108343	46.61	1.9	5.4	23532681	19831302	84.3
591126	602274	1515412	40.11	2.3	5.8	32479414	23610669	72.7
50342	33720	94819	48.86	1.0	2.9	1831213	1506595	82.3
25661	25478	62447	25.19	3.7	9.0	555213	250384	45.1
238	62	449	34.41	0.8	5.5	6240	5163	82.7
540	-53	335	14.82	-0.7	4.2	43465	28927	66.6
74993	91129	265497	33.26	3.4	10.0	4923097	4144046	84.2
271511	284786	774692	48.64	2.0	5.4	17756943	14962999	84.3
15213	7325	23266	34.85	1.4	4.5	632717	520712	82.3
152628	159827	293907	26.99	3.7	6.9	6730526	2191843	32.6
12	-38	-28	19.38	-15.1	-11.1	233	407	174.7
5107	-20	114	115.82			1884	381	20.2
257229	207635	557330	35.45	2.0	5.5	11052461	6383104	57.8
283657	300931	788580	45.88	2.2	5.7	19155373	15695857	81.9
29485	63184	114593	49.03	4.0	7.3	1551739	1076547	69.4
25874	30466	54995	31.12	3.0	5.4	721958	455949	63.2
223742	285191	700825	46.91	2.5	6.1	16173029	13669092	84.5
372503	317025	814673	36.92	2.1	5.5	16308502	9942365	61
516145	498256	1342466	42.77	2.1	5.6	30062607	21996841	73.2
16361	120989	277964	127.61	4.2	9.6	8840622	7523313	85.1
393335	295982	874047	42.32	1.7	4.9	17653291	12331265	69.9
84844	82362	165997	25.87	3.5	7.0	2809123	1522894	54.2
80100	103960	173032	28.07	4.0	6.7	2418924	1614616	66.7
54359	56067	100709	27.97	3.1	5.5	1597129	1112172	69.6
22748	42466	63105	29.47	6.8	10.1	605888	344986	56.9

14-5 施工总承包和专业承包建筑业企业财务状况（2015年）

指 标	Item	资产总计（万元） Total assets (10000 yuan)	流动资产合计（万元） Total current assets (10000 yuan)
总计	**Total**	**32481531**	**24721908**
#国有及国有控股	State-Owned and State Holding Majority Shares	23532681	19319543
一、按登记注册类型分	**Grouped by Registion Status**		
内资	Domestic Investment Enterprises	32479414	24719913
国有企业	State-owned Enterprises	1831213	1608271
集体企业	Collective-owned Enterprises	555213	423711
股份合作企业	Share-holding Corperative Enterprises	6240	5846
联营企业	Joint Ownership Enterprises	43465	41196
国有独资公司	State-owned Company	4923097	3991180
有限责任公司	Limited Liability Corporations	17756943	14574341
股份有限公司	Share-holding Corperation Ltd.	632717	531329
私营企业	Private Enterprises	6730526	3544039
其他企业	Others		
港澳台商投资企业	Enterprises with Funds from Hong Kong,Macao and Taiwan	233	219
外商投资企业	Enterprises with Foreign Investment	1884	1776
二、按国民经济行业分	**Grouped by Sector**		
房屋建筑业	Building Engineering Construction	11052461	7508778
土木工程建筑业	Civil Engineering Construction	19155373	15278726
建筑安装业	Installation of Construction	1551739	1327788
建筑装饰和其他建筑业	Architectural decoration and other Construction	721958	606616
三、按隶属关系分	**Grouped by Administrative Relationship**		
中央	Central	16173029	12925516
地方	Region	16308502	11796392
四、按企业资质等级分	**Grouped by Class of Enterprises**		
1. 施工总承包	Overall Contractor for Construction	30062607	22655739
#特级	Special Class	8840622	6600681
一级	First Class	17653291	13223412
二级	Second Class	2809123	2257986
2. 专业承包	Special Contractor	2418924	2066169
#一级以上	First Class	1597129	1377527
二级	Second Class	605888	483895

Financial Status of Overall Constructing Contractors and Professional Contractors（2015）

固定资产合计（万元）Total fixed assets (10000 yuan)	固定资产原价（万元）Original value of fixed assets (10000 yuan)	累计折旧（万元）Accumulated depreciation (10000 yuan)	本年折旧 Depreciation of this year	负债合计（万元）Total liabilities (10000 yuan)	流动负债合计（万元）Total current liabilities (10000 yuan)	非流动负债（万元）Non current liabilities (10000 yuan)	所有者权益合计（万元）Total owners' equity (10000 yuan)
1768977	**2949487**	**1571039**	**280931**	**23611457**	**21694134**	**1559745**	**8870073**
1067475	2179021	1284547	236154	19831302	18355047	1397550	3701380
1768906	2949309	1570889	280926	23610669	21693346	1559745	8868745
79740	152324	85619	8500	1506595	1339866	107980	324618
65268	77114	25589	4617	250384	240073	4400	304829
174	1283	1109	42	5163	5046		1077
1268	1369	966	382	28927	3100		14538
296631	687071	422704	88613	4144046	3907006	220889	779051
722610	1409143	812588	142163	14962999	13826389	1136466	2793944
33689	50173	21933	2476	520712	502112	14780	112006
569526	570832	200381	34133	2191843	1869754	75230	4538682
14	143	129	1	407	407		-174
57	35	21	4	381	381		1502
562332	679989	278834	35192	6383104	5880890	297523	4669356
1059068	2065379	1194432	231153	15695857	14343990	1206861	3459516
88554	122934	62147	8947	1076547	1029154	43148	475192
59023	81185	35626	5639	455949	440100	12213	266009
751486	1642767	987670	199361	13669092	12543191	1086305	2503937
1017491	1306720	583369	81570	9942365	9150943	473440	6366136
1555974	2708396	1446826	264484	21996841	20128856	1520317	8065766
222226	410674	231938	40058	7523313	6448987	1074325	1317310
958772	1792211	1001719	188665	12331265	11768337	384245	5322026
318642	385905	147651	26563	1522894	1301576	52777	1286229
213003	241091	124213	16447	1614616	1565278	39428	804307
144914	187703	98634	11607	1112172	1073126	32608	484958
62439	46969	21996	4308	344986	337134	6820	260902

14-5 续表

指 标	Item	实收资本（万元）Paid in capital (10000 yuan)	主营业务收入（万元）Main business income (10000 yuan)
总计	**Total**	**4851193**	**29524382**
#国有及国有控股	State-Owned and State Holding Majority Shares	2561388	23872070
一、按登记注册类型分	**Grouped by Registion Status**		
内资	Domestic Investment Enterprises	4849032	29520363
国有企业	State-owned Enterprises	233757	1957149
集体企业	Collective-owned Enterprises	281652	822259
股份合作企业	Share-holding Corperative Enterprises	847	11419
联营企业	Joint Ownership Enterprises	6612	8019
国有独资公司	State-owned Company	572833	5446573
有限责任公司	Limited Liability Corporations	1869523	16805825
股份有限公司	Share-holding Corperation Ltd.	67319	533631
私营企业	Private Enterprises	1816489	3935488
其他企业	Others		
港澳台商投资企业	Enterprises with Funds from Hong Kong,Macao and Taiwan	661	252
外商投资企业	Enterprises with Foreign Investment	1500	3767
二、按国民经济行业分	**Grouped by Sector**		
房屋建筑业	Building Engineering Construction	1964940	10131816
土木工程建筑业	Civil Engineering Construction	2354416	16856511
建筑安装业	Installation of Construction	321744	1720768
建筑装饰和其他建筑业	Architectural decoration and other Construction	210093	815287
三、按隶属关系分	**Grouped by Administrative Relationship**		
中央	Central	1640421	14761866
地方	Region	3210772	14762516
四、按企业资质等级分	**Grouped by Class of Enterprises**		
1. 施工总承包	Overall Contractor for Construction	4300778	27222137
#特级	Special Class	889789	6115181
一级	First Class	2206457	17912581
二级	Second Class	1087646	2355737
2. 专业承包	Special Contractor	550415	2302245
#一级以上	First Class	371213	1560678
二级	Second Class	131751	604838

continued 1

主营业务成本（万元）Main business costs (10000 yuan)	主营业务税金及附加（万元）The main business tax and surcharges (10000 yuan)	管理费用（万元）Management costs (10000 yuan)		营业利润（万元）Operating profit (10000 yuan)	利润总额（万元）Total profit (10000 yuan)	应付职工薪酬（万元）Payable to employees (10000 yuan)
			税金 taxes			
26624145	**878590**	**869383**	**38100**	**598808**	**602216**	**3549030**
21915033	698120	640381	25429	384794	395635	2800705
26620484	878450	869122	38095	598867	602274	3548697
1783374	59946	52789	1399	33474	33720	345172
604812	27080	31972	1852	33515	25478	145678
10844	384	115	3	62	62	85
6806	317	910	74	-56	-53	2746
4789154	165350	154623	6156	93991	91129	669394
15603987	484726	472423	18077	271889	284786	1822983
495711	16012	9480	359	6895	7325	34483
3325796	124635	146810	10175	159097	159827	528156
194	9	79	1	-38	-38	57
3467	131	182	4	-21	-20	276
8811546	326718	221014	17059	213553	207635	1541746
15561436	478559	556031	17962	292059	300931	1792910
1520191	49660	70053	2065	62868	63184	137192
730972	23653	22285	1014	30328	30466	77182
13459526	410786	446447	15660	274379	285191	1653341
13164619	467804	422936	22440	324429	317025	1895689
24644012	811986	750381	35274	495206	498256	3338289
5787080	158156	162967	6137	113671	120989	416440
16142997	559078	468689	21400	293569	295982	2480918
1951552	69588	92302	7153	89256	82362	367745
1980133	66604	119002	2826	103602	103960	210741
1372703	42444	62337	2021	56244	56067	144710
486132	20128	50643	696	42281	42466	52485

14-6 劳务分包建筑业企业生产经营情况（2015年）

单位：万元

指 标	Item	固定资产原价 Original value of fixed assets	本年折旧 Depreciation of this year
总计	**Total**	**256**	**67**
#国有及国有控股	State-Owned and State Holding Majority Shares		
一、按登记注册类型分	**Grouped by Registion Status**		
内资	Domestic Investment Enterprises	256	67
国有企业	State-owned Enterprises		
集体企业	Collective-owned Enterprises		
股份合作企业	Share-holding Corperative Enterprises		
联营企业	Joint Ownership Enterprises		
国有独资公司	State-owned Company		
有限责任公司	Limited Liability Corporations		
股份有限公司	Share-holding Corperation Ltd.		
私营企业	Private Enterprises	256	67
其他企业	Others		
港澳台商投资企业	Enterprises with Funds from Hong Kong,Macao and Taiwan		
外商投资企业	Enterprises with Foreign Investment		
二、按国民经济行业分	**Grouped by Sector**		
房屋建筑业	Building Engineering Construction	172	31
土木工程建筑业	Civil Engineering Construction	9	5
建筑安装业	Installation of Construction		
建筑装饰和其他建筑业	Architectural decoration and other Construction	75	31
三、按隶属关系分	**Grouped by Administrative Relationship**		
中央	Central		
地方	Region	256	67

Production and Management Situation of Subcontractor Construction Enterprises(2015)

(10 000yuan)

资产总计 Total assets	负债合计 Total liabilities	实收资本 Paid in capital	营业收入 Total Revenue	主营业务收入 Main business income	营业成本 Total Cost	主营业务收入 Main business income
30600	**27160**	**2764**	**60370**	**60361**	**56310**	**52590**
30600	27160	2764	60370	60361	56310	52590
30600	27160	2764	60370	60361	56310	52590
27732	25554	1509	31776	31767	29057	29057
1484	1284	200	915	915	869	869
587	310	300	3858	3858	3658	3658
797	12	755	23821	23821	22726	19006
30600	27160	2764	60370	60361	56310	52590

14-6 续表

单位：万元

指 标	Item	营业税金及附加 Taxs and Other Changes	主营业务税金及附加 Taxs and Other Changes on Principal Business
总计	**Total**	**2023**	**2023**
#国有及国有控股	State-Owned and State Holding Majority Shares		
一、按登记注册类型分	**Grouped by Registion Status**		
内资	Domestic Investment Enterprises	2023	2023
国有企业	State-owned Enterprises		
集体企业	Collective-owned Enterprises		
股份合作企业	Share-holding Corperative Enterprises		
联营企业	Joint Ownership Enterprises		
国有独资公司	State-owned Company		
有限责任公司	Limited Liability Corporations		
股份有限公司	Share-holding Corperation Ltd.		
私营企业	Private Enterprises	2023	2023
其他企业	Others		
港澳台商投资企业	Enterprises with Funds from Hong Kong,Macao and Taiwan		
外商投资企业	Enterprises with Foreign Investment		
二、按国民经济行业分	**Grouped by Sector**		
房屋建筑业	Building Engineering Construction	1066	1066
土木工程建筑业	Civil Engineering Construction	31	31
建筑安装业	Installation of Construction	130	130
建筑装饰和其他建筑业	Architectural decoration and other Construction	796	796
三、按隶属关系分	**Grouped by Administrative Relationship**		
中央	Central		
地方	Region	2023	2023

continued 1

(10 000yuan)

销售费用 Sale Expenses	管理费用 Management costs	税金 taxes	财务费用 Financial Expenses	营业利润 Operating profit	利润总额 Total profit	应付职工薪酬 Payable to employees
28	**1471**	**83**	**138**	**477**	**427**	**39939**
28	1471	83	138	477	427	39939
28	1471	83	138	477	427	39939
	1145	76	138	375	370	35103
	28			13	13	860
	74	4		-3	-3	3623
28	224	3		92	47	353
28	1471	83	138	477	427	39939

14-7 各区县建筑业主要经济指标（2015年）

Main Indicators of Construction Enterprises by Region（2015）

区 县	Region	企业个数 (个) Number of Enterprises (unit)	总产值 (亿元) Total Output Value (100 million yuan)	计算劳动生产率的平均人数(人) Average Number of Employed Persons in Calculation of Labor Productivity(person)	全员劳动生产率 (万元/人) Overall Labor Productivity (10 000 yuan/person)	利税总额 (亿元) Total Pre-tax Profits (100 million yuan)
合 计	**Total**	**697**	**2650.41**	**651272**	**40.70**	**151.55**
新城区	Xincheng	50	272.41	53056	51.34	12.22
碑林区	Beilin	101	662.59	104041	63.69	41.87
莲湖区	Lianhu	60	195.13	44506	43.84	10.70
灞桥区	Baqiao	33	96.44	38076	25.33	7.60
未央区	Weiyang	108	524.63	147291	35.62	33.18
雁塔区	Yanta	233	745.59	187038	39.86	34.99
阎良区	Yanliang	19	16.53	9140	18.09	0.79
临潼区	Lintong	23	12.09	5648	21.41	0.66
长安区	Chang'an	35	60.31	24130	24.99	3.45
高陵区	Gaoling	9	30.52	25904	11.78	3.67
蓝田县	Lantian	9	10.56	3747	28.17	1.19
周至县	Zhouzhi	11	9.83	3750	26.20	0.75
户 县	Huxian	6	13.78	4945	27.86	0.48

14-8 各区县建筑业房屋施工及竣工面积（2015年）

Floor Space of Buildings under Construction & Completed by Region（2015）

区 县	Region	房屋建筑施工面积（万平方米）Floor Space under Construction (10 000sq.m)	本年新开工面积 Newly Started This Year	房屋建筑竣工面积（万平方米）Floor Space of Buildings Completed (10 000sq.m)	竣工房屋价值（亿元）Value of Buildings Completed (100 million yuan)
合 计	**Total**	**11979.16**	**3123.78**	**2712.01**	**523.17**
新城区	Xincheng	1091.29	383.39	260.95	53.43
碑林区	Beilin	3914.92	1065.31	800.72	172.67
莲湖区	Lianhu	1649.89	317.03	357.43	80.48
灞桥区	Baqiao	131.98	49.74	52.34	9.72
未央区	Weiyang	2049.99	393.59	254.22	54.84
雁塔区	Yanta	2450.46	617.81	648.61	96.67
阎良区	Yanliang	85.08	29.05	28.47	4.36
临潼区	Lintong	53.47	24.09	25.47	3.59
长安区	Chang'an	195.72	62.75	100.41	18.13
高陵区	Gaoling	122.80	67.72	64.96	9.53
蓝田县	Lantian	42.51	23.54	16.35	2.45
周至县	Zhouzhi	67.36	34.98	41.64	6.75
户 县	Huxian	123.69	54.78	60.44	10.55

14-9 各区县建筑业企业主要经济效益指标（2015年）

Main Economic Benefit Indicators on Construction Enterprises by Region（2015）

区 县	Region	人均利润总额（元/人）Per Profit (yuan/person)	人均利税（元/人）Per Pre-tax Profits (yuan/person)	人均竣工产值（元/人）Per Output Value of Buildings Completed (yuan/person)	人均施工面积（平方米/人）Per Floor Space of Buildings Under Construcyion (sq.m/person)	人均竣工面积（平方米/人）Per Floor Space of Buildings Completed (sq.m/person)
合 计	**Total**	**9247**	**23270**	**80330**	**184**	**42**
新城区	Xincheng	7054	23033	100711	206	49
碑林区	Beilin	16632	40242	165965	376	77
莲湖区	Lianhu	9265	24045	180840	371	80
灞桥区	Baqiao	9935	19960	25532	35	14
未央区	Weiyang	9659	22529	37233	139	17
雁塔区	Yanta	6563	18710	51674	131	35
阎良区	Yanliang	4083	8690	47730	93	31
临潼区	Lintong	5540	11744	63481	95	45
长安区	Chang'an	5901	14302	75148	81	42
高陵区	Gaoling	5036	14156	36799	47	25
蓝田县	Lantian	23982	31633	65434	113	44
周至县	Zhouzhi	11165	19877	179912	180	111
户 县	Huxian	673	9606	213410	250	122

14-9 续表 continued

区 县	Region	产值利润率（%）Ratio of Profits to Output Value (%)	产值利税率（%）Ratio of Pre-tax Profits to Output Value (%)	资产利润率（%）Ratio of Profits to Assets (%)	资产利税率（%）Ratio of Pre-tax Profits to Assets (%)	资产负债率（%）Ratio of Debts to Assets (%)
合 计	**Total**	**2.3**	**5.7**	**1.9**	**4.7**	**72.7**
新城区	Xincheng	1.4	4.5	0.8	2.7	42.8
碑林区	Beilin	2.6	6.3	2.4	5.9	80.8
莲湖区	Lianhu	2.1	5.5	1.7	4.5	77.9
灞桥区	Baqiao	3.9	7.9	3.3	6.5	81.1
未央区	Weiyang	2.7	6.3	1.8	4.1	82.8
雁塔区	Yanta	1.6	4.7	1.6	4.5	74.5
阎良区	Yanliang	2.3	4.8	1.7	3.6	66.1
临潼区	Lintong	2.6	5.5	2.8	6.0	37.3
长安区	Chang'an	2.4	5.7	2.0	4.9	69.7
高陵区	Gaoling	4.3	12.0	2.9	8.3	9.7
蓝田县	Lantian	8.5	11.2	25.3	33.4	52.1
周至县	Zhouzhi	4.3	7.6	6.3	11.2	55.0
户 县	Huxian	0.2	3.4	0.6	8.3	46.8

主要统计指标解释

建筑业统计单位 指从事房屋、构筑物建造和设备安装活动的法人企业。建筑业法人企业应具有建筑业资质并能够独立核算，同时其应具备以下条件：①依法成立，有自己的名称、组织机构和场所，能够承担民事责任；②独立拥有和使用资产，承担负债，有权与其他单位签订合同；③独立核算盈亏，能够编制资产负债表。

建筑业总产值 是以货币形式表现的建筑业企业在一定时期内生产的建筑业产品和提供的服务的总和。建筑业总产值包括：

（1）建筑工程产值：指列入建筑工程预算内的各种工程价值。

（2）安装工程产值：指设备安装工程价值，不包括被安装设备本身的价值。

（3）其他产值：建筑业总产值中除建筑工程、安装丁程以外的产值。包括房屋构筑物修理产值、非标准设备制造产值、总包企业向分包企业收取的管理费以及不能明确划分的施工活动所完成的产值。

a. 房屋构筑物修理产值：指房屋和构筑物修理所完成的产值，但不包括被修理房屋、构筑物本身价值和生产设备的修埋价值。

b. 非标准设备制造产值：指加工制造没有定型的非标准生产设备的加了费和原材料价值（如化工厂、炼油厂用的各种罐、槽，矿井生产统一使用的各种漏斗、三角槽、阀门等）以及附属加工厂为本企业承建工程制作的非标准设备的价值。

建筑业增加值 指建筑业企业在报告期内以货币形式表现的建筑业生产经营活动的最终成果。

从2004年第一次全国经济普查开始，建筑业现价增加值按生产法和分配法（收入法）两种方法计算，以收入法的计算结果为准，即从收入的角度出发，根据生产要素在牛产过程中应得的收入份额计算。具体计算方法：经济普查年度建筑业增加值按照《经济普查年度GDP核算方案》计算，非经济普查年度建筑业增加值按照们≥经济普查年度GDP核算方案》计算。

房屋建筑施工面积 指在报告期内施过工的全部房屋建筑面积，包括本期新开工的房屋面积、上期施工跨入本期继续施工的房屋面积、上期停缓建在本期恢复施工的房屋面积、本期竣工的房屋面积及本期施丁后又停缓建的房屋面积。

房屋建筑竣工面积 指在报告期内房屋建筑按照设计要求全部完工，达到了使用条件，经验收鉴定合格，正式移交使用单位的房犀建筑面积。

Explanatory Notes on Main Statistical Indicators

Statistical Unit in the Construction Industry refers to a corporate enterprise engaged in the construction of buildings and structures and in the installation of equipment. A corporate construction enterprise should have qualification certificates with independent accounting system, and should meet the following 3 requirements: a) being set up in line with relevant legal basis, having its full name, organization and location, and capable of taking civil liabilities; b) independently possessing and using its assets and assuming its liabilities, and entitled to sign contracts with other institutions; and c) making independent accounts of its profits and losses, and capable of compiling its own balance sheet.

Gross Output Value of Construction refers to total of construction products and services, expressed in money terms, produced or rendered by construction and installation enterprises during a given period of time. It includes:

(1)Output value of construction projects: the value of projects covered by the project budgets;

(2) Output value of installation projects: the value of the installation of equipment, (excluding the value of the equipment to be installed);

(3)Other output values: the output value of construction industry apart from that of construction projects and installation projects. It includes: output value of repair of buildings and structures; output value of non-standard equipment manufacturing; overhead expenses received by contracted enterprises from the sub-contracted enterprises and the completed output value of construction activities for which there is no clear definition.

a. Output value of repair of buildings and structures: the value created through the repairs of buildings or structures. It does not include the value of buildings or structures being repaired and the value of the repair of production equipment;

b. Output value of manufactured non-standard equipment: the value of non-standard production equipment, including raw materials and manufacturing cost, made for the construction project (i.e., chemical plant; kettles or tanks used by refineries; various fillers, triangle tanks, valves used by mines). It also includes the output value of equipment manufactured by subsidiary workshops.

Value–added of Construction refers to the final result of the activities of production and operation of enterprises of the construction industry in monetary terms during the reference period.

Starting from the 2004 economic census, value-added of construction is calculated by both production approach and income approach, with the figures from the income approach as the final figures. Under the income approach, calculation starts from the perspective of income and is based on the share of income derived from the production process by the relevant factors of production. Specifically, value-added of construction for the Census years is calculated in accordance with the Programme of Compilation of GDP and National Accounts for the Year of Economic Census, and value-added of construction for other years is calculated in accordance with the Programme of Compilation of GDP and National Accounts for the Non Economic Census Years.

Floor Space of Buildings Under Construction refers to floor space of buildings under construction during the reference period, including the floor space of buildings for which construction has newly started; buildings for which construction has started earlier and is continuing during the reference period; and buildings for which construction has been suspended earlier but has restarted during the reference period; buildings completed during the reference period; and buildings under construction but construction has subsequently been during the reference period.

Floor Space of Buildings Completed refers to the floor space of buildings that are completed in the reference period in accordance with the requirements of the design, up to the standard for being put into use, and having been checked and accepted by departments concerned as qualified ones.

15 运输和邮电

TRANSPORT,POSTAL AND TELECOMMUNICATION SERVICE

资料整理：齐昆峰
Data management：Qi Kunfeng
数据审核：王金桂
Data audit：Wang Jingui

第十五部分　运输和邮电

一、简要说明

本章资料包括交通运输业和邮电通信业的基本情况，主要是交通运输工具、货物和旅客运输量、邮电业务、邮政局所及服务点等基本情况。资料由西安市统计局服务业和社会科技处根据有关部门提供资料整理。

二、主要指标

旅客周转量（亿人公里）	324.15	比上年增长	3.9%
货物周转量（亿吨公里）	643.01	比上年增长	2.9%
邮电业务总量（亿元）	331.53	比上年增长	13.5%
全社会车辆数（万辆）	239.41	比上年增长	11.9%
#民用小轿车	128.22	比上年增长	15.4%

15 TRANSPORT,POSTAL AND TELECOMMUNICATION SERVICES

Ⅰ.Brief Introduction

Data in this chapter consists of primarily basic data of communication, transportation and postal service industry, transportation facility, amount of goods and passenger transportation, basic data of postal service, post offices and service establishments of Xi'an City. Data in this chapter is compiled by Tertiary Industry and Social & Science and Technology Division of the Xi'an Bureau of Statistics according to the data provided by department concerned of the municipal government.

Ⅱ.Major Indicators

		Increase over Preceding Year
Passenger-Km (100 mil. Person-km)	324.15	3.9%
Freight Ton-Km (100 mil. Ton-km)	643.01	2.9%
Amount of Postal and Telecommunication Service(100 mil. Yuan)	331.53	13.5%
Number of Vehides in the whole Sciety(10 000 unit)	239.41	11.9%
Civil Car	128.22	15.4%

15-1 主要年份各种交通线路和桥梁

Transportation Routes and Number of Bridges in Representative Years

年 份 Year	公路里程 （公里） Length of Highways (km)	桥 梁 （座） Bridges (seat)	桥梁长度 （公里） length of Bridge (km)
1978			
1979			
1980			
1981			
1982			
1983			
1984			
1985			
1986			
1987			
1988			
1989	2563		
1990	2586		
1991	2785		
1992	2786		
1993	2801		
1994	2830		
1995	2852		
1996	2877		
1997	3026		
1998	3047		
1999	2789		
2000	3010		
2001	3298		
2002	7862	629	29799
2003	8360	629	29799
2004	8360	629	29799
2005	8500	634	46973
2006	9530	634	46973
2007	9672	1319	91412
2008	11895	1710	151996
2009	12378	1856	154866
2010	12378	1856	154866
2011	12599	1863	149743
2012	13127	2190	214978
2013	13135	2213	224962
2014	13251	2213	224949
2015	13328	2323	250910

注：本表数据来自市交通局、民航通航里程2013年统计口径发生较大变化。

15-1 续表 continued

年 份 Year	永久式桥梁 （座） Permanent Bridges (seat)	永久式桥梁 （公里） Length of Permanent Bridges (km)	民航通航里程 （重复航线）（公里） Length of Total Civil Aviation Routes(km)
1978			
1979			
1980			
1981			
1982			
1983			
1984			
1985			
1986			
1987			
1988			
1989			
1990			
1991			
1992			65007
1993			83215
1994			100800
1995			119753
1996			126433
1997			173010
1998			180000
1999			141284
2000			139764
2001			154614
2002	629	29799	211000
2003	629	29799	381800
2004	629	29799	386953
2005	632	46915	485749
2006	632	46915	418852
2007	1275	90716	553355
2008	1657	150980	515524
2009	1803	153850	587904
2010	1803	153850	742375
2011	1811	148810	898628
2012	2138	213985	981450
2013	2161	223970	70643568
2014	2171	224165	78626210
2015	2286	250175	93375419

15–2 各种交通线路里程和桥梁数（2015年）

Length of Transportation Routes and Number of Bridges（2015）

指　标	Item	2015
公路里程（公里）	**Length of Highways (km)**	**13328**
等级公路	Expressways and Class I to IV Highways	12805
高速	Expressway	532
一级	First Class	325
二级	Second Class	1476
三级	Third Class	1211
四级	Forth Class	9260
等外公路	Highways below Class IV	523
桥梁	Bridges	
永久式桥梁	Permanent	
座（座）	Seat (seat)	2286
长度（公里）	Length (m)	250175
民航通航里程（公里）（重复航线）	**Length of Total Civil Aviation Routes(km)**	**93375419**
国际航线	International routes	
民航航线条数（条）	**Length of Civil Aviation routes(Article)**	**276**
国际航线	International routes	36

注：本表数据来自市交通局。

15-3 主要年份全社会车辆数

Possession of Civil Vehicles in Representative Years

单位：辆、台 (unit)

年 份 Year	合计 Total	汽车 Motor	载客汽车 Passenget Vehicles	载货汽车 Ordinary Trucks	摩托车 Motorcycles	拖拉机 Tractors
1999	**279335**	133192	63772	44348		38023
2000	**310252**	138318	89783	44974		37177
2001	**369988**	172436	110744	55453		31355
2002	**454998**	206653	134527	64623	176960	36083
2003	**516719**	242599	163872	70781	191834	34733
2004	**512802**	276012	195524	74557	156709	34755
2005	**544586**	377628	240923	82463	131440	34741
2006	**608155**	393778	296078	89772	131449	33236
2007	**840376**	522616	360081	97614	284594	32028
2008	**875005**	595735	430472	89093	247079	30176
2009	**1012937**	754803	567326	113430	224121	31347
2010	**1253461**	961283	739038	145740	259239	29151
2011	**1445811**	1174874	928669	171649	241132	25600
2012	**1633257**	1380125	1123105	186412	224279	24458
2013	**1862063**	1634885	1372371	207058	200419	21898
2014	**2139024**	1926012	1658714	224409	190625	17484
2015	**2394052**	2191023	1929195	224322	179619	18099

注：本表数据来自市车管所。

15-4 全社会车辆数（2015年）

Possession of Civil Vehicles（2015）

指　标	Item	2015
合计（辆）	**Total (unit)**	**2394052**
民用汽车（辆）	Motor(unit)	2191023
#私人汽车拥有量	Possession of Private Vehicles	1974473
载客汽车	Passenget Vehicles	1929195
#大　型	Large	15736
轿　车	Car	1282225
普通载货汽车	Ordinary Trucks	224322
#重、中型	Heavy and Medium	59103
其他汽车	Others	37506
#三　轮	Three Wheelers	14613
拖拉机（台）	Tractors(unit)	18099
# 大中型	Large and Medium	
小　型	Small-sized	
摩托车（辆）	Motorcycle (unit)	179619
普通摩托车	Bicycle Motor	174379
挂车（辆）	Articulated Trailers (unit)	5241
其他类型车（辆）	Others (unit)	70

注：本表数据来自市车管所。

15-5 主要年份交通运输量及周转量

Passenger Traffic and Kilometers and Freight Traffic and Ton-kilometers in Representative Years

年 份 Year	客运量 （万人次） Passenger Traffic (10 000 person-times)	旅客周转量 （万人公里） Passenger-Km (10 000 person-Km)	货运量 （万吨） Freight Traffic (10 000 tons)	货物周转量（万吨公里） Freight Ton-Km (10 000 ton-Km)
1978	1334		3723	
1979	1420		3919	
1980	1508		3655	
1981	1839		3379	
1982	2340		4067	
1983	3054		4225	
1984	2899		4966	
1985	2404		5681	
1986	2186		5409	
1987	3781		6294	
1988	5721		6968	
1989	6092		8742	
1990	5748		6980	
1991	4193		3389	
1992	4368		8233	
1993	8036		8406	
1994	8321		8754	
1995	9069		9590	
1996	9854		10577	
1997	8922		9358	
1998	9223		9429	
1999	10311	2130383	9766	3452383
2000	10756	2507896	10191	3691963
2001	9078	2658037	7728	4229430
2002	12527	2524444	9484	4544040
2003	11413	2596402	9392	5037684
2004	10832	3112374	14845	5850029
2005	10479	1607568	12051	1249525
2006	11245	1721217	11832	1354318
2007	12466	1753464	15124	1473182
2008	26501	2529007	27560	3490707
2009	28693	2582025	30606	3766806
2010	30294	2942957	34323	4301680
2011	33375	3223544	39239	5212010
2012	36154	3387448	44924	5958742
2013	38289	3634915	50119	6471497
2014	25719	3091147	42039	6234128
2015	26904	3241463	46270	6430083

注：本表数据由市交通局、西安铁路局、咸阳机场、长安航空公司、东方航空公司西北分公司提供。
2014年陕西省公路运输统计方法制度改变，因此与往年数据不可比。

15-6 交通运输量及运输周转量（2015年）

Passenger Traffic and Kilometers and Freight Traffic and Ton-kilometers（2015）

指　标	Item	2015年	2015比上年增长（%）Increase over Preceding Year（%）
一、客运量合计（万人次）	**Passenger Traffic(10 000 person-times)**	**26904**	**4.3**
铁路	Railway	3982	11.1
公路	Highway	19625	1.8
民航	Civil Aviation	3297	12.7
二、旅客周转量合计（万人公里）	**Passenger-Km (10 000 person-Km)**	**3241463**	**3.9**
铁路	Railway	684134	-0.5
公路	Highway	1088896	2.0
民航	Civil Aviation	1468432	7.6
三、货运量合计（万吨）	**Freight Traffic(l0 000 tons)**	**46270**	**10.1**
铁路	Railway	848	-5.8
公路	Highway	45401	10.4
民航	Civil Aviation	21	13.5
四、货物周转量（万吨公里）	**Freight Ton-Kin (10 000 ton-Km)**	**6430083**	**2.9**
铁路	Railway	2164003	-8.9
公路	Highway	4254824	10.1
民航	Civil Aviation	11256	5.4

注：本表数据由市交通局、西安铁路局、咸阳机场、长安航空公司、东方航空公司西北分公司提供。

15-7 主要年份邮政电信情况

年份 Year	邮电业务总量（万元） Business Volume of Postal and Telecommunication Services(10 000 yuan)	电信业务总量 Business Volume of Telecommunication Services	#邮政业务总量 Business Volume of Postal Services
1978	1420		
1979	1616		
1980	1640		
1981	1713		
1982	2154		
1983	2250		
1984	2484		
1985	2972		
1986	3244		
1987	3911		
1988	5327		
1989	5973		
1990	7843		
1991	5700		
1992	6610		
1993	36581		
1994	54034		
1995	76450		
1996	104566		
1997	124601		
1998	204927		
1999	306457		
2000	461628		
2001	367620		
2002	515259	470492	44767
2003	820943	770673	50270
2004	1027415	975045	52370
2005	1320447	1261033	59414
2006	1867560	1796533	71027
2007	2267633	2191250	76383
2008	2646662	2564524	82138
2009	2989246	2900836	88410
2010	3231059	3167750	63309
2011	2005025	1944329	60696
2012	2162065	2098273	63762
2013	2479430	2313630	165800
2014	2922011	2695332	226679
2015	3315324	2983024	332300

注：2002年及以后，邮政电信机构分离；2001—2010年邮电业务总量按2000年不变价格计算；2011年后邮电业务总量按2010年不变价格计算，故与以往年份不可比。

Basic Statistic on Postal and Telecommunication Service in Representative Years

固定电话年末用户数（户） Number of Immobile Telephone at Year-end (subscriber)	农村电话用户数 Number of Telephone in Rural Areas at Year-end	移动电话用户年末数（户） Number of Mobile Phone at Year-end (subscriber)	互联网年末宽带用户数（户） Number of Broad Band Net User (subscriber)
12828	1062		
13487	1052		
14024	1086		
14497	1125		
15357	1129		
16922	1156		
18611	1203		
21624	1239		
26373	1235		
30200	1290		
34265	1357		
39506	1498		
45267	1668		
49516	2479		
60727	2613		
101327	2671		
197398	5067		
299485	8386		
430270	13654		
573244	21202		
736998	37863		
874586	74761		
1242637	170199		
1711500	259374	1277400	17183
2095230	358803	1964200	35230
2538393	415593	2412392	160900
2934424	480276	3500900	243448
3214806	500847	4199570	339280
3159639	467526	5510720	508775
3145819	419446	6645863	586213
3068807	383869	7377575	813987
2891009	358238	11200566	1167916
2617691	335048	14230800	1461804
2703640	320189	16141463	1841027
3110176	335864	18035397	2023059
3191112	330602	21606662	2670473
3066575	372823	20253157	2779458
2920773	306336	17669953	2899714

注：本表数据由市邮政管理局、市邮政局，中国联通、中国电信、中国移动和中国铁通等西安分公司提供。

15-8 邮政业务及服务网点

Postal Service and Branch Post Office

指 标	Item	2011	2012	2013	2014	2015
一、邮政业务总量（万元）	**Business Volume of Postal Services(10 000 yuan)**	**60696**	**63077**	**165800**	**226679**	**332300**
二、邮政业务收入（万元）	**Gross Income of Post Services (10 000 yuan)**	**65174**	**71778**	**177100**	**213893**	**307008**
其中：快递业务收入（万元）	Express delivery business income (10 000 yuan)			97100	134306	207451
三、函件（万件）	**Number of Letters (10 000 pcs)**	**3061**	**2769**	**2856**	**2112**	**1707**
四、包件（万件）	**Parcels (10 000 pcs)**	**91**	**50**	**89**	**71**	**69**
五、汇票（万张）	**Money Order (10 000 pcs)**	**112**	**90**	**148**	**81**	**48**
六、报纸订销累计份数（万份）	**Accumulated Newspaper Prescribing and** Sales Volume (10 000 pcs)	**12603**	**13052**	**14495**	**14338**	**14457**
七、杂志订销累计份数（万份）	**Accumulated Magazine Prescribing and** Sales Volume (10 000 pcs)	**564**	**613**	**1628**	**1572**	**1285**
八、特快专递类业务（万件）	**Express Mail Service Volume (10 000 pcs)**	**1901**	**129**	**138**	**107**	**61**
九、集邮业务量（万枚）	**Stamps For Collection (10 000 pcs)**	**1060**	**2312**	**1431**	**1477**	**1920**
十、邮政营销网点（处）	**Number of Post Office Branch Establishments (unit)**	**277**	**279**	**269**	**280**	**299**
#设在农村的局所	In it: number of post offices in rural area	50	115	110	123	140
十一、邮政信筒信箱（个）	**Number of Mailboxes(unit)**	**1108**	**1108**	**1108**	**1170**	**1170**

注：本表数据来自市邮政管理局和邮政局，2013年邮政数据统计口径变化。

15-9 电信业务情况

Telecommunication Service

指 标	Item	2011	2012	2013	2014	2015
一、电信业务总量（万元）	**Business Volume of Telecommunication Services (10 000 yuan)**	**1944329**	**2098274**	**2313630**	**2695332**	**2983024**
二、电信业务总收入（万元）	**Gross Income of Telecommunication Services (10 000 yuan)**	**1029629**	**1162257**	**1316435**	**1356705**	**1338203**
三、固定电话年末用户数（万户）	**Number of Immobile Telephone at Year-end (10 000 subscribers)**	**270.36**	**311.02**	**319.11**	**306.66**	**292.08**
#农村电话年末户数	Number of Telephone in Rural Areas at Year-end	**32.02**	**33.59**	**33.06**	**37.28**	**30.63**
四、电话交换机总容量（万门）	**Capacity (number) of Telephone Switchboard (10 000 lines)**	**441.49**	**420.38**	**378.02**	**230.01**	**145.08**
五、移动电话用户年末数（万户）	**Number of Mobile Phone at Year-end(10 000 subscribers)**	**1614.15**	**1803.54**	**2160.67**	**2025.32**	**1767.00**
#3G电话用户数	3G Mobile Phone Subscribers	177.37	394.97	666.36	638.96	495.69
六、互联网年末用户数（万户）	**Number of Broad Band Net User (10 000 subscribers)**	**184.10**	**202.31**	**267.05**	**277.95**	**289.97**

注：本表数据由中国联通、中国电信、中国移动和中国铁通等西安分公司提供。

主要统计指标解释

公路里程 指在一定时期内实际达到《公路工程技术标准JTJ01-88》规定的等级公路，并经公路主管部门正式验收交付使用的公路里程数。包括大中城市的郊区公路以及通过小城镇街道部分的公路里程和桥梁、隧道渡口的长度，不包括大中城市的街道、厂矿、林区生产用道和农业生产用道的里程。两条或多条公路共同经由同一路段，只计算一次，不得重复计算里程长度。它是反映公路建设发展规模的重要指标，也是计算运输网密度等指标的基础资料。

民用航空航线里程 指民航运输定期班机飞行的航线长度的总和。航线长度按机场之间的距离计算，通常有两种计算方法：一是将每条航线长度相加称为重复计算航线里程；一是将两线或两条以上航线经过同一区段里程，只计算一次航线长度称为不重复计算航线里程。一般常用的是后者，它能确切反映民航运输网的规模，是表明民航事业为国民经济服务和方便人民生活程度的主要指标。

货（客）运量 指在一定时期内，各种运输工具实际运送的货物（旅客）数量。它是反映运输业为国民经济和人民生活服务的数量指标，也是制定和检查运输生产计划、研究运输发展规模和速度的重要指标。货运按吨计算，客运按人计算。货物不论运输距离长短、货物类别，均按实际重量统计。旅客不论行程远近或票价多少，均按一人一次客运量统计；半价票、小孩票也按一人统计。

货物（旅客）周转量 指在一定时期内，由各种运输工具运送的货物（旅客）数量与其相应运输距离的乘积之总和。它是反映运输业生产总成果的重要指标，也是编制和检查运输生产计划，计算运输效率、劳动生产率以及核算运输单位成本的主要基础资料。计算货物周转量通常按发出站与到达站之间的最短距离，也就是计费距离计算。计算公式为：

货物（旅客）周转量=∑货物（旅客）运输量×运输距离

民用汽车拥有量 指报告期末，在公安交通管理部门按照《机动车注册登记工作规范》，已注册登记领有民用车辆牌照的全部汽车数量。汽车拥有量统计的主要分类：根据汽车结构分为载客汽车、载货汽车及其他汽车；根据汽车所有者不同分为个人（私人）汽车、单位汽车；根据汽车的使用性质分为营运汽车、非营运汽车；根据汽车大小规格不同载客汽车分为大型、中型、小型和微型，载货汽车分为重型、中型、轻型和微型。

邮电业务总量 指以价值量形式表现的邮电通信企业为社会提供各类邮电通信服务的总数量。邮电业务量按专业分类包括函件、包件、汇票、报刊发行、邮政快件、特快专递、邮政储蓄、集邮、公众电报、用户电报、传真、长途电话、出租电路、无线寻呼、移动电话、分组交换数据通信、出租代维等。计算方法为各类产品乘以相应的平均单价（不变价）之和，再加上出租电路和设备、代用户维护电话交换机和线路等的服务收入。它综合反映了一定时期邮电业务发展的总成果，是研究邮电业务量构成和发展趋势的重要指标。计算公式为：

邮电业务总量=∑（各类邮电业务量×不变单价）+出租代维及其他业务收入

移动电话用户 是指通过移动电话交换机进入移动电话网、占用移动电话号码的电话用户。用户数量以报告期末在移动电话营业部门实际办理登记手续进入移动电话网的户数进行计算，一部移动电话统计为一户。

电话用户 指接入国家公众固定电话网，并按固定电话业务进行经营管理的电话用户。1997年以前，电话用户分为市内电话用户和农村电话用户。“市内电话用户”是指接入县城及县以上城市的电话网上的电话用户；“农村电话用户”是指接入县邮电局农话台及县以下农村电话交换点，以县城为中心（除市话用户外）联通县、乡（镇）、行政村、村民小组的用户。从1997年起，电话用户数分组调整为以用户所在区域划分为“城市电话用户”和“乡村电话用户”，与过去的按市内电话和农村电话划分方法不同。而电话用户总数、电话机总部数统计范围不变。

农村电话用户 指县城关区以下的集镇和农村接入局用交换机的电话用户数。

局用交换机容量 是指安装在本地电信运营商内用于接续本地固定电话的电话交换机容量，有倍增设备按倍增后的数量计数。包括现用和备用的人工或自动交换机的全部容量。

互联网宽带接入端口 指用于接入互联网用户的各类实际安装运行的接入端口的数量，包括xDSL用户接入端口、LAN接入端口以及其他类型接入端口等，不包括窄带拨号接入端口。

Explanatory Notes on Main Statistical Indicators

Length of Highways refers to the length of highways which are built in conformity with the grades specified by the highway engineering standard formulated by the Ministry of Communications, and have been formally checked and accepted by the departments of highways and put into use. The length of highways includes that of the suburb highways at large and medium- sized cities,highways passing through streets at small cities and towns,and also the length of bridges, tunnel and ferries. It does not include the length of streets in big and medium-sized cities and highways built for the production purpose at factories, mines, forest areas and agricultural areas. If two or more highways go the same section of the way, the length of the section is only calculated for once and no duplication is allowed. The length of highways is an important indicator to show the development of the highway construction and to provide essential information to calculate the transport network density.

Length of Civil Aviation Routes refers to the length of all routes for regular civil aviation flights. There are usually two ways to calculate the distance between airports connected by the route length: one is to put the length of all air routes together, called duplicated calculation of the length of the routes; the other is not to allow the duplication in calculation when two or more routes passing the same section of aviation routes. The latter is usually used, as it can precisely show the size of the civil aviation network and indicate the extent of civil aviation serving the national economy and the people.

Freight (Passenger) Traffic refers to the volume of freight (passenger) transported with various means. Freight transport is calculated in tons and passenger traffic is calculated in the number of persons. Despite the type of freight and travelling distance, the freight transport is calculated in the actual weight of the goods: and despite the travelling distance and ticket price, the passenger traffic is calculated by the principle that one person can be counted only once in one travel. The passenger who travel with a half price ticket or a child ticket is also calculated as one person. The freight (passenger) traffic provides a quantitative measure to show how the transport industry serves the national economy and people, and is also an important indicator for planning the transport industry and for studying the development scale and speed of the transport industry.

Freight Ton–kilometers(Passenger–kilometers) refer to the sum of the products of the volume of transported cargo (passengers) multiplying by the transport distance, usually using ton-kilometer and passenger-kilometer as units for measurement. Normally, the shortest distance between the departure station and the destination station (i.e., the payable distance) is the basis to calculate the freight ton-kilometers. This is an important indicator to show the total results of the transport industry, to prepare and examine the transport plan and to measure the efficiency, the labour productivity and the unit cost of transport.

The formula is as follows:

Freight Ton-kilometers(Passenger-kilometers)=Σ {Freight (Passenger) Traffic × Distance of Transportation }

Measuring unit: ton-kilometer (person-kilometer)

Possession of Civil Motor Vehicles refer to the total numbers of vehicles that are registered and received vehicles license tags according to the Work Standard for Motor Vehicles Registration formulated by the Transport Management Office under the department of public security at the end of the reference period. They are divided into categories. According to the structure of motor vehicles, they are divided into passenger vehicles, trucks and others; according to ownership into private vehicles and vehicles for the unit' s use; according to kind of usage into working vehicles and non-working vehicles; and according to size of vehicles into large passenger vehicles, medium-sized passenger vehicles, small passenger vehicles and mini passenger vehicles,heavytrucks, light-heavy trucks, light trucks and mini-trucks.

Business Volume of Post and Telecommunications refers to the total amount of post and telecommunications services, expressed in value terms, provided by the post and telecommunications departments for the society. Post and telecommunication services can be classified asletters, parcels, remittance, issue of newspapers and magazines, fast mail service, express mail service, savings deposits, stamps for collection, public and individual telegraph service, facsimiles, long-distance telephone service,leasing of telephone lines, urban paging service, mobile telephone service, data transfer and transmission, etc. The accounting approach is to multiply the service products of all types with their average unit price (constant price) to get sum of business value, plus income from other services such as leasing of telephone lines and equipment, maintenance of telephone switchboards and lines on behalf of customers. This indicator reflects the overall results of post and telecommunications service during a given period, and is important to study the composition of business service and the development of post and telecommunications service.

The formula is as follows:

Business Volume of Post and Telecommunications=Σ (Transaction of Post and Telecommunication Service x Constant Price) + Income from Leasing, Maintenance and other Services

Mobile Telephone Subscribers refer to the persons who own mobile telephone numbers and are connected with the mobile telephone communication network through the mobile telephone switchboards. The number of subscribers is calculated by the subscribers who have completed registration at mobile communication business centers and entered into the mobile telephone network. One mobile telephone is taken as a subscriber.

Telephone Subscribers refer to subscribers that are connected to the public line telephone network provided with telephone services. Before 1997, telephone subscribers were classified as city subscribers and village subscribers. City subscribers referred to those connected to city telephone networks in county towns and cities, while village subscribers referred to those connected to village telephone stations at and below counties. Since 1997, the classification of telephone subscribers was modified on the basis of physical location of the subscribers as Urban telephone subscribers and rural telephone subscribers , which is different from the previous classification of categorizing local telephones and rural telephones , while the definition of total subscribers and total number of telephones remain unchanged.

Rural Telephone Subscribers refer to telephone subscribers, located at towns under county town and country, that are connected to the public line telephone network.

Capacity of Office Telephone Exchanges refers to the capacity (measured in gate) of telephone exchanges installed in the offices of local telecommunication service providers for communication between fixed telephones. It includes the capacity of both manual and automatic exchanges in use and for stand-by purpose. Equipment with expansion function is to be counted by the expanded capacity.

Broadband Connection Terminals refer to the connection terminals to internet users actually installed and put into operation, including connection terminals for xDSL, connection terminals for LAN, and other connection terminals for xDSL. N-ISDN connection terminals are not included.

16 国内贸易

DOMESTIC TRADE

资料整理：马晓庆　杨　骏　左　宇　赵琳瑛　胡树建
Data management: Ma Xiaoqing　Yang Jun　Zuo Yu　Zhao linying　Hu Shujian
数据审核：栾立森
Data audit: Luan Lisen

第十六部分　国内贸易

一、简要说明

本章资料主要包括社会消费品零售总额，批发零售贸易业商品购、销等情况，限额以上批发零售贸易业主要商品销售情况，限额以上批发零售贸易和住宿餐饮企业财务状况、经济效益，以及交易市场情况，由西安市统计局贸易外经处提供。

二、主要指标

社会消费品零售总额（亿元）	3405.38	比上年增长	10.1%
#批发零售贸易业零售额	3140.65	比上年增长	10.9%

16 DOMESTIC TRADE

Ⅰ.Brief Introduction

Content of this chapter consists of total retail sales of consumer goods, sails data on commodity purchasing and sails of wholesale and retail trade, sales data on primary goods exceeds quotation, financial, economic performance and market data on wholesale and retail trade and food services industry exceeds quotation. Data in this chapter is compiled and provided by Trade and Foreign Economy Division of the Xi'an Bureau of Statistics.

Ⅱ.Maior Indicators

		Increase over Preceding Year
Total Retail Sales of Consumer Goods (100 mil. yuan)	3405.38	10.1%
Retail Sales of Wholesale and Retail Enterprises	3140.65	10.9%

16-1 主要年份社会消费品零售额

Total Retail Sales of Consumer Goods in Representative Years

单位：亿元 (100 million yuan)

年 份 Year	社会消费品零售总额 Total Retail Sales of Consumer Goods	城镇 Urban	乡村 Village	批发和零售业 Wholesale Trades and Retail Trades	住宿和餐饮业 Accommodation and Catering Trade	其他行业 Others
1978	12.70	8.82	3.88	11.01	0.53	0.21
1979	13.94	9.88	4.06	11.88	0.60	0.21
1980	15.88	11.53	4.35	13.05	0.80	0.20
1981	17.41	12.85	4.56	14.31	0.80	0.19
1982	18.54	13.79	4.75	15.25	0.88	0.27
1983	20.82	15.14	5.68	16.95	1.03	0.32
1984	24.87	19.13	5.74	19.47	1.29	0.46
1985	32.92	26.09	6.83	25.04	1.69	0.48
1986	37.50	29.25	8.25	28.88	1.97	0.64
1987	43.86	34.62	9.24	33.32	2.50	0.49
1988	59.65	47.74	11.91	44.84	2.97	0.78
1989	68.05	54.60	13.45	54.41	2.98	0.76
1990	72.77	59.42	13.35	57.46	3.79	0.90
1991	81.04	66.93	14.11	60.35	4.43	1.26
1992	100.84	89.17	11.67	71.86	6.13	2.30
1993	115.38	104.41	10.97	75.99	7.49	2.71
1994	144.64	131.56	13.08	89.79	9.12	3.43
1995	186.60	165.98	20.62	115.46	11.97	3.73
1996	222.94	198.19	24.75	145.05	15.83	4.02
1997	264.47	238.17	26.30	169.08	22.12	4.17
1998	291.45	257.39	34.06	183.43	30.97	4.27
1999	323.37	283.32	40.05	207.96	34.78	4.85
2000	360.42	317.12	43.30	232.89	41.42	5.43
2001	406.21	358.97	47.24	265.25	48.87	5.86
2002	459.76	409.86	49.90	309.36	51.42	6.45
2003	502.65	449.62	53.03	440.28	53.30	9.07
2004	578.55	520.89	57.66	509.55	56.87	12.13
2005	670.56	604.63	65.93	592.77	63.59	14.20
2006	784.95	708.31	76.64	694.03	74.77	16.15
2007	936.21	845.59	90.62	828.63	89.32	18.26
2008	1176.58	1063.93	112.65	1033.00	122.90	20.68
2009	1398.37	1336.41	61.96	1250.41	147.96	
2010	1678.01	1610.88	67.13	1497.71	180.30	
2011	2039.24	1968.41	70.83	1825.79	213.45	
2012	2400.67	2326.84	73.83	2156.49	244.18	
2013	2742.89	2657.49	85.40	2494.74	248.15	
2014	3093.89	2996.43	97.46	2830.90	262.99	
2015	3405.38	3292.83	112.55	3140.65	264.73	

注：依据2008年第二次经济普查数据，对2005-2007年数据进行调整。
依据2013年第三次经济普查数据，对2009年—2013年数据进行调整。
2009年以前按经营单位所在地分为市和县及县以下。
2002年以前按行业分组中不包括制造业零售额和农业对非农业居民零售额。

16-2 社会消费品零售总额

Total Retail Sales of Consumer Goods

单位：亿元 (100 million yuan)

分 类	Classify	2014	2015
社会消费品零售总额	**Total Retail Sales of Consumer Goods**	**3093.89**	**3405.38**
（一）按销售单位所在地分	Grouped by Region		
（1）城镇	Urban	2996.43	3292.83
#城区	District	2596.00	2832.66
（2）乡村	Village	97.46	112.55
（二）按行业分	Grouped by Sector		
（1）批发业	Wholesale Enterprises	479.55	625.11
限额以上单位	Enterprises Above Designated Size	421.18	401.84
限额以下单位	Enterprises Below Designated Size and Self-employed Laborers	58.37	223.27
（2）零售业	Retail Enterprises	2351.35	2515.54
限额以上单位	Enterprises Above Designated Size	1761.41	1855.70
限额以下单位	Enterprises Below Designated Size and Self-employed Laborers	589.94	659.84
（3）住宿和餐饮业	Accommodation and Catering Trade	262.99	264.73
限额以下单位	Enterprises Above Designated Size	99.94	88.36
限额以上单位	Enterprises Below Designated Size and Self-employed Laborers	163.05	176.37
（4）其他行业	Others		

16-3 各区县社会消费品零售总额

Total Retail Sales of Consumer Goods by Region

单位：亿元 (100 million yuan)

区 县	Region	2004	2005	2006	2007	2008	2009	2010	2011	2012	2013	2014	2015
西安市	**xian**	**578.55**	**670.56**	**784.95**	**936.21**	**1176.58**	**1398.37**	**1678.01**	**2039.24**	**2400.67**	**2742.89**	**3093.89**	**3405.38**
新城区	Xincheng	114.56	129.00	146.70	169.95	207.01	241.56	285.41	342.48	397.08	446.06	499.78	557.59
碑林区	Beilin	115.65	131.09	149.07	172.55	206.80	241.48	285.45	342.56	395.07	445.11	505.87	561.46
莲湖区	Lianhu	105.97	116.34	128.71	144.57	169.62	198.10	234.84	282.08	325.93	368.62	413.00	451.82
灞桥区	Baqiao	15.72	17.89	20.06	22.79	27.01	36.26	50.18	68.02	95.43	132.26	154.28	173.26
未央区	Weiyang	48.79	64.38	85.21	114.53	164.14	200.54	245.41	301.10	361.75	423.72	480.79	515.21
雁塔区	Yanta	84.02	104.87	131.53	167.18	225.95	272.35	327.95	401.56	472.92	534.30	596.50	656.47
阎良区	Yanliang	7.12	8.25	9.58	11.29	13.85	16.41	19.67	23.91	27.87	31.37	34.93	37.90
临潼区	Lintong	19.50	20.37	22.45	25.04	29.02	34.29	40.95	49.72	57.75	64.08	72.63	77.99
长安区	Chang'an	31.69	37.36	44.13	52.44	64.67	76.80	91.86	111.41	130.09	144.94	164.00	183.37
高陵区	Gaoling	3.85	4.75	5.80	7.24	9.48	11.51	14.09	17.53	22.43	25.01	28.40	31.73
蓝田县	Lantian	11.93	13.53	15.41	17.83	21.44	25.00	29.70	35.64	41.18	45.74	51.57	56.40
周至县	Zhouzhi	7.50	8.54	9.94	11.69	14.38	16.75	19.86	23.84	27.68	30.71	34.63	38.47
户 县	Huxian	12.26	14.18	16.37	19.12	23.21	27.31	32.63	39.38	45.49	50.97	57.52	63.71

16-4 限额以上批发零售贸易企业财务状况（2015年）

单位：万元

分 类	Classify	单位数（个）Number (unit)	资产总计 Total Assets	流动资产合　计 Circulating Funds	固定资产合　计 Total Fixed Assets
总计	**Totai**	**858**	**16899856.9**	**12144910.9**	**1590940.1**
一、批发企业	**Wholesale Enterprises**	**361**	**8316541.9**	**6781756.6**	**432396.8**
1. 按登记注册类型分组	Grouped by Category of Commodities				
内资企业	Domestic Funded Enterprises	346	8032867.3	6529102.6	407885.2
国有	State-owned Enterprises	20	1116961.1	950789.3	96357.3
集体	Collective-owned Enterprises	1	1597.5	1496.0	101.5
股份合作	Corperative Enterprises				
联营	Joint Ownership Enterprises				
国有联营	State Joint Ownership Enterprises				
集体联营	Collective Joint Ownership Enterprises				
国有与集体联营	Joint State-collective Enterprises				
其他联营	Others Joint Ownership Enterprises				
有限责任公司	Limited Liability Corporrations	203	4527462.4	3936479.6	132055.3
国有独资公司	State Funded Corporations	11	1146100.3	953735.7	46913.2
其他有限责任公司	Other Limited Liability Corporrations	192	3381362.1	2982743.9	85142.1
股份有限公司	Other Limited Liability Corporrations	9	1248631.8	608887.1	155108.3
私营	Other Limited Liability Corporrations	111	1137389.5	1031240.6	23649.3
私营独资	Private-funded Enterprises	1	973.2	934.6	38.6
私营合伙	Private Partnership Enterprises				
私营有限责任公司	Private Limited Liability Corporations	107	1040902.2	951521.1	22364.6
私营股份有限公司	Private Share-holding Corporations Ltd.	3	95514.1	78784.9	1246.1
其他	Other Enterprises	2	825.0	210.0	613.5
港澳台商投资	Enterprises with Funds from Hong Kong, Macao &Taiwan	5	201057.0	192869.6	6833.7
外商投资	Foreign Funded Enterprises	10	82617.6	59784.4	17677.9
2. 按国民经济行业分组	Grouped by Sector				

Financial Stares of Enterprises above Designated Size in Wholesale and Retail（2015）

(10 000 yuan)

固定资产原价 Original Value of Fixed Assets	累计折旧 Accumulated Depreciation	负债合计 Total Liabilities	流动负债合计 Circulating Liabilities	非流动负债 Non-Circulating Liabilities	所有者权益合计 Total Owners' Equities	实收资本 Paid in Capital	营业收入 Total Revenue	主营业务收入 Revenue from Principal Business
2336091.4	**768620.3**	**12420711.7**	**11749848.8**	**670862.9**	**4479145.2**	**6385985.2**	**39882528.9**	**39500878.3**
692996.0	**260632.4**	**6496691.7**	**6269852.1**	**226839.6**	**1819850.2**	**1094349.7**	**23289752.8**	**23199359.2**
659791.2	251939.2	6269658.4	6042957.6	226700.8	1763208.9	1062728.1	22478340.8	22411806.6
159769.4	63412.1	739952.1	732740.3	7211.8	377009.0	50557.5	3296802.0	3288294.1
103.2	13.5	1489.7	896.8	592.9	107.8	110.8	2735.0	2735.0
221118.5	89076.3	3649636.7	3493914.8	155721.9	877825.7	488271.3	14090149.3	14067957.9
64612.4	17699.2	944833.2	931629.4	13203.8	201267.1	70823.0	3666497.0	3659276.3
156506.1	71377.1	2704803.5	2562285.4	142518.1	676558.6	417448.3	10423652.3	10408681.6
219073.9	63965.6	927803.6	887032.9	40770.7	320828.2	336242.3	2911213.1	2877086.9
59042.2	35401.2	950606.1	928202.6	22403.5	186783.4	186898.9	2164354.4	2162645.7
142.5	103.9	919.5	919.5		53.7	50.0	2915.8	2915.8
55941.9	33585.6	886228.2	873932.5	12295.7	154674.0	169938.4	1962087.9	1960379.2
2957.8	1711.7	63458.4	53350.6	10107.8	32055.7	16910.5	199350.7	199350.7
684.0	70.5	170.2	170.2		654.8	647.3	13087.0	13087.0
9242.9	2409.2	180212.5	180212.5		20844.5	8296.6	327582.2	326935.4
23961.9	6284.0	46820.8	46682.0	138.8	35796.8	23325.0	483829.8	460617.2

16-4 续表1

单位：万元

分 类	Classify	营业成本 Total Cost	主营业务成本 Cost of Principal Business	营业税金及附加 Taxs and Other Changes	主营业务税金及附加 Taxs and Other Changes on Principal Business
总计	**Totai**	**36389449.3**	**36261689.9**	**276387.4**	**271057.2**
一、批发企业	**Wholesale Enterprises**	**21998931.6**	**21930721.5**	**150007.6**	**148744.2**
1. 按登记注册类型分组	Grouped by Category of Commodities				
内资企业	Domestic Funded Enterprises	21255607.1	21199128.4	148387.3	147221.8
国有	State-owned Enterprises	2905154.8	2897367.2	124927.8	124882.6
集体	Collective-owned Enterprises	2588.0	2588.0		
股份合作	Corperative Enterprises				
联营	Joint Ownership Enterprises				
国有联营	State Joint Ownership Enterprises				
集体联营	Collective Joint Ownership Enterprises				
国有与集体联营	Joint State-collective Enterprises				
其他联营	Others Joint Ownership Enterprises				
有限责任公司	Limited Liability Corporrations	13578407.8	13572185.2	15841.8	14867.8
国有独资公司	State Funded Corporations	3622498.4	3619914.5	1618.2	1573.9
其他有限责任公司	Other Limited Liability Corporrations	9955909.4	9952270.7	14223.6	13293.9
股份有限公司	Other Limited Liability Corporrations	2683847.7	2642162.0	3757.1	3650.8
私营	Other Limited Liability Corporrations	2073508.8	2072726.0	3860.6	3820.6
私营独资	Private-funded Enterprises	2745.4	2745.4	1.1	1.1
私营合伙	Private Partnership Enterprises				
私营有限责任公司	Private Limited Liability Corporations	1890809.7	1890026.9	3112.0	3072.0
私营股份有限公司	Private Share-holding Corporations Ltd.	179953.7	179953.7	747.5	747.5
其他	Other Enterprises	12100.0	12100.0		
港澳台商投资	Enterprises with Funds from Hong Kong, Macao &Taiwan	277835.9	277726.8	1204.4	1204.4
外商投资	Foreign Funded Enterprises	465488.6	453866.3	415.9	318.0
2. 按国民经济行业分组	Grouped by Sector				

continued 1

(10 000 yuan)

销售费用 Sale Expenses	管理费用 Managenment Expenses	财务费用 Financial Expenses	营业利润 Business Profits	利润总额 Total Profits	应付职工薪酬 Salary Payable	本年应交增值税 Value Added Tax Payable
1440159.6	**658558.5**	**253458.1**	**901164.6**	**918633.3**	**714293.0**	**464687.0**
556324.0	**238154.9**	**65304.0**	**309915.9**	**326190.0**	**266467.0**	**172427.0**
519649.9	222561.6	66765.5	297177.4	312465.6	237416.0	168465.0
50685.2	56015.2	12753.0	106505.0	113955.7	54190.0	61669.0
74.0	88.5	13.8	-29.3		140.0	
275700.8	130672.8	33624.2	127916.7	133501.0	103388.0	44064.0
49592.3	34457.9	1009.9	-41636.5	-41112.9	18210.0	4141.0
226108.5	96214.9	32614.3	169553.2	174613.9	85178.0	39923.0
151608.4	9827.4	7077.6	52807.8	53363.9	53635.0	55067.0
41436.5	25837.7	13196.9	9355.2	11183.0	25552.0	7665.0
146.1	17.1	17.9	-11.8	-11.8	60.0	11.0
36006.7	23813.0	11381.2	-197.4	1549.3	16865.0	7047.0
5283.7	2007.6	1797.8	9564.4	9645.5	8627.0	607.0
145.0	120.0	100.0	622.0	462.0	511.0	
28283.8	9984.7	-2350.1	12438.7	12721.9	23122.0	2212.0
8390.3	5608.6	888.6	299.8	1002.5	5929.0	1750.0

16-4 续表2

单位：万元

分类	Classify	单位数（个）Number (unit)	资产总计 Total Assets	流动资产合计 Circulating Funds	固定资产合计 Total Fixed Assets
农、林、牧产品批发	Wholesale of Agricultural,Forestry and Animal Husbandry Products	5	77950.5	32872.0	14943.9
食品、饮料及烟草制品批发	Wholesale of food Beverages and Tobaccos	34	764305.2	628016.9	77731.4
纺织、服装及家庭服务器批发	Wholesale of Textiles, Garments and Daily Articles	28	728527.7	678301.2	33390.6
文化、体育用品及器材批发	Wholesale of Culture, Sports Applionces and Equipments	15	230089.0	133091.4	10727.0
医药及医疗器材批发	Wholesale of Medicines and Medical Appliances	64	1284852.2	1196897.5	23432.5
矿产品、建材及化工产品批发	Wholesale of Mineral Products, Building Materials and Chemical Products	134	3960056.3	2934174.2	236591.6
机械设备、五金产品及电子产品批发	Wholesale of Machinery, Hardware, and Electronic Equipment	73	1244001.7	1154981.9	33359.7
贸易经纪与代理	Trade Borker and Agency	2	11942.8	11261.4	338.9
其他批发	Other wholesale not Classified Elsewhere	6	14816.5	12160.1	1881.2
二、零售企业	**Retail Trade**	**497**	**8583315.0**	**5363154.3**	**1158543.3**
1. 按登记注册类型分组	Grouped by Category of Commodities				
内资	Domestic Funded Enterprises	452	6366616.9	3995688.2	913418.2
国有	State-owned Enterprises	10	190202.1	132921.2	38487.6
集体	Collective-owned Enterprises	18	10657.0	3387.4	5924.1
股份合作	Share-holding Cooperative Enterprises				
联营	Joint Ownership Enterprises				
国有联营	State Joint Ownership Enterprises				
集体联营	Collective Joint Ownership Enterprises				
国有与集体联营	Joint State-collective Enterprises				
其他联营	Others Joint Ownership Enterprises				
有限责任公司	Limited Liability Corporations	283	3697741.2	2436370.2	462616.1
国有独资	State Funded Corporations	7	125001.7	82579.5	26006.3

continued 2

(10 000 yuan)

固定资产原价 Original Value of Fixed Assets	累计折旧 Accumulated Depreciation	负债合计 Total Liabilities	流动负债合计 Circulating Liabilities	非流动负债 Non-Circulating Liabilities	所有者权益合计 Total Owners' Equities	实收资本 Paid in Capital	营业收入 Total Revenue	主营业务收入 Revenue from Principal Business
20536.8	5592.9	65185.1	37451.0	27734.1	12765.4	17357.0	13362.3	13362.3
127519.5	49788.1	195388.8	179620.2	15768.6	568916.4	51280.3	1717128.4	1714644.9
64930.7	31540.1	638927.0	633796.6	5130.4	89600.7	52656.6	2755022.9	2753251.4
18596.1	7869.1	144110.8	122464.2	21646.6	85978.2	43590.0	373668.1	371799.3
36677.4	13244.9	1178403.0	1116841.7	61561.3	106449.2	107728.9	2788066.1	2782699.7
361573.0	124993.2	3134107.2	3041558.6	92548.6	825949.1	743798.4	13433851.4	13387294.4
59713.2	26374.9	1122619.5	1120489.8	2129.7	121382.2	70096.4	2139305.1	2106965.4
405.1	66.2	10738.2	10417.9	320.3	1204.6	1251.1	29660.9	29660.7
3044.2	1163.0	7212.1	7212.1		7604.4	6591.0	39687.6	39681.1
1643095.4	**507987.9**	**5924020.0**	**5479996.7**	**444023.3**	**2659295.0**	**5291635.5**	**16592776.1**	**16301519.1**
1294460.6	404478.2	4650706.1	4279881.6	370824.5	1715910.8	4820041.0	12054712.5	11851343.0
47419.0	8931.4	90567.7	89665.6	902.1	99634.4	26307.0	316085.5	308849.5
6808.8	953.0	8708.9	7953.7	755.2	1948.1	1603.0	39225.9	39225.9
657423.0	218174.4	2681677.1	2526969.8	154707.3	1016064.1	4548882.1	8017978.3	7897829.9
39307.5	13301.2	84724.3	76868.9	7855.4	40277.4	24468.6	159074.1	157163.4

16-4 续表3

单位：万元

分 类	Classify	营业成本 Total Cost	主营业务成本 Cost of Principal Business	营业税金及附加 Taxs and Other Changes	主营业务税金及附加 Taxs and Other Changes on Principal Business
农、林、牧产品批发	Wholesale of Agricultural,Forestry and Animal Husbandry Products	11947.8	11947.8	35.8	35.8
食品、饮料及烟草制品批发	Wholesale of food Beverages and Tobaccos	1310697.7	1310135.2	124538.1	124513.5
纺织、服装及家庭服务器批发	Wholesale of Textiles, Garments and Daily Articles	2616896.0	2615815.3	7529.3	7527.0
文化、体育用品及器材批发	Wholesale of Culture, Sports Applionces and Equipments	316770.7	316642.7	2744.0	2720.3
医药及医疗器材批发	Wholesale of Medicines and Medical Appliances	2663994.2	2663994.1	3053.2	2632.5
矿产品、建材及化工产品批发	Wholesale of Mineral Products, Building Materials and Chemical Products	12988591.8	12938043.8	10112.9	9375.9
机械设备、五金产品及电子产品批发	Wholesale of Machinery, Hardware, and Electronic Equipment	2027015.1	2011124.3	1871.0	1815.9
贸易经纪与代理	Trade Borker and Agency	26629.8	26629.8	3.4	3.4
其他批发	Other wholesale not Classified Elsewhere	36388.5	36388.5	119.9	119.9
二、零售企业	**Retail Trade**	**14390517.7**	**14330968.4**	**126379.8**	**122313.0**
1. 按登记注册类型分组	Grouped by Category of Commodities				
内资	Domestic Funded Enterprises	10451285.2	10405256.7	107787.4	106623.0
国有	State-owned Enterprises	273077.4	272398.4	1282.9	1269.3
集体	Collective-owned Enterprises	34555.1	34555.1	811.2	811.2
股份合作	Share-holding Cooperative Enterprises				
联营	Joint Ownership Enterprises				
国有联营	State Joint Ownership Enterprises				
集体联营	Collective Joint Ownership Enterprises				
国有与集体联营	Joint State-collective Enterprises				
其他联营	Others Joint Ownership Enterprises				
有限责任公司	Limited Liability Corporations	6968604.2	6960150.7	74429.8	73393.3
国有独资	State Funded Corporations	137934.3	137877.7	224.5	178.9

continued 3

(10 000 yuan)

销售费用 Sale Expenses	管理费用 Management Expenses	财务费用 Financial Expenses	营业利润 Business Profits	利润总额 Total Profits	应付职工薪酬 Salary Payable	本年应交增值税 Value Added Tax Payable
1517.2	1539.2	397.6	-2075.3	123.0	882.0	297.0
74900.0	42185.5	-2181.0	231583.9	237061.0	55652.0	59120.0
58080.1	25782.0	-1163.4	48904.6	49610.3	44508.0	6883.0
10711.0	7651.1	-394.3	36127.9	36044.0	6813.0	1062.0
51002.4	35714.7	18907.7	13330.2	14050.5	31395.0	15667.0
297246.9	85844.1	48999.5	-27073.2	-21206.8	91200.0	79185.0
59458.9	37583.1	797.3	8105.1	9631.7	34647.0	9274.0
2103.9	523.5	-66.0	466.3	314.2	530.0	165.0
1303.6	1331.7	6.4	546.4	562.1	840.0	774.0
883835.6	**420403.6**	**188154.1**	**591248.7**	**592443.3**	**447826.0**	**292260.0**
549264.4	325593.4	162390.5	462960.6	487801.4	336152.0	187443.0
17881.3	16789.7	329.2	6484.5	6822.6	25130.0	30578.0
1096.5	1847.8	93.8	821.5	785.0	1664.0	103.0
389749.4	217244.2	48402.0	323275.4	336291.5	216458.0	122252.0
13355.5	6906.7	-521.8	1146.5	3127.1	12755.0	5313.0

16-4 续表4

单位：万元

分 类	Classify	单位数（个）Number (unit)	资产总计 Total Assets	流动资产合计 Circulating Funds	固定资产合计 Total Fixed Assets
其他有限责任公司	Other Limited Liability Corporations	276	3572739.5	2353790.7	436609.8
股份有限公司	Share-holding Corporations Ltd.	7	1411566.0	588606.0	286090.5
私营	Private Enterprises	131	1052541.8	831300.4	119883.4
私营独资	Private-funded Enterprises	3	4178.4	2882.3	966.4
私营合伙	Private Partnership Enterprises	2	1012.6	807.1	184.4
私营有限责任公司	Private Limited Liability Corporations	121	961058.8	778802.7	81598.8
私营股份有限公司	Private Share-holding Corporations Ltd.	5	86292.0	48808.3	37133.8
其他	Other	3	3908.8	3103.0	416.5
港澳台商投资	Enterprises with Funds from Hong Kong, Macao &Taiwan	24	1422134.4	975742.9	111240.3
外商投资	Foreign Funded Enterprises	21	794563.7	391723.2	133884.8
2. 按国民经济行业分组	Grouped by Sector				
综合零售	Integrated Retail	105	3102821.2	1791423.9	505900.9
食品、饮料及烟草制品专门零售	Food, Beverages and Tobaccos Special Retail Trade	30	656290.5	252187.7	146628.6
纺织、服装及日用品专门零售	Special Retail of Textiles,Garments and Daily Consumer Articles	32	450516.2	227972.7	33532.9
文化、体育用品及器材专门零售	Retail of Culture,Sports Appliances and Equipments	23	307747.0	203734.6	22576.6
医药及医疗器材专门零售	Retail of Medicines and Medical Appliances	21	161268.8	144894.1	7760.3
汽车、摩托车、燃料及零配件专门零售	Retail of Motor Vehicles,Motorcycles, Fuel and Parts	199	2861211.3	2041226.7	263346.8
家用电器及电子产品专门零售	Special Retail of Household Electric Appliances and Electronic Products	45	576373.6	434685.6	49385.3
五金、家具及室内装饰材料专门零售	Special Retail of Hardware,Furniture and Decoration Materials	32	360793.8	207410.7	85547.4
货摊、无店铺及其他零售业	Non-shop and Other Retail	10	106292.6	59618.3	43864.5

continued 4

(10 000 yuan)

固定资产原价 Original Value of Fixed Assets	累计折旧 Accumulated Depreciation	负债合计 Total Liabilities	流动负债合计 Circulating Liabilities	非流动负债 Non-Circulating Liabilities	所有者权益合计 Total Owners' Equities	实收资本 Paid in Capital	营业收入 Total Revenue	主营业务收入 Revenue from Principal Business
618115.5	204873.2	2596952.8	2450100.9	146851.9	975786.7	4524413.5	7858904.2	7740666.5
410561.9	124471.4	1107757.2	926073.4	181683.8	303808.8	96982.2	988770.4	927814.2
171683.2	51799.8	761434.2	728658.1	32776.1	291107.6	145541.7	2682989.3	2667960.4
1628.3	661.9	2152.7	2152.7	0.0	2025.7	1700.0	13707.1	13610.7
249.9	65.5	1142.6	1042.6	100.0	-130.0	130.0	6657.4	6657.4
130574.2	48975.4	734021.8	702070.7	31951.1	227037.0	142451.7	2464158.8	2449226.3
39230.8	2097.0	24117.1	23392.1	725.0	62174.9	1260.0	198466.0	198466.0
564.7	148.2	561.0	561.0	0.0	3347.8	725.0	9663.1	9663.1
160803.7	49563.4	842775.4	815721.5	27053.9	579359.0	205370.3	1775811.7	1705474.5
187831.1	53946.3	430538.5	384393.6	46144.9	364025.2	266224.2	2762251.9	2744701.6
686051.9	203517.6	2122056.4	1917373.4	204683.0	980764.8	422476.0	3234097.4	3033310.6
218598.5	71969.9	596802.8	523126.0	73676.8	59487.7	38522.5	290866.0	287050.3
58806.3	25341.7	197714.1	180603.0	17111.1	252802.1	101614.0	1163699.7	1160776.7
34425.1	11848.5	191048.9	167903.9	23145.0	116698.1	62961.1	294730.0	292525.0
11757.9	3997.6	138277.1	138261.1	16.0	22991.7	12818.9	178879.5	177803.8
383771.9	120425.1	2104466.7	2026282.0	78184.7	756744.6	4532612.4	6951966.0	6887309.5
72542.9	23157.6	282933.9	266794.2	16139.7	293439.7	56927.9	1976429.3	1961669.9
129609.8	44063.3	262637.7	232275.7	30362.0	98156.1	56145.2	1652944.4	1652630.1
47531.1	3666.6	28082.4	27377.4	705.0	78210.2	7557.5	849163.8	848443.2

16-4 续表5

分 类	Classify	营业成本 Total Cost	主营业务成本 Cost of Principal Business	营业税金及附加 Taxs and Other Changes	主营业务税金及附加 Taxs and Other Changes on Principal Business
其他有限责任公司	Other Limited Liability Corporations	6830669.9	6822273.0	74205.3	73214.4
股份有限公司	Share-holding Corporations Ltd.	809292.5	774407.3	5709.3	5709.3
私营	Private Enterprises	2358572.0	2356561.2	25489.6	25375.3
私营独资	Private-funded Enterprises	12461.4	12409.0	120.1	120.1
私营合伙	Private Partnership Enterprises	5961.4	5961.4	22.0	22.0
私营有限责任公司	Private Limited Liability Corporations	2200257.1	2198298.7	24989.0	24874.7
私营股份有限公司	Private Share-holding Corporations Ltd.	139892.1	139892.1	358.5	358.5
其他	Other	7184.0	7184.0	64.6	64.6
港澳台商投资	Enterprises with Funds from Hong Kong, Macao &Taiwan	1493023.6	1482558.0	10074.4	8384.4
外商投资	Foreign Funded Enterprises	2446208.9	2443153.7	8518.0	7305.6
2. 按国民经济行业分组	Grouped by Sector				
综合零售	Integrated Retail	2579979.6	2574683.3	29678.2	26398.6
食品、饮料及烟草制品专门零售	Food, Beverages and Tobaccos Special Retail Trade	186875.6	182415.9	1026.9	1026.4
纺织、服装及日用品专门零售	Special Retail of Textiles,Garments and Daily Consumer Articles	1002172.9	1002172.9	8527.8	8443.8
文化、体育用品及器材专门零售	Retail of Culture,Sports Appliances and Equipments	221678.2	221337.6	2435.2	2394.2
医药及医疗器材专门零售	Retail of Medicines and Medical Appliances	144567.3	142343.2	1653.7	1653.6
汽车、摩托车、燃料及零配件专门零售	Retail of Motor Vehicles,Motorcycles, Fuel and Parts	6476663.2	6434283.0	10550.7	10450.3
家用电器及电子产品专门零售	Special Retail of Household Electric Appliances and Electronic Products	1665282.1	1660952.0	35059.6	34585.1
五金、家具及室内装饰材料专门零售	Special Retail of Hardware,Furniture and Decoration Materials	1365191.3	1365119.8	35971.0	35884.3
货摊、无店铺及其他零售业	Non-shop and Other Retail	748107.5	747660.7	1476.7	1476.7

continued 5

(10 000 yuan)

销售费用 Sale Expenses	管理费用 Management Expenses	财务费用 Financial Expenses	营业利润 Business Profits	利润总额 Total Profits	应付职工薪酬 Salary Payable	本年应交增值税 Value Added Tax Payable
376393.9	210337.5	48923.8	322128.9	333164.4	203704.0	116939.0
25214.2	28537.2	96135.5	24386.4	33486.1	18451.0	3841.0
114878.4	60941.3	17427.5	106258.5	108681.9	74200.0	30669.0
503.5	276.1	130.0	216.0	216.0	240.0	52.0
487.6	130.4	0.0	56.0	93.9	443.0	92.0
109196.1	54550.2	17127.6	58616.8	61001.7	70477.0	28977.0
4691.2	5984.6	169.9	47369.7	47370.3	3041.0	1548.0
444.6	233.2	2.5	1734.3	1734.3	249.0	
146670.2	53340.7	15001.2	60904.8	64451.6	63357.0	92221.0
187901.0	41469.5	10762.4	67383.3	40190.3	48317.0	12596.0
357611.5	173583.9	28349.8	70343.3	79077.5	195538.0	43512.0
7432.2	4722.9	87725.8	3091.5	12326.1	6874.0	1074.0
63834.5	19197.7	314.5	70410.6	71042.1	27809.0	13694.0
23932.4	17976.8	4655.5	24044.7	24052.6	17737.0	2716.0
22034.1	7214.2	495.3	2911.9	4991.5	24681.0	4013.0
221896.3	114524.4	54476.1	73718.3	53590.0	124092.0	153442.0
113517.1	45435.6	2481.1	115308.7	113810.9	29072.0	35756.0
23409.3	28621.5	9550.3	191235.7	192310.6	11693.0	36408.0
50168.2	9126.6	105.7	40184.0	41242.0	10330.0	1645.0

16-5 限额以上住宿和餐饮企业财务状况（2015年）

单位：万元

分 类	Classify	单位数（个） Number (unit)	资产总计 Total Assets	流动资产合计 Circulating Funds	固定资产合计 Total Fixed Assets
总计	**Total**	**515**	**2973926.9**	**823523.3**	**1203959.5**
一、住宿业	**Hotel Services**	**228**	**2325732.5**	**526661.5**	**1022627.9**
1.按登记注册类型分组	Grouped by Type of Registration				
内资	Domestic Funded Enterprises	211	2016777.4	428189.4	841779.0
国有	State-owned Enterprises	25	166581.6	29186.2	122900.9
集体	Collective-owned Enterprises	2	2867.6	325.9	1414.0
股份合作	Cooperative Enterprises				
联营	Joint Ownership Enterprises				
国有联营	State Joint Ownership Enterprises				
集体联营	Collective Joint Ownership Enterprises				
国有与集体联营	Joint State-collective Enterprises				
其他联营	Others Joint Ownership Enterprises				
有限责任公司	Limited Liability Corporations	116	1174669.6	315659.9	647786.8
国有独资公司	State Sole Funded Corporations	4	53591.7	3884.5	42000.0
其他有限责任公司	Other Limited Liability Corporations	112	1121077.9	311775.4	605786.8
股份有限公司	Share-holding Corporations Ltd.	3	11949.6	1863.8	9465.3
私营	Private Enterprises	65	660709.0	81153.6	60212.0
私营独资	Private-funded Enterprises	3	4710.1	1725.1	1824.8
私营合伙	Private Partnership Enterprises				
私营有限责任公司	Private Limited Liability Corporations	61	655910.5	79340.4	58386.9
私营股份有限公司	Private Share-holding Corporations Ltd.	1	88.4	88.1	0.3
其他	Other Enterprises				
港澳台商投资	Enterprises with Funds from Hong Kong, Macao &Taiwan	7	152848.8	42037.7	90615.0
外商投资	Foreign Funded Enterprises	10	156106.3	56434.4	90233.9
2.按国民经济行业分组	Grouped by Sector				
旅游饭店	Tourist Hotel	167	2174645.2	475911.0	951049.4
一般旅馆	Normal Hotel	54	98229.2	43792.5	39222.4
其他住宿业	Others	7	52858.1	6958.0	32356.1

Finacial Status of Catering Eenterprises Above Designated Size（2015）

(10 000 yuan)

固定资产原价 Original Value of Fixed Assets	累计折旧 Accumulated Depreciation	负债合计 Total Liabilities	流动负债合　计 Circulating Liabilities	非流动负债 Non-Circulating Liabilities	所有者权益合计 Total Owners' Equities	实收资本 Paid in Capital	营业收入 Total Revenue	主营业务收入 Revenue from Principal Business
1881979.2	**685199.7**	**2113489.0**	**1573077.4**	**541427.5**	**860437.9**	**903399.7**	**1134218.4**	**1115917.9**
1589944.1	**567371.2**	**1592995.1**	**1109231.9**	**484762.9**	**732737.4**	**634099.3**	**526368.9**	**517745.7**
1228287.6	386563.6	1283853.4	963884.6	320968.5	732924.0	484929.1	434087.4	427498.0
188480.3	65579.4	111878.7	59747.2	53131.3	54702.9	37064.8	58470.9	57400.8
2965.7	1551.7	797.1	88.6	708.5	2070.5	2015.0	1836.7	1836.7
916749.1	269017.3	1009547.0	771881.1	237665.8	165122.6	348007.2	284151.6	280444.6
83336.4	41336.4	56771.8	40972.8	15799.0	-3180.1	29693.3	13679.5	12932.3
833412.7	227680.9	952775.2	730908.3	221866.8	168302.7	318313.9	270472.1	267512.3
15286.9	5821.6	6903.7	6903.7		5045.9	5483.0	5297.9	5297.9
104805.6	44593.6	154726.9	125264.0	29462.9	505982.1	92359.1	84330.3	82518.0
2107.5	282.7	792.9	716.6	76.3	3917.2	4000.0	1143.7	1143.7
102678.5	44291.6	153933.9	124547.3	29386.6	501976.6	88271.1	82896.6	81085.8
19.6	19.3	0.1	0.1		88.3	88.0	290.0	288.5
166572.0	75957.0	115425.5	66639.2	48786.3	37423.3	84598.3	37828.2	37493.3
195084.5	104850.6	193716.2	78708.1	115008.1	-37609.9	64571.9	54453.3	52754.4
1493767.3	542772.9	1476458.0	1006493.8	470964.1	698187.2	579667.2	453657.5	446350.0
60275.6	21053.2	64212.2	50413.2	13798.8	34017.0	47732.1	55549.4	54561.2
35901.2	3545.1	52324.9	52324.9		533.2	6700.0	17162.0	16834.5

16-5 续表1

单位：万元

分　类	Classify	营业成本 Total Cost	主营业务成本 Cost of Principal Business
总计	**Total**	**489953.5**	**483922.6**
一、住宿业	**Hotel Services**	**175203.4**	**172436.1**
1.按登记注册类型分组	Grouped by Type of Registration		
内资	Domestic Funded Enterprises	146956.6	144731.0
国有	State-owned Enterprises	23552.4	23398.5
集体	Collective-owned Enterprises	1332.8	1332.8
股份合作	Cooperative Enterprises		
联营	Joint Ownership Enterprises		
国有联营	State Joint Ownership Enterprises		
集体联营	Collective Joint Ownership Enterprises		
国有与集体联营	Joint State-collective Enterprises		
其他联营	Others Joint Ownership Enterprises		
有限责任公司	Limited Liability Corporations	88552.4	87523.8
国有独资公司	State Sole Funded Corporations	2840.1	2840.1
其他有限责任公司	Other Limited Liability Corporations	85712.3	84683.7
股份有限公司	Share-holding Corporations Ltd.	2428.7	2428.7
私营	Private Enterprises	31090.3	30047.2
私营独资	Private-funded Enterprises	753.5	753.5
私营合伙	Private Partnership Enterprises		
私营有限责任公司	Private Limited Liability Corporations	30156.8	29113.7
私营股份有限公司	Private Share-holding Corporations Ltd.	180.0	180.0
其他	Other Enterprises		
港澳台商投资	Enterprises with Funds from Hong Kong, Macao &Taiwan	12784.6	12631.4
外商投资	Foreign Funded Enterprises	15462.2	15073.7
2.按国民经济行业分组	Grouped by Sector		
旅游饭店	Tourist Hotel	150735.8	147978.9
一般旅馆	Normal Hotel	21734.3	21723.9
其他住宿业	Others	2733.3	2733.3

continued 1

(10 000 yuan)

营业税金及附加 Taxs and Other Changes	主营业务税金及附加 Taxs and Other Changes on Principal Business	销售费用 Sale Expenses	管理费用 Managenment Expenses	财务费用 Financial Expenses	营业利润 Business Profits	利润总额 Total Profits	应付职工薪酬 Salary Payable	本年应交所得税 Value Added Tax Payable
62740.9	**62181.8**	**380847.0**	**236678.9**	**35333.8**	**-67784.2**	**-63679.4**	**270131.5**	**4387.2**
30618.3	**30136.6**	**176890.4**	**163189.5**	**26824.3**	**-42099.9**	**-40521.3**	**140009.2**	**2601.5**
25519.0	25076.0	148256.6	135519.4	21508.0	-39424.2	-38536.3	117531.4	902.6
3067.6	2954.1	16009.4	17154.0	2752.5	-4672.8	-4305.9	15514.3	192.4
117.3	117.3	156.2	340.8	2.5	-125.0	-160.3	378.6	0.1
16313.3	16090.3	101035.2	92350.1	16145.4	-25834.1	-26282.7	80460.0	571.0
765.9	724.1	5522.2	5916.5	863.2	-2224.8	-1699.6	7310.0	45.2
15547.4	15366.2	95513.0	86433.6	15282.2	-23609.3	-24583.1	73150.0	525.8
307.6	270.3	1584.0	557.8	3.3	421.1	419.1	1625.8	
5713.2	5644.0	29471.8	25116.7	2604.3	-9213.4	-8206.5	19552.7	139.1
63.9	63.9	745.4	257.0	8.6	-684.7	-684.7	406.4	
5647.8	5578.6	28726.4	24747.4	2595.6	-8524.8	-7519.4	19124.5	139.1
1.5	1.5		112.3	0.1	-3.9	-2.4	21.8	
2019.9	2019.9	11959.3	12118.5	3662.9	-4683.0	-4179.3	9358.5	21.3
3079.4	3040.7	16674.5	15551.6	1653.4	2007.3	2194.3	13119.3	1677.6
26726.7	26273.2	151954.1	141608.1	20700.9	-39030.9	-36930.5	123366.4	2312.8
2933.7	2905.5	17718.8	14047.4	6023.6	-2069.0	-2226.0	13441.2	282.3
957.9	957.9	7217.5	7534.0	99.8	-1000.0	-1364.8	3201.6	6.4

16-5 续表2

单位：万元

分 类	Classify	单位数（个） Number (unit)	资产总计 Total Assets	流动资产合计 Circulating Funds	固定资产合计 Total Fixed Assets
二、餐饮业	**Catering Trade**	**287**	**648194.4**	**296861.8**	**181331.6**
1.按登记注册类型分组	Grouped by Type of Registration				
内资	Domestic Funded Enterprises	274	554554.4	267018.8	152860.6
国有	State-owned Enterprises	3	5372.7	1707.5	3565.1
集体	Collective-owned Enterprises				
股份合作	Cooperative Enterprises				
联营	Joint Ownership Enterprises				
国有联营	State Joint Ownership Enterprises				
集体联营	Collective Joint Ownership Enterprises				
国有与集体联营	Joint State-collective Enterprises				
其他联营	Others Joint Ownership Enterprises				
有限责任公司	Limited Liability Corporations	160	331416.7	161080.3	109836.0
国有独资公司	State Sole Funded Corporations	1	3237.7	312.9	2146.1
其他有限责任公司	Other Limited Liability Corporations	159	328179.0	160767.4	107689.9
股份有限公司	Share-holding Corporations Ltd.	2	113718.3	43968.0	20755.0
私营	Private Enterprises	106	103380.4	59819.8	18573.5
私营独资	Private-funded Enterprises	9	2021.0	972.3	578.9
私营合伙	Private Partnership Enterprises				
私营有限责任公司	Private Limited Liability Corporations	94	98169.1	55879.7	17772.1
私营股份有限公司	Private Share-holding Corporations Ltd.	3	3190.3	2967.8	222.5
其他	Other Enterprises	3	666.3	443.2	131.0
港澳台商投资	Enterprises with Funds from Hong Kong, Macao &Taiwan	7	34805.8	10901.7	13582.3
外商投资	Foreign Funded Enterprises	6	58834.2	18941.3	14888.7
2.按国民经济行业分	Grouped by Sdctor				
正餐服务	Dinner	278	573332.8	275303.4	142678.1
快餐服务	Fast Food	7	37757.8	15754.9	10905.4
饮料及冷饮服务	Beverages and Cold Drinks				
其他餐饮业	Other Catering Services	2	37103.8	5803.5	27748.1

continued 2

(10 000 yuan)

固定资产原价 Original Value of Fixed Assets	累计折旧 Accumulated Depreciation	负债合计 Total Liabilities	流动负债合计 Circulating Liabilities	非流动负债 Non-Circulating Liabilities	所有者权益合计 Total Owners' Equities	实收资本 Paid in Capital	营业收入 Total Revenue	主营业务收入 Revenue from Principal Business
292035.1	**117828.5**	**520493.9**	**463845.5**	**56664.6**	**127700.5**	**269300.4**	**607849.5**	**598172.2**
236331.2	90595.6	447276.2	398928.6	48363.8	107278.2	246383.4	468505.5	466710.0
4671.6	1106.5	3572.8	948.5	2624.3	1799.9	2067.0	7660.5	7660.5
161338.2	58423.2	293698.6	251841.2	41873.6	37718.1	157261.1	295936.6	294743.7
3731.6	1585.5	3137.7	3137.7		100.0	100.0	1302.6	1302.6
157606.6	56837.7	290560.9	248703.5	41873.6	37618.1	157161.1	294634.0	293441.1
31037.1	10282.1	40802.6	38692.2	2110.4	72915.7	50505.6	35768.3	35458.0
38620.3	20250.8	107845.7	106278.5	1567.2	-4465.3	36386.7	124270.0	123977.7
1430.6	851.7	1756.8	1756.8		264.2	1268.9	4578.8	4577.8
36624.0	19055.9	103857.7	102290.5	1567.2	-5688.6	33917.8	113211.4	112953.6
565.7	343.2	2231.2	2231.2		959.1	1200.0	6479.8	6446.3
664.0	533.0	1356.5	1168.2	188.3	-690.2	163.0	4870.1	4870.1
27931.8	14349.5	32118.8	29846.0	2272.8	2687.0	14369.4	39903.9	39903.9
27772.1	12883.4	41098.9	35070.9	6028.0	17735.3	8547.6	99440.1	91558.3
237263.8	101710.7	465887.7	414318.9	51585.0	107445.1	250433.6	557131.8	555167.4
21348.2	10442.8	24423.4	19343.8	5079.6	13334.4	10566.8	44274.8	36564.9
33423.1	5675.0	30182.8	30182.8		6921.0	8300.0	6442.9	6439.9

16-5 续表3

单位：万元

分 类	Classify	营业成本 Total Cost	主营业务成本 Cost of Principal Business
二、餐饮业	**Catering Trade**	**314750.1**	**311486.5**
1.按登记注册类型分组	Grouped by Type of Registration		
内资	Domestic Funded Enterprises	250602.1	249792.7
国有	State-owned Enterprises	5874.5	5874.5
集体	Collective-owned Enterprises		
股份合作	Cooperative Enterprises		
联营	Joint Ownership Enterprises		
国有联营	State Joint Ownership Enterprises		
集体联营	Collective Joint Ownership Enterprises		
国有与集体联营	Joint State-collective Enterprises		
其他联营	Others Joint Ownership Enterprises		
有限责任公司	Limited Liability Corporations	159467.8	158906.5
国有独资公司	State Sole Funded Corporations	822.8	822.8
其他有限责任公司	Other Limited Liability Corporations	158645.0	158083.7
股份有限公司	Share-holding Corporations Ltd.	21851.0	21851.0
私营	Private Enterprises	60595.9	60547.8
私营独资	Private-funded Enterprises	2325.7	2325.7
私营合伙	Private Partnership Enterprises		
私营有限责任公司	Private Limited Liability Corporations	56492.2	56456.2
私营股份有限公司	Private Share-holding Corporations Ltd.	1778.0	1765.9
其他	Other Enterprises	2812.9	2612.9
港澳台商投资	Enterprises with Funds from Hong Kong, Macao &Taiwan	19620.2	19620.2
外商投资	Foreign Funded Enterprises	44527.8	42073.6
2.按国民经济行业分	Grouped by Sdctor		
正餐服务	Dinner	290830.3	289970.2
快餐服务	Fast Food	22366.8	19963.3
饮料及冷饮服务	Beverages and Cold Drinks		
其他餐饮业	Other Catering Services	1553.0	1553.0

continued 3

(10 000 yuan)

营业税金及附加 Taxs and Other Changes	主营业务税金及附加 Taxs and Other Changes on Principal Business	销售费用 Sale Expenses	管理费用 Managenment Expenses	财务费用 Financial Expenses	营业利润 Business Profits	利润总额 Total Profits	应付职工薪酬 Salary Payable	本年应交所得税 Value Added Tax Payable
32122.6	**32045.2**	**203956.6**	**73489.4**	**8509.5**	**-25684.3**	**-23158.1**	**130122.3**	**1785.7**
25186.9	25109.5	153087.8	56993.6	7464.2	-24417.1	-21895.0	104090.5	975.4
393.7	393.7	704.3	1128.3	0.0	-440.3	-308.4	673.1	
15235.4	15182.9	92588.1	37496.4	6080.7	-14463.8	-12822.7	60815.4	888.7
75.3	75.3	18.1	342.5	3.8	40.1	33.4	211.8	
15160.1	15107.6	92570.0	37153.9	6076.9	-14503.9	-12856.1	60603.6	888.7
2002.7	1985.9	10295.1	3414.3	-92.7	-1940.6	-919.7	12766.3	
7294.5	7286.4	47617.2	14753.2	1465.9	-7474.2	-7744.5	29303.7	86.0
227.3	227.3	1652.8	283.4	10.7	27.9	74.9	1183.6	3.5
6705.2	6697.1	42291.7	13778.5	1452.6	-7475.2	-7791.5	27289.4	73.0
362.0	362.0	3672.7	691.3	2.6	-26.9	-27.9	830.7	9.5
260.6	260.6	1883.1	201.4	10.3	-98.2	-99.7	532.0	0.7
1995.1	1995.1	17761.7	3575.5	909.3	-4022.8	-3718.9	9190.2	19.0
4940.6	4940.6	33107.1	12920.3	136.0	2755.6	2455.8	16841.6	791.3
29915.8	29838.4	186576.8	65176.3	8198.7	-24431.7	-20352.0	119871.6	1166.5
1840.1	1840.1	15242.9	4336.0	231.2	423.9	-1135.9	8521.9	619.2
366.7	366.7	2136.9	3977.1	79.6	-1676.5	-1670.2	1728.8	

16-6 限额以上批发零售贸易业商品购进、销售、库存总额（2015年）

单位：个、万元

分类	Classify	单位数 Number of Enterprises	商品购进额 Total Purchases	进口 Exports
总计	**Total**	**885**	**40530858.6**	**959429.1**
一、批发企业	**Wholesale Enterprises**	**364**	**23747696.4**	**260405.3**
1.按登记注册类型分组	Grouped by Type of Registration			
内资企业	Domestic Funded Enterprises	349	23019459.8	250041.7
国有	State-owned Enterprises	20	3191336.3	781.1
集体	Collective-owned Enterprises	1	2625.0	
股份合作	Cooperative Enterprises			
联营	Joint Ownership Enterprises			
国有联营	State Joint Ownership Enterprises			
集体联营	Collective Joint Ownership Enterprises			
国有与集体联营	Joint State-collective Enterprises			
其他联营	Others Joint Ownership Enterprises			
有限责任公司	Limited Liability Corporations	204	14414692.6	194760.6
国有独资公司	State Sole Funded Corporations	11	3371433.5	14952.7
其他有限责任公司	Other Limited Liability Corporations	193	11043259.1	179807.9
股份有限公司	Share-holding Corporations Ltd.	11	3113400.5	
私营	Private Enterprises	111	2284905.4	54500.0
私营独资	Private-funded Enterprises	1	1418.6	
私营合伙	Private Partnership Enterprises			
私营有限责任公司	Private Limited Liability Corporations	107	2078618.4	46608.1
私营股份有限公司	Private Share-holding Corporations Ltd.	3	204868.4	7891.9
其他	Other Enterprises	2	12500.0	
港澳台商投资	Enterprises with Funds from Hong Kong, Macao &Taiwan	5	283860.9	
外商投资	Foreign Funded Enterprises	10	444375.7	10363.6
个体经营户	Individusl Enterprises			
2.按国民经济行业分组	Grouped by Economic Sector			
农、林、牧产品批发	Wholesale of Agricultural,Forestry and Animal Husbandry Products	5	10893.4	

Total Sales of Enterprises above Designated Size in Wholesale and Retail Trades Grouped by Category of Commodities（2015）

(unit，10 000 yuan)

商品销售额			批发额		零售额	期末商品库存额
	公共网络商品销售额	银行卡支付商品销售额		出口		Value of
Sales Value	Public Network Sales	Bank Card Paid Sales	Wholesale Trade	Exports	Retail Trade	Stock at Final goods
45199313.3	**2247128.0**	**4409144.3**	**22312693.3**	**784315.1**	**22886620.0**	**2258621.5**
25704903.1	**1359776.9**	**2085304.8**	**21921062.8**	**784315.1**	**3783840.3**	**899445.2**
24791002.7	1359776.9	1935341.7	21142483.7	761338.2	3648519.0	843146.3
3752494.5	1315987.0	1814431.1	3433553.1	17246.4	318941.4	142855.8
2735.0			2735.0			485.0
15269020.6	2215.1	90320.2	13048124.8	384278.9	2220895.8	489329.8
3686237.6			2695476.3	53716.7	990761.3	56199.1
11582783.0	2215.1	90320.2	10352648.5	330562.2	1230134.5	433130.7
3319685.4			2287709.5	162238.3	1031975.9	54829.1
2433980.1	41574.8	30590.4	2357274.2	197574.6	76705.9	155637.6
3360.4			3360.4			497.7
2221396.1	41574.8	30590.4	2179571.6	197574.6	41824.5	147638.8
209223.6			174342.2		34881.4	7501.1
13087.1			13087.1			9.0
360808.9		8026.1	225487.6		135321.3	36258.6
553091.5		141937.0	553091.5	22976.9		20040.3
13655.1		2057.6	9936.6		3718.5	5471.5

16-6 续表1

单位：个、万元

分 类	Classify	单位数 Number of Enterprises	商品购进额 Total Purchases	进口 Exports
食品、饮料及烟草制品批发	Wholesale of Food, Beverages and Tobacco Products	34	1518708.1	
纺织、服装及家庭服务器批发	Wholesale of Textiles, Garments and Daily Articles	29	3319897.1	9353.5
文化、体育用品及器材批发	Wholesale of Culture, Sports Articles and Equipments	15	393790.9	
医药及医疗器材批发	Wholesale of Medicines and Medical Appliances	64	2912734.8	136614.0
矿产品、建材及化工产品批发	Wholesale of Mineral Products, Building Materials and Chemical Products	134	13298852.8	43400.2
机械设备、五金产品及电子产品批发	Wholesale of Machinery, Hardwares, Transport Means and Electronic Products	75	2231012.3	70256.5
贸易经纪与代理	Trade Manage and Agent	2	28912.3	781.1
其他批发	Other Wholesales	6	32894.7	
3.按经营形式分组	Grouped by Means of Operation			
独立门店	Independent Shop	240	14591225.3	98500.8
连锁总店	Headquarter of Chain Store	4	1114844.6	
连锁门店	Chain Store	2	575514.4	
其他	Other	118	7466112.1	161904.5
二、零售企业	**Retail Trade**	521	16783162.2	699023.8
1.按登记注册类型分组	Grouped by Registration Status			
内资	Domestic Funded Enterprises	454	12100196.4	477926.0
国有	State-owned Enterprises	11	348711.4	
集体	Collective-owned Enterprises	18	37632.0	
股份合作	Cooperative Enterprises			
联营	Joint Ownership Enterprises			
国有联营	State Joint Ownership Enterprises			
集体联营	Collective Joint Ownership Enterprises			
国有与集体联营	Joint State-collective Enterprises			

continued 1

(unit, 10 000 yuan)

商品销售额			批发额		零售额	期末商品库存额
Sales Value	公共网络商品销售额 Public Network Sales	银行卡支付商品销售额 Bank Card Paid Sales	Wholesale Trade	出口 Exports	Retail Trade	Value of Stock at Final goods
1956560.0	1316021.3	1326913.3	1894559.6	154.9	62000.4	94577.2
3463071.1	31940.6	2782.3	2379635.7	230471.4	1083435.4	165030.1
389488.7			386781.1	3796.5	2707.6	35951.2
3093661.9	9919.0	24616.9	2903123.2	6463.4	190538.7	187351.6
14194247.8	1896.0	546779.0	12079606.4	61912.2	2114641.4	245196.2
2522113.3		154555.8	2195315.0	464270.3	326798.3	160753.2
26905.1			26905.1	17246.4		4433.7
45200.1		27599.9	45200.1			680.5
15553273.3	14062.4	557584.4	12318430.8	528213.5	3234842.5	482468.3
1506483.0	1315987.0	1319280.3	1506483.0			55191.8
617528.6		21064.9	377079.4		240449.2	51983.2
8027618.2	29727.5	187375.2	7719069.6	256101.6	308548.6	309801.9
19494410.2	887351.1	2323839.5	391630.5		19102779.7	1359176.3
13893140.0	126478.1	1758118.0	287193.1		13605946.9	1104632.4
360809.5	49.5	9276.9	808.5		360001.0	45194.8
39905.4			1493.9		38411.5	1640.1

16-6 续表2

单位：个、万元

分 类	Classify	单位数 Number of Enterprises	商品购进额 Total Purchases	进口 Exports
其他联营	Others Joint Ownership Enterprises			
有限责任公司	Limited Liability Corporations	285	8106300.5	376242.0
国有独资公司	State Sole Funded Corporations	7	160290.0	
其他有限责任公司	Other Limited Liability Corporations	278	7946010.5	376242.0
股份有限公司	Share-holding Corporations Ltd.	7	896237.7	17455.9
私营	Private Enterprises	130	2702508.4	84228.1
私营独资	Private-funded Enterprises	3	16356.2	
私营合伙	Private Partnership Enterprises	2	7886.1	
私营有限责任公司	Private Limited Liability Corporations	120	2472351.8	84228.1
私营股份有限公司	Private Share-holding Corporations Ltd.	5	205914.3	
其他	Other Enterprises	3	8806.4	
港澳台商投资	Enterprises with Funds from Hong Kong, Macao &Taiwan	24	1456178.2	199172.6
外商投资	Foreign Funded Enterprises	21	2662659.7	21925.2
个体经营户	Individusl Enterprises	22	564127.9	
2.按国民经济行业分组	Grouped by Registered Kind			
综合零售	General Retail Sales Trade	110	2665598.1	105.0
食品、饮料及烟草制品专门零售	Retail of Food, Beverage and Tobaccos	32	298695.1	497.0
纺织、服装及日用品专门零售	Retail of Textiles, Garments and Daily Articles	36	1337256.1	
文化、体育用品及器材专门零售	Retail of Culture, Sports Articles and Equipments	24	290765.3	170.0
医药及医疗器材专门零售	Retail of Medicines and Medical Appliances	21	183992.6	
汽车、摩托车、燃料及零配件专门零售	Retail of Motor Vehicles, Motorcycles, Feuls and Parts	205	7125455.6	698251.8
家用电器及电子产品	Retail of Household Electronic Equipments	48	2153068.1	

continued 2

(unit，10 000 yuan)

商品销售额 Sales Value	公共网络商品销售额 Public Network Sales	银行卡支付商品销售额 Bank Card Paid Sales	批发额 Wholesale Trade	出口 Exports	零售额 Retail Trade	期末商品库存额 Value of Stock at Final goods
9196288.2	31998.5	1100172.8	191981.3		9004306.9	801775.3
174408.2	3119.0	50662.2			174408.2	38785.0
9021880.0	28879.5	1049510.6	191981.3		8829898.7	762990.3
1116175.7		147868.9	47770.2		1068405.5	43752.1
3170298.1	94430.1	500799.4	45139.2		3125158.9	211802.8
16198.6		4352.0			16198.6	1192.7
7987.9					7987.9	556.2
2942944.1	94430.1	467706.2	44928.4		2898015.7	203823.3
203167.5		28741.2	210.8		202956.7	6230.6
9663.1					9663.1	467.3
1782441.7	1880.8	479888.3	20549.8		1761891.9	167641.4
3185208.0	758992.2	85833.2	68674.5		3116533.5	66819.5
633620.5			15213.1		618407.4	20083.0
3537812.4	5589.8	745946.9	1925.2		3535887.2	215877.1
462705.8	1493.3	5890.5	26827.6		435878.2	36845.9
1473788.9	1709.1	34194.0	51097.6		1422691.3	110742.9
307700.0	59.7	40320.9	44265.1		263434.9	86761.5
196478.5	500.0	1873.9	11149.0		185329.5	54141.0
8009920.9	20175.9	1120724.1	37236.3		7972684.6	741421.5
2480936.8	88283.8	215460.4	197023.5		2283913.3	79195.3

16-6 续表3

单位：个、万元

分 类	Classify	单位数 Number of Enterprises	商品购进额 Total Purchases	进口 Exports
专门零售	and Products			
五金、家具及室内装饰材料	etail of Hardwares, Furniture and Room	35	1807718.0	
专门零售	Decorative Building			
货摊、无店铺及其他零售业	No Fixed Stores and Other Retails	10	920613.3	
3.按经营形式分组	Grouped by Means of Operation			
独立门店	Independent Shop	435	12761389.0	699023.8
连锁总店	Headquarter of Chain Store	27	814024.3	
连锁门店	Chain Store	8	722677.4	
其他	Other	51	2485071.5	
4.按零售业态分组	Grouped by Retail Size			
有店铺	Retail of Shop	503	15771868.1	699023.8
食杂店	Grocery Store			
便利店	Convenience Store	7	34432.6	
折扣店	Dime Store			
超市	Supermarket	40	178355.8	
大型超市	Larget Supermarket	20	1217408.9	5.0
仓储会员店	Warehouse Club	2	9727.0	
百货店	Department Store	54	1361814.2	100.0
专业店	Special Store	175	5265391.9	325879.2
专卖店	Monopoly Store	157	4252806.3	373039.6
家居建材商店	Home-building Material Store	18	1302096.9	
购物中心	Shopping Center	14	1803550.2	
厂家直销中心	Factory Outlet Center	16	346284.3	
无店铺零售	Retail of No-shop	18	1011294.1	
电视购物	TV Shopping	2	159928.4	
邮购	Mail Order			
网上商店	Online Stores	6	735684.5	
自动售货亭	Vending Machine			
电话购物	Tele Shopping			

continued 3

(unit，10 000 yuan)

商品销售额			批发额		零售额	期末商品库存额
	公共网络商品销售额	银行卡支付商品销售额		出口		Value of
Sales Value	Public Network Sales	Bank Card Paid Sales	Wholesale Trade	Exports	Retail Trade	Stock at Final goods
2061265.7		159361.0	985.0		2060280.7	31689.8
963801.2	769539.5	67.8	21121.2		942680.0	2501.3
14848622.2	124182.0	1648983.4	174653.9		14673968.3	983679.0
977660.5	1390.8	154684.0			977660.5	106820.7
937557.3		385304.8	61645.1		875912.2	95331.5
2730570.2	761778.3	134867.3	155331.5		2575238.7	173345.1
18294302.3	115153.8	2323771.7	386895.7		17907406.6	1329524.1
41888.2		2490.5	1058.3		40829.9	2833.1
200326.1	729.0	10504.5	13939.8		186386.3	20283.1
1317172.0	197.1	165282.6			1317172.0	124352.3
9274.2					9274.2	685.0
2079214.6	4197.5	549125.3	1684.2		2077530.4	75020.1
6062465.8	99681.2	682920.1	131308.3		5931157.5	475199.5
4807084.0	5777.0	648035.1	127003.4		4680080.6	529993.7
1419188.4		20710.5	558.2		1418630.2	14860.2
1994245.2		162222.6	103150.2		1891095.0	35755.8
363443.8	4572.0	82480.5	8193.3		355250.5	50541.3
1200107.9	772197.3	67.8	4734.8		1195373.1	29652.2
160459.3		67.8	542.2		159917.1	129.1
773697.3	772197.3		800.0		772897.3	5595.8

16-7 限额以上住宿和餐饮业经营情况（2015年）

单位：个、万元

分　类	Classify	单位数 Number of Enterprises	营业额 Business Revenue	银行卡支付营业额 Bank Card Paid Turnover
总计	**Total**	**567**	**1277477.5**	**216509.0**
一、住宿业	**Lodging Services**	**239**	**579852.5**	**119590.0**
1. 按登记注册类型分组	Grouped by Registration Status			
内资企业	Domestic Funded Enterprises	221	472959.2	100108.1
国有	State-owned Enterprises	29	64793.2	6622.8
集体	Collective-owned Enterprises	2	1836.7	
股份合作	Cooperative Enterprises			
联营	Joint Ownership Enterprises			
国有联营	State Joint Ownership Enterprises			
集体联营	Collective Joint Ownership Enterprises			
国有与集体联营	Joint State-collective Ownership Enterprises			
其他联营	Other Joint Ownership Enterprises			
有限责任公司	Limited Liability Corporations	119	302066.6	69460.2
国有独资公司	State-funded Corporations	4	13139.8	501.2
其他有限责任公司	Other Limited Liability Corporations	115	288926.8	68959.0
股份有限公司	Stock Limited Corporation	5	17366.3	283.6
私营	Private Enterprises	66	86896.4	23741.5
私营独资	Private-funded Enterprises	3	1174.0	288.8
私营合伙	Private Partnership Enterprises			
私营有限责任公司	Private Limited Liability Corporations	62	85432.4	23452.7
私营股份有限公司	Private Share Holding Corporations	1	290.0	
其他	Others			
港澳台商投资	Enterprises Funded by Hong Kong, Macao and Taiwan	8	51742.4	5896.2
外商投资	Foreign Funded Enterprises	10	55150.9	13585.7
个体经营	Individual Enterprises			
2. 按国民经济行业分组	Grouped by Economic Sector			
旅游饭店	Tour Restaurant	176	501165.5	107299.5
一般旅馆	Common Hotel	56	61523.8	12264.5
其他住宿业	Others	7	17163.2	26.0

Statistic on Hotel Services and Catering Services above Designed Size（2015）

(unit, 10 000 yuan)

客房收入 From Hotel Room	公共网络客房收入 Public Network Room Revenue	餐费收入 From Meals	公共网络餐费收入 Public Network Catering Revenue	商品销售收入 From Commodities
349913.9	**25969.8**	**802402.5**	**17584.5**	**57387.3**
308240.7	**23252.1**	**214569.6**	**1881.5**	**13072.1**
249780.2	18939.2	178635.6	1576.6	9941.7
29982.5	1712.7	26251.4	44.9	2189.6
1049.2		190.2		157.9
156853.7	12233.1	118984.8	821.7	3992.8
5750.4	335.3	5943.8	32.6	157.1
151103.3	11897.8	113041.0	789.1	3835.7
6718.0	59.7	5738.2	0.8	2691.2
55176.8	4933.7	27471.0	709.2	910.2
554.6		334.0		53.2
54334.7	4928.7	27137.0	709.2	854.5
287.5	5.0			2.5
27161.9	2789.5	16773.6	267.2	1814.0
31298.6	1523.4	19160.4	37.7	1316.4
261751.2	21624.1	186358.9	1780.1	12090.5
37113.8	1428.0	21230.2	101.4	964.9
9375.7	200.0	6980.5		16.7

16-7 续表1

单位：个、万元

分 类	Classify	单位数 Number of Enterprises	营业额 Business Revenue	银行卡支付营业额 Bank Card Paid Turnover
二、餐饮业	**Catering Trade**	**328**	**697625.0**	**96919.0**
1. 按登记注册类型分	Grouped by Registration Status			
内资	Domestic Funded Enterprises	284	504667.5	92992.7
国有	State-owned Enterprises	4	11022.4	222.2
集体	Collective-owned Enterprises			
股份合作	Cooperative Enterprises			
联营	Joint Ownership Enterprises			
国有联营	State Joint Ownership Enterprises			
集体联营	Collective Joint Ownership Enterprises			
国有与集体联营	Joint State-collective Ownership Enterprises			
其他联营	Other Joint Ownership Enterprises			
有限责任公司	Limited Liability Corporations	167	318867.5	44591.8
国有独资公司	State-funded Corporations	1	1187.4	
其他有限责任公司	Other Limited Liability Corporations	166	317680.1	44591.8
股份有限公司	Stock Limited Corporation	1	35313.8	15041.4
私营	Private Enterprises	108	125823.7	33137.3
私营独资	Private-funded Enterprises	9	4578.7	1178.2
私营合伙	Private Partnership Enterprises			
私营有限责任公司	Private Limited Liability Corporations	97	119723.2	31959.1
私营股份有限公司	Private Share Holding Corporations	2	1521.8	
其他	Others	4	13640.1	
港澳台商投资	Enterprises Funded by Hong Kong, Macao and Taiwan	7	42750.7	1822.1
外商投资	Foreign Funded Enterprises	6	99440.1	1079.7
个体经营	Individual Enterprises	31	50766.7	1024.5
2. 按国民经济行业分	Grouped by Economic Sector			
正餐服务	Dinner Services	315	637997.8	92995.6
快餐服务	Fast Food Services	7	47121.7	68.1
饮料及冷饮服务	Beverage and Cold Beverage Services			
其他餐饮业	Other Catering Services	6	12505.5	3855.3

continued 1

(unit, 10 000 yuan)

客房收入 From Hotel Room	公共网络客房收入 Public Network Room Revenue	餐费收入 From Meals	公共网络餐费收入 Public Network Catering Revenue	商品销售收入 From Commodities
41673.2	**2717.7**	**587832.9**	**15703.0**	**44315.2**
40740.1	2717.7	408605.0	8686.9	39940.3
1112.1		7528.9		1599.9
31896.3	2661.6	247074.6	5248.0	31296.3
620.4		562.2		
31275.9	2661.6	246512.4	5248.0	31296.3
112.1		27850.6	692.4	2790.1
2544.9	56.1	117951.9	2746.5	4152.9
		4355.6	842.0	223.1
2544.9	56.1	112108.0	1904.5	3896.3
		1488.3		33.5
5074.7		8199.0		101.1
421.6		40226.2	1052.1	1471.6
		91558.4	5335.0	100.5
511.5		47443.3	629.0	2802.8
38864.1	2272.9	539545.1	15544.2	43497.8
		38607.9	129.9	803.9
2809.1	444.8	9679.9	28.9	13.5

16-8 限额以上批发和零售业主要商品分类销售额（2015年）

Sale Values of Enterprises above Designated Size of Wholesale and Retail Trades by Category of Main Commodities（2015）

单位：万元 (10 000 yuan)

分　类	Classify	销售合计 Total Sales Value	批发 Wholesale Value	零售 Retail Value
总计	**Total**	**42615994.3**	**20047171.7**	**22568822.6**
其中：通过公共网络实现的商品销售	Sales Achiered through the Prblis Network	2319103.5	1393214.8	925888.7
粮油、食品类	Cereals, Oils and Foodstuffs	1310558.8	255928.1	1054630.7
粮油类	Grain and Oil	479088.9	69104.1	409984.8
肉禽蛋类	Meat, Poultry and Eggs	154096.3	31447.6	122648.7
水产品类	Aquatic Products	193665.8	5172.4	188493.4
蔬菜类	Vegetables	149121.9	80290.1	68831.8
干鲜果品类	Fresh and Dried Fruit Category	92786.5	17885.2	74901.3
饮料类	Beverages	956053.7	418596.8	537456.9
烟酒类	Tobacco and Liquor	1622356.7	1366867.4	255489.3
服装、鞋帽、针、纺织品类	Clothing, Shoes, Hats and Textiles	5203621.1	1585073.9	3618547.2
#服装类	Clothing	4493088.9	1461939.4	3031149.5
鞋帽类	Shoes and Hats	443869.4	87495.6	356373.8
针、纺织品类	Knitwear and Textiles	266662.8	35638.9	231023.9
化妆品类	Cosmetics	399658.7	51139.2	348519.5
金银珠宝类	Gold,Silver and Jewelry	556258.5	150028.3	406230.2
日用品类	Articles for Daily Use	678507.8	96828.9	581678.9
#儿童玩具类	Children's Toys	80425.1	4092.3	76332.8
五金、电料类	Hardwear and Electrical Materials	228817.3	74241.1	154576.2
体育、娱乐用品类	Sports and Recreation Articles	369968.0	92740.8	277227.2
#照相器材类	Photography Equipment	89357.8	22729.1	66628.7
书报杂志类	Newspapers and Magazines	233044.2	144355.9	88688.3
电子出版物及音像制品类	E-journal and Video Products	50555.8	5373.0	45182.8
家用电器和音像器材类	Household Appliances and Video Products	1910441.0	740710.6	1169730.4
中西药品类	Traditional Chinese and Western Medicine	2941752.7	2466526.0	475226.7
#西药	Western Medicine	2418033.4	2007457.8	410575.6
中草药及中成药	Chinese Herbal Medicine and Traditional Chinese Medicine	233912.3	195195.3	38717.0
文化办公用品类	Cultural and Official Goods	922725.2	308606.9	614118.3
#计算机及其配套产品	Among Them: Computers and Ancillary Products	66973.8	4997.9	61975.9
家具类	Furniture	917482.3	1100.2	916382.1
通讯器材类	Communication Appliances	926153.7	141424.3	784729.4
煤炭及制品类	Coal and Related Products	3571318.1	2575627.4	995690.7
木材及制品类	Wood and Wooden Products			
石油及制品类	Petroleum and Related Products	6819136.3	4133690.2	2685446.1
化工材料及制品类	Raw Chemical Materials	291826.6	291826.6	
#化肥类	Chemical Fertilizers	64419.0	64419.0	
金属材料类	Metal Materials	3579676.2	3579676.2	
建筑及装潢材料类	Buildings and Decoration Materials	1155134.0	168967.1	986166.9
机电产品及设备类	Mechanical and Electrical Products	605296.7	597770.0	7526.7
#农机类	Agricultural Machinery			
汽车类	Automobile	6906362.2	704467.4	6201894.8
种子饲料类	Seeds and Feedstuff	2093.9	2093.9	
棉麻类	Cotton,Hemp	1278.0	1278.0	
其他类	Others	455916.8	92233.5	363683.3

16-9 亿元以上商品交易市场成交情况(2015年)

Basic Statistics on Commodity Exchange Markets of Transaction Value over 100 Million Yuan (2015)

分 类	Classify	年末出租摊位数(个) Number of Rental Booths at Year-end (unit)	成交额(万元) Turnover (10 000 yuan)
总计	**Total**	**26245**	**4590916**
粮油、食品类	Cereals, Oils and Foodstuffs	3289	1592317
#粮油类	Grain and Oil	569	303806
肉禽蛋类	Meat, Poultry and Eggs	717	22390
水产品类	Aquatic Products	439	16917
蔬菜类	Vegetables	529	48257
干鲜果品类	Fresh and Dried Fruit Category	1003	1081389
饮料类	Beverages	1994	84878
烟酒类	Tobacco and Liquor	153	2313
服装、鞋帽、针纺织品类	Clothing, Shoes, Hats and Textiles	7932	706879
#服装类	Clothing	5623	428852
鞋帽类	Shoes and Hats	1312	200685
针纺织品类	Knitwear and Textiles	997	77342
化妆品类	Cosmetics	91	2413
金银珠宝类	Gold,Silver and Jewelry	50	1200
日用品类	Articles for Daily Use	957	34320
#洗涤用品类	Bathing and Washing		
儿童玩具类	Children's Toys	87	2126
五金、电料类	Hardwear and Electrical Materials	979	24994
体育、娱乐用品类	Sports and Recreation Articles	75	1828
书报杂志类	Newspapers and Magazines	3	40
电子出版物及音像制品类	E-journal and Video Products	123	8947
家用电器和音像器材类	Household Appliances and Video Products	42	8074
中西药品类	Traditional Chinese and Western Medicine		
#西药	Western Medicine		
中草药及中成药	Chinese Herbal Medicine and Traditional Chinese Medicine		
文化办公用品类	Cultural and Official Goods	1204	304900
#计算机及其配套产品	Computer and Related Products	1110	301711
家具类	Furniture	313	12900
通讯器材类	Communication Appliances	1281	107240
煤炭及制品类	Coal and Related Products		
木材及制品类	Wood and Wooden Products		
石油及制品类	Petroleum and Related Products		
化工材料及制品类	Raw Chemical Materials	24	145600
#化肥类	Chemical Fertilizers		
金属材料类	Metal Materials	50	229700
建筑及装潢材料类	Buildings and Decoration Materials	4757	466438
机电产品及设备类	Mechanical and Electrical Products	815	159197
#农机类	Agricultural Machinery		
汽车类	Automobile	2023	692601
种子饲料类	Seeds and Feedstuff		
棉麻类	Cotton,Hemp		
其他类	Others	90	4137

16-10 批发和零售业连锁经营情况（2015年）

Basic Statistics on Chain Business of Wholesale and Retail Trades（2015）

指　标	Item	本年合计 Total	上年合计 Total Last Year	本年直营店 Regular Chain
一、门店总数（个）	**Number of Stores(unit)**	**1118**	**1090**	**990**
二、年末从业人员数（人）	**Employees at Year-end(person)**	**19312**	**19100**	**18721**
三、年末零售营业面积（平方米）	**Operating Area of Retail at Year-end(sq.m)**	**1179415**	**847259**	**1162225**
四、连锁门店商品购进额（万元）	**Purchases Value of Chain Stores(10 000 yuan)**	**3092930**	**3197010**	**3080345**
其中：统一配送商品购进额	Centralized Purchases and Delivery	2784762	2874520	2772177
其中：自有配送中心配送商品购进额	Self Centralized Purchases and Delivery	2584380	2686334	2571795
非自有配送中心配送商品购进额	Non-self Centralized Purchases and Delivery	177938	167994	177938
五、连锁门店商品销售额（万元）	**Sales Value of Chain Store(10 000 yuan)**	**3212677**	**3358371**	**3198153**
其中：零售额	Retail Value	1394722	1453840	1380198

16-10 续表 continued

指　标	Item	上年直营店 Regular Chain Last Year	本年加盟店 Franchise	上年加盟店 Franchise Last Year
一、门店总数（个）	**Number of Stores(unit)**	**929**	**128**	**161**
二、年末从业人员数（人）	**Employees at Year-end(person)**	**17548**	**591**	**1552**
三、年末零售营业面积（平方米）	**Operating Area of Retail at Year-end(sq.m)**	**827285**	**17190**	**19974**
四、连锁门店商品购进额（万元）	**Purchases Value of Chain Stores(10 000 yuan)**	**3179442**	**12585**	**17568**
其中：统一配送商品购进额	Centralized Purchases and Delivery	2856952	12585	17568
其中：自有配送中心配送商品购进额	Self Centralized Purchases and Delivery	2668766	12585	17568
非自有配送中心配送商品购进额	Non-self Centralized Purchases and Delivery	167994		
五、连锁门店商品销售额（万元）	**Sales Value of Chain Store(10 000 yuan)**	**3346734**	**14524**	**11637**
其中：零售额	Retail Value	1442203	14524	11637

16-11 住宿和餐饮业连锁经营情况（2015年）

Basic Statistics on Chain Business of Hotels and Catering Services（2015）

指 标	Item	本年合计 Total	上年合计 Total Last Year
一、门店总数（个）	**Number of Stores(unit)**	**199**	**189**
二、年末从业人员数（人）	**Employees at Year-end(person)**	**10364**	**12314**
三、年末餐饮营业面积（平方米）	**Operating Area of Retail at Year-end(sq.m)**	**89661**	**87481**
四、客房总数（间）	**Guest Rooms(room)**		
五、床位数（张）	**Guest Beds(bed)**		
六、餐位数（位）	**Dining Seats(set)**	**56554**	**56449**
七、连锁门店商品购进额（万元）	**Operating Area of Catering Services at Year end(room)(10 000yuan)**	**56322**	**60853**
其中：统一配送商品购进额	Centralized Purchases and Delivery	53720	57251
其中：自有配送中心配送商品购进额	Self Centralized Purchases and Delivery	46473	54245
非自有配送中心配送商品购进额	Non-self Centralized Purchases and Delivery	4242	
八、连锁门店商品营业额（万元）	**Sales Value of Chain Store(10 000 yuan)**	**125925**	**126330**
其中：餐费收入	Catering Revenues	124999	125333
商品销售额	Sales Value	926	997

16-11 续表 continued

指 标	Item	本年直营店 Regular Chain	上年直营店 Regular Chain Last Year
一、门店总数（个）	**Number of Stores(unit)**	**194**	**184**
二、年末从业人员数（人）	**Employees at Year-end(person)**	**10027**	**11967**
三、年末餐饮营业面积（平方米）	**Operating Area of Retail at Year-end(sq.m)**	**88961**	**86781**
四、客房总数（间）	**Guest Rooms(room)**		
五、床位数（张）	**Guest Beds(bed)**		
六、餐位数（位）	**Dining Seats(set)**	**56454**	**56355**
七、连锁门店商品购进额（万元）	**Operating Area of Catering Services at Year end(room)(10 000yuan)**	**55513**	**60056**
其中：统一配送商品购进额	Centralized Purchases and Delivery	53720	57251
其中：自有配送中心配送商品购进额	Self Centralized Purchases and Delivery	46473	54245
非自有配送中心配送商品购进额	Non-self Centralized Purchases and Delivery	4242	
八、连锁门店商品营业额（万元）	**Sales Value of Chain Store(10 000 yuan)**	**124513**	**124982**
其中：餐费收入	Catering Revenues	123587	123985
商品销售额	Sales Value	926	997

16-12 限额以上住宿和餐饮业经营情况（2015年）

单位：个、亿元

分 类	Classify	2013	
		单位数 Number of Enterprises	营业额 Business Revenue
总计	**Total**	**652**	**144.29**
一、住宿业	**Lodging Services**	232	61.02
1. 按登记注册类型分组	Grouped by Registration Status		
内资企业	Domestic Funded Enterprises	217	50.41
国有	State-owned Enterprises	37	8.02
集体	Collective-owned Enterprises	3	0.33
股份合作	Cooperative Enterprises		
联营	Joint Ownership Enterprises		
国有联营	State Joint Ownership Enterprises		
集体联营	Collective Joint Ownership Enterprises		
国有与集体联营	Joint State-collective Ownership Enterprises		
其他联营	Other Joint Ownership Enterprises		
有限责任公司	Limited Liability Corporations	119	33.15
国有独资公司	State-funded Corporations	4	1.48
其他有限责任公司	Other Limited Liability Corporations	115	31.67
股份有限公司	Stock Limited Corporation	3	0.63
私营	Private Enterprises	54	8.27
私营独资	Private-funded Enterprises	4	0.13
私营合伙	Private Partnership Enterprises	1	0.02
私营有限责任公司	Private Limited Liability Corporations	47	7.99
私营股份有限公司	Private Share Holding Corporations	2	0.12
其他	Others	1	0.01
港澳台商投资	Enterprises Funded by Hong Kong, Macao and Taiwan	6	4.62
外商投资	Foreign Funded Enterprises	8	5.97
个体经营	Individual Enterprises	1	0.02
2. 按国民经济行业分组	Grouped by Economic Sector		
旅游饭店	Tour Restaurant	187	55.43
一般旅馆	Common Hotel	39	4.78
其他住宿业	Others	6	0.81

Statistic on Hotel Services and Catering Services above Designed Size（2015）

（100 million yuan)

2014		2015	
单位数 Number of Enterprises	营业额 Business Revenue	单位数 Number of Enterprises	营业额 Business Revenue
602	**141.65**	**567**	**127.75**
237	63.05	239	57.99
220	51.51	221	47.30
32	7.38	29	6.48
2	0.24	2	0.18
119	31.79	119	30.21
4	1.62	4	1.31
115	30.18	115	28.89
4	1.49	5	1.74
63	10.61	66	8.69
3	0.14	3	0.12
1	0.06		
57	10.30	62	8.54
2	0.11	1	0.03
			0.00
7	5.25	8	5.17
10	6.29	10	5.52
181	55.93	176	50.12
51	5.93	56	6.15
5	1.19	7	1.72

16-12 续表1

单位：个、亿元

分 类	Classify	2013	
		单位数 Number of Enterprises	营业额 Business Revenue
二、餐饮业	**Catering Trade**	**420**	**83.27**
1. 按登记注册类型分	Grouped by Registration Status		
内资	Domestic Funded Enterprises	313	53.80
国有	State-owned Enterprises	5	1.38
集体	Collective-owned Enterprises	1	0.06
股份合作	Cooperative Enterprises		
联营	Joint Ownership Enterprises		
国有联营	State Joint Ownership Enterprises		
集体联营	Collective Joint Ownership Enterprises		
国有与集体联营	Joint State-collective Ownership Enterprises		
其他联营	Other Joint Ownership Enterprises		
有限责任公司	Limited Liability Corporations	179	32.91
国有独资公司	State-funded Corporations	3	0.40
其他有限责任公司	Other Limited Liability Corporations	176	32.51
股份有限公司	Stock Limited Corporation	4	4.96
私营	Private Enterprises	120	13.88
私营独资	Private-funded Enterprises	13	0.67
私营合伙	Private Partnership Enterprises	1	0.03
私营有限责任公司	Private Limited Liability Corporations	103	12.98
私营股份有限公司	Private Share Holding Corporations	3	0.20
其他	Others	4	0.61
港澳台商投资	Enterprises Funded by Hong Kong, Macao and Taiwan	7	8.13
外商投资	Foreign Funded Enterprises	8	10.02
个体经营	Individual Enterprises	92	11.32
2. 按国民经济行业分	Grouped by Economic Sector		
正餐服务	Dinner Services	396	72.61
快餐服务	Fast Food Services	15	9.69
饮料及冷饮服务	Beverage and Cold Beverage Services		
其他餐饮业	Other Catering Services	9	0.97

continued 1

(100 million yuan)

2014		2015	
单位数 Number of Enterprises	营业额 Business Revenue	单位数 Number of Enterprises	营业额 Business Revenue
365	**78.60**	**328**	**69.76**
310	53.40	284	50.47
5	1.14	4	1.10
177	33.12	167	31.89
2	0.38	1	0.12
175	32.74	166	31.77
3	4.28	1	3.53
121	14.18	108	12.58
12	0.63	9	0.46
106	13.32	97	11.97
3	0.23	2	0.15
4	0.68	4	1.36
7	6.88	7	4.28
7	10.04	6	9.94
41	8.27	31	5.08
351	69.49	315	63.80
7	7.74	7	4.71
7	1.38	6	1.25

主要统计指标解释

批发业 指批发商向批发、零售单位及其他企事业、机关单位批量销售生活用品和生产资料的活动，以及从事进出口贸易和贸易经纪与代理的活动。批发商可以对所批发的货物拥有所有权，并以本单位、公司的名义进行交易活动；也可以不拥有货物的所有权，而以中介身份做代理销售商。还包括各类商品批发市场中固定摊位的批发活动。

零售业 指百货商店、超级市场、专门零售商店、品牌专卖店、售货摊等主要面向最终消费者（如居民等）的销售活动。包括以互联网、邮政、电话、售货机等方式的销售活动，还包括在同地点，后面加工生产，前面销售的店铺（如前店后厂的面包房）。不包括：谷物、种子、饲料、牲畜、矿产品、生产用原料、化工原料、农用化工产品、机械设备（用车、计算机及通信设备等除外）等生产资料的销售（批发业）；非零售单位附带的零售活动（如汽车修理单位销售汽车零件）；商业零售单位所在商厦的物业管理（物业管理）；商业零售单位所在的商品市场、商业大厦的市场管理活动（市场管理）。

住宿业 指有偿为顾客提供临时住宿的服务活动，不包括提供长期住宿场所的活动（如出租房屋、公寓等）。

餐饮业 指在一定场所，对食物进行现场烹饪、调制，并出售给顾客主要供现场消费的服务活动。

社会消费品零售总额 指批发和零售业、餐饮业、新闻出版业、邮政业和其他服务业等，售予城乡居民用于生活消费的商品和社会集团用于公共消费的商品之总量。社会消费品零售总额包括：

一、批发和零售业企业（单位）售予城乡居民用于生活消费和社会集团用于公共消费的商品。包括：

1. 售予城乡居民的各种生活消费品；

2. 售予入境旅游的外国人、华侨、港澳台同胞的各类商品；

3. 售予行政事业单位、社会团体、军队和武警等机构的商品，以及以零售方式售予各类企业的商品。具体包括：用于非生产和社会交往的办公用品，如通讯设备、计算器具和设备、电讯网络设备、文印设备、音像视听器材和设备、纸张、本册、文具及装订文印材料、家具、日用电器、针纺织品、清洁卫生用品、文体用品、奖品、纪念品、礼品等；供内部人员乘坐的交通工具和燃料；用于办公设施修缮的各类配件、材料、工具等；用于取暖和防暑降温的设备、燃料、材料及食品等；专用于教学的用品和设备；非营利医疗机构的中、西药品、中药材和医疗设备器材；非专用的劳动保护用品；不对外营业的内部食堂用的餐具、炊具、设备、清洁卫生工具和食品、燃料等；军队、武警用于其人员生活的衣着品和个人用品；其他各类非生产性设备和用品。

二、餐饮业出售的主食、菜肴、烟酒饮料和其他商品。

三、新闻出版业、邮政业售予城乡居民、企事业单位、军队和武警等机构的书报杂志、音像制品、邮品等。

四、其他服务业出售的食品、烟酒饮料、服装鞋帽、日常生活用品、医药保健用品、艺术品、工艺美术品、玩具、殡葬用品以及其他消费品。

批发和零售业商品购进、销售、库存总额 指各种登记注册类型的批发和零售业企业（单位）以本企业（单位）为总体的，从国内、国外市场购进的商品总量，销售和出口的商品总量、库存的商品总量等情况。该指标可以反映商品流转过程中商品的购进、销售、库存之间的比例关系和存在的问题。

购进总额 指从本企业（单位）以外的单位和个人购进（包括从境外直接进口）作为转卖或加工后转卖的商品总额。它反映批发和零售业从国内、国外市场上购进商品的总量。商品购进包括：（1）从工农业生产者购进的商品；（2）从出版社、报社的出版发行部门购进的图书、杂志和报纸；（3）从各种登记注册类型的批发和零售业企业（单位）购进的商品；（4）从其他单位购进的商品，如从机关、团体、企业等单位购进的剩余物资，从住宿和餐饮业、其他服务业购进的商品，从海关、市场管理部门购进的缉私和没收的商品，从居民手中收购的废旧商品等；（5）从国（境）外直接进口的商品。不包括企业（单位）为自身经营用和未通过买卖行为而收入的商品以及销售退回、商品升溢等。

销售总额 指对本企业（单位）以外的单位和个人出售（包括对境外直接出口）的商品总额。它反映批发和零售业在国内市场上销售商品以及出口商品的总量。商品销售包括：（1）售给城乡居民和社会集团消费用的商品；（2）售给工业、农业、建筑业、运输邮电业、批发和零售业、住宿和餐饮业、其他服务业等作为生产、经营使用的商品；（3）售给批发和零售业作为转卖或加工后转卖的商品；（4）对国（境）外直接出口的商品。不包括出售本企业（单位）自用的废旧包装用品，未通过买卖行为付出的商品，经本单位介绍、由买卖双方直接结算、本单位只收取手续费的业务，购货退出的商品以及商品损耗和损失等。

库存总额 指报告期末各种登记注册类型的批发和零售业企业（单位）已取得所有权的商品。它反映批发和零售业企业（单位）的商品库存情况和对市场商品供应的保证程度。商品库存包括：（1）存放在批发和零售业经营单位（如门市部、批发站、经营处）仓库、货场、货柜和货架中的商品；（2）挑选、整理、包装中的商品；（3）已记入购进而尚未运到本单位的商品，即发货单或银行承兑凭证已到而货未到的商品；（4）寄放他处的商品，如因购货方拒绝承付而暂时存放在购货方的商品和已办完加工成品收回手续而未提回的商品；（5）委托其他单位代销（未作销售或调出）尚未售出的商品；（6）代其他单位购进尚未交付的商品。不包括所有权不属于本单位的商品、委托外单位加工生产尚未收回成品的商品、外贸企业代理其他单位从国外进口尚未付给订货单位的商品、代国家物资储备部门保管的商品等。

住宿和餐饮业营业额 指住宿和餐饮业法人企业（单位）在经营活动中因提供服务或销售商品等取得的收入。包括：客房收入、餐费收入、商品销售额和其他收入。客房收入指住宿和餐饮业法人企业（单位）在经营活动中因提供住宿服务取得的收入。餐费收入指住宿和餐饮业法人企业、（单位）因为顾客提供就餐服务取得的收入，包括经烹任、调制加工后出售的各种食品，如主食、炒菜、凉拌菜等的收入。商品销售额指住宿和餐饮业法人企业（单位）伴随服务而出售商品所取得的收入（含增值税）。其他收入指营业收入中除客房收入、餐费收入、商品销售额以外的其他收入，包括娱乐、健身和商务服务等。

连锁企业（或称连锁店、连锁公司） 指在核心企业或总店的领导下，由分散的、经营同类商品或服务的企业或活动单位，采取共同方针，实行集中采购和分散销售的有机结合，通过规范化经营，实现规模效益的经济联合组织形式。一般连锁店应由若干个分店组成。其经营特征：（1）经营同类商品；（2）使用统一商号；（3）统一采购配送，采购与销售相分离（部分商品可根据物流合理和保质保鲜原则，由供应商直接送货到门店，其余均由总部统一配送）。

连锁门店的形式分为直营连锁和加盟连锁。

直营连锁也叫正规连锁。指连锁门店均由总部独资或控股开设，在总部的直接领导下统一经营。总部采取纵深似的管理方式，直接下令掌管所有的零售门店，零售门店也必须完全接受总部指挥。这是大型垄断商业资本通过吞并、兼并或独资、控股等途径，发展壮大自身实力和规模的一种形式。

加盟连锁包括特许连锁和自由连锁两种形式。

特许连锁指各连锁门店（被特许人）通过合同形式，取得使用总部（特许人）商标、商号、经营技术和销售总部开发的商品的特许权，各加盟连锁门店为独立法人，在总部指导下统一经营。

自由连锁也称自愿连锁。指连锁公司的门店均为独立法人，各自的资产所有权关系不变，在公司总部的指导下共同经营。各成员店使用共同的店名，与总部订阅有关购、销、宣传等方面的合同，并按合同开展经营活动。在合同规定的范围之外，各成员店可以自由活动。根据自愿原则，各成员店可自由加入连锁体系，也可自由退出。

Explanatory Notes on Main Statistical Indicators

Wholesale Trade refers to the activities of wholesaler selling at wholesale commodities for daily use and capital goods to enterprises of wholesale and retail trades and other enterprises, institutions and government offices, including the activities of wholesaler engaged in import and export and acting as a trade agent. The wholesaler may have the right of ownership over the commodities of wholesale and trade in the name of its own or a company, the wholesaler may not have the right of ownership, only acts an agent. The wholesale trade also include the activities of wholesaler at the fixed stalls of the wholesale market of different commodities.

Retail Trade refers to the activities of department store,supermarket, franchised store, brand store, retail stall and on-the-spot-making-selling store selling commodities to the final consumers (citizens) by any means including internet, post, telephone, sales machine. Retail trade excludes the activities of sales of capital goods such a grain, seed, feed, livestock, mineral products, raw material for production, industrial chemicals, chemical products for farm, machine and equipment (vehicle, computer and communication equipment), and the activities of supplementary sales of non-retailer such as the sales of spare parts of car repair business

Hotel Services refer to the activities of enterprises providing paid services of lodging to the customer, excluding the activities of providing long period of services of lodging (such as leased house and apartments).

Catering Services refer to the activities of enterprises providing on-the-spot services of selling food cooked and prepared to the customer in certain sites

Total Retail Sales of Consumer Goods refer to the sum of retail sales of commodities sold by wholesale and retail trades, catering services, publishing, post and telecommunications and other service industries to urban and rural households for household consumption and to social institutions for public consumption. Retail sales of consumer goods include:

1) Sales sold by wholesale and retail trades to urban~thA and rural households for household consumption and to social institutions for public consumption.

a) of commodities to urban and rural households;

b) of commodities to foreigners, overseas Chinese and Chinese compatriots from Hong Kong, Macao and Taiwan visiting China;

c) of commodities to government agencies, institutions, social organizations, military and armed police units, and commodities to enterprises in the form of retail sales. More specifically, they include: office facilities and articles for non-production purposes such as communications equipment, computing equipment and instruments, TV and network equipment, printing and copying equipment, audio-visual equipment and instruments, paper, notebooks, stationeries, furniture, electric appliances, knitwear, sanitation and cleaning articles, cultural and sport articles, articles for prizes, souvenirs, etc.; transport vehicles and fuels for employees; materials, spare parts and tools for the maintenance of office facilities; equipment, fuels, materials and food for winter heating or summer cooling purposes; articles and equipment for teaching purpose; Chinese and western medicines and medical equipment and facilities purchased by non profit-making medical institutes; non- specialized work safety articles; cooking utensils, tableware, equipment, cleaning articles, food and fuels purchased by in-house cafeterias; clothes and personal articles purchased by military or armed police units for their officials and soldiers; and other equipment and articles for non-production purposes.

2) Sales of stable food, cooked dishes, beverages, tobaccos and other articles by catering units.

3) Sales of books, newspapers, magazines, audio-visual products and post products by publishing, post and telecommunications departments to urban and rural households and to enterprises, institutions, military and armed police units.

4) Sales of food, beverages, tobaccos, clothing, hats, footwear, articles for daily use, medicines, medical and health articles, work of art, handicrafts, toys, funeral articles and other articles by other service industries.

Purchase, Sales and Stock of Commodities by Wholesale and Retail Trades refer to the total volume of commodities purchased, total volume of sales and exports, and the stock of commodities by wholesale and retail enterprises (establishments) of different status of registration from domestic and overseas markets. This indicator reflects the relationship among purchase, sales and stock of commodities in the circulation of goods and reveals the existing problems.

Total Purchases of Commodities refer to the total value of purchases of commodities by enterprises (establishments)from other establishments or individuals (including direct import from abroad) for the purpose of re-selling, either with or without further processing of the commodities purchased. The commodities include: (1) commodities purchased from agricultural and industrial producer, wholesaler, retailer, publishing house and other service business; (2) commodities purchased from institutions and government departments; (3) confiscated goods purchased from the customs authorities or market management agencies; (4) second-hand goods and wastes purchased from residents; The commodities exclude 1 commodities purchased by enterprises (establishments) for use in their own business operation, commodities obtained without buying or selling procedures such as materials, consumable goods of low value, office appliances, etc. 2 received goods without trading, such as goods handed over from others, borrowed goods, preserved goods for others, donated goods from others, processed and retrieved goods, etc. 3. goods of direct settlement between buyer and seller with handling fees introduced by others, 4. goods returned or refused to pay by the buyer, 5. excessive goods.

Total Sales of Commodities refer to value of commodities sold by the establishments to other establishments and individuals (including goods sold for self consumption, including the value-added tax). The commodities include: (1) commodities sold to urban and rural residents and social groups for their consumption; (2) commodities sold to establishments in all industries for their production and operation, including agriculture, industry, construction, transportation, post and telecommunications, catering services, and public utility including commodities sold to wholesale and retail establishments for re-selling, with or without further processing; and (3) commodities for direct export to abroad.Excluded are (1) extended commodities without trading, such as goods handed over to other enterprises and institutions because of the change of organizations, lent goods, returned goods preserved for others, extended processing materials and samples donated to others, (2) goods of direct settlement between buyer and seller with handling fees introduced by others, (3)goods returned after purchase, (4) damaged and spoiled goods, (5) waste and used goods of selfuse,

Total Stock of Commodities refers to total commodities possessed by wholesaler and retailer of various types of registration status at the end of the reference period, reflecting the commodity stock level of various wholesaler and retailer and the potential for market supply. It includes: (1) commodities located in storage, garages, counters, and shelves of operating places (such as sale stores, wholesale centres, and operating offices) ; (2) commodities in the process of being selected, sorted, and packed; (3) commodities not arrived but recorded as purchase in the account, i.e. commodities not arrived but payment receipts for the commodities from the sellers or the banks arrived; (4) commodities deposited in other places rather than places mentioned above, for instance: commodities in the hold of purchasers temporarily due to the refusal of payment and commodities not taken back after going through the formalities; (5) commodities entrusted to other units to sell but not sold yet; (6) commodities purchased for other units but not delivered yet. Commodities not included as stock are those not owned by the enterprises (units), commodities on commission for processing but not yet delivered, imported commodities of agency of foreign trade enterprise but not yet delivered to ordering units and finally those put in stock on behalf of the state material reserves units.

Business Revenue of Hotels and Catering Services refers to revenue received from providing services or selling commodities by corporate enterprises and establishments engaged in hotels and catering services, including income from hotels, from catering services, from selling of commodities and from other services. Income from hotels refers to income of corporate enterprises and establishments engaged in hotels and catering services by providing lodging services. Income from catering services refers to income of corporate enterprises and establishments engaged in hotels and catering services by providing catering services, including selling of cooked or prepared foods such as staple food, cooked dishes or cold dishes. Income from selling of commodities refers to income of corporate enterprises and establishments engaged in hotels and catering services by selling commodities (including value-added tax) that accompany the services they provide. Income from other activities refers to income received other than income from hotels, catering services or selling of commodities, such as income from providing recreation, fitness or business services.

Chain Head Stores（headquarter） refer to the core leading stores responsible for development, allocation, administration and utilization of resources (name of stores, brand of stores, operation model, service standard, management way, ect.) of chain stores. Chain stores refers to the stores engaged in providing homogeneous commodities or services, with the central leadership of head store and guided by common policies, conduct centralized purchase and distributed selling of commodities, in order to gain better efficiency through standardized operation. The chain stores include regular chain stores, franchise chain stores and voluntary chain stores.

Regular Chain store refers to chain stores that are invested or controlled by the headquarters. They operate under direct and unified management from the headquarters.

Franchise chain store refers to the chain stores (franchisees) which are franchised with operation resources such as trade marks, names, patent and operation know-how by the franchisors in form of contract and pay the operation fees to the franchisors.

Voluntary chain store refers the stores operate jointly on the voluntary bases while maintaining their status of independent legal entities with full ownership of their assets. They sell goods of same brand from same channel of resource to the consumers.

17 对外经济贸易和旅游

FOREIGN TRADE AND ECONOMIC COOPERATION TOURISM

资料整理：马晓庆　赵琳瑛
Data management：Ma Xiaoqing Zhao linying
数据审核：栾立森
Data audit：Luan Lisen

第十七部分　对外经济贸易和旅游

一、简要说明

本章资料包括对外经济贸易、利用外资和旅游等方面资料，由西安市统计局贸易外经处根据西安市商务局、海关和旅游局提供资料整理。

二、主要指标

进出口总额（亿元）	1761.69	比上年增长	15.0%
#出　口	819.88	比上年增长	11.6%
实际利用外商直接投资额（亿美元）	40.08	比上年增长	8.2%

17 FOREIGN TRADE AND ECONOMIC COOPERATION,TOURISM

Ⅰ.Brief Introduction

Data in this chapter consists of data on foreign trade, using of foreign capital and fund and tourism. Data on foreign economy and trade and tourism are compiled and provided by Foreign Economy Division of the Xi'an Bureau of Statistics according to the data from Xi'an Bureau of Commerce, Xi'an Custom Office and Xi'an Bureau of Tourism.

Ⅱ.Major Indicators

		Increase over Preceding Year
Total Imports and Exports (100 mil.yuan)	1761.69	15.0%
#Exports	819.88	11.6%
Total Amount of Foreign Direst zwestment (USD 100 mil.)	40.08	8.2%

17-1 主要年份外资、外贸基本情况

Main Indicators on Foreign Investments,International Trading and International Tourism In Representative Years

指　标	Item	1990	1995	2000	2005	2008	2009
一、利用外资签定协议项目(个)	**Number of Projects of Foreign Capital Used through the Signed Agreements and Contracts (unit)**	**11**	**184**	**135**	**157**	**100**	**65**
利用外资签定协议金额（万美元）	Value of Foreign Capital Used through the Signed Agreements and Contracts(USD 10 000)	415	28956	54123	121499	118230	60027
外商实际直接投资额（万美元）	Value of Foreign Direct Investment (USD 10 000)	1154	18653	15633	57113	114738	121872
二、进出口总额（万美元）	**Total Imports and Exports (USD 10 000)**	**38229**	**137510**	**173696**	**390146**	**704029**	**724618**
#进口总额	Total Imports	9939	27347	67634	126705	256916	391504
出口总额	Total Exports	28290	110163	106062	263441	447113	333114
进出口差额(出口-进口)	Balance of Imports and Exports	18351	82816	38428	136736	190197	-58390
三、国际旅游者人数总计（万人次）	**Total Number of International Tourists (10 000 person-times)**	**25.88**	**41.35**	**65.03**	**77.56**	**63.20**	**67.29**
#外国人	Foreigners	15.40	37.11	54.65	65.86	53.58	59.09
港、澳、台同胞	Chinese Compatriot From Hong Kong, Macao and Taiwan	10.07	4.16	10.38	11.70	9.62	8.20
四、国际旅游者人天数总计（万人天）	**Total Number of Days of International Tourists (10 000 person/day)**	**55.03**	**84.44**	**162.69**	**224.93**	**162.93**	**195.14**
#外国人	Foreigners	33.48	75.71	131.44	190.99	138.72	171.36
港、澳、台同胞	Chinese Compatriot From Hong Kong, Macao and Taiwan	21.55	8.56	31.15	33.94	24.21	23.78
五、国际旅游收入（亿元）	**Earning of International Tourism (100 millon yuan)**	**1.96**	**10.38**	**22.41**	**33.54**	**28.72**	**31.05**
#商品收入	Income from Mercantile	0.44	2.57	7.71	11.25	9.74	8.94
劳务收入	Income from Labour Service	1.52	7.81	14.70	22.29	18.98	22.11
六、国际旅游者在西安人均停留天数　（天）	**Number of Days of Average Tourists Staying in Xi'an (day)**	**2.1**	**2.0**	**2.5**	**2.9**	**2.6**	**2.9**

注：2014年、2015年市旅游局未发布国际旅游统计数据。
本表来源于市商务局、西安海关、市旅游局。

17-1 续表 continued

指 标	Item	2010	2011	2012	2013	2014*	2015*
一、利用外资签定协议项目(个)	**Number of Projects of Foreign Capital Used through the Signed Agreements and Contracts (unit)**	**82**	**99**	**87**	**152**	**103**	**73**
利用外资签定协议金额（万美元）	Value of Foreign Capital Used through the Signed Agreements and Contracts(USD 10 000)	119689	120083	360264	251874	255321	193684
外商实际直接投资额（万美元）	Value of Foreign Direct Investment (USD 10 000)	156653	200522	247800	312994	370310	400833
二、进出口总额（万美元）	**Total Imports and Exports (USD 10 000)**	**1039273**	**1260179**	**1301446**	**1798534**	**15321514**	**17616896**
#进口总额	Total Imports	507544	677517	571568	950715	7974693	9418142
出口总额	Total Exports	531729	582662	729878	847819	7346822	8198754
进出口差额(出口-进口)	Balance of Imports and Exports	24185	-94855	158310	-102896	-627871	-1219388
三、国际旅游者人数总计（万人次）	**Total Number of International Tourists (10 000 person-times)**	**84.18**	**100.23**	**115.34**	**121.11**		
#外国人	Foreigners	73.21	88.63	101.40	106.89		
港、澳、台同胞	Chinese Compatriot From Hong Kong, Macao and Taiwan	10.97	11.60	13.94	14.22		
四、国际旅游者人天数总计（万人天）	**Total Number of Days of International Tourists (10 000 person/day)**	**241.67**	**287.09**	**334.44**	**351.11**		
#外国人	Foreigners	211.48	254.78	294.90	310.26		
港、澳、台同胞	Chinese Compatriot From Hong Kong, Macao and Taiwan	30.19	32.31	39.54	40.85		
五、国际旅游收入（亿元）	**Earning of International Tourism (100 millon yuan)**	**42.40**	**51.28**	**59.89**	**64.16**		
#商品收入	Income from Mercantile	11.87	11.38	14.19	14.69		
劳务收入	Income from Labour Service	30.53	39.90	45.70	49.47		
六、国际旅游者在西安人均停留天数 （天）	**Number of Days of Average Tourists Staying in Xi'an (day)**	**2.9**	**2.9**	**2.9**	**2.9**		

注：2014年以后进出口数据计量单位为万元。

17-2 主要年份利用外资情况

Utilization of Foreign Capital in Representative Years

单位：万美元 (USD 10 000)

年 份 Year	利用外资签订协议金额 Value of Foreign Capital Used through the Signed Agreements and Contracts	外商实际直接投资额 Direct Foreign Investment
1983	3500	800
1984	8	
1985	8361	1106
1986	19919	4010
1987	3218	5552
1988	2423	6758
1989	1645	11632
1990	415	1154
1991	591	1094
1992	24165	5200
1993	57289	8996
1994	20321	15240
1995	28956	18653
1996	35978	20510
1997	27214	22057
1998	40034	22286
1999	40390	13801
2000	54123	15633
2001	60736	17687
2002	70692	20281
2003	96380	25557
2004	78312	27595
2005	121499	57113
2006	182525	82463
2007	143978	111567
2008	118230	114738
2009	60027	121872
2010	119689	156653
2011	120083	200522
2012	360264	247800
2013	251874	312994
2014	255321	370310
2015	193684	400833

注：本表数据来源于市商务局。

17-3 外国和港澳台地区在西安直接投资（2015年）

Direct Investments from Foreign Countries and Hong Kong, Macao and Taiwan in Xi'an（2015）

分类	Classity	新签协议情况 New-signed Agreement Circumstances 合同数（个） Number of Constracts (unit)	利用外资签定协议金额（万美元） Value of Foreign Captial Used through the Signed (USD10 000)	外商实际直接投资额（万美元） Value of Foreign Direct Investment (USD 10 000)
合　计	**Total**	**73**	**193684**	**400833**
一、按投资方式分	**Grouped by Investment Mode**			
1.中外合资经营企业	Joint-venture Enterprises	20	36877	89081
2.中外合作经营企业	Cooperation Enterprises		2546	140
3.外资企业	Wholly Foreign-owned Enterprises	53	154262	311612
4.外资企业再投资	Re-investment from Foreign-funded Enterprises			
二、按国民经济行业分组	**Grouped by Sector**			
1.农、林、牧、渔业	Agriculture, Forestry, Animal Husbandry and Fishery	2	16	
2.采矿业	Mining		47	1976
3.制造业	Manufacturing	13	135143	353214
4.电力、燃气及水的生产供应业	Production and Distribution of Electricity,Gas and Water	1		3960
5.建筑业	Construction	1	113	1549
6.批发和零售业	Wholesale and Retail Trades	18	7359	10593
7.交通运输、仓储和邮政业	Traffic, Transport, Storage and Post	7	10084	8382
8.住宿和餐饮业	Hotels and Catering Services	7	75	680
9.信息传输、软件和信息技术服务业	Information Transmission,Software and Information Technology Services	3	-5	477
10.金融业	Financial Intermediation			1230
11.房地产	Real Estate	4	37408	12973
12.租赁和商务服务业	Leasing and Business Services	14	1186	1443
13.科学研究和技术服务业	Scientific Research and Technical Service		1	1093
14.水利、环境和公共设施管理业	Management of Water Conservancy,Environment and Public Facilities	1	1407	1163
15.居民服务、修理和其他服务业	Services to Households,Repairs and Other Services			131
16.教育	Education			
17.卫生和社会工作	Health and Social Work	1	515	1361
18.文化、体育和娱乐业	Culture, Sports and Entertainment	1	334	608
19.公共管理社会保障和社会组织	Public Management ,Social Security and Social Drganizations			
20.国际组织	International Organizations			
三、按投资国别、地区分组	**Grouped by Different Countries and Regions**			
香港	Hong Kong	32	80068	37734
澳门	Macao	1	12	3249
台湾省	Taiwan	3	-5	2732
日本	Japan		569	1341
泰国	Thailand			
马来西亚	Malaysia			5
新加坡	Singapore	3	9731	25846
韩国	Korea Rep	18	100206	313776
德意志联邦国	Germany			612
意大利	Italy	2	9	
法国	France	1	-10	55
英国	United Kingdom		1	106
捷克共和国	Czechoslovakia			
加拿大	Canada	3	38	40
美国	America	1	149	2283
澳大利亚	Australia	2	7	
维尔京群岛	Virgian Islands	1	245	1194
其它	Other	6	2666	11861

注：本表数据来源于市商务局。

17-4 各区县、开发区外商实际直接投资

Direct Investment by Foreign Entrepreneurs by Region and Development Zone

单位：万美元 (USD 10 000)

区县及开发区	Region and Economic Zone	2010	2011	2012	2013	2014	2015
区县合计	**Sum of Region**	**38855**	**49726**	**58119**	**45164**	**51423**	**59765**
新城区	Xincheng	4900	6765	7800	5012	6500	7775
碑林区	Beilin	5150	6273	7800	5103	5871	6873
莲湖区	Lianhu	5471	7405	7800	5100	5843	6873
灞桥区	Baqiao	5215	6001	7397	6124	6933	8148
未央区	Weiyang	5023	6202	7800	6000	6834	7870
雁塔区	Yanta	5488	6912	8190	6179	6847	8074
阎良区	Yanliang	1208	2070	2200	2200	2346	2555
临潼区	Lintong	1200	2000	2400	2400	2504	2765
长安区	Chang'an	1680	2300	2768	3003	3360	3961
高陵区	Gaoling	950	1089	1100	1100	1182	1478
蓝田县	Lantian	550	600	650	660	707	1283
周至县	Zhouzhi	970	1050	1100	1110	1210	773
户　县	Huxian	1050	1060	1115	1173	1288	1339
开发区合计	**Sum of Development Zones**	117798	150797	189681	267830	318887	311265
高新区	GaoXin	51130	64935	81776	132632	149387	167112
经开区	JingKai	42608	54201	68202	81423	103009	114538
曲江新区	Qujiang	17187	21002	26433	33870	41436	
浐灞生态区	Chanba Eco-District	3070	3856	4837	7266	8453	9800
航空基地	Aviation Industry Base	1239	1701	2072	2640	3082	3636
航天基地	Aerospace Base	1554	2030	2403	3000	3501	3980
国际港务区	International Trade&Logistic Park	1010	1571	2082	3469	5050	6429
沣东新城	FengDongXinCheng		1500	1876	3530	4970	5770

注：本表数据来源于市商务局。

17–5 主要年份进出口总额

Total Imports and Exports in Representative Years

单位：万美元 (USD 10 000)

年 份 Year	进出口总额 Total Imports and Exports	出口总额 Total Exports	进口总额 Total Imports
1987	13596	7540	6056
1988	36750	24632	12118
1989	32715	21564	11151
1990	38229	28290	9939
1991	55356	41511	13845
1992	70467	53060	17407
1993	93330	62393	30937
1994	104752	76897	27855
1995	137510	110163	27347
1996	143187	91745	51442
1997	150668	107753	42915
1998	180589	100492	80097
1999	172919	94495	78424
2000	173696	106062	67634
2001	169914	87948	81966
2002	186966	112479	74487
2003	230932	140327	90605
2004	309295	203539	105756
2005	390146	263441	126705
2006	415403	272862	142541
2007	536162	347133	189029
2008	704029	447113	256916
2009	724618	333114	391504
2010	1039273	531729	507544
2011	1260179	582662	677517
2012	1301446	729878	571568
2013	1798534	847819	950715
2014*	15321514	7346822	7974693
2015*	17616896	8198754	9418142

注：本表数据来源于西安海关。2014年以后数据计量单位为万元。

17-6 外贸商品进出口总额分国别和地区（2015年）

Total Value of Imports and Exports by Country and Region（2015）

单位：万元 (10 000 yuan)

国别和地区	Country and Region	进出口总额 Total Imports and Exports	出口 Exports
亚洲	**Asia**	**10896372**	**4925628**
#香港	Hong kong	1790305	1774958
台湾省	Taiwan	3665503	481736
日本	Japan	1091367	273917
菲律宾	Phiilippines	74135	30627
马来西亚	Malaysia	229402	121424
韩国	Korea	2382433	1159606
非洲	**Africa**	**455340**	**241159**
#埃及	Egypt	38234	38219
突尼斯	Tunisia	1501	1383
埃塞俄比亚	Ethiopia	40931	40930
博茨瓦纳	Botswana	837	699
南非	South Africa	174765	27214
欧洲	**Europe**	**2028919**	**1035469**
#德意志联邦国	Germany	346329	108019
法国	France	279182	220491
意大利	Italy	104462	48426
荷兰	Netherland	374628	157118
英国	England	250849	201477
瑞士	Switzerland	75268	5738
西班牙	Spain	27124	21203
俄罗斯联邦	Russia	106937	54158
拉丁美洲	**Latin America**	**477136**	**256119**
#哥伦比亚	Colombia	6379	6378
巴西	Brazil	101848	19163
阿根廷	Argentina	7652	7127
北美洲	**North America**	**3510087**	**1689257**
加拿大	Canada	91500	57815
美国	America	3418587	1631442
大洋洲及太平洋岛屿	**Oceanic and Pacific Islands**	**249011**	**51122**
#澳大利亚	Australia	240240	44229
新西兰	New Zealand	5199	3561

注：本表数据来源于西安海关。

17-7 主要商品分大类出口金额

单位：万美元

商品分类	HS Section and Division	2000	2004
食用蔬菜、根及块茎	Edible Vegetables, Certain,Roots amd Tubers	1095	1386
蔬菜、水果、坚果或植物其他部分的制品	Vegetables, Fruits, Nuts, or Products Made of Other Parts of Plants	2076	7786
矿砂、矿渣及矿灰	Ores,Slags and Ash	4083	30590
无机化学品；贵金属、稀土金属、放射性元素及其同位素的有机及无机化合物	Inorganic Chemicals,Organic or Inorganic Compounds of Precious Metals,of Rare Earth Metals,of Radioactive Elements or of Isotopes	3714	5806
有机化学品	Organic Chemicals	2367	4837
羊毛、动物细毛或粗毛、马毛纱线及其机织物	Wool ,Fine or Coarse Animal Hair; Horsehair Yarn and Woven Fabric	810	1640
棉花	Cotton	3197	3133
化学纤维短纤	Short Staple Chemical' Fibers	5061	1987
针织或钩编的服装及衣着附件	Articles of Apparel and Clothing Accessories, Knitted or Crocheted	6753	7465
非针织或非钩编的服装及衣着附件	Articles of Apparel and Clothing Accessories, not Knitted or Crocheted	7269	5543
其它纺织制成品；成套物品；旧衣着及旧纺织品	Other Made Up Textile Articles;Sets;Worn Clothing and Worn Textile Articles;Rags Articles	1649	2667
鞋靴、护膝和类似品及其零件	Footwear,Gaiters and The Like;Parts of Such Articles Headgear and Parts Thereof	1347	2687
玻璃及其制品	Glass and Glassware	3376	8083
钢铁	Iron and Steel	3534	5244
钢铁制品	Articles of Iron or Steel	5535	10398
铅及制品	Lead Areticles Thereof	1371	43
锌及制品	Zinc Areticles Thereof	4031	522
其他贱金属、金属陶瓷及其制品	Other Base Metals,Germets;Areticles Thereof	1066	6419
贱金属工具、器具、利口器、餐匙、餐叉及其零件	Tools,Implements,Cutlery,Spons and Forks, of Base Metal;Parts Thereof of Base Metal	2933	3406
核反应堆、锅炉、机器、机械器具及其零件	Nuclear Reactors ,Boilers, Machinery and Mechanical Appliances; and Parts Thereof	10915	24696
电机、电气设备及其零件；录音机及放声机、电视图象、声音的录制和重放设备及其零件、附件	Electrical Machinery and Equipment and Parts Thereof;Sound Recorders and Repreducers, Television Image and Sound Recordes and Repreducers, and Parts and Accessories of Such Articles	8339	19812
光学、照相、电影、计量、检验、医疗或外科仪器及设备、精密仪器及设备；上述物品的零配件、附件	Optical,Photographic,Cinematographic,Measuring, Checking,Precision Medical or Surgical Instruments and Apparatus;Parts and Accessories Thereof	2020	1847
家具、寝具、褥垫、弹簧床垫、软床垫及类似的填充制品；未列名灯具及照明装置；发光标志、发光名牌及类似品；活动房屋	Mattresses,Mattress Supports,Cushions and Similar Stuffed Furnishings;Lamps and Lighting Fittings, not Elsewhere Spcified or Included;Illumihated Signs,Illuminated	2587	4955

注：2014年、2015年数据计量单位为万元。

Export Value of Major Merchandise by Type

(USD 10 000)

2005	2006	2007	2008	2009	2010	2011	2012	2013	2014 *	2015*
1190	1136	1232	1374	803	4740	2016	1961	2699	2686	2039
10531	15374	37426	29270	21920	41289	36763	2576	49361	132663	112701
63247	52046	47378	40502	6141	325	4709	1679	1686	14977	96
10997	10916	16508	15882	9774	24875	11735	8911	12588	67764	44508
8569	11923	11182	13954	16294	982	20067	17890	28694	109986	109654
903	1400	1065	720	460	10133	796	562	2433	15782	3005
3240	3808	3255	3213	2346	98	2628	2185	5827	9252	14309
1471	1556	1767	1181	2217	479	2586	2375	8245	13685	11581
5736	5332	5345	4371	3617	3209	3366	12316	6491	29551	37030
5068	4078	3875	3623	2919	3394	3262	7050	4861	33872	23610
3000	3342	3090	3187	2813	544	2838	4412	4471	18906	15677
1368	216	348	380	367	150	1003	5252	6293	20186	5032
8576	8272	6246	6538	5574	928	8073	10995	13856	54453	45991
5314	4900	11366	11966	4254	18549	16681	8407	6730	31854	20390
13959	16903	17329	26568	11943	5998	25319	24259	33546	102720	88740
12	158	1650	2	1	10	2	4913	16	3	
135	4119	2470	46	78	28545	10	11	59	109	93
11233	17695	23414	27576	11276	3556	28092	21397	24030	106691	95442
3052	3607	3917	4083	2777	2893	3641	5176	5992	30653	25321
30832	36174	47381	75911	52372	130296	99631	127795	211009	1929864	2744726
23605	22801	33393	56758	53355	136	137105	183536	327931	3113155	3625079
2341	3521	4230	6348	5255	196	11066	14908	17879	112646	119117
4773	5086	8301	8296	4769	5328	3860	25644	23595	52352	42140

17-8 主要商品分大类进口金额

Import Value of Major Merchandise by Type

单位：万美元 (USD 10 000)

商品分类	HS Section and Division	2000	2005	2007	2008	2009
无机化学品；贵金属、稀土金属、放射性元素及其同位素的有机及无机化合物	Inorganic Chemicals,Organic or Inorganic Compounds of Precious Metals,of Rare Earth Metals,of Radioactive Elements or of Isotopes	1467	317	1039	6001	5040
有机化学品	Organic Chemicals	7257	15237	14536	15692	14186
塑料及其制品	Plastic and Articles Thereof	2559	4317	5149	2553	3134
钢铁	Iron and Steel	2467	752	1270	3888	2537
铜及制品	Copper and Articles Thereof	2367	689	22683	11097	41195
铝及制品	Aluminium and Articles Thereof	2652	3627	3223	4767	6505
核反应堆、锅炉、机器、机械器具及其零件	Nuclear Reactors ,Boilers, Machinery and Mechanical Appliances; and Parts Thereof	12990	38050	55243	68504	87493
电机、电气设备及其零件；录音机及放声机、电视图象、声音的录制和重放设备及其零件、附件	Electrical Machinery and Equipment and Parts Thereof;Sound Recorders and Repreducers, Television Image and Sound Recordes and Repreducers,and Parts and Accessories of Such Articles	5911	23337	25164	48008	113034
车辆及其零件、附件、铁道及电车道车辆除外	Vehicles Other Than Railway or Tramway Rolling-Stock, and Rarts and Accessories Thereof	1530	1387	1529	3789	1798
航空器、航天器及其零配件	Aircraft, Spacecraft and Parts Thereof	10443	8800	2463	26148	13057
光学、照相、电影、计量、检验、医疗或外科仪器及设备、精密仪器及设备；上述物品的零配件、附件	Optical,Photographic,Cinematographic,Measuring, Checking,Precision Medical or Surgical	3673	10424	17026	17737	24210

17-8 续表 continued

单位：万美元 (USD 10 000)

商品分类	HS Section and Division	2010	2011	2012	2013	2014*	2015*
无机化学品；贵金属、稀土金属、放射性元素及其同位素的有机及无机化合物	Inorganic Chemicals,Organic or Inorganic Compounds of Precious Metals,of Rare Earth Metals,of Radioactive Elements or of Isotopes	7513	19766	13329	11869	166549	185175
有机化学品	Organic Chemicals	13949	18100	12331	12504	98293	86359
塑料及其制品	Plastic and Articles Thereof	4091	3250	3107	8014	37082	54103
钢铁	Iron and Steel	10949	10643	5928	1802	11893	17403
铜及制品	Copper and Articles Thereof	43343	78482	11857	65170	169061	484480
铝及制品	Aluminium and Articles Thereof	3116	5913	8649	11758	45295	43935
核反应堆、锅炉、机器、机械器具及其零件	Nuclear Reactors ,Boilers, Machinery and Mechanical Appliances; and Parts Thereof	134753	135240	98802	186974	2017587	2021311
电机、电气设备及其零件；录音机及放声机、电视图象、声音的录制和重放设备及其零件、附件	Electrical Machinery and Equipment and Parts Thereof;Sound Recorders and Repreducers, Television Image and Sound Recordes and Repreducers,and Parts and Accessories of Such Articles	207937	230957	257444	444407	3919650	5011437
车辆及其零件、附件、铁道及电车道车辆除外	Vehicles Other Than Railway or Tramway Rolling-Stock, and Rarts and Accessories Thereof	3109	1527	2222	2966	17521	19700
航空器、航天器及其零配件	Aircraft, Spacecraft and Parts Thereof	3620	4654	8516	9179	43191	35164
光学、照相、电影、计量、检验、医疗或外科仪器及设备、精密仪器及设备；上述物品的零配件、附件	Optical,Photographic,Cinematographic,Measuring, Checking,Precision Medical or Surgical	37414	39317	48206	61727	452559	542812

注：本表数据来源于西安海关。2014年以后数据计量单位为万元。

17-9 按贸易方式分外贸出口总值

Total Value of Exports in Foreign Trade by Type of Trade

单位：万元 (10 000 yuan)

指 标	Item	2015	2015年比2014年增长（%） Growth Rate in 2015 over 2014(%)
出口总值	**Total Exports**	**8198754**	**11.6**
1.一般贸易	General Trade	2050972	-12.3
2.国家间、国际组织无偿援助	Between Countries, International Organizations	9155	5274.7
和赠送的物资	Aid and Donated Materials		
3.来料加工装配贸易	Assembly Processing Trade	38263	17.5
4.进料加工贸易	Processing With Imported Trade	5561457	15.4
5.对外承包工程出口货物	Exports Contracted Projects	138464	76.6
6.租赁贸易	Lease Trade		
7.易货贸易	Barter		
8.出料加工贸易	Material Processing	5	-91.6
9.保税监管场所进出境货物	Inward and Outward Goods of Free	142	-97.6
(保税仓库进出境货物)			
10.海关特殊监管区域物流货物	Re-export Goods of Free Trade Zone	397229	513.7
11.其他	Others	3067	2.0

17-10 按贸易方式分外贸进口总值

Total Value of Imports in Foreign Trade by Type of Trade

单位：万元　　　　(10 000 yuan)

指标名称	Item	2015	2015年比2014年增长（%） Growth Rate in 2015 over 2014(%)
进口总值	**Total Imports**	9418142	18.1
1.一般贸易	General Trade	1862893	22.7
2.国家间、国际组织无偿援助和赠送的物资	Between Countries, International s Organization Aid and Donated Materials	512	
3.华侨、港澳台同胞、外籍华人捐赠物资	The overseas Chinese, Hong Kong, Macao, Taiwan,Chinese of foreign Donated Materials	58	
4.来料加工装配贸易	Assembly Processing Trade	24468	-15.8
5.进料加工贸易	Processing With Imported Trade	4853431	13.3
6.来料加工装配进口的设备	Assembly Processing Trade Equipment	2054	
7.租赁贸易	Lease Trade	4	-79.2
8.外商投资企业作为投资进口的设备、物品	Foreign-invested Enterprises as the Import Investment of Equipment, Goods	25663	281.1
9.出料加工贸易	Material Processing	59	-79.3
10.易货贸易	Barter	121	
11.保税监管场所进出境货物（保税仓库进出境货物）	Inward and Outward Goods of Free	18384	-34.5
12.海关特殊监管区域物流货物（保税区仓储转口货物）	Re-export Goods of Free Trade Zone	626423	-60.2
13.海关特殊监管区域进口设备（出口加工区进口设备）	Export Processing Zones Imported	1982609	289
14.其他	Other	21463	-2.1

17-11 主要年份旅游人数及收入

Number of Tourists and Tourism Earnings in Representative Years

年 份 Year	接待旅游者人数（万人次） Number of Tourists (10 000 person-times)	国际旅游人数 Number of International Tourists	旅游总收入（万元） Total Tourism Earnings (10 000 yuan)	国际旅游收入 Earning of International Tourists	国际旅游者在西安人均停留天数（天） Number of Days of Average International Tourists Staying in Xi'an(day)
1980	4.00	4.00	1757	1757	3.8
1985	21.15	21.15	7029	7029	2.2
1990	25.88	25.88	19628	19628	2.1
1991	31.00	31.00	29051	29051	2.3
1992	40.16	40.16	40966	40966	2.2
1993	43.50	43.50	48951	48951	1.9
1994	41.49	41.49	82000	82000	2.2
1995	791.35	41.35	440000	103818	2.0
1996	925.39	45.39	470000	149400	2.6
1997	1010.53	48.53	510000	166359	2.6
1998	1105.80	47.98	560000	160244	2.6
1999	1260.40	55.41	830000	186282	2.5
2000	1567.00	65.03	1050000	224100	2.5
2001	1752.20	67.20	1130000	240700	2.4
2002	1984.13	74.13	1310000	260000	2.2
2003	1647.67	33.66	1064200	121200	2.5
2004	2149.03	65.03	1544000	273900	2.9
2005	2423.60	77.56	1785000	335380	2.9
2006	2738.70	86.73	2043000	378270	2.9
2007	3118.01	100.01	2372000	424263	2.9
2008	3232.20	63.20	2435200	287200	2.6
2009	3929.29	67.29	2974000	310500	2.9
2010	5285.18	84.18	4051800	424000	2.9
2011	6653.23	100.23	5301500	512800	2.9
2012	7978.35	115.35	6543900	598900	2.9
2013	10130.00	121.11	8114400	641600	2.9
2014	12000.00		9500000		
2015	13600.80		10736900		

注：本表数据来源于市旅游局。2014年、2015年市旅游局未发布国际旅游统计数据。

17-12 主要年份旅行社及A级景点

Statistics of Travel Agencies and Level-A Scenic Spots in Representative Years

项 目	Item	2008	2009	2010	2011	2012	2013	2014	2015
旅行社数（个）	Number of Travel Agencies (unit)	271	303	334	365	344	360	385	353
旅行社营业收入（亿元）	Revenue of Travel Agencies (100 million yuan)	17.85	21.34	31.22	44.31	49.49	57.93	45.7	59.54
旅游A级景点数（个）	Number of Level-A Scenic Spots(unit)	23	24	34	43	55	61	67	74
旅游A级景点年接待游客人次（万人次）	Number of Tourists Received at Level-A Scenic Spots (10 000 person times)	1420	1504	2726	4295	5306	7163	7462	8553

注：本表数据来源于市旅游局。

主要统计指标解释

进出口总额 指实际进出我国国境的货物总金额。包括对外贸易实际进出口货物，来料加工装配进出口货物，国家间、联合国及国际组织无偿援助物资和赠送品，华侨、港澳台同胞和外籍华人捐赠品，租赁期满归承租人所有的租赁货物，进料加工进出口货物，边境地方贸易及边境地区小额贸易进出口货物（边民互市贸易除外），中外合资企业、中外合作经营企业、外商独资经营企业进出口货物和公用物品，到、离岸价格在规定限额以上的进出口货样和广告品（无商业价值、无使用价值和免费提供出口的除外），从保税仓库提取在中国境内销售的进口货物，以及其他进出口货物。该指标可以观察一个国家在对外贸易方面的总规模。我国规定出口货物按离岸价格统计，进口货物按到岸价格统计。

商品经营单位所在地进、出口额 指在所在地海关注册登记的有进出口经营权的企业实际进、出口额。

商品目的地进口额和商品货源地出口额 目的地进口额指进口货物的消费、使用或最终抵运地的实际进口额；货源地出口额指出口货物的产地或原始发货地的实际出口额。

利用外资 指我国各级政府、部门、企业和其他经济组织通过对外借款、吸收外商直接投资以及用其他方式筹措的境外现汇、设备、技术等。

外商直接投资 指外国企业和经济组织或个人（包括华侨、港澳台胞以及我国在境外注册的企业）按我国有关政策、法规，用现汇、实物、技术等在我国境内开办外商独资企业、与我国境内的企业或经济组织共同举办中外合资经营企业、合作经营企业或合作开发资源的投资（包括外商投资收益的再投资），以及经政府有关部门批准的项目投资总额内企业从境外借入的资金。

旅游人数：

（1）入境旅游人数：指报告期内来我国观光、度假、探亲访友、就医疗养、购物、参加会议或从事经济、文化、体育、宗教活动的外国人、港澳台同胞等入境游客。统计时，外国人、港澳台同胞每入境一次统计1人次。

（2）出境人数：指中国（大陆）居民因公或因私出境前往其他国家、中国香港特别行政区、澳门特别行政区和台湾省观光、度假、探亲访友、就医疗养、购物、参加会议或从事经济、文化、体育、宗教活动的人数，即出境游客。统计时，按每出境一次统计1人次。

（3）国内旅游人数：指在报告期内在中国（大陆）观光游览、度假、探亲访友、就医疗养、购物、参加会议或从事经济、文化、体育、宗教活动的中国（大陆）居民人数，其出游的目的不是通过所从事的活动谋取报酬。统计时，国内游客按每出游一次统计1人次。

国际旅游（外汇）收入 指入境游客在中国（大陆）境内旅行、游览过程中用于交通、参观游览、住宿、餐饮、购物、娱乐等全部花费。

国内旅游收入 又称旅游总花费指国内游客在国内旅行、游览过程中用于交通、参观游览、住宿、餐饮、购物、娱乐等全部花费。

国际旅行社 指经营业务范围包括入境旅游业务、出境旅游业务和国内旅游业务的旅行社。

国内旅行社 指经营范围仅限于国内旅游业务的旅行社。

星级饭店 指设备、设施、服务符合《旅游饭店星级的划分与评定》（CB／T14308—2003），通过相关旅游管理部门评定，并取得星级饭店称号的饭店（含预备星级饭店）。

Explanatory Notes on Main Statistical Indicators

Total Imports and Exports at Customs refer to the real value of commodities imported and exported across the border of China. They include the actual imports and exports through foreign trade, imported and exported goods under the processing and assembling trades and materials, supplies and gifts as aid given gratis between governments and by the United Nations and other international organizations, and contributions donated by overseas Chinese, compatriots in Hong Kong and Macao and Chinese with foreign citizenship, leasing commodities owned by tenant at the expiration of leasing period, the imported and exported commodities processed with imported materials, commodities trading in border areas (excluding mutual exchange goods), the imported and exported commodities and articles for public use of the Sino-foreign joint ventures, cooperative enterprises and ventures with sole foreign investment. Also included is import or export of samples and advertising goods for which CIF or FOB value are beyond the permitted ceiling (excluding goods of no trading or use value and free commodities for export), imported goods sold in China from bonded warehouses and other imported or exported goods. The indicator of the total imports and exports at customs can be used to observe the total size of external trade in a country. In accordance with the stipulation of the Chinese government, imports are calculated at CIF, while exports are calculated at FOB.

Import Export Value by Location of China's Foreign Trade Managing Units refers to actual value of imports and exports carried out by corporations which have been registered by the local Customs house and are vested with right to run import export business.

Import Value of Commodities by Place of Destination and Export Value of Commodities by Place of Origin in China The former indicator refers to the value of import commodities of the places of their consumption, utilization or the places of their final destination. The latter indicator refers to the value of export commodities of the places of their origin or the places of the commodities dispatched.

Utilization of Foreign Capitals refers to remittance, equipment and technology financed from abroad, by loans, foreign direct investment and other forms undertaken by the Chinese governments at all levels, by various departments, enterprises and other economic units.

Foreign Borrowings refer to funds borrowed from abroad through formal signing of borrowing agreements with foreign institutions, including loans of foreign governments, loans of international financial institutions, commercial loans of foreign banks, export credit, and funds raised by Chinese bonds (and shares before 1996) issued abroad. It is an important part of China's utilization of foreign capitals.

Foreign Direct Investment refers to the investments inside China by foreign enterprises and economic organizations or individuals (including overseas Chinese, compatriots from Hong Kong, Macao and Taiwan, and Chinese enterprises registered abroad), following the relevant policies and laws of China, for the establishment of ventures exclusively with foreign own investment, Sino-foreign joint ventures and cooperative enterprises or for co-operative exploration of resources with enterprises or economic organizations in China.

Number of Tourists

(1) Visitor arrivals refer to the number of foreigners,Chinese compatriots from Hong Kong, Macao and Taiwan Chinese (mainland) who come to China (mainland) for sight-seeing,vacation,visiting relatives, medical treatment, shopping, attending conference, or to engage in economic, cultural, sports and religious activities. In compiling statistics, each time of entering China is counted as one person-time.

(2) Number of Chinese residents going abroad refer to the number of Chinese (mainland) residents going to other countries, Hong Kong Special Administrative region, Macao Special Administrative region and Taiwan for on official or private purposes, for sight-seeing, vacation, visiting relatives, medical treatment, shopping, attending conference, or to engage in economic, cultural, sports and religious

activities. In compiling statistics, each time of leaving is counted as one person-time.

(3) Number of domestic tourists refers to the number of Chinese (mainland) residents who travel within China (mainland) for sight-seeing, vacation, visiting relatives, medical treatment, shopping, attending conference, or to engage in economic, cultural, sports and religious activities. In compiling statistics, each time of travelling is counted as one person-time.

Foreign Exchange Earnings from International Tourism refer to the total expenditure of foreigners, overseas Chinese,Chinese compatriots from Hong Kong,Macao and Taiwan during their stay in the mainland of China on transportation,sighting,accommodation, food,shopping and entertainment.

Income from Domestic Tourism refer to expenditure of domestic tourists on transportation,sighting, accommodation, food, shopping and entertainment while they travel.

International Travel Agencies refer to travel agencies engaged in tourism entering China, Chinese residents going abroad and domestic tourism.

Domestic Travel Agencies refer to travel agencies only engaged in domestic tourism.

Star-rated Hotels refer to hotels rated with stars as assessed by the relevant tourism authorities according to GB/T14308-2003 standard with reference to their infrastructure, facilities and service levels.

18 服务业

TERTIARY INDUSTRY

资料整理：王家峰
Data management：Wang Jiafeng
数据审核：王金桂
Data audit：Wang Jingui

第十八部分　服务业

一、简要说明

本资料主要包括规模以上服务业（九个门类、四个中类）单位个数及主要经济指标，由西安市统计局服务业和社科处提供。

二、主要指标

单位数（个）	1056		
资产总计（亿元）	6232.20	比上年增长	7.9%
营业收入（亿元）	1562.28	比上年增长	2.5%
利润总额（亿元）	155.92	比上年下降	18.6%

18 FINANCIAL INTERMEDIATION

Ⅰ.Brief Introduction

The data in this chapter consists of the number of service units and main economic indicators of Service enterprises above designated size (Including nine categories, four Class) , data in this chapter is provided by Tertiary Industry and Social Science&Technology Division of Xi'an Bureau of Statistice.

Ⅱ.Major Indicators

		Increase over Preceding Year
Number of units(units)	1056	
Total assets (100 mil. yuan)	6232.20	7.9%
Operating income(100 mil. yuan)	1562.28	2.5%
The total profit (100 mil. yuan)	155.92	-18.6%

18-1 规模以上服务业按登记注册类型分主要经济指标

Main Economic Indicators for Services above the Designated Size grouped by Registration Type

单位：万元　　　　(10 000 yuan)

指　标	Item	单位数（个）Number of Enterprises (unit)	资产总计 Total Assets	固定资产原价 Original Value of Fixed Assets
总计	**Total**	**1056**	**62321993.9**	**34083410.8**
按登记注册类型分组	**Grouped by Registration Type**			
内资企业	Domestic Funded Enterprises	1008	61648517.8	33811013.7
国有	State-owned Enterprises	109	3564767.9	1324422.8
集体	Collective-owned Enterprises	17	65580.1	20675.8
股份合作	Corperative Enterprises	5	15242.7	4735.1
联营	Joint Ownership Enterprises			
国有联营	State Joint Ownership Enterprises			
集体联营	Collective Joint Ownership Enterprises			
国有与集体联营	Joint State-collective Enterprises			
其他联营	Others Joint Ownership Enterprises			
有限责任公司	Limited Liability Corporrations	536	51190861.4	28182475.5
国有独资公司	State Funded Corporations	58	27216317.3	13331784.8
其他有限责任公司	Other Limited Liability Corporrations	478	23974544.1	14850690.7
股份有限公司	Other Limited Liability Corporrations	49	4751429.7	3776456.7
私营	Other Limited Liability Corporrations	278	1961685.8	482773.5
私营独资	Private-funded Enterprises	10	12858.3	6671.8
私营合伙	Private Partnership Enterprises	6	51780.8	17264.8
私营有限责任公司	Private Limited Liability Corporations	247	1730345.7	452708.7
私营股份有限公司	Private Share-holding Corporations Ltd.	15	166701.0	6128.2
其他	Other Enterprises	14	98950.2	19474.3
港澳台商投资	Enterprises with Funds from Hong Kong, Macao &Taiwan	17	414454.8	141951.5
合资经营	Joint Ventures	8	241000.1	97880.1
合作经营	Cooperation Enterprises	2	84608.0	5606.2
港澳台商独资经营	Enterprises with Sole Investment from Hong Kong Macau and Taiwan	7	88846.7	38465.2
港澳台商投资股份有限公司	Share-holding Corporations Ltd. with funds from Hong Kong, Macao & Taiwan			
外商投资	Foreign Funded Enterprises	31	259021.3	130445.6
中外合资经营企业	Sino-foreign Joint Ventures Enterprises	8	50204.7	20269.0
中外合作经营企业	Sino-Foreign Cooperation Enterprises	2	5160.4	3813.0
外资企业	Foreign Owned Enterprises	18	195220.2	104065.6
外商投资股份有限公司	Limited Company Funded by Foreign Investment	1	1379.8	333.6
其他外商投资	Other Foreign Funded Enterprises	2	7056.2	1964.4

18-1 续表1

单位：万元

指　标	Item	负债合计 Total Liabilities	所有者权益合计 Total Owners' Equities	营业收入 Paid in Capital
总计	**Total**	**38612455.8**	**23706613.0**	**15622838.8**
按登记注册类型分组	**Grouped by Registration Type**			
内资企业	Domestic Funded Enterprises	38352595.4	23292997.3	15265556.5
国有	State-owned Enterprises	2356380.2	1208387.7	2463868.3
集体	Collective-owned Enterprises	40675.6	24904.5	43169.5
股份合作	Corperative Enterprises	7901.4	7341.3	6555.9
联营	Joint Ownership Enterprises			
国有联营	State Joint Ownership Enterprises			
集体联营	Collective Joint Ownership Enterprises			
国有与集体联营	Joint State-collective Enterprises			
其他联营	Others Joint Ownership Enterprises			
有限责任公司	Limited Liability Corporations	32728236.1	18462625.1	9906785.1
国有独资公司	State Funded Corporations	18562078.2	8654239.1	1540451.6
其他有限责任公司	Other Limited Liability Corporrations	14166157.9	9808386.0	8366333.5
股份有限公司	Other Limited Liability Corporrations	1881412.8	2870016.9	1964341.8
私营	Other Limited Liability Corporrations	1276829.0	681931.9	798507.2
私营独资	Private-funded Enterprises	7804.0	5054.3	12485.7
私营合伙	Private Partnership Enterprises	42707.3	9073.5	47434.6
私营有限责任公司	Private Limited Liability Corporations	1132572.6	594848.2	681319.7
私营股份有限公司	Private Share-holding Corporations Ltd.	93745.1	72955.9	57267.2
其他	Other Enterprises	61160.3	37789.9	82328.7
港澳台商投资	Enterprises with Funds from Hong Kong, Macao &Taiwan	164117.2	250337.6	161094.5
合资经营	Joint Ventures	104134.2	136865.9	97442.6
合作经营	Cooperation Enterprises	23194.4	61413.6	30521.3
港澳台商独资经营	Enterprises with Sole Investment from Hong Kong Macau and Taiwan	36788.6	52058.1	33130.6
港澳台商投资股份有限公司	Share-holding Corporations Ltd. with funds from Hong Kong, Macao & Taiwan			
外商投资	Foreign Funded Enterprises	95743.2	163278.1	196187.8
中外合资经营企业	Sino-foreign Joint Ventures Enterprises	17120.6	33084.1	31845.2
中外合作经营企业	Sino-Foreign Cooperation Enterprises	1703.8	3456.6	3144.4
外资企业	Foreign Owned Enterprises	74473.0	120747.2	139008.9
外商投资股份有限公司	Limited Company Funded by Foreign Investment	902.4	477.4	10421.3
其他外商投资	Other Foreign Funded Enterprises	1543.4	5512.8	11768.0

continued1

(10 000 yuan)

主营业务收入 Revenue from Principal Business	营业成本 Total Cost	主营业务成本 Cost of Principal Business	销售费用 Sale Expenses
14644510.4	**11094383.8**	**10471934.0**	**1138387.7**
14289279.7	10886385.4	10266049.9	1125251.4
2429729.4	2275301.3	2237443.4	40328.3
43032.7	20275.3	20239.4	6213.1
6139.4	2846.5	2817.6	284.2
9520575.6	6639378.6	6081320.6	880880.3
1530619.5	819093.6	803388.1	58058.6
7989956.1	5820285	5277932.5	822821.7
1416016.3	1360238.6	1348842.5	134812.2
791756.6	531951.2	519129.4	57355.2
12434.6	7405.9	7189.1	1818.4
47434.6	32191.6	32191.6	1209.5
674621.7	449643.9	437040.5	52262.7
57265.7	42709.8	42708.2	2064.6
82029.7	56393.9	56257.0	5378.1
159546.0	81443.3	81347.8	5988.0
97418.4	57723.4	57707.8	4388.7
29135.3	8662.3	8662.3	
32992.3	15057.6	14977.7	1599.3
195684.7	126555.1	124536.3	7148.3
31402.0	20577.8	20083.3	1001.4
3144.4	1490.7	1490.7	171.8
138968.7	85584.2	84059.9	5973.3
10401.6	8940.9	8940.9	
11768.0	9961.5	9961.5	1.8

18-1 续表2

单位：万元

指　标	Item	管理费用 Management Expenses	财务费用 Financial Expenses	投资收益 investment income
总计	**Total**	**1595009.8**	**974310.3**	**436577.4**
按登记注册类型分组	**Grouped by Registration Type**			
内资企业	Domestic Funded Enterprises	1514535.7	974140.0	436546.7
国有	State-owned Enterprises	263216.8	18214.6	24723.1
集体	Collective-owned Enterprises	15069.8	-225.0	127.0
股份合作	Corperative Enterprises	3822.7	-50.6	-115.1
联营	Joint Ownership Enterprises			
国有联营	State Joint Ownership Enterprises			
集体联营	Collective Joint Ownership Enterprises			
国有与集体联营	Joint State-collective Enterprises			
其他联营	Others Joint Ownership Enterprises			
有限责任公司	Limited Liability Corporrations	928608.7	889951.7	398204.9
国有独资公司	State Funded Corporations	134655.6	633511.9	307457.0
其他有限责任公司	Other Limited Liability Corporrations	793953.1	256439.8	90747.9
股份有限公司	Other Limited Liability Corporrations	144196.0	46237.5	10234.5
私营	Other Limited Liability Corporrations	147297.5	19840.6	3264.1
私营独资	Private-funded Enterprises	3090.1	79.9	
私营合伙	Private Partnership Enterprises	11810.3	677.9	147.6
私营有限责任公司	Private Limited Liability Corporations	125105.9	18841.9	3032.2
私营股份有限公司	Private Share-holding Corporations Ltd.	7291.2	240.9	84.3
其他	Other Enterprises	12324.2	171.2	108.2
港澳台商投资	Enterprises with Funds from Hong Kong, Macao &Taiwan	37051.5	2973.7	23.1
合资经营	Joint Ventures	24025.4	1176.0	14.0
合作经营	Cooperation Enterprises	2559.4	1159.6	
港澳台商独资经营	Enterprises with Sole Investment from Hong Kong Macau and Taiwan	10466.7	638.1	9.1
港澳台商投资股份有限公司	Share-holding Corporations Ltd. with funds from Hong Kong, Macao & Taiwan			
外商投资	Foreign Funded Enterprises	43422.6	-2803.4	7.6
中外合资经营企业	Sino-foreign Joint Ventures Enterprises	6388.0	238.2	1.9
中外合作经营企业	Sino-Foreign Cooperation Enterprises	718.5	-38.1	
外资企业	Foreign Owned Enterprises	34002.2	-2979.8	5.7
外商投资股份有限公司	Limited Company Funded by Foreign Investment	1006.2	-15.5	
其他外商投资	Other Foreign Funded Enterprises	1307.7	-8.2	

continued2

(10 000 yuan)

营业利润 Business Profits	利润总额 Total Profits	应付职工薪酬 Salary Payable	从业人员平均人数（人） Annual Average Employed Persons (person)
1256825.3	**1559208.3**	**2823540.9**	**335722**
1207819.3	1501732.9	2711021.4	325885
-79514.2	44935.6	531700.5	66590
1869.6	1865.2	25221.2	7273
-254.4	-79.7	2343.5	526
958417.9	1121212.9	1666467.0	178099
139316.4	165703.3	307743.6	33764
819101.5	955509.6	1358723.4	144335
288051.4	297540.6	292574.4	31998
33132.4	29775.6	175977.8	37352
225.7	221.0	2535.9	736
1301.8	1422.8	16392.5	1986
25849.6	22789.7	149339.9	33243
5755.3	5342.1	7709.5	1387
6116.6	6482.7	16737.0	4047
30804.5	33990.6	35432.6	3776
8797.4	11540.7	22343.7	2738
17032.0	16891.8	4130.4	261
4975.1	5558.1	8958.5	777
18201.5	23484.8	77086.9	6061
3446.5	3786.7	8124.0	792
650.0	650.0	730.7	170
13129.3	17741.4	55165.3	3922
481.4	542.4	4875.7	320
494.3	764.3	8191.2	857

18-2 规模以上服务业按规模分主要经济指标

单位：万元

指　标	Item	单位数（个） Number of Enterprises (unit)	资产总计 Total Assets	固定资产原价 Original Value of Fixed Assets
总计	**Total**	**1056**	**62321993.9**	**34083410.8**
按规模分组	**Grouped by Size of Enterprises**			
大型企业	Large-size	109	38524629.2	27288043.1
中型企业	Medium-size	228	7191828.5	1672203.2
小型企业	Small-size	625	14827909.2	4946992.8
微型企业	Microenterprise	94	1777627	176171.7

18-2 续表1

单位：万元

指　标	Item	销售费用 Sale Expenses	管理费用 Management Expenses	财务费用 Financial Expenses
总计	**Total**	**1138387.7**	**1595009.8**	**974310.3**
按规模分组	**Grouped by Size of Enterprises**			
大型企业	Large-size	914064.8	952078.0	686976.9
中型企业	Medium-size	106353.9	306867.7	35631.4
小型企业	Small-size	112118.2	308067.8	241143.7
微型企业	Microenterprise	5850.8	27996.3	10558.3

Main Economic Indicators for Services above the Designated Size grouped by Size of Enterprises

(10 000 yuan)

负债合计 Total Liabilities	所有者权益合计 Total Owners' Equities	营业收入 Paid in Capital	主营业务收入 Revenue from Principal Business	营业成本 Total Cost	主营业务成本 Cost of Principal Business
38612455.8	**23706613.0**	**15622838.8**	**14644510.4**	**11094383.8**	**10471934.0**
23842434.8	14682194.4	10390048.3	9535842.1	7009673.5	6712756.5
4725145.1	2466683.4	2280711.5	2252345.2	1755086.4	1659478.2
9277818.3	5547165.8	2758417.9	2667832.3	2178956.2	1952525.8
767057.6	1010569.4	193661.1	188490.8	150667.7	147173.5

continued 1

(10 000 yuan)

投资收益 investment income	营业利润 Business Profits	利润总额 Total Profits	应付职工薪酬 Salary Payable	从业人员平均人数（人） Annual Average Employed Persons (person)
436577.4	**1256825.3**	**1559208.3**	**2823540.9**	**335722**
66890.3	803563.6	1026340.2	1985120.0	197038
32382.0	101244.4	142544.0	490440.4	71313
85320.5	153003.2	190283.6	322003.8	62618
251984.6	199014.1	200040.5	25976.7	4753

18-3 规模以上服务业按行业分主要经济指标

单位：万元

指标	Item	单位数（个）Number of Enterprises (unit)	资产总计 Total Assets	固定资产原价 Original Value of Fixed Assets
总计	**Total**	**1056**	**62321993.9**	**34083410.8**
按国民经济行业大类分组	**Grouped by sector categories**			
铁路运输业	Railway transport industry	3	4146608.0	3989637.1
道路运输业	The road transport industry	86	21707872.7	13392867.1
水上运输业	Water transportation			
航空运输业	The air transport industry	6	2761754.6	1607020.6
管道运输业	Pipeline transportation	2	1057789.1	979035.7
装卸搬运和运输代理业	Handling and transport industry	17	44974.6	13204.4
仓储业	Warehousing industry	28	788211.2	156221.6
邮政业	The postal service	7	480480.3	437039.0
电信、广播电视和卫星传输服务业	Telecommunication, broadcasting and satellite transmission services	11	7503713.1	10311092.3
互联网和相关服务	The Internet and related services	7	29252.4	9124.4
软件和信息技术服务业	Software and information technology services	134	1677598.2	375497.6
物业管理	Property management	126	679794.1	209869.9
房地产中介服务	Real estate intermediary service	1	118.7	63.6
自有房地产经营活动	Owned Real Estate Business Activities	5	62140.8	32761.3
租赁业	Leasing industry	3	49222.7	36622.4
商务服务业	Business services	182	10893837.4	766341.2
研究和试验发展	Research and development	17	744586.3	271116.8
专业技术服务业	Professional and technical services	164	4304788.8	519570.5
科技推广和应用服务业	Promotion and application of science and technology services	17	804435.2	90790.2
水利管理业	Water resources management industry	2	1484.3	978.7
生态保护和环境治理业	Ecological protection and environmental control industries	4	146412.4	57778.6
公共设施管理业	Public facilities management industry	34	1396140.0	320415.9
居民服务业	Resident services	18	134751.3	70568.9
机动车、电子产品和日用产品修理业	Motor vehicles, electronics and household goods-repairing	18	66099.3	11242.5
其他服务业	Other service industries	8	12032.5	2236.7
教育	Education	13	45490.1	7182.1
卫生	Health	40	275141.7	166409.9
社会工作	Social work			
新闻出版业	Press and publishing industry	25	380284.8	70632.0
广播、电视、电影和影视录音制作业	Radio, television, film and video recordings	36	495912.4	59696.2
文化艺术业	Culture and arts	27	1565382.0	90935.8
体育	Physical education	6	39759.5	18312.3
娱乐业	The entertainment industry	9	25925.4	9145.5

Main Economic Indicators for Services above the Designated Size grouped by Industry

(10 000 yuan)

负债合计 Total Liabilities	所有者权益合计 Total Owners' Equities	营业收入 Paid in Capital	主营业务收入 Revenue from Principal Business	营业成本 Total Cost	主营业务成本 Cost of Principal Business
38612455.8	**23706613.0**	**15622838.8**	**14644510.4**	**11094383.8**	**10471934.0**
2682756.6	1463851.4	494945.0	494483.0	476943.0	333823.4
15200968.9	6506903.8	1322246.4	1304988.1	795349.8	789543.7
1010020.3	1751734.3	441301.5	393452.2	356224.1	327126.1
519714.2	538074.9	707704.6	171590.6	603108.4	598632.3
23971.6	21003.0	64664.5	64593.8	54047.7	53684.7
679409.5	108801.7	579413.3	590138.0	575823.2	573291.7
333255.5	147224.8	448044.8	430929.2	426652.0	425690.3
3448291.1	4055422.0	4001495.6	3782038.8	2353216.8	2122994.3
14145.6	15106.8	48859.1	48859.1	33328.4	32181.6
846022.4	828650.9	1475161.5	1462259.2	932650.5	918244.7
552937.4	126856.7	321368.6	309083.8	231685.4	221167.7
119.3	-0.6	991.0	991.0		
44708.2	17432.5	21741.5	20576.1	12856.6	12648.6
37020.2	12202.5	11669.5	11669.5	11566.3	11564.7
6678245.5	4215591.9	1403125.1	1369042.5	1039967.5	972537.7
265323.5	479262.8	342752.6	338797.8	243514.5	239919.1
2846397.2	1458391.5	2620199.4	2551261.8	2029269.6	1957884.2
477449.2	326986.0	85750.1	84388.7	57605.9	57468.6
1558.8	-74.5	2537.2	2418.8	2171.0	2111.7
101172.3	45240.1	30419.5	29591.8	16155.3	15968.6
1005639.7	390500.3	290841.5	289224.1	199296.6	198287.3
116539.5	18211.8	47300.2	47167.0	38284.5	34842.7
32229.9	33869.4	42865.1	42805.5	32342.8	31277.3
6605.3	5427.2	17638.0	17601.4	14299.7	12507.3
31279.8	14210.3	61933.7	61845.6	42741.8	42437.7
159393.2	115748.5	214910.7	213848.5	150220.4	147620.8
220480.6	159804.2	213737.8	210247.7	167633.9	150614.1
314852.5	181059.9	211329.1	207652.0	162736.4	153964.1
896456.7	668925.3	81560.6	76680.4	29536.1	28743.4
36679.5	3080.0	8462.4	8462.4	1407.2	1407.2
28811.8	-2886.4	7868.9	7822.0	3748.4	3748.4

18-3 续表1

单位：万元

指 标	Item	销售费用 Sale Expenses	管理费用 Management Expenses	财务费用 Financial Expenses
总计	**Total**	**1138387.7**	**1595009.8**	**974310.3**
按国民经济行业大类分组	**Grouped by sector categories**			
铁路运输业	Railway transport industry	1886.2	9541.0	138907.7
道路运输业	The road transport industry	2855.9	97013.0	615364.7
水上运输业	Water transportation			
航空运输业	The air transport industry	9340.0	29325.6	36115.9
管道运输业	Pipeline transportation	1025.5	14468.9	19781.4
装卸搬运和运输代理业	Handling and transport industry	2487.3	7113.2	272.8
仓储业	Warehousing industry	9416.7	19858.4	13793.2
邮政业	The postal service	511.7	67416.4	1503.1
电信、广播电视和卫星传输服务业	Telecommunication, broadcasting and satellite transmission services	758553.0	249204.1	15328
互联网和相关服务	The Internet and related services	1365.4	10963.8	-108.6
软件和信息技术服务业	Software and information technology services	50949.2	359769.9	8940.7
物业管理	Property management	9681.5	50227.8	11962.9
房地产中介服务	Real estate intermediary service	516.3	398.2	
自有房地产经营活动	Owned Real Estate Business Activities		9889.8	562.9
租赁业	Leasing industry	1136.2	1921.5	1257.8
商务服务业	Business services	77115.5	162475.1	88300.6
研究和试验发展	Research and development	6884.0	48234.8	1933.3
专业技术服务业	Professional and technical services	74513.8	268846.4	-7540.6
科技推广和应用服务业	Promotion and application of science and technology services	3543.3	18762.8	-1706.8
水利管理业	Water resources management industry	66.3	314.9	8.1
生态保护和环境治理业	Ecological protection and environmental control industries	6826.6	2957.9	1822.8
公共设施管理业	Public facilities management industry	15578.6	37303.0	11244.4
居民服务业	Resident services	3901.5	6846.6	212.7
机动车、电子产品和日用产品修理业	Motor vehicles, electronics and household goods-repairing	1875.1	4166.1	413.8
其他服务业	Other service industries	762.1	2038.4	-76.1
教育	Education	4513.0	7270.0	12.4
卫生	Health	11870.4	33072.8	2314.5
社会工作	Social work			
新闻出版业	Press and publishing industry	25443.3	31392.8	-30.4
广播、电视、电影和影视录音制作业	Radio, television, film and video recordings	18541.5	20269.5	8051.4
文化艺术业	Culture and arts	30151.1	19573.6	5150.5
体育	Physical education	4146.2	2880.8	227.4
娱乐业	The entertainment industry	2930.5	1492.7	289.8

continued 1

(10 000 yuan)

投资收益 investment income	营业利润 Business Profits	利润总额 Total Profits	应付职工薪酬 Salary Payable	从业人员平均人数（人） Annual Average Employed Persons (person)
436577.4	**1256825.3**	**1559208.3**	**2823540.9**	**335722**
	9886.6	8106.6	19093.0	2377
21165.4	-189314.6	-70882.8	338083.5	48413
17052.1	21593.6	25092.9	90866.3	8228
3745.6	71075.6	71773.2	34191.7	2110
	-461.4	992.5	9569.8	1747
70.9	-25609.1	762.7	18862.7	3466
203.8	-50349.0	-50607.3	150850.5	23507
2391.0	583956.1	649851.4	448477.3	43902
0.5	4073.5	4824.9	17488.6	2068
457.1	114464.6	163249.8	560966.3	35495
363.1	4796.5	5895.3	133733.3	35285
	19.9	19.9	308.4	58
66.4	-2824.6	-821.3	2356.9	405
	-4409.7	-2484.0	1828.5	366
338521.5	327075.6	319173.8	182069.6	33798
18418.3	58063.1	61346.9	84931.8	6257
17498.8	258455.5	254907.7	471802.6	42923
723.4	6055.4	8518.6	19321.0	2023
	-107.1	-102.6	481.4	96
	1748.7	2512.6	6563.1	843
79.4	38101.7	40956.1	50254.0	10073
13.6	-2312.3	-1798.5	19812.5	6202
	3799.0	3789.6	3931.7	868
	1550.5	1564.3	6900.8	1796
	5636.8	5593.7	11923.2	3091
-222.7	14945.9	15881.0	55988.2	9082
822.3	4034.3	10928.1	34316.5	3453
1384.8	7464.8	24629.6	15350.3	2397
13822.1	-2824.0	7295.1	27761.4	3811
	-608.2	-612.5	3388.2	819
	-1152.4	-1149.0	2067.8	763

18-4 规模以上服务业按隶属关系分主要经济指标

单位：万元

指标	Item	单位数（个） Number of Enterprises (unit)	资产总计 Total Assets	固定资产原价 Original Value of Fixed Assets
总计	**Total**	**1056**	**62321993.9**	**34083410.8**
按隶属关系分	**Grouped by affiliation**			
中央	Central	66	15612877.4	14780054.8
省（自治州、直辖市）	Province (autonomous prefectures, municipalities)	148	25378675.0	16398304.9
地（区、市、州、盟）	Land (District, municipal, State, Union)	140	10752496.5	1227833.9
县（区、市、旗）	Counties (districts, cities, flags)	75	2763585.6	242303
街道	Street	2	22747.2	17291.7
镇	Town	1	278.8	17.3
乡	Township			
（社区）居委会	(Community) neighborhood	1	774.3	28.1
村委会	Village	3	29107.3	5787.0
其他	Others	620	7761451.8	1411790.1

18-4 续表1

单位：万元

指标	Item	销售费用 Sale Expenses	管理费用 Management Expenses	财务费用 Financial Expenses
总计	**Total**	**1138387.7**	**1595009.8**	**974310.3**
按隶属关系分	**Grouped by affiliation**			
中央	Central	806266.1	484089.1	138182.0
省（自治州、直辖市）	Province (autonomous prefectures, municipalities)	91731.2	231805.0	603416.2
地（区、市、州、盟）	Land (District, municipal, State, Union)	82179.2	342858.2	150979.3
县（区、市、旗）	Counties (districts, cities, flags)	12295.3	40131.5	16111.3
街道	Street	885.4	1717.6	-0.5
镇	Town		69.8	0.7
乡	Township			
（社区）居委会	(Community) neighborhood	88.3	77.0	-4.0
村委会	Village	847.6	2488.1	-323.1
其他	Others	144094.6	491773.5	65948.4

Main Economic Indicators for Services above the Designated Size grouped by Affiliation

(10 000 yuan)

负债合计 Total Liabilities	所有者权益合计 Total Owners' Equities	营业收入 Paid in Capital	主营业务收入 Revenue from Principal Business	营业成本 Total Cost	主营业务成本 Cost of Principal Business
38612455.8	**23706613.0**	**15622838.8**	**14644510.4**	**11094383.8**	**10471934.0**
8737102.2	6875775.2	7005043.9	6768316.9	4912819.4	4512433.6
15871686.8	9506988.1	3626131.8	3006126.7	2632838.2	2525385.1
7384707.0	3367789.4	1651891.0	1624022.2	1263771.0	1239021.3
1542645.8	1220939.8	282019.5	273211.3	216529.0	214955.9
19050.6	3696.6	4601.8	4600.6	862.2	862.2
726.0	-447.2	365.1	365.1	312.3	312.3
518.9	255.4	492.7	492.7	256.4	256.4
29204.4	-97.1	7446.4	7313.9	4675.3	4639.4
5026814.1	2731712.8	3044846.6	2960061.0	2062320.0	1974067.8

continued 1

(10 000 yuan)

投资收益 investment income	营业利润 Business Profits	利润总额 Total Profits	应付职工薪酬 Salary Payable	从业人员平均人数（人） Annual Average Employed Persons (person)
436577.4	**1256825.3**	**1559208.3**	**2823540.9**	**335722**
17388.9	789174.0	878303.7	909820.4	82396
369255	356367.0	377291.3	475822.0	60659
10119.2	-162275.2	9313.6	613178.4	75567
2221.6	-6519.7	15525.1	57199.8	15408
16.8	1130.9	1157.5	915.3	241
	-38.4	-38.4	152.6	55
	47.4	47.3	335.1	111
-94.9	-129.7	-200.2	1686.8	332
37670.8	279069.0	277808.4	764430.5	100953

主 要 统 计 指 标 解 释

国家统计局规模以上服务业单位统计标准：辖区内年营业收入1000万元及以上，或年末从业人员50人及以上服务业法人单位。包括：交通运输、仓储和邮政业，信息传输、软件和信息技术服务业，租赁和商务服务业，科学研究和技术服务业，水利、环境和公共设施管理业，教育，卫生和社会工作；以及物业管理、房地产中介服务、自有房地产经营活动和其他房地产业等行业。

辖区内年营业收入500万元及以上，或年末从业人员50人及以上服务业法人单位。包括：居民服务、修理和其他服务业，文化、体育和娱乐业。

固定资产原价 指固定资产的成本，包括企业在购置、自行建造、安装、改建、扩建、技术改造某项固定资产时所发生的全部支出总额。根据会计“固定资产”科目的期末借方余额填报。

资产总计 指企业过去的交易或者事项形成的、由企业拥有或者控制的、预期会给企业带来经济利益的资源。资产一般按流动性（资产的变现或耗用时间长短）分为流动资产和非流动资产。其中流动资产可分为货币资金、交易性金融资产、应收票据、应收账款、预付款项、其他应收款、存货等；非流动资产可分为长期股权投资、固定资产、无形资产及其他非流动资产等。根据会计“资产负债表”中“资产总计”项目的期末余额数填报。

执行2006年《企业会计准则》或2011年《小企业会计准则》的企业：资产总计=流动资产合计+非流动资产合计；执行其他企业会计制度的企业资产包括流动资产、长期投资、固定资产、无形资产和其他资产等。

负债合计 指企业过去的交易或者事项形成的，预期会导致经济利益流出企业的现时义务。负债一般按偿还期长短分为流动负债和非流动负债。根据会计“资产负债表”中“负债合计”项目的期末余额数填报。

执行2006年《企业会计准则》或2011年《小企业会计准则》的企业：负债合计=流动负债合计+非流动负债合计；执行其他企业会计制度的企业负债包括流动负债和长期负债。

所有者权益合计 指企业资产扣除负债后由所有者享有的剩余权益。公司的所有者权益又称股东权益。包括实收资本、资本公积、盈余公积、未分配利润等。根据会计“资产负债表”中“所有者权益合计”项目的期末余额数填报。

营业收入 指企业经营主要业务和其他业务所确认的收入总额。营业收入合计包括“主营业务收入”和“其他业务收入”。根据会计“利润表”中“营业收入”项目的本期金额数填报。

主营业务收入 指企业确认的销售商品、提供劳务等主营业务的收入。根据会计“主营业务收入”科目的期末贷方余额（结转前）填报。执行2006年《企业会计准则》或2011年《小企业会计准则》的企业，如未设置该科目，以“营业收入”代替填报。

营业成本 指企业经营主要业务和其他业务所发生的成本总额。包括企业（单位）在报告期内从事销售商品、提供劳务等日常活动发生的各种耗费。包括“主营业务成本”和“其他业务成本”。根据会计“利润表”中“营业成本”项目的本期金额数填报。

主营业务成本 指企业经营主要业务所发生的成本总额。根据会计“主营业务成本”科目的期末借方余额（结转前）填报。执行2006年《企业会计准则》或2011年《小企业会计准则》的企业，如未设置该科目，以“营业成本”代替填报。

销售费用 指企业在销售商品和材料、提供劳务的过程中发生的各种费用，包括保险费、包装费、展览费和广告费、商品维修费、预计产品质量保证损失、运输费、装卸费等以及为销售本企业商品而专设的销售机构（含销售网点、售后服务网点等）的职工薪酬、业务费、折旧费等经营费用。建筑业企业销售费用指企业从事施工生产活动过程中发生的各项费用，包括应由企业负担的运输费、装卸费、包装费、保险费、维修费、展览费、差旅费、广告费和其他经费。房地产企业销售费用指企业在从事主要经营业务过程中所发生的各项销售费用，包括转让、销售、结算和出租开发产品等。执行2006年《企业会计准则》或2011年《小企业会计准则》的企业，根据会计“利润表”中“销售费用”项目的本期金额数填报。执行其他企业会计制度的企业，根据会计“利润表”中“营业费用（或经营费用）”项目的本期金额数填报。

管理费用 指企业为组织和管理企业生产经营所发生的费用，包括企业在筹建期间内发生的开办费、董事会和行政管理部门在企业经营管理中发生的，或者应当由企业统一负担的公司经费等。根据会计“利润表”中“管理费用”项目的本期金额数填报。

财务费用 指企业为筹集生产经营所需资金等而发生的筹资费用，包括企业生产经营期间发生的利息支出（减利息收入）、汇兑损失（减汇兑收益）以及相关的手续费等。根据会计“利润表”中“财务费用”项目的本期金额数填报。

投资收益 指企业确认的投资收益或投资损失，反映企业以各种方式对外投资所取得的收益。根据会计

"利润表"中"投资收益"项目的本期金额数填报。如为投资损失以"–"号记。

营业利润 指企业从事生产经营活动所取得的利润。执行2006年《企业会计准则》的企业，营业利润为营业收入减去营业成本、营业税金及附加、销售费用、管理费用、财务费用、资产减值损失，再加上公允价值变动收益和投资收益。执行2011年《小企业会计准则》的企业，营业利润为营业收入减去营业成本，营业税金及附加、销售费用、管理费用、财务费用，再加上投资收益后的金额；执行其他企业会计制度的企业，营业利润为主营业务收入减去主营业务成本、主营业务税金及附加，加上其他业务利润后，再减去销售费用、管理费用、财务费用后的金额。根据会计"利润表"中"营业利润"项目的本期金额数填报。

利润总额 指企业在一定会计期间的经营成果，是生产经营过程中各种收入扣除各种耗费后的盈余，反映企业在报告期内实现的盈亏总额。根据会计"利润表"中"利润总额"项目的本期金额数填报。执行2006年《企业会计准则》或2011年《小企业会计准则》的企业，利润总额为营业利润加上营业外收入，减去营业外支出后的金额；执行其他企业会计制度的企业，利润总额为营业利润加上投资收益、政府补助、营业外收入，再减去营业外支出后的金额。

应付职工薪酬 指企业为获得职工提供的服务而给予各种形式的报酬以及其他相关支出。包括职工工资、奖金、津贴和补贴，职工福利费，医疗保险费、养老保险费、失业保险费、工伤保险费和生育保险费等社会保险费，住房公积金，工会经费和职工教育经费，非货币性福利，因解除与职工的劳动关系给予的补偿，其他与获得职工提供的服务相关的支出。执行2006年《企业会计准则》或2011年《小企业会计准则》的企业，根据会计科目"应付职工薪酬"的本年贷方累计发生额填报；执行其他企业会计制度的企业，应将本年上述职工薪酬包含的科目归并填报。

从事服务业活动从业人员平均人数 指报告期内(年度、月度)平均拥有的人员数。按"谁用工，谁统计"的原则，包括正式人员，劳务派遣人员和临时聘用人员。

Explanatory Notes on Main Statistical Indicators

Statistical standard of the services unit above the designated size of the National Bureau of Statistics: The legal entitiesof the area whoseannual revenues are10 million yuan and above, or at the end of the service sector whose employees are more than 50 people.Including: transportation, storage and postal services, information transmission, software and information technology services, leasing and business services, scientific research and technological services, water conservancy, environment and public facilities management industry, education, health and social work as well as property management and real estate services industries.The legal entitiesof the area whoseannual revenues are5 million yuan and above, or at the end of the service sector whose employees are more than 50 people.Including: service, repair and other services, cultural, sports and entertainment.

Original value of fixed assets: It refers to the cost of fixed assets, including the enterprise itself costs on the acquisition, construction, installation, alteration, expansion, technological innovation of an asset for all expenditure. Depending on the "fixed assets" account debit balance at the end of filling.

Total assets: It refers to the resourcesformed bypast transactions or events, thatthe enterprise owns or controls, is expected to bring economic benefits to the enterprise. Asset is classified into current assets and non-current assets by its liquidity (realization of assets or spent time). Current assets can be divided into currency, tradable financial assets, notes receivable, accounts receivable, prepayments, other receivables and inventory; and non-current assets can be classified as equity investments, fixed assets, intangible assets and other non-current assets. It depends on the "balance sheet" of "total assets" closing balance number of items.

For business enterprisesthat implemented the 2006 accounting standard: total assets= total current assets +total non-current assets; for those who didn't implement the 2006 accounting standards, assets for business enterprises include current assets, long-term investments, fixed assets, intangible assets and other assets.

Total liabilities: It refers tothe present obligations of the enterprisethat formed by past transactions or events and are expected to lead to an outflow of economic benefits. Liability is divided into current and non-current liabilities according to the length of the repayment period. It depends onthe "balance sheets" in the "total" closing balance number of items.

For business enterprises that implemented the 2006 accounting standard: total liabilities = total current liabilities+ total non-current liabilities; for those who didn't implement the 2006 accounting standards, liabilities include current liabilities and long-term liabilities.

Totalowners ' equity: It refers to the residual rights and interests enjoyed by the owner after deducting the liabilities of an enterprise. The owner of the company is also called the shareholder's right. It includes the paid in capital, capital reserves, surplus reserves, undistributed profit and so on. According to the accounting "balance sheet", "the owner's equity total", the final balance of the project is reported.

Operating income: It refers to the total revenue recognized by the business and other business operations of the enterprise. Total operating income includes "main business income" and "other business income". It's reported according to the "business income" project of the "business income" in the accounting "profit statement".

The main business income: It refers to the income of the business of the main business, such as the sale of goods, services, etc..It's reported in accordance with the final credit balance of the accounts of the subject's "main business income" (before the transfer). For business enterprises that didn't implement the 2006 accounting standard, if not set up the subject, should fill the forms instead of the "operating income".

Operating cost: Itrefers to the total cost incurred by the business and other business of the enterprise. It includes a variety of costsof enterprises (units) in the reporting period to engage in sales of goods, services and other daily activities provided.It includes"the main business costs" and "other business costs". According to the "operating cost" of the "business cost" of the project in accordance with the accounting statement.

The main business cost: Itrefers to the total cost of the main business. It's reported in accordance with the final debit balance of the subject of accounting "main business cost". For business enterprises that didn't implement the 2006 accounting standard, if not set up the subject, should fill the forms instead of the "operating costs".

Selling expenses: It refers to the expenses of the enterprisein sales of goods and materials and providing services, including insurance, packing, exhibition fees and advertising fees, maintenance of commodity, expected to ensure product quality loss, transportation, loading and unloading charges and sales of the enterprise products and dedicated sales organizations (including sales network and after-sales service network) employee compensation, business expenses, depreciation charges and operating expenses. Construction enterprises selling expenses refers to expenses occurring in the process of production enterprises engaged in construction activities, including transportation fee shall be borne by the enterprise, handling, packing, insurance, maintenance, exhibition fees, poor travel costs, advertising costs and other expenses. Real estate enterprise sales cost refers to the business in the main business process of the sales costs, including transfer, sales, settlement and rental development products, etc.. According to the "sales expense" in accounting "profit statement", the amount of the item in this period of the project is reported. For business enterprises that didn't implement the 2006 accounting standard, according to the number of "operating expenses (or operating expenses)" of the project in accordance with the "profit statement".

Management expenses: Itrefers to the expenses for the organization and management of enterprise production and management of the enterprises, including costs in construction occurred during the start-up costs, the board of directors and administrative departments in enterprise management, or shall be made by the enterprise unified burden of company funds. According to the "management fee" in the accounting "profit table", the amount of this period of the project is reported.

Financial expenses: Itrefers tothe costsof the enterprise to raise the production and business operation required capital and funding, including occurred during the production and operation of enterprises interest payments (a reduction in interest income), exchange loss (less exchange gains) and related fees. It is reportedaccording to the amount of the "financial expense" in the project of "financial expense" in the accounting "profit statement".

Investment income: Itrefers to the enterprise confirming the investment income or investment losses, reflecting the foreign investment income of the enterprise in various ways. According to the "investment income" in the accounting "profit statement", the amount of this period of the project is reported. Such as investment losses to "-".

Operating profit: Itrefers tothe profits made by the enterprises in the production and operation activities. For business enterprises that implemented the 2006 accounting standard, operating profit is revenues minus operating costs, business taxes and surcharges, sales, management costs, financial costs, asset impairment loss and plus fair value changes in income and investment income. Without executing the 2006 "accounting standards for business enterprises" enterprises, operating profit equals the main business income minus the cost of major business, main business tax and surcharges, and plus profit from other operations, then minus the cost of sales and management costs, financial costs. It is reported according to the number of "operating profit" items in the accounting "profit table".

Total profit: Itrefers tothe business results of the enterprise in a certain accounting period, and it is the production and operation of various kinds of income after deducting the cost of earnings, reflecting the enterprise in the reporting period to achieve total profit and loss. According to the amount of the total amount of the total profit of the project in accordance with the accounting profit table. For business enterprises that implemented the 2006 accounting standard, the total profit is operating profit plus operating income, andminus operating expenses; while who didn't execute the 2006 "accounting standards for business enterprises", a total profit is operating profit plus return on investment, income subsidies, camp outside the industry income, andminus operating expenses.

Employee compensation: Itrefers tovarious forms of remuneration and other related expenses paid by the company for the services provided by the staff and workers. It includes wages, bonuses, allowances and subsidies, employee welfare benefit expenses, medical insurance, endowment insurance, unemployment insurance, work-related injury insurance premiums and maternity insurance fees social insurance, housing provident fund, the trade union funds and employee education funds, non-monetary benefits, for the solution in addition to give labor relations and workers compensation, and obtain a worker to provide other services related expenditure. For business enterprises that implemented the 2006 accounting standard, according to accounting subjects "to deal with workers' compensation" this year, the accumulated credits is filled; those who didn't execute the 2006 "accounting standards for business enterprises", it should be the employee compensation including the amalgamative course reportingthis year.

Average number of persons engaged in service

activities: It refers to the number of persons engaged in the service industry in the reporting period (annual, monthly). The principles of statistics is implemented according to the principle that "who labor, who statistics," including the official personnel, labor sent contingent personnel and temporaryemployeeswho take part in the enterprise service activities. And itdon't include employeeswho receive wages, dividends, bonusas well as not participate in the service activities of the enterprise.

19 金融业

FINANCIAL INTERMEDIATION

资料整理：刘　婷
Data management：Liu Ting
数据审核：陈　英
Data audit：Chen Ying

第十九部分　金融业

一、简要说明

本章资料包括金融、证券和保险业情况，由西安市统计局综合处根据人民银行西安分行营业管理部和市金融办提供资料整理。

二、主要指标

金融机构人民币（含外资）存款余额（亿元）	17796.38	比上年增长	17.3%
金融机构人民币（含外资）贷款余额（亿元）	13714.02	比上年增长	17.5%
保费收入（亿元）	263.02	比上年增长	19.8%

19　FINANCIAL INTERMEDIATION

Ⅰ.Brief Introduction

This chapter includes information of the financial, securities and insurance, compiled by Integration Division of the Xi'an Bureau of Statistics, according to data from Xi'an Branch Management Department of the People's Bank of China, Provincial Banking Bureau and Xi'an Financial Office.

Ⅱ.Major Indicators

		Increase over Preceding Year
Deposit in Financial Institution(100 mil. Yuan)	17796.38	17.3%
Loans in Financial Institutions(100 mil. Yuan)	13714.02	17.5%
Premiums(100 mil. Yuan)	263.02	19.8%

19-1 西安银行系统机构、人员数

Number of Institution and Employed Person in Finance System in Xi'an

机构名称	Name of Institution	2014		2015	
		机构数（个）Number of Institution (unit)	年末人数（人）Number of Staff and Workers (person)	机构数（个）Number of Institution (unit)	年末人数（人）Number of Staff and Workers (person)
合 计	**Total**	**1901**	**37311**	**1969**	**38882**
1. 人民银行西安分行营业管理部	Management Department of the People's Bank of China Xi'an Branch	1	386	1	364
2. 国家开发银行	National Development Bank	1	184	1	187
3. 中国进出口银行	Export Import Bank of China	1	64	1	83
4. 中国工商银行	Industrial and Commercial Bank of China	193	4976	193	4978
5. 中国农业银行	Agricultural Bank of China	173	3249	174	3306
6. 中国银行	Bank of China	126	3384	127	3488
7. 中国建设银行	Construction Bank of China	195	4255	197	4366
8. 交通银行	Bank of Communication	49	1169	55	1177
9. 中国邮政储蓄银行	The Postal Savings Bank of China	281	834	281	825
10. 中国农业发展银行	Agricultural Development Bank of China	10	258	11	264
11. 中信银行	CITIC Bank	26	869	29	902
12. 中国光大银行	China Everbright Bank	22	832	24	918
13. 华夏银行	China Huaxia Bank	14	467	18	613
14. 广发银行	China Guangfa Bank			1	104
15. 平安银行	Pingan Bank	4	331	11	408
16. 招商银行	China Merchants Bank	42	1340	54	1510
17. 上海浦东发展银行	Pufa Bank	19	656	19	702
18. 兴业银行	Fujian Industrial Bank	21	897	18	853
19. 中国民生银行	China Minsheng Banking	20	1136	21	1151
20. 恒丰银行	Evergrowing Bank	6	276	11	384
21. 浙商银行	China Zheshang Bank	5	290	6	329
22. 北京银行	Bank of Beijing	15	507	18	755
23. 齐商银行	Qi Commercial Bank	7	219	7	245
24. 成都市商业银行	Bank of Chengdu	4	165	5	169
25. 重庆银行	Bank of Chongqing	4	166	4	197
26. 宁夏银行	Bank of Ningxia	5	201	6	217
27. 昆仑银行	Bank of Kunlun	7	390	12	428
28. 西安银行	Bank of Xi'an	114	2595	131	2543
29. 长安银行	Bank of Changan	13	693	31	854
30. 秦农银行	Qinnong Bank			235	3401
31. 农村信用社联合社	Rural Credit Cooperatives Association	510	6080	251	2731
32. 西安高陵阳光村镇银行	Xi'an Gaoling sunshine village bank	1	21	4	39
33. 香港汇丰银行	Huifeng Bank of Hong Kong	3	50	3	46
34. 香港东亚银行	Dongya Bank of Hong Kong	7	293	7	278
35. 英国标准渣打银行	British Standard Chartered Bank	1	46	1	36
36. 韩亚银行	Hanya Bank	1	32	1	31

注：本表数据来源于人民银行西安营管部。

19-2 金融机构（含外资）本外币存贷款年末余额（2015年）

Financial institution Including Foreign-funded Balance of Bisic Currency and Foreign Currency at Year-end（2015）

单位：万元 (10 000 yuan)

指 标	Item	2015	比年初增减额 Increase or decrease compared with the beginning of the Year
一、各项存款	**All Deposits**	**180368994**	**23940608**
（一）境内存款	Domestic Deposits	180109245	23945360
1. 住户存款	Household Deposits	66403586	4694866
（1）活期存款	Demand Deposits	25419482	2579183
（2）定期及其他存款	Time and Other Deposits	40984103	2115682
2. 非金融企业存款	Non Financial Enterprises Deposits	71702723	12406691
（1）活期存款	Demand Deposits	34204465	8730765
（2）定期及其他存款	Time and Other Deposits	37498258	3675926
3. 广义政府存款	General Government Deposits	28999249	951826
（1）财政性存款	Fiscal Deposits	1184221	595551
（2）机关团体存款	Institution Deposits	27815028	356275
4. 非银行业金融机构存款	Non Banking Financial Institution Deposits	13003687	5891977
（二）境外存款	Foreign Deposits	259750	-4751
二、各项贷款	**All Loans**	**139656416**	**20765743**
（一）境内贷款	Domestic Loans	139489671	20765453
1. 住户贷款	Household loans	28578129	3168680
（1）短期贷款	Short-term Loans	4138515	114986
消费贷款	Consumer loans	1260606	252644
经营贷款	Business loans	2877909	-137658
（2）中长期贷款	Medium-term and Long-term loans	24439614	3053693
消费贷款	Consumer loans	21310557	2959103
经营贷款	Business loans	3129056	94590
2. 非金融企业及机关团体贷款	Non Financial Enterprises and Institution Loans	110894324	17661773
（1）短期贷款	Short-term Loans	24608312	2551466
（2）中长期贷款	Medium-term and Long-term loans	79037279	12556112
（3）票据融资	Bill Financing	7076220	2496892
（4）融资租赁	Financial Leasing	27901	-3051
（5）各项垫款	Various Advance Funds	144611	60353
3. 非银行业金融机构贷款	Non Banking Financial Institution Loans	17218	-65000
（二）境外贷款	**Foreign Loans**	**166745**	**290**

注：本表数据来源于人民银行西安营管部。

19-3　金融机构（不含外资）本外币存贷款年末余额（2015年）

Domestic Funded Financial institution balance of Bisic Currency and Foreign Currency at Year-end (2015)

单位：万元　　(10 000 yuan)

指　标	Item	2015	比年初增减额 Increase or decrease compared with the beginning of the Year
一、各项存款	**All Deposits**	**179066316**	**23777502**
（一）境内存款	Domestic Deposits	178828220	23786973
1. 住户存款	Household Deposits	66251287	4725477
（1）活期存款	Demand Deposits	25358084	2573413
（2）定期及其他存款	Time and Other Deposits	40893202	2152064
2. 非金融企业存款	Non Financial Enterprises Deposits	70825490	12387729
（1）活期存款	Demand Deposits	33944588	8636197
（2）定期及其他存款	Time and Other Deposits	36880902	3751533
3. 广义政府存款	General Government Deposits	28967759	921765
（1）财政性存款	Fiscal Deposits	1184221	595551
（2）机关团体存款	Institution Deposits	27783537	326214
4. 非银行业金融机构存款	Non Banking Financial Institution Deposits	12783685	5752001
（二）境外存款	Foreign Deposits	238096	-9470
二、各项贷款	**All Loans**	**138547681**	**20597520**
（一）境内贷款	Domestic Loans	138385064	20597691
1. 住户贷款	Household loans	28429994	3173986
（1）短期贷款	Short-term Loans	4129644	124875
消费贷款	Consumer loans	1259012	251062
经营贷款	Business loans	2870632	-126187
（2）中长期贷款	Medium-term and Long-term loans	24300350	3049110
消费贷款	Consumer loans	21218835	2951896
经营贷款	Business loans	3081515	97214
2. 非金融企业及机关团体贷款	Non Financial Enterprises and Institution Loans	109937852	17488705
（1）短期贷款	Short-term Loans	24366034	2522414
（2）中长期贷款	Medium-term and Long-term loans	78447138	12504793
（3）票据融资	Bill Financing	6954336	2405092
（4）融资租赁	Financial Leasing	27901	-3051
（5）各项垫款	Various Advance Funds	142443	59457
3. 非银行业金融机构贷款	Non Banking Financial Institution Loans	17218	-65000
（二）境外贷款	**Foreign Loans**	**162617**	**-170**

注：本表数据来源于人民银行西安营管部。

19-4 主要年份金融机构（含外资）人民币存款年末余额

Year-end Balance of Deposit in Financial Institutions Including Foreign-funded in Representative Years

单位：亿元　　　　(100million yuan)

年　份 Year	合计 Total	非金融企业存款 Non Financial Enterprises Loans	住户存款 Household loans
1978	12.82		3.72
1980	20.99		5.48
1985	40.68		16.70
1990	112.37	31.10	62.23
1995	359.51	114.54	230.63
1996	619.98	199.85	394.02
1997	602.50	227.61	358.78
1998	799.54	245.44	499.68
1999	1014.27	347.49	586.40
2000	1335.63	540.19	675.83
2001	1629.72	674.49	800.86
2002	2191.47	884.69	988.04
2003	2665.87	1041.43	1210.56
2004	3061.66	1159.98	1432.86
2005	3599.70	1237.37	1716.76
2006	4066.16	1374.91	1950.53
2007	4582.71	1702.12	2002.38
2008	5749.35	2213.67	2513.70
2009	7522.08	3077.99	3084.20
2010	8933.23	3556.78	3641.09
2011	10430.27	5997.60	4155.65
2012	12125.53	6927.84	4787.03
2013	13763.19	7759.61	5357.05
2014	15166.78	8604.03	5698.15
2015	17796.38	7031.75	6571.18

注：本表数据来源于人民银行西安营管部。

19-5 主要年份金融机构（含外资）人民币贷款年末余额

Year-end Balance of Loans in Financial Institutions Including Foreign-funded in Representative Years

单位：亿元 (100 million yuan)

年 份 Year	合计 Total	其 中：Among 短期贷款 Short-term Loans	中长期贷款 Medium-term&Long-term Loans
1978	23.56		
1980	26.40		
1985	48.60		
1990	131.67	101.13	23.78
1995	334.50	252.30	73.32
1996	477.97	333.88	90.12
1997	443.76	342.79	87.27
1998	597.34	448.74	118.42
1999	786.20	589.52	150.64
2000	972.51	652.00	241.27
2001	1185.97	666.41	387.82
2002	1598.42	780.69	502.03
2003	1954.18	946.64	743.72
2004	2052.33	950.50	850.01
2005	2158.10	830.68	1013.32
2006	2344.77	812.33	1310.57
2007	2683.77	883.32	1593.37
2008	3275.12	1031.62	1905.08
2009	4482.63	1155.83	2908.75
2010	6482.28	1097.60	5075.98
2011	7564.93	1431.29	5776.48
2012	8635.22	1917.51	6378.88
2013	10023.63	2326.63	7385.37
2014	11668.14	2516.78	8685.74
2015	13714.02	2768.31	10218.90

注：本表数据来源于人民银行西安营管部。

19-6　金融机构（含外资）人民币存贷款年末余额（2015年）

Year-end Balance of Deposit and Loans in Financial Institutionst Including Foreign-funded（2015）

单位：万元　　(10 000 yuan)

指　标	Item	2015	比年初增减额 Increase or decrease compared with the beginning of the Year
一、各项存款	**All Deposits**	**177963839**	**23089402**
（一）境内存款	Domestic Deposits	177842920	23083589
1. 住户存款	Household Deposits	65711826	4477292
（1）活期存款	Demand Deposits	25050170	2444207
（2）定期及其他存款	Time and Other Deposits	40661656	2033085
2. 非金融企业存款	Non Financial Enterprises Deposits	70317453	11881917
（1）活期存款	Demand Deposits	33390295	8337090
（2）定期及其他存款	Time and Other Deposits	36927159	3544827
3. 广义政府存款	General Government Deposits	28972631	942007
（1）财政性存款	Fiscal Deposits	1184221	595551
（2）机关团体存款	Institution Deposits	27788410	346456
4. 非银行业金融机构存款	Non Banking Financial Institution Deposits	12841010	5782373
（二）境外存款	Foreign Deposits	120920	5813
二、各项贷款	**All Loans**	**137140236**	**20356972**
（一）境内贷款	Domestic Loans	137127176	20351113
1. 住户贷款	Household loans	28576000	3168990
（1）短期贷款	Short-term Loans	4136553	115293
消费贷款	Consumer loans	1258644	252951
经营贷款	Business loans	2877909	-137658
（2）中长期贷款	Medium-term and Long-term loans	24439447	3053697
消费贷款	Consumer loans	21310391	2959106
经营贷款	Business loans	3129056	94590
2. 非金融企业及机关团体贷款	Non Financial Enterprises and Institution Loans	108533958	17247123
（1）短期贷款	Short-term Loans	23546548	2380433
（2）中长期贷款	Medium-term and Long-term loans	77749523	12277880
（3）票据融资	Bill Financing	7076220	2496892
（4）融资租赁	Financial Leasing	27901	-3051
（5）各项垫款	Various Advance Funds	133766	94968
3. 非银行业金融机构贷款	Non Banking Financial Institution Loans	17218	-65000
（二）境外贷款	**Foreign Loans**	**13060**	**5859**

注：本表数据来源于人民银行西安营管部。

19-7 金融机构（不含外资）人民币存贷款年末余额（2015年）

Year-end Balance of Deposit and Loans in Financial Institutions Not Including Foreign-funded（2015）

单位：万元 （10 000yuan）

指 标	Item	2015	比年初增减额 Increase or decrease compared with the beginning of the Year
一、各项存款	**All Deposits**	**176829448**	**22981857**
（一）境内存款	Domestic Deposits	176713236	22976484
1. 住户存款	Household Deposits	65586479	4516704
（1）活期存款	Demand Deposits	25002467	2443307
（2）定期及其他存款	Time and Other Deposits	40584012	2073397
2. 非金融企业存款	Non Financial Enterprises Deposits	69564609	11905437
（1）活期存款	Demand Deposits	33220140	8305698
（2）定期及其他存款	Time and Other Deposits	36344469	3599739
3. 广义政府存款	General Government Deposits	28941140	911946
（1）财政性存款	Fiscal Deposits	1184221	595551
（2）机关团体存款	Institution Deposits	27756919	316395
4. 非银行业金融机构存款	Non Banking Financial Institution Deposits	12621008	5642397
（二）境外存款	Foreign Deposits	116213	5373
二、各项贷款	**All Loans**	**136048934**	**20184156**
（一）境内贷款	Domestic Loans	136036969	20178557
1. 住户贷款	Household loans	28427865	3174296
（1）短期贷款	Short-term Loans	4127682	125182
消费贷款	Consumer loans	1257049	251369
经营贷款	Business loans	2870632	-126187
（2）中长期贷款	Medium-term and Long-term loans	24300184	3049114
消费贷款	Consumer loans	21218669	2951900
经营贷款	Business loans	3081515	97214
2. 非金融企业及机关团体贷款	Non Financial Enterprises and Institution Loans	107591886	17069262
（1）短期贷款	Short-term Loans	23305219	2349025
（2）中长期贷款	Medium-term and Long-term loans	77172832	12224123
（3）票据融资	Bill Financing	6954336	2405092
（4）融资租赁	Financial Leasing	27901	-3051
（5）各项垫款	Various Advance Funds	131598	94072
3. 非银行业金融机构贷款	Non Banking Financial Institution Loans	17218	-65000
（二）境外贷款	**Foreign Loans**	**11965**	**5598**

注：本表数据来源于人民银行西安营管部。

19-8 保险业务情况

Indicators of Insurance Business

指　标	Item	2011	2012	2013	2014	2015
保险金额（亿元）	**Amount Insured(100 million yuan)**	**44511**	**35199**	**42596**	**51454**	**62319**
保费收入（万元）	**Premiums(10 000 yuan)**	**1625666**	**1732089**	**2024067**	**2194924**	**2630158**
一、财产险（万元）	**Property Insurance(10 000 yuan)**	**449625**	**521619**	**629947**	**741762**	**835526**
（一）财产保险	Property Insurance	422739	484476	576666	668574	746317
1. 机动车辆及第三者责任	Motor Vehicle and Outside Person Liability	364585	431460	513634	602905	674555
2. 企业财产险	Enterprise Property Insurance	37452	41398	41140	41996	49949
3. 货物运输险	Freight Transport Insurance	4208	4312	3944	4427	5497
4. 家庭财产险	Family Property Insurance	366	323	296	584	754
5. 建工及安工保险及其责任险	Construction and Installation Projects Insurance and Related Libility Insurance	15004	5938	16133	16893	12325
6. 其他	Others	1124	1045	1519	1770	3237
（二）责任保险	Liability Insurance	8988	10719	13393	16328	23096
（三）信用保险	Export Credit Insurance	8188	8257	8648	8401	10449
（四）保证保险	Guarantee Insurance	8798	15421	21588	36868	45472
（五）农业保险	Agriculture Insurance	913	2747	9653	11590	10191
二、人身险（万元）	**Personnel Insurance(10 000 yuan)**	**1176041**	**1210469**	**1394120**	**1453162**	**1794632**
（一）人寿保险	Life Insurance	1072364	1077710	1221975	1238142	1506062
1. 非分红保险	Non Dividend Insurance	95292	99073	109810	444520	681952
2. 分红保险	Dividend Insurance	966024	967751	1099986	780653	810889
3. 投资连接保险	Insurance Connection Insurance	362	346	330	316	286
4. 万能保险	Universal Insurance	10687	10541	11849	12654	12935
（二）意外伤害险	Unforeseen Injury Insurance	37064	40433	49541	52963	63451
（三）健康保险	Health Insurance	66613	92326	122604	162057	225120
赔款支出和各项给付	**Indemnity and Other Expenditure**	**371421**	**475483**	**664905**	**807652**	**876182**
一、财产险（万元）	**Property Insurance(10 000 yuan)**	**199916**	**274285**	**339004**	**372906**	**406530**
（一）财产保险	Property Insurance	192900	263917	325128	360384	375449
1. 机动车辆及第三者责任	Motor Vehicle and Outside Person Liability	163878	235665	291390	327319	348185
2. 企业财产险	Enterprise Property Insurance	15151	18805	24870	22257	16753
3. 家庭财产保险	Freight Transport Insurance	130	66	93	107	112
4. 货物运输保险	Family Property Insurance	1342	1148	1224	2429	999
5. 建工及安工保险及其责任险	Construction and Installation Projects Insurance and Related Libility Insurance	11345	7893	6480	6719	8023
6. 其他	Others	1054	340	1070	1551	1377
（二）责任保险	Liability Insurance	3114	4713	5192	5695	6300
（三）信用保险	Export Credit Insurance	2324	5357	5414	1668	7884
（四）保证保险	Guarantee Insurance	579	-581	1450	2752	13129
（五）农业保险	Agriculture Insurance	999	878	1820	2406	3768
二、人身险（万元）	**Personnel Insurance(10 000 yuan)**	**171505**	**201198**	**325900**	**434746**	**469652**
（一）人寿保险	Life Insurance	140240	167146	268455	360895	379370
1. 非分红保险	Non Dividend Insurance	40017	50929	48680	44359	56908
2. 分红保险	Dividend Insurance	98169	113557	216911	313706	318993
3. 投资连接保险	Insurance Connection Insurance	595	327	32	33	48
4. 万能保险	Universal Insurance	1459	2334	2832	2797	3421
（二）意外伤害险	Unforeseen Injury Insurance Health Insurance	7572	9013	10685	11438	16795
（三）健康保险	Health Insurance	23694	25039	46760	62414	73486
退保金（万元）	**Withdrawal(10 000 yuan)**	**90546**	**107665**	**167446**	**405676**	**433227**
#人寿保险	Life Insurance	89150	105909	165303	403099	414260
1. 非分红保险	Ordinary Life Insurance	4303	5514	6192	20818	195551
2. 分红保险	Dividend Insurance	84804	100373	159077	382274	218693
3. 投资连接保险	Insurance Connection Insurance	2		9		
4. 万能保险	Universal Insurance	43	21	24	7	16

注：本表数据来源于市金融办。

19-9 西安地区证券期货系统机构、人员数

Number of Institution and Employed Person in Securities and Futures Systerm in Xi'an

机构名称	Name of Institution	2014		2015	
		机构数（个） Number of Institution (unit)	年末人数（人） Number of Staff and Workers (person)	机构数（个） Number of Institution (unit)	年末人数（人） Number of Staff and Workers (person)
证券经营机构	**Securities Company and the Sales Department**	188	5412	235	6446
一、证券公司	**Securities Company**	96	2760	130	3375
西部证券股份有限公司	Western Securities Company Ltd.	72	1995	80	2180
陕西开源证券经纪有限责任公司	KaiYuan Securities Company Ltd.	22	472	32	774
西安华弘证券经纪有限责任公司	Xi'an Huahong Securities Brokerage Co., Ltd.	2	293	18	421
二、证券营业部（含外地公司在西安营业部）	**Sales Department (include Xi'an departments of nonlocal companies.)**	**92**	**2652**	**105**	**3071**
期货经纪公司	**Futures Company**	**3**	**212**	**3**	**277**
迈科期货经纪有限公司	Maike Futures Company Ltd.	1	83	1	119
陕西长安期货经纪有限公司	Shanxi ChangAn Futures Company Ltd.	1	62	1	61
西部期货经纪有限公司	Western Futures Brokerage Co., Ltd.	1	67	1	97

注：证券公司包括三家公司及其在西安和外地的营业部。
本表数据来源于市金融办。

19-10 证券期货市场基本情况（2015年）

Basic Facts on Securities and Futures Markets（2015）

指　标	Item	2015
一、上市证券公司情况	Listed Securities Companies	
拥有上市股份公司（个）	Number of Listed Share-holding Companies(unit)	32
上市股份公司总股本（亿股）	Total Capital of Listed Share-holding Companies (100 millon shares)	401.19
#流通股(亿股)	Negotiable Shares(100 million shares)	286.29
总市值（亿元）	Total Market Capitalization(100 million yuan)	5818.36
累计证券市场筹措资金（亿元）	Accumulated Capital Raised by Securities Markets(100 millon yuan)	915.51
二、证券经营机构情况	Securities Trading Organizations	
拥有证券公司（个）	Number of Securities Companies(unit)	3
证券营业部（个）（含外地公司在西安营业部）	Number of Securities Business Departments(unit)	105
投资者开户数（万户）	Number of Investors Who have Opened an Account(10 000 accounts)	235.32
证券交易总额（亿元）	Total Turnover(100 million yuan)	54112.78
三、期货市场情况	Futures Market	
拥有期货经纪公司（个）	Number of Futures Business Management Companies(unit)	3
期货营业部（个）	Number of Futures Business,Departments(unit)	26
期货代理交易额（亿元）	Total Transaction Value in Futures Commissioning (100 million yuan)	69104.9
每个经纪公司平均拥有注册资金（万元）	Average Registered Capital of Each Business Management Company(10 000 yuan)	27600

注：本表数据来源于市金融办。

主要统计指标解释

信贷资金 指金融机构以信用方式积聚和分配的货币资金。金融机构信贷资金的来源有各项存款、金融债券、对国际金融机构负债、流通中现金、其他项目等；信贷资金的运用有各项贷款、有价证券及投资、金银占款、外汇占款、财政借款及在国际金融机构中的资产等。

存款 指企业、机关、团体或居民根据资金必须收回的原则，把货币资金存入银行或其他信贷机构保管并取得一定利息的一种信用活动形式。根据存款对象或性质的不同可划分为企业存款、财政存款、机关团体存款、城乡储蓄存款、农业存款、信托及委托类存款、其他存款等科目。它是银行信贷资金的主要来源。

贷款 指银行或其他信贷机构根据资金必须归还的原则，按一定利率，为企业、个人等提供资金的一种信用活动形式。我国银行贷款分为短期贷款、委托及信托类贷款、其他类贷款等。

保险公司 在中国境内的、经过保险监督管理部门批准设立，并依法登记注册的各类商业保险公司。

保险金额 指保险人承担赔偿或者给付保险金责任的最高限额。

保费 指投保人为取得保险人在约定范围内所承担赔偿责任而支付给保险人的费用。

赔款 指保险人根据保险合同的规定，向被保险人支付的赔偿保险责任损失的金额。

给付 包括死伤医疗给付和满期给付。死伤医疗给付是指保险人根据人寿保险及长期健康保险合同的规定，因被保险人在保险期内发生保险责任范围内的保险事故支付给被保险人（或受益人）的金额。满期给付是指被保险人生存期满，保险人按人寿保险合同规定支付给被保险人的满期保险金额。

Explanatory Notes on Main Statistical Indicators

Credit Funds refer to the monetary funds accumulated and distributed in the means of credit by the financial institutions. The sources of credit funds include various deposits, financial bonds, liabilities to international financial institutions, currency in circulation, other items. The uses of credit funds include loans, securities and investment, position for bullion and silver purchase, position for foreign exchange purchase, advances to treasury, and assets with international financial institutions..

Deposit is a form of credit by which enterprises, institutions, organizations or households can put money into banks and other credit institutions for safekeeping and interest earning under the principle of free withdrawal. According to different depositors, deposits are divided into enterprise deposits, fiscal deposits, deposits of government agencies and organizations, savings deposits of rural and urban households, agricultural savings deposits, entrusted deposits and other deposits. Deposits are major sources of the credit funds of banks.

Loan is a form of credit by which banks and other credit institutions provide funds at certain interest rate to enterprises and individuals in the light of the principle of unconditional repayment. Loans from Chinese banks include short-term loan, medium- term and long-term loans, entrusted loans, and other loans.

Insurance Companies refer to commercial insurance companies of various forms registered by law and established in China with the approval of insurance regulatory agencies.

Amount Insured refers to the maximum that the insurant will get for the claim of the case insured.

Premium is the fee paid by the insurant to the insurer to obtain the obligation of compensation from the insurance within the agreed terms.

Settled Claim is the compensation paid by the insurer to the insurant in accordance with the insurance contract.

Payment includes payment for death, injury or medical treatment and payment at maturity. Payment for death, injury or medical treatment refers to the money paid to the insurant (or the beneficiary) in accordance with the life or health insurance contract when the insurant encounters accidents within the insured period covered in the contract. Payment at maturity refers to the payment to the insurant in accordance with the life insurance contract at the end of the insured period.

20 教育和科技

EDUCATION,SCIENCE AND TECHNOLOGY

资料整理：郝　静　陈春光
Data management：Hao Jing Chen Chunguang
数据审核：王金桂
Data audit：Wang Jingui

第二十部分　教育和科技

一、简要说明

本章资料包括教育事业、科技事业基本情况，由西安市统计局服务业和社会科技处根据西安市教育局等有关部门提供资料整理。

二、主要指标

普通高等学校数（所）	63	与上年	持平
普通高等学校（本专科）在校学生（万人）	75.75	比上年减少	0.89万人
高等学校研究生在校人数（万人）	9.08	比上年增加	0.30万人

20　EDUCATION,SCIENCE AND TECHNOLOGY

Ⅰ.Brief Introduction

Data in this chapter consists of primarily data of educational undertakings, science and technology Activities of Xi'an city, compiled by Tertiary Industry and Social & Science and Technology Division of the Xi'an Bureau of Statistics according to data from Xi'an Bureau of Education concerned.

Ⅱ Major Indicators

		Increase over Preceding Year
Number of Schools Regular Institutions of Higher Education(unit)	63	essentially on a par with last year's
Student Enrollment of Regular Institutions of Higher Education(10 000 persons)	75.75	-0.89
Postgraduates(10 000 persons)	9.08	0.30

20-1 主要年份各类普通教育基本情况

Basic Statistics on Regular Eduction in Representative Years

指 标	Item	2010	2011	2012	2013	2014	2015
学校数（所）	**Number of Schools (units)**						
普通高等学校	Regular Institutions of Higher Educatior	50	61	62	63	63	63
普通中等专业学校	Regular Specialized Secondary Schools	28	24	24	22	22	20
普通中学	Regular Secondary School	436	423	419	418	421	422
小学	Primary Schools	1531	1424	1322	1291	1257	1234
幼儿园	Kindergarten	1004	1122	1239	1295	1343	1417
毕业生人数（万人）	**Graduates (10 000 persons)**						
普通高等学校	Regular Institutions of Higher Educatior	18.3	19.7	20.9	20.2	21.3	23.2
普通中等专业学校	Regular Specialized Secondary Schools	2.5	2.3	2.1	1.9	1.8	1.3
普通中学	Regular Secondary School	17.0	16.4	15.6	15.2	14.5	13.9
小学	Primary Schools	9.6	8.9	8.9	8.5	8.3	7.9
幼儿园	Kindergarten		6.4	7.6	8.4	8.9	10.0
招生数（万人）	**New Enrollment (10 000 persons)**						
普通高等学校	Regular Institutions of Higher Educatior	21.7	23.1	25.2	23.9	23.6	23.4
普通中等专业学校	Regular Specialized Secondary Schools	2.1	2.0	1.7	1.4	1.3	1.0
普通中学	Regular Secondary School	16.2	15.4	15.0	14.5	14.0	13.4
小学	Primary Schools	8.6	8.8	8.9	9.6	10.1	10.5
幼儿园	Kindergarten	8.4	10.0	11.6	11.0	9.6	12.0
在校学生数（万人）	**Total Enrollment (10 000 persons)**						
普通高等学校	Regular Institutions of Higher Educatior	73.3	76.6	80.7	83.8	85.4	84.8
普通中等专业学校	Regular Specialized Secondary Schools	6.8	6.1	5.4	4.7	4.1	3.5
普通中学	Regular Secondary School	48.9	47.2	45.3	43.7	42.6	41.4
小学	Primary Schools	51.6	51.4	50.9	52.0	53.8	56.6
幼儿园	Kindergarten	18.4	24.0	27.1	28.6	29.0	30.9
教职工数（人）	**Staff and Teachers (persons)**						
普通高等学校	Regular Institutions of Higher Educatior	72247	72739	74041	74993	74954	74857
普通中等专业学校	Regular Specialized Secondary Schools	3249	2868	2733	2599	2315	1991
普通中学	Regular Secondary School	39207	41135	41197	41003	40576	40689
小学	Primary Schools	34118	32457	32208	31863	32162	32585
幼儿园	Kindergarten	18710	23680	27735	31989	33062	36004
专任教师（人）	**Number of Full-time Teachers (persons)**						
普通高等学校	Regular Institutions of Higher Educatior	42098	42734	44487	46436	46766	47768
普通中等专业学校	Regular Specialized Secondary Schools	1845	1723	1595	1474	1346	1228
普通中学	Regular Secondary School	31506	33122	31526	31419	32615	33014
小学	Primary Schools	29944	28453	29651	29421	28395	28395
幼儿园	Kindergarten	10638	12577	14293	16238	17337	19096

注：本表数据来源于市教育局。

本表中普通高等学校毕业生、招生、在校生数含研究生及普通高等学校中普通本、专科学生数。

本表中小学的学校数是指独立小学个数，其在校生、教职工等指标均为普通初等教育；幼儿园的校数是指独立的幼儿园个数，其在校生、教职工等指标均为学前教育。（下表同）

20-2 各级各类学校校数、教职工、专任教师数（2015年）

Basic Facts on Regular Education Teacher by School Type（2015）

指 标	Item	学校数（所）Number of Schools (units)	教职工数（人）Number of Staff and Teachers (persons)	专任教师数（人）Full-time Teachers (persons)
一、高等教育	**Higher education**	**76**	**77512**	**49172**
（一）研究生培养机构	Postgraduate training institutions	(43)		
1、高等学校	Institutions of Higher Schools	(22)		
2、科研机构	Scientific Research Institution	(21)		
(二)普通高等学校	Regular Institutions of Higher Schools	63	74857	47768
1、 本科院校	Universities and Colleges of Undergraduate Course	42	64636	40843
其中：独立学院	Non-university Tertiary	11	7171	4534
2、专科院校	Higher Vocational Colleges	21	10221	6925
其中：高等职业学校	Higher Vocational College	19	8696	6115
(三)成人高等学校	Adult Higher Schools	13	2655	1404
二、中等职业教育	**Secondary Occupation Education**	**189**	**11828**	**8426**
1、普通中等专业学校	Regular Specialized Secondary Schools	20	1991	1228
2、成人中等专业学校	Adult Secondary Specialized Schools	4	1390	929
3、职业高中学校	Vocational Hight Schools	80	3239	2214
其中：市属	Municipal schools	79	3016	2118
4、技工学校	Technical Schools	85	5208	4055
其中：市属	Municipal schools	40	1556	1180
三、基础教育	**Elementary Education**	**3082**	**109673**	**81131**
（一）普通中等教育	Regular Institutions Education	422	40689	33014
1、高中	Senior High Schools	157		18099
完全中学	Complete Secondary Schools	97	12547	10274
高级中学	Senior Secondary Schools	49	7568	6147
十二年一贯制学校	Twelve-year Consistency Schools	11	2213	1678
2、初中	Junior Middle Schools	265		14915
初级中学	Junior Middle Schools	227	15370	12528
九年一贯制学校	Nine-year Consistency Schools	38	2991	2387
完全中学	Complete Secondary school	(97)		
十二年一贯制学校	Twelve-year Consistency schools	(11)		
附设普通初中班的学校	Senior Secondary Schools with Regular Junior Secondary Classes	(1)		(6)
（二）普通初等教育	Regular Primary Education		32585	28748
独立小学	Independent Primary Schools	1234		28135
教学点	Teaching Points	(107)		613
九年一贯制学校	Nine-year Consistency schools	(38)		
十二年一贯制学校	Twelve-year Consistency schools	(11)		
附设小学班的学校	Schools with Primary Classes	(4)		(56)
（三）特殊教育	Special Education Schools		352	240
特殊教育学校	Special Education Schools	8	352	240
附设特教班的学校	Schools with Special Edution Classes	(1)		
（四）工读学校	Reformatory Schools	1	43	33
（五）学前教育	Preschool Education		36004	19096
幼儿园	Kindergarten	1417	36004	19096
附设幼儿班的学校	Schools with Nursery Classes	(108)		(88)
另有：技术培训机构	Technique Training Institution	1594	13244	8530

注：本表数据来源于市教育局。
本表为西安市行政区划内各级各类学校全口径数据（不含军事院校、党校）。
技工学校数据由西安市人力资源和社会保障局提供。
按照事业统计主体校原则，完全中学、十二年一贯制学校的学校数计入普通高中，九年一贯制学校的校数计入普通初中。
教职工数按照办学类型划分，为使用方便，专任教师同时按照办学层次列出。
( ) 内数据不计入总计。(下表同)

20-3 各级各类教育学生情况（2015年）

Basic Facts on Education Student by School Type（2015）

单位：人 (persons)

指 标	Item	毕业生数 Number of Graduates	招生数 New Enrollment	在校学生数 Total Enrollment	女生 Female Students
一、高等教育	**Higher education**	**341028**	**364136**	**1135726**	**549103**
(一)研究生	Postgraduates	25322	29487	91448	39490
1、高等学校	Institutions of Higher Schools	25104	29293	90790	39339
2、科研机构	Scientific Research Institution	218	194	658	151
（二）普通高等教育	Regular Institutions of Higher Schools	207192	204853	757510	383782
1、本科	Universities Course Schools	127323	123293	522931	266224
2、专科	Junior Colleges	79869	81560	234579	117558
（三）成人高等教育	Higher Vocational Colleges	48681	42474	130563	61781
其中：成人高等学校	Contains:Adult Higher Education	9871	8737	24043	9065
（四）网络本专科生	Network Undergraduate and clooege students	59833	87322	156205	64050
1、本科	Universities Course Schools	25733	38050	67408	29087
2、专科	Junior Colleges	34100	49272	88797	34963
二、中等职业教育	**Secondary Occupation Education**	**56664**	**51738**	**161498**	**42728**
1、普通中等专业学校	Regular Specialized Secondary Schools	13194	9471	34714	17487
2、成人中等专业学校	Adult Secondary Specialized Schools	1783	89	2713	631
3、职业高中学校	Vocational high Schools	18565	15060	49092	24610
其中：市属	Municipal schools	18353	15060	48708	30405
4、技工学校	Technical Schools	23122	27118	74979	
其中：市属	Municipal schools	7025	8704	23228	
三、基础教育	**Elementary Education**	**318003**	**359086**	**1290373**	**603959**
(一)普通中等教育	Regular Institutions Education	139199	134115	413725	192863
1、高中	Senior High Schools	53077	53498	164324	80442
完全中学	Complete Secondary Schools	23633	24931	73561	36884
高级中学	Senior Secondary Schools	27947	26642	85456	41066
十二年一贯制学校	Twelve-year Consistency schools	1497	1925	5307	2492
2、初中	Junior Middle Schools	86122	80617	249401	112421
初级中学	Junior Middle Schools	48268	42978	135410	60591
九年一贯制学校	Nine-year Consistency Schools	4329	5311	15944	7269
十二年一贯制学校	Twelve-year Consistency Schools	3286	3472	10062	4477
完全中学	Complete Secondary school	30239	28856	87985	40084
(二)普通初等教育	Regular Primary Education	78532	105063	566229	263197
小学	Pricmary Schools	73021	96493	524490	243918
九年一贯制学校	Nine-year Consistency schools	3677	6319	30787	14256
十二年一贯制学校	Twelve-year Consistency Schools	1834	2251	10952	5023
（三）特殊教育	Special Education Schools	168	338	1373	541
1、特殊教育学校	Special Education Schools	63	163	782	301
2、小学附设特教班	Primary Schools with Special Education Classes			5	1
3、小学随班就读	Elementary Inclusive	84	85	418	170
4、初中随班就读	Junior Mainstreaming	21	90	168	69
（四）工读学校	Reformatory Schools	19	17	26	11
（五）学前教育	Preschool Education	100085	119553	309020	147347
1、独立幼儿园	Independent Kindergartens	91635	117902	306615	146163
2、附设幼儿园	Attached Kindergartens	8450	1651	2405	1184
另有：职业技术培训机构	Vocational and Technical Institutions	410395		474608	252242

注：本表数据来源于市教育局。

20-4 主要年份普通高等学校和科研机构研究生情况

Basic Statistics on Regular Institutions Schools and Post-graduates of Scientific Research Institution in Representative Years

单位：人 (person)

年份 Year	毕业生数 Number of Graduates	高等学校 Higher Schools	招生数 New Enrollment	高等学校 Higher Schools	在校学生数 Total Enrollment	高等学校 Higher Schools
1978					232	232
1980					651	651
1985					4799	4799
1990	2051	2051	1662	1662	5275	5275
1995	1769	1769	2712	2712	7974	7974
1998	2316	2316	3888	3888	10833	10833
1999	2903	2903	5020	5020	12986	12986
2000	3236	3236	6924	6924	16620	16620
2001	3881	3770	9274	8966	22564	21855
2002	4103	3952	11282	10882	28446	27471
2003	5971	5765	14322	13882	36936	35790
2004	8384	8127	17310	16871	45402	44169
2005	10416	10127	18583	18106	52699	51310
2006	12914	12552	19581	19105	58433	56951
2007	15506	15124	20570	20167	64137	62801
2008	17234	16788	21892	21443	67296	65834
2009	19025	18574	24879	24400	72366	70908
2010	19526	19129	25971	25477	76993	75483
2011	20965	20605	26686	26256	81696	80332
2012	22963	22578	28065	27618	84712	83306
2013	24778	24385	28786	28333	87002	85570
2014	24092	23881	28636	28436	88518	87826
2015	25322	25104	29487	29293	91448	90790

注：本表数据来源于市教育局。

20-5 主要年份普通高等学校基本情况

Baisc Statistics on Regular Higher Education in Representative Years

单位：所、万人 (units 10 000 persons)

年 份 Year	学校数 Number of Schools	毕业生数 Number of Graduates	招生数 New Enrollment	在校学生数 Total Enrollment	教职工数 Number of Staff and Teachers	专任教师数 Full-time Teachers
1978	21	0.60	1.31	2.88	2.24	0.87
1980	24	0.21	1.08	4.17	2.55	0.97
1985	28	1.17	2.28	6.49	3.40	1.28
1990	31	2.11	2.00	7.50	4.15	1.56
1995	32	2.87	3.13	10.07	4.21	1.59
1998	29	2.61	3.30	11.58	3.91	1.50
1999	29	2.84	5.12	13.79	3.95	1.52
2000	25	2.71	6.79	17.75	3.81	1.57
2001	32	3.31	8.31	23.24	4.30	1.75
2002	35	3.82	10.75	30.15	4.67	2.06
2003	37	5.89	12.21	36.42	4.92	2.21
2004	41	7.66	13.17	40.29	5.45	2.69
2005	44	10.08	14.68	47.79	5.73	2.95
2006	47	11.75	15.15	51.40	6.14	3.29
2007	48	14.33	16.96	56.03	6.56	3.67
2008	48	15.82	19.31	60.10	6.90	3.89
2009	49	15.04	18.84	63.22	7.08	4.06
2010	50	16.33	19.16	65.74	7.22	4.21
2011	61	17.68	20.52	68.52	7.27	4.27
2012	62	18.64	22.46	72.40	7.40	4.45
2013	63	17.73	21.05	75.27	7.50	4.64
2014	63	18.88	20.74	76.64	7.50	4.68
2015	63	20.72	20.49	75.75	7.49	4.78

注：本表数据来源于市教育局。
本表仅包括本、专科。
历史年份个别数据有调整，以此表数据为准。

20-6 主要年份普通中等专业学校基本情况

Baisc Statistics on Regular Specialized Secondary Schools in Representative Years

年 份 Year	学校数（所） Number of Schools (units)	毕业生数（万人） Number of Graduates (10 000 persons)	招生数（万人） New Enrollment (10 000 persons)	在校学生数（万人） Total Enrollment (10 000 persons)	教职工数（人） Number of Staff and Teachers(person)	专任教师数（人） Full-time Teachers(person)
1978	19	0.19	0.45	0.82	3937	1110
1980	31	0.18	0.42	1.50	3895	1474
1985	37	0.43	0.76	1.70	6071	2363
1990	44	0.56	0.68	2.09	7136	2891
1995	46	0.97	1.37	3.74	5903	2533
1996	47	1.15	1.61	4.18	5940	2573
1997	47	1.20	1.65	4.63	6124	2731
1998	47	1.26	1.62	5.08	6181	2840
1999	46	1.42	2.11	5.75	6385	2865
2000	47	1.63	1.90	6.02	6964	3172
2001	47	1.70	1.58	5.63	5252	2467
2002	46	1.60	1.69	5.57	5170	2508
2003	34	1.62	1.80	5.28	4562	2302
2004	35	1.40	2.09	5.71	4676	2388
2005	32	1.44	2.26	6.16	3924	2130
2006	31	1.84	2.61	7.30	3621	2014
2007	30	2.03	2.91	7.97	3548	2011
2008	29	2.58	2.55	8.06	3278	1814
2009	28	2.70	2.15	7.44	2965	1720
2010	28	2.45	2.08	6.75	3249	1845
2011	24	2.34	1.96	6.11	2868	1723
2012	24	2.15	1.67	5.43	2733	1595
2013	22	1.93	1.35	4.66	2599	1474
2014	22	1.76	1.25	4.07	2315	1346
2015	20	1.32	0.95	3.47	1991	1228

注：本表数据来源于市教育局。
历史年份个别数据有调整，以此表数据为准。

20-7 主要年份普通中学基本情况

Baisc Statistics on Regular Secondary Schools in Representative Years

年 份 Year	学校数（所） Number of Schools (units)	毕业生数（万人） Number of Graduates (10 000 persons)	招生数（万人） New Enrollment (10 000 persons)	在校学生数（万人） Total Enrollment (10 000 persons)	教职工数（人） Number of Staff and Teachers(person)	专任教师数（人） Full-time Teachers(person)
1978	962			44.16	27380	20660
1980	1002	12.33	14.03	44.08	29867	22530
1985	563	10.72	13.05	38.24	30063	22050
1990	518	9.11	10.49	30.03	30739	22386
1995	485	8.13	12.40	32.32	30423	21984
1996	462	8.67	13.03	35.25	30902	22478
1997	466	9.96	13.83	37.16	31682	23129
1998	467	10.64	15.00	39.79	32371	23884
1999	469	11.21	16.58	43.49	33387	25114
2000	466	12.01	17.88	48.31	34385	26230
2001	470	13.85	18.98	52.50	35442	27190
2002	467	15.76	19.68	55.36	36706	28335
2003	467	16.76	18.78	56.44	38252	29887
2004	461	18.01	18.85	56.54	39121	30600
2005	460	18.82	18.83	55.74	39456	31094
2006	457	18.04	18.61	56.11	39341	31203
2007	453	18.37	17.96	54.68	39171	31373
2008	442	17.99	17.16	52.83	39088	31425
2009	439	17.80	16.57	50.63	39002	31415
2010	436	17.01	16.15	48.89	39207	31506
2011	423	16.44	15.42	47.20	41135	31675
2012	419	15.64	14.98	45.33	41197	31526
2013	418	15.24	14.47	43.73	41003	31419
2014	421	14.54	13.97	42.57	40576	32615
2015	422	13.92	13.41	41.37	40689	33014

注：本表数据来源于市教育局。

20-8 各区县普通中学基本情况（2015年）

Baisc Statistics on Regular Secondary Schools by Region（2015）

单位：所、人 (unit, person)

区 县 Region	学校数 Number of Schools	毕业生数 Number of Graduates	高中 Senior	招生数 New Enrollment	高中 Senior	在校学生数 Total Enrollment	女生 Female Students	高中 Senior	教职工数 Number of Staff and Teachers	专任教师数 Full-time Teachers
合 计 Total	**422**	**139199**	**53077**	**134115**	**53498**	**413725**	**192863**	**164324**	**40689**	**33014**
新城区 Xincheng	25	11540	3587	10906	3806	34188	16247	11353	2483	2035
碑林区 Beilin	35	16161	6209	16055	6867	47955	22380	19878	3847	2956
莲湖区 Lianhu	20	11327	3704	10669	3741	33074	15717	11266	2860	2233
灞桥区 Baqiao	26	7582	2407	7654	2142	23355	11128	6979	2338	1864
未央区 Weiyang	32	9814	4194	10968	4351	31440	15281	13003	3620	2933
雁塔区 Yanta	47	15577	5061	15985	5863	48347	22836	16846	5064	4124
阎良区 Yanliang	12	3925	1608	3350	1356	10830	5384	4474	1120	945
临潼区 Lintong	32	10893	4122	9931	4386	31225	15526	13449	3338	2769
长安区 Chang'an	50	14075	6309	13194	5872	40725	18916	18107	4091	3493
高陵区 Gaoling	15	3702	1543	3349	1285	10636	5136	4176	1148	984
蓝田县 Lantian	45	10195	4051	9249	3783	30258	14472	13084	3314	2612
周至县 Zhouzhi	35	11221	5016	9991	4594	31761	12698	14556	3276	2514
户 县 Huxian	36	10094	4348	9284	4374	29830	12543	14237	3051	2649
沣东新城 Fengdongxincheng	12	3093	918	3530	1078	10101	4599	2916	1139	903

注：本表数据来源于市教育局。
本表中教职工数按照办学类型划分，专任教师数按照办学层次划分。

20-9 主要年份职业高中基本情况

Baisc Statistics on Vocational Secondary Schools in Representative Years

单位：所、人 (unit, person)

年 份 Year	学校数 Number of Schools	毕业生数 Number of Graduates	招生数 New Enrollment	在校学生数 Total Enrollment	教职工数 Number of Staff and Teachers	专任教师数 Full-time Teachers
1985	40	1661	8346	17621	1375	868
1990	58	5936	8095	20151	2674	1574
1995	71	8976	12490	32673	2394	1877
1996	67	9235	10563	25955	3098	1735
1997	73	8756	13390	29068	2993	1709
1998	89	7753	13949	31264	3152	1823
1999	91	8480	13062	31973	3217	1908
2000	95	9949	13903	32188	3311	1997
2001	85	10300	15591	34336	3517	2113
2002	78	8659	17231	39428	3461	2192
2003	87	10755	17310	44033	4036	2458
2004	83	12177	17865	46358	4101	2515
2005	91	15092	20603	51766	4750	2892
2006	96	14887	21158	53828	5193	3126
2007	86	14881	24434	56012	4899	3064
2008	84	15813	30201	62963	4878	3008
2009	84	14691	31042	72388	5129	3179
2010	84	18100	30042	78244	5222	3178
2011	78	22493	27641	75108	4849	3173
2012	77	24048	24995	67969	4775	3148
2013	74	21243	23043	61968	4699	3085
2014	81	19156	19508	60024	4860	3186
2015	80	18565	15060	49092	3239	2214

注：本表数据来源于市教育局。

20-10 各区县职业高中基本情况（2015年）

Basic Statistics on Vocational Secondary Schools by Region（2015）

单位：所、人 (unit, person)

区 县	Region	学校数 Number of Schools	毕业生数 Number of Graduates	招生数 New Enrollment	在校学生数 Total Enrollment	女生 Female Students	教职工数 Number of Staff and Teachers	专任教师数 Full-time Teachers
合 计	**Total**	**79**	**18353**	**15060**	**48708**	**24535**	**3016**	**2118**
新城区	Xincheng	10	3619	4914	12276	6171	542	332
碑林区	Beilin	7	2015	429	3824	1696	202	136
莲湖区	Lianhu	6	2465	1921	6712	3743	287	182
灞桥区	Baqiao	11	939	568	2361	1756	208	153
未央区	Weiyang	6	756	822	2411	1330	152	103
雁塔区	Yanta	13	1736	1587	5944	2464	330	243
阎良区	Yanliang	2	600	711	2261	1299	171	125
临潼区	Lintong	5	1230	726	2610	1078	250	178
长安区	Chang'an	6	1437	1261	4477	2104	457	296
高陵区	Gaoling	1	745	589	1695	1023	70	65
蓝田县	Lantian	2	269	575	1155	523		
周至县	Zhouzhi	5	1922	533	1828	943	134	103
户 县	Huxian	5	620	424	1154	405	213	202
沣东新城	Fengdongxincheng							

注：本表数据来源于市教育局。
本表仅包括市属部分。

20-11 主要年份小学基本情况

Basic Statistics on Primary Schools in Representative Years

年 份 Year	学校数（所） Number of Schools (units)	毕业生数 （万人） Number of Graduates (10 000 persons)	招生数 （万人） New Enrollment (10 000 persons)	在校学生数 （万人） Total Enrollment (10 000 persons)	教职工数（人） Number of Staff and Teachers(person)	专任教师数 （人） Full-time Teachers(person)
1978	2667	13.07	14.10	74.03	29744	26428
1980	2337	11.91	12.57	73.36	31770	28360
1985	2337	11.21	9.57	62.16	31075	26430
1990	2343	8.67	10.85	61.87	37788	29090
1995	2360	9.93	14.09	79.36	35568	30270
1996	2362	10.48	13.63	81.81	35821	30267
1997	2368	10.98	12.48	82.67	35767	30117
1998	2361	12.18	11.88	82.03	35576	30089
1999	2354	13.65	11.61	79.81	35639	30196
2000	2323	13.83	11.51	77.81	35336	30215
2001	2277	14.20	11.07	74.51	34257	29281
2002	2137	13.89	10.13	70.78	34143	29428
2003	2084	12.97	9.28	66.78	34080	29531
2004	2016	12.37	9.12	63.75	33794	29367
2005	1980	11.92	8.47	60.47	33907	29674
2006	1929	11.53	9.16	59.33	34460	30018
2007	1872	11.38	8.67	56.83	34901	30533
2008	1781	10.58	8.33	54.66	34653	30382
2009	1666	9.96	7.84	52.52	34389	30334
2010	1531	9.61	8.64	51.56	34118	29944
2011	1424	8.92	8.77	51.39	32457	29900
2012	1322	8.88	8.88	50.85	32208	29651
2013	1291	8.51	9.56	51.95	31863	29421
2014	1257	8.29	10.13	53.79	32162	28395
2015	1234	7.85	10.51	56.62	32585	28395

注：本表数据来源于市教育局。

20-12　各区县小学基本情况（2015年）

Basic Statistics on Primary Schools by Region（2015）

单位：所、人　　　　(unit, person)

区　县	Region	学校数 Number of Schools	毕业生数 Number of Graduates	招生数 New Enrollment	在校学生数 Total Enrollment	女生 Female Students	教职工数 Number of Staff and Teachers	专任教师数 Full-time Teachers
合　计	**Total**	**1234**	**78532**	**105063**	**566229**	**263197**	**32585**	**28748**
新城区	Xincheng	35	5756	5854	36920	17235	1771	1537
碑林区	Beilin	43	5989	7065	42754	19902	2413	1992
莲湖区	Lianhu	47	6801	8892	51522	24215	2526	2228
灞桥区	Baqiao	75	5447	8914	43391	20287	2097	1702
未央区	Weiyang	60	7556	13962	65326	30100	2450	2231
雁塔区	Yanta	73	10728	16950	86177	40178	4084	3680
阎良区	Yanliang	24	2071	2649	14401	7016	982	888
临潼区	Lintong	130	6195	6433	36807	17254	2882	2531
长安区	Chang'an	153	7184	11280	56023	26251	3615	3093
高陵区	Gaoling	70	2137	3329	17429	8320	1458	1311
蓝田县	Lantian	213	5483	4115	29041	13584	2692	2477
周至县	Zhouzhi	149	5365	6180	32768	14398	2293	2078
户　县	Huxian	115	4797	4798	29871	13562	2094	1921
沣东新城	Fengdongxincheng	47	3023	4642	23799	10895	1228	1079

注：本表数据来源于市教育局。
　　本表中教职工数按照办学类型划分，专任教师数按办学层次划分。

20-13 主要年份学前教育基本情况

Basic Conditions of Pre-school Education in Representative Years

年　份 Year	幼儿园（所） Number of Kindergartens (units)	班数（个） Number of Class (unit)	在园幼儿园数（万人） Student Enrollment (10000 persons)	教职工数（人） Number of Staff and Teachers(person)	专任教师数（人） Full-time Teachers(person)
1978	363		4	3568	1315
1980	186		10	5525	2657
1985	310	3135	10	6887	2770
1990	256	3816	14	6123	2058
1995	257	4464	16	6173	2659
1996	244	4313	15	5918	2661
1997	228	4243	15	6065	2748
1998	235	4195	13	6272	2910
1999	234	4222	13	6329	2982
2000	367	4142	13	6346	2995
2001	366	4306	12	6224	3069
2002	378	4186	12	6541	3397
2003	610	4470	12	8959	4853
2004	660	4507	12	9870	5577
2005	737	4712	13	10528	5959
2006	863	5037	13	12335	7106
2007	830	5081	14	13468	7951
2008	905	5506	15	14932	8704
2009	896	5710	16	15928	9240
2010	1004	6420	18	18710	10638
2011	1122	8010	24	23680	12577
2012	1239	8729	27.1	27735	14293
2013	1295	9408	28.56	31989	16238
2014	1343	9782	28.95	33062	17337
2015	1417	10457	30.90	36004	19096

注：本表数据来源于市教育局。
幼儿园在园人数中包括学前班。

20-14 主要年份特殊教育基本情况

Basic Statistics on Special Education in Representative Years

单位：所、人 (unit, person)

年份 Year	学校数 Number of Schools	毕业生数 Number of Graduates	招生数 New Enrollment	在校学生数 Total Enrollment	教职工数 Number of Staff and Teachers	专任教师数 Full-time Teachers
1980	1	48	64	315	66	43
1985	2	14	36	318	94	59
1990	5	35	111	451	142	96
1995	5	27	147	1363	204	141
1996	5	60	164	1520	210	150
1997	5	153	164	1655	210	148
1998	5	266	140	2145	232	157
1999	5	349	115	1912	235	160
2000	5	269	145	1880	230	156
2001	5	237	209	1915	238	162
2002	5	216	148	1661	232	157
2003	5	156	161	1380	237	166
2004	5	137	142	1290	236	167
2005	5	184	182	1445	240	169
2006	6	171	143	1425	254	178
2007	6	169	114	1342	259	190
2008	6	83	96	1286	259	190
2009	7	311	202	1523	335	234
2010	8	214	402	1529	340	235
2011	8	280	222	1393	343	231
2012	8	197	220	1392	352	248
2013	8	194	212	1174	338	243
2014	8	172	222	1225	345	238
2015	8	168	338	1373	352	240

注：本表数据来源于市教育局。

包括盲、聋、哑、弱智儿童教育在内。

20-15 基础教育监测评价情况（2015年）

Monitoring and Evaluation of Basic Education（2015）

指　标	Item	2015
入学率(%)	Enrollment Rate(%)	
小学	Primary Schools	99.98
初中	Junior Middle Schools	99.79
重读率(%)	Restduy-Rate(%)	
小学	Primary schools	0.09
初中	Junior Middle Schools	0.05
巩固率(%)	The Consolidation Rate (%)	
小学(六年)	Primary Schools (six years)	97.22
初中(三年)	Junior Middle Schools (three years)	95.94
毕业率(%)	The Graduate Rate(%)	
小学	Primary school	99.64
初中	Junior middle school	98.31
专任教师学历合格率(%)	Qualified Rate Of Full-time Teacher Education (%)	
小学	Primary Schools	99.73
初中	Junior Middle Schools	99.75
高中	Senior Middle Schools	98.13
幼儿园	Kindergartens	96.35
小学教师专科以上学历达到率(%)	Rate of Primary School Teachers with College degree or Above (%)	95.53
初中教师本科以上学历达到率(%)	Rate of Junior Middle SchoolTeachers with Bachelor degree or Above (%)	88.99
高中教师研究生以上学历达到率(%)	Rate of Senior Middle School Teachers with Postgraduate degree or Above (%)	12.85

注：本表数据来源于市教育局。

20-16 主要年份平均每万人口在校学生数及构成

单位：人、%

年 份 Year	平均每万人 高等学校在校学生 Per 10000 people on average Hight Education Students in the school	平均每万人 高中阶段在校学生 Per 10000 people on average Number of Senior high School Students in the school	平均每万人 初中在校学生 Per 10000 people on average Number of Junior Secondary School Students in the school
1978	58		
1980	84		
1985	117		
1990	123		
1995	168		
1996	177		
1997	180		
1998	189		
1999	224		
2000	282		
2001	366		
2002	470		
2003	560		
2004	618	463	517
2005	715	492	489
2006	760	534	484
2007	817	543	466
2008	863	571	444
2009	901	619	413
2010	939	635	361
2011	1090	576	337
2012	1132	541	319
2013	1146	448	307
2014	1157	414	301
2015	1125	374	286

注：本表数据来源于市教育局。

The Number of Students in the School Average every 10000 Individuals in Representative Years

(persons,%)

平均每万人 小学在校学生 Per 10000 people on average Number of Primary School Students in the school	普通高等学校在校学生 占学生总数比重 Senior high School Students in the school in accounting for the proportion of the total number of students	中等学校在校学生 占学生总数比重 Junior Secondary School students in the school in accounting for the proportion of the total number of students	小学在校学生 占学生总数比重 Primary School students in the school in accounting for the proportion of the total number of students
1486	2.3	34.9	58.6
1434	3.1	33.2	55.3
1124	5.3	31.3	50.9
1016	6.7	25.1	51.7
1224	7.3	28.0	53.6
1249	7.6	28.8	53.5
1249	7.6	29.8	53.1
1228	8.0	31.3	52.0
1183	9.3	33.2	49.2
1131	11.5	34.8	46.0
1072	14.6	35.9	42.6
1007	18.2	36.4	39.0
932	20.1	33.8	33.5
879	22.2	35.2	31.6
815	26.4	36.2	30.1
788	27.7	37.1	28.7
744	29.3	36.3	26.7
708	30.8	36.1	25.2
672	31.8	36.5	23.7
660	33.0	35.0	23.2
604	29.8	30.1	19.9
595	31.0	28.2	19.5
605	32.6	25.3	20.2
626	33.2	23.8	20.9
650	32.8	22.2	21.9

20-17 民办教育情况（2015年）

Private Education Situation（2015）

单位：所、人 (unit, person)

指 标	Item	学校数 Number of Schools	毕业生数 Number of Graduates	招生数 New Enrollment
一、民办高等教育(民办高校）	**Private higher Education (Institutions)**	**16**	**77301**	**73140**
二、民办中等教育	**Private Secondary Education**	98	36967	38504
民办普通高中	Ordinary High School	27	5700	6472
民办中等专业学校	Specialized Secondary School	1	1095	448
民办职业高中	Vocational hight school	47	7754	8941
民办普通初中	Ordinary Junior middle school	23	19555	20486
民办的附设中职班	Private primary school class	(9)	2863	2157
三、民办普通小学	**Private Primary School**	**57**	**7727**	**15006**
四、民办幼儿园	**Private kindergarten**	**881**	**57318**	**83565**
另有：民办培训机构	Private Training Institutions	585	217914	

注：本表数据来源于市教育局。
毕业生数中幼儿园为离园人数。
民办高等教育在校生为民办高校普通、成人本专科学生数。
聘请校外教师中，小学、中学、幼儿园为代课教师和兼任教师之和。
民办普通高中含完全中学15所、高级中学5所、12年一贯制7所；民办普通初中含初级中学14所,9年一贯制9所。

20-17 续表 continued

单位：所、人 (unit, person)

指标	Item	在校学生数 Total Enrollment	教职工数 Number of Teachers and Staff	专任教师 Full-time Teachers	聘请外校教师 Teachers hired from Outside Schools
一、民办高等教育(民办高校）	**Private higher Education (Institutions)**	**266234**	**20857**	**13406**	
二、民办中等教育	**Private Secondary Education**	117447	7907	5952	150
民办普通高中	Ordinary High School	18834	3950	3015	138
民办中等专业学校	Specialized Secondary School	1775	265	160	
民办职业高中	Vocational hight school	26522	1128	681	12
民办普通初中	Ordinary Junior middle school	61597	2564	2096	
民办的附设中职班	Private primary school class	8719			
三、民办普通小学	**Private Primary School**	**69326**	**3218**	**2734**	**2**
四、民办幼儿园	**Private kindergarten**	**217910**	**26076**	**13210**	
另有：民办培训机构	Private Training Institutions	285631	8168	4428	5377

20-18　研究与试验发展（R&D）情况（2015年）

Research and Experiment Development Facts（2015）

指　标	Item	2015
一、单位数（个）	**Number of Units(unit)**	**1805**
科研单位	Units of Scientific Research	63
高等院校	Institutions of Higher Education	69
规模以上工业企业	Industrial Enterpries above Designated Size	1151
#有R&D活动单位数	The number of R&D active units	506
科研单位	Units of Scientific Research	48
高等院校	Institutions of Higher Education	64
规模以上工业企业	Industrial Enterpries above Designated Size	316
二、科技活动人员（人）	**Personnel Eagaged in Scientific and Technical Activities (person)**	**160629**
科研单位	Units of Scientific Research	39874
高等院校	Institutions of Higher Education	45825
规模以上工业企业	Industrial Enterpries above Designated Size	57896
三、R&D经费内部支出（万元）	**R&D Intramural Expenditure (10000 yuan)**	**3037122**
科研单位	Units of Scientific Research	1616544
高等院校	Institutions of Higher Education	336808
规模以上工业企业	Industrial Enterpries above Designated Size	924793
四、R&D项目（课题）（个）	**Project（Issue）**	**32239**
科研单位	Units of Scientific Research	2207
高等院校	Institutions of Higher Education	29397
规模以上工业企业	Industrial Enterpries above Designated Size	2058

注：本表数据来源于省统计局反馈。
　　2015年数据不含省直管5家企业。

20–19 科研院所研究与试验发展（R&D）情况（2015年）

Research and Experiment Development Facts in Scientific Research Institutions（2015）

指　标	Item	2015
一、基本情况	**Basic Facts**	
单位数（个）	Number of Unit(unit)	63
#有R&D活动的单位数	The number of R&D active units	48
科技活动人员（人）	Number of Personnel Engaged in Scientific Research (person)	39874
# R&D人员	R&D personnel	29858
其中：女性	Female	9060
其中：博士毕业	Doctor	1559
硕士毕业	Master	10083
本科毕业	Undergraduate	11287
二、R&D人员折合全时当量（人年）	**R&D staff equivalent to full-time equivalents (person--year)**	**28096**
其中：研究人员	Personnel Engaged in Research	18964
其中：基础研究	Basic Research	2168
应用研究	Applied Research	10179
试验发展	Experiment Development	15749
二、R&D经费内部支出（万元）	**Intramural Expenditure for R & D(10000 yuan)**	**1616544**
在支出中：1、基础研究	Expenditure on: Basic Research	53146
2、应用研究	Applied Research	470296
3、试验发展	Experiment Development	1093102
在支出中：1、日常支出	Expenditure on: Daily Expenditure	1306234
#人员劳务费	Service Fees of Personnel	241475
2、资产性支出	Assets Expenditure	310310
#仪器和设备	Instruments and Equipment	172493
在支出中：1、政府资金	Expenditure on: Government Funds	1515756
2、企业资金	Enterpreises Funds	23136
3、境外资金	Overseas Funds	89
4、其他资金	Others	77563
四、R&D产出	**R&D outputs**	
专利申请数（个）	Number of Patent Applications (item)	2962
#发明专利	Number of Invention Patents	2415
专利授权数（个）	Number of Patents Awarded (item)	1743
#发明专利	Number of Invention Patents	1269
有效发明专利数（件）	Number of Effective Invention Patents(item)	4046
发表科技论文（篇）	Scientific and Technical Thesis (piece)	5061
出版科技著作（种）	Scientific and Technical Works Published (book)	78

注：本表数据来源于省统计局反馈。

20-20 大专院校研究与试验发展（R&D）情况（2015年）

Research and Experiment Development Facts in Universities（2015）

指　标	Item	2015
一、基本情况	**Basic Facts**	
单位数（个）	Number of Unit(unit)	69
#有R&D活动的单位数	The number of R&D active units	64
科技活动人员（人）	Number of Personnel Engaged in Scientific Research (person)	58092
# R&D人员	R&D personnel	17291
其中：女性	Female	
其中：博士毕业	Doctor	5474
硕士毕业	Master	6588
本科毕业	Undergraduate	4408
二、R&D人员折合全时当量（人年）	**R&D staff equivalent to full-time equivalents (person--year)**	**7545**
其中：研究人员	Personnel Engaged in Research	
其中：基础研究	Basic Research	4064
应用研究	Applied Research	2567
试验发展	Experiment Development	914
三、R&D经费内部支出（万元）	**Intramural Expenditure for R & D(10000 yuan)**	**336808**
在支出中：1、基础研究	Expenditure on: Basic Research	113790
2、应用研究	Applied Research	165682
3、试验发展	Experiment Development	57336
在支出中：1、日常支出	Expenditure on: Daily Expenditure	285714
#人员劳务费	Service Fees of Personnel	39626
2、资产性支出	Assets Expenditure	51094
#仪器和设备	Instruments and Equipment	4923
在支出中：1、政府资金	Expenditure on: Government Funds	195683
2、企业资金	Enterpreises Funds	135194
3、境外资金	Overseas Funds	664
4、其他资金	Others	5267
四、R&D产出	**R&D outputs**	
专利申请数（个）	Number of Patent Applications (item)	8270
#发明专利	Number of Invention Patents	4873
专利授权数（个）	Number of Patents Awarded (item)	6224
#发明专利	Number of Invention Patents	3251
有效发明专利数（件）	Number of Effective Invention Patents(item)	11551
发表科技论文（篇）	Scientific and Technical Thesis (piece)	43247
出版科技著作（种）	Scientific and Technical Works Published (book)	1056

注：本表数据来源于省统计局反馈。

20-21 规模以上工业企业研究与试验发展（R&D）情况（2015年）

Research and Experiment Development Facts in Large-size and Medium-size Industrial Enterprises（2015）

指　标	Item	2015
一、基本情况	**Basic Facts**	
单位数（个）	Number of Unit(unit)	1151
有R&D活动的单位数	The number of R&D active units	316
从事科技活动人员（人）	Number of Personnel Engaged in Scientific Research (person)	57896
# R&D人员	R&D personnel	35609
其中：女性	Female	9958
二、R&D人员折合全时当量（人年）	**R&D staff equivalent to full-time equivalents (person--year)**	**26236**
其中：研究人员	Personnel Engaged in Research	9552
其中：基础研究	Basic Research	7
应用研究生	Applied Research	962
试验发展	Experiment Development	25267
三、R&D经费内部支出（万元）	**Intramural Expenditure for R & D(10000 yuan)**	**924793**
在支出中：1、基础研究	Expenditure on: Basic Research	248
2、应用研究	Applied Research	31877
3、试验发展	Experiment Development	892668
在支出中：1、日常支出	Expenditure on: Daily Expenditure	863615
#人员劳务费	Service Fees of Personnel	213311
2、资产性支出	Assets Expenditure	61178
#仪器和设备	Instruments and Equipment	59503
在支出中：1、政府资金	Expenditure on: Government Funds	325451
2、企业资金	Enterpreises Funds	594704
3、境外资金	Overseas Funds	1272
4、其他资金	Others	3366
四、R&D产出	**R&D outputs**	
专利申请数（个）	Number of Patent Applications (item)	4292
#发明专利	Number of Invention Patents	1732
有效发明专利数（件）	Number of Effective Invention Patents(item)	4877
发表科技论文（篇）	Scientific and Technical Thesis (piece)	2443

注：本表数据来自于省统计局反馈。
2015年数据不含省直管5家企业。
2015年研发报表制度变化导致部分指标波动较大。

20-22 规模以上工业企业研究与试验发展（R&D）人员和经费支出情况（2015年）

指标	Item	R&D人员（人）R&D personnel（person）	#研究人员 #Researchers
总计	**Total**	35609	13038
按企业规模分	**Grouped by Size of Enterprises**		
大型企业	Large-size	25238	8653
中型企业	Medium-size	6069	2529
小型企业	Small-size	4292	1851
微型企业	microenterprise	10	5
按登记注册类型分组	**Grouped by Registion Status**		
内资企业	Domestic Investment Enterprises	33661	12148
国有企业	State-owned Enterprises	10237	3946
集体企业	Collective-owned Enterprises		
股份合作企业	Stock cooperative enterprises	12	6
联营企业	Affiliated companies		
有限责任公司	Limited Liability Corporations	18990	6394
股份有限公司	Share-holding Corperation Ltd.	3460	1377
私营企业	Private Enterprises	962	425
其他	Other Domestic Funded Enterprises		
港澳台商投资	Enterprises with Funds from Hong Kong,Macao and Taiwan	172	72
外商投资企业	Foreign Funded Enterprises	1776	818
按工业行业大类分	**Grouped by Sector**		
采矿业	Mining	785	393
煤炭开采和洗选业	Mining and Washing of Coal		
石油和天然气开采业	Extraction of Petroleum and Natural Gas		
黑色金属矿采选业	Mining of Ferrous Metal Ores		
有色金属矿采选业	Mining of Non-ferrous Metal Ores		
非金属矿采选业	Mining and Processing of Nonmetal Ores		
开采辅助活动	Mining of Other Ores	785	393
制造业	Processing of Food from Agricultural Products	34824	12645
农副食品加工业	Manufacture of Foods	6	1
食品制造业	Manufacture of Beverages	117	37
酒、饮料和精制茶制造业	Manufacture of Tobacco	58	29
烟草制品业	Manufacture of Textile		
纺织业	Manufacture of Textile Wearing Apparel, Footware and Caps	179	90
纺织服装、服饰业	Manufacture of Leather, Fur, Feather and Related Products		
皮革、毛皮、羽毛及其制品和制鞋业	Processing of Timber,Manufacture of Wood, Bamboo,Rattan, its Froducts and Footwear	27	7

R&D Personnel and Expenditure Conditions of Industrial Enterprises above Designated Size（2015）

R&D经费内部支出（万元） R&D Intramural Expenditure (10000 yuan)	#政府资金 # Government funds	#企业资金 # Enterprise funds	#境外资金 # Foreign funds
924793	325451	594704	1272
736754	305018	430518	1179
105972	10310	94267	93
81978	10123	69830	
89		89	
788275	322978	460752	1179
233333	69739	163585	
154		154	
473131	242944	226534	1179
65419	7710	57402	
16238	2585	13077	
4541	661	3880	
131977	1812	130072	93
21595	4101	17494	
21595	4101	17494	
903198	321350	577210	1272
80		80	
1613	14	1366	
1454	355	1100	
2634	142	2492	
108		108	

20-22 续表1

指标	Item	R&D人员（人） R&D personnel（person）	#研究人员 #Researchers
木材加工和木、竹、藤、棕、草制品业	Plam and Straw Products and Straw Products		
家具制造业	Manufacture of Furniture		
造纸及纸制品业	Manufacture of Paper and Paper Products	18	3
印刷和记录媒介复制业	Printing,Reproduction of Recording Media	100	46
文教、工美、体育和娱乐用品制造业	Manufacture of Articles For Culture, Education and Sport Activities	11	1
石油加工业、炼焦和核燃料加工业	Processing of Petroleum, Coking, Processing of Nuclear Fuel		
化学原料及化学制品制造业	Manufacture of Raw Chemical Materials and Chemical Products	2399	1001
医药制造业	Manufacture of Medicines	1301	568
化学纤维制造业	Manufacture of Chemical Fibers		
橡胶和塑料制品业	Manufacture of Rubber and Manufacture of Plastics	192	54
非金属矿物制品业	Manufacture of Non-metallic Mineral Products	95	49
黑色金属冶炼和压延加工业	Smelting and Pressing of Ferrous Metals		
有色金属冶炼和压延加工业	Smelting and Pressing of Non-ferrous Metals	856	330
金属制品业	Manufacture of Metal Products	2076	737
通用设备制造业	Manufacture of General Purpose Machinery	1072	439
专用设备制造业	Manufacture of Special Equipment	1542	693
汽车制造业	Manufacture of Motor Vehicle	3966	1112
铁路、船舶、航空航天和其他运输设备制造业	Railways,Shipbuilding,Aerospace and Other Transportation Equipment Manufacturing Industry	11001	3192
电气机械和器材制造业	Manufacture of Electric Equipment and Machinery	3489	1396
计算机、通讯和其他电子设备制造业	Manufacture of Communication Equipment, Computers and other Electronic Equipment	4599	2030
仪器仪表制造业	Manufacture of Measuring Instruments and Machinery	1649	794
其他制造业	Other Manufacturing	66	33
金属制品、机械和设备修理业	Metal Products,Machinery and Equipment Repair Industry	5	3
电力、热力、燃气及水生产和供应业	Production and Distribution of Electricity,Gas and Water		
电力、热力的生产和供应业	Production and Supply of Electric Power and Heat Power		
燃气生产和供应业	Gas mining and supplying industry		
水的生产和供应业	Production and Supply of Water		

continued 1

R&D经费内部支出（万元） R&D Intramural Expenditure (10000 yuan)	#政府资金 # Government funds	#企业资金 # Enterprise funds	#境外资金 # Foreign funds
253	31	111	
2634		2634	
26	1	25	
57702	5352	52350	
52236	1403	50826	
6236	325	5911	
4059	2167	1891	
15360	2662	12698	
42241	9142	33098	
16422	511	15584	
33392	6624	26609	84
45172	3761	41382	
345192	263711	80293	1188
87666	4596	81672	
150995	18656	132150	
36721	1843	33882	
730	54	676	
272		272	

20-23　规模以上工业企业研究和试验发展（R&D）项目情况（2015年）

指标	Item	项目数（项）The number of items（item）
总计	**Total**	2058
按企业规模分	**Grouped by Size of Enterprises**	
大型企业	Large-size	999
中型企业	Medium-size	523
小型企业	Small-size	532
微型企业	microenterprise	4
按登记注册类型分组	**Grouped by Registion Status**	
内资企业	Domestic Investment Enterprises	1951
国有企业	State-owned Enterprises	542
集体企业	Collective-owned Enterprises	
股份合作企业	Stock cooperative enterprises	2
联营企业	Affiliated companies	
有限责任公司	Limited Liability Corporations	953
股份有限公司	Share-holding Corperation Ltd.	319
私营企业	Private Enterprises	135
其他	Other Domestic Funded Enterprises	
港澳台商投资	Enterprises with Funds from	14
	Hong Kong,Macao and Taiwan	
外商投资企业	Foreign Funded Enterprises	93
按工业行业大类分	**Grouped by Sector**	
采矿业	Mining	97
煤炭开采和洗选业	Mining and Washing of Coal	
石油和天然气开采业	Extraction of Petroleum and Natural Gas	
黑色金属矿采选业	Mining of Ferrous Metal Ores	
有色金属矿采选业	Mining of Non-ferrous Metal Ores	
非金属矿采选业	Mining and Processing of Nonmetal Ores	
开采辅助活动	Mining of Other Ores	97
制造业	Processing of Food from Agricultural Products	1961
农副食品加工业	Manufacture of Foods	1
食品制造业	Manufacture of Beverages	8
酒、饮料和精制茶制造业	Manufacture of Tobacco	2
烟草制品业	Manufacture of Textile	
纺织业	Manufacture of Textile Wearing	8
	Apparel, Footware and Caps	
纺织服装、服饰业	Manufacture of Leather, Fur,	
	Feather and Related Products	
皮革、毛皮、羽毛及其	Processing of Timber,Manufacture of Wood,	7
制品和制鞋业	Bamboo,Rattan, its Products and Footwear	

R&D Project Status of Industrial Enterprises above Designated Size（2015）

参加项目人员（人） Personnel participating in the project（person）	项目人员折合全时当量（人年） Personnel participating in the project equivalent to full-time equivalents（person--years）	项目经费内部支出（万元） Intramural Expenditure（10 000 yuan）
32249	23433	832648
23062	17761	661854
5309	3474	98623
3868	2194	72097
10	4	74
30411	21984	704752
8750	6492	227891
12	12	154
17743	12931	407965
3057	2040	54629
849	508	14114
169	97	4201
1669	1353	123694
722	343	19504
722	343	19504
31527	23091	813144
6	3	80
115	21	1393
47	9	994
124	26	2634
17	6	97

20-23 续表1

指标	Item	项目数（项）The number of items（item）
木材加工和木、竹、藤、棕、草制品业	Plam and Straw Products and Straw Products	
家具制造业	Manufacture of Furniture	
造纸及纸制品业	Manufacture of Paper and Paper Products	1
印刷和记录媒介复制业	Printing,Reproduction of Recording Media	10
文教、工美、体育和娱乐用品制造业	Manufacture of Articles For Culture, Education and Sport Activities	1
石油加工业、炼焦和核燃料加工业	Processing of Petroleum, Coking, Processing of Nuclear Fuel	
化学原料及化学制品制造业	Manufacture of Raw Chemical Materials and Chemical Products	290
医药制造业	Manufacture of Medicines	127
化学纤维制造业	Manufacture of Chemical Fibers	
橡胶和塑料制品业	Manufacture of Rubber and Manufacture of Plastics	26
非金属矿物制品业	Manufacture of Non-metallic Mineral Products	10
黑色金属冶炼和压延加工业	Smelting and Pressing of Ferrous Metals	
有色金属冶炼和压延加工业	Smelting and Pressing of Non-ferrous Metals	85
金属制品业	Manufacture of Metal Products	105
通用设备制造业	Manufacture of General Purpose Machinery	107
专用设备制造业	Manufacture of Special Equipment	153
汽车制造业	Manufacture of Motor Vehicle	107
铁路、船舶、航空航天和其他运输设备制造业	Railways,Shipbuilding,Aerospace and Other Transportation Equipment Manufacturing Industry	241
电气机械和器材制造业	Manufacture of Electric Equipment and Machinery	435
计算机、通讯和其他电子设备制造业	Manufacture of Communication Equipment, Computers and other Electronic Equipment	147
仪器仪表制造业	Manufacture of Measuring Instruments and Machinery	79
其他制造业	Other Manufacturing	8
金属制品、机械和设备修理业	Metal Products,Machinery and Equipment Repair Industry	3
电力、热力、燃气及水生产和供应业	Production and Distribution of Electricity,Gas and Water	
电力、热力的生产和供应业	Production and Supply of Electric Power and Heat Power	
燃气生产和供应业	Gas mining and supplying industry	
水的生产和供应业	Production and Supply of Water	

continued 1

参加项目人员（人） Personnel participating in the project（person）	项目人员折合全时当量（人年） Personnel participating in the project equivalent to full-time equivalents（person--years）	项目经费内部支出（万元） Intramural Expenditure（10 000 yuan）
18	1	245
100	84	2016
11	1	26
2108	1660	48283
1187	837	43450
126	67	5334
82	37	3291
816	614	14990
2044	1854	41169
860	352	12957
1389	943	31224
3940	2642	44200
9957	8271	291960
3335	1802	85505
4100	3314	146828
1085	503	35713
55	41	483
5	3	272

20-24 规模以上工业企业新产品开发、生产及销售情况（2015年）

指标	Item	新产品开发项目数（项）Number of new product development projects（item）
总计	**Total**	2535
按企业规模分	**Grouped by Size of Enterprises**	
大型企业	Large-size	1102
中型企业	Medium-size	644
小型企业	Small-size	783
微型企业	microenterprise	6
按登记注册类型分组	**Grouped by Registion Status**	
内资企业	Domestic Investment Enterprises	2379
国有企业	State-owned Enterprises	715
集体企业	Collective-owned Enterprises	
股份合作企业	Stock cooperative enterprises	3
联营企业	Affiliated companies	
有限责任公司	Limited Liability Corporations	992
股份有限公司	Share-holding Corperation Ltd.	424
私营企业	Private Enterprises	245
其他	Other Domestic Funded Enterprises	
港澳台商投资	Enterprises with Funds from Hong Kong,Macao and Taiwan	18
外商投资企业	Foreign Funded Enterprises	138
按工业行业大类分	**Grouped by Sector**	
采矿业	Mining	52
煤炭开采和洗选业	Mining and Washing of Coal	
石油和天然气开采业	Extraction of Petroleum and Natural Gas	
黑色金属矿采选业	Mining of Ferrous Metal Ores	
有色金属矿采选业	Mining of Non-ferrous Metal Ores	
非金属矿采选业	Mining and Processing of Nonmetal Ores	
开采辅助活动	Mining of Other Ores	52
制造业	Processing of Food from Agricultural Products	2482
农副食品加工业	Manufacture of Foods	3
食品制造业	Manufacture of Beverages	15
酒、饮料和精制茶制造业	Manufacture of Tobacco	2
烟草制品业	Manufacture of Textile	
纺织业	Manufacture of Textile Wearing Apparel, Footware and Caps	8
纺织服装、服饰业	Manufacture of Leather, Fur, Feather and Related Products	
皮革、毛皮、羽毛及其制品和制鞋业	Processing of Timber,Manufacture of Wood, Bamboo,Rattan, its Froducts and Footwear	8

New Product Development, Production and Sales of Above-scale Industrial Enterprises（2015）

新产品开发经费支出（万元） New Product Development Expenditure （10 000 yuan）	新产品产值 （万元） New product output value （10 000 yuan）	新产品销售收入 （万元） Sales of new products （10 000 yuan）
997143	7241100	5931680
741496	5670785	4613168
133171	1101297	873617
121875	464443	440288
601	4575	4607
846669	5721990	4764916
220690	1251481	1060289
251	2797	2796
520131	3829495	3144177
78363	569096	486025
27234	69121	71628
5362	358503	253196
145113	1160607	913569
12162	62483	780
12162	62483	780
984942	7176424	5922718
177	415	311
3825	42938	40834
1455	1744	882
2634	7756	7759
127	7318	7318

20-24 续表1

指标	Item	新产品开发项目数（项） Number of new product development projects（item）
木材加工和木、竹、藤、棕、草制品业	Plam and Straw Products and Straw Products	
家具制造业	Manufacture of Furniture	
造纸及纸制品业	Manufacture of Paper and Paper Products	
印刷和记录媒介复制业	Printing,Reproduction of Recording Media	7
文教、工美、体育和娱乐用品制造业	Manufacture of Articles For Culture, Education and Sport Activities	1
石油加工业、炼焦和核燃料加工业	Processing of Petroleum, Coking, Processing of Nuclear Fuel	
化学原料及化学制品制造业	Manufacture of Raw Chemical Materials and Chemical Products	405
医药制造业	Manufacture of Medicines	148
化学纤维制造业	Manufacture of Chemical Fibers	1
橡胶和塑料制品业	Manufacture of Rubber and Manufacture of Plastics	20
非金属矿物制品业	Manufacture of Non-metallic Mineral Products	11
黑色金属冶炼和压延加工业	Smelting and Pressing of Ferrous Metals	
有色金属冶炼和压延加工业	Smelting and Pressing of Non-ferrous Metals	121
金属制品业	Manufacture of Metal Products	100
通用设备制造业	Manufacture of General Purpose Machinery	120
专用设备制造业	Manufacture of Special Equipment	236
汽车制造业	Manufacture of Motor Vehicle	164
铁路、船舶、航空航天和其他运输设备制造业	Railways,Shipbuilding,Aerospace and Other Transportation Equipment Manufacturing Industry	241
电气机械和器材制造业	Manufacture of Electric Equipment and Machinery	524
计算机、通讯和其他电子设备制造业	Manufacture of Communication Equipment, Computers and other Electronic Equipment	203
仪器仪表制造业	Manufacture of Measuring Instruments and Machinery	134
其他制造业	Other Manufacturing	7
金属制品、机械和设备修理业	Metal Products,Machinery and Equipment Repair Industry	3
电力、热力、燃气及水生产和供应业	Production and Distribution of Electricity,Gas and Water	1
电力、热力的生产和供应业	Production and Supply of Electric Power and Heat Power	
燃气生产和供应业	Gas mining and supplying industry	1
水的生产和供应业	Production and Supply of Water	

continued 1

新产品开发经费支出（万元） New Product Development Expenditure （10 000 yuan）	新产品产值 （万元） New product output value （10 000 yuan）	新产品销售收入 （万元） Sales of new products （10 000 yuan）
1918		
26		
54305	154725	153321
50118	250792	193282
80		
4237	64390	54950
6505	30087	27038
20988	217886	214207
39781	198760	185898
17936	189532	154264
51973	224670	186000
63012	1876064	1477469
392880	1284550	1115815
100844	995211	925327
154482	1435395	1112790
16967	185548	56611
402	2242	2242
272	6402	6402
39	2193	8182
39	2193	8182

20-25 主要年份企事业单位知识产权情况

Intellectual Property Right of Enterprises and Institutions in Representative Years

指 标	Item	2010	2011	2012	2013	2014	2015
一、科技活动情况	**Science and technology activities**						
科技活动人员（人）	People involved into activities(person)	128559	147814	162232	161004	173320	160629
科技活动机构数（个）	units involved into activities(unit)	490	625	616	634	656	646
二、知识产权拥有量情况	**Number of IPR**						
1. 专利情况（件）	Patents(item)						
（1）累计申请专利	Accumulated patent applications	74694	102411	139290	186401	233435	294421
当年申请专利	Patent applictions in this year	19486	27717	36983	47111	47034	60986
#发明专利	Invention patents	7176	11689	15029	23534	21189	14024
（2）累计授权专利	Accumulated patents awarded	31999	41273	53118	69368	86639	103910
当年授权专利	Patents awarded in this year	8037	9274	11862	16250	17271	25103
#发明专利	Invention patents	1651	2738	3475	3708	4272	5873
2. 商标情况（件）	Trade marks(item)						
（1）当年注册商标申请	Trade mark registration claimed in this year	21562	15620	18230	12372	10023	23000
（2）累计注册商标	Accumulated trade mark registrations	52387	39381	65733	69915	75515	80150
#当年注册商标	Trade mark registrations in this year	18107	12278	12120	8850	8875	9600
三、民事知识产权维权情况（件）	**IPR controversy(item)**	**241**	**512**	**631**	**476**	**385**	**813**
1. 专利纠纷	Patent controversies	69	104	107	77	48	130
2. 商标纠纷	Trade mark controversies	29	49	107	209	173	277
3. 著作权纠纷	Copyright controversies	110	315	365	141	126	327
4. 技术合同纠纷	Technological contract controversies	6	15	9	16	7	12
5. 其他知识产权纠纷	Others IPR controvers	27	29	43	33	31	67

注：本表数据由省统计局、市科技局、市工商局、市中级人民法院等提供。

20–26 主要年份高新技术产业开发区情况

Basic Statistics of Hi-Tech Development Zone in Representative Years

指　标	Item	2010	2011	2012	2013	2014	2015
1. 高新技术企业数 （个）	Number of High-tech Enterprises(unit)	672	774	690	802	878	1008
2. 年末从业人员（人）	Number of Persons Employed at year-end (person)	287140	296723	320259	328707	346679	399403
从事技术开发人数	Number of Persons Engaged in Technology Development	67708	78636	81787	88179	101479	117176
3. 技术开发经费支出总额（万元）	Expenditures on Technology Development(10 000 yuan)	1031223	1322923	1768282	1926100	3125766	3841817
研究与发展支出	Expenditures on Research and Development	669083	831822	1273311	1666389	2049769	3271000
4. 利润总额（万元）	Total Profits (10 000 yuan)	1707925	2224850	2905877	3539526	3896038	4101017
5. 上缴税费总额（万元）	Sum of tax (10 000 yuan)	1964820	2586712	3383678	4465587	4640297	5125209
6. 出口创汇总额（千美元）	Foreign Exchange Earnings of Exports(USD 1 000)	4951265	6447050	6591977	7880206	9488010	12141353

注：2015年数据未经科技部评估。

20–27 高新技术产业开发区发展规模（2015年）

Development Status of Hi-Tech Development Zone（2015）

指　标	Item	合计 Total	新建区 Newly constructed Zone
累计已开发面积（平方公里）	Accumulated Areas Developed (sq.km)	55	55
高新区工商注册（个）	Registered Enterprises in Hi-tech Zones (unit)	33640	33640
#工业型技术开发技术服务型企业数	Number of industrial technology developing enterprises	12966	12966
#三资企业数	Enterprises of Joiut Venture,Cooperation and Foreign-funded	1145	1145
已认定的高新技术企业数（个）	Hi-tech Enterprises Designated (unit)	1215	1215

注：本表数据来源于西安市高新技术开发区。

20-28 主要年份高新技术产业开发区建设与集资情况

Capital Construction and Funds-Raising of Hi-Tech Development Zone in Representative Years

指　标	Item	2010	2011	2012	2013	2014	2015
一、基建投资（亿元）	**Investment on Capital Construction (100 million yuan)**						
本年基建投资	Investment on Capital Construction of this year	255.57	266.51	350.88	432.38	601.01	615.33
二、开发面积	**Area Developed**						
新建区累计开发土地面积（平方公里）	Accumulated Area Developed in Newly Constructed Zone (sq.km)	35	35	40	50	55	55.13
#当年新开发土地面积	Area Developed in this year			5	10	5	1.84
累计竣工建筑面积（万平方米）	Accumulated Floor Space Completed (10 000 sq.m)	2419.9	2748.1	3095.1	3433.89	3773.89	4127.39
#当年竣工建筑面积	Floor Space Completed in this year	334.2	328.22	347	338.8	340	353.5
三、吸引外资（亿美元）	**Foreign Investment(100million USB)**						
年末累计境外客商协议投资额	Contracted Foreign Investment Accumulated at Year-end	52.76	56.71	74.11	150.61	170.61	192.82
年末累计境外客商实际投资额	Actual Foreign Investment	29.75	36.24	45.02	58.28	72.78	89.39
#当年实际投资额	Actual Investmen in this year	5.11	6.49	8.18	13.26	14.5	16.71

注：本表数据来源于西安市高新技术开发区。

主要统计指标解释

普通高等学校 指按国家规定的设置标准和审批程序批准举办的，通过全国普通高等学校统一招生考试，招收高中毕业生为主要培养对象，实施高等学历教育的全日制大学、独立设置的学院和高等专科学校、高等职业学校及其他机构（独立学院和分校、大专班）。

大学、独立设置的学院主要实施本科层次以上教育。高等专科学校、高等职业学校实施专科层次教育。其他机构是承担国家普通招生计划任务不计校数的机构，包括独立学院、普通高等学校分校、大专班和批准筹建的普通高等学校等。独立学院指由普通本科高校按新机制、新模式举办的本科层次的二级学院，一些普通本科高校按公办机制和模式建立的二级学院，“分校”或其他类似的二级办学机构不属此范畴。

成人高等学校 指按照国家规定的设置标准和审批程序批准举办的，通过全国成人高等教育统一招生考试，招收具有高中毕业或同等学历的人员为主要培养对象，利用函授、业余、脱产等多种形式对其实施高等学历教育的学校。包括职工高等学校、农民高等学校、管理干部学院、教育学院、独立函授学院、广播电视大学、其他机构等。其他机构是承担国家成人招生计划任务不计校数的机构。

小学学龄儿童净入学率 指调查范围内已入小学学习的学龄儿童占校内外学龄儿童总数（包括弱智儿童，不包括盲聋哑儿童）的比重。计算公式为：

小学学龄儿童净入学率（%）=已入学的小学学龄儿童数／校内外小学学龄儿童总数×100%

研究与试验发展（R&D） 指在科学技术领域，为增加知识总量，以及运用这些知识去创造新的应用进行的系统的创造性的活动，包括基础研究、应用研究、试验发展三类活动。国际上通常采用R&D活动的规模和强度指标反映一国的科技实力和核心竞争力。

基础研究 指为了获得关于现象和可观察事实的基本原理的新知识（揭示客观事物的本质、运动规律，获得新发现、新学说）而进行的实验性或理论性研究，它不以任何专门或特定的应用或使用为目的。其成果以科学论文和科学著作为主要形式。用来反映知识的原始创新能力。

应用研究 指为获得新知识而进行的创造性研究，主要针对某一特定的目的或目标。应用研究是为了确定基础研究成果可能的用途，或是为达到预定的目标探索应采取的新方法（原理性）或新途径。其成果形式以科学论文、专著、原理性模型或发明专利为主。用来反映对基础研究成果应用途径的探索。

试验发展 指利用从基础研究、应用研究和实际经验所获得的现有知识，为产生新的产品、材料和装置，建立新的工艺、系统和服务，以及对已产生和建立的上述各项作实质性的改进而进行的系统性工作。其成果形式主要是专利、专有技术、具有新产品基本特征的产品原型或具有新装置基本特征的原始样机等。在社会科学领域，试验发展是指把通过基础研究、应用研究获得的知识转变成可以实施的计划（包括为进行检验和评估实施示范项目）的过程。人文科学领域没有对应的试验发展活动。主要反映将科研成果转化为技术和产品的能力，是科技推动经济社会发展的物化成果。

R&D人员 指参与研究与试验发展项目研究、管理和辅助工作的人员，包括项目（课题）组人员，企业科技行政管理人员和直接为项目（课题）活动提供服务的辅助人员。反映投入从事拥有自主知识产权的研究开发活动的人力规模。

R&D人员全时当量 指全时人员数加非全时人员按工作量折算为全时人员数的总和。例如：有两个全时人员和三个非全时人员（工作时间分别为20%、30%和70%），则全时当量为2+0.2+0.3+0.7=3.2人年。为国际上比较科技人力投入而制定的可比指标。

R&D经费内部支出 合计指调查单位用于内部开展R&D活动（基础研究、应用研究和试验发展）的实际支出。包括用于R&D项目（课题）活动的直接支出，以及间接用TR&D活动的管理费、服务费、与R&D有关的基本建设支出以及外协加工费等。不包括生产性活动支出、归还贷款支出以及与外单位合作或委托外单位进行R&D活动而转拨给对方的经费支出。

R&D经费内部支出中政府资金 指R&D经费内部支出中来自各级政府部门的各类资金，包括财政科学技术拨款、科学基金、教育等部门事业费以及政府部门预算外资金的实际支出。

R&D经费内部支出中企业资金 指R&D经费内部支出中来自本企业的自有资金和接受其他企业委托而获得的经费，以及科研院所、高校等事业单位从企业获得的资金的实际支出。

R&D项目（课题）数 指在当年立项并开展研究工作、以前年份立项仍继续进行研究的研发项目（课题）数，包括当年完成和年内研究：工作已告失败的研发项目（课题），但不包括委托外单位进行的研发项目（课题）数。

R&D项目（课题）人员全时当量 指实际参加研发项目（课题）活动人员折合的全时当量。

R&D项目（课题）经费内部支出 指调查单位内部在报告年度进行研发项目（课题）研究和试制等的实际支出。包括劳务费、其他日常支出、固定资产购建费、外协加工费等，不包括委托或与外单位合作进行项目（课题）研究而拨付给对方使用的经费。

新产品产值 指报告期企业生产的新产品的产值。新产品是指采用新技术原理、新设计构思研制、生产的全新产品，或在结构、材质、工艺等某一方面比原有产品有明显改进，从而显著提高了产品性能或扩大了使用功能的产品。新产品产值、新产品销售收入既包括经政府有关部门认定并在有效期内的新产品，也包括企业自行研制开发，未经政府有关部门认定，从投产之日起一年之内的新产品。

新产品销售收入 指报告期企业销售新产品实现的销售收入。

专利 是专利权的简称，是对发明人的发明创造经审查合格后，由专利局依据专利法授予发明人和设计人对该项发明创造享有的专有权。包括发明、实用新型和外观设计。反映拥有自主知识产权的科技和设计成果情况。

发明（专利） 指对产品、方法或者其改进所提出的新的技术方案。是国际通行的反映拥有自主知识产权技术的核心指标。

Explanatory Notes on Main Statistical Indicators

Regular Institutions of Higher Education refer to educational establishments set up according to the government evaluation and approval procedures, recruiting graduates from senior secondary schools as the main target by National Matriculation TEST. They include full-time universities, colleges, institutions of higher professional education, institutions of higher vocational education, institutions of higher vocational education and others (non-university tertiary, branch schools and undergraduate classes) .

Universities and colleges primarily provide undergraduate courses; institutions of higher professional education and institutions of higher vocational education primarily provide professional trainings; and others refer to educational establishments, which are responsible for enrolling higher education students under the State Plan but not enumerated in the total number of schools, including: branch schools of universities and colleges, and universities and colleges that have been approved and under plan for construction. Non-university tertiary refers to the regular undergraduate branch college which is running in new mechanism and mode, excluding the branch schools and other similar branches of educational institutions.

Institutions of Higher Education for Adults refer to educational establishments, set up in line with relevant rules approved by the government, enrolling staff and workers with senior secondary school or equivalent education, and providing higher education courses in many forms of correspondence, spare time, or full time for adults. Professionals thus trained receive a qualification equivalent to graduates studying regular courses at regular universities, colleges and professional colleges. Institutions of higher learning for adults include schools of higher education for staff and workers, schools of higher education for peasants, colleges for management cadres, pedagogical colleges, independent correspondence colleges, Radio and TV universities and other educational establishments. Other educational establishments have undertakings to enrol adult students but not enumerated in the schools under the State Plan.

Net Enrolment Ratio of Primary Schools refers to the proportion of school age children enrolled at schools to the total number of school age children both in and outside schools (including retarded children, but excluding blind, deaf and mute children) . The formula is:

$$\text{Net Enrolment Ratio Of Primary Schools} = \frac{\text{Total Primary School-age Children at Schools}}{\text{Total Primary School-age WnerdlihChether or Not Attending School}} \times 100\%$$

Research and Development (R&D) refers to systematic and creative activities in the field of science and technology aiming at increasing the knowledge and using the knowledge for new application. R&D includes 3 categories of activities: basic research, applied research and experimentation for development. The scale and intensity of R&D are widely used internationally to reflect the strength of S&T and the core competitiveness of a country in the world.

Basic Research refers to empirical or theoretical research aiming at obtaining new knowledge on the fundamental principles regarding phenomena or observable facts to reveal the intrinsic nature and underlying laws and to acquire new discoveries or new theories. Basic research takes no specific or designated application as the aim of the research. Results of basic research are mainly released or disseminated in the form of scientific papers or monographs. This indicator reflects the innovation capacity for original knowledge.

Applied Research refers to creative research aiming at obtaining new knowledge on a specific objective or target. Purpose of the applied research is to identify the possible uses of results from basic research, or to explore new (fundamental) methods or new approaches. Results of applied research are expressed in the form of scientific papers, monographs, fundamental models or invention patents. This indicator reflects the exploration of ways to apply the results of basic research.

Experiments and Development refer to systematic activities aiming at using the knowledge from basic and applied researches or from practical experience to develop new products, materials and equipment, to establish new production process, systems and services, or to make substantial improvement on the existing products, process or services. Results of experiment and development activities are embodied in patents, exclusive technology, and monotype of new products or equipment. In social sciences, experiment and development activities refer to the process of converting the knowledge from basic or applied researches into feasible programmes (including conduct of demonstration projects for assessment and evaluation) . There are no experiment and development activities in the science of humanities. This indicator reflects the capability of transferring the results of S&T into technique and products, and measures the realization of S&T in spearheading the economic and social development.

R&D Personnel refer to persons engaged in research, management and supporting activities ofR & D, including persons in the project teams, persons engaged in the management of S&T activities of enterprises and supporting staff providing direct service to the research projects. This indicator reflects the size of personnel engaged in R&D activities with independent intellectual property.

Full-time Equivalent of R&D Personnel refers to the sum of the full-time persons and the full-time equivalent of part-time persons converted by workload. For instance, if there are 2 full-time persons and 3 part-time workers (20%, 30% and 70% of working hours respectively on R&D activities) , the full-time equivalent are 2+0.2+0.3+0.7=3.2 person-years. This is an internationally comparable indicator of S&T manpower input.

Total Internal Expenditure of Funds on R&D refers to the real expenditure of surveyed units on their own R&D activities (basic research, application study, test and development) including direct expenditure on R&D activities, indirect expenditure of management and services on R&D activities, expenditure on capital construction and material processing by others. Excluding the expenditure on production activities, return of loan, and fees transferred to cooperated and entrusted agencies on R&D activities.

Internal Expenditure of Government Funds refersto the expenditure of funds on R&D activities from government agencies at different levels, including appropriate funds on science and technology from financial departments, scientific funds, operating expenses from education departments and the real expenditure of extra budgetary funds from government agencies.

Internal Expenditure of Funds of Enterprises refers to the expenditure of funds on R&D activities from self-raised funds of enterprises and funds from other enterprises through entrustment, and the expenditure of funds of institutions, such as institution of scientific research and universities, from enterprises.

Number of R&D Projects (subjects) refers to the number of R&D projects (subjects) set up and implemented at the reference year, and the number of R&D projects (subjects) set up in former years and under implementation, including the projects (subjects) finished and failed at the reference year, excluding the projects (subjects) implemented by others through entrustment.

Full-time Equivalent of R&D Personnel refers to the full-time equivalent of persons actually engaged in R&D projects. (subjects)

Internal Expenditure of Funds on R&D Projects (subjects) refers to the real expenditure of internal funds of the surveyed units on research and test of R&D projects (subjects) at the reference year, including service fee, other daily expenditure, cost for capital goods, cost of external process; excluding expenditure of funds transferred to other cooperated and entrusted units of the projects.

Output Value of New Products refers to the output value of new products during the reporting period. The new products refer to brand new products produced with new technology and new design, or product that represent noticeable improvement in terms of structure, material, or production process for improving significantly the character of function of the older versions. The output value and sales income of the new products include those of new products certified by relevant government agencies within the period of certification, as well as new products designed and produced by enterprises within a year without certification by government agencies.

Sales Income of New Products refers to the real sales income of new products of the enterprises at the reporting period.

Patent is an abbreviation for the patent right and refers to the exclusive right of ownership by the inventors or designers for the creation or inventions, given from the patent offices after due process of assessment and approval in accordance with the Patent Law. Patents are granted for inventions, utility models and designs. This indicator reflects the achievements of S&T and design with independent intellectual property.

Patented Inventions refer to new technical proposals to the products or methods or their modifications. This is universal core indicator reflecting the technologies with independent intellectual property.

21 文化、体育、卫生、社会福利和其他

CULTURE,SPORTS,PUBLIC HEALTH,SOCIAL WELFARE INSTITUTIONS AND OTHER SOCIAL ACTIVITIES

资料整理：郝　静
Data management：Hao Jing
数据审核：王金桂
Data audit：Wang Jingui

第二十一部分　文化、体育、卫生、社会福利和其他

一、简要说明

本章资料主要包括文化、卫生、民政、体育、计划生育、共青团、妇联以及公检法等方面的内容，由西安市统计局服务业和社会科技处根据西安市文广新局、卫计委、民政局、体育局、妇联、共青团市委以及公安局、检察院、法院等部门提供资料整理。

二、主要指标

图书馆藏量（千册件）	6522	比上年增加	237千册件
医院数（个）	295	比上年增加	14个
医院床位数（万张）	4.98	比上年增加	4269张

21 CULTURE,SPORTS,SANITATION,SOCIAL WELFARE INSTITUTIONS AND OTHER SOCIAL ACTIVITIES

Ⅰ.Brief Introduction

Data in this chapter primarily consists of data of culture, sanitation, civil administration, physical education, family planning, Communist Youth League, the Women's Federation, public security organs, procuratorial organs and people's court, compiled by Tertiary Industry and Social Science & Technology Division of Xi'an Bureau of Statistics according to data from Xi'an Bureau of Cuture, health and Family Planning Commision, Bureau of Civial Adnimistration, Bureau of PE, the Women's Federation, Municipal Committee of Communist Youth League, Bureau of Public Security, Procuratorate, People's Court and other department concerned.

Ⅱ.Major Indicators

		Increase over Preceding Year
Number of Collections in Libraries(1 000 vol.)	6522	237
Number of Hospitals(unit)	295	14
Number of Beds(10 000 units)	4.98	4269 units

21-1 文化事业机构和人数（2015年）

Number of Institutions and Personnel in Culture and Art（2015）

项　　目	Item	机构数（个） Number of Institutions （unit）	人员数（人） Number of Personnel （person）
一、电影事业	**Career of Film**		
制片厂	Studio	1	900
发行放映管理机构	Number of Film Projection and Publication Administrating Institutions	2	8
电影放映单位	Unit of Film shows	197	2433
#电影院	Cinema	65	2217
影剧院	Theaters	5	69
放映队	Film Projection Team	127	147
二、艺术事业	**Art**		
艺术表演团体	Art Performance Troupes	18	2313
艺术表演场所	Art Centers	17	338
三、艺术科研机构	**Art Scientific Research Institution**	**2**	**56**
四、图书馆事业	**Libraries**	**13**	**542**
五、群众文化事业	**Mass Culture**		
群众艺术馆	Activities of Mass Art Centres	2	123
文化馆	Cultural Centers	14	233
文化站	Culture Stations	183	732
农村文化室	Rural Cultural Center	2671	
六、文化部门教育机构	**Educations Institution of Culture Department**	**2**	**117**

注：在2015年公共图书馆统计中取消了碑林、新城两家没有机构设置和人员编制的公共图书馆。
本表数据来源于市文广新局。

21-2 文化事业发展情况（2015年）

Basic Statistics on Culture Development（2015）

指　标	Item	2014	2015
电影放映场数（千场）	Number of Film Shows (1 000 shows)	487.1	702.0
电影观众人数（千人次）	Number of Spectators (1 000 person-times)	16620	24664
电影票房收入（万元）	Box-office Receipts(10 000 yuan)	56599	81087
艺术表演团体演出场次（场）	Number of Art Performance Troupes Performers (shows)	5451	5059
#国内演出场次	Number of domestic Performance	5190	5010
艺术表演观众人次（千人次）	Number of Spectators(1 000 person-times)	5978	6824
图书馆藏量（千册件）	The library collection (thousand of books）	6285	6522
电子图书（千册）	E-books (1 000 volumes)	1300	1453
书刊文献外借人次（千人次）	Books, Journals and Documents Borrowing (1 000 person-times)	1020	1087
书刊文献外借册次（千册次）	Books, Journals and Documents Borrowing (1 000 Volume-time)	2617	2850
县以上公共图书馆购书经费（万元）	Book-purchase Fund of Public Library above the County Level(1 000yuan）	1596	1974

注：图书馆藏量因统计口径调整，2014年数据以此表为准。
本表数据来源于市文广新局。

21-3 主要年份群众艺术馆、文化馆（站）活动情况

Basic Statistics on Activities of Mass Art Centers and Cultural Centers in Representative Years

指　标	Item	2010	2011	2012	2013	2014	2015
机构数（个）	Number of Insititutions (units)	197	196	197	198	199	199
举办展览个数（个）	Number of Exhibitions (units)	705	592	652	658	627	606
举办展览参观人次（千人次）	Number of Exhibition Visitors(1 000 person-times)		375	416	301	326	289
组织文艺活动次数　（次）	Art Performances and Story-telling Sessions (times)	3729	4544	3273	4114	3617	3811
组织文艺活动参加人次（千人次）	Number of Culture Activities attendees (1 000 person-times)		1778	1377	1633	1576	1574
举办训练班班次（个）	Number of Training Courses (units)	3018	2224	1798	1616	1872	2126
举办训练班结业人次（千人次）	Number of Certificate Trained Persons (1 000 person-times)	133	115	143	155	156	207
组织各类理论研讨和讲座次数（次）	Number of Theoretical Discussion and Seminars(1 000 person-times)		106	78	122	254	216
组织各类理论研讨和讲座参加人次（千人次）	Number of Persons in Theoretical Discussion and Seminars(1 000 person-times)		15	14	19	28	25
本年收入（千元）	Income of this year (1 000 yuan)	42937	55367	88475	101365	89520	102567
本年支出（千元）	Expenditure of this year (1 000 yuan)	45160	62368	84522	93485	84827	100749

注：本表数据来源于市文广新局。

21-4　文物保护业基本情况（2015年）

Basic Statistics on Cultural Relics Protection（2015）

指　标	Item	机　构（个）Insititution (unit)	人　员（人）Personnel (person)	文物藏品 实际数量（件）Factual Number of Collections (piece)	一级品（件）Grade One (piece)	举办陈列展览次数(次) Times of exhibition (times)	参观人员（千人次）Number of Visitors (1000 person-times)
文物保护管理机构	Cultural Relics administrative Departments	27	553	28523	32	19	2257
其他文物机构	Other Agencies	8	199	40457			
博物馆	Museums	100	4194	1060639	4803	440	21269
#免费开放馆	Museums Open Free	76	1662	857557	3845	273	8125
文物科研机构	Scientific Research of Historical Relics Preservation	3	224	34347	186		

注：本表数据来源于市文物局。

21-5　主要年份广播电台及节目制作情况

Basic Statistics of Broadcasting Stations and Program Production in Representative Years

指　标	Item	2010	2011	2012	2013	2014	2015
省、地广播电台（座）	Broadcasting Stations at the Province and District Level(set)	2	1	1			
省、地广播电视台（座）	Broadcasting Station at Province and District Level(set)		1	1	2	2	2
县级广播电视台（座）	Number of Wire Broadcasting Stations and TV Relaying Stations(set)	6	6	6	6	6	6
中、短波转播发射台（座）	Medium and Short Wave Broadcast Transmitting Station (base)	55	54	59	57	57	13
节目套数（套）	Number of Programs(set)	18	19	20	20	20	20
全年播出时间(时：分)	Broadcasting Hours annually(hour)	124100	121723	129856	138278	143873	137075
广播节目综合人口覆盖率（%）	Broadcasts comprehensive population coverage	99.4	99.42	99.45	99.47	99.49	99.55
制作广播节目(时：分)	Productions of Broadcasting(hour)	110639	83368	104300	106554	104459	116603
#新闻资讯类	News Programs	13786	13821	14025	14355	13208	12208
专题服务类	Special Subject Programs	24451	16318	21891	30181	26884	21864
综艺类	Variety Programs	37720	28679	28096	24516	27148	37885
广播剧类	Literature Programs	2406	2014	1720	3083	3712	6674
广告类	Advertisements	28339	14202	19547	20552	18465	15777
其他类	Service Programs	3937	8334	19021	13867	15042	22195

注：中、短波转播发射台2014年之前统计口径为中短波、调频发射台及转播台。数据变化因指标含义变化所致。
本表数据来源于市文广新局。

21-6　主要年份电视台及节目制作情况

Basic Statistics of TV Stations and Production of TV Program in Representative Years

指　标	Item	2010	2011	2012	2013	2014	2015
调频电视转播发射台（座）	FM Television Relay Station (base)	10	10	11	11	11	48
无线电视节目（套）	Program Productions of Non-cable television Stations (set)	6	6	6	6	6	6
有线电视节目（套）	Program Productions of cable television Stations (set)	16	16	16	16	16	16
全年播出时间（时：分）	Broadcasting Hours annually(hour)	141856	147003	137936	140927	143000	141839
电视节目综合人口覆盖率（%）	TV shows comprehensive population coverage(%)	98.57	98.60	98.83	98.84	98.96	99.01
制作电视节目（时：分）	Earth Stations of Satellite TV (set)	29626	43925	30091	46614	35182	43563
#新闻资讯类	News and Information Programs	8930	10656	11169	13360	11797	11839
专题服务类	Special Subject Programs	7762	19191	7689	7751	8289	8073
综艺类	Variety Programs	3942	5202	5458	6508	5014	6242
广播剧类	Literature Programs	1729	3781	113	1820	110	462
广告类	Advertisement	3313	3200	3663	8066	3491	7921
其他类	Service Programs	3950	1894	1997	9109	6479	9026
有线电视用户（万户）	Users of Cable television Stations (10 000 households)	164.64	179.29	188.71	207.48	216.55	229.00
有线广播电视干线网总长度(公里)	The total length of cable broadcasting and television arteries of communication(km)		62494	62494	37126	37551	37613
有线电视入户率(%)	The Rate of Cable Television(%)		79.08	80.53	86.62	88.20	91.51

注：调频电视转播发射台2014年之前统计口径为发射台及转播台。数字变化因指标含义变化所致。
　　本表数据来源于市文广新局。

21-7　体育事业基本情况(2015年)

The Basic Situations of Sport（2015）

单位：人、枚　　　　(person, unit)

指　标	Item	2015
一、体育部门职工人数	**Number of Staffs and Workers in Physical Education System**	**612**
#运动员	Athletes	46
教练员	Coaches	161
二、等级裁判员发展人数	**Number of the Development of Grade Referees**	**970**
三、等级运动员发展人数	**Number of the Development of Grade Athletes**	**180**
四、全年获得国家级、省级金牌和银牌情况	**Basic Situations of Aquiring National, Provincial Gold and Silver Medals through The Year**	
#国家级金牌	National Gold	14
国家级银牌	National Silver	11
省级金牌	Provincial Gold	216
省级银牌	Provincial Silver	151

注：本表数据来源于市体育局。

21-8 少年儿童分项业余体校情况（2015年）

Basic Statistics of Youth Part-time Physical Training School（2015）

单位：人 (person)

指　　标	Items	2015
一、在读学生数	**Total Enrollment**	**8826**
田径	Track and Field	2100
游泳	Swimming	1400
体操	Gymnastics	130
举重	Weightlifting	75
国际式摔跤	Wrestling	88
柔道	Judo	70
射击	Shooting	340
射箭	Archery	210
足球	Football	730
篮球	Basketball	1800
排球	Volleyball	230
乒乓球	Table Tennis	850
拳击	Boxing	40
武术	Wu Shu	420
跆拳道	Kickboxing	160
跳水	Diving	88
棒球	Baseball	95
二、职工数	**Number of Staff and Workers**	**1340**

注：本表数据来源于市体育局。

21-9 群众体育事业（2015年）

Mass Sports（2015）

指　　标	Items	2015
社会体育指导员（人）	Social Sports Instructor(persons)	17898
晨晚健身站点（个）	Morning and Evening Fitness sites(units)	1600
社区建有体育组织比重(%)	The community has a sports organization proportion (%)	98.9
全国、全省体育先进社区（个）	National, provincial advanced sports community (units)	25
体育人口(万人)	Sports population(10 000 persons)	420

注：本表数据来源于市体育局。

21-10 主要年份卫生机构、床位、人员情况

Number of Health Care Institutions, Beds and Employed Persons in Health Care Institutions in Representative Years

年份 Year	卫生机构数（个） Number of Health Care Institutions (unit)	医院数（个） Number of Health Care Hospital (unit)	卫生机构床位数（张） Number of Health Care Bed (unit)	医院床位数（张） Number of Hospital Bed (unit)	卫生技术人员数（人） Number of Medical Technical Personnel (person)
2008	2239	276	34618	30582	47433
2009	2162	261	36849	32371	51641
2010	2385	258	39407	34274	56579
2011	5554	268	41010	35976	61281
2012	5576	276	44239	39213	66899
2013	5503	281	47867	42753	71134
2014	5554	281	51065	45561	76005
2015	5802	295	54708	49830	81462

注：本表数据来源于市卫计委。
2008年及以后为新的统计口径、分类。

21-11 卫生机构、床位及人员情况（2015年）

卫生机构	Health Care Institutions	机构数（个）Number of Institutions (unit)	床位数（张）Number of Beds (unit)
总计	**Total**	**5802**	**54708**
一、医院	**Hospitals**	**295**	**49830**
综合医院	General Hospitals	205	36797
中医医院	Hospitals Specialized in Traditional Chinese Medicine	43	5782
中西医结合医院	Hospitals Integrating Traditional Chinese Medicine with Western Therapeutics in Practice	3	289
民族医院	Nationalities Hospitals		
专科医院	Specialized Hospitals	44	6962
护理院	Nursing Centets		
二、基层医疗卫生机构	**Commuting health care service centre**	**5245**	**3386**
社区卫生服务中心(站)	Community Health Care Center(Station)	209	1808
社区卫生服务中心	Community Health Care Center	119	1805
社区卫生服务站	Community Health Care Station	90	3
卫生院	Health Center	100	1515
街道卫生院	Urban Health-center	5	45
乡镇卫生院	Rural Health-center	95	1470
村卫生室	Village clinics	2958	
门诊部	Outpatient department	205	63
诊所、卫生所、医务室	Clinic, health center, Infirmary	1773	
三、专科公共卫生机构	**College of public health institutions**	**238**	**1478**
疾病预防控制中心	Center for Disease Control and Prevention	16	
专科疾病防治院（所、站）	Specialized disease prevention and cure center (place, station)	1	800
健康教育所（站、中心）	Health Education Institute (station, center)	2	
妇幼保健院（所、站）	Maternal and Child Health Hospital (Station)	14	678
急救中心（站）	Emergency Center	1	
采供血机构	Blood Collection Agencies	1	
卫生监督所（中心）	Health Supervision Agencies (Center)	14	
计划生育技术服务机构	Institutions of Technical Service for Family Planning	189	
四、其他卫生机构	**Other Health Institution**	**24**	**14**
疗养院	Nursing Centres	1	14
卫生监督检验(监测、检测)所(站)	Health Supervision and inspection Agencies		
医学科学研究机构	Medical scientific research institutions	3	
医学在职培训机构	Medical training institutions	5	
临床检验中心（所、站）	Clinical testing center (place, station)		
统计信息中心	Statistical information center	1	
其他	other	14	

注：本表数据来源于市卫计委。
本表人员合计中包括乡村医生3588人和卫生员244人。

Number of Health Care Institutions, Beds and Employed Persons in Health Care Institutions（2015）

人员合计（人）Total Number of Employed Persons (person)	卫生技术人员（人）Medical Technical Personnel (person)	执业（助理）医师数 Licensed (Assistant) Doctors	#执业医师 Chartered Doctors
102684	**81462**	**26626**	**23818**
73603	**60170**	**17936**	**17059**
56585	46679	14089	13432
6893	5676	1723	1592
206	189	72	68
9919	7626	2052	1967
23291	**17551**	**7687**	**5889**
5858	4855	1560	1179
5082	4167	1307	959
776	688	253	220
2833	2335	583	366
112	96	20	15
2721	2239	563	351
4757	925	786	254
2981	2718	1241	1065
6862	6718	3517	3025
5120	**3383**	**879**	**755**
1070	812	300	273
475	369	88	84
70	28	5	5
1530	1229	327	269
119	55	34	32
143	93	16	14
555	447		
1158	350	109	78
670	**358**	**124**	**115**
70	37	12	12
147	82	45	44
189	75	6	6
6			
258	164	61	53

21-11 续表1

卫生机构	Health Care Institutions	人员合计（人）	
		卫生技术人员中	
		注册护士 Registered Nurses	药师（士） Junior Paramedics
总计	**Total**	**34819**	**3957**
一、医院	**Hospitals**	**28132**	**2801**
综合医院	General Hospitals	21680	2046
中医医院	Hospitals Specialized in Traditional Chinese Medicine	2533	411
中西医结合医院	Hospitals Integrating Traditional Chinese Medicine with Western Therapeutics in Practice	88	13
民族医院	Nationalities Hospitals		
专科医院	Specialized Hospitals	3831	331
护理院	Nursing Centets		
二、基层医疗卫生机构	**Commuting health care service centre**	**5727**	**1042**
社区卫生服务中心(站)	Community Health Care Center(Station)	1599	379
社区卫生服务中心	Community Health Care Center	1314	320
社区卫生服务站	Community Health Care Station	285	59
卫生院	Health Center	574	159
街道卫生院	Urban Health-center	22	9
乡镇卫生院	Rural Health-center	552	150
村卫生室	Village clinics	139	
门诊部	Outpatient department	966	168
诊所、卫生所、医务室	Clinic, health center, Infirmary	2449	336
三、专科公共卫生机构	**College of public health institutions**	**878**	**104**
疾病预防控制中心	Center for Disease Control and Prevention	58	12
专科疾病防治院（所、站）	Specialized disease prevention and cure center (place, station)	185	19
健康教育所（站、中心）	Health Education Institute (station, center)	1	
妇幼保健院（所、站）	Maternal and Child Health Hospital (Station)	521	54
急救中心（站）	Emergency Center	15	2
采供血机构	Blood Collection Agencies	27	4
卫生监督所（中心）	Health Supervision Agencies (Center)		
计划生育技术服务机构	Institutions of Technical Service for Family Planning	71	13
四、其他卫生机构	**Other Health Institution**	**82**	**10**
疗养院	Nursing Centres	18	2
卫生监督检验(监测、检测)所(站)	Health Supervision and inspection Agencies		
医学科学研究机构	Medical scientific research institutions	13	4
医学在职培训机构	Medical training institutions		
临床检验中心（所、站）	Clinical testing center (place, station)		
统计信息中心	Statistical information center		
其他	other	51	4

continued 1

Total Number of Employed Persons (person)					
Among:Medical Technical Personnel			其他技术人员 Other Technical Personnel	管理人员 Administrative Personnel	工勤技能人员 Logistics Technical Workers
技师（士） Technicians	#检验师 Laboratory Technicians	其他 Other			
4690	**3338**	**11370**	**816**	**8248**	**8326**
3452	**2428**	**7849**	**537**	**6159**	**6737**
2628	1877	6236	427	4575	4904
339	191	670	82	563	572
13	11	3		11	6
472	349	940	28	1010	1255
786	**519**	**2309**	**37**	**910**	**961**
359	233	958	30	471	502
319	197	907	27	416	472
40	36	51	3	55	30
195	119	824	7	250	241
11	6	34	2	8	6
184	113	790	5	242	235
174	124	169		141	122
58	43	358		48	96
406	**355**	**1116**	**173**	**1009**	**555**
213	205	229	13	135	110
31	21	46		59	47
		22	23	18	1
105	79	222	1	183	117
		4		37	27
24	24	22	2	40	8
		447	2	47	59
33	26	124	132	490	186
46	**36**	**96**	**69**	**170**	**73**
2	2	3		16	17
18	14	2	13	33	19
2	2	67	46	48	20
				6	
24	18	24	10	67	17

21-12 各区县卫生机构、床位及人员情况（2015年）

Number of Health Care Institutions, Beds and Employed Persons in Health Care Institutions By Region（2015）

区 县	Region	机构（个） Number of Health Care Institutions (unit)	床位（张） Number of Beds (unit)	人员合计（人） Total Number of Employed Persons (person)	#卫生技术人员 Total Number of Medical Technical Personnel
合 计	**Total**	**5802**	**54708**	**102684**	**81462**
新城区	Xincheng	271	6964	13697	10893
碑林区	Beilin	388	7486	14259	11946
莲湖区	Lianhu	349	7350	13208	10856
灞桥区	Baqiao	453	3059	5163	4212
未央区	Weiyang	385	4873	9352	7728
雁塔区	Yanta	492	8726	17457	14353
阎良区	Yanliang	162	1422	2593	2007
临潼区	Lintong	534	2331	3810	2648
长安区	Chang'an	810	4953	8246	6083
高陵区	Gaoling	230	1632	3024	2322
蓝田县	Lantian	640	1256	2710	1900
周至县	Zhouzhi	475	1517	3864	2637
户 县	Huxian	613	3139	5301	3877

注：本表数据来源于市卫计委。

21-13 各区县农村村级卫生组织情况（2015年）

Village Level Health Organization in the Rural Area by Counties（2015）

区 县	Region	村卫生室（个）Village health room（unit）	乡村医生和卫生员（人）Rural doctors and health workers（person）	#乡村医生 Rural doctors	#卫生员 health workers
全 市	**Total**	**2958**	**3832**	**3588**	**244**
新城区	Xincheng				
碑林区	Beilin				
莲湖区	Lianhu				
灞桥区	Baqiao	213	272	270	2
未央区	Weiyang	110	195	195	
雁塔区	Yanta	64	159	156	3
阎良区	Yanliang	80	110	110	
临潼区	Lintong	351	499	403	96
长安区	Chang'an	594	635	630	5
高陵区	Gaoling	143	230	207	23
蓝田县	Lantian	534	454	454	
周至县	Zhouzhi	372	750	642	108
户 县	Huxian	497	528	521	7

21-14 各区县社区卫生服务中心（站）情况（2015年）

Situations of Community Health Service Center (Station) by Region (2015)

区 县 Region	社区卫生服务中心（站）（个）Community Health Care Center(Station) (unit)	床位数（张）Number of Beds (unit)	人员数（人）Personnel number (person)	卫生技术人员（人）Medical Technical Personnel (person)	执业（助理）医师 Licensed (Assistant) Doctors	注册护士 Registered Nurses
全 市 Total	**209**	**1808**	**5858**	**4855**	**1560**	**1599**
新城区 Xincheng	17		310	241	92	80
碑林区 Beilin	18	60	474	374	166	120
莲湖区 Lianhu	19	110	632	515	187	186
灞桥区 Baqiao	24	408	864	727	239	270
未央区 Weiyang	35	91	770	630	195	252
雁塔区 Yanta	32	60	857	747	216	255
阎良区 Yanliang	8	66	160	143	42	50
临潼区 Lintong	27	487	618	515	130	117
长安区 Chang'an	22	526	1073	874	272	218
高陵区 Gaoling	7		100	89	21	51
蓝田县 Lantian						
周至县 Zhouzhi						
户 县 Huxian						

21-15 主要年份卫生机构各类人员情况

Number of Employed Persons in Health Care Institutions in Representative Years

单位：人 (person)

指 标	Item	2010	2011	2012	2013	2014	2015
人员合计	**Total**	**71230**	**79999**	**86096**	**90129**	**95633**	**102684**
卫生技术人员	Medical Technical Personnel	56579	61281	66899	71134	76005	81462
执业（助理）医师	Licensed (Assistant) Doctors	18763	21551	23051	23885	24820	26626
#执业医师	Chartered Doctors	16613	18904	20414	21205	22145	23818
注册护士	Registered Nurses	22640	25043	27837	29967	32136	34819
药师(士)	Junior Paramedics	3030	3127	3380	3551	3709	3957
技师（士）	Technicians	4589	3622	3953	4089	4276	4690
#检验师	Laboratory Technicians	2439	2622	2830	2974	3108	3338
其他	Other	7557	7938	8678	9642	11064	11370
其他技术人员	Other Technical Personnel	1156	895	633	590	621	816
管理人员	Administrative Personnel	6416	6769	6939	7160	7355	8248
工勤技能人员	Logistics Technical Workers	7079	6789	7555	7437	7944	8326

注：本表数据来源于市卫计委。
本表2011年人员合计中包括乡村医生3856人和卫生员409人；2012年人员合计中包括乡村医生3611人和卫生员459人。
2013年人员合计中包括乡村医生3477人和卫生员331人；2014年人员合计中包括乡村医生3327人和卫生员381人。
2015年人员合计中包括乡村医生3588人和卫生员244人。

21-16 医疗卫生机构门诊、住院及病床使用情况（2015年）

指 标	Item	总诊疗人次数 总计 Total
总计	**Total**	**51750662**
一、医院	**Hospitals**	**29415781**
综合医院	General Hospitals	22548732
中医医院	Hospitals Specialized in Traditional Chinese Medicine	2464938
中西医结合医院	Hospitals Integrating Traditional Chinese Medicine with Western Therapeutics in Practice	81749
民族医院	Nationalities Hospitals	
专科医院	Specialized Hospitals	4320362
护理院	Nursing Centets	
二、基层医疗卫生机构	**Commuting health care service centre**	**21440568**
社区卫生服务中心（站）	Community Health Care Center(Station)	4052814
社区卫生服务中心	Community Health Care Center	3246917
社区卫生服务站	Community Health Care Station	805897
卫生院	Health Center	1293962
街道卫生院	Urban Health-center	52029
乡镇卫生院	Rural Health-center	1241933
村卫生室	Village clinics	9806839
门诊部	Outpatient department	1549212
诊所、卫生所、医务室	Clinic, health center, Infirmary	4737741
三、专科公共卫生机构	**College of public health institutions**	**893415**
专科疾病防治院（所、站）	Specialized disease prevention and cure center (place, station)	37983
妇幼保健院（所、站）	Maternal and Child Health Hospital (Station)	723092
急救中心（站）	Emergency Center	132340
四、其他卫生机构	**Other Health Institution**	**898**
疗养院	Sanatorium	898

注：本表数据来源于市卫计委。

Medical and Health Institutions Outpatient, Inpatient and Utilization of Beds（2015）

Total Number of Clinics (person time)				观察室 Observation Room	
门、急诊人次数合计 Total number of people in outpatient and emergency department	门诊人次数(人次) Number of Outpatients (person time)	急诊人次数小计(人次) The number of emergency subtotal (person time)	死亡人数（人） Number of Deaths (persons)	留观病例数(人次) Number of Patients Receiving (person time)	死亡人数（人） Number of Deaths (persons)
50853941	**48000545**	**2853396**	**2968**	**29161**	**52**
29239372	**26706933**	**2532439**	**2962**	**28753**	**52**
22400563	20301639	2098924	2892	28409	52
2452517	2376383	76134	28	61	
81749	73492	8257	4		
4304543	3955419	349124	38	283	
20720992	**20598945**	**122047**	**6**	**336**	
3986247	3887322	98925	6		
3192430	3110858	81572	6		
793817	776464	17353			
1291501	1268379	23122		336	
52008	51679	329			
1239493	1216700	22793		336	
9259450	9259450				
1518148	1518148				
4665646	4665646				
892679	**693769**	**198910**		**72**	
37983	37937	46			
722356	655832	66524		72	
132340		132340			
898	**898**				
898	898				

21-16 续表1

指 标	Item	急诊死亡率（%）Emergency Mortality (%)	入院人数合计（人）Total Number of Admission Patients (person)
总计	**Total**	**0.10**	**103736**
一、医院	**Hospitals**	**0.12**	**90501**
综合医院	General Hospitals	0.14	71132
中医医院	Hospitals Specialized in Traditional Chinese Medicine	0.04	19369
中西医结合医院	Hospitals Integrating Traditional Chinese Medicine with Western Therapeutics in Practice	0.05	
民族医院	Nationalities Hospitals		
专科医院	Specialized Hospitals	0.01	
护理院	Nursing Centets		
二、基层医疗卫生机构	**Commuting health care service centre**		**5600**
社区卫生服务中心（站）	Community Health Care Center(Station)	0.01	
社区卫生服务中心	Community Health Care Center	0.01	
社区卫生服务站	Community Health Care Station		
卫生院	Health Center		5600
街道卫生院	Urban Health-center		
乡镇卫生院	Rural Health-center		5600
村卫生室	Village clinics		
门诊部	Outpatient department		
诊所、卫生所、医务室	Clinic, health center, Infirmary		
三、专科公共卫生机构	**College of public health institutions**		**7635**
专科疾病防治院（所、站）	Specialized disease prevention and cure center (place, station)		
妇幼保健院（所、站）	Maternal and Child Health Hospital (Station)		7635
急救中心（站）	Emergency Center		
四、其他卫生机构	**Other Health Institution**		
疗养院	Sanatorium		

continued 1

出院人数合计（人）Total Number of Discharge Patients (person)	死亡人数（人）Number of Hospital Csualty (person)	病床周转次数（次）Nnumber of Bed Rumover (time)	病床使用率（%）Bed occupancy rate (%)	出院者平均住院日（天）Average Stay Days in Hospital (day)
103346	**258**	**31.9**	**82.99**	**9.5**
90063	**257**	**33.3**	**86.17**	**9.4**
70742	244	35.5	87.14	8.9
19321	13	23.9	80.53	12.4
		29.8	84.30	10.1
		28.7	85.70	10.8
5635		**16.0**	**36.51**	**8.1**
		16.8	37.89	7.9
		16.8	37.95	7.9
5635		14.8	34.91	8.6
		1.8	3.91	8.1
5635		15.1	35.86	8.6
7648	**1**	**23.4**	**81.12**	**12.6**
		7.1	89.26	46.1
7648	1	42.8	71.51	6.0
		10.3	**41.19**	**14.6**
		10.3	41.19	14.6

21-17 提供住宿的社会服务机构（2015年）

Social Welfare Insititutions Providing Accommodation（2015）

指 标	Item	机构数（个）Number of Institutions	年末职工人数（人）Number of Staff and Workers at the end of year	#女性 female	床位数（张）Number of Beds	年末在院人数（人）Number of Persons Housed at the Year-end
合 计	**Total**	**137**	**2820**	**1678**	**25365**	**13500**
1、养老服务机构	Pension Service Institutions	125	2484	1540	22965	12187
其中：城市养老服务机构	Among Them:Urban Pension Service Institutions	75	1746	1108	15800	7822
农村养老服务机构	Rural Pension Service Institutions	29	362	250	3827	1422
社会福利院	Social Welfare Homes	3	68	31	1215	814
军干所	Army Cadre Institutions	18	308	151	2123	2129
2、儿童福利院	Baby Welfare Homes	1	70	44	900	675
3、社会福利医院	Social Welfare Hospitals	1	127	49	650	455
4、救助站	Rescue Station	9	119	42	849	183
5、军事供应站	Military Supply Station	1	20	3	1	

注：本表数据来源于市民政局。

21-18 主要年份社会福利事业单位机构及人员情况

Number of Social Welfare Institutions and Employed Persons

单位：个、人 (unit, person)

指 标	Item	2010	2011	2012	2013	2014	2015
一、机构	**Insititutions**						
烈士纪念建筑物管理单位	Institutions Managing Memorial Buildings of Martyrs	2	2	2	2	2	2
救助类单位	Units Providing Assistance	8	8	8	8	9	9
殡仪服务单位	Funeral Service Units	22	21	22	25	26	26
殡仪馆	Funeral Homes	4	5	4	4	3	3
公墓	Cemeteries	14	12	12	15	16	16
殡葬管理单位	Funeral Management Units	4	4	6	6	7	7
二、人员	**Staff**						
烈士纪念建筑物管理单位	Institutions Managing Memorial Buildings of Martyrs	37	38	40	42	44	42
救助类单位	Units Providing Assistance	116	119	130	137	139	119
殡仪服务单位	Funeral Service Units	1371	1313	1400	1430	1392	1510
殡仪馆	Funeral Homes	375	408	442	491	470	497
公墓	Cemeteries	939	838	869	855	838	929
殡葬管理单位	Funeral Management Units	57	67	89	84	84	84

注：本表数据来源于市民政局。

21-19 全市及各区县福利企业单位基本情况（2015年）

Basic Statistics on Social Welfare Insititutions（2015）

单位：个、人 (unit, person)

区 县	Region	单位数 Number of Enterprise	年末职工人数 Number of Staff and Workers at the end of year	年末残疾职工人数 Number of Disabled Staff and Workers at the end of year	年末职工人数中女性 The number of female workers At the end of year
合 计	**Total**	**60**	**3427**	**1349**	**1275**
市本级	City Level	13	1137	428	505
新城区	Xincheng	6	282	150	99
碑林区	Beilin				
莲湖区	Lianhu	6	253	100	90
灞桥区	Baqiao	1	25	10	8
未央区	Weiyang	6	211	143	72
雁塔区	Yanta	2	114	11	76
阎良区	Yanliang	3	141	67	37
临潼区	Lintong				
长安区	Chang'an	8	387	132	110
高陵区	Gaoling				
蓝田县	Lantian	2	162	64	34
周至县	Zhouzhi	2	108	38	42
户 县	Huxian	11	607	206	202
沣东新城	Fengdongxincheng				

注：本表数据来源于市民政局。

21-20 社会保障基本情况（2015年）

Basic Sitiation of Social Security（2015）

单位：万人、万户 （10 000 persons、10 000 households）

指 标	Item	2015
基本养老保险参保人数	Number of Basic Old-age Insurance	590.66
1. 城镇企业职工养老保险参保人数	Number of Town Enterprise Worker Old-age Insurance	306.99
其中：离退休人员	Retired Personnel	63.84
2. 机关事业单位养老保险参保人数	Number of Institution Old-age Insurance	28.38
其中：离退休人员	Retired Personnel	9.59
3. 城乡居民养老保险参保人数	Number of Rural Residents Old-age Insurance	255.29
城镇基本医疗保险参保人数	Number of urban basic medical insurance	419.52
失业保险参保人数	Number of unemployed insurance	149.62
生育保险参保人数	Number of Maternity insurance	110.04
工伤保险参保人数	Number of industrial injury insurance	149.22
城镇居民最低生活保障户数	The Number of Minimum Living Guarantee for Urban Resident Households	3.32
城镇居民最低生活保障人数	The Number of Minimum Living Guarantee for Urban Residents	5.93
农村居民最低生活保障户数	The Number of Minimum Living Guarantee for Rural Resident Households	4.33
农村居民最低生活保障人数	The Number of Minimum Living Guarantee for Rural Residents	13.12

注：本表数据来源于市人社局。

21-21 全市及各区县新型农村合作医疗情况（2015年）

Situation of the New Rural Cooperative Medical Care of the Whole City and Area County（2015）

区 县	Region	参加新型农村合作医疗人数（万人） Participate in the new rural cooperative medical Population（10 000 persons）	新型农村合作医疗参合率（%） Participate in the new rural cooperative medical care ration（%）
合 计	**Total**	**406.11**	**99.22**
新城区	Xincheng		
碑林区	Beilin		
莲湖区	Lianhu		
灞桥区	Baqiao	29.58	99.95
未央区	Weiyang	11.29	100.00
雁塔区	Yanta	13.92	100.00
阎良区	Yanliang	17.00	99.73
临潼区	Lintong	56.92	99.99
长安区	Chang'an	73.74	97.35
高陵区	Gaoling	23.40	100.00
蓝田县	Lantian	56.58	99.41
周至县	Zhouzhi	58.19	99.22
户 县	Huxian	47.61	99.66
沣东新城	Fengdongxincheng	17.88	99.16

注：本表数据来源于市卫生局。

21-22 全市及各区县优抚对象人员情况（2015年）

Statistics on Persons Enjoying Favoured Treatment by Region（2015）

单位：人 (person)

区　县	Region	革命伤残人员 Number of Disabled Veterans	烈军属人员 Number of Family Members of Martyrs and Soldiers	在乡复员军人 Demobilized Soldiers in Hometown	在乡退伍军人 Veterans in Hometown
合　计	**Total**	**4956**	**1021**	**3822**	**1792**
市本级	City Level	51			
新城区	Xincheng	630	30	9	
碑林区	Beilin	614	43	8	1
莲湖区	Lianhu	737	53	33	2
灞桥区	Baqiao	261	52	215	210
未央区	Weiyang	195	53	117	3
雁塔区	Yanta	734	70	80	10
阎良区	Yanliang	105	49	273	66
临潼区	Lintong	267	80	506	270
长安区	Chang'an	357	93	418	123
高陵区	Gaoling	137	64	319	172
蓝田县	Lantian	207	80	404	173
周至县	Zhouzhi	337	241	901	212
户　县	Huxian	255	80	368	100
沣东新城	Fengdongxincheng	69	33	171	450

注：本表数据来源于市民政局。

21-23 全市及各区县计划生育和婚姻登记情况（2015年）

Conditions of Birth Control and Marriage Registration by Region（2015）

区 县	Region	计划生育率（%） Family Planning Rate(%)	节育率(%) Birth control Rate(%)	独生子女领证率(%) Only-child Certificate Rate (%)
合 计	**Total**	**94.3**	**91.2**	**45.1**
新城区	Xincheng	98.6	85.8	48.9
碑林区	Beilin	98.8	87.9	54.6
莲湖区	Lianhu	96.9	89.1	58.8
灞桥区	Baqiao	95.2	93.9	61.8
未央区	Weiyang	94.9	91.4	59.6
雁塔区	Yanta	93.9	90.7	52.3
阎良区	Yanliang	94.4	93.4	66.9
临潼区	Lintong	92.6	93.0	28.3
长安区	Chang'an	94.1	94.2	33.9
高陵区	Gaoling	95.3	91.5	44.3
蓝田县	Lantian	92.5	91.1	22.1
周至县	Zhouzhi	93.0	92.6	13.3
户 县	Huxian	90.6	93.2	28.6
沣东新城	Fengdongxincheng	95.4	94.7	49.6

注：本表数据来源于市计生委、市民政局、市法院。

21-23 续表1 continued 1

区 县	Region	结婚对数（对） Marriages (couple)	再婚人数（人） Remarriages (person)	离婚对数（对） Divorced Couple (couple)
合 计	**Total**	**80790**	**27143**	**22748**
新城区	Xincheng	5115	2013	1811
碑林区	Beilin	10029	3001	2336
莲湖区	Lianhu	6735	2878	2338
灞桥区	Baqiao	5177	1815	1462
未央区	Weiyang	4784	1876	1851
雁塔区	Yanta	8977	3084	2788
阎良区	Yanliang	2935	1288	992
临潼区	Lintong	6175	1957	1938
长安区	Chang'an	9275	2985	2636
高陵区	Gaoling	3231	1316	1112
蓝田县	Lantian	5519	1406	1102
周至县	Zhouzhi	6867	1718	1099
户 县	Huxian	5954	1801	1267
沣东新城	Fengdongxincheng	17	5	16

21-24 全市及各区县妇幼卫生保健情况（2015年）

Care Health Conditions of Women and Child by Region（2015）

区 县	Region	5岁以下儿童死亡率（‰） Mortality rate of Children under 5-year-old(‰)	新生儿死亡率（‰） Infant Mortality Ratio in 2012(‰)	婴儿死亡率（‰） Neonatal Mortality Ratio (‰)
合计	**Total**	**3.92**	**1.79**	**2.77**
新城区	Xincheng	1.90	1.14	1.52
碑林区	Beilin	1.33	1.33	1.33
莲湖区	Lianhu	4.66	1.86	3.73
灞桥区	Baqiao	1.52	0.61	0.91
未央区	Weiyang	3.41	1.02	2.39
雁塔区	Yanta	6.13	3.20	5.06
阎良区	Yanliang	5.40	2.25	2.70
临潼区	Lintong	2.21	0.92	1.66
长安区	Chang'an	5.41	2.53	3.85
高陵区	Gaoling	4.06	1.01	2.70
蓝田县	Lantian	3.46	2.38	2.38
周至县	Zhouzhi	4.90	2.45	3.37
户 县	Huxian	3.76	1.33	2.88
沣东新城	Fengdongxincheng	3.94	1.18	1.97

注：本表数据来源于市卫生局。

21-24 续表1 continued 1

区 县	Region	孕产妇死亡率（1/10万） Maternal Mortality Ratio (one in hundred thousandth)	产妇住院分娩比例（%） Proportion of maternal Hospital Births (%)
合计	**Total**	**12.93**	**99.99**
新城区	Xincheng		100
碑林区	Beilin		100
莲湖区	Lianhu		100
灞桥区	Baqiao	30.43	100
未央区	Weiyang		100
雁塔区	Yanta	26.65	100
阎良区	Yanliang	44.98	99.96
临潼区	Lintong	36.89	100
长安区	Chang'an		100
高陵区	Gaoling		100
蓝田县	Lantian	21.63	99.96
周至县	Zhouzhi		100
户 县	Huxian		100
沣东新城	Fengdongxincheng	39.39	100

21-25 主要年份律师、公证及调解情况

Basic Statistics on Lawyer, Notaries and Mediation in Representative Years

指 标	Item	2010	2011	2012	2013	2014	2015
一、律师工作	**Lawyers**						
律师事务所（个）	Number of Law Offices (unit)	95	97	105	116	122	149
律师（人）	Lawyers(person)	1202	1347	1522	1639	1846	2198
#专职	Full-time	1139	1275	1439	1560	1738	2092
兼职	Part-time	63	68	73	77	88	91
刑事诉讼辩护及代理（件）				2438	3267	3118	3524
民事诉讼代理（件）				8848	10754	9985	15308
行政诉讼代理（件）				170	319	374	532
非诉讼法律事务（件）				1965	2265	2352	2780
二、公证工作	**Notarization**						
公证处（个）	Number of Notary Offices (unit)	14	14	14	14	14	14
公证人员（人）	Notarial Personnel (person)	202	233	235	222	298	307
#公证员	Notaries	112	118	116	115	118	121
办理公证件数（件）	Number of Notarized Documents Issued (case)	106491	108120	119605	136471	135413	135622
国内	Domestic	72670	68239	79167	98572	90171	86589
涉外	Foreign-related	33410	39545	39888	37444	44773	49033
港澳台	Hong Kong. Macao and Taiwan related	411	336	550	455	469	373
三、人民调解工作	**Number of People Mediations**						
已建调委会数（个）	Number of Mediation Committees (unit)	3911	4031	4053	4040	4059	4052
调解人员数（人）	Number of Mediators (person)	15717	12848	15080	15240	15793	14838
调解纠纷数（件）	Number of Civil Disputes Mediated (case)	22247	33851	39230	33651	33641	31696
#调解成功数	Number of Cases Successfully Mediated	22164	32109	37510	32368	32537	30590

注：本表数据来源于市司法局。

2015年开始，统计制度上将港澳台并入国内，办理公证件数中港澳台数据为国内的其中数，2014年前为并列关系。

21-26 主要年份共青团组织情况

Basic Facts on Communist Youth League in Representative Years

单位：个、人 (unit, person)

指 标	Item	2010	2011	2012	2013	2014	2015
一、基层团组织	**Grass-root Youth League Organisations**	**7006**	**11248**	**9097**	**10770**	**10152**	**10074**
二、共青团员	**Youth League Members**	**308141**	**345682**	**336156**	**344096**	**343121**	**331261**
#女团员	Female Youth League Members	142379	159725	157924	158287	153212	146213
三、专职团干部	**Full-time Youth League Cadre**	**311**	**270**	**680**	**737**	**659**	**496**

注：本表数据来源于共青团西安市委员会。

21-27 妇联组织情况（2015年）

Women's Organizations Status（2015）

单位：个 (unit)

指 标	Item	2015
一、妇联组织	**Women's Organizations**	
市级妇联	Municipal Women's Federation	1
街道妇联	Street Women's Federation	103
社区妇联	Community Women's Federation	719
县（区）妇联	County (district) Women's Federation	13
乡（镇）妇联	Township (town) Women's Federation	76
村妇代会	Village Women's Representative Conference	2827
二、非公有制经济组织中妇女组织	**Women's Organizations in Non-public Economic Organizations**	
个体劳动者协会中的妇女组织	Women's Organizations in Association of Individual Workers	4
专业市场中的妇女组织	Women's Organizations in the Professional Market	8
私营企业中的妇女组织	Women's Organizations in the Private Sector	84
三资企业中的妇女组织	Foreign-funded Enterprises in the Women's Organizations	25
三、机关事业单位妇女组织	**Women's Organizations in Government Departments and Institutions**	
直属机关妇委会（妇工委）	Women's Committee of Direct-affiliated Departments	54
部门机关妇委会（妇工委）	Women's Committee of Affiliated Departments	274
事业单位妇委会（妇工委）	Women's Committee of Government Institutions	50
四、民主党派妇女组织	**Women's Organizations of Democratic Parties**	
民主党派妇委会	Women's Committee of Democratic Parties	7
五、团体会员	**Members of Organisation**	
工会女职工委员会	Women Staff Committee of Labor Unions	3432
民政部门登记注册的妇女社团	Women's Communities Registered at Civil Administration Departments	7

注：本表数据来源于市妇联。

21-28 妇联工作情况（2015年）

Basic Facts on Women's Federation（2015）

单位：个、人　　(unit, person)

指　标	Item	2015
一、双学双比活动	**Double Learning and Double Competition Activities**	
（一）科技培训	Scientific and Technical Training	
接受技术培训人数	Number of People Receiving Technical Training	8568
获得绿色证书人数	Number of People Gaining Green Certificates	325
女农民技术员人数	The number of female farmer technician	339
妇代会主任中农民技术员数	Number of Farmer in Women's Head Technicians	226
（二）巾帼扶贫	Women Aid-the-poor Project	
脱贫户数（户）	Households out of Poverty（households）	212
扶贫项目数	Number of Poverty Alleviation Projects	19
二、巾帼建功活动	**Women Make Achievements**	
（一）巾帼建功	Women Make Achievements	
评选巾帼建功标兵数	Number of Pacemakes	122
巾帼建功先进工作者数	Number of Advanced Workers	59
巾帼文明示范岗数	Number of Model Workers	88
（二）下岗失业妇女再就业	Re-employment of Laid-off and Unemployed Women	
妇女就业服务机构数	Number of Institutions for Women's Employment Services	13
三、三八红旗手	**Models of Women**	**58**
四、三八红旗集体	**Models of Women Group**	**25**
五、实施春雷计划	**Carrying out of CHUNLEI Project**	
资助女童入学或返校数	Helping Women Children Enter School or Back School	40
社会捐资总额（万元）	Amount of Money That Social Attributes (10 000yuan)	6
六、来信来访情况（件）	**Conditions of Letters and Visits(case)**	
女职工劳动保护信访案件	Cases about Labor Protection of Employed Women through Letters and Visits	55
侵犯妇女财产权利信访案件	Cases about Encroachment of Women's Property through Letters and Visits	142

注：本表数据来源于市妇联。

21-29 主要年份交通、火灾及安全生产情况

Transportation, Fire and Safety Production in Representative Years

指　标	Item	2010	2011	2012	2013	2014	2015
全市合计	**Sum of Entire City**						
事故数(起)	Number of Cases (case)	4173	4199	5029	6329	5203	5039
死亡人数（人）	Number of Deaths (person)	568	566	553	505	516	513
受伤人数（人）	Number of Injuries (person)	2529	2271	2492	2223	1840	2332
损失（万元）	Economic Loss (10 000 yuan)	3666.8	2780.5	4524.8	4432.8	6122.6	4294.7
道路交通事故	**Road Accidents**						
事故数(起)	Number of Traffic Accident (case)	2323	2264	2446	2252	1970	2392
死亡人数（人）	Number of Deaths (person)	531	531	516	460	483	481
受伤人数（人）	Number of Injuries (person)	2520	2260	2486	2217	1832	2318
损失（万元）	Economic Loss (10 000 yuan)	736.6	611.9	1011.1	1143.9	1264.0	1470.2
火灾事故	**Fire Accidents**						
事故数(起)	Number of Cases (case)	1825	1920	2568	4062	3199	2590
死亡人数（人）	Number of Deaths (person)	13	8	16	26	17	20
受伤人数（人）	Number of Injuries (person)	7	3	4	6	5	7
损失（万元）	Economic Loss (10 000 yuan)	2224.2	1587.2	2793.7	3011.9	4381.1	2401.5
农机事故	**Farm Machinery Accidents**						
事故数(起)	Number of Cases (case)	5		2	1	24	47
死亡人数（人）	Number of Deaths (person)			2	1	1	1
受伤人数（人）	Number of Injuries (person)	2				3	7
损失（万元）	Economic Loss (10 000 yuan)	3.1		12.4	7.0	7.3	5.0
工矿商贸事故	**Accidents in Industry,Mine,Business and Trade**						
事故数(起)	Number of Cases (case)	20	15	13	14	10	10
死亡人数（人）	Number of Deaths (person)	24	27	19	18	15	11
受伤人数（人）	Number of Injuries (person)		8	2			
损失（万元）	Economic Loss (10 000 yuan)	703.0	581.5	707.7	270.0	470.2	418.0

注：本表数据来源于市公安局及安监局。其中交通、火灾数据2011年及以前年份来自于市安监局，2012年以后数据来自于市公安局。2014年农机及工矿商贸事故发生起数统计口径变化，数据与以前年份不可比。

21-30 主要年份刑事案件情况

Data on Criminal Cases in Representative Years

指 标	Item	2010	2011	2012	2013	2014	2015
一、案件数情况	**Data on Number of Cases**						
立案数（起）	Number of Registered Cases(case)	48566	71499	61071	72611	77051	108955
破案数（起）	Number of Cleared up Cases(case)	18906	17585	20788	26587	25830	28629
破案率（%）	Percent of Cleared up Cases(%)	38.9	24.6	34.0	36.6	33.5	26.3
抓获作案成员(人)	Number of Criminals Caught(person)	13104	14672	16980	14255	14184	12827
二、查获犯罪集团情况	**Data on Hunted down and Seized Criminal Gangs**						
查获犯罪集团个数（个）	Number of Hunted down and Seized Criminal Gangs (person)	186	209	853	695	359	153
查获犯罪集团人数（人）	Number of Members of Hunted down and Seized Criminal Gangs (person)	939	970	3332	2632	1508	680
涉及案件（起）	Number of Cases Involved(case)	1172	485	2039	2439	1111	291
三、涉枪案件情况	**Data on Cases with Guns Involved**						
立案数（起）	Number of Registered Cases(case)	16	13	30	17	13	9
破案数（起）	Number of Cleared up Cases(case)	11	10	25	16	8	6
破案率（%）	Percent of Cleared up Cases(%)	68.8	76.9	83.3	94.1	61.5	66.7

注：本表数据来源于市公安局。

21-31 主要年份治安案件情况

Data on Public Order Cases in Representative Years

指 标	Item	2010	2011	2012	2013	2014	2015
受理数（起）	Number of Accepted Cases(case)	58968	63289	60747	94853	108780	104553
查处数（起）	Number of Investigated and Prosecuted Cases(case)	57151	62647	59949	93546	106811	100954
查处率（%）	Percent of Investigated and Prosecuted Cases(%)	96.9	99.0	98.7	98.6	98.2	96.6
查处违法人数（人）	Number of Investigated and Prosecuted Law-breakers and Crime Committer(person)	45856	44199	34346	46253	52922	40838

注：本表数据来源于市公安局。

21-32 主要年份西安市人民检察院案件办理情况

Data on Acceptance of Cases of Xi'an People's Procuratorate

指 标	Item	2010	2011	2012	2013	2014	2015
一、贪污贿赂案件立案人数（人）	**Number of Persons Invovled in Case about Corporation and Bribery(person)**	**184**	**166**	**175**	**172**	**207**	**220**
二、渎职侵权案件立案人数（人）	**Number of Persons Invovled in Case about Misprison and Toetious(person)**	**40**	**33**	**38**	**42**	**56**	**46**
三、审查逮捕案件受理件数（件）	**Examination and Arresting(case)**	**4229**	**5741**	**5024**	**5748**	**6443**	**6545**
四、逮捕各类案件人数（人）	**Arresting of Criminals of each kind(person)**	**6183**	**8787**	**7168**	**7177**	**7534**	**6692**
决定逮捕贪污贿赂犯罪嫌疑人（人）	Suspects of Corporation and Bribery to be Arrested (person)	51	34	43	49	64	100
决定逮捕渎职、侵权犯罪嫌疑人（人）	Suspects of Misprision and Tortious to be Arrested (person)	2		6		18	4
批准逮捕刑事犯罪嫌疑人（人）	Suspects of Criminal to be Arrested (person)	6130	8753	7119	7128	7452	6588
五、刑事立案监督、侦查活动监督（件）	**Supervision of Acceptance of Criminal Cases and Investigation (case)**	**623**	**89**	**263**	**368**	**284**	**162**
六、审查起诉案件受理件数（件）	**Examination and Prosecution (case)**	**4662**	**6298**	**6747**	**6371**	**7278**	**6922**
七、起诉各类案件人数（人）	**Prosecution of Criminals of each kind(person)**	**5946**	**8276**	**7307**	**7615**	**8399**	**8018**
起诉贪污贿赂犯罪被告人（人）	Prosecution of Criminals of Corruption and Bribery to be Defendants(person)	163	129	157	151	123	153
起诉渎职、侵权犯罪被告人（人）	Prosecution of Misprision and Tortious to be Defendants (person)	22	13	29	24	44	17
起诉刑事犯罪被告人（人）	Prosecution of Criminal to be Defendants (person)	5761	8134	7121	7440	8232	7848

注：本表数据来源于市检察院。

21-33 西安市中级人民法院案件基本情况（2015年）

Xi'an Intermediate People's Court Basic Data of the Law Cases（2015）

单位：件、万元 (case,10 000 yuan)

指 标	Item	合计 Total		中级人民法院theIntermediate People's Court	
		结案 Number of Case	诉讼标的总金额 Subject Matter of Litigation the Total Amount	结案 Number of Case	诉讼标的总金额 The Intermediate People's Court Litigation Total Amount
合 计	**Total**	**119166**	**3086197.39**	**15716**	**1995694.36**
一、刑事	**Criminal**	**7752**	**13486.32**	**1083**	**1235.85**
二、民商事	**Civil and Commercial Matters**	**77750**	**1347046.93**	**10286**	**757993.83**
三、行政	**Administration**	**3117**	**73.71**	**1072**	
四、申诉、申请再审	**Appeals, Apply for Retrial**	**3085**		**1043**	
五、司法赔偿	**Judicial Indemnification**	**17**	**10.05**	**14**	**10.05**
六、执行	**Execution**	**27445**	**1725580.38**	**2218**	**1236454.63**

21-33 续表 continued

单位：件、万元 (case,10 000 yuan)

指 标	Item	基层人民法院 the Basic People's Court		人民法庭 People's Tribunal	
		结案 Number of Case	诉讼标的总金额 Litigation Total Amount	结 案 Number of Case	诉讼标的总金额 Total Number of Litigation
合 计	**Total**	**103450**	**1090503.03**	**22434**	**130061.21**
一、刑事	**Criminal**	**6669**	**12250.47**		
二、民商事	**Civil and Commercial Matters**	**67464**	**589053.10**	**22434**	**130061.21**
三、行政	**Administration**	**2045**	**73.71**		
四、申诉、申请再审	**Appeals, Apply for Retrial**	**2042**			
五、司法赔偿	**Judicial Indemnification**	**3**			
六、执行	**Execution**	**25227**	**489125.75**		

注：本表数据来源于市中级人民法院。

主要统计指标解释

艺术表演团体 指由文化部门主办或实行行业管理（经文化行政部门审批并领取营业性演出许可证），专门从事表演艺术等活动的各类专业艺术表演团体，含民间职业剧团。（不包括群众业余文艺表演团队）

艺术表演场馆 指由文化部门主办或实行行业管理（向文化行政部门备案或领取合资（合作）演出场所许可证），有观众席、舞台、灯光设备，公开售票、专供文艺团体演出的文化活动场所。附属于文化部门机构内非独立核算的剧场、排演场，公开营业的也应单独统计。

图书馆 指各类图书馆的管理与服务（对文献和信息的搜集、整理、存储、利用和管理，向社会公众开放并提供科学、文化等各种知识普及教育）。包括公共图书馆和各类机构内部举办的或单独举办的图书馆的管理与服务。不包括部队系统以及文化馆（文化中心、群众艺术馆）、文化站内设的图书室。

群众文化活动 指开展群众文化活动的场所的管理和组织活动。包括文化馆（含综合性文化中心、群众艺术馆）、文化站、文化宫、少年宫等群众文化活动。在本制度中，目前暂不统计文化部门以外的文化宫和少年宫。

文化馆 （含综合性文化中心、群众艺术馆）、文化站：指专门从事群众文化活动的群众文化场馆。不包括临时抽调人员组成、没有编制的农村和街道文化工作队、服务站等。

广播节目综合人口覆盖率 根据国家广电总局制定的《广播电视人口覆盖率统计技术标准和方法》进行统计调查的，分别反映中央、省级、地市级、县级广播节目在本行政区域的综合覆盖情况，反应以无线方式传输的广播节目综合覆盖情况，综合反映广播公共服务覆盖的规模、能力、水平。

电视节目综合人口覆盖率 根据国家广电总局制定的《广播电视人口覆盖率统计技术标准和方法》进行统计调查的，分别反映中央、省级、地市级、县级电视节目在本行政区域的综合覆盖情况，反应以无线方式传输的电视节目综合覆盖情况，综合反映广播公共服务覆盖的规模、能力、水平。

博物馆 指为了研究、教育、欣赏的目的，收藏、保护、展示人类活动和自然环境的见证物，向公众开放，非盈利性、永久性社会服务机构，包括以博物馆（院）、纪念馆（舍）科技馆、陈列馆等专有名称开展活动的单位。

等级运动员人数 指经考核正式批准授予等级运动员称号的人数。运动员等级分为国际级运动健将、运动健将、一级运动员、二级运动员、三级运动员、少年级运动员。

等级裁判员人数 指经考核正式批准授予等级裁判员称号的人数。裁判员等级分为国际裁判、国家级裁判、一级裁判、二级裁判、三级裁判。

卫生机构 指从卫生行政部门取得《医疗机构执业许可证》，或从民政、工商行政、机构编制管理部门取得法人单位登记证书，为社会提供医疗保健、疾病控制、卫生监督服务或从事医学科研和教育等工作的单位。卫生机构包括医院、疗养院、社区卫生服务中心（站）、卫生院、门诊部、诊所（卫生所、医务室）、急救中心（站）、采供血机构、妇幼保健院（所、站）、专科疾病防治院（所、站）、疾病预防控制中心（防疫站）、卫生监督所、卫生监督监测机构、医学科研机构、医学在职培训机构、健康教育所（站）等其他卫生机构。

社区卫生服务中心（站） 指为本社区居民提供预防、医疗、保健、康复、健康教育、计划生育技术服务等的基层卫生机构。包括社区卫生服务中心和社区卫生服务站。

卫生人员 指在医疗、预防保健、医学科研和在职教育等卫生机构工作的职工，包括卫生技术人员、其他技术人员、管理人员和工勤人员。

卫生技术人员 包括执业（助理）医师、注册护士、药师（士）、检验和影像人员等卫生专业人员。不包括从事管理工作的卫生技术人员。

执业医师 指《医师执业证》“级别”为“执业医师”且实际从事医疗、预防保健工作的人员，不包括实际从事管理工作的执业医师。执业医师类别分为临床、中医、口腔和公共卫生四类。

执业助理医师 指《医师执业证》“级别”为“执业助理医师”且实际从事医疗、预防保健工作的人员，不包括实际从事管理工作的执业助理医师。执业助理医师类别同样分为临床、中医、口腔和公共卫生四类。

死亡率（疾病） 指在一定时期内，在一定人群中，死于某病的频率。

死亡率=某期间内（因某病）死亡总数／同期平均人口数×100%

社会福利企业 指以集中安置有一定劳动能力的残疾人员就业为目的（残疾职工占生产人员10%以上）、带有社会福利性质的企业总称。主要包括福利工厂、假肢厂和其他福利企业。

公证人员 指在国家公证机关依法办理公证事务的司法人员，包括公证员、助理公证员和在公证处工作的其他人员。

办理公证文书 指公证处在一定时期内办结的公证文书件数。公证文书按司法部规定或批准的格式制作，包括国内公证和涉外公证两部分。国内公证分为经济合同公证和民事法律关系公证两大类。

调解人员 指在人民调解委员会担负调解民间一般民事纠纷和轻微违法行为引起纠纷的工作人员，包括调解委员会的委员和调解小组的调解员。

立案 指检察机关对犯罪线索进行初步调查后，认为存在职务犯罪事实并需要追究刑事责任时，依法决定作为刑事案件进行侦查的诉讼活动，是追究犯罪的开始。

Explanatory Notes on Main Statistical Indicators

Arts Performance Troupes refer to the various professional performing arts groups, which sponsored by the cultural sectors or guided by the cultural society (Receive commercial performance license approved by the cultural administration authority),including non-governmental troupes. (The mass amateur arts performance troupes are not included.)

Arts Performance Places refer to the various sites for cultural activities, which sponsored by the cultural sectors or guided by the cultural society (approved by the cultural market administration, or receive joint/cooperative venues permit), with the facility of auditorium, stage and lighting, and selling tickets in public, including the opera halls and rehearse sites, etc. which are affiliated to the culture sectors without independent financial accounts and open to the public.

Library refers to all types of library management and services(collection, collation, storage, use and management of literature and information, open and provide scientific, cultural and other literacy education to the public). Including the management and services of public libraries and the libraries internally or separately organized by various sectors. Excluding the libraries in troops system and cultural palaces (cultural centers, mass art centers),cultural stations.

Mass Culture Center refers to the management and organization of the places where mass culture activities hold. Including cultural palace (cultural center ,mass art center), cultural stations, cultural palaces ,youth palaces and other mass cultural activities. In this system ,cultural palaces and youth palaces beyond cultural sectors are not counted at present.

Cultural Palaces (Cultural Centers, Mass Art Centers),Cultural Stations refers to the mass cultural venues specialized in mass cultural activities. Excluding rural and street cultural teams, service stations which made up by temporary without authorized strength.

Radio Coverage of Population refers to the comprehensive coverage which respectively reflected central ,province, city, prefecture and county radio programs by wireless in the administrative region, and comprehensively reflect the size, capacity, level of the public broadcasting services, according to Statistical Standard and Method on Television and Radio Coverage of Population established by the State Administration of Broadcasting ,Film and Television

Television Coverage of Population refers to the comprehensive coverage which respectively reflected central, province, city, prefecture and county television programs by wireless in the administrative region, and comprehensively reflect the size, capacity, level of the public broadcasting services, according to Statistical Standard and Method on Television and Radio Coverage of Population established by the State Administration of Broadcasting , Film and Television

Museum refers to the non-profit, permanent society service sectors which collect ,protect ,show human activities and the witnesses of natural environment, including the units that organize activities with the proper name such as museum, memorial hall , science and technology museum, exhibition hall, etc.

Number of Athletes in Grades refers to the number of athletes who have been given titles through examination. The titles of athletes include international masters of sports, masters of sports, first-grade, second-grade and third-grade sportsmen and young athletes.

Number of Referees in Grades refers to the number of referees who have been given titles after examination. They are classified as international referees, national referees and referees of the first, second and third grades.

Health Care Institutions refer to the units which have been qualified the Certification of Health Care Institution by the administration of public health, or qualified the Certification of Corporate Unit by the civil affairs, administration for industry and commerce, commission office for public sector reform, and engaging in medical care, disease prevention and control, health supervision and inspection, medicine research and health education, etc., including: hospitals, sanatoriums, community health service centers （stations）, health centers, clinics （health stations and infirmaries）, first-aid centres (stations）, blood gathering and supplying institutions, women and children care agencies （centres and stations), special disease prevention and curing agencies(centres and stations), disease prevention and control centres (epidemic prevention stations), health supervision and inspection agencies, sanitary inspection institutions, medicinal scientific research and on-job training institutions, health education centres and so on.

Community Health Service Centres (stations) refer to the primary units that provide the health care for community residents, such as disease prevention and control, medical treatment, health care, rehabilitation, health education, family planning technical services, including community health service centres and community health service stations.

Health Care Employee refer to all employee engaged in the health care institutions, such as medical organizations, disease prevention and control centres, health care agencies, medicinal scientific research and on-job training institutions, including medical technical personnel, other technical personnel, manager and labour.

Medical Technical Personnel refer to the professional staff engaged in health care, including licensed (assistant) doctors, registered nurse, pharmacists, laboratory technician, and imaging staff, excluding the medical technical personnel engaged in management job.

Licensed Doctors refer to the medical workers who have obtained the licenses of qualified doctors and are employed in medical treatment, disease prevention or healthcare institutions, excluding the licensed doctors engaged in management job. The licensed doctors are divided into 4 categories: clinician, Chinese medicine physicians, dentist and public health physicians.

Licensed Assistant Doctors refer to the medical workers who have obtained the licenses of qualified assistant doctors and are employed in medical treatment, disease prevention or healthcare institutions, excluding the licensed assistant doctors engaged in management job. The classification of licensed assistant doctors is cliniciam Chinese medicine, dentist and public health.

Mortality Rate refers to the ratio of deaths causedby diseases at reference period to the certain group of population.

Mortality Rate = total deaths （caused by diseases） at reference period/average population at same period x 100%.

Social Welfare Enterprises refers to those welfare-oriented enterprises employing a significant number of handicapped people with certain labour ability (handicapped employees shall exceed 10% of the production staff), including welfare factories, artificial limb plants as well as other welfare enterprises.

Notary Personnel refers to judicial workers of the state notary offices handling notarization work according to law. They include notaries, assistant notaries, and other people working for notary offices.

Notarized Documents refer to the documents settled by notary offices in a year. The notary documents are drawn up in accordance with the regulations of the Ministry of Justice, including domestic documents and foreign-related documents. Domestic documents are divided into two major categories, documents on economic contracts and documents on civil legal relations.

Mediators refer to workers on peoples mediation committees responsible for mediating in civil disputes and cases of slight infraction of the law. They include members of the mediation committees and mediators of mediation groups.

Acceptance of Case refers to the decision made by the procurators office to confirm the act of crime after initial investigation and to start legal proceedings of the case as criminal case.

22 企业调查

ENTERPRISES INVESTIGATION

资料整理：薛　燕
Data management：Xue Yan
数据审核：黄雪冰
Data audit：Huang Xuebing

第二十二部分　企业调查

一、简要说明

本章资料主要包括各行业企业景气调查指数和企业家信心指数等，由西安市统计局社会经济调查中心提供。

二、主要指标

企业景气指数（第四季度）	102.8
企业家信心指数（第四季度）	98.5

22 ENTERPRISES INVESTIGATION

Ⅰ.Brief Introduction

Data in this chapter consists prosperity survey indices of various industries and Entrepreneur Expectation Indicator, provided by Xi'an Municipal Bureau of Statics .

Ⅱ.Major Indicators

Business Climate Index（Fourth Quarter）	102.8
Entrepreneur Expectation Indicator（Fourth Quarter）	98.5

22-1 企业景气指数（2015年）

Business Climate Index（2015）

指 标	Item	一季度 First Quarter	二季度 Second Quarter	三季度 Third Quarter	四季度 Fourth Quarter
企业景气指数	**Business Climate Index**	**119.2**	**113.1**	**105.8**	**102.8**
按行业门类分	**Grouped by Sector**				
工业	Industry	122.5	118.1	116.8	113.8
建筑业	Construction	116.9	110.8	104.6	107.7
交通运输、仓储及邮政业	Transport, Storage and Post	102.7	106.4	105.9	109.6
批发和零售业	Wholesale and Retail Sales	100.0	94.3	96.4	91.0
房地产业	Real Estate	94.8	92.2	90.4	77.0
社会服务业	Social Services	140.0	123.5	102.6	98.7
信息传输、计算机服务和软件业	Information Transmission, Computer Service and Safeware Service	114.0	130.0	102.0	101.3
住宿和餐饮业	Hotels and Catering Services	96.3	95.0	95.8	87.5
按企业(单位)登记注册类型分组	**Grouped by Registration**				
国有企业	State-owned Enterprises	117.7	119.2	121.5	116.2
集体企业	Collective-owned Enterprises	105.0	120.0	112.5	120.0
股份合作企业	Share-holding Cooperative Enterprises	46.7	80.0	100.0	113.3
联营企业	Joint Ownership Enterprises	100.0	100.0	100.0	100.0
有限责任公司	Limited Liability Corporations	114.7	107.4	103.6	101.9
股份有限公司	Share-holding Corporations Ltd.	122.5	128.8	118.4	120.6
私营企业	Privately Owned Enterprises	116.2	108.5	105.6	92.9
港澳台商投资企业	Enterprises Invested by Foreigners or Investors from Hongkong,Macro and Taiwan	116.2	107.6	103.8	95.2
外商投资企业	Foreign Funded Enterprises	132.9	118.6	120.0	118.1
按企业规模分	**Grouped by Size of Enterprises**				
大型企业	Large-size	120.9	119.4	125.5	121.0
中型企业	Medium-size	126.0	120.4	111.6	111.3
小型企业	Small-size	114.1	113.8	105.9	100.6

22-2 企业家信心指数（2015年）

Entrepreneur Expectation Indicator（2015）

指　标	Item	一季度 First Season	二季度 Second Season	三季度 Third Season	四季度 Fourth Season
企业家信心指数	**Entrepreneur Expectation Indicator**	**112.8**	**108.8**	**98.7**	**98.5**
按行业门类分	**Grouped by Sector**				
工业	Industry	116.1	111.0	111.4	107.2
建筑业	Construction	97.4	90.3	85.5	87.7
交通运输、仓储及邮政业	Transport, Storage and Post	111.8	101.8	99.3	115.6
批发和零售业	Wholesale and Retail Sales	95.7	94.0	94.1	96.9
房地产业	Real Estate	81.7	91.3	76.3	70.4
社会服务业	Social Services	129.6	125.2	96.4	97.1
信息传输、计算机服务和软件业	Information Transmission, Computer Service and Safeware Service	140.0	140.0	108.0	110.7
住宿和餐饮业	Hotels and Catering Services	107.5	101.3	92.7	87.5
按企业（单位）登记注册类型分组	**Grouped by Registration**				
国有企业	State-owned Enterprises	106.1	105.9	103.0	109.4
集体企业	Collective-owned Enterprises	97.5	125.0	100.0	107.5
股份合作企业	Share-holding Cooperative Enterprises	100.0	100.0	70.0	93.3
联营企业	Joint Ownership Enterprises	0.0	100.0	100.0	100.0
有限责任公司	Limited Liability Corporations	111.3	103.2	99.5	97.5
股份有限公司	Share-holding Corporations Ltd.	117.5	126.3	120.3	116.6
私营企业	Privately Owned Enterprises	116.5	107.7	100.7	95.8
港澳台商投资企业	Enterprises Invested by Foreigners or Investors from Hongkong,Macro and Taiwan	97.2	91.4	98.1	97.1
外商投资企业	Foreign Funded Enterprises	121.0	111.4	110.8	110.8
按企业规模分	**Grouped by Size of Enterprises**				
大型企业	Large-size	121.4	113.3	119.5	121.5
中型企业	Medium-size	121.9	117.4	111.7	115.4
小型企业	Small-size	113.7	114.1	105.2	105.0

主要统计指标解释

企业景气指数：是根据企业家对本企业综合生产经营情况所作的判断与预期（通常是对“良好”、“一般”、“不佳”的选择）而编制的指数，用以综合反映企业的生产经营状况。企业景气指数也称“企业综合生产经营景气指数”。

企业家信心指数：是根据企业家对企业外部市场经济环境与宏观政策的认识、看法判断和预期（通常是对“乐观”、“一般”、“不乐观”的选择）而编制的指数，用以综合反映企业家对宏观经济环境的感受与信心。企业家信心指数也称“宏观经济景气指数”。

景气指数的表示方式：景气指数的表示范围在0~200之间，其含义：100为景气指数的临界值，表明景气状况变化不大；100~200为景气区间，表明景气状况趋于上升或改善，越接近于200，状况越景气；0~100为不景气区间，表明经济状况趋于下降或恶化，越接近于0，状况越不景气。

Explanatory Notes on Main Statistical Indicators

Business Climate Index it is an index worked out according to the judgment and anticipation (normally a choice from good, ordinary, not good) of entrepreneurs made based on synthetic productive and operational situation of the enterprise. It is used to reflect synthetically the productive and operational situation of the enterprise. It is also referred to as synthetic and productiveoperational prosperity index of enterprise.

Confidence index of entrepreneur it is an index worked out according to the judgment and anticipation (normally a choice from optimistic , ordinary , not optimistic) of entrepreneurs made based on their understandings and views of the market and economic environment outside the enterprise and the macro policies. It is used to reflect synthetically the confidence and feelings of the entrepreneurs to the macro economic environment. It is also referred to as macro-economy prosperity index.

The way to express prosperity index the range of prosperity index is from 0 to 200; 100 is the critical value, and means economic situation didn't change largely; from 100 to 200 is the interval of prosperity; and from 0 to 100 is the interval of not prosperity, meaning economic situation is going down or worse, the closer to 0, the worse the economic situation.

中国统计出版社最新图书简目

(仅供参考，以实际出版为准)

统计资料

中国统计年鉴 中国统计摘要 中国发展报告
中国经济普查年鉴2013 国际统计年鉴 金砖国家联合统计手册
中国-东盟国家统计手册 中国农村统计年鉴 中国县域统计年鉴
中国城市统计年鉴 中国对外直接投资统计公报 中国地区经济监测报告
中国贸易外经统计年鉴 中国零售和餐饮连锁企业统计年鉴 中国商品交易市场统计年鉴
大中型批发零售和住宿餐饮企业统计年鉴 中国农产品价格调查年鉴 中国住户调查年鉴
中国价格统计年鉴 中国能源统计年鉴 全国农产品成本收益资料汇编
中国环境统计年鉴 中国建筑业统计年鉴 国外资源、能源和环境统计资料汇编
中国工业统计年鉴 中国城乡建设统计年鉴 中国房地产统计年鉴
中国城市建设统计年鉴 中国科技统计年鉴 中国第三产业统计年鉴
中国证券期货统计年鉴 中国劳动统计年鉴 中国高技术产业统计年鉴
工业企业科技活动资料 中国社会统计年鉴 中国人口和就业统计年鉴
中国人才资源统计报告 中国教育经费统计年鉴 中国文化及相关产业统计年鉴
文化及相关产业统计概览 中国民政统计年鉴 中国民族统计年鉴
中国残疾人事业统计年鉴 中国妇女儿童状况统计资料（英） 中国乡镇街道行政区域简册
中国基本单位统计年鉴

省级综合统计年鉴系列

北京 天津 河北 山西 内蒙古 辽宁 吉林 黑龙江 上海 江苏 浙江 安徽 福建 江西 山东 河南 湖北 湖南
广东 广西 海南 重庆 四川 贵州 云南 西藏 陕西 甘肃 青海 宁夏 新疆 新疆生产建设兵团

市(县)级综合统计年鉴系列

天津滨海新区 石家庄 唐山 邯郸 保定 沧州 邢台 廊坊 承德 衡水 秦皇岛 张家口 太原 大同 阳泉 长治 晋城
朔州 晋中 运城 忻州 临汾 呼和浩特 呼和浩特新城区 鄂尔多斯 包头 沈阳 大连 长春 延吉 四平 通化 哈尔滨
齐齐哈尔 黑龙江垦区 上海浦东新区 南京 无锡 徐州 常州 苏州 南通 连云港 淮安 盐城 扬州 镇江 泰州
宿迁 江阴 丹阳 杭州 宁波 温州 嘉兴 湖州 绍兴 金华 衢州 舟山 台州 丽水 合肥 安庆 马鞍山 福州 厦门
宁德 漳州 南昌 九江 上饶 新余 抚州 萍乡 赣州 吉安 景德镇 济南 青岛 潍坊 枣庄 日照 滕州 郑州 洛阳
平顶山 三门峡 商丘 信阳 济源 武汉 十堰 荆州 宜昌 荆门 咸宁 长沙 广州 深圳 惠州 东莞 南宁 柳州 桂林
来宾 海口 三亚 成都 贵阳 昆明 西安 安康 兰州 庆阳 银川 乌鲁木齐 兵团一师 兵团十师

调查年鉴系列

天津 山西 内蒙古 辽宁 吉林 上海 福建 江西 河南 湖北 湖南 广西 重庆 四川 云南 甘肃 宁夏 新疆

统计方法应用/实用手册

实用SAS统计分析教程 马克威统计分析与数据挖掘应用案例
乡镇统计人员岗位知识培训系列教材：辅助调查员岗位基础知识 乡镇统计人员岗位基础知识
县级统计人员岗位知识培训系列教材：Excel在统计工作中的应用 简明统计分析
EXCEL在基层统计工作中的应用 统计公文知识问答

统计通俗读物/统计科普图书

漫话诺贝尔经济学大师与数学情缘 魅力统计 漫话信息时代的统计学 统计使人更聪明
漫游数据王国 探访随机世界 新中国统计工作历史流变1949-1999 无处不在的统计

重点图书

新编英汉汉英统计大词典 中华医学统计百科全书
挑大学选专业2016—考研择校指南 挑大学选专业2016—高考志愿填报指南